THE DERIVATION SYSTEM SD+

All the rules of SD and

Modus Tollens

MT i, j	i	$\alpha \rightarrow \beta$
	j	$\neg \beta$
	k	$\neg \alpha$

Hypothetical Syllogism

HS i, j	i	$\alpha \rightarrow \beta$
	j	$\beta \rightarrow \delta$
	k	$\alpha \rightarrow \delta$

Disjunctive Syllogism

DS i, j	i	$\alpha \vee \beta$
	j	$\neg \alpha$
	k	β

DS i, j	i	$\alpha \vee \beta$
	j	$\neg \beta$
	k	α

Commutation (CM)

$\alpha \,\&\, \beta :: \beta \,\&\, \alpha$
$\alpha \vee \beta :: \beta \vee \alpha$
$\alpha \equiv \beta :: \beta \equiv \alpha$

Association (AS)

$\alpha \,\&\, (\beta \,\&\, \delta) :: (\alpha \,\&\, \beta) \,\&\, \delta$
$\alpha \vee (\beta \vee \delta) :: (\alpha \vee \beta) \vee \delta$
$\alpha \equiv (\beta \equiv \delta) :: (\alpha \equiv \beta) \equiv \delta$

De Morgan (DM)

$\neg(\alpha \,\&\, \beta) :: \neg\alpha \vee \neg\beta$
$\neg(\alpha \vee \beta) :: \neg\alpha \,\&\, \neg\beta$

Idempotence (ID)

$\alpha :: \alpha \,\&\, \alpha$
$\alpha :: \alpha \vee \alpha$

Implication (IM)

$\alpha \rightarrow \beta :: \neg\alpha \vee \beta$

Double Negation (DN)

$\alpha :: \neg\neg\alpha$

Transposition (TR)

$\alpha \rightarrow \beta :: \neg\beta \rightarrow \neg\alpha$

Exportation (EX)

$\alpha \rightarrow (\beta \rightarrow \delta) :: (\alpha \,\&\, \beta) \rightarrow \delta$

Distribution (DI)

$\alpha \,\&\, (\beta \vee \delta) :: (\alpha \,\&\, \beta) \vee (\alpha \,\&\, \delta)$
$\alpha \vee (\beta \,\&\, \delta) :: (\alpha \vee \beta) \,\&\, (\alpha \vee \delta)$

Equivalence (EQ)

$\alpha \equiv \beta :: (\alpha \rightarrow \beta) \,\&\, (\beta \rightarrow \alpha)$
$\alpha \equiv \beta :: (\alpha \,\&\, \beta) \vee (\neg\alpha \,\&\, \neg\beta)$

THE DERIVATION SYSTEM PD

All the rules of SD and

∀-Introduction

∀I x/a i	i	α
	j	$(\forall x)\alpha(x/a)$

∀-Elimination

∀E a/x i	i	$(\forall x)\alpha$
	j	$\alpha(a/x)$

∃-Introduction

∃I x/a i	i	α
	j	$(\exists x)\alpha(x/a)$

∃-Elimination

ASSUMPTION	i	$(\exists x)\alpha$
	j	$\alpha(a/x)$
	k	β
∃E a/x i, j-k	l	β

Restrictions:
1. **a** must not occur in a premise or undischarged assumption.
2. **a** must not occur in $(\forall x)\alpha(x/a)$.

Restrictions:
1. **a** must not occur in a premise or undischarged assumption.
2. **a** must not occur in $(\exists x)\alpha$.
3. **a** must not occur in β.

THE DERIVATION SYSTEM PD+

All the rules of SD+ and

Quantifier Negation (QN)

$\neg(\exists x)\alpha :: (\forall x)\neg\alpha$
$\neg(\forall x)\alpha :: (\exists x)\neg\alpha$

LOGIC WITH SYMLOG
Learning
Symbolic Logic
by Computer

Frederic D. Portoraro
University of Toronto

Robert E. Tully
University of Toronto

Prentice Hall, Englewood Cliffs, New Jersey 07632

Library of Congress Cataloging-in-Publication Data

Portoraro, Frederic D.
  Logic with Symlog : learning symbolic logic by computer / Frederic
D. Portoraro, Robert E. Tully.
    p.   cm.
  Includes bibliographical references and index.
  ISBN 0-13-327628-7
  1. Symlog. 2. Logic, Symbolic and mathematical—Study and
teaching. I. Tully, Robert E. II. Title.
BC135.P69 [date]
160′.285′5369—dc20   93-14976

Acquisitions editor: *Ted Bolen*
Editorial/production supervision and interior design: *Edie Riker*
Cover design: *Wendy Alling Judy*
Production coordinator: *Mary Ann Gloriande*
Editorial assistant: *Nicole Gray*

 © 1994 by Prentice-Hall, Inc.
A Paramount Communications Company
Englewood Cliffs, New Jersey 07632

Printed in the United States of America

10 9 8 7 6 5 4 3 2 1

ISBN 0-13-327628-7

Prentice-Hall International (UK) Limited, *London*
Prentice-Hall of Australia Pty. Limited, *Sydney*
Prentice-Hall Canada Inc., *Toronto*
Prentice-Hall Hispanoamericana, S. A., *Mexico*
Prentice-Hall of India Private Limited, *New Delhi*
Prentice-Hall of Japan, Inc., *Tokyo*
Simon & Schuster Asia Pte. Ltd., *Singapore*
Editora Prentice-Hall do Brasil, Ltda., *Rio de Janeiro*

To our parents

Contents

APPENDICES

Foreword

In their new textbook on logic Frederic Portoraro and Robert Tully have taken a significant step in a direction that will surely be followed by almost everyone in the future. They have prepared computer software to accompany the text in a way that makes doing exercises, especially proofs, with an automatic check of validity by the computer program, a natural and almost inevitable part of a modern course in logic. Within philosophy the introductory course in logic is the obvious one to be augmented by software for handling exercises. Other courses, however, should soon follow this trend, especially courses in logic and the philosophy of science.

The use of computer technology can benefit both student and teacher. The student can expect prompt and objective evaluation of the work done, as well as potentially greater individualization in the choice of exercises. The teacher can be relieved of the tedium of evaluating hundreds of elementary exercises. Equally important, the formal concepts of logic, so important to our modern view of the subject, are realized in a concrete way that can be highly instructive. Many of my own students tell me that they never really understood what formal proofs were all about until they had constructed them themselves in a computer framework.

It is also important to recognize that today's undergraduates to a large extent have already acquired an easy familiarity with computers during their high school years. In many cases the use of such software programs as *Symlog* is what they expect as an extension of their earlier experience. This expectation will be even more true of future undergraduates.

Patrick Suppes
Institute for Mathematical Studies
in the Social Sciences
Stanford University

Acknowledgements

Symlog is a system for learning symbolic logic which comprises both a computer program and textbook, each intended to mesh with the other. The program was designed and written by Frederic D. Portoraro. The text was coauthored by Frederic D. Portoraro and Robert E. Tully. *Symlog* was developed at the University of Toronto as an innovative approach to the teaching of introductory symbolic logic, and its success there as well as at other universities has not only vindicated this approach but also encourages its extension to intermediate areas of logic.

Although *Symlog* will continue to evolve, we are now able to look back and appreciate those people whose advice, support and encouragement guided this project in its earlier stages and helped bring it to fulfillment. Chief among these is Arthur B. Portoraro, Frederic's brother, without whose contribution the *Symlog* project would almost certainly have never existed. Although it was necessary for him to leave the project, he took a major role in writing a suitable set of notes to accompany the program when it was first introduced to University of Toronto students. Those who are familiar with introductory logic textbooks will easily discover our considerable indebtedness to the work of Frederic B. Fitch as it is presented in his *Symbolic Logic: An Introduction* (Ronald, 1952) but also to a text which has become a standard in the field, *The Logic Book*, by Bergmann, Moor and Nelson (2nd ed., McGraw-Hill, 1990). Although our presentation of formal logic runs parallel to theirs, *Symlog*'s rules deviate somewhat from those of *The Logic Book*, owing mainly to the constraints of a computerized approach. The original inspiration for the design of the *Symlog* software was the well-known EXCHECK/VALID system of Patrick Suppes, an interactive theorem-proving program used in computer-aided instruction courses at Stanford University. Unlike EXCHECK/VALID, however, *Symlog* was designed to run on personal computers and (following the practice of most introductions to symbolic logic) was restricted to the propositional and predicate calculus.

Since its inception, the *Symlog* project has been warmly supported by the Department of Philosophy at the University of Toronto, which for years has taken pride in the quality of its logic courses. We have drawn the expertise and experience of many members of this department, particularly Peter J. Apostoli, Hans G. Herzberger, Robert A. Imlay, Andrew D. Irvine (now at the University of British Columbia), Bernard D. Katz and John G. Slater. We are especially grateful to James R. Brown and Alasdair I. Urquhart for their continuous and warm support. We are also grateful to Frank Cunningham, former chair of the department, who first advanced the cause of *Symlog* for us in the university community; to Wayne Sumner, the current chair, who has continued that support; and to John J. Hartley, former undergraduate coordinator of the department, who made necessary administrative arrangements when *Symlog* was getting started. The division of our philosophy department which is housed at St. Michael's College has been very instrumental in the advancement and implementation of *Symlog* in our campus: Fruitful negotiations with the Department of Computer Science have resulted in the installation of *Symlog* in several of their large microcomputer networks, making *Symlog* easily accessible to hundreds of students every year. The *Symlog* project also benefited from the skills and good will of many professionals outside the Department of Philosophy. We thank Ian Lancashire, director of the Centre for Computing in the Humanities (CCH) at the University of Toronto. Armed with the support of on-going projects such as *Symlog*'s, he was able to complete an agreement between the university and IBM Canada, from which the *Symlog* project, in particular, has benefited but also CCH and the university in general; IBM Canada itself, whose donation of personal computers and related equipment made possible the original implementation of *Symlog*; we are indebted to our editors, Joe Heider, who initiated the project at Prentice Hall, and particularly Ted Bolen who brought it to its successful completion. We are also in debt to Edie Riker of East End Publishing Services, for her project management services in producing this book and to the team at Interactive Composition Corporation for meeting our exacting needs in the composition of the book. We are expecially thankful for their patience throughout the duration of the project. Any user of *Symlog*, including ourselves, should be grateful to the anonymous reviewers of Prentice Hall for their valuable criticisms on both the text and software.

Frederic personally thanks Steve A. Cook, of the Department of Computer Science, University of Toronto, for granting him access to the computing facilities of the Artificial Intelligence Laboratory, where some experiments on automated reasoning were conducted and where work on natural deduction theorem provers continues. For their advice and help when he was writing the program, but especially for sharing their views on computer-assisted logic instruction, Frederic cordially thanks James Moor and Mark Bedau, Department of Philosophy, Dartmouth College; John Etchemendy, Center for the Study of Language and Information, Stanford University; Richard Scheines, Department of Philosophy and Center for Design of Educational Computing (CDEC), Carnegie Mellon University, for his highly valuable suggestions on searching natural deduction proofs; Leslie Burkholder, Robert Cavalier and Jonathan Pressler, also at CDEC; Peter Carruthers of the Department of Philosophy, University of Essex, who 'test ran' an earlier version of the program; Alan Dow, Claude Laflamme (to whom I am especially indebted) and Jonathan Ostroff, Mathematics and Computer Science, York University, for their invaluable suggestions at both the pedagogical and technical level; Andrew McCafferty at the Department of Philosophy of Louisiana State University for his fruitful suggestions on implementing *Symlog*'s theorem prover; Stephen Read at the Department of Logic and Metaphysics of the University of St. Andrews, Scotland, for putting us in contact with several researchers at the other side of the Atlantic and initiating an exchange of ideas from which *Symlog* has benefited; Joseph Hanna and Herbert Hendry at the Department of Philosophy at Michigan State University; Don Jones at the Department of Philosophy at the University of Central Florida; Mohammed Dahroug, formerly of the Department of Mathematics, University of Toronto, and now in private industry, who patiently answered nondenumerably many questions about computer hardware and software, as well as about symbolic logic; Geoff B. Keene, Department of Philosophy, University of Exeter; Greg Scott, Department of Philosophy, St. Mary's University; David Owen, Department of Philosophy, University of Arizona; and Keith J. Cooper, Pacific Lutheran University. Frederic is also grateful to his brothers Mario, who spent many long hours testing several parts of the program and checking proofs, and Andrew, for his expert technical advice on PC memory and disk management; to the Toronto-based firm Vision Computer Associates, Inc.—in particular, its president Louis Florence—for letting me use their computers as backup systems; to Peter Turney and Pamela Reeve, who tested the program here at our home university as teachers and indicated where it needed improvement; and not least, to the vast number of students on whom *Symlog* was tested, many of whom took an active interest in the project.

We reserve our deepest gratitude to our families whose love, patience, understanding and encouragement have endured during what certainly was for them an ordeal. From the earliest moments when the *Symlog* project was conceived, Frederic's parents, Dominic and Isabel Portoraro, have been a source of strength and enthusiasm. Our lives are richer, and so too our work, because of our wives, Montse and Anne. They have sustained us and we shall never forget.

Frederic D. Portoraro
Robert E. Tully
Toronto, spring of 1993

Introduction

. . . when controversies arise, there will be no more need for disputation between two philosophers than between two specialists in computation. It will be enough for them to take pen in hand, sit down at the abacus and, having called in a friend if they want, say to each other: Let us calculate!

G. W. von Leibniz

About Logic

The science of logic is the formal study of reasoning. Logic is a science because it aims to offer a systematic account of reasoning—chiefly what is known as *deductive reasoning*. It is formal because, unlike an empirical science such as psychology, logic does not study the beings who do the reasoning or their thought processes but the structure of reasoning itself. Formal logic is sometimes described as a preparation for other studies. In one sense this is true, for logic provides a set of tools for the detailed analysis and appraisal of arguments, no matter what their subject matter. An argument might be about astronomy, art, biochemistry, baseball, politics or mathematics, yet what interests the logician is different than what we ordinarily think of as the content of an argument. Instead, attention is drawn to the *structure* of the statements comprising the argument and to the question of whether its premises *entail* the conclusion. For the logician, form is the content of an argument.

1

Reasoning is sometimes thought to involve great effort; in fact, it is humanity's original labor-saving device. By applying logic, we extract new information from other information already in our possession. This process of extraction is called inference. The focus of logic is on the different *patterns of inference*, which give shape to reasoning; on *arguments*, which express and communicate reasoning; on *techniques* for determining whether the relation between the premises and conclusion of an argument is one of entailment and on *rules* that both govern and guarantee valid inference. Striving not only for rigor but also for comprehensiveness, logic includes a formal account of its own scope and its limits as a science. This area of investigation is known as metalogic.

In Roman art and mythology, Janus was the guardian of gateways and was commonly represented as a head with two faces looking in opposite directions. The head of Janus is an appropriate icon for any science which directs its gaze toward theory as well as toward practice, toward pure research as well as toward its application. Logic is perhaps the most Janus-like of the sciences. Its gaze extends in one direction to the abstract realm of infinite sets and to the exploration of relations, functions and the formal properties of languages, including languages that no one but logicians would find interesting. But in the opposite direction, the gaze of logic is fixed on the nuts and bolts of everyday language in which we make claims and draw inferences. In this book you will be carried in both directions, though not to extremes. The terrain to be examined in greatest detail is the middle ground: the classification of statements, their deployment in arguments, and the analysis of arguments. To make this investigation precise and clear we will introduce a few of the tools of metalogic, but our discussion will never drift into abstraction. As for what lies in the opposite direction, the raw material of ordinary language, although we want to show you how logic converts familiar sentences into new forms of expression which can be more easily manipulated, we will not go beyond this point in order to collect and catalog specimens of everyday language or to analyze conversations for argumentative content.

Logic did not invent arguments any more than physics invented gravity. Arguments, along with the human capacity to appraise them, existed for thousands of years before the head of Janus was ever placed over a gateway. So the raw material of logic is not just language itself but certain logical notions or concepts which are central to our human birthright. Notice that in explaining generally what logic is and what it does, we have relied on words whose meaning you already understand intuitively, such as 'statement,' 'argument' and 'conclusion.' The meaning of some other words was bound to be less clear, however, such as 'inference,' 'deductive,' 'entailment' and 'valid.' Logic engages in the process of refining the concepts associated with all such words and of forging methods which put these improved concepts to use. The need for precision in dealing with arguments was probably the original impetus for developing logic into a science. The first major codification of logical concepts and rules of inference was accomplished by

Aristotle (384–322 B.C.). So influential in Western thought was the Aristotelian system of logic that it was not until the late nineteenth century, in the work of the German mathematician Frege (1848–1925), that a new and far more comprehensive method of exploring logic was finally devised. Some two hundred years earlier, a fellow German, Leibniz (1646–1716), had become convinced of the need for a rigorous language to state and solve disputed questions. Although Leibniz was unsuccessful in his attempts to devise such a language, his vision of the possibilities of logic remains compelling even today, and it is for this that we pay him tribute in the preceding quotation.

Adapting mathematical techniques, Frege introduced a battery of special symbols to express the formal content in which logicians are interested, symbols representing a statement's essential ingredients, relations between statements and various patterns of inference. His method also included techniques for the construction of valid inferences from a set of necessary truths, called axioms, from which an infinite number of further necessary truths was derivable. The result was a genuine system of logic, into which the traditional Aristotelian account was fully absorbed, a system which could be expounded with precision and objectivity by the help of metalogical symbols. Perhaps it is just an accident of history that the axiomatic method, which had been known to the ancient Greeks for geometry, was not successfully applied to logic before Frege; but because of the advances made by him and, less than 25 years later, by the British logician Bertrand Russell (1872–1970), a new age began for the science of logic from which it has not looked back, and as with nearly every other science in the twentieth century, changes have been both remarkable and rapid. In the chapters that follow we will mention a few of these developments in passing, and at the end of the book you will find a brief bibliography of further readings on logic.

Because of the enormous influence of Aristotle in Western thought, logic has been customarily associated with philosophy, and although there is no essential connection between these two fields, the relationship continues to be a strong one. Not surprisingly, a hybrid specialty called philosophical logic has come into being. Because formal logic offers rigorous standards of precision in conceptual analysis, it is equally unsurprising that it has taken root and grown steadily in other fields of study, such as mathematics (set theory and the foundations of mathematics and discrete mathematics) and computer science (theoretical computer science and artificial intelligence).

The material covered in this book is usually called symbolic logic, although sometimes, because of its origins in the work of Frege and Russell, it is described as mathematical logic (Russell himself was a mathematician before finding his way into philosophy through logic). However, the specific variety of symbolic logic to be presented here differs from theirs in two significant ways. The practice in logic for many years now has been to expound what is called the method of natural deduction instead of the axiomatic method. In natural deduction, the emphasis is on applying deductive rules to *construct* valid arguments, and because this method (unlike the axiomatic method) is not restricted to necessary truths, it applies to a wider range of arguments, especially ones drawn from ordinary language. Another difference between present and vintage practice concerns the use of decision procedures, which are mechanical methods for detecting the presence or absence of logical properties. Validity, for instance, is a logical property of arguments which can be tested for. Decision procedures were invented after the pioneering work of Frege and Russell was finished.

About *Symlog*

Decision procedures and natural deduction make up what has become the canonical version of modern introductory logic. The chapters which follow are now going to present this version to you in a new and enterprising way. They are designed to be read and assimilated with the help of the logic program called *Symlog*, which will provide the means of harnessing the power of a personal computer to learn formal logic. *Symlog* has a lot to offer, as you will discover in the coming chapters. Because *Symlog* is an interactive computer program, you will increase your chances of learning deductive logic quickly, thoroughly, skillfully and with far greater assurance than you could gain by merely studying a logic textbook. *Symlog* will be your electronic guide and tutor—the 'friend' mentioned by Leibniz whom you can summon. The program will not only tell you where you have made a mistake in solving a problem but also describe the mistake. If you cannot see the next step when constructing a valid argument, using the rules of natural deduction, *Symlog* will suggest a step and even explain why the suggestion makes sense. It also has the capacity of generating an endless stream of problems to work on at a level which you select. This feature will enable you to challenge yourself and build confidence, so that you can correctly judge when you have mastered the concepts of each new chapter. Instead of having to hand in logic exercises and wait for your teacher to mark them, you will get results in a matter of seconds, and if there are mistakes the program will describe them. In short, *Symlog* will work hard and tirelessly for you, but it will not do the work that you should do yourself.

Both this book and the computer program, then, are integral to learning formal logic effectively. The book will introduce and progressively refine your understanding of the basic concepts of deductive logic, and *Symlog* will help embed that knowledge by guiding you through practical routines meant to sharpen the analytical skills needed. Remember, logic is a science which is both theoretical and applied. One side enlarges your understanding; the other engages it through practice. Do not consider *Symlog*, therefore, to be a mere illustration of what is explained in the book, nor the book itself to be little more than a computer manual whose job is to introduce the program. In principle, although you could come to know much about formal logic simply by reading this book, your powers of analysis, which are essential to a full understanding, would remain poorly developed. So it is clearly in your interest to get this program working for you; the book will show how to get the most out of it, with its illustrations and step-by-step instruction. Working with *Symlog* requires no knowledge of computer theory or programming. It is not even necessary for you to have worked on a personal computer (PC) already. Before long, however, you will be impressed by your own efforts when you see logic problems growing toward their solution on the computer screen. The more practice, the better you will become at formal logic. Even though you will not want to give up pencil and paper while working on problems, there is a good chance that you will come to rely on the program itself as a more efficient way of doing logic.

Even after you have mastered all the chapters of this book, the program remains available for putting your logical expertise to work. For instance, it will tell you promptly whether an argument that intrigues you is deductively valid, and it will also assist in constructing proofs for your own arguments in case you get stuck. We hope you will come to think of *Symlog* as a handy tool for deductive reasoning—a genuine logic calculator—a device that would have probably impressed Leibniz and anyone of his time who used the abacus.

Preliminaries to the Text

Exercises

The concepts of formal logic are best learned through examples, and the only way to develop skills to apply these concepts is by doing exercises. This book has many examples to study and problems to solve, both sorts making good use of your computer and *Symlog*. As far as examples are concerned, here is the procedure to expect: All the main stages of an example are keyed to illustrations in the text. You will be not only studying each example in the text but also working interactively with *Symlog* while reading. (Or you may prefer reading the material in the text first and then working with *Symlog*.) Once a concept or technique has been introduced, you will be given problems to work on—simpler ones within each section, more challenging exercises at the end of each section. Many of the problems (identified by name) are also stored on disk so that you can call them up and begin working without having to copy (more about this in Chapter 1, '*Symlog*'s Tools'). Answers to odd-numbered exercises (1, 3, 5. etc.; a, c, e etc.) will be found at the end of the book. Most of the exercises were solved with *Symlog* (the text clearly suggests which ones should not be attempted with the program—e.g., theory related); actually, many of the derivations were solved by *Symlog*'s natural deduction theorem prover.

Typography

The font for most of the text—the text you are now reading—is Aster. We write in Helvetica that text which would appear on your computer's screen or which refers to special terms used for the description of the software. We also use this device to avoid constant quoting (i.e., we write P & Q instead of 'P & Q'). Finally, we formally introduce important terms and phrases by writing them in **boldface.**

Getting Started

If you have a basic working knowledge of computers and want to install *Symlog* in your PC, please turn to Appendix A. (This appendix also contains information about hardware requirements and the installation of *Symlog* on a network for multiple users.) If you are new to computers, please read Appendix B. This appendix gives an overview of the workings of personal computers and some essential information about computer files, which will help you to navigate with *Symlog*. Appendix B also describes the keyboard assignments used by *Symlog*. Having found what you wanted or needed to know in appendices A and B, you are ready to find out more about *Symlog* itself by reading Chapter 1, '*Symlog*'s Tools.' We wish you success with *Symlog* and, above all, with your study of formal logic!

1

Symlog's Tools

Symlog is a computer program designed to help you master the fundamentals of symbolic logic. What symbolic logic is and what it does will become clear as you work your way through the program itself, guided by the examples and the accompanying discussion that you will find in the chapters that follow. In this chapter, however, we want to tell you something about how you are going to be learning symbolic logic. It will make you familiar with some of *Symlog*'s features and routines. You will find yourself becoming quickly comfortable with them, especially if you are able to move back and forth between the textbook and your computer, so we suggest that you keep this textbook open on your lap or next to your keyboard and that you pause from time to time for some practice on the screen. This is the best way to begin learning *Symlog*. In fact, practice is the key to success in learning symbolic logic. You will learn this subject well if you apply its rules to the exercises we give; if you build up your knowledge steadily by learning only a bit at a time, instead of trying to force-feed yourself large chunks of material just before a test; and above all if you are honest with yourself in discovering where your weaknesses lie. The knowledge of symbolic logic that you will be gaining from *Symlog* is similar to that which you could acquire from any good text in the area. It consists mainly of a set of skills rather than a collection of facts or an abstract theory, which is why practice is so important. Aristotle once said that there are some subjects that are best learned by doing. He used the example of learning to play the cithara, which was a stringed instrument much liked by the ancient Greeks. To become an accomplished player, a person does not have to know how citharas are manufactured or even to study musical theory. The right way to learn the cithara is by playing it. Much the same holds true for symbolic logic. With *Symlog*, however, your learning will be much easier than it would be with just a textbook. You will be able to write your work on the screen in front of you and have it checked immediately by the program. You will be able to get help from *Symlog* when you need it and keep a record of the work you have completed. The program will serve you like a personal assistant. By the way, history does not record whether Aristotle himself knew how to play the cithara, but we do know that he was an accomplished logician. We think he would have been delighted with *Symlog*, and we hope you will be too.

1.1 *Getting Started*

We assume that *Symlog* is ready to run on your personal computer (PC). If it is not, you will have to read Appendix A, which describes how to install *Symlog*, or else consult your course instructor. We also assume that you already possess the basic information about PCs and computer keyboards that you will need to start using *Symlog*. If you are new to computers or simply want to refresh your memory, you will find this information in Appendix B, together with some useful details about DOS, the disk operating system used by the many different software programs (including *Symlog*) that run on PCs. You will be operating *Symlog* through a standard PC keyboard and seeing the results on your computer screen. Most of the key assignments are probably familiar to you already: the alphanumeric keys, Space Bar, Backspace, Enter and Esc (escape) keys, Caps Lock, cursor keys, and so on, all function in the usual way for DOS programs. The special key assignments which *Symlog* gives to the Ctrl (control) key and to the Function keys, F1 to F10, will be introduced as needed in the text. (A complete summary of these assignments can be found in Appendix C.) When you call up *Symlog*, the program displays the screen depicted in Figure 1.1. This display remains in view for a few seconds and is then replaced by the Entry Point screen, which is similar to Figure 1.2, except that here we identify for you the different parts of the Entry Point screen.

Symlog's screen is divided into four parts. Mostly it consists of the Workspace, where you will be doing logic problems of many different kinds later on. Notice that there are two narrow bands which serve as the top and bottom borders of the Workspace. The top band is called the Information Line. This is where *Symlog* will show you, for example, the name of the particular problem you happen to be working on as well as other details which will be described in later chapters. The bottom band is called the Error Line. Whenever you set up a problem and follow it through, you will be following the same set of logical rules that *Symlog* knows by heart and never forgets. (After all, *Symlog* is not human!) Once in a while, however, you may make a

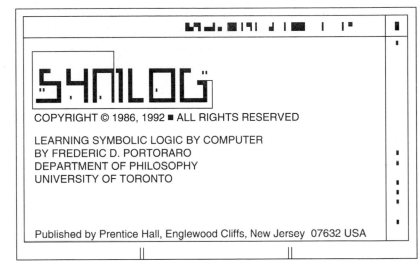

Figure 1.1

COPYRIGHT © 1986, 1992 ■ ALL RIGHTS RESERVED

LEARNING SYMBOLIC LOGIC BY COMPUTER
BY FREDERIC D. PORTORARO
DEPARTMENT OF PHILOSOPHY
UNIVERSITY OF TORONTO

Published by Prentice Hall, Englewood Cliffs, New Jersey 07632 USA

move which breaks one of these rules, in which case the program will quickly tell you. That is one of the purposes of the Error Line. There are a few others which you will see later on. The Message Line, located immediately below the Error Line, is used as a means of communication between you and *Symlog*. For instance, sometimes *Symlog* displays there explanatory messages that help clarify some of the program's features. Also, if *Symlog* needs confirmation to execute a certain command you have issued, it will ask you

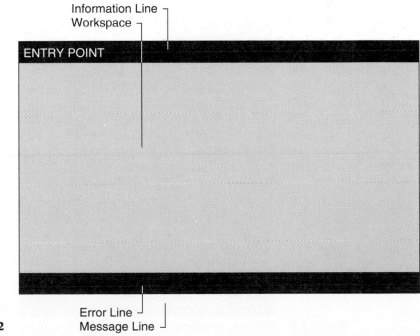

Figure 1.2

to confirm. Such questions, and other warning messages, will be displayed in the Message Line. Finally, when you are working on logic exercises, this line will display commands available to you.

1.2   *The OPTIONS Menu*

The Entry Point screen remains still until you invoke *Symlog*'s OPTIONS menu by pressing the function key F1. Pressing this key (please do so now) changes the display to *Symlog*'s OPTIONS menu, from which you will be able to select the type of work you want to do in logic or the sort of routine you want the program to carry out for you (Figure 1.3).

     By pressing the F1 key, you can summon the OPTIONS menu at virtually any time while you are operating *Symlog*. *Symlog*'s OPTIONS are selected by a two-step movement which will soon become automatic to you: Locate the specific OPTION you want by the keyboard's Arrow keys (also known as the Cursor keys) and then declare your choice to the program by the keyboard's Enter key. The **cursor** itself is simply a location marker on your screen. There are four Arrow keys, two for opening menus to the right or left and two for moving the cursor up or down. *Symlog* offers seven different menu OPTIONS (listed on your screen's Information Line). Notice that the one it has automatically chosen for you when you pressed F1 is called Environment, which would normally be the preferred option whenever you begin a session with *Symlog*. Directly underneath Environment are the specific areas—environments—of the program in which you can work (such as Truth-Tables and the Derivation Systems). There you can test out whether a certain compound statement is

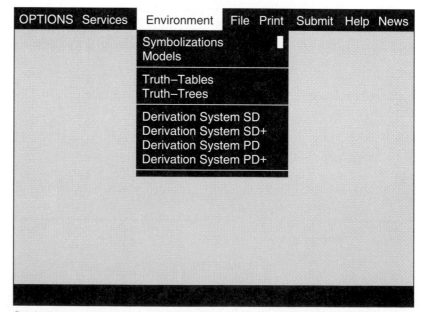

Figure 1.3   Symbolize statements, sets of statements, and arguments in symbolic logic

true or construct a valid argument according to the rules that apply to a given environment. Of course, we shall be describing the different environments in great detail in the following chapters. These various possibilities make up what is called a **pull-down menu.** Each of the main OPTIONS has its own menu. Notice that the flashing cursor stands just to the right of the first of the choices listed beneath the Environment menu. If you wanted to work in the Symbolizations environment, you would simply press the Enter key. If you wanted to choose one of the other environments, you would use the Up/Down Arrow keys and then press Enter. If you wanted to select another of the main OPTIONS altogether, you would first use the Right/Left Arrow keys to select it, then move the flashing cursor down its menu to the specific option you are interested in and then press Enter.

This is the way in which you will get *Symlog* to do a lot of useful work in a direct and easy manner that should make it unnecessary for you to remember a lot of commands or to take your eyes off the screen, once you have become familiar with the position of the Arrow keys (in computerese, the program is said to be 'menu driven'). It would be a good idea to take a few moments now to begin experimenting with these keys to see what changes they make on your screen. Notice that as you change the position of the cursor to a different item on the menu, a brief description of that item appears on the screen's Message Line. Use the Arrow keys to scroll up and down the menu and to switch back and forth between menus. If you press the wrong key by mistake and find yourself facing something you do not recognize, we suggest at this stage that you ask your instructor for help. If no help is available, you can always switch off your computer and start again.[1] Feel free now to experiment until you feel at home with *Symlog*'s OPTIONS menu.

Now that you have had a brief look at the Environment menu, it is time to find out a little bit more about *Symlog*'s other options as well as about the different environments of logic in which you will work. These remarks will be brief since we merely want to give you a quick tour of the program. When we speak of invoking one of these options we mean the sequence of moving to the menu you want, scrolling to that option and pressing the Enter key.

1.3 Services

The Services option offers a variety of useful services, all of which are identified in its pull-down menu, as shown in Figure 1.4. At any time while working in *Symlog* you can request these services and then, simply by pressing the Esc—escape—key, you will be returned to your work. (Note: the only time this action obviously will not occur is when the service Quit is selected.)

---

[1] You can 'reboot'—switch off and back on—your computer from the keyboard with the following key combination: Press first the Shift and Alt keys and then, while keeping them down, press the Del key.

```
┌─────────────────────────────────────────┐
│ Services                                  │
├───────────────────────────────────────────┤
│ Date/Time                              ▪  │
│ Note Pad                                  │
│ Environment Status                        │
│ Interactive/Noninteractive Mode           │
├───────────────────────────────────────────┤
│ Progress Report                           │
├───────────────────────────────────────────┤
│ Quit                                      │
└───────────────────────────────────────────┘
```

Figure 1.4

Date/Time

Date/Time makes *Symlog* display the computer's date and time at the top of your screen. You can request this service from *Symlog* whenever you wish.

Note Pad

The second service you can request is an electronic 'pad' on which to write brief notes about logic, reminders and so on. The Note Pad, when invoked, appears as in Figure 1.5 (with some sample notes). Once the Note Pad has been selected, you can jot down notes for yourself on it, 'hide' them and then resume working. If you have not exited from *Symlog*, your notes will reappear the next time you select the Note Pad. Try a sample note. We encourage you to make full use of it, especially when you have no pencil or paper on hand.

Environment Status

Symlog's Environment Status gives you information concerning the logical environment (i.e., the specific area of logic) in which you are working at the time and whether or not your mode of working is interactive (see below).

Interactive/Noninteractive Mode

By default, *Symlog* is in interactive mode, which partly means that if, for instance, you are working in one of the logical environments (Symbolizations, Models, Truth-Trees, Truth-Tables or any of the Derivation Systems) and you make a mistake, *Symlog* issues an error or a warning message. Thus, so to speak, *Symlog* is awake and alert when it is in its interactive mode. However, if *Symlog* is in its noninteractive mode, error messages, some warning messages and several other capabilities are turned off. You can still work in any of the logical environments, but *Symlog* will then become a silent partner. This noninteractive mode is useful, for example, if you want to see how well you know the subject being studied without getting any help from *Symlog*. Later you can have all your work checked and marked with notes and error messages by *Symlog* (this is the purpose of the Submit option).

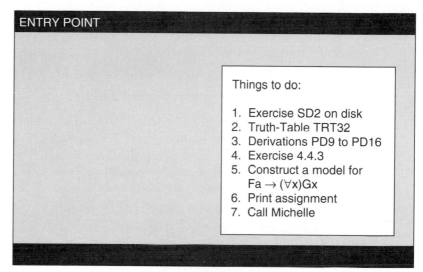

Figure 1.5

If *Symlog* is in the interactive mode and you select Interactive/Noninterac-tive Mode in the Services pull-down menu, the noninteractive mode is acti-vated. In contrast, selecting the Interactive/Noninteractive Mode when *Symlog* is in the noninteractive mode activates the interactive mode. That is, this par-ticular selection process operates as an on-off switch. If at any time you wish to know in what mode *Symlog* is working, you have only to select the Environment Status selection from the Services pull-down menu.

Progress Report

Symlog has many exercises stored on disk. Some of these form the basis of your Progress Report (they are the files called PR001 to PR150). Invoking this option makes *Symlog* display information about how many Progress Report Exercises have been successfully completed. The Progress Report is updated any time you sucessfully submit a 'PR' exercise with *Symlog*'s Submit option (described below). After you exit the Progress Report, you return to the point you left.

Quit

Quit allows you to exit the current environment or to exit *Symlog* altogether. Suppose you are working in the Derivation System SD environment and you decide to exit it. Open the Services pull-down menu and select Quit. *Symlog* warns you then that quitting the environment will destroy any work which you have not yet saved on your disk. Once you have confirmed that you want to quit the current environment, *Symlog* returns you to the Entry Point; if you change your mind and do not wish to quit, you can cancel your request.

However, if you are not in any of the environments but at the Entry Point itself, selecting Quit abandons *Symlog* and delivers you to the operating system of your computer. To return to *Symlog* then, you will have to restart the program.

1.4   *Environment*

The Environment option is the core of *Symlog*. This is the place where you do most of your work in symbolic logic. Like other disciplines, symbolic logic is divided into specific areas. *Symlog* allows you to work in these areas, or as they are called in *Symlog*, environments. (See Figure 1.6.)

Symbolizations

Symbolizations are translations of sentences of natural language (in this case, English) into the rigorously defined symbols of logic. *Symlog* presents the language of logic in two levels: sentential logic (SL) and predicate logic (PL). A module of the program—Symbolizations—is devoted to translations into SL and PL. A comprehensive discussion and further practice in symbolizing at both levels will be found in the textbook. Symbolizations are treated in Chapters 2 and 3 (SL) and Chapter 6 (PL).

Models

To test PL sentences for truth or falsity, *Symlog* makes it possible to construct 'experimental worlds' by using its Models environment. First, you decide what objects will belong to such a world and what their relationships will be; next, you proceed to investigate this world by asking *Symlog* questions formulated in the language of predicate logic (PL). Through its answers, the program will reveal facts about the world you have designed and help provide insight into the meaning of PL sentences. Models are covered in Chapter 9.

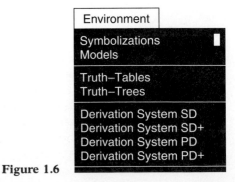

Figure 1.6

Truth-Tables

Truth-tables are a method of investigating the sentences of sentential logic (SL) to determine whether they are true or false or to find out whether arguments consisting of such sentences are valid or invalid. The method consists in assigning what are called truth-values to the simplest components of SL sentences to see how these affect the truth-values of the larger sentences to which they belong. In Chapter 2, you will learn how to construct and evaluate truth-tables. All your work can be done on the screens provided by *Symlog*. Truth-tables are covered in Chapters 2 and 3.

Truth-Trees

Truth-trees is a systematic method of analyzing sentences or sets of sentences into their simplest components. Although the objective is similar to that of truth-tables (to determine the validity or invalidity of arguments, say), the method of truth-trees is more comprehensive, because it applies to the sentences of both SL and PL. Your trees will be constructed on *Symlog*'s screen. Compound sentences will be 'deconstructed' before your eyes, with the help of the program's commands. Truth-trees are covered in Chapter 4 (SL) and Chapter 7 (PL).

Derivation Systems

Perhaps the heart of logic itself consists of doing proofs or, as it is known in *Symlog*, constructing derivations. The program and this text will guide you in acquiring this skill. Derivations are constructed according to clear rules of procedure. *Symlog* provides rules for derivations in both sentential and predicate logic. Within each area, there is a core set of rules (called system SD and system PD). Most of your efforts in proof construction will focus on these core rules. Once you have mastered them, you can work with an enriched set of rules, called SD+ and PD+, which will enable you to take shortcuts when constructing derivations. In all of these areas, you will want to work with *Symlog* interactively. Derivations are covered in Chapter 5 (SD, SD+) and Chapter 8 (PD, PD+).

1.5   *File*

If the OPTIONS menu is not already on your screen, press F1 to redisplay it and then use your Right/Left Arrow keys to move over to the File menu. Anyone already familiar with other programs written for PCs will recognize the items on this menu as being all file-handling routines. Think of a file as the computer equivalent of pages of paper. It is designed to hold data such as text, pictures or graphs. In *Symlog*, your data will take the form of logic problems, one problem per file. The program offers a full selection of problems to work on, and as your work progresses, you will create new files and store them on your disk, just as you would keep pages of completed problems in a loose-leaf binder. The File option gives you control over these documents, which are stored in your computer's file cabinet, the disk. The pull-down menu of File is depicted in Figure 1.7.

When stored on your disk, each file must have a unique name; that is, no two files in the same storage area may share the same name. *Symlog* follows certain conventions for naming files which are common to programs using DOS (please see Appendix B for details). Since some of the exercises in the text are already stored on disk, we have adopted a specific scheme for naming these files. For a given chapter, you will find two types of (disk) exercises: Learn Exercises and Progress Report Exercises. At specific points in the chapter you will be advised to solve one or more of the Learn problems; as the name indicates, their purpose is to reinforce the material being learned. All the Learn Exercises are already stored on disk, and their names will be given to you at the right time during the reading of the material. The Progress Report Exercises are drawn from the more challenging end-of-section exercises in the textbook.

Name

By invoking the Name option, you get *Symlog* to assign a name to your current work. A name can be given before you start working on a given problem or at any point after, but before such work can be stored as a file on your disk, it must be named. *Symlog* will prompt you about this, so do not worry. The name which you give to your current work is displayed on the top left of the screen.

Save

When Save is selected, *Symlog* records your current work on disk under the file name and returns you to where you were, so that you can continue working. Never forget, all your current work—*until it is saved*—exists only in the computer's temporary memory, called RAM (see Appendix B). Conse-

Figure 1.7

quently, if your computer is turned off (by accident, say, or because of a blackout) *before* your work is saved, it will disappear into thin air and you will have to restart the computer and redo the work. Try to develop the habit of saving your work at regular intervals; that way, if your computer loses power suddenly, you will have lost only a small portion of current work.

Saving a file under a name that belongs to a file already on disk will make *Symlog* overwrite the file in the disk with the one being saved; however, before *Symlog* overwrites the one on disk, it asks you to confirm. For instance, suppose that you are working with a file called PROOF26 and that you save it and continue working with it. Suppose that later you decide to save it again. *Symlog* notices that in the disk there is already a file called PROOF26 and that you are asking the program to save a file with the same name. *Symlog* asks you whether you are sure you want to get rid of the old PROOF26 and save instead the updated one. If you confirm your request, *Symlog* will overwrite the file PROOF26 in the disk with the one in your screen (i.e., with the one in the main memory of your computer system). If you cancel your request, *Symlog* will return you to where you were previously without saving your file.

Retrieve

The selection Retrieve allows you to bring back a particular file from the disk. When this option is selected, *Symlog* displays a list of files on the screen from which you can 'point and shoot'—choose—the file to be retrieved. The method also allows you to obtain a (blank) new file, in which case *Symlog* asks you for the name of the new file. (If the name corresponds to a file which already exists on the disk, *Symlog* will load it into the memory of your computer system. This feature, in effect, allows you to retrieve files by typing their names too.) When *Symlog* asks you for the name of the file but you do not specify one, *Symlog* will load the blank file with no name; you will need to name it before it can be saved, however. Note that to retrieve a file from the disk, you must first be in one of *Symlog*'s environments. If you attempt to retrieve a file without being in any environment (i.e., from the Entry Point), *Symlog* will display a message reminding you of this need. As the key combination Ctrl-R is the keyboard shortcut for Retrieve, pressing Ctrl-R immediately followed by Enter is all it takes to retrieve the 'next' exercise from the disk.

Create

By doing the end-of-section exercises you will increase your command of symbolic logic, yet sooner or later you will finish these and (we hope) look for more. That is when *Symlog* comes to the rescue with a particularly helpful service. Using its Create option you can request a fresh problem to work on—a problem which the program will think up for you on the spot. In principle, *Symlog* will supply an unending series of new exercises randomly generated in your computer (so you will never be at a loss for something to do). Create works at both the SL and PL levels of symbolic logic: It will serve up problems related to Truth-Tables, Truth-Trees, and all four of the Derivation Systems (SD and SD+, PD and PD+). Before creating an exercise for you, *Symlog* will ask you to choose the level of difficulty.

Directory

The selection Directory is used to obtain a directory—a listing—of the files contained on your disk. Selecting this option prompts *Symlog* to display a screen similar to Figure 1.8. *Symlog* will then ask you to type in a 'mask' for the directory. This is an optional step. If you type nothing but simply press the Enter key, the program will immediately give you a list of all the files you have saved so far. However, the purpose of the mask option is to narrow down the list somewhat by specifying just those files whose names match a particular mask—that is, a pattern. *Symlog* adds specific 'extensions' to the names you give to your files: TTB for truth-tables, TTR for truth-trees, DER for derivations and so on. To see just the truth-table files you have on your disk, simply enter the mask *.TTB; it stands for all those files which have the extension TTB. Similarly, to get a listing of all the derivations on your disk you would enter *.DER. Note that entering *.* would give you a listing of all the files on your disk regardless of either name or extension. As mentioned previously, if you do not enter anything when prompted for the Dir mask, *Symlog* will give you a directory of all the files in your disk, as if you had entered *.*

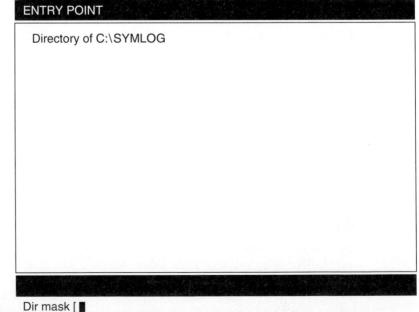

ENTRY POINT

Directory of C:\SYMLOG

Figure 1.8   Dir mask [▮

Copy

This selection allows you to duplicate any file stored on the disk. For instance, you could make a backup copy of all the exercises you have completed for safekeeping—not a bad idea, when you think of all the work you have put into it. To obtain a backup, invoke the Copy option and follow *Symlog*'s instructions on the Message Line.

Rename

If you want to change the name of a file on the disk, select the Rename option. Note that the difference between Name and Rename is that whereas the former allows you to change the name of your current work, the latter applies to files already on disk, not to the one on your screen (i.e., in the main memory of your computer). To rename a file, select the Rename option and follow *Symlog*'s instructions on the Message Line.

Erase

By invoking Erase you are, in effect, crumpling up a whole file and throwing it into the wastebasket. You would do so when you wanted to get rid of old work you no longer need. If your floppy disk becomes too full and you do not have another disk handy, you could make room for new files in this way. Be warned, though: Invoking Erase is an irreversible step. Thus, when you select this item and give the name of the file to be erased, *Symlog* will ask you on the Message Line to confirm your intention. If you do confirm, the file will be discarded.

Access

The Access option allows you to switch to other disk drives or directories. That is, it enables you to save or retrieve your work to or from other disk drives or directories. This option also allows multiple users of *Symlog* to communicate with a common external drive (sometimes called a file server) in a network of PCs. Such an arrangement would allow homework problem sets to be transferred directly to your own PC more quickly and efficiently than by handing out paper. Similarly, your course instructor may require you to hand in your homework assignment by saving it in a specific disk or directory. To illustrate, suppose that from now on you wanted to store and retrieve all your work to and from the floppy disk which is placed in your second disk drive (usually called the B: drive). Select Access, and when *Symlog* asks for the 'data directory,' enter the name of your drive, namely, B: (yes, the colon is part of the name). Similarly, if you wanted to access a hard disk whose name is F: (which forms part of a computer network), just enter F: at *Symlog*'s prompt.

Important tip: If you cannot retrieve any of the exercises already stored on disk once *Symlog* is up and running (e.g., selecting Retrieve displays a blank screen with no exercises listed), it is because they are probably on a different disk or directory. To gain access to them, use the Access option.

1.6 *Print*

Symlog offers two options for printing out your work (Figure 1.9): on paper—a so-called hard copy—or on disk.

To Printer

Invoking To Printer allows you to send your current work to the printer. Before printing your work, however, *Symlog* will offer two options regarding the quality of your printout: Draft or High Quality. Draft will give you a fast, readable copy containing everything essential in your work. Since printing with Draft Print is faster than using High-Quality Print, you may want to use it to get printouts of your rough work, or even of finished work if many people happen to be waiting to use the printer. High-Quality Print will deliver a more finished-looking version of your work. To get such results takes more of the printer's time, however, and sometimes is unnecessary. For example, you may have an unfinished problem that you want to complete on paper, or you may merely want copies of files for you own records rather than to hand in for credit.[2]

To Disk

Invoking To Disk allows you to 'print' your current work to a so-called ASCII text file on disk. (The name of the text file will be the name of your work with the extension TXT, as in PROOF5.TXT.) You can use this feature for obtaining files to be 'imported' into your word processor, perhaps for a customized printing, or to be sent via modem to a remote system for printing. As with the preceeding option, *Symlog* allows you to select the 'print' quality of the data sent to the text file.

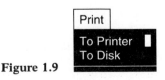

Figure 1.9

---

[2] Technical note: You may be forced to use the Draft Print option if the printer you are using does not support the so-called extended ASCII character set. In draft mode, the logic symbol ¬ is printed as ~, → as >, ≡ as =, ∃ as E, and ∀ as A.

1.7   *Submit*

Symlog does a lot more than manage files. Consider it as primarily a personal assistant or tutor in logic whose role is to be available to look over your work and check it for any errors. This role is the essence of *Symlog*. The first thing to keep in mind is that the program gives you control over when to ask for a check. When you are just beginning to work in one of the environment areas, you will probably want *Symlog* to check each step as you make it—just press the Enter key. Then, if you make a mistake, you will learn about it instantly on the Error Line and be able to correct it before proceeding. This way of working is called the interactive mode. *Symlog* is set up to run in the interactive mode whenever you invoke one of the options from the Environment menu. When you start using *Symlog* to learn logic symbolizations or truth-tables in Chapter 2, we will describe the kind of information the program gives you on the screen whenever it detects a mistake. For now, however, let us consider the other typical way of getting your work checked: the Submit Work option.

Submit Work

As mentioned, we recommend that you work with *Symlog* in the interactive mode; in that way, the program will warn you as soon as you make a mistake in the process of solving an exercise. However, once the exercise is completed, we strongly recommend that you submit it in its entirety with the Submit Work option. The program will then go to work at high speed and report the results on the Message Line. If there are no mistakes you will be told so, and any that it does discover will be flagged and given appropriate error messages. The Submit option can be invoked at any time during your work regardless of your working mode (interactive or nonineractive).

Alternatively, once you have built up your confidence, you may want to do one or two problems on your own—that is, without having *Symlog* look over your shoulder as you work. You are bound to be familiar with this method from completing problem sets and then handing them in to be corrected. The Submit option enables you to do much the same thing (Figure 1.10). Here is how you would proceed: First you would select an environment in which to work, then turn off the interactive mode (using Interactive/ Noninteractive Mode in Services), proceed to complete your problem and finally invoke Submit. As before, *Symlog* will flag and report any errors your work may contain. You may also want to follow the same procedure when practicing for a test.

Figure 1.10

1.8   *Help*

Four items available on the Help menu are intended to close any gap between *Symlog*'s program and the accompanying textbook (Figure 1.11). At first, you will be using the textbook to launch your work in one of the program's eight environments; eventually you will have enough momentum to explore that environment by doing problems on your PC; but even so, you may need some review or clarification about the scope of a rule of logic or the right combination of keys to press while doing a problem. The same need might arise when you switch from one environment to another in the course of a session or when you return to an environment covered earlier. The Logic Booklet and Reference Guide options are meant to assist you at such times. They provide summaries of what you have already studied in the textbook. Of course, they cannot replace your text, but there are bound to be times when you will find these options handy. With the third option, Proof Advisor, you can request expert advice when solving problems in *Symlog*'s derivation environments. The information available through these three options is restricted to what will help reinforce your work at your PC, but there are many interesting details of logic which are discussed only in the text. You will need to determine for yourself whether the on-screen Help is sufficient for your purposes or whether you have to return to the text. In many cases, the on-screen Help will be sufficient. Do not forget that it stands ready to be summoned. Finally, System Tour provides a good way to quickly become acquainted with the different parts of *Symlog*, especially the environments.

The Logic Booklet

The Logic Booklet selection—whose name alludes to *The Logic Book* by Bergmann, Moor, and Nelson—is a glossary of the fundamental concepts in symbolic logic. For instance, The Logic Booklet has information about functional connectives, truth-values, rules of logic and other concepts that you will learn in forthcoming chapters. When you select The Logic Booklet, *Symlog* will try to guess what kind of help you need, depending on the context; that is, *Symlog* offers what is called context-sensitive help. More precisely, *Symlog* presents in your screen information—definitions, rules of logic and so on—related to the environment you are currently working in. If you need it, you can ask for a table of contents so that you can choose other sections of The Logic Booklet you may be interested in.

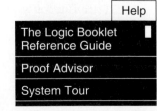

Figure 1.11

Reference Guide

You can invoke the Reference Guide whenever you have forgotten how a particular command in *Symlog* is to be executed. For instance, if you forget how to issue the Erase command while constructing a derivation in the Derivation System SD+, the Reference Guide has the needed information. Similarly, the Reference Guide explains what the different keyboard keys are used for. By the way, these commands can be more conveniently and quickly displayed by pressing the key F2.

Proof Advisor

Proof Advisor is one of *Symlog*'s jewels. This option is a so-called 'expert system,' which is capable of analyzing your derivation—proof—up to the point you have reached—up to the point, say, where you have gotten stuck—and then suggesting how to go on. Not only does Proof Advisor indicate the appropriate rule to apply (i.e., move to make), but it will also explain why its choice is a suitable one. In Proof Advisor, *Symlog* acts in the role of experienced tutor or guide. We believe it is priceless. But aim to use this option wisely: Invoke it only when you are *really* stuck; otherwise, you will simply be relying on the program's knowledge of logic instead of acquiring your own, and you will have merely learned how to be dependent. Proof Advisor can be more conveniently invoked within a derivation environment by pressing the function key F3.

System Tour

The System Tour is an ideal way to quickly become familiar with the multiple options that *Symlog* offers, especially the different logical environments you will study. Take the whole tour now to gain a sense of how you will be using *Symlog* in your learning of logic; take one part at a time later when the text introduces you to each of the environments.

1.9 *News*

News is the last option in the OPTIONS menu, and as you can see in Figure 1.12, its pull-down menu contains four selections. The various items on this menu are especially useful when *Symlog* is installed in a local area network. Mailbox enables you to read messages sent to you by the teacher or other people using the network. Newsletter contains items of interest to all the users, such as the announcement of a special lecture, the course schedule, details about office hours and so on. Bibliography could list further information about a topic in the course or supplementary readings on logic. Just how these options would be employed would depend on the person responsible for implementing *Symlog* in your institution.

Figure 1.12

Mailbox

Symlog allows you to read messages sent to you by other people using *Symlog* (or other programs) in the same computer network. For instance, the Mailbox can be used to read important notices left by the person in charge of your course; thus, it is advisable to check your mail often.

Suggestions

The Suggestions feature is useful to let instructors know how *Symlog* could be improved or what other features you would like to see implemented in the program. Also, it is a good means of reporting any errors in the text or malfunctionings in the program. For this use, invoke the Suggestions option and follow *Symlog*'s instructions.

Newsletter

The Newsletter keeps you up to date about developments in logic you might find interesting, about logic-related conferences held at your university or at other universities, about new logic or logic-related books and journals in the market and so forth.

Bibliography

The Bibliography is a listing of books or papers on logic and related fields. This option is useful in case you want further references or secondary readings to expand your knowledge of logic.

We hope that by now you are acquainted with the different parts of *Symlog* and its features. Remember, to make use of them, they must be accessed through the OPTIONS menu. Recall that at any time, pressing F1 will summon the OPTIONS menu and pressing Esc will make it disappear. If you are familiar with the system of pull-down menus, you can now begin to study symbolic logic with the help of *Symlog*. To be sure, *Symlog* has some other capabilities that have not been explained yet; they will be introduced in the chapters that follow.

2

Sentences and Truth-Tables

The study of formal logic begins with statements. Everyone is already familiar with the idea of a statement in ordinary language. What logic does is to make it more precise. Statements and their relations are the subject matter of propositional logic, also known as sentential logic. In this chapter we start to examine them, first while reading the text and then on the screen with the help of *Symlog*. These two methods of study reinforce each other, so that by the end of the chapter you should have a clearer understanding of how logic looks at statements as well as some experience in using the truth-table technique to analyze them. This same technique will be used in the next chapter to look at arguments and their properties. We begin by giving a rough description of statements in general and of the difference between simple and compound statements, aiming as we proceed for greater degrees of exactness. Thus, both this chapter and the next conclude with a set of formal definitions of SL concepts.

2.1 What Statements Are

Ordinary language uses sentences for an enormous number of purposes. Take a moment to think of some of the ways you might have used sentences just today. Perhaps you wished someone 'Good Morning,' complained about your breakfast (or about not having had it), made an agreement to meet a friend, passed on the latest news about another friend, asked a question in

class, maybe tried to answer one or wondered to yourself what you were going to be doing this evening. The list may not be endless, but if you stopped
to mark down each case of using a sentence in an average day, the list
would be very, very long. However, it takes special effort to focus our attention on just *how* we use a particular sentence. Daily life usually does not require such effort, but formal logic does.

To bring out some of the differences in sentence use which logic finds
important, let us look at a few examples. In each of the following cases,
imagine yourself either using the sentence or hearing someone else using it:

(a) Please close the door!
(b) Your car has a flat tire.
(c) I name this kayak Titanic!
(d) Are you going to the surprise party for Marianne?
(e) I'm bored.

These examples can be sorted out by considering what the words do in a
typical case. For instance, example (a) would count as a request or perhaps,
depending on circumstances, as a politely given command. However, the
sort of thing that (a) does strikes us as quite different from that which is
happening in (e). Someone would use (e) to express a particular feeling. In
contrast, asking a question—which is what (d) does—need not involve expressing any feeling at all, and the same holds for (b). You can inform someone about a flat tire, and you can even do so emphatically, without expressing any feeling about the matter. What (b) aims to do is to give information.
In this respect it is like (e), despite their difference in expressing feeling. As
for sentence (c) it does not provide information or give a command or ask a
question. When you name your kayak you might well have certain feelings
at the same time, but that certainly is not the real point of using such
words. The point is to christen the boat, to bestow on it the name by which
your kayak is to be known.

So far, then, we have seen three important differences in sentence use.
First, sentences can be used to perform actions like making requests, giving
commands, asking questions, christening boats, and so on. Second, they can
be expressed with a greater or lesser degree of feeling. Third, they make
claims. Since formal logic takes no interest in *how* language is used to express feelings, we are going to remove that use from our discussion. True,
arguments are often advanced with strong feeling and logic is supposed to
be concerned with arguments, but from the standpoint of formal logic, feelings are just something that accompany arguments: They are incidental,
not part of their substance. That leaves two different sorts of use, concerning actions and claims. At first glance, the difference between these may not
seem to be great; in fact, it may not seem clear where the line is to be
drawn. What is the difference between giving an order and giving information? Cannot someone make a request as well as make a claim?

The best way to sharpen the difference is to distinguish between the act of giving information and the content of that information, between speaking the words of a sentence and what we use the words to say. Just as there are lots of different kinds of actions that can be performed by words, there are many different ways of making a claim. For instance, you could inform someone that he has a flat tire or remind him of the fact if he already knows it or even deceive him by saying that he has a flat tire when he does not. However, these different intentions are not what primarily interests logic. When sentences are used to make claims, logic strives to isolate their content; that is, it strives to isolate *what* the sentence states, not *how* it is stated or the *purpose* of stating it. One reason for this distinction is that several sentences can be used to make the same claim; they can have identical content. For example, suppose I am waiting at a red light when another driver pulls up alongside me, rolls down her window and shouts, 'Your car has a flat tire!' My wife asks me what the matter is and I reply, 'We have a flat tire' and then pull off to the side of the road for repair. Being a hapless academic, easily confused by events outside logic, I yield the tire wrench to my able wife, explaining to another driver who stops to offer help, 'Our car has a flat tire.' Each of these three sentences performs a different task, being directed to different people; yet each says the same thing. This sort of fact, namely, that each sentence states the same thing, is important to formal logic. What mainly interests logic when sentences are used are the claims they might contain. Logic calls these claims **statements.**

Let us glance back for a moment at the five examples given earlier and examine them from this selective viewpoint. We can see that (b) involves a statement. By the same standard, the only other claim-making sentence is (e). Saying 'I'm bored' makes a claim, however strong the feeling expressed by these words. Perhaps what is crucial to you when you utter this sentence is making sure that everyone around knows how you feel. No matter. What logic notices is the claim. This example also reveals that a statement can be about something private or personal as well as about something as public as a flat tire. Statements can be about things in the past or future as well as the present and also about abstract things like numbers and sets. No limits are set by logic itself to our claims, although it can show that some statements are 'illogical' and that others do not deserve to be called statements at all because they are really pieces of nonsense.

To avoid detouring into matters less important to formal logic, we will not pursue the topic of *how* sentences make claims. The examples we present will be noncontroversial. To illustrate, the following are examples of claim-making sentences:

The earth goes around the sun.
Grass is blue.
Ottawa is the capital of Canada.
$1 + 1 = 2$
Electrons have no charge.

It is useful to keep in mind that formal logic did not discover statements. Nor did it invent them. The concept of a statement merely emphasizes a particular role played by sentences and thus helps filter out other aspects of language use. Focusing on the content of a claim, on the statement being made, is an everyday practice which logic has raised to the level of a science. Formal logic aims to build a certain picture of language which, although much simplified, is an accurate, rigorous and informative account of statements and their relations. Think of natural language as a modern, congested city and of logic as a road map that helps you locate where things are. Even if you have lived there all your life you are likely to find the map useful. It gives the names of the streets and shows you how these are related, but it tells you nothing about the buildings or about the way the inhabitants live. A good map does not have to provide that sort of information to help you navigate through the city.

Exercises

2.1.1 Which of the following are claim-making sentences?
  a. Do you have the time, please?
  b. I have a headache.
  c. There is no business like show business.
  d. If I were rich . . .
  e. $E = mc^2$
  f. Rome is the capital of France.
  g. Attention!
  h. Beware of the dog.
  i. $1 + 1 = 7$
  j. It is not the case that it isn't raining.
  k. Suzy and Peter are in love.
  l. 1, 2, 3, Go!
  m. Grass is not blue but the moon is made of cheese.
  n. Bob Wilson
  o. God exists.

2.2   Truth-Values

When a sentence is used to make a claim, we can say that the claim is either **true** or **false.** That is, the statement is either true or false, not the sentence that expresses the claim. By itself, a sentence is just a string of words which only begins to say something true or false when it is applied. This requirement is quite familiar to us from everyday language. The words 'The car has a flat tire!' do not count as a claim until we know what car is being referred to, even though we understand what every word in the sentence means; but when we do know what car is being referred to, then we could begin to find out whether the statement is true or not. The result depends entirely on whether the car in question does have a flat tire. This example illustrates the relationship between statements and what they aim to describe. Statements identify possible situations: If the situation is the case then the statement describing it is true; otherwise it is false. The truth or falsity of each of our two examples depends on what the situation is. The woman who says, 'I'm bored' speaks the truth if and only if she is bored.

Situations are often called **facts,** and as is commonly said, facts are what make statements true or false. However, it is important to realize that not all facts are neat and simple like having a certain feeling or a tire being flat. Take a moment to think about the following examples. It is a fact that the earth revolves around the sun, that the earth is experiencing a warming trend, that the average North American couple has (let us say) 2.15 children and that the force of gravity between two bodies increases or decreases proportionally with the square of their distance. As you can see from such examples, facts can be rather complicated. The average couple, for instance, is a mathematical construct. Real children are not made up of decimal parts. Sometimes, therefore, the statements which are used to express facts need to be unpacked to make it clear to us what their truth really depends on. However, the job of unpacking statements for the sake of actually finding out whether they are true does not belong to formal logic. The methods people use for discovering facts range from simple ones such as inspecting a car's tires to sophisticated ones such as statistically analyzing a whole mass of sociological data. Logic does not study such methods. It assumes that in cases like these there is some fact or group of facts which would determine whether the corresponding description is true or false. (Of course, there is no attempt to prove this assumption—it is merely assumed.) Another thing worth noticing is that the truth of a particular statement does not depend on whether someone actually knows or even believes it to be true. If this assertion seems puzzling to you, perhaps you are thinking of examples like the flat tire, where it is hard to imagine how a person on the scene could fail to know whether or not the particular statement is true. All the same, there is an important difference between a statement's being true and our finding out that it is, even when we cannot help finding out. This difference is not any more real, it just becomes more obvious whenever we happen to be ignorant of what the facts are and do not know what to believe. Consider this example: Was Mozart poisoned to death? We can be sure of at least three things here and probably no more: that the facts give a decisive answer to this question, that the answer is true or false and that we have no idea which it is.

Statements, be they true or false, are the bedrock of SL. SL—which is short for sentential language—is a formal language specifically designed to represent statements, which are further classified as either simple or compound. In SL, the basic units are called **simple statements:** We leave these unanalyzed. They help form compound statements, which will be discussed in the next section. All the examples of statements given so far are simple statements. So,

> Your car has a flat tire.
> Ottawa is the capital of Canada.
> The earth goes around the sun.
> I'm bored.

are cases of simple statements, whereas, as we will soon discover,

> Ottawa is the capital of Canada and the earth goes around the sun.
> Either your car has a flat tire or it hasn't.

are examples of compound statements. In SL, simple statements are always referred to by letters of the alphabet, a different letter for each distinct statement. In *Symlog*, we will use only uppercase letters, such as A, B, C and so on. Where convenient, you can select a letter which serves to abbreviate some key word or other in the statement it stands for. For instance, you could make the letter T stand for 'Your car has a flat tire,' B for 'I'm bored' and C for 'The average couple has 2.15 children.' Or you could have C represent the first of these statements. Just remember that you need to be consistent. When used in the same context, a letter—say C—cannot represent more than one statement. Hence, in a given context, C cannot represent both 'Your car has a flat tire' and 'The average couple has 2.15 children.' To use these letters correctly, however, it is not necessary to have a specific context in mind. An instance of P by itself, unassociated with a particular statement, will stand for any simple statement whatever; if it happens to occur along with Q (which has not been assigned to a statement either), then Q will likewise be understood to represent any particular statement. An analogy will perhaps clarify this point. When working with numbers, you can let the variables x and y stand for, say, the numbers 2 and 5, respectively. However, to study algebraic equations such as $x + y = y + x$, it is not necessary to have x and y take on specific values.

The symbols A, B, C, P, Q and so on are all sentences of SL and are meant to represent simple statements. Just how many statements are there? Actually, there are infinitely many, but in this text and while working with *Symlog* we will mainly deal with small clusters of them at one time; and since the letters themselves can be reassigned to represent different simple statements in different contexts, we will not run out of ready vocabulary for the work we want to do. (Later we will describe an infinite list of distinct letters; this detail would only get in the way here.) Also, as you will see, SL is restricted to compound sentences of finite length, that is, to sentences which are capable of being both explicitly represented and completely analyzed. This restriction is not peculiar to *Symlog*, however.

We are now going to give the first details of a **semantic** account of simple statements. Here is how *Symlog*—and formal logic generally—looks at such statements: Every simple statement has one of two **truth-values;** that is, it is either true or false. No simple statement can lack a truth-value or have both at the same time. It is possible, of course, for circumstances to change to the point where a particular statement's truth-value must be revised. An example will make this clear. Consider the simple statement 'I am bald,' which you express about yourself. Right now, you may declare this statement an outright falsehood. However, in 40 years' time the truth-value (like the appearance of your head) may be quite different. What we are able to do for a simple statement like this is to imagine circumstances in which it would have the same or a different truth-value from the one it has now. But there are many statements whose truth-value now we do not know; in fact, formal logic does not even need to know the actual truth-value. To describe any statement, there is a general way which covers all the possible truth-values it can have. For simple statements denoted by A or B and so on, *Symlog* uses the following truth-value schema:

A
T
F

Here the symbol T stands for the truth-value of being true and F for that of being false. Together, they cover all possible situations since whatever simple statement A represents and whatever the circumstances happen to be, it is going to be either true or false. Hence, a given sentence of SL can take on either the truth-value T or the truth-value F (but not both), and this covers all the possibilities for truth-value assignments to a sentence of SL. In the next section, this semantic account will be extended to compound sentences. Before you read on, however, we suggest that you turn to the exercises for this section; these will give you some practice at distinguishing statements from nonstatements and at recognizing when different sentences make the same statement.

Exercises

2.2.1 Which of the following have a truth-value?
   a. Open the door, please.
   b. I still have a headache.
   c. The winning number for next week will be 630456.
   d. 2 is even but 6 is not.
   e. Is π an irrational number?

     f. What about the square root of 2?

     g. The digit in the five millionth place in the decimal expansion of π is a 7.

     h. Don't do this ever again.

     i. Your answer to question (c) above is probably correct.

     j. I am quite confident that you will enjoy studying logic.

2.2.2 Recall that a statement purports to make a claim. Which of the following are statements and which are not?

     a. The capital of France is Paris.

     b. Whoever invests in gold is making a sound financial decision.

     c. $2 + 3 = 7$

     d. Can anybody help me with this question?

     e. Hallelujah!

     f. No news is good news.

     g. Rome is the capital of Bulgaria.

     h. Is cold fusion possible?

     i. One, two, three . . .

     j. Although Gina likes dancing, she will not go to Bill's birthday party.

2.2.3 Explain what is being expressed by the following statements. Which are making the same claim?

     a. Only Peter eats apples.

     b. Peter only eats apples.

     c. Peter eats only apples.

     d. Only Peter eats only apples.

     e. Peter eats apples.

2.2.4 Place the sentences which make the same statement in the same group.

     a. Arthur smokes and Fred does not smoke.

     b. Arthur smokes but Fred doesn't.

     c. At least one of them smokes.

     d. Both are smokers.

     e. Arthur smokes all he wants but Fred won't even touch it.

     f. Fred isn't a smoker but Arthur is.

     g. Neither of them smokes.

     h. If someone is polluting the atmosphere, Arthur and Fred are the ones.

     i. Fred smokes or Arthur does.

     j. Fred doesn't smoke, and fortunately, Arthur doesn't either.

2.2.5 Place the sentences which make the same statement in the same group.

     a. John is happy.

     b. Lucy is happy; however, John is not.

    c. If John is happy then so is Lucy.

    d. John isn't sad.

    e. Lucy is happy assuming that John is.

    f. Lucy and John are happy.

    g. John is sad.

    h. John is sad but Lucy isn't.

    i. It isn't the case that John isn't sad.

    j. John is happy and Lucy feels the same.

2.3 Compound Statements

Two or more simple statements are said to be **logically independent** of one another in the sense that the truth or falsity of any one of them has no bearing on the truth or falsity of any other. In SL, all simple sentences are logically independent. Another way of putting this, which can be succinctly shown for two simple sentences A and B, is that it is possible for them to have any combination of truth-values together. Schematically,

A	B
T	T
T	F
F	T
F	F

This is a comprehensive schema of truth-values for any two simple statements represented (by this pair of sentence letters). It covers the whole range of possibilities—whatever the facts happen to be. The schema can be extended to cover any finite number of sentence letters (the method for doing so will be given later on). Here, for instance, is the schema for a group of three:

A	B	C
T	T	T
T	T	F
T	F	T
T	F	F
F	T	T
F	T	F
F	F	T
F	F	F

    The schematic display of truth-values makes it easy to define the five different kinds of compound sentences—to represent **compound state-**

ments—which are built up from simpler ones by what are called **logical connectives.** These compounds depend on the truth-values of their constituents. They are the main subject matter of SL and are the counterparts of sentences which are quite familiar from ordinary language. The compounds are identified in terms of their logical connectives: **negation, conjunction, disjunction, conditional** and **biconditional.** All five will now be described briefly in terms of their distinctive patterns of truth-values, with a few points added as we go along regarding their meaning in ordinary language. However, in the next chapter you will find a much fuller discussion of how to translate these compounds from ordinary language into symbolic notation and back. Right now, our concern is with what is sometimes called the semantics of compound statements, namely, their **truth-conditions.** The distinctive pattern of truth-values which characterizes each of the five is commonly referred to as a **truth-table.** For the sake of uniformity and to highlight important differences, we are going to use only two sentence letters, A and B, which might as well stand for the statements 'Anne is going to the zoo' and 'Bob is going to the zoo.'

Negation

Symbolic Form:[1]   ¬A

Truth-table:

A	¬A
T	F
F	T

Translations: not A; it is false that A

Using the ¬ symbol in front of a sentence forms the negation of that sentence. Whichever truth-value a given sentence has, negating it produces a compound sentence, namely, its negation, with the other truth-value. In other words, as you can see in the preceding table, negating 'flips' the truth-value of the sentence it applies to. If it is false that Anne is going to the zoo (i.e., if A has the truth-value F), then ¬A has the truth-value T. Negating a sentence always has this effect. To continue this example: Since ¬A has the truth-value T, ¬¬A (like A itself) is F. Any compound sentence of any of the five types (negation, conjunction, disjunction, conditional and biconditional), however long it is, is able to be negated, but the ultimate or 'atomic' component(s) of a negation will always be sentence letters.

   The negation symbol (sometimes called a **tilde**) always precedes the sentence it negates; it is never meaningfully used after a sentence (as in A¬) or by itself. The following expressions do not meet these requirements and

---

[1] ~A, A̅ and -A are alternative notations used in some textbooks but they are not recognized by *Symlog.*

are therefore counted as meaningless by *Symlog:* A¬, ¬¬¬, ¬A¬, ¬a. To be clear about these requirements, you should ask yourself what is wrong in each of these cases. Note that ¬ only needs one sentence (say A) to form a negated sentence (namely, ¬A); thus the tilde ¬ is said to be a **unary** or **monadic** connective. The rules for using the negation symbol in formal logic are much narrower than those found in ordinary language. You will find this situation recurring throughout your study of logic. Ordinary language offers a great variety of ways of expressing the same thing, whereas formal logic makes do with as small a number of expressions as possible and restricts them to well-defined limits. For example, here are some alternatives for translating the sentence ¬A of SL into ordinary language:

> Anne is not going to the zoo.
> That Anne is going to the zoo isn't true.
> It's not a fact that Anne is going to the zoo.
> No, Anne isn't going to the zoo.

Notice that the last case, unlike ¬¬A, is not a double negative.

Conjunction

Symbolic Form:[2]   A & B

Truth-table:

A B	A & B
T T	T
T F	F
F T	F
F F	F

Translations: A and B; both A and B

Unlike negation, conjunction requires two sentences, called **conjuncts,** to make up a compound; the same also holds for the next three logical connectives that we will discuss. For this reason the four are sometimes called **binary** or **dyadic** connectives, meaning that their role is to bring together a pair of sentences to form a compound. The two need not be different sentences—for example, A & A is a legitimate (though uncommon) example of a conjunction. The special differences among the four types of binary compound appear in sharp contrast when their truth-tables are compared.

Take a moment to inspect the truth-table for conjunction. A short while back you saw the same pattern of truth-values for a pair of simple sentences (namely, the pattern TT-TF-FT-FF). This pattern is what occupies

---

[2] A ∧ B, A   B and AB are alternative notations but are not recognized by *Symlog.*

the left-hand side of the table. It represents the set of all possible combinations of truth-values for the pair of sentences A and B. These are called **truth-value assignments.** A compound sentence A & B is T on just one truth-value assignment: when both of the conjuncts are T. In all other cases (i.e., where one or both of the conjuncts are F), the compound sentence itself is F. The right-hand side of the table represents the truth-values of A & B relative to these assignments. Together, they constitute the truth-conditions for conjunction. Compare them with the truth-conditions for any atomic sentence by itself, such as B, which is T in only one case; similarly, A & B is T in one case alone, when both of its components are T.

Whenever a conjunction is T, therefore, its conjuncts are also T. But what sorts of sentences can be conjuncts in a conjunction? The answer is that any sentence of SL can be, whether atomic or compound. Thus, we will need to use punctuation in the language of SL to mark off clearly what the component sentences of a compound are when the components themselves are compounds. There is a convention in formal logic which *Symlog* follows of using parentheses (and brackets) for the punctuation of compound sentences. These rules for punctuation are to be given later in full detail, and all we want to do now is to give you a feel for how to use them. You can easily see the important difference parentheses make in the following example: Whereas ¬A & B represents the statement

Anne isn't going to the zoo but Bob is.

the sentence ¬(A & B) represents the statement

It's false that both Bob and Anne are going to the zoo.

The first of these compound sentences is a conjunction, one of whose conjuncts is a negation; the second sentence is the negation of a conjunction. Let us assume that both sentences are T. Then, according to the first sentence, ¬A and B are both T. But since ¬(A & B) is also T, the conjunction which it negates, A & B, has to be F. Remember that a conjunction can be F on any of three different truth-value assignments. So the second sentence does not tell you that B is T, whereas the first one does; therefore, the two sentences do not have the same meaning. Of course, you already recognized this difference when you understood the two English statements. One purpose of using parentheses is to preserve distinctions that we often take for granted in ordinary language because we can make these distinctions with such ease. Now let us bring together the two sentences into a conjunction:

(¬A & B) & ¬(A & B)

As you can see, another pair of parentheses is required to set off the conjunction of ¬A and B as a conjunct in a larger conjunction. This example helps show that the use of parentheses follows commonsense rules, the most fundamental of which is that in every compound sentence containing more than one connective, only one connective can be dominant. In this example, the ampersand connecting the sentences ¬A & B and ¬(A & B) is the dominant connective. Even when three simple sentences are conjoined, one of the connectives has to rank over the others. For example, take the famous saying of Julius Caesar, 'I came, I saw, I conquered.' Let these statements be represented by C, S, and Q, respectively. Then, if Caesar were using the language SL, he could have written C & (S & Q); or he could have written (C & S) & Q. (It does not matter which since formal logic treats them as saying the same thing.) But if Caesar had written C & S & Q he would have broken a grammatical rule of SL, which is a pretty serious thing for a famous Roman general to do.

The grammatical rules of SL amount to a very simple requirement. No matter how complicated the structure of a compound, it must be possible to identify it unambiguously as either a negation or conjunction or one of the other compounds. Also, its components must be clearly identifiable, with no confusion about what their structure is, right down to the level of atomic sentences. But sentences like A, B and ¬A do not need to be surrounded by parentheses because no ambiguity arises from omitting them. Neither are parentheses needed to separate the negation signs in a double (or more) negation. Each of the following examples (with one exception) breaks one or another of the rules we have been describing. Ask yourself, What's wrong with it? (You will find the answers in the footnote below, but try first to figure them out before looking.) (1) A¬ & B; (2) B & A; (3) & B; (4) A & ¬(BC); (5) ¬¬(A & B & ¬C).[3] Here, finally, are a few alternative translations to the sentence A & B:

Anne and Bob are both going to the zoo.

Anne is going to the zoo; so is Bob.

Anne is going to the zoo; Bob is going to the zoo.

Although Anne is going to the zoo, Bob is too.

There will be a fuller discussion of translations involving conjunctions in the next chapter.

---

[3] Answer: (1) ¬& is a meaningless sequence of connectives; (2) this one is correct; (3) a sentence is missing to the left of &; (4) an ampersand is missing between B and C in (BC); and (5) either A & B or B & ¬C should be surrounded by parentheses.

Disjunction

Symbolic Form:[4]   A ∨ B

Truth-table:

A B	A ∨ B
T T	T
T F	T
F T	T
F F	F

Translations: A or B; either A or B

The component sentences in a disjunction (the two sentences flanking the ∨—also known as the **wedge**) are called **disjuncts.** In ordinary language, we use two different senses of 'either . . . or,' although this rarely causes any confusion. You can detect this difference in the following two examples:

(1) John Glenn or Neil Armstrong was an astronaut.
(2) John Glenn or Neil Armstrong was the first man to walk on the moon.

In the case of (1), it is possible for both of the disjuncts to be true: That John Glenn was an astronaut and Neil Armstrong was an astronaut are (as a matter of fact) true. But the two disjuncts in example (2) cannot both be true. The truth of one would exclude that of the other. (Thus, strictly speaking, the disjuncts in (2) cannot be counted as simple statements because they are not logically independent.) In effect, what (2) says is that at least one of its two disjuncts is true but not both; this is often referred to as the **exclusive** sense of disjunction. What example (1) says is that at least one of its disjuncts is true and possibly both; this is called the **inclusive** sense. We recognize this difference as soon as it is pointed out. Almost always we take it into account automatically in ordinary language. However, in formal logic, a decision had to be made about which sense of 'either . . . or' was to be assigned to the wedge ∨. If you now look back at the truth-table for disjunction given previously, you will see that it expresses disjunction in the inclusive sense. A disjunction is T in any of three different cases, namely, when at least one of the disjuncts is T. Only in the fourth case, when both disjuncts are F, is the disjunctive sentence itself F. This choice makes sense. If what you mean to say is that Anne or Bob is going to the zoo but not both, in other words if what you mean is the exclusive sense of disjunction, the symbolic form would be

(A ∨ B) & ¬(A & B)

---

[4] A + B and A | B are alternative notations (but not recognized by *Symlog*).

You can use this sentence as a model for formulating exclusive disjunctions. Notice how the two binary connectives function together with negation to express this sense. In terms of form alone, this sentence is a conjunction.

The grammatical rules for disjunction run parallel to those for conjunction, so nothing needs to be added on this score. However, ordinary language uses a negative form of disjunction ('neither . . . nor') for which there is no regular counterpart in the case of conjunction. The statement

Neither Anne nor Bob is going to the zoo.

has two equivalent translations: $\neg(A \vee B)$ as well as $\neg A \,\&\, \neg B$. The reason why these translations are said to be equivalent is that their truth-tables are identical, which is a matter we shall return to later in the chapter.

Conditional

Symbolic Form:[5] $A \rightarrow B$

Truth-table:

A B	$A \rightarrow B$
T T	T
T F	F
F T	T
F F	T

Translations: if A then B; B if A

Comparing the truth-conditions for conjunction and disjunction brings out a pattern of resemblance: If at least one conjunct is F, the conjunction is F; if at least one disjunct is T, the disjunction is T. Notice that the truth-conditions do not need to be described more specifically than this. The F conjunct (or T disjunct) can stand on the left or right side of the logical connective. In other words, where it stands in the compound makes no difference. When you have a moment, work out the truth-tables for the two sentences B & A and B ∨ A. What you will find is that the columns of truth-values underneath the connectives exactly match the ones given earlier for A & B and A ∨ B, respectively. Now inspect the truth-table for the conditional. You can see there that position makes a big difference, that is, whether a sentence is to the left or to the right of the horseshoe symbol →. Whenever A is T and B is F, the conditional $A \rightarrow B$ is F; but if you were to reverse the positions of A and B without altering their truth-values, the newly obtained sentence, $B \rightarrow A$, would be T. Because of this fact, it is useful to have separate names for the left- and right-hand components of a conditional. Logic has

---

[5] $A \supset B$ and $A \Rightarrow B$ are alternative notations, but they are not recognized by *Symlog*. (B :- A, read as B if A, is widely used by the 'logic programming' community.) The symbol $\supset$ is called the **horseshoe.** To remain consistent with other logic textbooks, we will still call → a horseshoe.

adopted names that are probably already familiar to you. In the sentence A → B, A is called the **antecedent,** B the **consequent.** Keep in mind that these names concern only the position of the components in the symbolic sentence. If A occurred on the right-hand side, it would be called the consequent. Having these names makes it easier to summarize the truth-conditions for the conditional: Any conditional sentence has the truth-value T whenever its antecedent is F or its consequent is T (or both). (It does not matter whether these components are atomic or compound.) There is only one truth-value assignment on which a conditional takes on the truth-value F, and that is when the antecedent is T and the consequent is F.

A conditional statement is more guarded in what it asserts than either of the last two types of statements we have considered. In natural language, conjunctions assert that both of their components are true. Disjunctions (i.e., inclusive ones) claim that at least one of their components is true. But a true conditional statement merely rules out one particular combination of truth-values for its antecedent and consequent. It does not say how the conditional is itself true. Since a conditional can be T in any of three different ways, as you can see from the preceding table, any claim that it does make may strike you as downright weak. A more accurate way of describing the claim would be to say that it is noncommittal about every combination of truth-values except the one that would take you from a true antecedent to a false consequent, which is the one combination that renders any conditional statement false. This is the core of meaning that logic assigns to the conditional, and as with all the other connectives, the meaning is expressed entirely in terms of the truth-values of the component sentences. In ordinary language, the meaning of conditional sentences is usually richer than this, as we shall see in the next chapter. For instance, if someone says,

If Bob isn't going to the zoo then neither is Anne.

it is natural to suppose that Bob's not going the zoo would be a *cause* or a reason for Anne's not going. But the corresponding expression of this meaning in symbols, ¬B → ¬A, aims to capture only that part of the conditional's meaning that involves truth-values. Further aspects of meaning which the statement might be understood to have in ordinary usage are ignored in the symbolic translation. In other words, whether an antecedent happens to express a cause or reason for a consequent is never part of the meaning expressed by the conditional in symbolic logic.

We could justify the truth-table for the conditional by looking at the following situation: Suppose that I say to you, 'If it rains then we go to the movies.' Now, let us further suppose that it is actually raining and that we do go to the movies. Then, I was certainly speaking the truth when I said, 'If it rains then we go to the movies.' This situation justifies the first row in the truth-table for the conditional. But what if it rains and we do not go to the movies? In this case, you can certainly call me a liar for I stated that we would go to the movies if it rained; but it is raining and we are not going.

This situation gives us the second row in the truth-table. Finally, I am also speaking the truth (when I say, 'If it rains then we go to the movies') if it does not rain, regardless of whether we go to the movies or not, for I said that we would go to the movies *it if rained;* I did not say what we would do if it did not rain. This situation justifies the last two rows in the truth-table.

Yet another way of justifying the truth-table for the conditional runs as follows: A ∨ B states the same as ¬A → B and, consequently, ¬A ∨ B must state the same as ¬¬A → B or, equivalently, A → B. Therefore, the truth-table for A → B is that of ¬A ∨ B which, if you care to construct it, you will see that it is no other than the one we have given to define the conditional.

By looking at the truth-table which defines the conditional, we can determine its truth-value when the truth-values of its antecedent and consequent are given. So, if the antecedent happens to be T but the consequent is F, that is enough to determine that the symbolic sentence is F. This last remark shows an important characteristic of all five types of compound sentences: Once you know the truth-values of A and B, you can determine at once the truth-values for ¬A and ¬B and then go on to figure the value for the conditional, ¬B → ¬A. With the same information, you can also determine the truth-values for the conjunction and disjunction of the same two negative statements. Such compounds are often called **truth-functional,** which just means that the truth-values of any compound sentence are completely and unambiguously determined by the truth-values assigned to their atomic components (and of course, by the syntactic structure of the sentence). As you will see, the whole theory of truth-table testing for compound sentences depends on this characteristic.

Here now is a further sample of different ways in which conditional statements can be expressed. Keep in mind that all of them would be translated by the same symbolic form, A → B:

> Assuming that Anne is going to the zoo, so is Bob.
> Bob is going to the zoo, provided that Anne is.
> Granting that Anne is going to the zoo, Bob is going too.

Notice that in ordinary language we have the freedom to put the antecedent after the consequent (in the form B if A) without changing the meaning of the conditional. (It does not matter whether we say, 'I'll go if you go' or 'If you go, I'll go.') But when it comes to symbolic form the order is rigid: Antecedent always before consequent.

'If-then' can also be used to paraphrase statements involving 'unless': 'Unless Anne buys his ticket there is no way that Bob will go to the zoo' says that 'If Anne does not buy his ticket then there is no way that Bob will go to the zoo.' That is, A unless ¬B is symbolized as ¬A → ¬B.[6]

---

[6] More generally, A unless B is to be symbolized as ¬A → B or, equivalently, as A ∨ B.

Biconditional

Symbolic Form:[7]   A ≡ B

Truth-table:

A B	A ≡ B
T T	T
T F	F
F T	F
F F	T

Translations: B if and only if A (or B iff A); A if and only if B (or A iff B)

The syllable 'bi' in the word 'biconditional' means 'two'. A biconditional compound is really a pair of conjoined conditional sentences whose form can be read in either of the two ways just given, which are, in fact, equivalent. For the moment, however, we will concentrate on just the first of these, B if and only if A. Note that this is actually a conjunction, namely, B if A *and* B only if A. One of the conjuncts in this pair you met in the last section—the conditional statement B if A (i.e., A → B). The other half of the biconditional is B only if A. The obvious question is this: How is this second conjunct to be represented in SL? The answer will be clear once we have seen how the two connectives 'if' and 'only if' are related.

The first thing to notice is that the words 'if' and 'only if' do not mean the same thing, as a few brief examples will show. Both of the following statements are true:

A (geometrical) figure is a square only if it has four sides.
Combustion takes place only if oxygen is present.

However, if you remove the word 'only' in these two examples the resulting statements are false:

A (geometrical) figure is a square if it has four sides.
Combustion takes place if oxygen is present.

For a figure to be a square, four sides are not enough; the sides have to be equal and the angles they form have to be 90-degree angles. Having four sides is indispensable, of course, but more is required since there are many kinds of four-sided figures that are not squares. In the same way, the presence of oxygen is essential for combustion to take place, but other factors are essential too, which makes it false to say that if oxygen is present com-

---

[7] A ↔ B and A ⇔ B are alternative notations not recognized by *Symlog*.

bustion occurs. So the word 'only' makes an important difference when used alongside 'if,' and the best advice is to think of 'only if' as though it were a single word ('onlyif'), clearly different from 'if,' with a distinct role to play in the forming of conditional compounds. Let us look now at what that role is.

The component statements introduced by 'only if' are described by logic as expressing **necessary conditions.** In the first example, having four sides is a necessary condition for being a square. In the second, the presence of oxygen is a necessary condition for combustion. Statements which express necessary conditions are identified by logic as the consequents of conditional statements. With this statement as a guide, the two examples we started with can easily be reformulated as conditional compounds ready for translation into symbols:

> If a (geometrical) figure is a square, then it has four sides.
>
> If combustion takes place, then oxygen is present.

Not only are these statements true, they also succeed in expressing necessary conditions without the need for logic to introduce a special symbol to capture the meaning of 'only if.' You will recall that every conditional compound has a fixed order: antecedent → consequent. As far as the structure of conditional statements is concerned, the role of 'only if' is simply to introduce the consequent, just as the role of 'if' is to introduce the antecedent. The symbolic translation of B only if A, then, is B → A. The translation of A only if B is A → B. These follow the familiar pattern of conditional sentences. The connective →, then, can be read in one of two ways, using either 'if' or 'only if.' It is equally correct to read A → B either as 'If A then B' or as 'A only if B'. This statement may seem ambiguous but it is not. As far as symbolic logic goes, there is no difference in meaning between these two readings because they correspond to the very same conditional statement. They have identical truth-conditions, which are the ones given earlier for A → B.

Let us get back to the biconditional, A ≡ B (A if and only if B). You can see that this compound does two things at once: It uses 'if' to introduce B as the antecedent (as in B → A) and 'only if' to introduce it also as the consequent of A (as in A → B). The biconditional should be seen as a compact way of conjoining these two different conditional statements. As you will be able to show later on, it is truth-functionally equivalent to the conjunction (B → A) & (A → B). This equivalence, better than anything we can say here, will explain why A ≡ B has the specific truth-table definition given previously.

Logic uses another term to designate the antecedents of conditional statements. It calls them **sufficient conditions.** (Think of sufficient conditions as the statements introduced by 'if.') This term will help us to complete our explanation of the biconditional. What the biconditional says, with regard to a pair of statements, is that one of them is both a necessary and a sufficient condition of the other. If you glance back at the conjunction just given, (B → A) & (A → B), you will see that the statement A is both a necessary condition of B (the left-hand conjunct) and a sufficient condition of B (the right-hand conjunct). But now look at it again and recall that there are two different ways of reading any conditional. The same conjunction says that B is both a necessary condition (right-hand) as well as a sufficient condition (left-hand) of A. Really, because these readings correspond to the same truth-functional statement (the conjunction), it does not matter which you choose. That is why we gave the two different readings at the outset, B iff A as well as A iff B. It may seem odd that whereas the order of a conditional statement is fixed, that of the biconditional is not, but this is a result of the fact that a biconditional is a conjunction of two conditionals, and as we saw earlier, the truth-functional ordering of conjuncts and disjuncts is immaterial. However, when you consider just the conditional, it will often make a crucial difference—the difference between a true and a false statement—on which side of the horseshoe → you place the component sentences. Recall, for instance, that having four sides is necessary for a figure to be a square but it is not sufficient.

There is a bit more to be said about the matter of necessary and sufficient conditions, but it can wait until the next chapter, where we will be discussing translations from ordinary language into symbols. The only point worth stressing now is that the **triple-bar,** ≡, does not mean the same as the mathematical symbol, =, for equality. To illustrate,

John = Peter.

('John' = 'Peter,' to be more precise) means that the individual whose name is 'John' is the same individual whose name is 'Peter.' But,

John ≡ Peter

(or even 'John' ≡ 'Peter') makes no sense since John or Peter is not a statement. A ≡ B expresses a compound (bi)conditional relationship between A and B and nothing more. It does not say that A 'equals' B or that A 'means the same as' B. The only respect in which A and B are the same is that each of them is both antecedent and consequent of the other in a pair of conditional statements.

As you proceed through the rest of this chapter, you may find it helpful to have the following summary of the truth-value definitions of the five connectives. To present them, however, we will use a different kind of symbol from the A's and B's—the atomic sentences—which have figured so far in the discussion. We will use the Greek letters α and β to stand for any sentence whatever, whether atomic or compound. This use allows the definitions to cover as wide an area as possible in an uncomplicated way. (As used here, α and β are sometimes called **metalogical symbols**—or **metasentences,** in the present case.) The tables of truth-value assignments for α and β remain the same, in the sense of covering the full range of possible truth-values.

α	$\neg\alpha$
T	F
F	T

α β	$\alpha \,\&\, \beta$
T T	T
T F	F
F T	F
F F	F

α β	$\alpha \lor \beta$
T T	T
T F	T
F T	T
F F	F

α β	$\alpha \to \beta$
T T	T
T F	F
F T	T
F F	T

α β	$\alpha \equiv \beta$
T T	T
T F	F
F T	F
F F	T

You have reached the point at which *Symlog* can help sharpen your logical focus on statements. In the rest of this section and in the following ones you will be moving back and forth from textbook to screen, so try to have these conveniently close to each other. Our first goal is to transform simple statements of English into the language SL. To assist, *Symlog* will present a screen divided into sections, like the one displayed in Figure 2.1. Notice that the SYMBOLIZATION section contains a 'lexicon' of sentence letters and the atomic statements they represent; these are the only sentence letters you should use when entering your symbolized SL sentence in the ANSWER section. Initially, the English statement or statements to be symbolized will be presented in the CURRENT section. On request (by using the Down Arrow or PgDn keys), these can be moved to the PREVIOUS section, and a new stage of the sentence being translated appears in the CURRENT section. (See Appendix C for details under the heading Symbolization Pad Commands.) Until you have gained experience with translations, it is preferable to proceed in such stages, whether or not you are working in this particular environment. For instance, it is useful to paraphrase the statement

John smokes if Lucy doesn't.

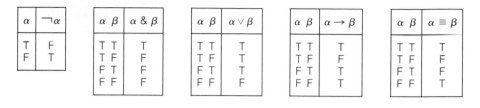

Figure 2.1

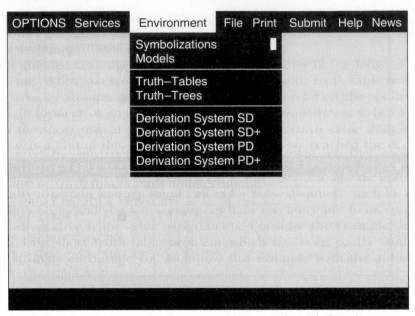

Figure 2.2   Symbolize statements, sets of statements, and arguments in symbolic logic

as

>   If Lucy doesn't smoke then John smokes.

before you attempt its full representation in logical notation, $\neg L \rightarrow J$. This method helps to reveal the logical structure of the statement at hand in a way that conforms more clearly with the standards of SL, and this was our main consideration in designing these exercises. By means of the PREVIOUS and CURRENT portions of your screen, *Symlog* enables you to cycle back and forth from the original sentence to its 'full-dress' version in symbols. The intermediate stages are partial translations which emphasize logically relevant features of the sentence: the overall form, together with the structure of its components. As you can see in the CURRENT section in Figure 2.1, these preliminary stages may contain a mixture of English and SL symbols. The program keeps two adjacent stages of translation on screen so that you can compare them. You progress through these stages at your own pace.

   To work on symbolizations, select Environment from the OPTIONS menu and invoke Symbolizations (Figure 2.2). After selecting the Symbolizations environment, *Symlog* produces a screen similar to the one depicted in Figure 2.3, and it waits for you to choose a symbolization to work on.[8] Select the exercise SL01. Once *Symlog* has retrieved the exercise from your disk, study the statement given in the CURRENT section. Once you think you have the

---

[8] If on the screen you do not see any exercises being listed, it is because they probably are on a different disk or DOS directory. To access them use Access (in the File menu). When you select this option *Symlog* asks for the name of the directory where the exercises are located.

SYMBOLIZATIONS

<newFile>	SL01.SLS	SL02.SLS	SL03.3LS	SL04.SLS
SL05.SLS	SL06.SLS	SL07.SLS	SL08.SLS	SL09.SLS
SL10.SLS	SL11.SLS	SL12.SLS	SL13.SLS	SL14.SLS
SL15.SLS	SL16.SLS	SL17.SLS	SL18.SLS	SL19.SLS
SL20.SLS	SL21.SLS	SL22.SLS	SL23.SLS	SL24.SLS
SL25.SLS	SL26.SLS	SL27.SLS	SL28.SLS	SL29.SLS
SL30.SLS	SL31.SLS	SL32.SLS	SL33.SLS	SL34.SLS
SL35.SLS	SL36.SLS	SL37.SLS	SL38.SLS	SL39.SLS
SL40.SLS	SL41.SLS	SL42.SLS	SL43.SLS	SL44.SLS
SL45.SLS				

Figure 2.3 DIRECTORY C:\SYMLOG   45 FILES READ

answer, enter it into the ANSWER section (and hit the Enter key). *Symlog* will indicate whether it agrees with your answer.[9] If you need a hint, ask *Symlog* to display a further stage of the translation (again, with the Down Arrow or PgDn keys). Try also the exercises SL02 to SL15 on your disk (call the OPTIONS menu, choose File and then select Retrieve; alternatively, issue the 'retrieve next exercise' command: Ctrl-R).

Exercises

2.3.1 Characterize each of the following statements as either simple or compound; if compound, specify whether the statement is a negation, conjunction, disjunction, conditional or biconditional.

a. John is happy.
b. Mary isn't happy at all.
c. If Lucy is happy so is Mary.
d. Either John is happy or Lucy isn't.
e. Mary is happy if and only if John and Lucy are.
f. John is sad.
g. Peter is sad but so is Lucy.
h. Lucy, Mary and Peter are happy.
i. It is not the case that Lucy isn't sad.
j. John is sad only if Mary is.
k. It's false that if Lucy is happy Mary is too.
l. Neither Lucy, Mary nor Peter is happy.

[9] Your answer does not have to be syntactically identical to *Symlog*'s to be correct; *Symlog* checks for truth-functional—semantical—equivalence. For instance, if you enter A & (B & C) instead of (A & B) & C, or ¬A & ¬B as opposed to ¬ (A ∨ B), *Symlog* will still recognize your answer as valid.

2.3.2   Let the sentence letters J, L, M and P stand for 'John is happy,' 'Lucy is happy,' 'Mary is happy' and 'Peter is happy,' respectively. Express in SL each of the statements of exercise 2.3.1 and give their truth-value, assuming that J is T, L is F, M is T and P is T.

2.3.3   Given the following symbolization,

A : Anne likes music.

B : Bob likes music.

C : Carol likes music.

express in SL the following statements.

a. Anne dislikes music.

b. Carol doesn't like music and neither does Anne.

c. It is not the case that both Anne and Bob are music lovers.

d. Carol likes music and so does Anne.

e. Either Anne doesn't like music or Carol does.

f. Neither Bob nor Carol likes music.

g. If Bob hates music then so do both Carol and Anne.

h. Bob doesn't like music if Anne doesn't either.

i. Carol likes music only if Bob does not.

j. Anne hates music if and only if it is not the case that both Bob and Carol do.

2.3.4   Assume that it is true that Anne likes music, that it is false that Bob likes music and that it is also false that Carol likes music. What are the truth-values of each of the statements of exercise 2.3.3 above?

2.3.5   Do as in 2.3.4 if it is false that Anne likes music, it is true that Bob likes music and it is false that Carol likes music.

2.3.6   Given the following symbolization,

C : Canada will win the race.

F : France will win the race.

I : Italy will win the race.

S : USA will win the race.

express in SL the following statements.

a. Either Canada or France will win the race but not Italy.

b. USA will win the race if Italy does not.

c. Neither Canada, France nor Italy will win the race.

d. Italy will not win if and only if USA will not either.

e. Canada will win only if neither Italy nor France wins.

f. France will win but not Canada.

g. If USA does not win neither does Italy, and vice versa.

h. Canada will win the race only if France does not win.

i. France will win.

j. Even though Canada will not win, USA will not win either.

2.3.7   Given that A is T, B is F, C is T and D is T find the truth-values of the following.

a. A & ¬A

b. ¬(B & ¬C)

c. ¬(¬A ∨ D) → ¬B

d. (D ≡ ¬¬A) → (B ≡ C)

e. ¬(B & ¬C) ∨ ¬(C ∨ ¬A)

2.3.8   Repeat as in exercise 2.3.7 if A is F and B, C and D are each T.

2.3.9   Given the following symbolization,

D : I will go dancing.

P : I will pass the test.

S : I will study hard.

T : I will play tennis.

express in SL the following statements.

a. I'll pass the test if I study hard.

b. If I play tennis and I don't study hard then there is no way that I'll pass that test.

c. I will not play tennis and I'll study hard.

d. I will fail the test if either I play tennis or don't study hard.

e. I will fail the test if and only if I don't study hard.

f. Either I study hard and pass the test or I play tennis and I fail it.

g. If I play tennis and go dancing and study hard then I will pass the test.

h. I will fail the test if I go dancing or play tennis.

i. If I study hard and either play tennis or go dancing then I will pass the test.

j. If I go dancing or play tennis then I will pass the test if and only if I study hard.

2.3.10 Given the following symbolization,

A : Light A is green.

B : Light B is green.

C : Light C is green.

P : The pressure is high.

T : The temperature is high.

express in SL the following statements, knowing that these are all the lights there are and that a light can be only in green or red.

a. If light A is red then the temperature is high.

b. The pressure is low if and only if both lights A and C are red.

c. If lights B and C are green then the temperature is low and so is the pressure.

d. The temperature is high if and only if the pressure is also high.

e. If all the lights are green then the pressure is low.

f. If light C is red and the temperature is high then light B is red too.

g. Either lights B and C are red or light A is green.

    h. If the pressure is high then either lights A and C are red or the temperature is high.

    i. If light C is red and the temperature is low then light A is green and the pressure is high.

    j. If no light is green then both the temperature and the pressure are high.

    k. If light A is red then no other light is red also.

    l. The pressure is low if and only if no light is red.

    m. If the temperature is high and the pressure is low then either lights A and C are red or lights B and C are green.

    n. The temperature is high if and only if all the lights are red or if the pressure is low and lights B and C are green.

    o. If all the lights are green except light B then the pressure is low or the temperature is high.

    p. If lights A and B are green and the temperature is low then light B is red.

    q. If a light is green then the pressure is low.

    r. If a light is green and it's not A then the temperature is low.

    s. The temperature is high if the pressure is high also.

    t. If light A is green then light C is red, and if light B is red then light A is green.

2.4   Formation Rules of SL

From time to time in the last section we mentioned the importance of excluding all ambiguity from the formal representation of sentences of SL. However complicated a compound may be, it must be clearly one or another of the five types (negation, conjunction, disjunction, conditional and biconditional); in the same way, its immediate components must either be atomic sentences or, once again, clearly one of the five types. This requirement holds at each level in the structure of the sentence, right down to the level at which there are no longer any compounds but only atomic sentences. In short, although compound sentences can be (in principle) of any finite size whatever, their structure will always be hierarchical—assuming they have been properly constructed. To make sure that a string of symbols forms a genuine sentence and not a piece of nonsense that merely looks like a sentence, SL uses a set of so-called formation rules. These are a bit like the grammatical rules for a foreign language which can help you to distinguish real sentences from nonsentences. If English is your native language, you never learned its grammatical rules separately but instead absorbed them and learned to follow them unconsciously. However, if you have ever studied a foreign language, you already have some experience of keeping to a set of rules which govern the construction of sentences and phrases, especially at the early stages. SL's formation rules serve that kind of purpose. Although you will learn to read and write SL sentences very quickly, you will probably need to refer to these rules once in a while to find out whether an expression has been formulated correctly.

To set out these rules we will use the two metalogical symbols (α and β) which were introduced at the end of the last section. The remaining symbols, standing for atomic sentences, the five connectives and left- and right-hand parentheses, will be already quite familiar, except in one respect. When we were discussing simple statements earlier, all we needed were a few instances of atomic letters, like A and B, to represent them. But in logic there is no theoretical limit to the number of different simple statements; it assumes, in fact, that simple statements are endless in number. How, then, are these to be symbolized in SL, supposing that we wanted to say something about all of them at once? If you start at the beginning of the alphabet it is easy to see that you will exhaust the supply of letters pretty quickly. The problem is solved in the following way. The series of letters, A, B, C, . . . , can be continued indefinitely by attaching whole numbers to the letters in the following way: A_1, B_1, C_1, . . . , A_2, B_2, C_2, . . . , A_3, B_3, C_3, . . . and so on. Since you cannot run out of whole numbers, this method guarantees an infinite supply of symbols for different simple statements. As you will see later, it is theoretically important that any number of simple statements can be represented in symbolic language, but for practical purposes (whether or not you are working in *Symlog*), the number of simple statements to be handled is so small that it will not be necessary to use whole-number subscripts when doing problems. It will not even be necessary to use more than a handful of letters at one time. In fact, because logic reserves the letters at the end of the alphabet for a different purpose, *Symlog* uses the shorter series A through T as its source of sentence letters. Thus, the letters U through Z will never occur in *Symlog* as sentence letters. Keep in mind that *Symlog*'s sentence letters are always capitalized (uppercase).

There is one very good reason why it is important to know these formation rules: *Symlog* itself follows them. If you happen to write a symbolic expression which conflicts with the rules, *Symlog* will not try to guess what you meant to write or give you the benefit of the doubt but will simply tell you that the expression is not a sentence of SL and wait for your next move. In other words, to play this game, you are going to have to play by the program's rules (which are actually logic's rules). These rules of formation, whose purpose is to allow you to decide whether a given expression is a sentence of SL or not, constitute what is called the **syntax** of SL. The specification begins by laying out the alphabet—basic classes of symbols—of SL: the sentence letters, the truth-functional connectives and the punctuation marks.

1. **Sentence letters:** The sentence letters—or **atomic sentences**—of SL are the capital letters of the Roman alphabet from A to, and including, T with or without positive integer numerical subscripts.
2. **Truth-functional connectives:** $\neg$, &, $\vee$, $\rightarrow$, $\equiv$.
3. **Punctuation symbols:** (,).

We can now give the nesessary rules to construct, and recognize, sentences of SL (note that below we let α and β stand for any sentences of SL).

1. All the sentence letters of SL are sentences of SL.
2. If α is a sentence of SL, then $\neg\alpha$ is a sentence of SL.
3. If α and β are sentences of SL, then $(\alpha \& \beta)$, $(\alpha \vee \beta)$, $(\alpha \rightarrow \beta)$ and $(\alpha \equiv \beta)$ are sentences of SL.
4. Anything that cannot be constructed by finitely many applications of one or more than one of rules 1 to 3 is not a sentence of SL.

These rules are comprehensive: They are meant to cover every sort of expression which is a sentence of SL. Also, the rules are exclusive: Only expressions which satisfy the rules will be regarded as sentences of SL. Finally, they are **recursive:** They can be applied repeatedly in the construction of any size of compound sentence; and—going the other way—they can be used to analyze any size of compound sentence to determine whether each of its component parts is itself an SL sentence, right down to the level of the atomic sentences. Sentences which conform to the rules are sometimes referred to as **well-formed formulas** (of SL), or **wffs,** for short. These rules are quite precise and strict; for one thing, as they stand, they do not allow the use of square brackets, although for *practical* reasons we will loosen this restriction in a moment; but before we do so, let us consider some examples of expressions, some of which are sentences of SL and some of which are not. According to the rules, the following expressions are sentences of SL:

G
G_{34}
$(G \& \neg B)$
$\neg((G \& \neg B) \equiv (A \vee \neg(B \vee \neg T)))$
$(\neg((G \& \neg B) \equiv (A \vee \neg(B \vee \neg T))) \rightarrow (\neg A \& (A \vee H)))$

But the following are not:

(G)
$G_{1.5}$
g & $\neg$B
$\neg(G \& \neg B) \equiv (A \vee \neg(B \vee \neg T)$
$((G \& \neg B) \rightarrow (\neg A \& A \vee H))$

Let us examine these bogus sentences one by one to see what is wrong with them. The rules of formation specify parentheses for compound sentences only but not for either atomic sentences or negated sentences. Hence, (G) is not a sentence of SL. As for the second case, 1.5 is not an integer and it cannot be used as a subscript. In the third example, since uppercase letters only are used to represent atomic sentences in SL, the use of the letter g in g & ¬B is not legal. That takes care of the first three cases. The next two illustrate common problems in the use of parentheses. In the fourth example, first, there is one parenthesis too few on the right-hand side of the biconditional. That side should read (A ∨ ¬(B ∨ ¬T)); second, the entire biconditional expression should be surrounded by parentheses. In the fifth case, which is a conditional 'sentence,' the problem lies in the consequent. When that part of the expression is taken by itself, you can see that the punctuation fails to show whether the expression is supposed to be the conjunction, (¬A & (A ∨ H)), or the disjunction, ((¬A & A) ∨ H). These are truth-functionally—but also syntactically—different sentences, but which of these two is meant cannot be guessed from the expression itself. SL sentences do not write themselves—they are written by someone intending to say something, and if a rule of formation is violated in the process, the result is not a sentence in this language.

As mentioned earlier, parentheses help to identify the structure of any compound sentence as one of the five types. If you look at the sentence (¬¬¬P ∨ ¬¬(Q → (R ≡ ¬Q))), you will see that it is a disjunction; its disjuncts are ¬¬¬P (a triple negation) and ¬¬(Q → (R ≡ ¬Q)) (a double negation). The disjunction sign, ∨, is called the **main connective,** also known as the **main logical operator,** of this sentence, and the disjuncts are the sentence's immediate components. Its ultimate components are P, Q and R, its atomic components. The main connective is the last connective introduced in the process of constructing a compound sentence of SL (using the rules of formation).

There is one final detail regarding parentheses that has to be mentioned. It may sometimes strike you that there are too many to make the reading of a sentence easy. We agree. So, to handle this problem, you may use square brackets in the construction of sentences of SL; also, you may drop the outermost set of parentheses in sentences of SL to improve readability. Let us go back to the last example, (¬¬¬P ∨ ¬¬(Q → (R ≡ ¬Q))). After the adoption of these two conventions, ¬¬¬P ∨ ¬¬[Q → (R ≡ ¬Q)] is considered a sentence of SL. Whenever you find it clearer to mix brackets with parentheses to set off the structure of a sentence, please feel free to do so. *Symlog* will not mind, and we shall often be using them in the text from now on. Only be sure of two things regarding the punctuation of your formulas: Always use parentheses and brackets in pairs, and never pair up a single bracket with a single parenthesis. To get familiar with the syntax of SL, and before reading any further, you should try some of the exercises at the end of this section.

Exercises

2.4.1 According to the formation rules of SL, determine which of the following are sentences of SL. (Note: In this exercise, strict adherence to the rules of formation is required.)

    a. P
    b. (C)
    c. (D ∨ E)
    d. ¬(K ∨ ¬A)
    e. A → M
    f. (¬A)
    g. (A & B & C)
    h. ((A ∨ B) ∨ ¬(C ∨ D))
    i. (((K & ¬L) ∨ (D → M)) ≡ ((D → M) → ¬(L ∨ ¬K)))
    j. ¬[(M & ¬A) → K]

2.4.2 Determine the main connective of each of the following sentences of SL. (Note that the syntax has been relaxed.)
    a. A → ¬B
    b. ¬¬B
    c. ¬(P → Q)
    d. ((H ≡ L) → M) ∨ H
    e. ¬A ≡ (¬B → ¬C)
    f. ¬(P ∨ (¬Q & ¬R))
    g. [¬(¬M ≡ K) ≡ J] & [(L ∨ ¬H) → J]
    h. ¬(A ∨ B) ∨ (C ∨ D)
    i. ¬(¬K & (D → M)) ≡ ¬((D → M) → ¬K)
    j. [(E & ¬A) → (C ≡ B)] → [C → (¬A → (B ≡ E))]

2.4.3 Which of the following sentences are of the form ¬α ∨ β?
    a. A ∨ B   b. ¬P ∨ Q   c. ¬(H ∨ K)
    d. ¬¬P ∨ Q   e. ¬C ∨ ¬D   f. A ∨ ¬B
    g. ¬P & Q   h. ¬¬K ∨ ¬L   i. ¬¬M ∨ (R & K)

2.4.4 Answer true or false (but not both) to each of the following questions.
    a. SL has infinitely many sentence letters.
    b. ¬P is a wff (well-formed formula) of SL.
    c. A & B ∨ C is a wff of SL.
    d. There are some sentences in SL which are infinitely long.
    e. ¬(¬P → Q) is a wff of SL.
    f. Every wff has a main connective.
    g. A wff has at most one main connective.
    h. The main connective of (¬P ≡ Q) is ≡.
    i. ¬ is the main connective of the consequent of ((H ≡ ¬K) → ¬M).
    j. The main connective of the antecedent of ((¬(P ≡ Q) ∨ S) → ¬R) is ¬.
    k. ¬(¬(¬(P ≡ Q) ∨ ¬(S & T)) → ¬R) is a sentence of SL.
    l. (α → β) is a well-formed formula of SL.
    m. If α and β are wffs of SL, then (α → β) is a wff of SL.
    n. There is a sentence in SL with infinitely many sentence letters.
    o. If A is T then ¬A → B will be T regardless of the truth-value of B.

2.4.5 The **subwffs** of a wff of SL are defined as follows:

(i) α has only one subwff, namely, α itself, if α is an atomic wff (i.e., a sentence letter).

(ii) The subwffs of $\neg\alpha$ are $\neg\alpha$ itself plus the subwffs of α.

(iii) If we let $*$ stand for either &, $\vee$, $\rightarrow$ or $\equiv$, then the subwffs of $(\alpha * \beta)$ are $(\alpha * \beta)$ itself, the subwffs of α plus the subffws of β.

Define the **length of a wff** as the number of subwffs it has. State the subwffs and the length of

a. $\neg P$

b. $(A \,\&\, \neg B)$

c. $((P \equiv \neg\neg Q) \vee R)$

d. $\neg(\neg\neg R \vee S)$

e. $\neg(\neg(A \rightarrow B) \rightarrow \neg(A \vee B))$

2.4.6 Which of the following sentences are of the form $\alpha \rightarrow \neg\beta$?

a. $\neg A \rightarrow B$ b. $P \rightarrow Q$ c. $\neg(H \rightarrow \neg K)$

d. $P \rightarrow \neg Q$ e. $\neg C \vee \neg\neg D$ f. $A \rightarrow \neg\neg B$

g. $\neg H \rightarrow \neg\neg K$ h. $\neg C \rightarrow \neg D$ i. $(H \equiv K) \rightarrow \neg C$

2.5 *Symlog's Truth-Tables*

By this time, you have gained a basic familiarity with symbolization. You will be returning to this environment of *Symlog* later for the treatment of more complicated examples. Right now, however, you are going to deepen your understanding of SL's sentences by investigating their semantical character, that is, the properties which depend on the truth or falsity of these sentences. For this purpose we move to another of *Symlog*'s environments.[10] With the program active, select Environment from the OPTIONS menu and invoke Truth-Tables. After selecting the Truth-Tables environment, open a *new file; Symlog* asks you to enter the name of the truth-table to construct. To name your truth-table, enter the name, say, POST.[11] If there is no file with that name in the disk, *Symlog* realizes that POST is a new file, and it produces on your screen a clean sheet from the Truth-Table Pad for you to use.

Take a moment to become acquainted with the truth-table screen. Here is a brief description which you can follow by referring to Figure 2.4 in the text.

Every page from the Truth-Table Pad is divided into areas called fields, some of which are used by the program and some by yourself. The three so-called mark fields come under the former heading and their use will be described in the course of the first problem. The Sentence Field is the space in

---

[10] In this and the following discussions, ideally, you would have a computer by your side running *Symlog*. This, of course, may not always be possible (you may be reading this in a crowded bus!). Yet you can still read ahead without loss of continuity: All our illustrations (with some obvious exceptions) are actual *Symlog* screen samples reflecting (a) the logical concepts being discussed and (b) what you would see in a real computer screen if you had it in front of you.

[11] Most of our files are named after people who made important contributions to symbolic logic.

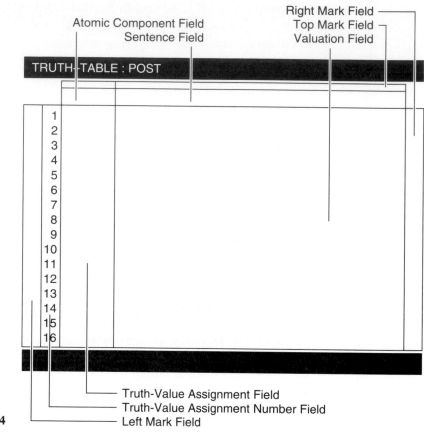

Figure 2.4

which you will enter an SL sentence that you want to test by the truth-table method; *Symlog* will list its atomic components for you in the area called Atomic Component Field. The space beneath this (called the Truth-Value Assignment Field) is where you will set out all the logically possible truth-value assignments for the atomic components of the sentence; and the actual truth-table you construct will occupy the space underneath the sentence itself, called the Valuation Field. The lines in these last two fields will always be numbered by the program. Sixteen is the maximum number of lines for a 'workable' problem in the Truth-Tables environment. As you will see, this corresponds to an SL sentence having four atomic components and will be more than enough for our purposes here.

Now let us start to work on the problem POST. The first thing needed is an SL sentence, and the one we have chosen should be familiar to you from the discussion of the biconditional. Enter the sentence (A → B) & (B → A) in the Sentence Field.[12] Your screen should look like Figure 2.5a.

---

[12] If you happen to make a typing mistake at this stage, you can use the editing keys described in Appendix C (in the section Truth-Table Pad Commands). This section gives all the commands needed to operate this environment properly. The information is also available on-line (in the Reference Guide under the Help menu).

```
┌──────────────────────────────────────────────────────────────┐
│ TRUTH–TABLE : POST                                          ■  │
├──────────────────────────────────────────────────────────────┤
│        A B   │ (A → B) & (B → A)                              │
│     1 ■                                                        │
│     2                                                         │
│     3                                                         │
│     4                                                         │
│     5                                                         │
│     6                                                         │
│     7                                                         │
│     8                                                         │
│     9                                                         │
│    10                                                         │
│    11                                                         │
│    12                                                         │
│    13                                                         │
│    14                                                         │
│    15                                                         │
│    16                                                         │
└──────────────────────────────────────────────────────────────┘
```

Figure 2.5a

```
┌──────────────────────────────────────────────────────────────┐
│ TRUTH–TABLE : POST                                          ■  │
├──────────────────────────────────────────────────────────────┤
│          ■ ■                                                   │
│          A B   │ (A → B) & (B → A)                            │
│  ■   1   T T                                                   │
│  ■   2   T F                                                   │
│  ■   3   F T                                                   │
│  ■   4   F F                                                   │
│      5                                                        │
└──────────────────────────────────────────────────────────────┘
```

Figure 2.5b

```
┌──────────────────────────────────────────────────────────────┐
│ TRUTH–TABLE : POST                                          ■  │
├──────────────────────────────────────────────────────────────┤
│          ■ ■        ■    ■    ■    ■                          │
│          A B   │ (A → B) & (B → A)                            │
│  ■   1   T T     T    T    T    T                          ■  │
│  ■   2   T F                                                   │
│  ■   3   F T                                                   │
│  ■   4   F F                                                   │
│      5                                                        │
└──────────────────────────────────────────────────────────────┘
```

Figure 2.5c

```
┌──────────────────────────────────────────────────────────────┐
│ TRUTH–TABLE : POST                                            │
├──────────────────────────────────────────────────────────────┤
│          A B   │ (A → B) & (B → A)                            │
│      1   T T     T    T    T    T                             │
│      2   T F     T    F    F    T                             │
│      3   F T     F    T    T    F                             │
│      4   F F     F    F    F    F                             │
│      5                                                        │
└──────────────────────────────────────────────────────────────┘
```

Figure 2.5d

TRUTH–TABLE : POST

	A B	(A → B) & (B → A)	
1	T T	T T T	T T T
2	T F	T F F	F T T
3	F T	F T T	T F F
4	F F	F T F	F T F
5			

Figure 2.5e

TRUTH–TABLE : POST

	A B	(A → B) & (B → A)
1	T T	T T T T T T T
2	T F	T F F F F T T
3	F T	F T T F T F F
4	F F	F T F T F T F
5		

Figure 2.5f

OPTIONS	Services	Environment	File	Print	Submit	Help	News

	A B	(A → B) & (B → A)	Name
1	T T	T T T T T T T	Save ■
2	T F	T F F F F T T	Retrieve
3	F T	F T T F T F F	Create
4	F F	F T F T F T F	
5			Directory
6			Copy
7			Rename
8			Erase
9			
10			Access
11			
12			
13			
14			
15			
16			

Figure 2.5g   Save current work and continue working

We will construct the truth-table for this conjunction and see why it has the same truth-values assigned to A ≡ B. You probably noticed that as soon as you entered this sentence, *Symlog* extracted the atomic components A and B and set them in the Atomic Component Field. (The program does this step routinely; not only that, it always arranges the atomic sentences in alphabetical order from left to right.) The next step is to represent all of the possible permutations of truth-values for this pair of atomic sentences; you already know something about this task from our earlier discussion of the logical connectives. We are going to duplicate the pattern of truth-values that appeared under A and B for each of the four binary connectives. This is not the only possible pattern but it is the only type that *Symlog* will recognize; we call it the **standard pattern of truth-value assignments.** (You will see how to construct larger patterns in just a while.) Begin duplicating the pattern of T's and F's you see under A and B in Figure 2.5b. As you type in T's and F's, square markers appear in the top mark and the left mark fields as well as some messages in the Error Line. These are just a reminder that so far, these entries have not been checked by *Symlog* (and may contain errors). You can ask *Symlog* to check your work—either a single entry in the truth-table, a whole column or the entire piece of work—at any time.[13]

Let us stop for a moment to find out what these markers are all about. The field that you are working in—for the moment it is the Truth-Value Assignment Field, but this explanation also applies to the Valuation Field—is divided by *Symlog* into units called cells. Think of them as forming an invisible grid in which each cell has a precise location known to the program. A cell can either be empty or have a letter in it (here, a T or F). For a given sentence of SL, like the one in this example, *Symlog* knows how the cells should be filled, and when you type in a letter, for example, T or F, the program responds by posting three markers. One of these is located at the upper right-hand corner of the Top Mark Field, and it will always appear whenever any cell has been typed but not justified (i.e., checked) by *Symlog* or entered incorrectly. The other two are intended to work in tandem to help you locate a particular—usually offending—cell. The marker on the left or right side gives a cell's vertical location; the one at the top, its horizontal location. (It may help you to imagine the cell as the place where lines drawn from these two markers would intersect.) *Symlog* evaluates your chosen letter, that is, truth-value, as soon as you press the Enter key. If the markers disappear, the truth-value entered is the correct one for that cell; if the marks remain, the program will tell you what is wrong in a message at the bottom of the screen. You can then go back to the cell and try again. When a number of markers are on at the same time, you may want to find out what the program is trying to tell you; just bring your cursor back to each corresponding cell one by one and read the messages at the bottom of the screen. Messages change to fit the cell the cursor is on (assuming the cell has markers corresponding to it). If, for instance, you have entered a T or F underneath a parenthesis or bracket, *Symlog* will tell you so.[14]

Back to POST. Now that you have completed the pattern of truth-value permutations and understand what the markers mean, we can construct the

---

[13] Again, see Appendix C under Truth-Table Pad Commands or the on-line commands.

[14] As you will quickly realize, about the best way to use *Symlog* to construct truth-tables is to fill in a whole column of truth-values and then have the program check your work before going on to the next column. Besides getting immediate feedback on your recently completed column, this method also avoids spreading errors through your work.

truth-table for our conjunction. Whenever you do one of these problems, you will be drawing on the pool of truth-functional definitions given earlier, so be sure you have these clearly in mind (look back at the summary at the end of section 2.3 whenever necessary—or in The Logic Booklet under the Help menu). Every sentence of SL is truth-functional. This statement means, for instance, that this conjunction will be T when and only when both of its conjuncts are T. But the conjuncts are conditionals, and each of these will be T except when its antecedent is T and its consequent F. In both cases, the components of the conditionals are atomic sentences, and we now have a list of all of their possible truth-values in the Truth-Value Assignment Field. So the first step in the Valuation Field is to carry over the columns of truth-values that appear under A and B. Move the cursor over to the Valuation Field and enter a T directly under each of these two atomic statements wherever you find them in our sentence, as shown in Figure 2.5c. These values correspond to the first of the four rows in the Truth-Value Assignment Field.

You should now duplicate the remaining three rows. Then, ask *Symlog* to check all your work—the four columns—completed so far (using Ctrl-C). If there are no errors your screen should appear as in Figure 2.5d. (If there are errors, locate them with the help of the marks in the mark fields and correct them as suggested by *Symlog*'s messages.)

Now we are in a position to calculate the truth-values for each of the conditionals, row by row. (It does not matter which conjunct you begin with, but we shall go from left to right.) In the first row, both antecedent and consequent are T, so the value of A → B is T for that row; using the definition of →, you can calculate the truth-values for the remaining three rows as F, T and T, respectively. Notice that the column of truth-values under A → B exactly matches what was given earlier in the definition of →. In a sense, this is coincidental, because what we are doing now is using the definition of the conditional, not merely repeating it. The point will be clearer when you move over to the other conjunct, B → A, and begin to calculate its truth-values. Applying the definition of → once again gives you the column of truth-values for this right conjunct. After your work is checked by *Symlog* your screen should look like Figure 2.5e. Note that the sentence B → A is F only in the one case (row 3), where B is T and A is F, but T for all the other truth-value assignments to A and B.

At this point, we can begin to calculate the truth-values for the conjunction itself. Recall that a conjunction is T just when both of its immediate components are T. In the present case, this situation occurs in just the first and fourth rows, so the column of truth-values under the main connective, &, which is the column that presents the truth-table for the sentence itself, will read as in Figure 2.5f (after your work is checked by *Symlog*).

This is the same column that appeared earlier under the definition of ≡, only now we have obtained it by constructing a truth-table that uses two other logical connectives, namely, → and &. This exercise helps show all over again what ≡ basically means in truth-functional terms, and also takes some of the strangeness out of saying that a biconditional statement is true whenever its immediate components[15] are either both true or both false. By the way, you may be wondering whether other logical connectives like ∨ and → can be expressed truth-functionally in terms of each other or in terms of other connectives. The answer is 'yes,' but only with the help of the negation operator, ¬. This topic is taken up in one of the exercises.[16] At this point you should save the work you have just done. Summon the OPTIONS menu, scroll over to File and then scroll down and invoke Save (Figure 2.5g).

Symlog will record your work on disk under the name you have given it, POST, where it will remain for you to retrieve (until you erase it). Admittedly, this truth-table problem is a lot simpler than others you will be working on, so that you may never see the need of calling it up again. You can always erase it if you need the space. What is important is that you get into the habit of saving your work on disk, so we urge you now to take a minute to go through the routine of saving this problem.[17]

Let us move on to a sentence containing three atomic sentences: ¬(G → E) ≡ (¬L ∨ ¬E). First, call up a fresh page from your Truth-Table Pad by selecting Retrieve under the File menu, give the name RUSSELL to it and then enter the sentence in the Sentence Field. If *Symlog* accepted your sentence, it has extracted the three atomic sentences, arranged them at the top of the Truth-Value Assignment Field and has stationed the cursor at the point where you will enter the first truth-value in that field (Figure 2.6a).

But what is the right pattern of truth-value permutations to use when there are three atomic sentences? Here is the routine that *Symlog* follows. The number of rows needed in the Truth-Value Assignment Field, which is actually the number of rows your truth-table is going to take, is 2^n, where n stands for the number of different atomic sentences in the sentence being analyzed. In the present case, the number is 3, so 2^3 (or $2 \times 2 \times 2$) will give a total of 8 truth-value assignments. If there were 4 different atomic sentences, the number of possible truth-value assignments would be 16 (= 2^4). (This formula can be used to calculate how many rows would be needed for any number of atomic sentences.[18]) Once that has been determined, begin filling in the T's and F's from right to left, column by column, in the following way (see Figure 2.6b): Under the right-most atomic sentence, alternate single T's and single F's all the way down to the eighth row. Moving to the next atomic sentence on the left, alternate two T's followed by two F's straight down to the eighth row. Finally, under the left-most atomic sentence, alternate four T's followed by four F's. The resulting pattern is sometimes called a **matrix** of logically possible truth-value assignments for the

---

[15] In contrast with the other binary connectives, there is no conventional name in logic for the immediate components of a biconditional.

[16] See the exercises at the end of section 3.5.

[17] By the way, to check that your work was actually saved to the disk, you may want to invoke Directory under the File menu. (Note: *Symlog* will then ask to enter a 'Dir mask'; just hit the Enter key). The name of your work, possibly among others, will be listed on the screen.

[18] Later we shall be speaking of sets of sentences, and n will stand for the number of distinct atomic sentences in the set being analyzed.

TRUTH–TABLE : RUSSELL

	E G L	¬(G→E) ≡ (¬L ∨ ¬E)
1		
2		
3		
4		
5		
6		
7		
8		
9		

Figure 2.6a

TRUTH–TABLE : RUSSELL

	E G L	¬(G→E) ≡ (¬L ∨ ¬E)
1	T T T	
2	T T F	
3	T F T	
4	T F F	
5	F T T	
6	F T F	
7	F F T	
8	F F F	
9		

Figure 2.6b

TRUTH–TABLE : RUSSELL

	E G L	¬ (G → E) ≡ (¬L ∨ ¬E)
1	T T T	F T T T T FT F FT
2	T T F	F T T T F TF T FT
3	T F T	F F T T T FT F FT
4	T F F	F F T T F TF T FT
5	F T T	T T F F T FT T TF
6	F T F	T T F F T TF T TF
7	F F T	F F T F F FT T TF
8	F F F	F F T F F TF T TF
9		

Figure 2.6c

number of atomic sentences involved. The pattern for the matrix of truth-value assignments is easily extended for larger numbers. For four atomic sentences, the matrix would show eight T's followed by eight F's in the left-most column down to the sixteenth row. It may seem laborious to fill in all the cells one after another, but the practice will help you to learn the routine.[19]

Each column of truth-values should now be carried over to the Valuation Field and repeated under the appropriate atomic sentence. Notice that C occurs twice. Once that is done, the work of constructing the truth-table for RUSSELL can proceed. (As you enter work at the screen you may want to check your results with the completed problem as shown in Figure 2.6c.) It does not matter which side of the biconditional sign you start with, but we will start with the right-side component. This is a disjunction both of whose disjuncts are negations, so the truth-values of these two immediate components will have to be calculated first, from row 1 to 8. In each case you will be applying the definition of $\neg$: Wherever there is a T or an F under L or E you will put an F or a T, respectively, next to it in the column under the negation sign. This step will give you the set of all possible truth-values for $\neg$L and $\neg$E, which you need in order to determine the truth-values of their disjunction, $\neg$L $\vee$ $\neg$E. Now, row by row, calculate the truth-values for the disjunction, keeping in mind that such a sentence is T except when both of its components are F.[20] Once you have finished the column under $\vee$, you will have obtained the truth-values for the right-hand side of the biconditional and can shift over to the other side, where the sentence is a negated conditional. You already have the values for the antecedent and consequent, so the first task is to calculate the values under $\rightarrow$ and then under $\neg$, which will complete the work on the left side. Finally, the truth-values for the biconditional itself can be obtained. You will recall from the last example that such a sentence is T whenever both components are either both T or both F. Apply this definition row by row under $\equiv$, relating the values already found for its immediate components. To learn how these logical concepts fit together, it is important that you work out the values step by step for yourself and not merely copy what you see in Figure 2.6c.

You have now tabulated all of the logically possible conditions under which this biconditional is true (or false); you have obtained a truth-functional profile of this sentence. In the next section there will be more to say about the interpretation of truth-tables, but at this time you should take a moment to admire your work—and then, considering all your effort, save it!

---

[19] Once you learn the routine you can ask *Symlog* to fill in the truth-values for you. See Appendix C.

[20] The following is worth repeating: When using *Symlog*, as illustrated here, you will find it far more convenient to construct a truth-table as follows. Choose a connective in your sentence and then fill in its entire column with truth-values (according, of course, to the definition of the connective). Then, have the column checked by *Symlog* using Ctrl-C. If everything is correct, move on. Working in this way is not only faster but also you avoid compounding errors through your table.

For now we strongly suggest that you work through the Learn Exercises TABLE01 to TABLE06 which are stored on your disk. However, we want to make it a little easier for you to set up some of these problems on the screen. After doing the last two problems, you probably began to feel a certain tedium from entering all the truth-values for the matrix of truth-value assignments and then repeating these same columns under each atomic component of the sentence. This was, in fact, only the manual method, and you will be happy to know that *Symlog* gives you the option of an automatic procedure. The details can be found in Appendix C. The automatic procedure enables you to have the program rapidly generate the entire column of truth-values under an atomic statement or compound; by using it you can build the required matrix quickly and then import the columns of truth-values under all the atomic sentences in the Valuation Field. Then you are ready to begin calculating the truth-values of whatever compound sentences happen to be components of the sentence you are testing. The procedure is *Symlog*'s Generation command. In fact, by using this command you would be able, in effect, to have *Symlog* do a whole problem for you by getting it to present the truth-values not only of atomic sentences but of any compound as well. The program's designers thought that you should have this facility in case you ever wanted to use the truth-table technique for a quick check of a sentence in order to find out what truth-functional characteristics it has. However, when you are learning what truth-tables are, we urge you to use the Generation command wisely, such as when setting up a problem in the way just described. You will learn nothing of real benefit unless you apply the rules of the truth-functional connectives yourself at all the crucial points in a problem. It is worth repeating that another facility in the program which you will find very useful is its Justification command, which justifies, that is, checks, an entire column for you.[21] Both commands are issued with the Ctrl-C key combination.

As we said at the beginning of the text, the kind of logic you are learning with the help of *Symlog* is best thought of as a skill that you acquire by practice. This textbook can only give you information. The experience you need will develop naturally as you work with the program. The next section is going to draw on some of that newly acquired experience. Hence, after you have solved the Learn Exercises TABLE01 to TABLE06, we encourage you to increase your experience by trying some of the exercises for this section.

Exercises

We suggest that for at least some of the exercises below, you make use of *Symlog*'s Submit option. That is, complete a truth-table without evaluating any cells at the time of constructing it; that is, simply type in the entries you think are correct without pressing the Enter key. Once the truth-table is finished and you are satisfied with it, submit it for *Symlog* to check by in-

---

[21] This is the last time that we mention that these and all other commands can be found in Appendix C as well as on-line in the Reference Guide, under the Help menu.

voking *Symlog*'s OPTIONS menu, opening the Submit pull-down menu and selecting Submit Work from it. This will be good practice for your upcoming tests (where you will not have immediate feedback on any mistakes you make).

2.5.1 Using *Symlog*, construct truth-tables for each of the following sentences. (Note: If the name of a file begins with PR, as in PR11 below, *Symlog* will update your Progress Report when the exercise is successfully submitted.)

    a. $\neg P \vee \neg (Q \mathbin{\&} \neg P)$
    b. $\neg(P \mathbin{\&} \neg P)$
    c. $(H \rightarrow M) \rightarrow (\neg H \vee M)$
    d. $\neg(H \equiv G) \rightarrow \neg J$
    e. $\neg((A \rightarrow B) \equiv (\neg B \rightarrow \neg A))$
    f. $((P \vee Q) \rightarrow R) \equiv (Q \rightarrow (\neg R \mathbin{\&} \neg P))$
    g. $\neg(\neg P \equiv (Q \vee \neg R)) \rightarrow \neg S$
    h. $[A \vee [B \vee (C \vee D)]] \equiv [(A \vee B) \vee (C \vee D)]$
    i. $\neg[(P \mathbin{\&} (P \rightarrow Q)) \rightarrow Q]$
[PR11] j. $[(N \mathbin{\&} \neg B) \rightarrow (C \equiv L)] \rightarrow [N \rightarrow [\neg B \rightarrow (C \equiv L)]]$

2.5.2 Use the Create option under *Symlog*'s File menu to ask the program to generate sentences (randomly) whose truth-tables you should then construct. Submit your work when done.

2.6   *Formal Properties of Sentences of SL*

By this time you have completed and saved a cluster of problems from the truth-table exercises and (we hope) have used *Symlog*'s Generation and Justification commands to help speed your work. You should now have a clearer idea of what an SL sentence is and how to go about finding its truth-value for a given truth-value assignment. If the sentence under analysis is compound, you know that its truth-value depends on those of its immediate and subordinate components. Any truth-table that you have constructed on the screen displays a functional relationship between the SL sentence being tested and the set of truth-value assignments to its atomic components, each of which uniquely determines a truth-value. Consequently, you can see why SL sentences should be described, not simply as having the truth-value T or F, period, but rather as being T or F *on a given truth-value assignment*. In formal logic, a given truth-value assignment is said to satisfy a particular sentence if and only if the sentence is T on that assignment. We can express this succinctly in the following definition:

> **Definition.** A truth-value assignment, τ, **satisfies** a sentence, α, of SL if and only if α has the truth-value T on τ.

If τ satisfies α we then write $\tau \models \alpha$, and $\tau \not\models \alpha$ otherwise. The Greek letter τ used here is another metalogical symbol and stands for any truth-value assignment. Recall that for any sentence of SL having n atomic components there are 2^n possible truth-value assignments to its atomic components; τ is meant to signify any one of these, arbitrarily chosen. Notice that the preceding definition uses the terminology of necessary and sufficient conditions. If (let us suppose) τ fails to satisfy α, α has the value F on τ. It is important to recall that a sentence is neither T nor F by itself but always relative to some truth-value assignment. There is a concise way of representing particular truth-value assignments by using T's and F's together with commas and parentheses. For instance, (T, T) and (F, F, T) represent possible assignments for compounds consisting of, respectively, two and three atomic sentences. Think of these patterns as being identical to the various horizontal rows found in a truth-value assignment field, with the T's and F's (from left to right) matching the alphabetical order of sentences in the atomic component field. To illustrate, the assignment (F, F, T) corresponds to the penultimate assignment for any three atomic components. This particular assignment satisfies the sentences (G ∨ ¬M) → D as well as (¬A & C) & ¬B but does not satisfy the sentence ¬A → (C ∨ ¬D). A sentence of SL is **satisfiable** if and only if there is at least one truth-value assignment on which it is T. The logical concept of satisfaction, which is thus semantical in character, will now be used to classify the most important properties of SL sentences.

When you were working through the truth-table exercises you must have noticed that the main column of truth-values—the one underneath the main connective—took many different forms. Some columns consisted entirely of T's, others of all F's, and still others had a mixture of both sorts of truth-value. Take just a moment now to reflect on what these different sorts of columns reveal about the sentences corresponding to them. If the main connective has nothing but T's underneath, the tested sentence is T no matter what truth-values are assigned to its atomic components. It is T on every possible truth-value assignment; in short, it is 'always' T. However, if a column contained nothing but F's, the sentence would be 'never' T. These words 'always' and 'never' mean something quite definite in truth-functional terms. They relate a sentence concisely to the truth-values of its atomic components by indicating uniform results from a truth-table test, and such results are of considerable interest to logic because they help specify an important pair of properties. The first of these properties is that of truth-functional truth.

> **Definition.** A sentence α of SL is **truth-functionally true** if and only if it is satisfied by every truth-value assignment.

This definition specifies what it means for α to count as a logical truth of SL: Given any truth-value assignment τ, $\tau \models \alpha$. For instance, the sentence

P → (Q → P)

is truth-functionally true, as shown in the truth-table depicted in Figure 2.7.

```
 TRUTH–TABLE : TURING
                P Q     P → (Q → P)
              1 T T     T T   T T T
              2 T F     T T   F T T
              3 F T     F T   T F F
              4 F F     F T   F T F
              5
```

Figure 2.7

As you can see, every truth-value assignment makes the sentence take on the truth-value T; that is, there are no F's under the main connective of the sentence (the first occurrence of →).

The second property is that of truth-functional falsehood.

> **Definition.** A sentence α of SL is **truth-functionally false** if and only if it is satisfied by no truth-value assignment.

That is, given any truth-value assignment τ to α, $\tau \not\models \alpha$. For instance, the sentence

$$[(H \vee M) \rightarrow K] \equiv \neg[(M \vee H) \rightarrow K]$$

is truth-functionally false, as shown in the truth-table depicted in Figure 2.8. As you can see, there is no truth-value assignment that makes the sentence take on the truth-value T; that is, there are no T's under its main connective (the connective ≡).

Sentences with either one of these properties, namely, that of being truth-functionally true or truth-functionally false, are sometimes described, respectively, as being **logically true** or **logically false**.[22] There are also sentences which are neither truth-functionally true nor truth-functionally false, sentences whose main column in a truth-table test would contain at least one T and one F. Sentences of this sort are said to be truth-functionally indeterminate—or, simply, **contingent**—and are defined as follows:

> **Definition.** A sentence α of SL is **truth-functionally indeterminate** if and only if there is at least one truth-value assignment which satisfies α and at least one truth-value assignment which does not.

Note that to apply this definition you must find—there must be—two truth-value assignments, τ_1 and τ_2, such that $\tau_1 \models \alpha$ and $\tau_2 \not\models \alpha$. For instance, the sentence

$$(G \equiv E) \vee (B \ \& \ \neg N)$$

---

[22] The expression 'logically' applies more widely than 'truth-functionally,' as you will see later when we begin to look at the sentences of the language PL. Nevertheless, when the context makes it clear that we are speaking of SL sentences, we use the two expressions interchangeably.

TRUTH–TABLE : SKOLEM

	H K M	[(H v M) → K] ≡ ¬[(M v H) → K]
1	T T T	T T T T T F F T T T T T
2	T T F	T T F T T F F F T T T T
3	T F T	T T T F F F T T T T F F
4	T F F	T T F F F F T F T T F F
5	F T T	F T T T T F F T T F T T
6	F T F	F F F T T F F F F F T T
7	F F T	F T T F F F T T T F F F
8	F F F	F F F T F F F F F F T F
9		

Figure 2.8

is truth-functionally indeterminate, as the truth-table depicted in Figure 2.9 shows. There is at least one truth-value assignment for which the sentence takes on the truth-value T (any of the truth-value assignments in lines 1, 2, 4, 6, 7, 8, 9, 10, 15 and 16 satisfies the sentence), and there is at least one truth-value assignment for which it takes on the truth-value F (in fact, any of the truth-value assignments in lines 3, 5, 11, 12, 13 and 14 do so).

A contingent sentence, therefore, is sometimes T and sometimes F, depending on the actual truth-value assignment used. For the record, it does not matter to logic how many T's as opposed to F's the sentence happens to have under its main connective. Even with 15 out of 16 T's it would still fail to be logically true and hence would be classified as contingent (as would

TRUTH–TABLE : TARSKI

	B E G N	(G ≡ E) v (B & ¬N)
1	T T T T	T T T T T F F T
2	T T T F	T T T T T T T F
3	T T F T	F F T F T F F T
4	T T F F	F F T T T T T F
5	T F T T	T F F F T F F T
6	T F T F	T F F T T T T F
7	T F F T	F T F T T F F T
8	T F F F	F T F T T T T F
9	F T T T	T T T T F F F T
10	F T T F	T T T T F F T F
11	F T F T	F F T F F F F T
12	F T F F	F F T F F F T F
13	F F T T	T F F F F F F T
14	F F T F	T F F F F F T F
15	F F F T	F T F T F F F T
16	F F F F	F T F T F F T F

Figure 2.9

its negation). One sentence of SL is not 'more true' than another because it has more T's under its main connective. However, logic pays particular attention to logically true and logically false sentences. For one thing, the statements represented by these sentences are always true or always false, regardless of how the world is. But if a sentence is a contingent one, it becomes necessary to go outside of logic—say, by appealing to physics or history—to find out whether the statement it represents happens to be true in a given situation. For this reason alone it is not surprising that logic should be interested in statements which are either always true or always false. But there are other, more important reasons, as we shall see both in the next section and in the next chapter.

If a sentence of SL fails to be T for a given truth-value assignment, it has to be F for that truth-value assignment (there is no other possibility); but if it fails to be logically true, you cannot infer that it is logically false since there is indeed another possibility, namely, that of being contingent. However, since a contingent sentence fails to be either logically true or logically false, there is an alternative way to express the preceeding definition:

> **Alternative Definition.** A sentence α of SL is **truth-functionally indeterminate** if and only if it is neither truth-functionally true nor truth-functionally false.

This way of putting things may be more succinct but you may find the previous definition more immediately informative. Whichever definition you prefer, it is important to avoid thinking that contingent sentences are somehow an imperfect or irregular type of sentence. The language of SL abounds with them. Note that, for instance, every atomic sentence of SL is contingent. So too are all the sentences used earlier (such as A → B) to set out the definitions of the five connectives.

However, even though a sentence such as A ≡ B is contingent, there are sentences of the same form, $\alpha \equiv \beta$, which belong to the other two categories. Here is an example of each, where we give only the main column of truth-values (Figure 2.10). The biconditional on the left is logically true, which means that it is T on every truth-value assignment to its atomic components; but whenever a biconditional is T, its two immediate components must have the same truth-value (either both are T or both are F) on every truth-value assignment to their atomic components. As you will recall, the

TRUTH–TABLE : CARNAP			
	A B	(A → B) ≡ (¬A ∨ B) ,	(¬A ∨ B) ≡ (A & ¬B)
1	T T	T	F
2	T F	T	F
3	F T	T	F
4	F F	T	F
5			

Figure 2.10

	A B	A → B, ¬A ∨ B
1	T T	T T T FT T T
2	T F	T F F FT F F
3	F T	F T T TF T T
4	F F	F T F TF T F
5		

TRUTH–TABLE : BROWN

Figure 2.11

statement A → B is contingent and thus is T on at least one truth-value as-signment and F on at least one other. What follows, then, is that the other component of this biconditional, ¬A ∨ B, must be T or F on exactly the same truth-value assignments as A → B. (We invite you to verify this statement by filling in the missing entries in the truth-table.) In cases of this kind, A → B and ¬A ∨ B, or more generally, α and β, are said to be truth-functionally (or logically) equivalent. This does not mean that the two sentences equal each other; what it means is given in the following definition:

> **Definition.** Two sentences α and β of SL are **truth-functionally equiva-lent** if and only if every truth-value assignment which satisfies (fails to satisfy) one of the sentences also satisfies (fails to satisfy) the other.

For instance, as stated above, the two sentences A → B and ¬A ∨ B are truth-functionally equivalent, as the truth-table in Figure 2.11 shows. (Note that in *Symlog* you can enter in the Sentence Field more than one sentence—actu-ally a set of sentences; more on this later.)

A more succinct way of expressing this matter of truth-functional equivalence uses the previously defined concept of truth-functional truth:

> **Alternative Definition.** Two sentences α and β of SL are **truth-functionally equivalent** if and only if their biconditional, $\alpha \equiv \beta$, is truth-functionally true.

Sentences which are logically equivalent will play a significant role later in the exploration of SL. Basically, the importance of such sentences lies in the idea that if the truth-functional characteristics of α and β exactly match, one of them could be substituted for the other without altering the charac-teristics of any sentence to which it belongs. We mentioned in the last sec-tion that the connectives → and ∨ can be truth-functionally defined in terms of each other, but only with the help of ¬. The biconditional just discussed provides the basis for such a definition.[23]

No further definitions are required at this time. Before going on, how-ever, you should be confident that you grasp the sense of these definitions—

---

[23] You may have wondered whether the other biconditional, (¬A ∨ B) ≡ (A & ¬B), which illus-trates a truth-functionally false sentence, has a particular use in SL. The answer is no. Truth-functionally false sentences like these are not accorded a name or a role, except insofar as they are logical falsehoods.

that is, that you understand how they relate to the truth-tables that *Symlog* has been helping you to construct. Try to express the concepts in your own words. Understanding them in this way is much more valuable than merely committing the definitions to blind memory as though they contained secret formulas. Expressions such as 'contingent' or 'logical truth' are meant to describe something of the essential character of an SL sentence. As you have seen, SL sentences do not show what particular character they have on their surface. The form of a statement, say $\alpha \rightarrow \beta$, will not always tell you whether it is logically true, logically false or contingent. To find that information, you need to do some (truth-table) testing. But if it is true that $\alpha \rightarrow \beta$ is, say, contingent, then by understanding these definitions you would know what the results of a truth-table test done on it would have to look like. In the following section we will describe a method which will make testing much easier. But before you move on, we strongly suggest that you now try the Learn Exercises TABLE07 to TABLE12 on your disk, which deal with the truth-functional concepts just discussed.

Exercises

2.6.1 Answer yes or no to the following (i.e., determine whether the given truth-value assignment satisfies the given sentence or not).

   a. (T,F) $\models$ A & $\neg$B

   b. (T,F) $\models$ B $\vee \neg$(B $\vee$ A)

   c. (F,T,T) $\models$ K $\rightarrow$ ($\neg$H $\vee \neg$G)

   d. (F,T,F,F) $\models$ ($\neg$J & H) $\vee$ ($\neg$G & $\neg$F)

   e. (F,T,F) $\models$ (J $\vee \neg$G) & ($\neg$H $\rightarrow$ J)

2.6.2 Use *Symlog* to determine which of the following sentences are satisfiable, and when the sentence is satisfiable, give the truth-value assignments which satisfy it.

   a. A & $\neg$A

   b. B

   c. K $\rightarrow$ ($\neg$H $\vee \neg$K)

   d. $\neg$[($\neg$P & (P $\vee$ Q)) $\rightarrow$ Q]

   e. (C $\vee \neg$G) & ($\neg$G $\rightarrow$ B)

2.6.3 Determine by means of a (long) truth-table in *Symlog* whether each of the following sentences is truth-functionally true, truth-functionally false or truth-functionally indeterminate.

   a. (G $\equiv$ M) $\equiv \neg$(M $\equiv$ G)

   b. $\neg$[[(A $\rightarrow$ B) & (B $\rightarrow$ A)] $\rightarrow$ (A $\equiv$ B)]

   c. (M & B) $\rightarrow$ D

   d. (A $\rightarrow$ B) $\equiv$ ($\neg$B $\rightarrow \neg$A)

   e. (A $\rightarrow$ M) $\rightarrow$ ($\neg$A $\vee$ M)

   f. [(H $\equiv$ G) $\rightarrow \neg$D] $\vee$ (P $\equiv$ P)

   g. (A $\vee$ H) $\rightarrow \neg$(A $\vee$ H)

   h. $\neg$[[$\neg$A & $\neg$(B $\vee$ C)] $\vee$ [C $\vee$ (B $\vee$ A)]]

    i. A & ¬A

    j. M

    k. ¬G → (H ≡ D)

    l. [(D ∨ E) → Q] ≡ [Q ∨ (¬E & ¬D)]

    m. (A ∨ B) ≡ ¬(M ≡ ¬J)

    n. ¬[(H ≡ G) → ¬D] & ¬(P ≡ P)

    o. (M & (M → G)) → (G & M)

2.6.4 Construct appropriate truth-tables with *Symlog* to show that the sentences in each of the following pairs are truth-functionally equivalent.

    a. P ∨ P and P & P

    b. ¬(A → B) and ¬(¬A ∨ ¬¬B)

    c. ¬(¬J & K) and J ∨ ¬K

    d. ¬(P & (Q & R)) and ¬P ∨ (¬Q ∨ ¬R)

    e. (E ∨ F) & ¬G and ¬[¬(¬E & ¬F) → G]

    f. (¬L → ¬N) & (L ∨ Q) and (Q & ¬N) ∨ L

    g. (C ≡ ¬(B ∨ ¬E)) and (C → (¬B & E)) & ((B ∨ ¬E) ∨ C)

    h. ¬¬(¬A ∨ D) and ¬D → ¬A

    i. P ≡ ¬P and ¬(L ∨ ¬L) ∨ (Q & ¬Q)

    j. R → (¬S ∨ N) and (S & ¬N) → ¬R

2.6.5 Answer true or false to each of the following and explain your answer.

    a. If α is truth-functionally true then $\neg\alpha$ is truth-functionally false.

    b. If α is truth-functionally indeterminate then so is $\neg\alpha$.

    c. The conjunction of any two truth-functionally false sentences is itself truth-functionally false.

    d. The conjunction of any two truth-functionally indeterminate sentences is itself truth-functionally indeterminate.

    e. If α and β are truth-functionally equivalent then $\alpha \equiv \beta$ is truth-functionally true.

    f. Any sentence of the form $(\alpha \rightarrow \beta) \equiv (\neg\beta \rightarrow \neg\alpha)$ is truth-functionally true.

2.6.6 Use the Create option under *Symlog*'s File menu to ask the program to generate sentences (randomly) whose truth-functional status (truth-functional truth, falsehood or indeterminacy) you should then determine. Submit your work when done.

2.7   Short Truth-Table Tests

Let us say that you are asked to determine whether or not the following sentence is truth-functionally true:

$$[(P \rightarrow Q) \& (R \rightarrow S)] \rightarrow [\neg(P \vee R) \vee (Q \vee S)]$$

It is a big problem. Just by counting the different atomic sentences it contains, you can tell there will be a matrix of 16 different possible truth-value assignments (which you already know is quite a screenful). But before you set out to answer the question in the usual way by constructing a full truth-table, let us do some reasoning about the question itself because there is in fact a different way of answering it which often proves to be much quicker.

First, the question has a narrow focus: You have to find out only whether this sentence is a logical truth; so, if you happen to find it is not, you are not being asked to say which of the two remaining categories—logical falsehood or contingency—it belongs to. Now, ask yourself this: What would the main column of truth-values look like if it is a logical truth? Here is a hint. It would consist of exactly 16 T's. But if it is not a logical truth? Then, there would have to be at least 1 F. So, what would happen if you assumed that this sentence is not logically true; that is, what would happen if you copied it down and then placed an F under the main connective? Well, nothing would happen until you began to follow the consequences of this assumption and tried to find a truth-value assignment to its atomic components on which it is F. If the sentence is F (on some truth-value assignment) there must be—obviously enough—at least one such assignment, and what we shall do is work 'backward' in search of it. Since the sentence is a conditional and is assumed to be F for some truth-value assignment, its antecedent must be T and its consequent F (on the same truth-value assignment). This reasoning leads us on. Since the antecedent takes a T (on this assumption) and it is a conjunction, then so are both of its conjuncts; likewise, since the consequent takes an F and is a disjunction, both of its disjuncts would also take an F. We can continue figuring out what truth-values the immediate components of these components would have on the assumption that the original statement itself is F on some truth-value assignment. Only, the more you go on in this way, the easier it becomes to get lost in a forest of truth-values. We need to keep a record of what we are doing, and that is where *Symlog* can be a great help. So let us pause for a moment to set up this problem on the screen and carry out our reasoning with the aid of *Symlog*. Be sure not to lose sight of the forest itself: We want to learn whether the sentence we began with is truth-functionally true. The procedure to be followed is called the **short truth-table test,** and you are likely to use it often.

We need a name for this problem. We suggest you use the name given in the text: WANG. Take a fresh sheet of 'paper' from *Symlog*'s Truth-Table Pad, name your work, enter the original sentence in the Sentence Field, then (instead of beginning to construct the usual matrix) scroll over to the cell directly underneath the main connective in the Valuation Field and—according to our assumption—enter an F in that cell (Figure 2.12a).

Now we can put the program to work. *Symlog* has a command called the Goal Analysis command (fully described in Appendix C), which will assist in tracking truth-values through a sentence. It was designed to be part of the short truth-table test. Here is how it works. Place the cursor over the F which you just entered under the horseshoe → and issue the Goal Analysis—Shift-Tab—command; immediately, *Symlog* will place a T under the main connective of the antecedent and an F under that of the consequent. The program can readily do so because these are the truth-value assignments which the antecedent and consequent must have whenever a conditional sentence takes an F (Figure 2.12b).

Now move over to the consequent side of the sentence, place the cursor on the F and give the Goal Analysis command again. *Symlog* at once puts an F under each of the disjuncts (since both disjuncts have to be F if the disjunction itself is). Since the right-hand disjunct itself is a disjunction, if you place your cursor over its truth-value and, once again, give the Goal Analysis command, a pair of F's will appear under its two atomic components, Q and S. Applying the Goal Analysis routine to each of these in turn makes their truth-values turn up in the appropriate places in the Truth-Value Assignment Field (Figure 2.12c).

The truth-value of the left-hand disjunct of the consequent is F. When you place your cursor on top and issue the Goal Analysis command, you will see a T appear under the disjunction, P ∨ R (Figure 2.12d). But when you repeat this move on the T itself something different happens: On the Message Line *Symlog* offers you a choice since a disjunction is T on any of three different truth-value assignments. Not only are these three choices listed but a fourth and a fifth are listed as well—Branch and None, respectively—each identified by number. At this point choose 'none' and move the cursor to the main connective—the ampersand—of the antecedent (we will talk about these choices later). The Goal Analysis routine will produce T's under both of the conjuncts, but each of these contains an atomic sentence whose truth-value has already been found (look back at the Truth-Value Assignment Field). So your next move is to enter an F under both Q and S. This step leads immediately to another pair of moves. If you apply the goal method to each conjunct separately you should see *Symlog* placing an F under their corresponding antecedents P and R. The reason is that both of these conjuncts have the value T and both are conditionals whose consequents, we know, must have the value F. But that means that their antecedents, P and R, must also have the value F because if you were to assign a T to either antecedent you would produce an impossible truth-value assignment: According to SL's truth-table definitions, every conditional with an antecedent which is T and a consequent which is F can only be F. Be sure to issue the Goal Analysis command on each P and R to make these values surface in the Truth-Value Assignment Field (Figure 2.12e). Incidentally, these four F's in the Truth-Value Assignment Field are listed in row 1, whereas in a 16-row matrix they would turn up in the final row. Thus, if you try separately to justify each of these F's by hitting the Enter key, *Symlog* will deliver an error message at the bottom of the screen. To avoid this message, be sure to use the Goal Analysis routine to make the program display the truth-values for you.[24]

We have now come to the point at which we can complete the job of filling in truth-values since there is an entry for each of the atomic sen-

---

[24] The fact that these values are listed in row 1 is of no consequence. What we are looking for is a truth-value assignment (sometimes there will be more than one) on which the sentence being tested is F, and if this is found, the row number corresponding to it is irrelevant. The numbering of rows in a matrix is related only to *Symlog*'s long truth-tables.

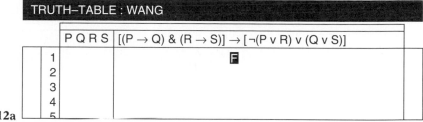

TRUTH–TABLE : WANG

	P Q R S	[(P → Q) & (R → S)] → [¬(P v R) v (Q v S)]
1		F
2		
3		
4		
5		

Figure 2.12a

TRUTH–TABLE : WANG

	P Q R S	[(P → Q) & (R → S)] → [¬(P v R) v (Q v S)]
1		T F F
2		
3		
4		
5		

Figure 2.12b

TRUTH–TABLE : WANG

	P Q R S	[(P → Q) & (R → S)] → [¬(P v R) v (Q v S)]
1	F F	T F F F F F F
2		
3		
4		
5		

Figure 2.12c

TRUTH–TABLE : WANG

	P Q R S	[(P → Q) & (R → S)] → [¬(P v R) v (Q v S)]
1	F F	T F F T F F F F
2		
3		
4		
5		

Figure 2.12d

TRUTH–TABLE : WANG

	P Q R S	[(P → Q) & (R → S)] → [¬(P v R) v (Q v S)]
1	F F F F	F T F T F T F F F T F F F
2		
3		
4		
5		

Figure 2.12e

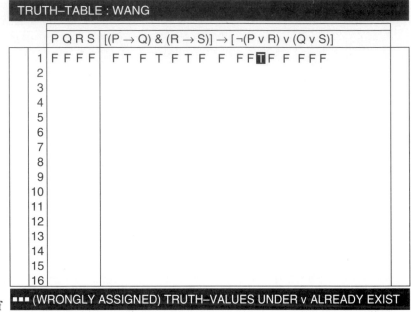

Figure 2.12f   ▪▪▪ (WRONGLY ASSIGNED) TRUTH–VALUES UNDER ∨ ALREADY EXIST

tences in the Truth-Value Assignment Field. Remember that we had left two blanks under P and R in the sentence ¬(P ∨ R). We since found that both of these must carry the value F, so we need to scroll back to this disjunction and enter these values. At this point, however, *Symlog* issues a complaint on the Error Line (whether you apply the goal method to ∨ or try to justify its truth-value T). The truth-value assignment you have just entered is an impossible one (Figure 2.12f).

No disjunction can be T when both of its disjuncts are F. And yet, this impossible assignment was unavoidable: We found that both P and R have to be F, and before that we also knew their disjunction has to be T. It is no use going back and changing the truth-value of either atomic sentence, for that would only produce an impossible truth-value assignment in the antecedent. And of course there is no point in saying that P or R is both T and F. So, what has happened? We have been led into an impossible situation—a logical contradiction—by our original assumption that the sentence is not truth-functionally true, that it is F on some truth-value assignment or other. Our attempt to discover such an assignment has been unsuccessful. What we have found instead is that there isn't any. In other words, we have found that WANG is a truth-functional truth.

Here is a very brief summary of the kind of reasoning that was just carried out. Suppose you want to find out whether a certain sentence of SL, call it α, is a logical truth. Assume that α is not logically true by assigning the value F to its main connective. From this assumption it follows that there must be some truth-value assignment to the atomic components of α on which it is F. Set out to discover such an assignment by working downward from the truth-value of α itself to those of its immediate components, and keep on until you reach the bedrock of atomic sentences, always maintaining consistency with the semantic rules of SL, that is, with the rules for truth-table construction. At some point in this journey you may be driven into unavoidable conflict with those rules (this can occur even before you reach any or all of the atomic sentences). If so, your original assumption was false and you can rightly conclude that α is truth-functionally true. If no conflict arises, you have indeed found a truth-value assignment on which α is F and you will be justified in concluding that it fails to be a truth-functional truth.

This kind of reasoning is common in formal logic. A person succeeds in proving that a claim is true (in this case, that α is logically true) by showing that a contradiction inescapably follows from the assumption of its denial. In logic, no less than in other areas of reasoning, a contradiction is just about the worst thing to fall into. It amounts to saying that some statement and its denial are both true at the same time, and no course in formal logic is needed to enable you to recognize the absurdity in this, for such a combination is bound to be always false. But logic is able to use contradictions to its advantage. If you wish, think of them as a kind of powerful force which reasoning is able to harness for the sake of a cogent proof. We will be using this style of proof often, referring to it as the method of **indirect proof.**[25]

The same method of reasoning can serve to discover whether a given statement, α, is logically false or else contingent. If your goal is the former, make the assumption that α has the value T on some truth-value assignment and construct a short truth-table for it in the manner previously described. If the test encounters an inescapable contradiction, your assumption has to be rejected (and you will have shown that α is logically false); if it does not, the assumption that α is not logically false is confirmed. Finding out whether a sentence is contingent is more complicated since it amounts to showing that the sentence is neither logically true nor logically false, and this proof would involve a pair of short truth-table tests. You must show that there is a truth-value assignment which satisfies the sentence. You also must show there is one which does not.

The short truth-table test has both advantages and disadvantages over the long-form test, which you should be aware of before approaching the exercises for this section. First, the advantages: The short test is able to give you answers to crucial questions quickly. If the question being asked is 'Is some particular sentence logically true?' the short test can obtain, in many cases, an answer with less effort than that required by the long one. If you find that your sentence is not logically true, you will be able to cite a truth-value assignment to prove it. Typically, you would not be interested in citing all such assignments—one is enough to establish the absence of logical truth. Apart from this, the process of obtaining the answer is somewhat 'less mechanical' and engages your reasoning in a more challenging and interesting way than is possible with a long test. Although *Symlog* gives you facility

---

[25] This method is also known as *reductio ad absurdum*, where the 'absurdity' is a derivable contradiction.

with both kinds of test, you will most likely find the short one the preferable route to follow. This will become quite apparent in the next chapter, which will describe techniques for assessing arguments.

Now for the disadvantages: The mechanical character of the long test is also its virtue. When you have finished constructing your truth-table row by row you have an absolute assurance of being able to read off the results under the main connective. In contrast, no mechanical *regularity* is to be expected from the short test in your hunt for a possible truth-value assignment. There was a hint of this in problem WANG. When we reached the disjunction P∨R the first time and applied the goal analysis routine, we were offered multiple choices of truth-values for the disjuncts. Although we managed eventually to obtain a single set of values for these disjuncts, such luck does not always occur and you will sometimes have no choice but to investigate all the alternative truth-value assignments. Consider the example, in Figure 2.13a, of a short truth-table problem which has been partly completed. (We strongly encourage you to follow this example with the aid of *Symlog*.)

As before, the goal here is to find out whether this conditional statement is a logical truth—which is why an F stands under the main connective. The goal analysis method immediately determines the truth-values of the antecedent and consequent, and since the consequent itself is a conditional (with truth-value F), the values for P and R are quickly obtained too: T and F, respectively. However, these truth-values are of no immediate help in working out the remaining ones of the antecedent, as you can see for yourself, so let us see how the program can help us. When you place the cursor over the truth-value T of the antecedent and give the Goal Analysis command, *Symlog* will offer five numbered choices—three pairs of truth-values, a 'branch' option and a 'none of these' option. (The reason for the three alternatives should be obvious: They reflect the truth-conditions for any conditional which carries the value T.) At this point, the only way to make progress is to try all of these possibilities. As you can see, your analysis branches at this point in three possible directions, all of which must be considered in turn to see if any one of them leads to a truth-value assignment which makes the sentence F. If this is not the case, that is, no branch leads to a truth-value assignment which makes the sentence F, we know that no truth-value assignment will falsify it and, therefore, it is logically true. Choosing Branch will allow you to do just this, namely, to consider all the possibilites in turn in a systematic way (Figure 2.13b).[26]

Let us consider the first branch, that is, possibility. Applying the goal method to the antecedent Q → R, we make this current branch branch still further (Figure 2.13c). The problem with this new current branch (i.e., the first row in the short truth-table) is that R has been assigned two distinct truth-values, which is absurd. Hence, delete this row (with Ctrl-Y) and con-

---

[26] In case you have not guessed yet, a branch could branch even further. All branches can be considered in turn—systematically and without loosing track of your work—by always working in the first row of the Truth-Table Pad. A branch can be conveniently discarded by simply deleting its row.

TRUTH–TABLE : PEANO

	P	Q	R	[(Q → R) → (P → Q)] → (P → R)
1	T		F	🆃 F T F F
2				
3				
4				
5				
6				

Figure 2.13a

TRUTH–TABLE : PEANO

	P	Q	R	[(Q → R) → (P → Q)] → (P → R)
1	T		F	T 🆃 T F T F F
2	T		F	F T T F T F F
3	T		F	F T F F T F F
4				
5				
6				

Figure 2.13b

TRUTH–TABLE : PEANO

	P	Q	R	[(Q → R) → (P → Q)] → (P → R)
1	T		F	T 🆃 T T T F T F F
2	T		F	F T T T T F T F F
3	T		F	F T F T T F T F F
4	T		F	F T T F T F F
5	T		F	F T F F T F F
6				

Figure 2.13c

TRUTH–TABLE : PEANO

	P	Q	R	[(Q → R) → (P → Q)] → (P → R)
1	T		F	F 🆃 F T T F T F F
2	T		F	F T T F T F F
3	T		F	F T F F T F F
4				
5				
6				

Figure 2.13d

sider the next branch (which is the new row 1 since *Symlog* moves your short truth-table up when you delete one row). The same problem applies here: R has been assigned two distinct truth-value assignments; so discard this branch too (Figure 2.13d). You may want to apply the goal method to the consequent P → Q, but a quick look at the truth-values assigned to the atomic components shows that this new current branch can be discarded: Since P is T and Q is F, P → Q cannot be T. Hence, delete this branch. Two more branches to go (Figure 2.13e).

TRUTH–TABLE : PEANO

	P Q R	[(Q → R) → (P → Q)] → (P → R)
1	T F	**F** T T F T F F
2	T F	F T F F T F F
3		
4		
5		
6		

Figure 2.13e

TRUTH–TABLE : PEANO

	P Q R	[(Q → R) → (P → Q)] → (P → R)
1	T F	T **F** F T T F T F F
2	T F	F T F F T F F
3		
4		
5		
6		

Figure 2.13f

TRUTH–TABLE : PEANO

	P Q R	[(Q → R) → (P → Q)] → (P → R)
1	T F	T F F T T **T** T F T F F
2	T F	T F F T F T T F T F F
3	T F	T F F T F T F F T F F
4	T F	F T F F T F F
5		
6		

Figure 2.13g

At this point you may spot a possible truth-value assignment which will falsify the sentence: Q → R can only be F if Q is T and R if F, which is consistent with our previously assigned truth-values to P and R. But if P is T and Q is T then P → Q is T, also consistent with the truth-value assigned to this conditional. In short, it seems that the assignment (T,T,F) will do the job. More systematically, apply the goal method to Q → R (Figure 2.13f) and then to P → Q by branching (Figure 2.13g). These steps complete the job. You have found a truth-value assignment on which the original statement is false (which shows that it is not a logical truth).

This example illustrates an important point about the short truth-table method, namely, that sometimes you will face multiple possibilities of truth-value assignments (and testing out some of these might produce further sets of possibilities);[27] once you have embarked on the short method for

---

[27] This is inevitable whenever a biconditional is being tested, whatever truth-value is initially assigned to it.

testing a sentence, you should commit yourself to following through to discovering whether or not there is a decisive truth-value assignment. Only delete a branch, that is, a truth-table row, when the branch leads to an absurdity. Then, consider the next one. The best way to gain the experience you need from short truth-tables is by first doing the Learn Exercises TABLE13 to TABLE23 on your disk and then continuing with the exercises for this section, which are designed to be neither ridiculously easy nor impossibly long.

Exercises

2.7.1 Use *Symlog* to construct a short truth-table for each sentence to show that it is truth-functionally true.

    a. $[(E \vee F) \rightarrow R] \equiv [R \vee (\neg F \,\&\, \neg E)]$

    b. $[J \equiv (K \vee \neg A)] \rightarrow [[\neg(\neg A \vee K) \rightarrow \neg J] \,\&\, [(K \vee \neg A) \rightarrow J]]$

    c. $[A \vee [B \vee (C \vee D)]] \equiv [(A \vee B) \vee (C \vee D)]$

    d. $[\neg(K \,\&\, \neg L) \vee (D \rightarrow M)] \equiv [\neg(D \rightarrow M) \rightarrow (L \vee \neg K)]$

    e. $[(M \,\&\, \neg A) \rightarrow (B \equiv K)] \rightarrow [M \rightarrow [\neg A \rightarrow (B \equiv K)]]$

2.7.2 Use *Symlog* to construct a short truth-table for each sentence to show that it is truth-functionally false.

    a. $\neg[(A \equiv B) \vee (\neg A \equiv B)]$

    b. $\neg[[(M \equiv R) \rightarrow E] \equiv [E \vee \neg(R \equiv M)]]$

    c. $[\neg(A \,\&\, B) \vee \neg(D \vee M)] \,\&\, \neg[\neg[(A \,\&\, B) \,\&\, (D \vee M)]]$

    d. $[A \vee (B \,\&\, \neg H)] \,\&\, \neg[(B \vee A) \,\&\, (\neg H \vee A)]$

    e. $\neg[(\neg H \,\&\, M) \rightarrow A] \,\&\, [M \rightarrow (\neg H \rightarrow A)]$

2.7.3 Use *Symlog* to construct short truth-tables for each sentence to show that it is truth-functionally indeterminate.

    a. $[K \vee (J \equiv L)] \rightarrow \neg K$

    b. $\neg[(L \,\&\, \neg M) \vee H] \rightarrow E$

    c. $\neg\neg[(M \vee A) \,\&\, \neg(D \rightarrow \neg B)]$

    d. $[A \vee (B \vee C)] \,\&\, (C \vee M)$

    e. $[\neg A \equiv (H \vee \neg\neg G)] \rightarrow K$

2.7.4 Use *Symlog*'s short truth-table test to determine whether each pair of sentences in exercise 2.6.4 is a truth-functional equivalence.

2.7.5 Show that $(\alpha \vee \beta) \vee \delta$ and $\alpha \vee (\beta \vee \delta)$ are truth-functionally equivalent (so that it would be 'permissible' to write $\alpha \vee \beta \vee \delta$ in **SL**). Do the same for $\alpha \,\&\, \beta \,\&\, \delta$ and $\alpha \equiv \beta \equiv \delta$. (Note: If you want to solve this problem with *Symlog*, use, respectively, A, B and D instead of α, β and δ.)

2.8   *Extensions of the Truth-Table Method*

Symlog sets a maximum of four atomic sentences per problem. This limit allows enough variety and richness for learning the techniques of both the long and short truth-table methods and makes it unnecessary for you to carry over work from one screen to another. Nevertheless, these techniques can easily be applied independently of *Symlog* to problems having more than four atomic sentences. In theory, there is no limit to the number, although in practice the 'pay off' in experience and logical knowledge which you could gain from attacking larger problems is likely to be about the same as from working within *Symlog*'s framework.

Here is how you would proceed. For any statement α to be tested, count up the number of different atomic sentences and then apply the formula 2^n to determine the number of logically possible truth-value assignments. Such numbers increase geometrically. For sentences having 5, 6 or 7 atomic components, there would be 32, 64 or 128 different truth-value assignments, respectively, so that the higher you go the more desirable it becomes to use the short truth-table test. When you attempt a problem of any size on 'real' paper, try to preserve the general look of *Symlog*'s screen. Allow room on the left-hand side to list atomic components and their truth-value assignments and sufficient space underneath the sentence to deal with any multiple possibilities which might turn up.

As far as this textbook is concerned, however, you will not be forced to switch away from electronic paper. Whenever possible, think of ways to get *Symlog* to help you. Here is a final suggestion. When constructing long truth-tables, you may want to invoke *Symlog*'s Noninteractive Mode under the Services menu. *Symlog* will then assume a passive role until called upon. Once you have completed your work you can use the program's Submit option to have your work checked. The program will then inform you at the bottom of the screen whether any errors have been found and at the same time will post markers for them. You will be impressed by how little time it takes *Symlog* to look over your work, so much so that you may wish to complete and save a whole batch of problems first and then submit them one by one.

Exercises

2.8.1 How many rows does the long truth-table have for each of the following sentences?

  a. A ∨ (B ∨ C)

  b. [P → (R ∨ P)] & (Q ∨ R)

  c. H ∨ [(K ∨ L) & (J ∨ N)]

  d. ¬C ∨ (C → ¬B)

  e. [¬P ≡ (¬P → P)] & ¬(P ≡ ¬¬P)

2.8.2 Give an example of a sentence which, when tested for logical truth, has the same number of rows in the short truth-table test as in the long truth-table test.

2.8.3 Assume that you could construct a whole row in a truth-table in one second. How long would it take you to construct the truth-table for a sentence with 35 sentence letters?

3

Translating and Analyzing Arguments

In this chapter our main concern will be arguments, not in the sense of disputes or verbal battles but in the sense of 'pieces of reasoning.' We are going to use truth-functional logic to represent their structure and to devise ways of sorting out 'strong' arguments from 'weak' ones. For a while, this investigation is going to take us away from symbolic logic and back to ordinary language because that is the native home of arguments. Not even logicians argue merely in symbols; like everyone else, whatever the topic, they construct arguments by using statements expressed in the medium of natural language. So the logical study of arguments needs to take into view the various ways in which statements in ordinary language are compounded and then assembled into the familiar patterns of reasons and conclusions. Here is the plan to be followed. The first thing is to look at the sense that words like 'and' and 'or' have in ordinary language and to catalog some of the ways in which this sense is conveyed. Although the truth-table definitions introduced earlier capture what is essential to their meaning, some details that are useful to know had to be ignored at the time. The next job is to consider what arguments are and how they are expressed in natural language. Once that is done, we can return to the framework of symbolic logic in order to present ways of representing and assessing them. Some new concepts of truth-functional logic are going to be needed here, but you will find them closely related to the ones introduced in the last chapter and easily understood by means of *Symlog*'s truth-table tests.

   The final section of this chapter will discuss SL as the foundation of a logical analysis of language and will suggest a few ways of consolidating that foundation. This brief discussion is meant to serve as an example of what is called metalogic, or the systematic reasoning about logic itself.

3.1   *Translating Logical Compounds*

The last chapter described how truth-functional logic interprets each of the five compound-forming symbols, $\neg$, &, $\vee$, $\rightarrow$, and $\equiv$, but it touched only briefly on the different ways in which these logical concepts are expressed in ordinary language. Even though we cannot hope to list here all of these various ways, it is still possible to call your attention to some obvious ones, and a few which are less obvious, so that you can identify examples of these connectives more easily. That is the aim of the present section. We will cover each of the connectives in the same order as before and use different instances of simple statements as we go along. To symbolize them we will choose sentence letters which correspond to key words in the statements.

Negation Revisited

The negation of a sentence is sometimes called its **denial.** The sentence $\neg\alpha$ would then be described as the denial of α. However, these two notions do not always coincide. Imagine the situation in which an angry father says to a young man, 'You never intended to marry my daughter!' to which the accused replies, 'But I did, I did!' What these last words express is the simple statement 'I intended to marry her,' which would be symbolized in SL by a symbol such as I (or M if you prefer); however, in this context the young man's words would be understood as a denial of the father's accusation, even though it lacks a negative word like 'not.' Such an example shows that it is sometimes necessary to distinguish the actual work that a statement does from its overt logical form in order to estimate more fully what is being communicated. Concerns of this sort belong to a branch of logic called pragmatics, but the account of SL being given here belongs to a different branch, which restricts itself to overt logical forms. Our aim is to relate SL to ordinary language without making ordinary language itself the main object of study. Consequently, we will speak of negations rather than denials and focus on linguistic signs alone, for the most part avoiding any reference to an imagined context.

Let us take a fresh example—and one which involves very little in the way of personal dynamics. Did the famous pirate Bluebeard really have a beard that was blue? Here are some ways in which it is possible to reply in the negative:

Bluebeard did not have a blue beard.
It's false that Bluebeard had a blue beard.
Bluebeard lacked a blue beard.

It isn't the case that Bluebeard had a blue beard.

There's no truth in saying that Bluebeard had a blue beard.

The idea that Bluebeard's beard was blue is ridiculous.

Bluebeard had a blue beard? That's nonsense!

SL looks on all these sentences as expressing the negation of the simple statement 'Bluebeard had a blue beard,' which we will represent by the atomic sentence B. In using any of them, a speaker might also show surprise or impatience or some other feeling, but as you already know, the symbolism of SL never takes account of such features of language use. The critical question to ask yourself is whether a statement seems to be meant as a negation, whatever else is conveyed. If so, make ¬ the main operator, and the result will be a sentence of SL that will include as much of the meaning of the original statement as we need.

A natural language like English is grammatically rich in ways of forming negative statements. Here is a handful of illustrations for the negation of the statement that Bluebeard had friends:

Bluebeard didn't have any friends.

Bluebeard had no friends.

Bluebeard was without friends.

Bluebeard was friendless.

Bluebeard was never befriended.

There are still other ways of bringing in negation, which you can easily recognize in the following examples:

Bluebeard was incapable of generosity.

Bluebeard was thoroughly impolite.

Bluebeard was disloyal to his country.

But when you reach cases like these, it becomes a matter of choice whether they are to be treated as simple statements or as negations. In other words, you could either symbolize the whole of the third example just given as, say, D (Bluebeard was disloyal to his country) or represent the sentence as a negation, ¬L (It is false that Bluebeard was loyal to his country).[1] There is no line which clearly separates statements of this sort into one or another group, nor is any such line really needed. You simply have to decide what your simple statement is to be, assign an appropriate symbol to it and then use it consistently. This means, for instance, that if you choose L as an atomic sentence to represent the simple satement 'Bluebeard was loyal to his

---

[1] Two different sentence letters have been used in this example for the sake of clarity. It would be possible to use the same letter in either of the two ways described, though not of course in both.

country,' and then happen to meet a statement such as 'It isn't true that Bluebeard was disloyal to his country,' your symbolization in SL will be ¬¬L.[2]

Keep a sharp lookout for the scope of a negation (i.e., what sentences
the negation sign applies to). In ordinary language, as well as in SL, negation can encompass a good deal of complicated structure. In fact, sometimes you might even find yourself wishing that natural language would
adopt SL's method of punctuation. Compare, for instance, the following
sentence and its more orderly looking symbolic translation:

> It's false that if Bluebeard had neither friends nor a blue beard, then
> he didn't fail to have a happy childhood.
>
> ¬[¬(F ∨ B) → ¬¬H]

Conjunction Revisited

In natural language there is a fundamental, universally recognized convention about conjoining statements which has no counterpart in SL. This is
the practice of listing conjuncts one after the other without any explicit use
of a connective. When Julius Caesar summed up his wartime experiences in
Gaul[3] with the words 'I came, I saw, I conquered,' people did not puzzle
over how he meant to combine these three statements. The same holds true
for us today. We know that what Caesar meant was that he came and saw
and conquered. Caesar stopped at three statements, though it is easy to
imagine a passage containing many more, such as the description of someone's appearance or beliefs. An SL translation of Caesar's words, however,
would need to use the & symbol explicitly, along with appropriate punctuation, to yield a well-formed formula, for instance, (C & S) & Q.[4] This is one
important difference between the rules for & and 'and.' Let us look at some
others.

As you know from *Symlog*'s truth-tables, the symbol & is purely truth-
functional and the order of conjuncts is immaterial. That is, in the translation just given the order of the atomic sentences could be rearranged in any
way one chooses without affecting its truth-functional character. But supposing Caesar had said, 'I conquered, I saw, I came'; what would we think
he meant? Maybe that after conquering, he saw what he had done and has
only just arrived. This thought would leave us quite confused, although
what would be confusing is not so much the conjunction of these statements
as their order. We take Caesar to be reporting events that follow a temporal
order in which, according to another convention of natural language, the

---

[2] Since the statement 'Bluebeard was loyal to his country' and 'It isn't true that Bluebeard was
disloyal to his country' are logically equivalent, either L or ¬¬L would serve to symbolize 'It
isn't true that Bluebeard was disloyal to his country.' The double negation was used to make a
point about keeping track of simple statements.

[3] Roughly, the territory of France and Belgium.

[4] The alternative version, C & (S & Q), is logically equivalent.

earliest event is listed first. In short, Caesar's statements are linked by an implicit 'and then,' which makes rearranging them awkward if not impossible.

However, the sense of 'and' as 'and then' is only an occasional feature of conjunctions in ordinary language. It appears in narratives of events but not in descriptions of how things appear. A newspaper article about a catastrophe would use this sense more than a newspaper editorial. The word 'then' is often used by itself for just this purpose. We all recognize this temporal sense of 'and' without needing to have it pointed out to us but would find it hard to come up with a precise rule for its use. Fortunately, one is not needed here. The existence (whether explicit or not) of a temporal connection between a pair of conjuncts is never part of the meaning of & in SL.

Conjunctive sentences in English are often more concise than their SL counterparts. For example, the sentence 'Caesar and Brutus were Romans' would have to be translated as a conjunction of two sentences: C & B. However, be on your guard not to be deceived because although conjunctions in SL always mean what they appear to mean, the same does not hold true in natural language. Compare the sentence just given with this one: 'Caesar and Brutus were enemies.' This is not a conjunctive statement, despite having the same form, for its actual meaning is that Caesar and Brutus were enemies *of each other*. So the only accurate translation in SL would be as an atomic sentence, such as E. This example shows that there is no simple correspondence between the compound forms of SL and grammatical forms of natural language, in which degrees of compression allow for variety of style.

Let us move on to a related topic. Suppose for a moment that Roman history was a little different. Caesar writes to his compatriots about the Gauls: 'I came but although I saw well enough I'm afraid I fell short of conquering them.' A satisfactory SL translation would be (C & S) & ¬Q. Retranslated into English as 'truth-functionally' as possible, this would read, 'I came and I saw well enough and I did not conquer them.' You can see at once what has been left out: the contrast and emphasis that Caesar was able to gain by the words 'but' and 'although.' These are very effective tools for shaping the thoughts we wish to express, but they form no part of the logical meaning of conjunction. Here is a brief list of such words—all of them conjunctive in a logical sense but far from being merely so when they are used in ordinary language:

(1) moreover, in addition, also, too, not only that but
(2) but, nevertheless, however, nonetheless, despite that, all the same, even so, yet
(3) although, though, even though, while

These conjunctive expressions have been arranged into three different groups. As an exercise, use them to make up conjunctions from the following set of statements about Caesar. You will find that the meaning of the statements you construct shifts, more or less, as you move from group to group because of the rhetoric of these conjunctive expressions, the stylistic enrichment they give to the statements without altering their truth-functional core.

> He was a fine general.
> He was an ambitious politician.
> He bragged too much.

The words 'neither' and 'nor' (along with the closely related phrase 'not either . . . or') are often used in English to make a conjoined denial. Let us suppose that someone wanted to defend Caesar against the last two claims just made about him. This reply could take the form 'He wasn't an ambitious politician and he didn't brag too much either.' Symbolized, it would look like ¬A & ¬B. Another version of the reply would be 'He was neither too ambitious nor too much of a braggart.' The reason why disjunctive expressions are so closely associated in our language with negation and conjunction is the existence of an underlying logical equivalence which you have already met in a previous exercise: $(\neg\alpha \mathbin{\&} \neg\beta) \equiv \neg(\alpha \vee \beta)$.[5]

Disjunction Revisited

As you know from Chapter 2, SL defines $\alpha \vee \beta$ in the inclusive sense. But on many occasions, one also uses 'or' in an exclusive sense. To illustrate, let us represent the simple statements 'With the hamburger you get french fries' and 'With the hamburger you get baked potato' by F and B, respectively. Consider now the compound statement 'With the hamburger you get french fries or baked potato.' In most cases (i.e., in most restaurants), a safe reformulation of this sentence would be 'With the hamburger you get french fries or with the hamburger you get baked potato, but not both,' which would be symbolized in SL as $(F \vee B) \mathbin{\&} \neg(F \mathbin{\&} B)$. In this way, we can deal with examples in which the exclusive 'or' is present.

In natural language, we often know that two statements could not both be true, and therefore we would understand their disjunction in the exclusive sense. An example is 'Caesar was either assassinated or died of natural causes,' a full SL rendering of which would be the sentence $(A \vee D) \mathbin{\&} \neg(A \mathbin{\&} D)$. It is not the word 'or' that signals the need for this interpretation but the meaning of the two disjuncts, which partly depends on our background knowledge that people die only once. This knowledge is what accounts for the inclusion of the right-hand conjunct. For practical reasons, SL interprets 'or' in the inclusive sense. Otherwise, too much would be made to depend on the kind of knowledge which has nothing to do with logic. But

---

[5] This equivalence has many variations, which traditionally are called De Morgan equivalences (after a British logician of the nineteenth century). They will turn up later in the course of our treatment of deductive inference.

there is a theoretical side to this matter which also has practical consequences. All simple statements, you remember, are logically independent,
which means (in part) that it is at least possible for any pair of them to be
true together. Consequently, it seems strange to relate a pair of simple
statements by exclusive disjunction, which assigns the value false in the
case whenever both disjuncts are true. This fact now casts a shadow over
the SL sentence given previously, which was intended to reflect the fact that
A and D are incompatible. If they are, and that is what they certainly appear
to be, they are not really sentences denoting simple statements; but if they
are not simple statements, then why were the sentence letters A and D used
in the first place?

There are two ways of dealing with this complication. One is to analyze the statements 'Caesar was assassinated' and 'Caesar died of natural
causes' down to a level consisting of nothing but simple statements.[6] The
other is, in effect, to pretend that sentences such as these are not incompatible and to treat them as simple statements. Of these two alternatives the
second is far simpler and is the one we are going to choose. The reason is
that the job of analyzing statements which are only apparently simple
would take us too far from logic itself into the study of meanings in natural
language, and such a job is not a requirement for doing formal logic. SL
bases itself on simple statements, and ordinary language offers so many examples of them that it becomes unnecessary to stop in order to examine the
credentials of doubtful ones. Doubtful ones will be classified as simple.
What is important in SL is to distinguish simple from compound statements, not the more simple from the less simple. Consequently, we will continue to treat 'Caesar was assassinated' and 'Caesar died of natural causes'
as simple statements. Whenever you are faced with an example like this
one, you have the alternative of symbolizing the sentence as either an inclusive or an exclusive disjunction. In other words, the Caesar example can be
rendered in the way given above or, more simply, as A ∨ D. In both cases the
statements A and D are treated as though they were simple. Adding the conjunct, ¬(A & D), does not change things, for it does not claim that these
statements cannot both be true, or that they are fundamentally incompatible, but only that as a *matter of fact* they are both false. Remember that a
conjunction in SL can involve no other relation between its conjuncts than
what is given by its truth-functional definition.

We turn now to look at some of the ways in which disjunctions are expressed in ordinary language. As with conjunctions, sentences are often
compressed. 'Either Brutus or Caesar wanted to be emperor of Rome' would
be translated in SL as B ∨ C. "The famous Roman who said, 'The die is cast'
was either Antony or Brutus or Caesar" becomes A ∨ (B ∨ C).[7] On the whole

---

[6] These 'simpler' statements would assert (separately) that Caesar was disposed to die from
natural circumstances, Caesar was the target of political violence and Caesar died. These are
logically independent, and the real story about 'the' cause of Caesar's death would end up being a compound statement.

[7] Note that the sentence letters have been reassigned in this second example; and note too that
parentheses are required.

there is not as great variety in the ways of expressing disjunction because the connective is used much less often than conjunction to express emphasis and contrast. However, there are some expressions which almost amount to formulas for expressing disjunction, for example, words like 'choices,' 'possibilities,' 'options' and 'alternatives.' Whenever you meet one of these in a sentence, consider whether an SL disjunction might be involved. For instance, let us examine the following sentence: 'There were three options facing Caesar on his return to Rome: (a) pursue his secret desire to become the greatest leader the country had ever known; (b) make peace with the Senate by upholding the traditional form of government; (c) retire honorably from the army with a large pension and make wine at a country villa.' Notice that (a) through (c) are arranged one after another without a connective in between. By themselves, they might well be taken as conjuncts, but the overriding word in the sentence is 'options,' which sets them in contrast to one another as alternatives. So it should be read as a disjunction having the structure 'Caesar could do (a) on his return to Rome or he could do (b) or he could do (c).' From here it is easy to move on to an SL translation, namely, $P \lor (M \lor (R \ \& \ C))$.

This example indicates the general method it is sometimes necessary to apply when translating sentences into SL, which measures ordinary language against a rather broad scale. Basically, the method asks, which of the five compounds seems to fit best what is being said? (If it is not an atomic sentence, it has to be one of the five compounds, or it is not a sentence of SL.) Once that question is answered, the method can be applied repeatedly to the components of the statement. Do not forget that translating into SL is not like trying to capture a sentence's full meaning (or as much of it as possible) in another natural language like French or Russian. The only thing that matters to SL is its truth-functional content. Symbolic translation isolates and clearly frames that content, though, as a result, it allows other aspects of meaning to slip from view. As you will see in the next section, conditional statements offer the best illustration of this point.

Conditional Revisited

In natural language, conditional sentences can be used to express relationships that are sometimes quite complicated between antecedent and consequent. Here are the most important:

(a) *Causal relations between individual things.* The sentence 'If you press that button now the alarm will sound' means that pressing the button at this moment will cause the alarm to go off immediately after. The antecedent expresses a causal or a sufficient condition of the consequent.

(b) *Causal laws.* Sometimes causal relations are expressed in the form of generalizations or laws: 'If untreated iron is exposed to water then it rusts.' Here the relationship holds not merely for this or that piece of iron but for any piece of iron whatever, at any time.

(c) *Noncausal regular connections.* Sometimes, one class of events is regularly associated with another class, without any suggestion of a causal link between the two. Think of the symptoms of an illness, for example. We imagine many of them simply as being found together—all effects of the underlying cause of the illness but not causes and effects of one another. 'If the patient has symptom x, then symptom y is also likely to be found.' Other examples are found in descriptions of behavior, such as 'If Jack drinks alone, he gets very, very drunk.' Here, a pattern is indicated: one circumstance regularly followed by the other.

(d) *Criteria.* An antecedent might express a sign or criterion in relation to the consequent. 'If the customer over there always looks nervously toward the door, he is afraid of someone or something' does not mean that this way of sitting causes the customer to be afraid; what it does is to show or give evidence that he is afraid.

(e) *Necessary connections.* With each of the four other kinds of conditionals, it is possible for the antecedent to be true and the consequent false. This relationship is so even for causal laws. However unlikely it is that a well-established law of physics could be false, at least the possibility remains that somewhere, under certain circumstances, what is expected to happen in terms of this law does not happen. To put the matter another way, causal laws are not logically or truth-functionally true. However, logical truth is the distinctive characteristic of each of the following examples:

> If she is divorced, then she used to be married.
>
> If a figure is a square, then it has four sides.

To understand why these are truth-functionally true, it is necessary to ask what each antecedent means in relation to its consequent. The question is not an abstract one—it concerns only how the statements would be understood by us in ordinary language. Consider the two examples. Part of what we mean when someone is said to be divorced is that the person was at one time married. In other words, having once been married forms part of the meaning of being divorced, just as having four sides is part of what it means for a figure to be a square. A woman might be married and never divorced, but it would be nonsense to describe her as 'divorced but never married,' just as it would be nonsense to call some figure a square which did not have four sides. Such notions are self-contradictory. In both examples the consequent expresses an important part of the meaning of the antecedent, so if the antecedent happens to be true, the consequent not only may be true but also must be true; otherwise a contradiction results. There is a logical term for this sort of relation: The antecedent is said to **entail** the consequent, and the relation itself is called **entailment.**

In terms of truth-tables, an SL conditional whose antecedent entails its consequent would be T on every truth-value assignment to its simple components. After the recent discussion of disjunctions, it should be obvious at once that no simple statement entails another (although every simple statement entails itself). Consequently, in the two preceding examples ('If she is divorced, then she used to be married'; 'If a figure is a square, then it has four sides'), the antecedent and consequent could not each be translated by an atomic sentence without sacrificing a crucial logical detail, and some ingenuity is therefore required to produce a suitable translation which preserves this detail. Once again, however, we shall make a detour and avoid the problem of fully analyzing sentences in ordinary language which merely look simple but are really compound.[8] There are plenty of other examples of SL conditionals whose antecedents (usually a truth-functional compound) entail the consequents. You have met a number of these already in the exercises, and there will be quite a few more later in this chapter when we get to the truth-functional analysis of arguments.

Which of the four kinds of conditionals just described matches the use of $\rightarrow$ in the language SL? In fact, none of them do. The *assertion* of a sentence of the form $\alpha \rightarrow \beta$ does not attach a truth-value to either the antecedent or the consequent, other than to exclude one particular combination: that α is true and β is false. Moreover, it is neutral with regard to any more specific way in which antecedent might be related to consequent, such as by means of a causal link. Also, if α happens to entail β, this is never shown by $\rightarrow$ itself but would be revealed by truth-table testing. It is best to think of an SL conditional as expressing no more than a core of meaning which is common to all conditionals. The name given to it by formal logic is the **material conditional**.[9] Its purely truth-functional meaning was described in the last chapter. Examples of sentences in ordinary language which have just this sense or, in other words, which have just the meaning that $\rightarrow$ has are relatively uncommon, but here are a few examples to give you an idea of what they are like:

> If the president knew he was ill, then he didn't tell anyone.
> If music is the food of love, her voice will put you on a diet.
> If you become a programmer, there are plenty of good jobs available.

So far, all the examples of conditional sentences were constructed with the familiar words 'if . . . then' (or just 'if' by itself). The reason was to emphasize the important role played by the component sentences themselves in determining whatever fuller meaning a conditional might have in ordinary language. But 'if . . . then' is just one of many conditional expressions in our language, some of which are tailored to fit one or another of the kinds of conditional sentences listed above. For instance, each of the following expressions could be substituted for 'if' in the examples given without a change of meaning:[10]

---

[8] The SL translation would have to show the antecedent as a conjunction of 'simpler statements,' one of which also occurs as the consequent. As will be seen later, a translation in the language called PL can achieve this requirement with greater ease.

[9] Another name commonly used is '**material implication**.' The word 'material' in both names is meant to contrast with 'logical,' where '**logically imply**' means the same as 'entail.'

[10] Whether 'then' would need to be retained is a matter of stylistic choice.

supposing that, provided that, assuming that, on condition that, given that

Expressions like 'whenever' and 'at any time that' are very often used to assert generalizations about classes of events. To illustrate,

Whenever untreated iron is exposed to water it rusts.

Any time Jack drinks alone, he gets very, very drunk.

It will come as no surprise to learn that conditional sentences sometimes assume a compact form which needs to be unpacked for translation into SL symbols:[11]

Pressing that button now will make the alarm sound.

The exposure of untreated iron to water causes it to rust.

Any patient who has symptom x is likely to show symptom y as well.

Always looking nervously toward the door—that shows the customer over there is afraid of someone or something.

Necessary connections are often expressed with the help of words like 'entail,' 'imply' and 'must':

Being divorced entails having once been married.

To be a square implies having four sides.

To be a square, a figure must have four sides.

However, these particular words are sometimes used (loosely) to indicate only that one statement is a necessary condition of another. We will return to this matter in the next section.

Biconditional Revisited

From earlier discussions, you know that any biconditional asserts of its two components, α and β, that each is both a necessary and a sufficient condition of the other; also, that when some statement plays the role of necessary condition, it appears as the consequent in an SL conditional; and finally, that SL aims to translate only the core of meaning found in the conditional sentences of ordinary language. In the case of an SL sentence like A → B, it does not matter whether you call A the sufficient condition of B or B the necessary condition of A because in truth-functional terms these mean the same thing. However, there is not the same freedom of choice with some of the types of conditional sentences described in the previous section. For example, 'Whenever it rains, the streets become wet' asserts a causal relation,

---

[11] The best way to go about unpacking these is to rephrase them explicitly by means of 'if . . . then,' which is the form in which they were first presented.

but it would be odd to describe the statement as asserting that wet streets are a necessary condition of rain. It makes a lot more sense to describe rain as a sufficient condition for streets becoming wet. Why the discrepancy? The answer is that when causal relations are involved, both the necessary and the sufficient conditions of an event take place before (or at least simultaneously with) that event. Consequently, when you treat A as a causally sufficient condition of B, you mean that it precedes B; whereas if you treat B as a causally necessary condition of A, you still mean that it takes place (or needs to occur) first. For instance, oxygen is a causally necessary condition for combustion—but it must be already present if combustion is to occur, though it is not the only thing required. However, streets do not have to be wet in order for it to rain. The only cause mentioned is rain, and it is a sufficient condition of the streets becoming wet. In short, when we assert causal conditionals, the notion of a temporal sequence that forms no part of what → means is included, and that is why we cannot 'read' them in a way that stresses only the formal role of antecedent and consequent. The same consideration about time (that events are arranged in a temporal sequence) helps explain why it would be strange to say that Jack's getting very, very drunk is a necessary condition of his drinking alone. Jack's being alone is certainly not the cause of his getting so drunk but is what happens first.

In ordinary language, sentences which express necessary conditions are often causal or at least involve some idea of temporal sequence. The other major alternative is a logically necessary condition, which is merely another way of referring to the consequent of any conditional whose antecedent entails it. Having four sides is a logically necessary condition of being a square, just as having once been married is logically necessary for being divorced. There is a family of expressions commonly used for this purpose. It includes words like 'entails,' 'requires,' 'implies' and 'presupposes,' whose substitution gives (for instance), 'Being a square entails having four sides' and 'Being divorced presupposes having once been married.' Note the inversion of the component statements. If β is a logically necessary condition of α, it is a logical consequent of α. Hence, α entails (requires, implies, etc.) β. However, these words are sometimes used to mean a causally necessary condition rather than a logically necessary one, as in 'Combustion requires the presence of oxygen.' Which sense is meant will often be clear from the meaning (the content) of the antecedent and consequent.

Biconditional sentences in ordinary language—like their counterparts in SL—are conjunctions of two conditionals and therefore convey the same meaning as their components, although without nearly as much linguistic variety. 'If and only if' and 'If but only if' are the most common connectives. Occasionally, biconditionals are asserted with the help of the word 'otherwise,' as in the following example: 'A journalist can get into the country if she bribes the border guard but not otherwise.' What this means can be unpacked into two conditionals: If the journalist bribes the border guard, she can enter the country and if she does not then she cannot, or in SL symbols, (B → G) & (¬B → ¬G). Let us take a closer look at the right-hand conjunct because it holds an important key to an alternative translation. You may recall from the truth-table exercises that any sentence having the form $(\alpha \rightarrow \beta) \equiv (\neg\beta \rightarrow \neg\alpha)$ is truth-functionally true. In other words, two conditionals corresponding to these patterns are logically equivalent (i.e., true and false under the same truth-value assignments to their atomic components). Thus the right-hand conjunct, $\neg B \rightarrow \neg G$, is logically equivalent to $G \rightarrow B$, so the SL translation given above can be seen as just a variation on the standard form of the biconditional. Accordingly, a logically equivalent translation of the original sentence is $B \equiv G$.

The phrase 'just in case' sometimes has a biconditional sense, as in this example: 'You are entitled to receive a full refund just in case you can produce the original receipt of purchase.' An SL translation of this would be $R \equiv P$ ('You are entitled to a full refund if but only if you can produce the original receipt of purchase'). However, there is a different and probably more common meaning of 'just in case,' which will be taken up in the next section.

Exercises

As promised before, we now visit again *Symlog*'s Symbolizations environment to work on more complex symbolizations. After solving some of the following exercises (no need to use *Symlog* with these), try the exercises SL16 to SL30 on your disk.

3.1.1 Identify each of the following sentences in truth-functional terms as either a simple statement or as one of the five types of compound (negation, conjunction, disjunction, conditional and biconditional).
   a. Wynton and Branford Marsalis are trumpeters.
   b. Although Branford is older, Wynton is better known.
   c. Wynton and Branford Marsalis are brothers.
   d. Either they both will play or neither will.
   e. If Wynton won't play then neither will Branford.
   f. That Wynton likes playing only jazz is just plain false.
   g. They both play the trumpet or just one does.
   h. Neither Wynton nor Branford sings.

3.1.2 Provide a truth-functional translation of each of the following sentences, using the symbols given in parentheses.
   a. If Wynton won't play then neither will Branford. (T, B)
   b. The king was pleased, whereas the queen wasn't. (K, Q)
   c. Supposing Joe calls, I am not at home. (J, H)
   d. I don't have either the time or the money. (T, M)
   e. If she apologizes, I'll talk to her; otherwise not. (A, T)
   f. If she apologizes, then if she's sincere, I'll talk to her. (A, S, T)
   g. Either Wynton and Branford both play the trumpet or just one of them does. (T, B)

      h. I'll bet on the Mets and the Blue Jays or, if the Yankees swing a big trade, then I'll bet on them and the Mets. (M, B, S, K)

3.1.3 Provide a truth-functional translation of each of the following conditional sentences, using the symbols given in parentheses.

      a. I am not at home in case Joe calls. (H, J)

      b. I'll talk to her only if she apologizes. (T, A)

      c. If the king was pleased, whereas the queen wasn't, then should the jester show his head in court, he will lose it. (K, Q, J, L)

      d. I won't talk to her unless she apologizes. (T, A)

      e. I get depressed whenever I think of winter. (D, T)

      f. Success in politics depends on having a lot of money. (S, M)

      g. Having a lot of money is necessary for political success. (M, S)

[PR1] h. If the king was pleased, whereas the queen wasn't, then should the jester show his head in court, he will lose it unless he throws himself on the ground and begs for mercy. (K, Q, J, L, G, B)

3.1.4 A, B and C are three simple sentences. Each of the following sentences describes a truth-functional relationship for them. Represent each of these descriptions as a truth-functional compound. (As an illustration, 'A is a sufficient condition for B' should be represented as A → B.)

      a. It is false that A is a sufficient condition for B.

      b. A and C are both necessary conditions of B.

      c. A is a necessary condition of C but not a sufficient one.

      d. The falsity of C is a sufficient condition of the falsity of B.

      e. C implies itself.

      f. C is true if but only if either A or B is.

      g. Unless A is false, both B and C are false.

      h. Not all three are true.

3.1.5 Answer true or false (but not both) to each of the following claims.

      a. Every sentence of SL is either true or false in the exclusive sense.

      b. The negation of a contingent sentence is either truth-functionally true or truth-functionally false.

      c. If one sentence logically implies another, then it is logically equivalent to it.

      d. Any two logical truths are logically equivalent.

      e. The **converse**, $\beta \to \alpha$, of any conditional sentence, $\alpha \to \beta$, is logically equivalent to it.

      f. To be a sufficient condition doesn't exclude the possibility of also being a necessary condition.

      g. Negating a biconditional sentence is truth-functionally the same as negating both of the conditional sentences that it conjoins.

      h. The **contrapositive**, $\neg\beta \to \neg\alpha$, of any conditional sentence, $\alpha \to \beta$, is logically equivalent to it.

3.1.6 Each of the following sentences in the list is logically equivalent to one other sentence. Using the symbols T and B, represent each sentence and then match it with its logical equivalent (do a truth-table test to check your work if necessary).

a. If Wynton won't play then neither will Branford.
b. It's false that if Branford plays Wynton will too.
c. Either Wynton plays or Wynton doesn't.
d. It's false that Wynton will play but Branford won't.
e. Either Wynton won't play or Branford will.
f. If Branford plays then so will Wynton.
g. If Branford plays then Branford plays.
h. It's false that if Wynton doesn't play then Branford won't either.

3.1.7 Provide a truth-functional translation of each of the following sentences, using the symbolization:

C : The train passengers will complain.
F : We will get free wine with our lunch.
L : I will be on time for my lecture at Queen's University.
S : There will be a snowstorm.
T : The train will be on time.

a. There will be a snowstorm, the train will be late, and I won't be on time for my lecture at Queen's.

b. Regardless of whether there is a snowstorm or not, the train will be on time.

c. If there is a snowstorm then either I will be late for my lecture at Queen's or the train will be late.

d. Even though there will be no snowstorm the train will be late, and although we will get free wine with our lunch the passengers will still complain.

e. The train will be late but we will all get free wine with our lunch. However, I will be late for my lecture at Queen's.

f. The train won't be on time but if we get free wine with our lunch the passengers won't complain.

g. Only if the train is late we will get free wine with our lunch.

h. I'll be on time for my lecture at Queen's unless there is a snowstorm, in which case the train will be late.

i. If there's a snowstorm and the train is late then we won't get free wine with our lunch, but we will if there's no snowstorm and the train is late.

j. The passengers will complain unless we get free wine with our lunch. But we will get free wine only if there is a snowstorm and the train is late.

k. Regardless of whether the train is late or not, the passengers won't complain. They will complain only if we don't get free wine with our lunch.

l. The train will be late if and only if there is a snowstorm. But if so, that is, the train is late, I'll be late for my lecture at Queen's.

m. Neither there will be a snowstorm nor the train will be late. I'll be on time for my lecture at Queen's but, unfortunately, we won't get free wine with our lunch.

n. I'll be on time for my lecture at Queen's University only if there isn't a snowstorm and the train is on time.

o. There won't be a snowstorm, the train will be late, I won't be on time for my lecture at Queen's University and, on top of that, we won't get free wine with our lunch. However, incredible as it may sound, the passengers won't complain.

3.2 Arguments

Simple statements—but more often than not, compound ones—are the foundation of the most important logical operation of all in sentential logic: **inference**. By means of this operation, a particular statement is supported by one or more other ones; it is said to follow from them, and they are said to constitute its basis. The typical form that inference takes in ordinary language is called an **argument**. The supporting statements are termed **premises**; the statement which follows from them, the **conclusion**. The nature of the support that inference gives to the conclusion of an argument is semantical and involves degrees of strength. The premises make it certain that a conclusion is true or nearly certain or merely probable. Although logic in general is concerned with any degree of inference which makes it more likely than not that the conclusion is true, SL's first aim in examining arguments is to determine whether or not their conclusions follow with *certainty*, that is, whether the premises give (or fail to give) an absolute guarantee that the conclusion must be true *if the premises are true*. This standard of analysis, which is followed by sentential logic and similar systems of formal logic, is sometimes called the **deductive** standard, and consequently they are often referred to as systems of **deductive logic**.

The next section will show you how the truth-table theory of SL can be applied to the analysis of arguments when these have been translated into symbolic form. You will also see there the close relation between deductive inference and entailment. The purpose of the present section is to say something about the 'look' of arguments as they occur in ordinary language.

So familiar to us are arguments in our reading, talking and thinking that their structure often goes unnoticed. Nevertheless, it is easy to recognize the telltale signs of an argument. Words like 'therefore,' 'and so,' 'consequently,' 'it follows that,' 'I conclude' and 'thus' serve to introduce a statement (simple or compound) as the conclusion. Words like 'because,' 'for,' 'since' and 'for the following reasons' play the role of introducing premises. Both kinds will be referred to here as **inference indicators**.[12] Although these

---

[12] This term is used by Stephen Thomas, *Practical Reasoning in Natural Language* (Prentice Hall, 1986), pp. 12–13.

two groups of expressions function in distinct ways, choosing between them when constructing an argument in ordinary language is arbitrary, in the sense that it does not make any logical difference. The conclusion of an argument can be either stated first or presented after the premises have been listed without changing its structure, as you can see by comparing the following two examples:

(a) The present government isn't likely to be reelected because the unemployment rate is already high and getting higher, the party hasn't kept its promise to reform the bureaucracy, taxes keep going up, the currency keeps declining in value and, not least, there have been a few juicy scandals.

(b) The unemployment rate is already high and getting higher, the party hasn't kept its promise to reform the bureaucracy, taxes keep going up, the currency keeps declining in value and, not least, there have been a few juicy scandals, all of which makes it quite clear that the present government isn't likely to be reelected.

A few other points should be kept in mind regarding the 'style' of presenting an argument. Sometimes the arguer may place the conclusion in the midst of the reasons which support it. The argument just given could be reworked in this way:

The unemployment rate is already high and getting higher, taxes keep going up and so does inflation, while the currency keeps declining in value. This suggests the unlikelihood of the present government being reelected, and the fact the party hasn't kept its promise to reform the bureaucracy, not to mention a few juicy scandals, only increases that prospect.

A further point is that strictly speaking, an argument can be presented without an inference indicator. Often this is done in very brief arguments such as 'The raffle has had to be canceled; not enough tickets were sold.' Between these two sentences an inference indicator like 'since' or 'because' could have been inserted, yet its presence would not have made it any clearer how the two statements are supposed to be related. The content of the two statements themselves makes that clear enough. As an experiment, however, go back to example (a) above and (mentally) remove the word 'because' as you reread it. You will see that even in larger passages like this it is possible to grasp that an argument is being presented and what its structure is, despite the absence of an inference indicator. Nevertheless, a good rule to follow in ordinary language arguments is to include an inference indicator whenever there is a chance that others might fail to notice that you want to make an inference.

Arguments in ordinary language are sometimes combined in one passage. An example building on the one just given would be

> The raffle has had to be cancelled because not enough tickets were sold. So, some other way of raising the money will have to be found.

In this passage, not only is the first statement supported by the second but also it is used to support the third. Rewritten in order to bring this relationship out, we have

> Not enough tickets were sold. Therefore, the raffle has had to be cancelled. Therefore, some other way of raising the money will have to be found.

Rewriting makes it clear that there are two arguments here, with the same statement occurring first as conclusion and then as premise. Often this technique is required when analyzing ordinary language, but in the exercises (for SL as well as PL) you will not find more than one argument per passage.

Here are a few additional pointers that might help you to recognize the structure of an argument in ordinary language. Expressions like 'since,' 'just in case that,' 'so' and 'as a result that' can play a role other than indicating inferences. Our language would be easier to describe if this were not the case, but since it is, the best antidote is to be well prepared to recognize the differences. Perhaps the best way of showing these differences is through contrasting examples. In each of the following pairs of sentences you will find one of these expressions working, first, in the role of an inference indicator and, second, in a quite different role that you will easily recognize (answers are given in a footnote below, but try to identify this other role before looking):

(1a) Since the boss wouldn't give me a raise, I quit.

(1b) Since last spring, I haven't had a job.

(2a) I tape the teacher's lectures just in case I can't understand my own notes.

(2b) A triangle is called 'isosceles' just in case two of its sides are equal.

(3a) The boss wouldn't give me a raise, so I quit.

(3b) I thought she loved me, but it wasn't so.

(4a) He deliberately violated the school's rules and as a result he must be punished.

(4b) She went on a heavy diet and as a result she became very ill.[13]

As you have seen, inference indicators come in many different shapes and sizes. It is worthwhile remembering that by themselves they add nothing in the way of logical strength to any argument. The only difference between saying, 'A therefore B' and 'A so any intelligent person is compelled to recog-

---

[13] Answers: (1b) The word 'since' is used in a temporal sense to mean 'dating from the time of'; (2b) 'just in case' expresses a necessary and sufficient condition (that is, 'iff'); (3b) 'so' here means 'the case' or 'true'; (4b) 'as a result' means 'as a consequence' or 'it had the effect that.'

nize the truth of B′ is one of style or rhetoric, which has no bearing on the logical issue of whether A provides a strong basis for B. Whether it does or not is determined by analysis, not by degree of emphasis.

One final point: Not every time the word 'argument' is used can you expect to find an argument (in the logical sense). Suppose you read in a newspaper story, 'The president of the company argued that the advertising campaign was doing more harm than good.' This sentence does not express an argument; there are no premises and conclusion here. We can assume that what the president contended—that the advertising campaign was doing more harm than good—was indeed argued for, but in the context of the newspaper report it is no more than an assertion. An argument has to have at least one expressed premise.[14]

In contrast with the variety found in ordinary language, SL has only one pattern for displaying arguments which have been translated into symbols: The premises are given in a column and the conclusion is written underneath, separated from them by a horizontal line. Here is that pattern in schematic form using the familiar metalogical symbols (but with subscript numbers under the premises to indicate that they can be of any finite number, n):

$$\alpha_1$$
$$\alpha_2$$
$$.$$
$$.$$
$$.$$
$$\frac{\alpha_n}{\beta}$$

In the following section, some new tools will be introduced for the truth-functional analysis of the entailment relation as well as of arguments translated into SL. Before moving on, however, you may find it a helpful review of the present section to work through the textbook's exercises dealing with arguments in ordinary language. In particular, you may want to use *Symlog*'s Symbolizations to try the exercises SL31 to SL45 on your disk.

Exercises

3.2.1 In the following sentences, pick out any word or words which play the role of inference indicator (if a sentence contains no inference indicator, write 'None').

a. She wanted to see Paris, I wanted to see London, so we compromised and went to Rio instead.

b. Because he was so ambitious, Caesar was assassinated.

---

[14] Some arguments do not express all their premises, and others do not make their conclusions explicit—but these are different matters which will not concern us.

    c. Since the dinosaurs died out, no colossal reptiles have roamed the earth.

    d. The party really began to get noisy; consequently I left.

    e. Wynton and Branford are brothers; that's why they receive equal billing.

    f. Why she paid so much for a new hair style I'll never know.

    g. The judge declared a mistrial in view of the fact that the jury was split.

    h. Inasmuch as I have no money saved, the problem of deciding where to spend my holidays this year is solved.

3.2.2 None of the following passages contains an inference indicator. Read each with care and then decide whether it contains an argument; if it does, identify the premises and conclusion.

    a. The day before yesterday Larry asked me whether I could help him put starch in his white shirts. I asked him whether he was looking for a maid or a mother, and that made him sulk for a while and then he started talking about how he wanted to sell a lot of magazine subscriptions. He asked me if I liked *Mechanix Illustrated.* Is that a body-building magazine?

    b. Larry gets on my nerves. Yesterday he wanted me to buy a magazine subscription. The day before that he wanted to know whether I could help him put starch in his white shirts. You know what he did today? Sent me two red roses.

    c. Since I met Sheila I've begun to wear clean shirts and I've even started to lose interest in my male-bonding seminars. If I can earn some money from magazine subscriptions then I can take her to that vegetarian dinner she keeps talking about. And the roses! I just sent her two roses. It all points to just one thing. I'm a fool for love!

3.2.3 Organize the following arguments according to the standard pattern (premises—dividing line—conclusion); then translate them into SL by using the symbols provided.

    a. We are going to either Paris, London or Rio. But Paris is out. So is London. So the only alternative is to go to Rio. (P, L, R)

[PR2] b. The judge will declare a mistrial because, if the jury is split then he will declare a mistrial and if he declares a mistrial then there will have to be a retrial and it's true that there has to be a retrial. (M, S, R)

    c. Wynton won't play for a very simple reason. He'll play only if Branford receives the same amount of money and gets equal billing besides. But it's clear that while their billing is the same Branford will get paid less. (T, M, B)

[PR3] d. The judge will declare a mistrial if but only if the jury is split or there has been a procedural flaw in the trial but since neither of these things has happened he will certainly do no such thing. (M, S, F)

[PR4] e. If I have money, then I spend it, in which case I don't have any. Therefore, I don't have any. (H, S)

    f. If I have money, then I spend it. However, if I give money to charity, then even though I don't spend it I don't have it either. So I have money if and only if I don't give any to charity. (H, S, G)

g. It's altogether clear to me that if I give money to charity then I don't have it. Here's why. If I have money, then I spend it, and if I spend it, then I don't have it; but neither do I have money if I give it to charity. Now, either I don't spend money or I have it. (H, S, G)

h. If I have money, then I spend it, but if I give money to charity, then I feel good. But since if I have money I don't give it to charity, the consequence is that if I spend it I don't feel good. (H, S, G, F)

3.2.4 Answer true or false to each of the following claims.

a. An argument's inference indicator need not be given explicitly.

b. In an argument, the premises must always be given before the conclusion.

c. In a deductive argument, if all the premises are true then the conclusion will also be true.

d. In a deductive argument, if one of the premises is false then the conclusion will also be false.

e. The premises of an argument always form a conjunction.

f. In an argument, the word 'since' plays the role of introducing the premises.

g. In an argument, the word 'therefore' plays the role of introducing the conclusion.

h. Arguments in SL can have only finitely many premises.

3.2.5 Using the symbols provided, translate the following prose arguments into SL arguments.

[PR5] a. Either the Blue Jays or the Red Sox will be in the playoffs because of the following detailed analysis. If the Red Sox are in the playoffs, then the Yankees won't be. If the Blue Jays are in the playoffs, then Detroit won't be. But already we know that it's false that the Yankees and Detroit will be in the playoffs. (B, R, K, D)

[PR6] b. If the Blue Jays are in the playoffs but the Yankees are not, then if Detroit isn't in the playoffs either, Boston will win all their remaining games, which is impossible. So, if Detroit is not in the playoffs but the Blue Jays are, then so will the Yankees. (B, K, D, T)

c. The king is pleased if and only if the queen isn't. If the jester is vulgar then the king is pleased. So if the jester is not vulgar then the king is not pleased but the queen is. (K, Q, J)

[PR7] d. To please the king it is necessary for the jester to be vulgar, whereas to displease the queen it is enough that the king is pleased. Therefore, if the queen is pleased and the jester is not vulgar then the king is displeased. (K, J, Q)

[PR8] e. If the king was pleased, whereas the queen wasn't, then should the jester show his head in court, he will lose it. The king is displeased only if the queen is pleased, however, and she is not. So it is false that the jester has shown his head in court without losing it. (K, Q, J, L)

[PR9] f. If you love someone then you show it. However, the converse is not true. If you hate someone, you are sad, but the converse of this is false too. It follows that you do not love someone and do not hate someone. (L, S, H, D)

g. I love her, yet I don't love her; therefore God exists. (L, G)

[PR10] h. He loves her. But if he loves her he never shows it, and if he never shows it then he never thinks about her, and it's clear that he never thinks about her. So, he loves her; yet he doesn't think about her. (L, S, T)

3.3 Sets of Sentences and Their Basic Properties

An argument is not a new form of compound statement. It also is not a conjunction or negation or one of the other kinds of compounds met earlier. Words like 'therefore' and 'because' perform a different sort of job by signaling that an inference is in process of being made, which means that one or more statements (the premises) are being used in support of another (the conclusion). This is quite a different matter from merely asserting that a particular statement is true. You can spot this difference at once in the following one-premise argument:

> Mars is a planet.
> Earth is a planet.

Both of these statements happen to be true, but that fact alone does not make the argument itself a strong one. What is needed is a way of determining whether or not any inference consisting of sentences of SL is deductively strong, which involves more than just finding out what their truth-values are. Fortunately, the tools of truth-table analysis can be adapted to meet this need.

To deal with the formal properties of arguments and with some important related concepts, we must first outline what is meant by a **set of sentences**.[15] By a set here is meant any collection or group of sentences of SL (finite in number). Each member of a set is either a simple or compound sentence, although it is possible for a set to have no members at all, in which case it is called the **empty** or **null set**. It is important to remember that a set is no more than a collection of sentences; that is, no logical relations whatever are indicated among its members beyond their being part of the same collection. A set (like an argument) is not a compound statement or sentence. Thus it is useful to adopt a simple way of representing sets of sentences by ordinary punctuation symbols such as the comma, as in the following pattern, where metalogical symbols stand for SL sentences:

$$\{\alpha_1, \alpha_2, \alpha_3, \ldots, \alpha_n\}$$

---

[15] In logic the word 'set' has a much wider meaning, which you will see in Appendix D. To simplify matters here, the word is used in a narrower sense that can be dispensed with later.

A set of sentences of SL will be usually denoted by the Greek letter Γ (gamma). Sets are easy to form. The one-premise argument given above can be converted into a set with two members:

{Mars is a planet, Earth is a planet}

Notice that this is just a set, not another way of writing the argument. Nothing in the set corresponds to the word 'therefore.' As sets go, this one is pretty simple—two members, each of which is a simple statement. There is no limit to the number of members of an SL set, as long as the number, *n*, is finite.

SL sets exhibit truth-functional properties because their member sentences do. For instance, an SL set is either consistent or inconsistent depending on the truth-functional characteristics of its members. Earlier we introduced the definition of satisfiability as it applied to sentences of SL. We now extend this definition to sets of sentences of SL as well.

> **Definition.** A truth-value assignment τ (to the atomic components of the members of a set Γ of sentences of SL) **satisfies** Γ if and only if τ satisfies every sentence in Γ.

If τ satisfies Γ we write τ ⊨ Γ, and τ ⊭ Γ otherwise. For instance, the truth-value assignment (T,F)—which assigns T to G and F to M—satisfies the set {¬M, G ∨ ¬G} since both members, ¬M and G ∨ ¬G, come out T under this truth-value assignment. However, (T,F) does not satisfy the set {¬M & G, ¬G}. To give a longer example, you should verify for yourself that (T,F,T,T,T,F) satisfies the set {A & ¬B, (S ≡ G) ∨ D, ¬¬H}. We are now ready to introduce a pair of fundamental definitions:

> **Definition.** An SL set Γ is **truth-functionally consistent**—or simply **consistent** or **satisfiable**—if and only if there is at least one truth-value assignment to the atomic components of its members which satisfies Γ.

Similarly,

> **Definition.** An SL set Γ is **truth-functionally inconsistent**—or simply **inconsistent** or **nonsatisfiable**—if and only if there is no truth-value assignment to the atomic components of its members which satisfies Γ.

To illustrate, the set {¬M, G ∨ ¬G} is consistent since there is at least one truth-value assignment—(T,F), for instance—which satisfies it. As you can see, these definitions are complementary. The crucial question regarding an SL set is whether there is some truth-value assignment to the atomic components of its member sentences on which all of those members are T. This question is answered by means of truth-table analysis, and in particular by *Symlog*. Here is the routine to follow (you may want to refer to the

```
TRUTH–TABLE : RAMSEY                    TRUTH–TABLE : URQUHART

    A B G │ A, G ≡ (A v B), B → G           D G H │ H ≡ ¬G, H & D, D → G

  1 T T T │ T  TT TT T  TT T            1 T T T │ TFFT  TTT  TTT
  2 T T F │ T  FF TT T  TF F            2 T T F │ FTFT  FFT  TTT
  3 T F T │ T  TT TT F  FT T            3 T F T │ TTTF  TTT  TFF
  4 T F F │ T  FF TT F  FT F            4 T F F │ FFTF  FFT  TFF
  5 F T T │ F  TT FT T  TT T            5 F T T │ TFFT  TFF  FTT
  6 F T F │ F  FF FT T  TF F            6 F T F │ FTFT  FFF  FTT
  7 F F T │ F  TF FF F  FT T            7 F F T │ TTTF  TFF  FTF
  8 F F F │ F  FT FF F  FT F            8 F F F │ FFTF  FFF  FTF
  9                                     9
```

Figure 3.1

screens given in Figure 3.1):

(a) On a fresh sheet from *Symlog*'s Truth-Table Pad, enter the members of the set to be tested in the Sentence Field, according to the pattern given above (the use of curly braces, { and }, is optional but you have to include the commas).

(b) Enter the values in the Truth-Value Assignment Field in the usual way and then repeat these columns underneath the atomic statements in the Valuation Field.

(c) Determine the truth-values for each of the members, α_1 to α_n, from the values assigned to their atomic components. That is, construct a truth-table for each member in the set.

The set will be consistent if and only if there is some truth-value assignment on which all of the member sentences carry the value T; otherwise the set is inconsistent. One such assignment from the 2, 4, 8 or 16 possibilities is all that is required (there might, of course, be more than one). You will find it easy to spot the assignment on the screen, and if you are experienced with truth-tables already your work will be much simplified by using *Symlog*'s Generation command.[16]

Here are two problems similar to those you will find in the exercises: Are the following sets consistent or inconsistent?

(i) {A, G ≡ (A ∨ B), B → G}

(ii) {H ≡ ¬G, H & D, D → G}

Once all the truth values have been entered, your screens would look like those in Figure 3.1. It is easy now to find out whether each of the sets is consistent. Check the rows in the truth-tables one by one to see whether there is a truth-value assignment on which all three members of the set are true. In the case of (i) your search stops almost as soon as it starts because on the

---

[16] The routine described in the text is readily adapted to any problem involving more than four atomic components (*Symlog*'s limit).

assignment of T to the atomic sentences A, B and G, all three members, A, G ≡ (A ∨ B) and B → G are T, so the set is consistent. (Note that there is another assignment on which all the members are T, namely, the one in row 3. Either one will do; it is unnecessary to cite both.[17]) However, there is no truth-value assignment to D, G and H on which all the members of set (ii) are T, so that set is inconsistent. Before continuing, we suggest that you start up *Symlog* to work through the Learn Exercises TABLE24 to TABLE30, which relate to consistency. That will be your best preparation for the discussion that follows. In case you are wondering, the short truth-table method described in the last chapter will prove very convenient in dealing with sets of sentences, and we shall get to it shortly.

Exercises

3.3.1 Answer yes or no to the following (i.e., determine whether the given truth-value assignment satisfies the given set or not).

    a. (T,F) ⊨ {A , ¬B}

    b. (F,T) ⊨ {P ∨ Q, ¬P, ¬Q ≡ P}

    c. (F,T,F) ⊨ {¬P ∨ Q, ¬R, P}

    d. (F,T,T,F) ⊨ {I & (G → H), (¬¬G ∨ ¬I) & K, K → (¬H ∨ ¬G)}

    e. (F,F,T,F) ⊨ {H, ¬(R ∨ S) ≡ ¬H, (¬D & ¬S) & ¬R}

3.3.2 Determine, using *Symlog*, which of the following sets are satisfiable, and when the set is satisfiable, give the truth-value assignments which satisfy it.

    a. {A, ¬A}

    b. {A, ¬B, C}

    c. {K ∨ M, ¬K ∨ ¬M}

    d. {¬P, P ∨ Q, ¬Q}

    e. {¬P → Q, ¬R ∨ P}

3.3.3 Construct truth-tables with *Symlog* to determine whether the following sets are truth-functionally consistent or inconsistent.

    a. {R ≡ ¬R}

    b. {I & (G → H), (¬¬G ∨ ¬I) & K, K → (¬H ∨ ¬G)}

[PR12] c. {F ∨ G, (¬J & H) ∨ (¬G & ¬F), (J ∨ ¬G) & (¬H ∨ J)}

    d. {A ≡ ¬¬¬B, B → ¬M, (A ∨ B) & M}

    e. {¬(S ∨ J) ≡ D, D & ¬¬M, M → ¬¬J}

    f. {¬K ∨ M, ¬(K ∨ M) ≡ R, R & S}

    g. {(A → B) → C, ¬B ∨ ¬A, ¬C}

    h. {H, ¬(R ∨ S) ≡ ¬H, (¬D & ¬S) & ¬R}

3.3.4 Answer true or false and explain why to each of the following.

    a. If {α} is truth-functionally consistent then so is {¬α}.

    b. If {α} and {β} are truth-functionally consistent then so is {α, β}.

---

[17] The property of consistency does not come in degrees. A set is either consistent or inconsistent; one set is not more consistent than another.

    c. If $\{\alpha\}$ and $\{\beta\}$ are truth-functionally inconsistent then so is $\{\alpha, \beta\}$.

    d. Any set with a truth-functionally true sentence as one of its members must be truth-functionally consistent.

    e. Any set with a truth-functionally false sentence as one of its members must be truth-functionally inconsistent.

3.3.5 Use the Create option under *Symlog*'s File menu to ask the program to generate sets of sentences (randomly) whose truth-tables you should then construct to determine their truth-functional consistency or inconsistency. Submit your work when done.

3.4 *Further Properties of Sets of Sentences*

The properties of consistency and inconsistency are central to a family of logical concepts, and between these two it is inconsistency that plays the more important role. Let us take a moment to see why. Suppose you have three sentences, α_1, α_2 and α_3, which we assume to be of different truth-functional types: α_1 is logically true, α_2 is logically false and α_3 is contingent. (To simplify matters, we are going to treat α_1 here as if it were a sentence, even though strictly it stands for any SL sentence which is logically or truth-functionally true, and we will do the same with α_2 and with α_3.) Now, let us make up three sets, each having one of these sentences as its sole member, called, respectively, Γ_1, Γ_2 and Γ_3. It is easy to see that both Γ_1 and Γ_3 are consistent sets since α_1 is T on every truth-value assignment and α_3 (being contingent) is T on at least one. However, Γ_2 is inconsistent because there is no assignment on which α_2 is T. So, merely testing for consistency will not distinguish between sentences which are logically true and those which are contingent. However, finding that a set is inconsistent can tell us a lot when the set has been constructed with a clear purpose in mind. As you will see in a moment, getting the answer you need depends on asking the right kind of question, and that in turn requires knowing how to put the concept of inconsistency to work.

Entailment

Earlier in this chapter, we saw a type of conditional statement involving a necessary connection between antecedent and consequent, by means of which it is impossible for an antecedent to be true and the consequent false. This relation is called entailment. Here are two examples of SL conditional sentences in which the antecedent entails the consequent:

(1) $P \rightarrow P$
(2) $(P \vee Q) \rightarrow (Q \vee P)$

One way of establishing this fact is by showing that each sentence is a logical truth. This procedure is already familiar. Another way, which we are about to focus on, uses the method of indirect proof (described in Chapter 2) to test for inconsistency. Here is an outline of the procedure. Suppose you want to determine whether a sentence α entails a sentence β. You know that if it does, it is impossible for α to be T and β to be F—in other words, that on every truth-value assignment to their atomic components on which α is T, β is also T. To get the answer, form the hypothesis that α does not entail β, which means that there is some truth-value assignment on which α is T and β is F. From this it follows that there is some truth-value assignment to their atomic components on which α and $\neg\beta$ are both T and that therefore the set consisting of just these two statements, $\{\alpha, \neg\beta\}$, is consistent. Test this set for consistency. If it is consistent, then indeed there is a truth-value assignment on which α is T but β is F, and so α does not entail β. But if the set is inconsistent then there is no such assignment, which means that α does entail β. In short, your hypothesis is either confirmed or overturned, and this tells you whether the entailment relation is absent or present. The whole procedure centers on a special set consisting of α and $\neg\beta$. A set constructed in this way is called a **test set**. It is the test set which you should enter in the Sentence Field from now on whenever you want to test for entailment.

Now we can apply this method to sentences (1) and (2) above. Does P entail P? Assume that it does not. Form the test set $\{P, \neg P\}$ and find out whether it is consistent. You will quickly see that this test set is inconsistent, and that therefore P does entail itself. Does $P \vee Q$ entail $Q \vee P$? Well, is the test set $\{P \vee Q, \neg(Q \vee P)\}$ consistent? You will find that it is not.

Let us take a fresh example. Does $P \rightarrow Q$ entail its converse,[18] $Q \rightarrow P$? Taking the same appproach as in the previous example, form the test set $\{P \rightarrow Q, \neg(Q \rightarrow P)\}$ and enter it in the Sentence Field. This time, however, we are going to analyze it by means of a short truth-table test, which, you recall, makes use of *Symlog*'s Goal Analysis command. To test the set for consistency, assign the truth-value T to each of the two main connectives of the members in the set (since you are assuming that the test set is consistent). (See Figure 3.2a.) From this it follows right away that $Q \rightarrow P$ is F, and hence that P is T and Q is F. Here, then, is a truth-value assignment on which both members of the set are T (Figure 3.2b).

This result shows that the test set is consistent and that $P \rightarrow Q$ does not entail $Q \rightarrow P$. From this it also follows that the conditional sentence $(P \rightarrow Q) \rightarrow (Q \rightarrow P)$ is not a logical or truth-functional truth.

So far, the examples have concerned cases of single sentences entailing (or failing to entail) a given sentence. But this idea can be extended to sets of sentences entailing (or failing to entail) a given sentence.

> **Definition.** An SL set Γ **truth-functionally entails**—or simply **entails**— a sentence β if and only if there is no truth-value assignment which satisfies Γ and does not satisfy β.

---

[18] The **converse** of any conditional, $\alpha \rightarrow \beta$, has the form $\beta \rightarrow \alpha$. Its **contrapositive** has the form $\neg\beta \rightarrow \neg\alpha$.

TRUTH–TABLE : LEIBNIZ ◾

	P Q	P → Q, ¬(Q → P)
1		T **T**
2		
3		
4		
5		

Figure 3.2a

TRUTH–TABLE : LEIBNIZ ◾

	P Q	P → Q, ¬(Q → P)
1	F T	F **T** T T T F F
2		
3		
4		
5		

Figure 3.2b

TRUTH–TABLE : QUINE

	B M R S	B → ¬M,	B,	S & R,	¬M & R
1	T T T T	T F F T	T	T T T	F T F T
2	T T T F	T F F T	T	F F T	F T F T
3	T T F T	T F F T	T	T F F	F T F F
4	T T F F	T F F T	T	F F F	F T F F
5	T F T T	T T T F	T	T T T	T F T T
6	T F T F	T T T F	T	F F T	T F T T
7	T F F T	T T T F	T	T F F	T F F F
8	T F F F	T T T F	T	F F F	T F F F
9	F T T T	F T F T	F	T T T	F T F T
10	F T T F	F T F T	F	F F T	F T F T
11	F T F T	F T F T	F	T F F	F T F F
12	F T F F	F T F T	F	F F F	F T F F
13	F F T T	F T T F	F	T T T	T F T T
14	F F T F	F T T F	F	F F T	T F T T
15	F F F T	F T T F	F	T F F	T F F F
16	F F F F	F T T F	F	F F F	T F F F

Figure 3.3

In other words, Γ entails β if and only if there is no truth-value assignment on which all the sentences in Γ take the value T and β takes the value F. If Γ entails β then we write Γ ⊨ β. To give an example, the set {B → ¬M, B, S & R} entails the sentence ¬M & R. Figure 3.3 shows why. Note that when Γ ⊨ β, any truth-value assignment which satisfies Γ—here there is only one, namely, (T,F,T,T)—also satisfies β.

    The method of forming test sets combined with short truth-tables can be now extended to cover this broader range where the relation of entailment holds between a set of sentences and a given sentence. For example, the set {A → (B → C), ¬C, ¬¬B} entails the sentence ¬A ∨ B because, as you will find with the help of *Symlog*, the test set {A → (B → C), ¬C, ¬¬B, ¬(¬A ∨ B)} proves to be inconsistent. (Why not take a moment to verify this?) This procedure has no theoretical limit. If there is an entailment relationship between a finite set of sentences and a given sentence, the formation of a test set and the method of testing it for consistency will reveal this fact, and if there is no relation of entailment, the same method will establish it also. This finding can be generalized:

> **Test for Entailment.** An SL set {$\alpha_1, \alpha_2, \ldots, \alpha_n$} truth-functionally entails a sentence β if and only if the test set {$\alpha_1, \alpha_2, \ldots, \alpha_n, \neg\beta$} is inconsistent.[19]

This statement could be expressed more succinctly by using some of the symbolism we now have available: $\Gamma \models \beta$ if and only if $\Gamma \cup \{\neg\beta\}$ is inconsistent, where Γ is a set, β is a sentence and $\Gamma \cup \{\neg\beta\}$ is the corresponding test set.

Validity and Cogency

Earlier in the chapter, arguments were described from the viewpoint of ordinary language. They can also be characterized in the language of sets:

> **Definition.** An **argument** is a group of sentences, one of which, called the **conclusion**, is presented as being supported by the remaining sentences, called the **premises**.

The premises of an argument aim to support the conclusion, to provide reasons for concluding that the conclusion is true. When deductive logic examines an argument, its goal is to determine whether the premises provide conclusive reasons, that is, whether it is impossible for the conclusion to be false if the premises themselves are true. In short, the question which deductive logic seeks to answer is whether the premises as a group entail the conclusion. If they do, the argument is classified as valid; if not, invalid.

> **Definition.** An argument is **truth-functionally valid**—or simply **valid**—if and only if its set of premises entails the conclusion.[20]

---

[19] The symbols α and β, which are used in this definition and others, are meant to represent any sentences of SL but not necessarily distinct sentences. So, it is possible to say that the sentence P entails itself since the test set {P, ¬P} is inconsistent.

[20] This definition specifies the meaning of deductive validity, according to which the premises of an argument give conclusive reasons for the conclusion. Arguments may contain good but not conclusive reasons for their conclusions. The standards for investigating them, however, belong to a branch of logic called inductive logic, in which criteria other than entailment are used to define validity.

The question of validity in SL can thus be settled by truth-table means, and in particular by testing a test set for consistency, following the new procedure. The test set formed from an argument will consist of its premises plus the negation of its conclusion. Bear in mind that the test set will not look like an argument nor in fact will be an argument, but only a set of sentences. Nevertheless, as sets go, its role is of great importance since testing it will reveal the relation between premises and conclusion on which validity depends. An argument of SL is valid if and only if its test set proves to be inconsistent.

With the help of *Symlog*, let us now follow an example from start to finish as a kind of dress rehearsal for some of the exercises. We want to find out whether the following argument is valid or invalid. Here is the text:

> Either Anne or Bob will be going to the zoo. If Anne goes, then if the dogs don't get fed at home the cats won't be able to sleep. But the dogs getting fed depends on Bob's not going to the zoo. Therefore, if Bob goes to the zoo, then either Anne won't go too or the cats won't be able to sleep.

Here is a useful procedure you might want to adopt:

1. Isolate the simple statements in the argument and assign sentence letters to them. In the present case, there are four and they just happen to be best represented by the sentence letters A, B, C and D.

2. Write down the components of the argument, beginning with the first premise you encounter and ending with the conclusion (using a horizontal line to separate all the premises from the conclusion):

$A \vee B$
$A \rightarrow (\neg D \rightarrow \neg C)$
$D \rightarrow \neg B^{21}$
_____
$B \rightarrow (\neg A \vee \neg C)$

3. Take a fresh sheet from *Symlog*'s Truth-Table Pad, enter the components of the argument in the form of a test set, and then test it for consistency. (Remember: An argument is valid if and only if its test set is inconsistent.)

Especially when there are more than two simple statements (i.e., atomic sentences), you will find *Symlog*'s goal analysis approach and the short truth-table method the best combination to work with, and that is how the present problem has been done. You should match your own results with the following four illustrations, which begin with the initial truth-value assignment of T to each member of the test set and move on

---

[21]'The dogs getting fed depends on Bob's not going to the zoo' expresses the fact that if Bob goes to the zoo then the dogs won't get fed, and this, when translated in SL, gives $B \rightarrow \neg D$. Here we use the (truth-functional) equivalent form $D \rightarrow \neg B$.

through successive derivations of truth-values to their components (Figures 3.4a–d). By the time you reach the fourth stage (Figure 3.4d), you have become saddled with a truth-value assignment (highlighted) which is both inescapable and impossible. The second premise ends up with a component, namely, A, which is both T and F. So the test set is inconsistent, the premises do entail the conclusion and the original argument is therefore valid.

Discovering that an argument is valid only tells you that it is impossible for the premises to be true and the conclusion false. So you know that if the premises are true the conclusion must be too. But this discovery does not tell you whether the premises are as a matter of fact true. Are the

TRUTH–TABLE : HEMPEL	■

	A B C D	A ∨ B , A → (¬D → ¬C) , D → ¬B , ¬[B → (¬A ∨ ¬C)]
1		T T T T
2		
3		
4		
5		

Figure 3.4a

TRUTH–TABLE : HEMPEL	■

	A B C D	A ∨ B , A → (¬D → ¬C) , D → ¬B , ¬[B → (¬A ∨ ¬C)]
1	T T T	T T T T T F F T F F F**T**
2		
3		
4		
5		

Figure 3.4b

TRUTH–TABLE : HEMPEL	■

	A B C D	A ∨ B , A → (¬D → ¬C) , D → ¬B , ¬[B → (¬A ∨ ¬C)]
1	T T T F	T T **F** T FT T T F F T F F T
2		
3		
4		
5		

Figure 3.4c

TRUTH–TABLE : HEMPEL	■

	A B C D	A ∨ B , A → (¬D → ¬C) , D → ¬B , ¬[B → (¬A ∨ ¬C)]
1	T T T F	T T T **F** T TF F FT F T FT T T F F T F F T
2		
3		
4		
5		

Figure 3.4d

premises about Bob and Anne and the cats true? You cannot look to logic for an answer; the truth here lies outside of logic. Nevertheless, people have an understandable interest in learning whether the premises of a valid argument are true because it is on this particular combination that the practical force of any argument depends. An argument which is invalid lacks conclusive grounds for its conclusion; but a valid argument with one or more false premises does not compel acceptance that its conclusion is true. The argument about Bob and Anne would be no less valid even if all of its premises happened to be false since its test set would remain inconsistent. However, it would not be a cogent argument: It would offer no good reason for accepting that its conclusion is true. Thus it is necessary to distinguish between validity and cogency.

> **Definition.** A **deductively cogent** argument is a valid argument all of whose premises are *in fact* true.[22]

It follows automatically that the conclusion of a cogent argument is true, whereas it is not possible to infer this from the sole knowledge that an argument is valid. The same valid argument might combine one or more false premises with a false conclusion or even with a true conclusion. Suppose that as a matter of fact, Anne is going to the zoo but Bob is not. Now consider this argument (using the familiar abbreviations):

$$A \vee B$$
$$\frac{\neg A}{B}$$

A test will quickly show that this argument is valid. However, because of the assumptions we have made, it is not a cogent argument. Now let us imagine the facts to be different: Anne has just changed her mind and is not going to the zoo either (for the sake of the dogs and cats, of course). The argument retains the same form yet still is not cogent because now the first premise is false (besides the conclusion). This brief example is meant to illustrate the important difference between validity and cogency. You might want to think of this difference in the following way. Although validity and cogency are both semantical concepts, they differ in terms of the amount of information given about an argument. Knowing that an argument is valid tells you that one of four possible combinations of truth-value is excluded (true premises and false conclusion), whereas knowing that an argument is cogent tells you which one of the remaining three applies. Obtaining this extra information, however, is a *practical* rather than a *logical* matter.

An Alternate Method for Testing Validity

The first examples of entailment we saw took the form of conditional sentences—logically true conditionals whose antecedents entail their conse-

---

[22] Cogent arguments are sometimes referred to as **sound** arguments.

quents. These were sentences, not arguments. Nevertheless, valid arguments could easily be constructed which correspond to them. One of the examples we considered was the sentence $(P \vee Q) \to (Q \vee P)$. The valid argument corresponding to this logical truth is

$$\frac{P \vee Q}{Q \vee P}$$

Conversely, logically true conditionals can be constructed from valid arguments. In general, whenever a sentence α entails a statement β there is a valid argument of the form

$$\frac{\alpha}{\beta}$$

as well as a logical truth of the form $\alpha \to \beta$. An argument with many premises would be treated no differently, except for the fact that the set of premises, Γ, would be replaced by the iterated conjunction[23] of all the premises. To illustrate, here is the conditional that corresponds to the Anne and Bob example above: $[(A \vee B) \, \& \, ((A \to (\neg D \to \neg C)) \, \& \, (D \to \neg B))] \to [B \to (\neg A \vee \neg C)]$. Notice that this is neither an argument nor a test set. In fact, it is not a set at all but a truth-functional compound (a conditional sentence) constructed according to the rules of formation given in Chapter 2, which explains the presence of all the conjunction signs and the parentheses. But it is a fair specimen of a type of sentence into which any SL argument can be converted by following a few simple steps:

1. Form the iterated conjunction of all the premises, $\alpha_1, \alpha_2, \ldots, \alpha_n$, observing SL's rules of formation.
2. Make this conjunction the antecedent of a conditional sentence whose consequent is β, the conclusion of the argument.

A sentence formed in this way from an argument is called the **conditional analogue** of that argument and it can be used to determine its validity. For if the argument is valid, there will be no truth-value assignment to the simple components of the conditional analogue on which it is F; if the argument is invalid, there will be such an assigment. In other words,

> **Alternative Definition.** An argument is **valid** if and only if its conditional analogue is logically true.

The best way of testing a conditional analogue is none other than *Symlog*'s short truth-table test, using the Goal Analysis command. Indeed, if you stop

---

[23] For example, the iterated conjunction of the sentences in the set {A, B, C} is the sentence (A & B) & C.

for a moment to think about the truth-table exercises you have completed earlier, you will now recognize that any conditional statement found to be logically (truth-functionally) true could be converted into a valid argument, and any conditional that failed to be logically true would produce an invalid one.

The method of constructing and testing conditional analogues is an alternative to the method of test sets. Although more complicated by the need for additional punctuation, it is just as effective for determining whether or not the premises of an SL argument entail its conclusion. The choice is yours. We suggest that before deciding, however, you work through the Learn Exercises TABLE31 to TABLE35 on the screen.

Entailment and Validity Revisited

The method of conditional analogues brings out how closely knit the formal concepts of SL are. Chapter 2 contained a set of definitions of logical truth, logical falsity and so on, all expressed in terms of satisfaction. Clearly, these truth-functional properties of sentences can have a direct bearing on whether an SL set is consistent or not. For instance, if a sentence α is logically false, any set of sentences containing it is bound to be inconsistent, no matter what other sentences are found in that set since α itself is false on every truth-value assignment.[24] This relationship makes it possible to express logical falsity in terms of inconsistency.

> **Alternative Definition.** A sentence α of SL is **logically false** if and only if $\{\alpha\}$ is inconsistent.

The fact that the negation of a logical truth is logically false makes it possible to offer a closely related definition:

> **Alternative Definition.** A sentence α of SL is **logically true** if and only if $\{\neg\alpha\}$ is inconsistent.

In effect, $\{\neg\alpha\}$ is a 'test set' for a single sentence α which is to be tested for logical truth. Finally, the fact that truth-functionally contingent sentences are neither logically true nor logically false forms the basis of a definition which combines the two preceding ones:

> **Alternative Definition.** A sentence α of SL is **contingent** if and only if neither $\{\alpha\}$ nor $\{\neg\alpha\}$ is inconsistent.

These three definitions have been included more for ornamental than practical purposes: They are meant to show the interweaving of SL concepts. If you wanted to find out whether some particular sentence α was, say, logi-

---

[24] The converse of this does not hold. A set's being inconsistent does not establish that some one of its members is logically false, except where the set itself contains only one member.

cally true, it would only be an added step to make up a test set for it, and in practical terms such a step is unnecessary.

However, since validity itself has been defined in terms of entailment, you may have wondered what purpose is served by distinguishing these two concepts—validity and entailment—in the first place. There are two reasons for making this distinction, both of which reflect the fact that entailment is a broader concept than validity. Sometimes a person is interested only in what follows from a statement *if it is true*, not with whether the statement itself is true. In such cases, the focus is on entailment rather than on making an argument; and when an entailing statement is not treated as a premise an argument is not involved, and so the question of validity does not arise. That is the first reason.

The second one is more theoretical. In each case of entailment met so far there have always been two sentences at the minimum, α and β. It seems to be a matter of common sense that a set of entailing sentences needs to have at least one sentence. But recall that there is such a set as the null or empty set. Does it make any sense to say of a statement β that it is entailed by the null set? In fact it does, in one case alone. A set of statements Γ entails a sentence β if and only if the corresponding test set is inconsistent. When Γ happens to be empty (in other words, when there is no α), the test set will have only one member and will take this form: $\{\neg\beta\}$. Such a set will be inconsistent when but only when the sentence $\neg\beta$ is logically false (i.e., β is logically true). Hence the null set can be said to entail any sentence β which is a logical truth.

What makes sense in terms of entailment, however, makes no sense at all in terms of validity. The set of premises of an argument may be incomplete but is never completely empty since a sentence is identifiable as a conclusion only when some other sentence (or group of sentences) is presented in support.[25] If a particular sentence α happens to be logically true it may be useful to explain or clarify it for someone, but α does not stand in any logical need of a supporting argument. Accordingly, the concept of validity applies to arguments alone, whereas the concept of entailment applies more widely to cases in which no argument at all is intended.

Exercises

3.4.1   Construct long truth-tables using *Symlog* to determine, by using the definition of truth-functional entailment, whether each of the following is true or false (i.e., whether the given set truth-functionally entails the corresponding sentence).

a. $\{G \,\&\, D, D \rightarrow R\} \vDash H \rightarrow (R \,\&\, G)$

b. $\{M \rightarrow R, H \equiv (\neg M \,\&\, S), R\} \vDash \neg D$

---

[25] A supporting statement for β might be β itself. An argument of this kind is sometimes called 'circular' because the very same statement occurs in the double role of both supporting and following from itself. It would indeed be a valid argument, though whether it would also be a cogent one would depend on β's being true.

[PR13] c. $\{K \equiv (K \rightarrow M), M \rightarrow \neg E\} \models (K \rightarrow \neg E) \vee G$

d. $\{(A \& B) \rightarrow (\neg M \vee D)\} \models A \rightarrow [B \rightarrow (\neg M \vee D)]$

e. $\{L \vee \neg Q, (Q \vee L) \rightarrow R, H\} \models R \& H$

3.4.2   Repeat as in 3.4.1 by using the test for entailment.

3.4.3   Use *Symlog* to determine whether the test sets in 3.4.1 are truth-functionally consistent or inconsistent by means of short truth-tables.

3.4.4   Using *Symlog,* determine whether the following arguments are truth-functionally valid or invalid.

a. $K \vee S$
   $\neg G \rightarrow \neg S$
   $\neg \neg \neg G$
   ———————
   $H \vee K$

b. $P \vee \neg P$
   ———————
   P

c. $P \equiv \neg P$
   ———————
   Q

d. $P \equiv \neg P$
   ———————
   $\neg Q$

e. $P \rightarrow Q$
   $\neg Q$
   ———————
   $\neg P$

f. $\neg(A \& B)$
   ———————
   $\neg A \vee \neg B$

3.4.5   Express in SL the following arguments, and using the test for entailment and with the help of *Symlog,* determine whether they are truth-functionally valid or invalid.

[PR14] a. The space shuttle mission will be a success if the on-board computers work properly. But the on-board computers will work if they are properly programmed and there is no transmission problems between them and the one at the control center. Although the on-board computers systems were properly programmed they will not work. Therefore, the shuttle mission will fail. (S, B, P, T)

b. Having four sides is a necessary condition for being a square. Hence, not having four sides is sufficient for not being a square. (F, S)

[PR15] c. If it rains we will go to the movies and if it doesn't rain we will still go to the movies. We are definitely not going to the movies. From all this it follows that my uncle Bernie will have a heart attack sometime next week. (R, M, B)

d. If it rains then we go to the movies. It isn't raining. Hence, we are not going to the movies. (R, M)

e. Being rich is neither a necessary nor a sufficient condition for be-ing happy in this life. So, one can be happy without being rich and one can be rich without being happy. (R, H)

3.4.6   Use *Symlog* to test each of the arguments in exercise 3.2.3 for validity by means of a short truth-table test.

3.4.7   Use *Symlog* to test each of the arguments in exercise 3.2.5 for validity by means of a test set.

3.4.8   Answer true or false and explain your answer to each of the fol-lowing.

a. If α is truth-functionally true then $\{\neg\alpha\}$ is truth-functionally in-consistent.

b. If α and β are truth-functionally indeterminate then $\{\alpha,\ \beta\}$ is truth-functionally consistent.

c. If $\{\alpha\}$ and $\{\beta\}$ are truth-functionally inconsistent then so is $\{\alpha \equiv \beta\}$.

d. Any argument with a truth-functionally inconsistent set of premises is truth-functionally valid.

e. Any set entails any truth-functionally true sentence.

3.4.9   Let us call a set of sentences Γ of SL **truth-functionally independent** if and only if for each sentence $\alpha \in \Gamma$ there is a truth-value assign-ment τ such that $\tau \vDash \Gamma - \{\alpha\}$ but $\tau \nvDash \alpha$. (a) Show that the set $\{$P & Q, P $\rightarrow$ R, $\neg$R $\vee$ S$\}$ is truth-functionally independent. (b) Also, show that any set that has as one of its members a truth-functionally true sen-tence is truth-functionally dependent (i.e., it is not truth-functionally independent). Use *Symlog* on a few specific examples to gain some in-sight before proving the more general case.

3.4.10   Call a set Γ of SL **minimally inconsistent** if and only if (1) Γ is truth-functionally inconsistent and (2), for any $\alpha \in \Gamma$, $\Gamma - \{\alpha\}$ is truth-functionally consistent. (a) Is the set $\{$S $\vee$ (P $\rightarrow$ Q), P, $\neg$Q & $\neg$S$\}$ mini-mally inconsistent? (b) Give an example of a minimally inconsistent set having exactly four members.

3.4.11   Show that if $\Gamma \vDash \alpha$ and $\Gamma \vDash \neg\alpha$, then Γ is truth-functionally incon-sistent.

3.4.12   Use the Create option under *Symlog*'s File menu to ask the program to generate sets of sentences (randomly) whose truth-tables you should then construct to determine if, for a given set, any sentence in the set is entailed by the remaining ones.

3.5   *SL Viewed as a Formal System*

In this section we invite you to take a step back for a moment to survey the whole of SL in order to gain some idea of its logical strength. To start with, think of the sort of building materials which were used in the construction of SL: five compound-forming connectives, a few punctuation marks and a set of sentence symbols which can be enlarged as the need arises. Yet de-spite this small stock of materials it is possible to analyze a passage of lan-guage of any length as a structure of statements which, whether simple or compound, are unambiguously related to one another and to capture within that structure the all-important linguistic chores of assertion, denial and inference. Using the concept of truth-values, we have given statements an interpretation which runs parallel to ordinary language and we have used it to pin down a wide range of logical concepts including, most important, entailment. Thus, SL forms the foundation of a logical analysis of language. As you will see when we examine predicate logic (PL), many of its pieces will remain firmly in place.

On several occasions already we have emphasized that SL does not really aim to translate our natural language into formal symbols in the way that one natural language attempts to translate another. Instead, SL's goal is limited to capturing the linguistic stratum of assertions and arguments. Its success in analyzing this stratum is more modest than that of PL because some of the statements which SL classifies as simple are in fact capable of further analysis and because it makes no attempt in any case to delineate the inner structure of simple statements. Nevertheless, in terms of what it does attempt, SL is quite systematic. We would like now to give you a brief indication of what we mean by this.

In the course of using *Symlog* to do truth-tables, you came upon the following two logical equivalences:

$$(A \rightarrow B) \equiv \neg(A \,\&\, \neg B)$$
$$(A \rightarrow B) \equiv (\neg A \lor B)$$

These can be compared with another logical equivalence, which is already quite familiar:

$$(A \equiv B) \equiv [(A \rightarrow B) \,\&\, (B \rightarrow A)]$$

Recall that when two sentences are logically equivalent, they have the same truth-values on all assignments to their simple components. This fact would justify a *substitution rule,* if we wanted to have one in SL, to the effect that any sentence of SL could be replaced by a logically equivalent sentence, without altering the truth-table 'fingerprints' of the original. By means of such a rule, any conditional sentence could be replaced by its logical equivalent in either of the two forms given above and the resulting sentence would have exactly the same pattern of truth-values under its main connective. It would make no difference whether the substitution was carried out for an entire sentence or just part, as long as the replacing sentence and whatever it replaces are logically equivalent. For instance, the left-hand conjunct of $(A \rightarrow B) \,\&\, (B \rightarrow A)$ could be replaced by $\neg A \lor B$ (since these are equivalent) and the resulting sentence, $(\neg A \lor B) \,\&\, (B \rightarrow A)$, would be equivalent to the original (as a quick check with *Symlog* will confirm). In principle, then, just as any biconditional may be replaced by a conjunction of two conditionals, any conditional sentence itself could also be replaced by an equivalent nonconditional. The rule itself would read somewhat like the following:

Rule for Substitution of Equivalents. A sentence of SL, or any of its well-formed parts, may be replaced by any logically equivalent sentence.

In keeping with the general scope of this rule, and for ease of reference, it is convenient to represent the logical equivalences (LE) just given by metalogical symbols and to assign name tags:

LE1: $(\alpha \equiv \beta) \equiv [(\alpha \to \beta) \,\&\, (\beta \to \alpha)]$

LE2: $(\alpha \to \beta) \equiv (\neg\alpha \vee \beta)$

LE3: $(\alpha \to \beta) \equiv \neg(\alpha \,\&\, \neg\beta)$

The list continues with this further group of equivalences, which are useful to have on hand:

LE4: $\alpha \equiv \neg\neg\alpha$

LE5: $(\alpha \,\&\, \beta) \equiv \neg(\neg\alpha \vee \neg\beta)$

LE6: $(\alpha \vee \beta) \equiv \neg(\neg\alpha \,\&\, \neg\beta)$

LE7: $\neg(\alpha \to \beta) \equiv (\alpha \,\&\, \neg\beta)$

Why have a rule of substitution? Where does all this lead? It leads to a kind of simplification of the building materials used to construct SL in the first place. All the equivalences listed above are strategically important because, theoretically, it would be possible to reexpress every SL sentence in terms of negation, conjunction and disjunction; negation and conjunction alone; negation and disjunction; or negation and the conditional. In other words, instead of five connectives, it would be possible to get by with three or even just two.[26]

As an example, let us transform $(\neg A \vee B) \,\&\, (B \to A)$ a few more stages. By applying LE2 to the right-hand conjunct this sentence becomes $(\neg A \vee B)$ $\&\, (\neg B \vee A)$, a conjunction of disjunctions, and by applying LE5 in turn to the whole of this result we get $\neg[\neg(\neg A \vee B) \vee \neg(\neg B \vee A)]$, a sentence compounded in terms of $\neg$ and $\vee$ alone. For another example, let us start with $\neg(A \equiv B)$. This time, we will number the sentences in one column and, right alongside, the logical equivalence which has been applied to obtain the sentence on that line. Try to follow the transformations as they develop line by line:

1. $\neg(A \equiv B)$ — Given
2. $\neg[(A \to B) \,\&\, (B \to A)]$ — LE1
3. $\neg[\neg\neg(A \to B) \,\&\, \neg\neg(B \to A)]$ — LE4 (twice)
4. $\neg(A \to B) \vee \neg(B \to A)$ — LE6
5. $(A \,\&\, \neg B) \vee (B \,\&\, \neg A)$ — LE7 (twice)

---

[26] Actually, we can get by with one single connective: the **alternative denial**, whose truth-table is $\neg(\alpha \,\&\, \beta)$'s. See exercise 3.5.3 (but also 3.5.2).

By means of the substitution rule and a core of logical equivalences, any sentence from SL's infinite number can be reexpressed in terms of a small number of connectives. This feature is important for theoretical purposes: It means that any question about SL as a whole, that is, as a system of sentences, or about the formal or semantical properties of its sentences could be investigated in terms of just two (or three) chosen connectives, and it would be certain that no type of sentence was being left out of the investigation. Which set of connectives was chosen would depend on how someone wanted to organize the system.

Questions about SL as a system of sentences belong to the area of logic called **metalogic,** an area which begins with redesigning the system itself on a simpler but adequate basis of connectives in the way just shown. Although this subject does not fall within the scope of our text, there is already a well-developed metalogic for sentential logic. At the end of the last chapter on sentential logic, we shall mention some of the results of metalogic which apply to it.

Exercises

3.5.1 Express the sentences (a) A $\equiv$ B, (b) A & (B & C) and (c) (P $\rightarrow$ Q) $\rightarrow$ P in terms of $\neg$ and $\vee$ alone. (Note: Your answer will be correct if it is truth-functionally equivalent to the one being simplified. Construct a truth-table with *Symlog* to verify your work.)

3.5.2 The truth-table for the **joint denial,** $\alpha \downarrow \beta$, of α and β is identical to that of $\neg(\alpha \vee \beta)$. (a) Construct the truth-table for $\alpha \downarrow \beta$, and (b) express $\neg\alpha$, $\alpha \& \beta$ and $\alpha \vee \beta$ in terms of $\downarrow$ alone.

3.5.3 The truth-table for the **alternative denial**—also known as the Sheffer's stroke, $\alpha \mid \beta$—of α and β is identical to that of $\neg(\alpha \& \beta)$. (a) Construct the truth-table for $\alpha \mid \beta$, and (b) express $\neg\alpha$, $\alpha \& \beta$ and $\alpha \vee \beta$ in terms of $\mid$ alone.

3.5.4 Express the sentence (P $\equiv$ Q) $\rightarrow$ (P & S) in terms of $\neg$ and $\vee$ alone. (Note: Your answer will be correct if it is truth-functionally equivalent to the one being simplified. Construct a truth-table with *Symlog* to verify your work.)

4

SL Truth-Trees

In this chapter we take a fresh approach in determining whether a given set of SL sentences is truth-functionally consistent or inconsistent. As we have seen, the property of being inconsistent plays an important diagnostic role in formal logic: It enables us to detect that an argument is valid, that one sentence entails another, that a particular sentence is logically true and so on. Such matters were first examined by the method of long truth-tables and afterward, more succinctly, by the short truth-table test. We will now see how questions of validity, entailment, logical truth and so on can be answered effectively by a quite different method, which concentrates on the syntax of sentences, that is, on their truth-functional structure. This new procedure is called the **truth-tree method.** We will begin with a brief, general account of the method and then introduce the rules by which it is applied. Since these rules are designed for use in *Symlog*, the best way to learn them and to discover how the new diagnostic tool works is through examples. We encourage you therefore to follow our examples on your own screen and to solve the suggested problems.

4.1   The Logic and the Look of Truth-Trees

Tree testing is a method of transforming a set of one or more compound sentences into a collection of sets whose members are nothing but **literals.**[1]

---

[1] The term 'literal,' which is adapted here from computer theory, stands for any atomic sentence or its negation. For example, A, J, ¬A and ¬K are all literals.

This resulting collection of sets—the **truth-tree**—makes it easy to test the original set for inconsistency.[2] If a set is inconsistent, this fact can be 'read off' from the collection at a glance without having to refer to truth-values; if a set is consistent, that too can be seen in the resulting collection. The truth-tree analysis of sets relies on two facts about SL: (1) any compound sentence is logically equivalent to a sentence which uses no more than three sentence-forming operators: &, ∨ and ¬; (2) any negated compound sentence is logically equivalent to a sentence in which the scope of ¬ is restricted to atomic sentences alone. These two facts are reflected in a list of logical equivalences:

(1) $\neg\neg\alpha \equiv \alpha$

(2) $\neg(\alpha \vee \beta) \equiv (\neg\alpha \,\&\, \neg\beta)$

(3) $\neg(\alpha \rightarrow \beta) \equiv (\alpha \,\&\, \neg\beta)$

(4) $\neg(\alpha \,\&\, \beta) \equiv (\neg\alpha \vee \neg\beta)$

(5) $(\alpha \rightarrow \beta) \equiv (\neg\alpha \vee \beta)$

(6) $(\alpha \equiv \beta) \equiv ((\alpha \,\&\, \beta) \vee (\neg\alpha \,\&\, \neg\beta))$

(7) $\neg(\alpha \equiv \beta) \equiv ((\alpha \,\&\, \neg\beta) \vee (\neg\alpha \,\&\, \beta))$

(Notice that on the right-hand side of each biconditional there is no occurrence of either → or ≡; notice also that each negated compound on the left-hand side is equivalent to an unnegated one on the right.) To each of these logical equivalences there corresponds a specific tree-testing rule, called a **decomposition rule**, which is designed to simplify the syntactical structure of a compound sentence. A truth-tree grows from a given set of sentences by means of these rules (to be listed in the next section). A tree is **complete** when it has no sentences still to be decomposed.

You may find it helpful to keep in mind the image of a real tree when approaching truth-trees for the first time. A real tree has roots, a trunk and branches, and it bears fruit. Think of the set of sentences to be analyzed as the roots of the tree, and the simpler sentences which appear from the analysis of each member of the set as constituting its trunk and branches. The fruit on the branches are the atomic components of the set, whether negated or unnegated. A truth-tree grows in just two ways: by straight, undivided growth or by branching. These are the two ways in which the truth-tree method graphically represents the truth-functional conjunctions and disjunctions of SL. A conjunction of sentences is a straight, undivided growth, whereas a disjunction always appears as a branching of sentences. In *Symlog*'s truth-trees, every set of sentences will be interpreted as a conjunction, and every such conjunction will appear as a boxed-in stack of sentences—a **branch**—having the following form:

---

[2] *Symlog*'s truth-trees are, in essence, Smullyan's **analytic tableaux** (R. M. Smullyan, *First-Order Logic*, Springer-Verlag, 1968).

Every disjunction will always show up as a pair of boxes forming a pair of branches:[3]

$$\boxed{\begin{array}{c}\alpha_1\\\alpha_2\\.\\.\\.\\\alpha_n\end{array}}\quad\boxed{\begin{array}{c}\beta_1\\\beta_2\\.\\.\\.\\\beta_n\end{array}}$$

This is the essential look of a truth-tree. In place of an explicitly truth-functional disjunction of conjunctions, the tree method produces branches of conjoined sentences having the same logical form as the truth-functional compound. Because of the decomposition rules, the ultimate elements to be found on the branches are literals, that is, negated and unnegated atomic sentences.

The property of inconsistency assumes a distinct appearance in the truth-tree method. Any boxed-in stack of sentences containing both a sentence, α, and its negation, $\neg\alpha$, will be called a **closed** or **dead branch**. It is easy to see why these names are appropriate. A pair of sentences like this is formally the same as the conjunction, $\alpha\ \&\ \neg\alpha$, and hence the conjunction of this logically false compound with however many other sentences there might be on that branch would be itself logically false. A dead branch therefore is formally the same as a logically false conjunction of SL. In applying the decomposition rules you will regularly encounter dead branches. It makes no difference whether α is a compound sentence or an atomic one; as long as the sentence is matched by its contradictory, $\neg\alpha$, somewhere on the same branch, the branch is a dead one and can be removed at once from the tree on which it grew.

Symlog provides a quick and efficient way of clipping dead branches from a tree whenever they appear. This is called the **close branch** (CB) routine, which causes any dead branch to vanish from the screen. Use CB as often as necessary in the course of analyzing a set of sentences. In this way, the tree is kept to a manageable size, and what is more important, you will be able to determine whether the particular set you have been analyzing is

---

[3] You are already familiar with the device of conjoining sentences by arranging them vertically. This is the way in which the premises of an argument are given. In the tree method, a vertical stack of sentences is enclosed in a box because a typical truth-tree contains at least one pair of branches and, therefore, at least two different stacks to be distinguished from one another.

consistent or not. We come here to the heart of the truth-tree method. Suppose that every branch of the tree grown from the set is dead: Then the tree itself is dead, and the set of sentences from which it grew is declared inconsistent. Suppose, however, that one or more living branches remain after you have analyzed all the members of the set into their atomic—actually, literal—components: In this case, the tree is a living tree and the set from which it grew is declared consistent. The decomposition rules will enable you to carry out the analysis of any set of SL sentences to the point of getting one of these two results. The logical properties detected by the tree method will be discussed in section 4.4.

4.2 The Decomposition Rules

The aim of this section is to present *Symlog*'s decomposition rules for compound sentences. The mechanics of applying the rules to make trees will be learned through the examples given in the next section. For the moment, just concentrate on the particular 'look' of these rules, for they represent what you will soon be observing on your screen when you do the examples. All of the rules will be identified in a standard way, using symbols for the logical operators of SL combined with the letter D. There are three basic decomposition rules: one for conjunctions α & β, one for disjunctions $\alpha \vee \beta$ and one for sentences preceded by a double negation $\neg\neg\alpha$. These rules will be identified as &D, $\vee$D and $\neg\neg$D, respectively. The first of these, &D, is used for decomposing any compound sentence whose main operator is &. For instance, a set containing the sentence $\neg\neg(P \rightarrow Q)$ & $(P \vee \neg R)$,

$$\boxed{\neg\neg(P \rightarrow Q)\ \&\ (P \vee \neg R)}$$

will have the following appearance when decomposed into its conjuncts:

$$\boxed{\begin{array}{l} \neg\neg(P \rightarrow Q) \\ P \vee \neg R \end{array}}$$

The second rule, $\vee$D, applies to any compound whose main operator is $\vee$, such as P $\vee$ Q. The decomposition of this sentence (as well as of any disjunction) involves branching:

For a further example of $\vee$D, let us decompose the disjunction P $\vee$ $\neg$R, which occurs in the preceding box. In a case like this, where a box includes sentences other than the one to be decomposed, the new branches carry over these other sentences too. From now on we will keep the original boxes in the 'background' so that you can compare them with the ones which result by applying the rules.[4] The truth-tree grown so far looks like the top half of Figure 4.1.

The third basic rule, ¬¬D, has the effect of eliminating a double negation. We will apply this to each of the branches in the tree: The ¬¬D rule should be applied each time a double negation turns up on a branch. As you can see, the rule itself does not produce branching, nor does it increase the number of sentences in a box (Figure 4.1).

Let us now state, more formally, each of the rules we have introduced so far:

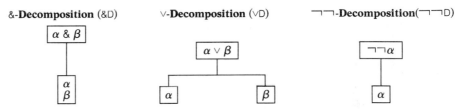

The six decomposition rules still to be presented are, in a sense, variations on &D and ∨D because every compound sentence of SL whose main operator is → or ≡, as well as the negation of a compound sentence, is logically equivalent to a sentence whose main operator is either & or ∨. Take a moment to review the list of logical equivalences given in section 4.1. There you will see that (1) corresponds to ¬¬D. We will now give the decomposition rules for (2) through (7), and to make the correspondence even closer, we will state these six rules, as we did above with the other three, by using the metalogical symbols, α and β.

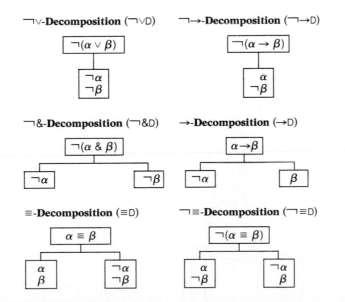

[4] The graphical representation of the sequence of rule applications and their effect on branches (a 'history') looks like an upside-down tree—hence the name for the method.

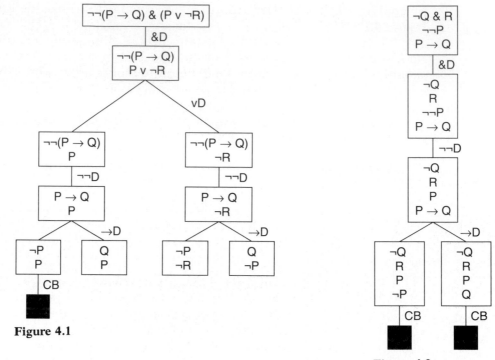

Figure 4.1

Figure 4.2

We can now complete the truth-tree we were working on. Since P → Q appears in both branches, we apply →D to each. After doing so, one of the resulting branches can be closed since it contains two contradictory sentences, P and ¬P. The completed tree is shown in Figure 4.1. Note that for clarity, we have identified the decomposition rules used in producing the tree; each label indicates that a new branch (below) was obtained from the previous one (above) by using the mentioned rule. Note how one of the branches in the tree of Figure 4.1 has been closed with the CB 'rule' (this is indicated with a black box; in *Symlog*'s screen, the branch will literally vanish). Also note that the sentences in all the remaining branches cannot be decomposed any further: They are all literals. Since the tree is not dead, that is, not all of its branches are dead, the original set is consistent. By comparison, Figure 4.2 shows that the set {¬Q & R, ¬¬P, P → Q} is inconsistent. Every stage in the growing—and dying—process of the tree is marked by a corresponding decomposition rule. Since this is a dead tree, the original set is inconsistent.

4.3   Growing Trees with Symlog

Managing a full-blown tree—including all its past history—on your computer screen is a bit cumbersome; hence, you will appreciate the simplicity of *Symlog*'s representation of branches as 'pop-up windows.' Once a decom-

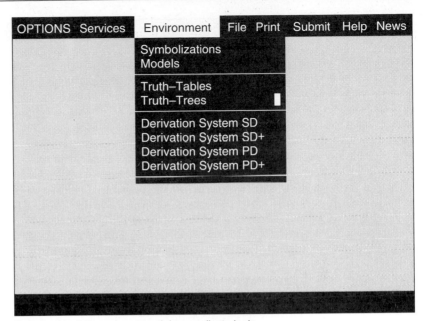

Figure 4.3   Construct truth-trees in sentential or predicate logic

position rule is applied to a molecular sentence there is no need to keep track of it anymore. *Symlog* will simply replace the sentence in a branch by the ones resulting from the application of the rule (*Symlog*, of course, will automatically generate new branches if necessary). Similarly for whole branches: Once a branch has been closed there is no need to keep track of it (as you will soon see, the branch itself vanishes from the screen).

We are ready to work through an example by using *Symlog*. Begin by selecting from the Environment menu the option Truth-Trees (Figure 4.3). After you tell *Symlog* you want to work on a new file—select <newFile> on the screen—and enter the name of the tree, WANG, *Symlog* will then present the Truth-Tree Pad, where you should enter the sentences as shown in Figure 4.4a. After entering the sentences, issue the command to begin constructing the tree (Ctrl-T). If all the sentences in the set are well formed, your screen will look like Figure 4.4b.

We are going to discover whether this set is inconsistent. Let us begin by applying a decomposition rule to the first sentence in the branch. Place the cursor next to the sentence H ≡ ¬G and hit the Enter key. *Symlog* will then display a window listing all the decomposition rules (Figure 4.4c).[5] Since the sentence we want to decompose is a biconditional, select the ≡D rule by placing the cursor next to it (and then hitting the Enter key). This is a branching rule; your screen should look like Figure 4.4d. As a result of applying the ≡D rule, you now have the sentences H and ¬G in the left-hand

---

[5] Four of the decomposition rules in the window will be new to you. These are used in PL and will be introduced in a later chapter; for the time being you can safely ignore them.

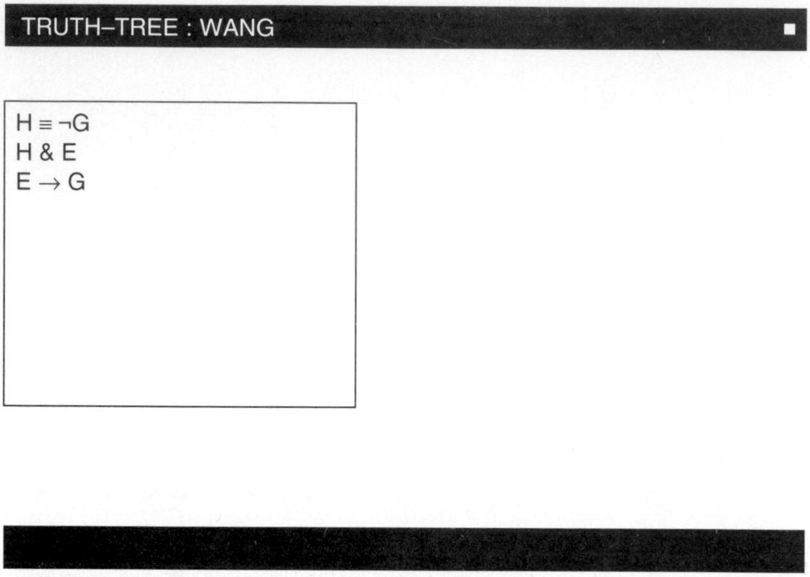

TRUTH–TREE : WANG

H ≡ ¬G
H & E
E → G

Figure 4.4a

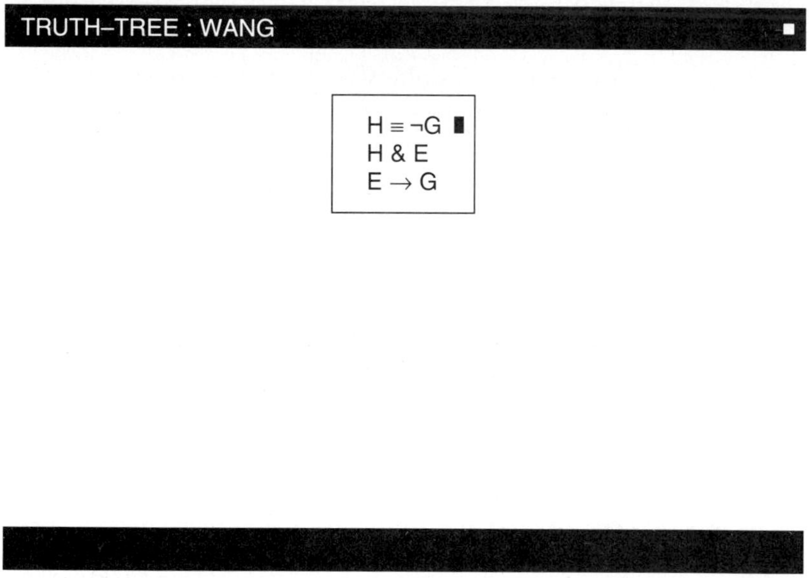

TRUTH–TREE : WANG

H ≡ ¬G ▮
H & E
E → G

Figure 4.4b

side branch, and in the branch to the right you have ¬H and ¬¬G. Let us work on the left-most branch. There are two sentences you could choose at this stage: H & E and E → G. Let us choose E → G and apply →D to it. The truth-tree looks like Figure 4.4e. By the way, you can jump from one branch to another simply by using your right and left cursor keys. Let us select now the sentence H & E in the left-most branch and apply &D to it (Figure 4.4f). Note that this branch has both a sentence, E, and its contradictory, ¬E. Place the cursor next to either one and, by applying the CB routine, close the branch. Now you are left with only two open branches (Figure 4.4g).

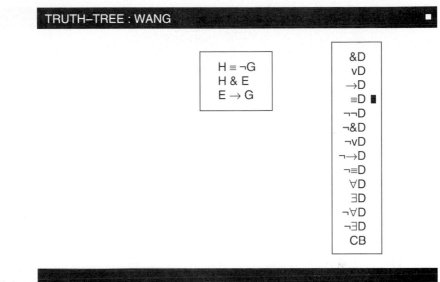

Figure 4.4c

As mentioned before, a branch that has been discarded (by using the close branch routine) because it contains a sentence and its negation is called a **closed branch**, or a dead branch. As soon as a branch is closed it vanishes from *Symlog*'s screen. Any branch still on the screen is termed **open**. Actually, there are two kinds of open branches: those that are open because you are still working on them; that is, one or another decomposition rule could still be applied to its sentences; and those open branches to which no rule can be applied, which occurs when all the sentences in the

TRUTH–TREE : WANG

H ∎	¬H
¬G	¬¬G
H & E	H & E
E → G	E → G

Figure 4.4d

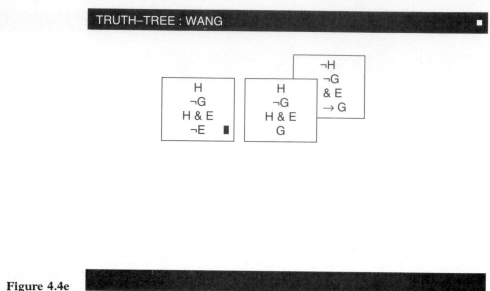

Figure 4.4e

branch are literals and no sentence and its negation are present. In this second case the branch is said to be a **completed open branch**. A tree with at
least one completed open branch is called a **completed open tree**. When
testing a tree, the objective is to attempt to close all the branches or to find
a completed open branch. If you manage to close all the branches in a tree,
the result is a **closed**, or dead, **tree**. This fact is important because it marks
the presence of an inconsistent set of sentences.

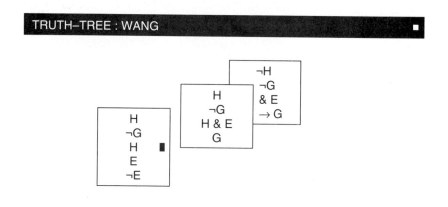

Figure 4.4f

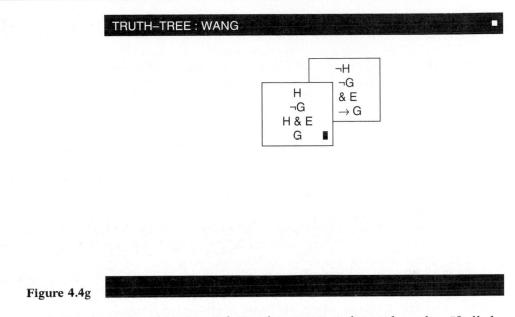

TRUTH–TREE : WANG

Figure 4.4g

You can now continue with *Symlog:* Keep applying the rules. If all the branches on the screen become closed, *Symlog* will confirm by a message that the original set is inconsistent. By the way, you can submit a partially constructed truth-tree for *Symlog* to check (with the Submit option). *Symlog* will tell you then whether more work can be done on the tree or not (Figure 4.5). Since a set is consistent if and only if it is not inconsistent, it follows that a set is consistent if and only if its tree has at least one completed open branch, that is, if it has a completed open tree. For example, Figure 4.5

TRUTH–TREE : DeMORGAN

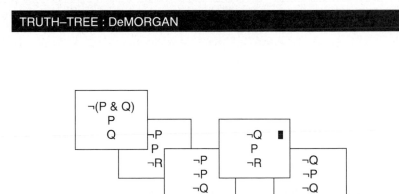

Figure 4.5   Completed open branch: Set is consistent

shows that the set $\{\neg(P \& Q), P \equiv (Q \lor \neg R)\}$ is consistent since there is at least one completed open branch—the one the cursor is on—in its tree.[6]

The following is worth repeating: If you manage to close a branch on the tree, but there are still open branches in the tree, your work must go on. Keep working on the tree until either all the branches have been closed (in which case the initial set is inconsistent) or a completed open branch is encountered (in which case the set is consistent).

Before you try the Learn Exercises SLTREE01 to SLTREE06, which are on your disk, please note some other points about truth-trees. We suggested earlier that truth-trees somewhat resemble real trees. Of course, the analogy has only a limited use. The trees of logic grow downward, they cannot be watered, branches are either fully dead or living but never half dead and sometimes the 'fruit'—literals—is found among the roots or on the 'trunk' itself; that is, the original set of sentences to be analyzed might contain an atomic sentence (or its negation) or one of these might turn up in the first application of a decomposition rule, such as $\neg\neg D$. Wherever such fruit occurs, it always forms part of all the branches subsequently grown. The decomposition rules can be applied in any chosen order.[7] Nevertheless, it is a useful strategy to try to grow a trunk before growing the branches of a truth-tree. That is, you should try to apply those rules which involve single, undivided growth before using any that involve branching. In other words, if possible, use &D, $\neg\neg D$, $\neg \lor D$ and $\neg \rightarrow D$ before applying the remaining decomposition rules. These four rules give 'conjunctive' rather than 'disjunctive' growth and will ensure a more compact, smaller, tree. Sometimes, however, initial branching may be unavoidable; then again, trees with double trunks are occasionally found in nature also.

Exercises

At some point when solving some of the following exercises with *Symlog*, you may want to use the Submit option so that *Symlog* can check your work. *Symlog* will let you know whether more work can be done on the tree. Also, when constructing a tree, do not blindly apply rules; to reinforce your learning, before selecting—applying—a decomposition rule from the rule window you should ask yourself this question: How will this rule affect my branch? A good exercise which makes you appreciate the effect of a rule on a tree is to try to complete the tree by using the least number of rule applications.

---

[6] Although the set $\{\alpha, \alpha\}$ is the same as the set $\{\alpha\}$, *Symlog* will still display in a branch on the screen both occurrences of α (this can be noticed in some of the branches in Figure 4.5). There is a pedagogical reason to do so: If you were to apply a rule to a branch and one of the resulting sentences were to disappear, because it already occurs somewhere in the branch (which could contain many sentences), you would probably become confused.

[7] It is a fact (which we state without proof) that in whatever order the decomposition rules are applied, they will all lead to the same destination, namely, to a closed tree if the initial set is inconsistent or to a tree having a completed open branch if the initial set is consistent. In this respect, it is theoretically irrelevant what tree you construct, and it is for this reason that we will continue to speak of *the* truth-tree for a given set (instead of *a* truth-tree).

4.3.1 Answer true or false (but not both) to each of the following.

    a. If the truth-tree for Γ is closed, then Γ is a truth-functionally inconsistent set.

    b. If a set is truth-functionally consistent, then its truth-tree has at least one closed branch.

    c. If a set is truth-functionally consistent, then its truth-tree has at least one completed open branch.

    d. If Γ_1 and Γ_2 are both truth-functionally consistent, then $\Gamma_1 \cup \Gamma_2$ has a completed open truth-tree.

    e. If Γ_1 and Γ_2 have both closed truth-trees, then $\Gamma_1 \cap \Gamma_2$ has a closed truth-tree as well.

    f. A truth-tree with a completed open branch cannot be closed.

4.3.2 Construct truth-trees by using *Symlog* to determine whether the following sets are truth-functionally consistent or inconsistent.

    a. $\{\neg(\neg P \vee Q) \vee R, \neg B \rightarrow \neg P, \neg R\}$

    b. $\{B \equiv \neg B\}$

    c. $\{F \vee G, (\neg J \& H) \vee (\neg G \& \neg F), (J \vee \neg G) \& (\neg H \vee J)\}$

    d. $\{\neg(L \vee C) \equiv D, \neg\neg D \& B, \neg B \vee C\}$

    e. $\{P \rightarrow Q, \neg(K \vee Q) \equiv R, R \& S\}$

    f. $\{G \rightarrow H, (G \vee \neg I) \& K, \neg K \vee (\neg H \vee \neg G)\}$

    g. $\{H, \neg(R \vee S) \equiv \neg H, (\neg D \& \neg S) \& \neg R\}$

    h. $\{A \equiv B, B \rightarrow \neg C, (A \vee B) \& C\}$

4.3.3 Use the Create option under *Symlog*'s File menu to ask the program to generate (randomly) SL sets of sentences whose truth-trees you should then construct to determine whether they are consistent or inconsistent.

4.4   *Tree Testing for Logical Properties*

Like truth-tables, tree testing is a method for deciding the consistency of SL sets; it is sometimes called a **decision procedure**. What this means is that given any SL set you can determine—decide—whether it is consistent or not by constructing its truth-tree. This is an important and highly desirable property of the technique. There is a formal statement of this property (whose proof is beyond the scope of this text) known as the completeness and soundness theorems for the truth-tree method:[8]

> **The Completeness Theorem.**   If an SL set Γ is truth-functionally inconsistent, then Γ has a closed truth-tree.

> **The Soundness Theorem.**   If an SL set Γ has a closed truth-tree, then Γ is truth-functionally inconsistent.

---

[8] Later we will meet systems of logic which although complete and sound lack a full decision procedure.

Given these two important results, we now consider how the truth-tree technique can also be used as a test for entailment and validity. Likewise, other truth-functional properties of sentences can be decided, such as truth-functional truth, falsehood, indeterminacy and equivalence, if we express all of these semantical concepts in terms of the consistency of sets. As you can see, logic is (once again) using the concept of inconsistency to its advantage.

Let us begin with entailment. Recalling that a set Γ entails a sentence α if and only if $\Gamma \cup \{\neg\alpha\}$ is inconsistent, and that a set is inconsistent if and only if it has a closed tree, the test for entailment that we introduced for truth-tables can now be adapted for truth-trees, as follows:

> **Test for Entailment.** An SL set $\{\alpha_1, \alpha_2, \ldots, \alpha_n\}$ **truth-functionally entails** a sentence β if and only if the test set $\{\alpha_1, \alpha_2, \ldots, \alpha_n, \neg\beta\}$ has a closed truth-tree.

Again, since an argument is **truth-functionally valid** if and only if its set of premises truth-functionally entails the conclusion, the test for entailment serves as a test for validity. To illustrate with an example, consider the following argument:

> Either Bob goes to the party or Suzy doesn't. If Bob goes to the party so does Suzy. Therefore, Suzy will go to the party if and only if Bob goes too.

To test for validity, we first symbolize the argument:

$$B \vee \neg S$$
$$B \rightarrow S$$
$$\overline{S \equiv B}$$

Next, we form the test set, $\{B \vee \neg S, B \rightarrow S, \neg(S \equiv B)\}$, which we test for inconsistency by constructing the truth-tree shown in Figure 4.6. Since the tree is closed it follows that the argument is valid.[9] To become further acquainted with these concepts, you should now try the exercises SLTREE07 to SLTREE11 on your disk.

So far the truth-tree method has been used to test the properties of sets of sentences and arguments. It can also be applied to determine the truth-functional status of sentences. More precisely,

> **Theorem.** A sentence α of SL is **truth-functionally true** if and only if the set $\{\neg\alpha\}$ has a closed tree.

---

[9] The validity of the argument can also be checked by testing that the set $\{\neg[((B \vee \neg S)$ & $(B \rightarrow S)) \rightarrow (S \equiv B)]\}$—its sole member is the negation of the argument's conditional analogue—is inconsistent. In this respect, truth-trees constitute a **refutation method**.

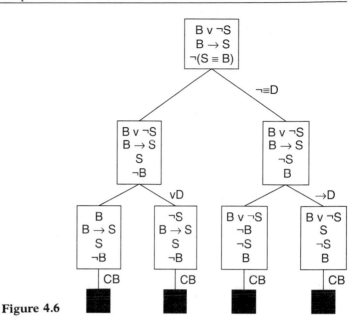

Figure 4.6

Theorem. A sentence α of SL is **truth-functionally false** if and only if the set $\{\alpha\}$ has a closed tree.

These two theorems depend on the fact that a sentence α is truth-functionally false if and only if the set $\{\alpha\}$ is inconsistent and that the negation of any truth-functionally true sentence is truth-functionally false. Figure 4.7 shows that the sentence $(A \rightarrow B) \equiv (\neg A \vee B)$ is truth-functionally true since the set containing its negation, namely, $\{\neg[(A \rightarrow B) \equiv (\neg A \vee B)]\}$, has a closed truth-tree. Since a sentence is truth-functionally indeterminate if and only if it is neither truth-functionally true nor truth-functionally false, the preceding two theorems can be combined to obtain a compact statement of truth-functional indeterminacy:

Theorem. A sentence α of SL is **truth-functionally indeterminate** if and only if neither $\{\neg\alpha\}$ nor $\{\alpha\}$ has a closed tree.

In Figure 4.8, the sentence $(P \vee \neg(P \vee Q)) \rightarrow \neg Q$ is shown to be truth-functionally indeterminate by means of two truth-trees—one constructed for the sentence, the other for its negation. Note that each tree contains at least one completed open branch. Finally, recall that two sentences α and β are truth-functionally equivalent if and only if $\alpha \equiv \beta$ is truth-functionally true. Combining this with our previous theorem for truth-functional truth we obtain

Theorem. Two sentences α and β of SL are **truth-functionally equivalent** if and only if $\{\neg(\alpha \equiv \beta)\}$ has a closed tree.

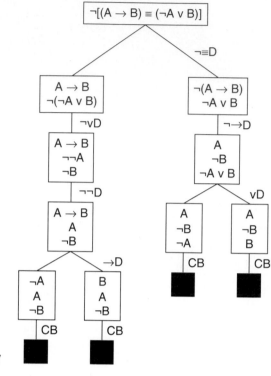

Figure 4.7

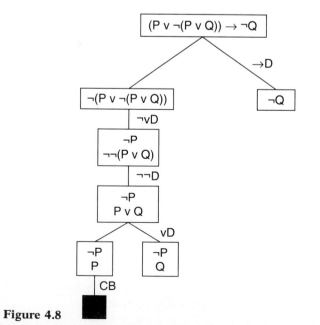

Figure 4.8

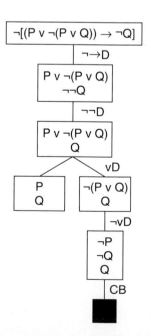

Glance back at Figure 4.7. In terms of this last theorem, you will see that A → B is truth-functionally equivalent to ¬A ∨ B. (At this point try to solve the exercises SLTREE12 to SLTREE16 on your disk.)

Truth-trees provide more information than meets the eye. For instance, the presence of a completed open branch in a truth-tree not only flags the set being tested as consistent but also makes it possible to obtain a truth-value assignment which satisfies the set. To obtain such a truth-value assignment from a completed open branch, proceed as follows:

1. Assign the truth-value T to any atomic sentence which appears on the branch and the truth-value F to any atomic sentence which appears negated on the branch.
2. Arbitrarily assign the truth-value T or F to any atomic sentence which belongs to the set being tested but is not found on the branch itself.

For an illustration, consider the completed open branch marked by the cursor in Figure 4.5. For this branch we can construct a truth-value assignment which assigns T to P, F to Q and F to R. Here is another illustration. From any of the completed open branches in the trees of Figure 4.8 we can recover truth-value assignments which satisfy their corresponding sets. For example, from the bottom right-hand completed open branch of the tree for (P ∨ ¬(P ∨ Q)) → ¬Q we obtain the truth-value assignment which assigns F to P (since the branch contains ¬P) and T to Q (since it contains Q). And from the upper right-hand branch containing only ¬Q, we can obtain two assignments since P does not occur in the branch: T to P and F to Q, as well as F to P and F to Q. You should verify that each of these assignments indeed satisfies (P ∨ ¬(P ∨ Q)) → ¬Q. Now look at the separate tree for ¬[(P ∨ ¬(P ∨ Q)) → ¬Q] and devise the appropriate truth-value assignment (only one is possible). Then, verify that it satisfies ¬[(P ∨ ¬(P ∨ Q)) → ¬Q].

Exercises

4.4.1   Using *Symlog,* construct a truth-tree by using the test for entailment to determine whether each of the following is true or false (i.e., whether each given set truth-functionally entails the corresponding sentence).

a. {¬E ∨ F, G ≡ (¬F & H), G} ⊨ ¬E
b. {(A & B) → (¬M ∨ D)} ⊨ A → [B → (¬M ∨ D)]
c. {L ∨ Q, (Q ∨ L) → R, H} ⊨ R & H
d. {B & K, ¬K ∨ J} ⊢ ¬L & (J & B)
e. {P ≡ (P → O), ¬(O & N)} ⊨ ¬(P → ¬N) → Q

4.4.2   Use *Symlog* to determine whether the following arguments are truth-functionally valid or invalid.

a.   (P → S) → R
     (¬N & L) & Q
     ――――――――――――――
     ¬(P → S)

b. P & ¬P

Q

c. ¬M & H

S ≡ H

A → [B → ¬(¬S & ¬M)]

d. A & B

P ≡ (P ∨ P)

e. Q

P ≡ P

f. A → B

¬C → ¬B

C ∨ D

¬E → ¬D

A ∨ E

g. ¬(P ∨ Q)

¬P & ¬Q

[PR16] h. P ∨ S

Q ∨ ¬S

¬Q

H ∨ P

i. (M & ¬S) ∨ ¬¬A

D ≡ (R ∨ G)

H ∨ ¬(¬B ∨ J)

P ≡ R

j. P ∨ ¬P

P → (Q → P)

4.4.3   Express in SL the following arguments and determine, using *Symlog*'s truth-trees, whether they are truth-functionally valid or invalid.

a. If I take math then I will take biology. I will not take biology. Therefore, I will not take math. (B, M)

b. Either I will study physics or chemistry but not both. I will certainly not take physics. Therefore, I will enroll in chemistry. (C, P)

c. I will not study both chemistry and math. However, if I take math I will also take either physics or logic. There is no way I can take physics. Hence, I will study either math or logic. (C, L, M, P)

[PR17] d. I will take neither biology nor physics. However, if I study logic then I will take both math and computer science. But I can't take both math and computer science. Hence, I won't take logic either. (B, C, L, M, P)

e. If I take both logic and math then I can also do computer science. But I can't study computer science unless I do physics too. For sure I am not taking physics. That simply means that I will be able to study neither logic nor math. (C, L, M, P)

4.4.4   Use *Symlog* to test each of the arguments in exercise 3.2.3 for validity by means of the truth-tree method.

4.4.5   Use *Symlog* to test each of the arguments in exercise 3.2.5 for validity by means of the truth-tree method.

4.4.6   Answer true or false (but not both) to each of the following.

   a. If α is truth-functionally true, then $\{\neg\alpha\}$ has a closed truth-tree.

   b. If α is truth-functionally true, then $\{\alpha\}$ has a completed open truth-tree.

   c. If α is truth-functionally false, then $\{\alpha\}$ has a closed truth-tree.

   d. If α and β are truth-functionally true, then $\{\neg\alpha, \neg\beta\}$ has a closed truth-tree.

   e. Any set with a truth-functionally false sentence as one of its members must have a closed truth-tree.

   f. Any set with a truth-functionally true sentence as one of its members must have a completed open truth-tree.

   g. If α and β are truth-functionally equivalent, then $\{\neg(\alpha \equiv \beta)\}$ has a closed truth-tree.

   h. If α is truth-functionally indeterminate, then $\{\alpha\}$ has a completed open tree.

   i. If α is truth-functionally indeterminate, then $\{\neg\alpha\}$ has a completed open tree.

   j. If $\{\alpha\}$ has a completed open truth-tree, then α is truth-functionally indeterminate.

4.4.7   Using *Symlog*, construct a truth-tree for each sentence to show that it is truth-functionally true.

[PR18]   a. $\neg[L \equiv (K \vee \neg N)] \vee [[(\neg N \vee K) \vee \neg L] \,\&\, [(K \vee \neg N) \rightarrow L]]$

   b. $[(P \,\&\, \neg A) \rightarrow (B \equiv K)] \rightarrow [P \rightarrow [\neg A \rightarrow (B \equiv K)]]$

   c. $[\neg(P \vee Q) \vee R] \equiv [R \vee (\neg Q \,\&\, \neg P)]$

   d. $[\neg(S \,\&\, \neg P) \vee (N \rightarrow R)] \equiv [\neg(N \rightarrow R) \rightarrow \neg(\neg P \,\&\, S)]$

[PR19]   e. $[A \equiv [B \equiv (C \equiv D)]] \equiv [(A \equiv B) \equiv (C \equiv D)]$

4.4.8   Using *Symlog*, construct a truth-tree for each sentence to show that it is truth-functionally false.

   a. $\neg[(\neg Q \,\&\, P) \rightarrow R] \,\&\, [P \rightarrow (\neg Q \rightarrow R)]$

   b. $\neg[[(P \equiv R) \rightarrow S] \equiv [S \vee \neg(R \equiv P)]]$

[PR20]   c. $[E \vee (F \,\&\, \neg H)] \,\&\, \neg[(F \vee E) \,\&\, (\neg H \vee E)]$

   d. $\neg[(P \equiv Q) \vee (\neg P \equiv Q)]$

   e. $[\neg(L \,\&\, J) \vee \neg(K \vee M)] \,\&\, \neg\neg[(L \,\&\, J) \,\&\, (K \vee M)]$

4.4.9   Using *Symlog*, construct appropriate truth-trees for each sentence to show that it is truth-functionally indeterminate.

   a. $\neg[\neg L \equiv \neg(J \vee G)] \rightarrow \neg K$

   b. $(B \vee C) \,\&\, \neg(D \rightarrow \neg A)$

   c. $[P \vee (Q \vee \neg R)] \,\&\, (R \vee Q)$

   d. $[(C \,\&\, \neg B) \vee D] \vee C$

   e. $\neg[(B \vee (C \equiv D)) \,\&\, B]$

4.4.10 Determine with *Symlog's* truth-trees which of the following sentences are satisfiable and, when the sentence is satisfiable, recover a truth-value assignment which satisfies it.

    a. ¬[(¬P & (P ∨ Q)) → Q]

    b. (P → Q) ≡ (¬Q → ¬P)

    c. ¬[(C ∨ ¬J) ≡ (¬J → B)]

    d. (A → B) & ¬(B ∨ ¬A)

    e. (C ∨ B) → (¬B ∨ ¬C)

4.4.11 Determine, by constructing a truth-tree with *Symlog,* whether each of the following sentences is truth-functionally true, truth-functionally false or truth-functionally indeterminate.

    a. ¬[¬(A ≡ C) ∨ ¬D] & ¬(B ≡ B)

    b. (R ∨ S) → ¬T

    c. (J → L) ≡ (¬L → ¬J)

    d. [(Q ≡ R) → ¬S] ∨ ¬(R ≡ ¬R)

    e. (A ∨ H) → ¬(A & H)

    f. ¬[(¬A & ¬(B ∨ C)) ∨ (C ∨ (B ∨ A))]

    g. (K → M) ≡ (¬K ∨ M)

    h. S ∨ T

    i. ¬(J → ¬(L ≡ F))

    j. [(P ∨ R) → Q] → [Q ∨ (¬R & ¬P)]

    k. P & ¬P

    l. (N ∨ O) ≡ ¬(L ≡ ¬G)

    m. ¬[((¬A ∨ B) & (¬B ∨ A)) → (A ≡ B)]

    n. (J & (J → K)) → (K & J)

    o. (P ≡ Q) ≡ ¬(Q ≡ P)

4.4.12 Construct appropriate truth-trees with *Symlog* to show that the sentences in each of the following pairs are truth-functionally equivalent.

    a. ¬(J & ¬J) and J ∨ ¬J

    b. L → (J → H) and (J & ¬H) → ¬L

    c. ¬(B ≡ C) and ¬(¬B ∨ C) ∨ ¬(¬C ∨ B)

    d. P ∨ P and P

    e. ¬T ≡ ¬¬R and (R ∨ T) & (¬T ∨ ¬R)

    f. (L ∨ K) & ¬J and ¬(¬L & ¬K) & ¬J

    g. ¬¬(¬P ∨ Q) and ¬P ∨ Q

    h. ¬B ≡ B and ¬(C ∨ ¬C)

    i. ¬S ∨ T and ¬(S & ¬T)

    j. (¬Q → S) & (¬R ∨ Q) and ¬Q → (S & ¬R)

4.4.13 Determine which of the following sets are satisfiable and, when the set is satisfiable, recover a truth-value assignment which satisfies it.

    a. {P, ¬Q, R}

    b. {K ∨ M, ¬K ∨ ¬M}

    c. $\{\neg B \rightarrow Q, \neg R \vee B\}$

    d. $\{P, P \rightarrow \neg R, \neg(Q \vee \neg R)\}$

    e. $\{\neg L, L \vee K, \neg K\}$

4.4.14 Give an example of a set that when tested for truth-functional inconsistency, has this property: The number of times that rules must be applied to construct its smallest truth-tree is the same as the number of rows in its truth-table.

4.4.15 Let us suppose that we were to replace the rule of ∨-decomposition by the one that follows:

Show that, by incorporating this new rule, some truth-functionally consistent SL sets would be rendered by the truth-tree method as truth-functionally inconsistent.

4.4.16 Design a rule to decompose sentences of the form $\alpha \oplus \beta$, where $\oplus$ is the exclusive-or connective. (Hint: Express $\oplus$ in terms of the more familiar connectives.)

4.4.17 Design a rule to decompose sentences of the form $\alpha \downarrow \beta$, where $\downarrow$ is the joint denial connective. (Hint: See exercise 3.5.2.)

4.4.18 Use the Create option under *Symlog*'s File menu to ask the program to generate (randomly) sentences of SL whose truth-functional status (truth-functional truth, falsehood and indeterminacy) you should then determine by constructing appropriate truth-trees.

5

Natural Deduction in Propositional Logic

In this chapter we take an entirely different approach to SL. So far, our emphasis has been on decision procedures (like truth-tables and truth-trees), which enable us to *determine* whether a statement is logically true, logically false or neither and whether an argument is valid or invalid. Our attention now will shift to **proof procedures**, that is, to the *building* of valid arguments. In this new approach, an argument is considered to be more than a set of premises plus a conclusion; it also consists of all the statements which lead, logically, from the premises to that conclusion. Proving an argument's validity takes a form analogous to forging a chain. The links of the chain are sentences which join the premises to the final and most important link, the conclusion. Each link, obtained by a rule of deductive inference, is said to be a **derived sentence**, and the procedure of proving an argument's validity amounts, in short, to deriving its conclusion from the premises. A similar procedure serves to prove logical truths. You will discover that *Symlog* is an expert when it comes to building these chains of deduction. We call the rules of deductive inference to be used in this chapter **SD rules**. Together, these form the derivation system known as **SD** (for sentential, or propositional, deduction), which forms the core of larger derivation systems. Further rules will be added to SD to form the system **SD+**. Later, the rules of SD will be incorporated in a system of quantificational logic called PD. The enriched version of PD is called PD+.

5.1   *The Derivation System SD*

Each derivation rule of SD is also a rule of entailment. Thus, every derived sentence (including the conclusion) will be true *if* the sentences from which they are obtained (the premises as well as all the intermediate links) are true. The rules of SD illustrate what are often called **natural deduction** rules. Such rules attempt to capture and make precise a variety of patterns of deductive inference, patterns which are encountered many times in arguments expressed in natural language. You already know many of these deductive rules, although probably you are unfamiliar with their names in formal logic. Rules of deductive inference are certainly not the only kind used in reasoning. Sound inferences often point to conclusions that are probably true rather than certainly true, and in such cases the support which a set of premises gives to a conclusion is classified as inductive. Nevertheless, deductive rules are an important part of the fabric of reasoning. To see how a few of these patterns work, take a moment to read the following example with care:

> If it rains tonight then we will watch the Blue Jay's game on TV and have dinner at home. If we have dinner at home, then if we're not going to have Kentucky Fried chicken again we'll have sushi. It is indeed raining tonight, but we're not going to have Kentucky Fried chicken again. So for dinner we're going to have sushi.

The conclusion and premises of this argument are easily spotted, and with hardly more effort it is easy to see that there is a connection among the premises which leads deductively to that conclusion. First, let us list the three premises (simplifying them a bit):

1. If it rains, then we will watch the game and eat at home.
2. If we eat at home, then if it's not chicken it will be sushi.
3. It is raining, but we won't have chicken.

Next, let us assume that each of the premises is true. Since premise 3 is a conjunction, BOTH of its conjuncts must be true, and in particular the left-hand sentence, 'It is raining.' Premise 1 says that IF it is raining THEN we will watch the game AND we will eat at home, and we already know that the antecedent has to be true. So the consequent also must be true. But this too is a conjunction. Consequently both conjuncts must be true, and in particular the right-hand conjunct, 'We will eat at home.' This same sentence occurs in premise 2 as the antecedent. Hence the consequent, IF not chicken THEN sushi, has to be true. However, from premise 3 (the right-hand conjunct this time) we know that we will NOT have chicken. Therefore, we will have sushi—which, in fact, is the stated conclusion of the argument. We have worked our way down to this statement by a series of entailments which now show us that if the premises are true then so too is the conclusion. The steps have been marked by words written in capital letters: the familiar sentence connectives. Take another moment to review these steps. If you are puzzled by one or another of the moves, you may find it helpful to recall the truth-functional meaning of compound sentences like conjunctions and conditionals which were studied in Chapter 2. Natural deduction rules, including those of SD, reflect this meaning.

Perhaps you have been asking yourself this: Do we really need another way of showing arguments to be valid? Why aren't truth-tables and truth-trees enough? The answer is that natural deduction systems are more fundamental and are presupposed by those two decision procedures. Recall how you use the short truth-table test to test the validity of any given argument. First, a conditional analogue formed from that argument is assumed to be false, so the truth-value F is placed under the main operator (the conditional sign). But then it follows right away that the antecedent is true and the consequence false. Why? Because IF a conditional statement is false (as here), THEN those must be the truth-values of its immediate components. Is the antecedent a conjunction (i.e., does the argument have more than one premise)? If so, both of the conjuncts are true, as well as all the premises. Why? Because IF a conjunction is true, THEN so are its conjuncts. Ultimately, does the search for a truth-value assignment lead to an inescapable contradiction? If so, the assumption of the argument's invalidity is overturned. Why? Because no statement can be true if it leads deductively to a logical impossibility (in which one statement must be both true and false).

In all this step-by-step reasoning about truth values, natural deduction rules are used for making the connections, and their use is so frequent that we tend to take them for granted. The purpose in having a system like SD is to isolate a basic, working set of rules which will acquaint us directly with patterns of deductive inference. By applying the rules we become more familiar with the rules themselves. The reason for introducing SD, therefore, is not to give us just another means of showing the validity of arguments. The two decision procedures of truth-table and truth-tree construction are quite enough. The reason is to guide us through the process of deductive reasoning itself. Valid arguments and logical truths are the means to that end. This last point may help explain how a proof procedure differs from a decision procedure. Our aim is not to find out whether an argument is valid but rather, by using derivation rules, to forge the logical connections that show the necessary connection between premises and conclusion. Thus we are shown why a valid argument is valid, and of course that cannot be done for invalid arguments. Think of a valid argument appearing in its usual or standard form—the set of premises plus the conclusion—as something highly compressed or condensed. The business of SD is to unpack that standard form and to display how the conclusion actually *follows* from the premises.

Although SD limits itself to valid arguments and although its rules are few, it is a powerful and complete system of natural deduction for SL:

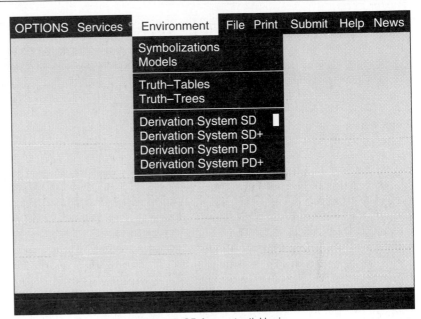

Figure 5.1   Construct derivations in the system SD for sentential logic

Given any set of sentences, Γ, which entails a particular sentence, α, a proof (forged with the rules of SD) is constructible showing α to be derivable from Γ.[1] Thus, every valid argument of SL has a proof in SD. With the help of *Symlog*, we turn now to those rules.

In *Symlog*, the derivation system SD is reached through the pull-down Environment menu (Figure 5.1). By selecting it, you will be given a fresh sheet from what we call the Derivation Pad (Figure 5.2). The work area of the Derivation Pad contains four different fields: (1) the Line Number Field, next to which you will enter the sentences of a derivation; the program provides up to 100 lines—more than enough for our purposes; (2) the Theorem Field, where you will enter the sentences of SL, one per line; in the case of an argument, you would begin by listing the first premise on line 1, the second premise on line 2 and so on; (3) the Justification Field, in which you set down the particular rule of SD which warrants the entering of each sentence in a derivation, from the premises to the conclusion; and last (4) the Mark Field, where the program places a checkmark next to every sentence not yet evaluated—checked—by it; this particular feature is very similar to that which you found when working on truth-table pads. Constructing a derivation in SD involves conventions similar to those of other *Symlog* environments. For instance, since each derivation is a computer file it must be given a unique name, which will then be listed in the upper left-hand corner. Also, you will be able to ask the program to check your work either one line at a time or one whole derivation at a time, and *Symlog* will respond with appropriate

---

[1] The proof of this claim belongs to metalogic and will not be covered in this text.

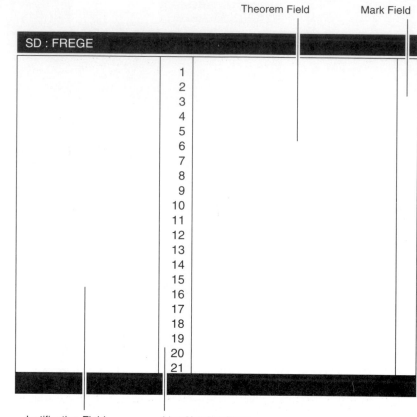

Theorem Field   Mark Field

Figure 5.2   Justification Field   Line Number Field

messages at the bottom of your screen. See Appendix C for a complete list of commands available for the Derivation Pad. Since all sentences of SL are written in capital letters, we advise that you continue the practice of keeping the Caps Lock key toggled on.

With the help of *Symlog*, the rules of SD will now be set out and illustrated one by one. To assist you, we have provided several practice problems on disk, which we urge you to try as you read through the text. These problems will acquaint you with basic routines common to all derivations as well as with important details which are specific to each rule. Once all the rules of SD have been introduced, we can begin to tackle more challenging derivations. For now, however, the focus will be on the rules themselves, and so the problems will be simpler. Each SD rule has a schematic presentation in which familiar metalogical symbols like α and β stand for sentences of SL (whether simple or compound) and lowercase letters like i, j, k and l represent line numbers. The majority are identified as either 'introduction' rules or 'elimination' rules. An introduction rule is a routine which results in a sentence of one of the five truth-functional types found in SL (negation, conjunction, etc.), and an elimination rule is a routine meant to be applied to sentences of one or another of those types. Each rule also car-

SD : SUSHI		
PREMISE	1	R → (G & E)
PREMISE	2	E → (¬C → S)
PREMISE	3	R & ¬C
	4	
	5	
	6	
	7	
	8	
	9	
	10	

Figure 5.3

ries a 'name tag' (given in parentheses) which identifies its use in the Justification Field; this is the name by which *Symlog* knows the rule, so it is important to become familiar with these tags.

Premise (PREMISE)

PREMISE	i	α

Restriction: A premise cannot be entered within a subderivation.

This is the rule by which the **premises (primary assumptions** or **axioms)** of an argument whose conclusion is to be derived are formally introduced into the derivation. The word PREMISE in the Justification Field identifies the role of each of these sentences as being given, and no further justification is needed. PREMISE is not so much a rule of derivation in **SD** as a routine for furnishing sentences to which the other rules are to be applied. *Symlog* will recognize these sentences as forming the basis for a derivation.[2] Previously, we discussed an argument about eating sushi for dinner. Here now are the premises of that argument (Figure 5.3), introduced as just such a basis.

Reiteration (R)

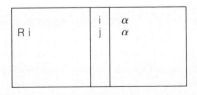

---

[2] The restriction against using this rule in what is called a subderivation will be explained later in connection with a related rule known as ASSUMPTION.

SD : SUSHI		
PREMISE	1	R → (G & E)
PREMISE	2	E → (¬C → S)
PREMISE	3	R & ¬C
R 1	4	R → (G & E)
R 3	5	R & ¬C
R 4	6	R → (G & E)
	7	
	8	
	9	
	10	

Figure 5.4

The reiteration rule licenses the following move: Any sentence already occurring in a derivation may be subsequently repeated in that derivation.
For instance, any of the three premises just listed is available for reiteration, as would be any sentence derived from one or more of them. Reiteration always produces a new line at a later stage in a proof; it is contrary to
the rules of proof making to reiterate a later sentence to an earlier stage. In
Figure 5.4, the rule R is applied three times.

   As will be seen in connection with some later rules, such as ASSUMP-
TION, both premises and the sentences derivable from them may also be reiterated in any subderivation of a given derivation. In a practical sense, this
is the primary role of the rule R. However, details regarding subderivations
can be ignored for the present. As an exercise with *Symlog*, turn to the sample derivation called SD01 on your disk and justify the theorems by filling
in the missing entries in the Justification Field. Then have *Symlog* check your
work.

&-Introduction (&I)

	i	α
	j	β
&I i, j	k	α & β

The rule &-introduction is SD's rule for constructing new conjunctions, as
needed, in the course of a derivation. The conjuncts must come from earlier
stages in the derivation; they may be premises or other sentences already
derived. The sentences which are to serve as the conjuncts do not have to be
reiterated first. However, in an actual derivation, those sentences (taking
the place of α and β) would each be justified by an SD rule in the Justification
Field. In Figure 5.5, &I is used four different times. It would be rare for a

```
SD : SUSHI

PREMISE              1   R → (G & E)
PREMISE              2   E → (¬C → S)
PREMISE              3   R & ¬C
&I  3, 1             4   (R & ¬C) & (R → (G & E))
&I  1, 3             5   (R → (G & E)) & (R & ¬C)
&I  3, 5             6   (R & ¬C) & ((R → (G & E)) & (R & ¬C))
&I  2, 2             7   (E → (¬C → S)) & (E → (¬C → S))
                     8
                     9
                    10
```

Figure 5.5

derivation to apply this rule so often in succession; lines 4 to 7 are meant rather to illustrate different possible uses.

Please note that when you appeal to the rule &I you must cite two line numbers indicating where the conjuncts originate. In addition, you must also make sure that the order of these numbers corresponds to the place-ment of the left- and right-hand conjuncts. Notice how the difference be-tween the conjunctions on lines 4 and 5 is matched by the ordering of line numbers in the Justification Field. There is a good reason for this practice. Later, you will see how *Symlog* offers a nice shortcut when you are con-structing a derivation: Instead of having to retype sentences in the Theorem Field, the program allows you to type in just the justification for a sentence you want to derive and it then proceeds to enter that very sentence. But right now the important thing is to gain more familiarity with the rules in-troduced so far, so call up exercise SD02, complete the work called for in the Justification and Theorem Fields and then submit your work for a quick check by *Symlog;* do the same for SD03 and SD04.

&-Elimination on the Left (&EL)
&-Elimination on the Right (&ER)

The next two rules complement &I. They enable you to unpack a conjunc-tion into one or another of its conjuncts. Since the only real difference be-tween these two rules concerns which of the two conjuncts—the left or the right—is to be extracted, they will be presented together.[3]

```
              i   α & β                          i   α & β
&EL i                            &ER i
              j   α                              j   β
```

---

[3] The word 'elimination' in the names of the rules applies to the main connective—& here—not to its immediate sentence components. Thus, in &EL one eliminates the ampersand while keep-ing its left conjunct.

Clearly, the sentence 'It is raining but we won't have chicken' entails the sentence 'It is raining'; just as clearly it entails 'We won't have chicken.' Conversely, the two sentences together would entail their formal conjunction. We mention this fact to remind you that each rule of derivation in SD runs parallel to an entailment relation. It may help to keep that fact in mind when encountering any derivation rule for the first time. Figure 5.6 is an illustration of the two new rules applied to one of the three premises.

It is worth emphasizing that an SD rule such as &EL applies to the entire sentence occupying a given line, never to a mere component of that sentence. For instance, the rule cannot be legitimately applied to premise 1, which is a conditional sentence; R → (G & E) does not entail the conjuncts G and E. If you attempt to make this illegal move, *Symlog* will quickly warn you (Figure 5.7).

SD : SUSHI			
PREMISE	1	R → (G & E)	
PREMISE	2	E → (¬C → S)	
PREMISE	3	R & ¬C	
&ER 3	4	¬C	
&EL 3	5	R	
	6		
	7		
	8		
	9		
	10		

Figure 5.6

SD : SUSHI			■
PREMISE	1	R → (G & E)	
PREMISE	2	E → (¬C → S)	
PREMISE	3	R & ¬C	
&ER 1■	4	E	■
	5		
	6		
	7		
	8		
	9		
	10		
	11		
	12		
	13		
	14		
	15		
	16		
■■■ MAIN CONNECTIVE OF THE LINE CITED IS NOT AN AMPERSAND			

Figure 5.7

SD : SUSHI		
PREMISE	1	R → (G & E)
PREMISE	2	E → (¬C → S)
PREMISE	3	R & ¬C
&EL 3	4	R
→E 1,4	5	G & E
&ER 5	6	E
→E 2,6	7	¬C → S
&ER 3	8	¬C
→E 7,8	9	S
	10	

Figure 5.8

Try now to construct the derivations in exercises SD05 and SD06 on disk. Again, submit each derivation once it is completed.

→-Elimination (→E)

→E i, j	i	α → β
	j	α
	k	β

Reasoning based on a conditional sentence plus the antecedent of that conditional is probably the most familiar rule of natural deduction arguments.[4] Suppose that you are contentedly eating sushi. Suddenly, an old warning from your mother occurs to you—that if you eat sushi you are definitely going to get indigestion—and you realize with a chill that here you are, eating sushi. With the speed of lightning you make an inference: I am sure to get indigestion! The entailment is unavoidable. However, perhaps what your mother said was false. Your only hope now is that it was.

The essence of such reasoning is captured in the SD rule, →-elimination (→E). Please glance back at the schema just given. Although a derivation must contain the two key sentences, α and α → β, the particular order in which they occur does not matter. Either way, β is clearly entailed: β cannot be false whenever both α and α → β are true. Take a moment to confirm that fact. You can expect to rely on this rule frequently in the course of derivations. We are now going to illustrate the use of →E by including it in the complete derivation for our sushi argument (Figure 5.8). Watch how the derivation develops step by step; the final sentence in the

---

[4] In some systems of natural deduction, this pattern of inference is known by its medieval Latin name of **modus ponens**. (This familiar pattern of reasoning itself is much older than the Middle Ages, however.)

derivation is of course the conclusion of the original argument, 'We are go-ing to have sushi for dinner.'

Before we leave this particular argument behind, a few remarks may be helpful. The rule →E was used three different times in this derivation, and in each case the order of sentences was just the same: $\alpha \rightarrow \beta$ before α. The order might have been different, in part at least. For instance, the sen-tence ¬C might have been obtained right after the sentence R was, instead of later at line 8. In general, the steps followed in constructing a derivation do not follow an absolute order. Thus there are often several different ways of going about the job. Each rule of SD specifies what is both necessary and sufficient for its application but not when to apply it. A sense of timing in these matters will grow with experience, which is one of the reasons why it is so important to concentrate on the exercises we have provided: Besides il-lustrating how a rule works they will also show you how several SD rules cooperate in the course of a derivation. Hence, without much ado, we ask you to solve the exercises SD07 to SD11 on your disk. Do not forget to submit your work for *Symlog* to check.

Assumption (ASSUMPTION)

A derivation constructed with the rules of SD introduced up to this point in-volves the construction of a single sequence of sentences written one under another. Several other SD rules will give derivations a distinctly different look, however. They require an auxiliary sequence of sentences which is sub-ordinate to the derivation. For this reason, such rules are said to involve what is called a subordinate derivation, or more simply, a **subderivation**. Es-sentially, this is a proof within the framework of a larger proof. The deriva-tion headed by the premises of an argument will now be called the **main derivation**. Every complete derivation consists of at least the main deriva-tion, whether or not there are any subderivations, but no proof is complete unless its final derived sentence occurs in the main derivation. In the case of an argument, that sentence would be, of course, the conclusion. If the conclu-sion of the argument simply occurs within a subderivation headed by an as-sumption, α, then one cannot say that the conclusion has been derived from the set of premises, Γ, but only that it has been derived from Γ *on the assump-tion that* α. The proof of any argument thus begins and ends in the main derivation, and any subordinate derivations should be thought of as tempo-rary stages within the course of a proof. A typical proof might well consist of several levels of subderivations, as shown in Figure 5.9.[5]

ASSUMPTION is SD's rule for initiating a subderivation. It compares closely with PREMISE in supplying sentences for other SD rules to operate on, but even so there are crucial differences. PREMISE applies exclusively to

---

[5] It is not the case that every proof has to begin with a nonempty set of premises, however. SD rules can be deployed to proving logical truths from no premises, as you will see later. The dis-cussion in the text concentrates on arguments in order to avoid needless qualifications regard-ing the rules themselves.

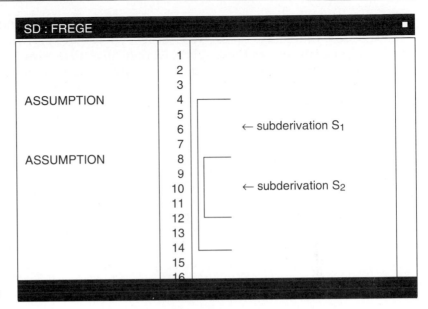

Figure 5.9

main derivations, whereas ASSUMPTION restricts itself to subordinate derivations. Again, an argument may begin with any (finite) number of premises, whereas ASSUMPTION introduces only one sentence (whether simple or compound) each time it is used; finally, since every subordinate derivation is temporary and must be terminated before the proof can move back toward the main derivation, assumptions (but also all the other sentences within the subderivation) have a brief life span. Each rule of SD which makes use of a subderivation includes a routine for terminating that derivation. Whenever a subordinate derivation is terminated, the assumption heading that derivation is said to be **discharged**. In any complete proof of an argument, all assumptions must be discharged. By contrast, premises themselves are never discharged.

Let us now see how the ASSUMPTION rule works in *Symlog*.

ASSUMPTION	i	$\lceil \alpha$
	j	$\lfloor$

When you ask the program to begin a subderivation, *Symlog* will respond by opening up a blank five-line sequence delimited by a **scope line**. Your work will then proceed within this subderivation, headed by the sentence you want to assume. Into this new subderivation you may reiterate premises or previously derived sentences, and of course you may also apply any of the other rules discussed earlier, such as →E and &I. You can even initiate a further subordinate derivation by means of the ASSUMPTION rule, which would thus involve a subderivation within the preceding subderivation. *Symlog* is able to manage up to five levels of subordinate derivations at one time. The program places these subderivations in a hierarchy.

Suppose that you had two unterminated subordinate derivations on your screen (Figure 5.9). For the sake of this example, call them S_1 and S_2, and suppose that S_1 is immediately subordinate to the main derivation and that S_2 is immediately subordinate to S_1. S_2 is the lowest member of this hierarchy. It is subordinate both to S_1 and to the main derivation, whereas S_1 is subordinate only to the main derivation. However, the lowest in the hierarchy is always the first to be terminated. The assumption heading up S_2 is discharged before the others; only then may S_1's assumption be discharged, which brings you back to the main derivation.[6] Besides premises and previously derived sentences, an undischarged assumption may also be reiterated or appealed to into any sequence which is subordinate to it. Once an assumption has been discharged, however, this sentence but also all the other sentences within the scope line of its subderivation become unavailable for use at later stages of the proof: *They may no longer be reiterated, nor may they be appealed to by any other rule of SD.* Incidentally, do not be concerned about the number of lines the program gives you within a subderivation. The initial five lines which *Symlog* supplies whenever ASSUMPTION is invoked can easily be added to, and the program provides simple routines for deleting unwanted empty lines from a derivation as well as for 'erasing' particular sentences and even entire subderivations. See Appendix C (under Derivation Pad Commands); you will need to be familiar with these details when constructing subderivations within a proof. Let us now proceed to the rules of SD which require a subderivation.

→-Introduction (→I)

ASSUMPTION	i	α
	j	β
→I i-j	k	$\alpha \rightarrow \beta$

The rule →-introduction (→I) is the SD rule for constructing conditional sentences of the form $\alpha \rightarrow \beta$ via a subderivation in which the antecedent, α, is assumed and the consequent, β, derived. The natural deduction reasoning which underlies this rule is intuitively clear. Suppose that you want to show that if you eat sushi, you will get indigestion. You already know— these are your premises—that if you eat sushi you are eating raw fish and that by eating raw fish you will get indigestion. Assume, then, that you do

---

[6] By this we do not mean to imply that when working with *Symlog* you will have to finish all your work in S_2 before you can move to S_1. *Symlog* gives you considerable freedom in this respect but, ultimately, all the subderivations must be terminated by some rule of SD.

SD : FREGE		
PREMISE	1	(A v B) & G
PREMISE	2	¬H
ASSUMPTION	3	⌐ M
R 1	4	│ (A v B) & G
&ER 4	5	│ G
R 2	6	│ ¬H
&I 5,6	7	└ G & ¬H
→I 3-7	8	M → (G & ¬H)
	9	
	10	

Figure 5.10

eat sushi. Then, by →E and the first premise, you can infer that you are eating raw fish, and by →E once again and the other premise you can derive
that you will get indigestion. Consequently, you are justified in claiming
that if you do eat sushi you will get indigestion, which is just what you set
out to show. Quite probably you would not stop to reason out all of these
steps. That does not matter. The rules of SD show you what connections
there are, all the same. In particular, the new rule →I provides a framework
in which you proceed to reason on the basis of a separate assumption supplied by yourself.

    The procedure required by →I is always the same: First, use ASSUMP-
TION to introduce α at the top of a subderivation; next, apply successively
whatever SD rules might be necessary to derive β within that subderivation; finally, invoke the rule →I in the Justification Field, together with the appropriate line numbers.[7] Let us see how the rule works in a specific example
(Figure 5.10), in which you have to derive the sentence M → (G & ¬H) from
the two given premises. Note how the justification given on line 8 mentions
the entire subderivation which runs from line 3 through line 7. So much for
this particular example. To gain more experience in using the two conditional rules, we urge you to turn now to exercises SD12 through SD15 on
disk.

¬-Introduction (¬I)

ASSUMPTION	i	⌐α
	j	│ β
	k	└ ¬β
¬I i-j, i-k	l	¬α

[7] Note the use of a hyphen ('-', as in →I i-j) for identifying the line numbers in the schema for →I.
The subderivation begins with α on line i and ends with β on line j. There may be any number
of lines in between, each containing a derived sentence. The identification 'i-j' stands for all the
lines of the subderivation, beginning with α and running up to and including β.

The rule ¬-introduction (¬I) is the SD rule which incorporates the technique of reasoning identified in earlier chapters as **reductio ad absurdum** or **indirect proof**.[8] This technique builds on the fact that in any valid argument, the premises entail the conclusion. Consequently, given the premises of such an argument, further assuming the opposite of what the conclusion asserts is bound always to result in a logical contradiction. As you can see from the schematic diagram for the rule ¬I, incompatibility in SD takes the form of a self-contradictory pair of derived sentences, β and $\neg\beta$, which occur within the same subderivation. However, the use of this rule is not restricted to assuming the opposite of conclusions only. ¬I is a routine which delivers the negation of any assumption whatever, on condition that the subderivation headed by that assumption contains a self-contradictory pair of sentences. (The order in which the two members of the pair occur does not matter, although they must occur in the same subderivation.) ¬I is always used in combination with ASSUMPTION: The main derivation of an argument, you recall, is never discharged. The following example employs ¬I in indirect proof fashion to derive the conclusion of an argument. Other examples using this rule will be found on disk as Learn Exercises SD16 to SD20. Be sure to try them.

Here now is a valid argument together with its symbolization:

Both Germany and Mexico will win a gold medal.
If Austria and Belgium win a gold medal then Mexico won't.
Austria will win a gold medal.

Belgium will not win a gold medal.

G & M
(A & B) → ¬M
A

¬B

The conclusion of this argument can be obtained from the premises by assuming the sentence B and then by deriving the required contradictory sentences within the subderivation, as shown in Figure 5.11. Note how the line numbers have been identified at line 9 in the Justification Field. Two sequences of sentences are mentioned, each beginning with B (line 4) and ending with one member of the contradictory pair (M and ¬M).

¬-Elimination (¬E)

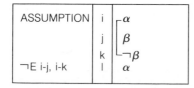

---

[8] See the section 'Short Truth-Tables Tests' in Chapter 2.

SD : FREGE		
PREMISE	1	G & M
PREMISE	2	(A & B) → ¬M
PREMISE	3	A
ASSUMPTION	4	⌐ B
R 1	5	G & M
&ER 5	6	M
&I 3,4	7	A & B
→E 2,7	8	⌐ ¬M
¬I 4-6, 4-8	9	¬B
	10	

Figure 5.11

The ¬-elimination (¬E) rule is similar to ¬I: If by assuming ¬α it proves possible to derive both β and ¬β, then α itself may be derived. The main and obvious difference is that ¬E is used when the sentence being assumed, which is meant to lead to a contradiction, is the negation of the conclusion. Like ¬I, the rule ¬E can be used to derive a conclusion by the method of indirect proof, as we shall now illustrate. Suppose you are given the two premises, M & [¬(D ∨ P) & C] and C → (D ∨ P), from which you are to derive the conclusion, S. You could proceed by assuming ¬S and then deriving two contradictory sentences, such as D ∨ P and ¬(D ∨ P), as shown in Figure 5.12. Further examples of ¬E will be found in exercises SD21, SD22 and SD23. Once you have solved each of the problems, let *Symlog* check your work.

∨-Introduction on the Left (∨L)
∨-Introduction on the Right (∨R)

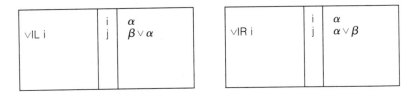

The rule ∨-introduction on the left (∨L) says that if a sentence α has been derived in line i, then the sentence β ∨ α can be derived in line j, where β is any sentence whatsoever of SL. Intuitively, it is clear that since the sentence 'a triangle has three sides' is true, the new sentence 'a square has four sides or a triangle has three sides' is also true (if you are not convinced, you can always construct the necessary truth-tables). Equally, if α is the sentence 'a triangle has four sides,' then β ∨ α would also be entailed, no matter what sentence is used in place of β. Remember that the relation of entailment does not require the entailing sentences (in this case, α) to be true.

The rule ∨-introduction on the right (∨R) is similar to ∨L. The only difference is that here you can add a sentence to the right of a previously

SD : FREGE		
PREMISE	1	M & [¬(D v P) & C]
PREMISE	2	C → (D v P)
ASSUMPTION	3	┌─ ¬S
&ER 1	4	¬(D v P) & C
&ER 4	5	C
→E 2, 5	6	D v P
&EL 4	7	└─ ¬(D v P)
¬E 3-6, 3-7	8	S
	9	
	10	

Figure 5.12

SD : FREGE		
PREMISE	1	M → (B & ¬D)
PREMISE	2	B → (G & H)
ASSUMPTION	3	┌─ M
→E 1, 3	4	B & ¬D
&EL 4	5	B
→E 2, 5	6	G & H
&EL 6	7	└─ G
→I 3-7	8	M → G
vIR 8	9	(M → G) v (¬S ≡ P)
	10	

Figure 5.13

derived sentence. Let us illustrate the new rule. Suppose that you want to derive (M → G) ∨ (¬S ≡ P) starting with M → (B & ¬D) and B → (G & H) as premises. One way of constructing an appropriate derivation is displayed in Figure 5.13. ∨IL and ∨IR are reminiscent of &EL and &ER in schematic form. Do be aware, though, that ∨-introduction is a rule for constructing sentences, whereas &-elimination is a rule for deconstructing them, and that the logical properties of the two connectives on which the rules are based are quite different. This fact is easy to see. Whereas any conjunction entails either of its conjuncts, disjunctions enjoy no such privilege regarding their components. Consider the following little example. It is true that you will either pass this course on symbolic logic or fail it; in symbols, P ∨ ¬P. Sorry to say, it is impossible to deduce from this sentence that you will pass. But it is easy to find consolation; just recall that it is equally impossible to deduce that you will fail.

The exercises SD24, SD25 and SD26 on disk illustrate the use of these rules. We encourage you to solve them at this point.

∨-Elimination (∨E)

	i	$\alpha \vee \beta$
ASSUMPTION	j	α
	k	δ
ASSUMPTION	l	β
	m	δ
VE i, j-k, l-m	n	δ

Let us begin with an informal illustration of the deductive reasoning reflected in the rule ∨-elimination (∨E). Suppose that Jim is going to buy either a new car or a new motorcycle (C ∨ M). Also, you know that if Jim buys the car, you will both celebrate the event by having dinner out tonight (C → D). But you also know that if he purchases the motorcycle, you will celebrate this event too by eating out tonight (M → D). Either way, you conclude, you will be eating out tonight (D). At first, this new rule might seem less intuitive than the others, especially when you recall that a disjunction does not entail either of its disjuncts, but the reasoning involved is deductively valid, and by taking a moment to examine the schema you will find it easy to grasp. Suppose you have a disjunction, $\alpha \vee \beta$ (line i), to which you wish to apply the rule ∨E. The key to it is to reason from each disjunct separately—*proving by cases*. That is why you see two separate assumptions in the schema, one headed by α (line j) and the other by β (line l). The rule says, in effect, that if you can derive the same sentence δ from each of these assumptions, you are entitled to claim that δ is derivable from $\alpha \vee \beta$ itself (line n). Think of the two subordinate derivations as necessary detours which proceed from $\alpha \vee \beta$ to δ. And note how these two sequences are displayed in the schema: The subderivation headed by β is directly underneath the one headed by α. In SD these are called parallel subderivations. The important thing to remember here is that although each of them is a subderivation, neither one is a subderivation of the other. What this means in practice and how parallel subderivations are discharged are best seen through an example. Suppose you are asked to derive the sentence C from the following premises: A, B and [(A & B) → C] ∨ [B → [A → (C & D)]]. Your proof might take the form shown in Figure 5.14.

Let us see how the strategy for deriving the conclusion develops. Clearly, the sentence, C, cannot be obtained from the first two premises alone. The solution depends on premise 3, which, being a disjunction, brings the rule ∨E into play. That is why we begin by assuming the left-hand disjunct on line 4. From this assumption, together with the first two premises, it is easy to derive the conclusion, C, although the proof cannot end there since this sentence occurs within a subderivation which has yet to be discharged. At this point (in compliance with ∨E) ASSUMPTION is used again, this time to introduce the right-hand disjunct in order to initiate a parallel subderivation in which C is once again obtained (line 13). At this

SD : FREGE

PREMISE	1	A
PREMISE	2	B
PREMISE	3	$[(A \& B) \to C] \vee [B \to [A \to (C \& D)]]$
ASSUMPTION	4	⌐ $(A \& B) \to C$
R 1	5	A
R 2	6	B
&I 5, 6	7	A & B
→E 4, 7	8	⌊ C
ASSUMPTION	9	⌐ $B \to [A \to (C \& D)]$
R 2	10	B
→E 9, 10	11	$A \to (C \& D)$
→E 1, 11	12	C & D
&EL 12	13	⌊ C
vE 3, 4-8, 9-13	14	C
	15	
	16	

Figure 5.14

point, it is possible to invoke the rule ∨E officially and declare C to have been derived from the disjunction itself. The justification given for line 14 identifies the disjunction followed by the two parallel subderivations, each headed by one of its disjuncts (note the use of hyphens). It is worth emphasizing that, although parallel subderivations are always deployed in tandem, they are handled in isolation from each other. Each of these two specimens is a subderivation of the main derivation, but neither one is subordinate to the other. Consequently, it would be an error to reiterate the first assumption (line 4) into the second subderivation (starting on line 9) or, in general, to appeal in one member of the pair to any sentence that occurs in the parallel subderivation.

We urge you now to increase your familiarity with the rule ∨E by doing exercises SD27 through SD30.

≡-Introduction (≡I)

ASSUMPTION	i	⌐ α
	j	⌊ β
ASSUMPTION	k	⌐ β
	l	⌊ α
≡I i-j, k-l	m	$\alpha \equiv \beta$

The rule ≡-introduction (≡I), which makes it possible to construct biconditional sentences, is the only other rule of SD whose format includes parallel subderivations. Why they are necessary will be evident from the structure of the biconditional itself. Since $\alpha \equiv \beta$ is logically equivalent to $(\alpha \to \beta)$ &

SD : FREGE		
PREMISE	1	(C v M) → (A & B)
PREMISE	2	C & D
PREMISE	3	(C v D) → (M & ¬S)
ASSUMPTION	4	A
&ER 2	5	D
vIL 5	6	C v D
→E 3, 6	7	M & ¬S
&EL 7	8	M
ASSUMPTION	9	M
&EL 2	10	C
vIR 10	11	C v M
→E 1, 11	12	A & B
&EL 12	13	A
≡I 4-8, 9-13	14	A ≡ M
	15	
	16	

Figure 5.15

($\beta \rightarrow \alpha$), this new rule can be thought of as a compact way of bringing together two subordinate (and separate) proofs: the derivation of α from the assumption of β, and the derivation of β from the assumption of α. The restrictions affecting parallel subderivations just mentioned for vE apply to the rule ≡I as well.

Let us put this rule to work in an example, first in prose and then in an SD proof (Figure 5.15):

> If Carol or Mike passed the test then both Anne and Bob did too.
> Carol and David did pass the test.
> If Carol or David passed the test then Mike did too but not Suzy.
> _____
> Anne passed the test if and only if Mike did.

Exercises SD31 through SD34 will give you more practice with ≡I.

≡-Elimination (≡E)

		i	$\alpha \equiv \beta$
≡E i, j		j	α
		k	β

		i	$\alpha \equiv \beta$
≡E i, j		j	β
		k	α

This final rule of SD, ≡-elimination (≡E) is a close logical cousin of →E. Given any biconditional plus a sentence identical to its left- or right-hand component, the other component is immediately derivable. (The two schematic drawings cover the range of possibilities.) Knowing both that Mike

SD : FREGE		
PREMISE	1	A ≡ (B ≡ C)
PREMISE	2	A & C
&EL 2	3	A
≡E 1, 3	4	B ≡ C
&ER 2	5	C
≡E 4, 5	6	B
	7	
	8	
	9	
	10	

Figure 5.16

passed the test and that Anne passed if and only if Mike did, you can infer at
once that Anne passed too. (To make the inference even clearer, think of this
biconditional as unpacked into its two conditionals.) Figure 5.16 illustrates
≡E in use, and by doing exercises SD35 to SD38 right afterward you will increase your familiarity with this rule.

   This was the last rule of SD. Before we examine some lengthier problems and discuss strategies for constructing proofs in SD, it may be helpful
to point out a few common misapplications of the rules. *Symlog* watches for
false moves and will identify errors in the form of a warning message at the
bottom of the screen. Figure 5.17 shows what happens when a sentence is
cited which occurs within a subderivation that has already been discharged. (Remember that the sentences of a discharged subderivation are
no longer available later in the proof.) At line 14 there is a mistaken use of
reiteration.

SD : FREGE			■
PREMISE	1	P ≡ T	
PREMISE	2	S	
PREMISE	3	(T & S) → (Q & ¬R)	
	4		
ASSUMPTION	5	P	
	6		
≡E 1, 5	7	T	
&I 7, 2	8	T & S	
→E 3, 8	9	Q & ¬R	
	10		
&EL 9	11	Q	
→I 5-11	12	P → Q	
	13		
R 7■	14	T	■
	15		
	16		
■■■ LINE BEING APPEALED TO IS NOT ACCESSIBLE FROM HERE			

Figure 5.17

SD : FREGE ■

Justification	Line	Sentence
PREMISE	1	A → B
PREMISE	2	(A & C) → ¬¬M
PREMISE	3	G & A
PREMISE	4	C ≡ B
&ER 3	5	A
→E 1, 5	6	B
≡E 4, 6	7	C
&I 5, 7	8	A & C
→E 8, 2	9	¬¬M
¬¬E 9 ■	10	M	■
	11	
	12	
	13	
	14	
	15	
	16	

Figure 5.18   ■■■ RULE NOT AVAILABLE IN THIS DERIVATION SYSTEM

SD : FREGE ■

Justification	Line	Sentence
PREMISE	1	S
PREMISE	2	(S & Q) → T
PREMISE	3	Q v (T ≡ S)
PREMISE	4	T → ((P & Q) & R)
	5	
ASSUMPTION	6	⌐ Q
	7	
&I 1, 6	8	S & Q
→E 2, 8	9	⌐ T
ASSUMPTION	10	⌐ T ≡ S
	11	
≡E 1, 10	12	⌐ T
vE 3, 6-9, 10-12	13	T
→E 13, 4	14	(P & Q) & R
&EL 14 ■	15	P	■
	16	

Figure 5.19   ■■■ THIS IS NOT THE LEFT CONJUNCT OF THE LINE BEING CITED

Figure 5.18 involves a different sort of mistake. From your earlier work in SL you know that the two sentences ¬¬M and M are logically equivalent. This fact, however, does not correspond to any rule of SD; that is, no rule of SD licenses the derivation of M from ¬¬M *in one step*.[9] SD is not an open set of rules which can be added to as needed. This is what *Symlog* is trying to say when it evaluates the justification given in line 10.

Figure 5.19 shows what happens when someone tries to telescope the use of an SD rule, in this case to derive the sentence P at one go from the sentence (P & Q) & R. Such a move is a mistaken use of the rule &EL. The derivation of P requires two separate uses of this rule.

[9] There is a derivation of M from ¬¬M in SD but it takes more than one step. The next section shows how it can be done.

165

Exercises

5.1.1 By now you should have solved *all* the SD Learn Exercises, SD1 to SD38, on your disk. In case you have not done so, now is the time to do it.

5.1.2 The following derivation has three errors. Find them.

SD : ERRORS			■
PREMISE	1	(P→ (S & Q)) ≡ R	■
PREMISE	2	T → (R v P)	■
PREMISE	3	(¬¬S ≡ T) & Q	■
ASSUMPTION	4	⌐ P	■
vIL 4	5	R v P	■
→E 2, 5	6	T	■
&EL 3	7	¬¬S ≡ T	■
≡E 6, 7	8	¬¬S	■
¬E 8	9	S	■
&ER 3	10	Q	■
&I 9, 10	11	└ S & Q	■
→I 4-11	12	P → (S & Q)	■
≡E 1, 12	13	R	■
&I 6, 13	14	T & R	■
vIR 14	15	(T & R) v M	■
	16		
	17		
	18		

5.1.3 In the following derivation replace the question marks (?) with appropriate connectives and justifications. Submit your answer to *Symlog*.

SD : REPLACE			■
PREMISE	1	M ? (J ? N)	■
PREMISE	2	(L? M) ? (J ? K)	■
PREMISE	3	(L ? H) ? (K ? H)	■
?	4	J ? K	■
?	5	⌐ J	■
?	6	J ? N	■
?	7	M	■
?	8	L ? M	■
?	9	└ L	■
?	10	⌐ K	■
?	11	K ? H	■
?	12	L ? H	■
?	13	└ L	■
?	14	L	■
?	15	L ? M	■
?	16	M	
	17		
	18		

5.1.4 Use *Symlog* to derive the given sentence from the given set of premises.

a. {(A & B) & C, B → D, (A ∨ M) → F}, D & F
b. {(G → E) & (G & F), (B & C) ≡ ¬A, D → C, (E ∨ ¬F) ≡ (B & (F→ D))}, ¬A & F
c. {A ∨ B, (C ∨ B) ≡ D, A ≡ D}, D
d. {P ∨ Q, P → (M & S), Q → (S ≡ (Q & R)), R & T}, S
e. {P → Q, ¬M → (P & ¬Q)}, M

5.2   *Constructing Derivations in SD*

In all the examples seen thus far, the derivations have been constructed from top to bottom, from the premises to the conclusion. This is the best way of showing the logical links in a derivation, but since it displays a proof as a *finished* piece of work, it indicates nothing about how to begin *constructing* a proof when you are given only the premises and the conclusion to be reached. And that is just the situation in which you may desire some enlightenment. For example, although it can be easily seen that the sentence M is derivable from the set {M & ¬G, S ∨ D} by a single application of the rule &EL to M & ¬G, it might not be nearly so evident how to go about deriving the sentence (Q & N) → R from the set of premises {Q → ¬T, (T ∨ R) ∨ ¬N}. In this section and the next, we will discuss methods and strategies for constructing proofs. To begin, we suggest that you take a blank 'sheet' from *Symlog*'s Derivation Pad (Figure 5.20) and open up a new file. We have called ours BOOLE (Figure 5.21).

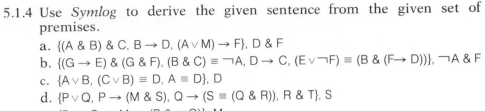

SD				
\<newFile\> ■	PD01.DER	PD02.DER	PD03.DER	PD04.DER
PD05.DER	PD06.DER	PD07.DER	PD08.DER	PD09.DER
PD10.DER	PD11.DER	PD12.DER	PD13.DER	PD14.DER
PD15.DER	PD16.DER	PD17.DER	PD18.DER	PD19.DER
PD20.DER	PD21.DER	PD22.DER	PD23.DER	PD24.DER
PD25.DER	PD26.DER	PDPLUS01.DER	PDPLUS02.DER	PDPLUS03.DER
PDPLUS04.DER	PDPLUS05.DER	PR01.DER	PR02.DER	PR03.DER
PR04.DER	PR05.DER	PR06.DER	PR07.DER	PR08.DER
PR09.DER	PR10.DER	PR11.DER	PR12.DER	PR13.DER
PR14.DER	PR15.DER	PR16.DER	PR17.DER	PR18.DER
PR19.DER	PR20.DER	PR21.DER	PR22.DER	PR23.DER
PR24.DER	PR25.DER	PR26.DER	PR27.DER	PR28.DER
PR29.DER	PR30.DER	PR31.DER	PR32.DER	PR33.DER
PR34.DER	PR35.DER	PR36.DER	PR37.DER	PR38.DER
PR39.DER	PR40.DER	PR41.DER	PR42.DER	PR43.DER

DIRECTORY C:\SYMLOG   195 FILES READ

Figure 5.20

```
SD : BOOLE

  ■                                 1
                                    2
                                    3
                                    4
                                    5
                                    6
                                    7
                                    8
                                    9
                                   10
                                   11
                                   12
                                   13
                                   14
                                   15
                                   16
```

Figure 5.21

Besides the Justification command, the Derivation Pad offers two other commands which we will pause for a moment to describe, for you will find them quite useful tools to have on hand for proof making. We will compare them to the Justification command, with which you have already become familiar. When you issue the Justification command (by pressing the Enter key) for a particular sentence, *Symlog* checks to find out whether your sentence is legitimate by the standards of SD. If it is, the mark—the little square in the Mark Field—disappears; if not, *Symlog* will display an error message which is *associated* to the line in question. Thus you are able to return to any marked line to read its message by placing the cursor on the line; the message will reappear on the Error Line.

Generation Command

Issuing the Generation command (by pressing the Tab key) will make *Symlog* display (if it can) a desired theorem in the Theorem Field. For instance, suppose that you have A and B as premises in lines 1 and 2 of a derivation. If, in the Justification Field for line 3, you then type &I 1,2 and issue the Generation— Tab—command, *Symlog* will produce the sentence A & B in the Theorem Field. Also, if you type PREMISE in the Justification Field in a line and issue the Generation command, *Symlog* asks you in the Message Line to enter your premise; after you do so, *Symlog* displays the sentence you chose as your premise in the Theorem Field in the corresponding line. When necessary, *Symlog* will display an appropriate error message in the Error Line.

Goal Analysis Command

The Goal Analysis command (issued by pressing Shift-Tab) enables you to take a **goal analysis** approach to proof construction. This is a powerful feature of *Symlog* which, when combined with the strategies outlined in the next section, will allow you to handle long and complex proofs. Let us see how the method works. Suppose you have to derive the conclusion [(M & G) & E] & H from the following premises: E, G, H and M. The conclusion is of course the goal. To reach it, you need (M & G) & E, which, together with the premise H, will yield the desired sentence by one application of &I; but to obtain (M & G) & E, you first need M & G and E. E is easy to obtain—it is one of the premises. Your immediate goal is then M & G, which can be obtained from the premises M and G. What you are doing here is to break down the main problem (to obtain [(M & G) & E] & H) into *subgoals*. Each of these subgoals becomes for a while your main concern because not until all these subgoals have been achieved will your derivation be complete. *This is the way derivations are usually constructed.* (Actually, they consist of a mix of both forward and (mostly) backward moves which 'meet at the middle.') Issuing the Goal Analysis command in *Symlog* allows you to work more easily when moving upward, starting from the bottom of your derivation, in order to derive, subgoal after subgoal, the sought conclusion.[10] Of course, when necessary, *Symlog* will display appropriate error messages in the Error Line.

Consider another example. Suppose you are asked to show that J can be derived from the set {($\neg$S $\rightarrow$ J) & M, K $\equiv$ M, K $\rightarrow$ $\neg$S}. This means that you must construct a derivation—using nothing but the rules of SD—whose premises consist of the members of the set {($\neg$S $\rightarrow$ J) & M, K $\equiv$ M, K $\rightarrow$ $\neg$S} and in which the sentence at the bottom of the derivation is J.

Place the cursor in the left-most position of the Justification Field in line 1, type PREMISE and then issue the Generation command (by pressing the Tab key). *Symlog* will ask you in the Message Line to enter your first premise, which is ($\neg$S $\rightarrow$ J) & M. When you do so, your screen should look like Figure 5.22a.[11]

To get your second premise, type PREMISE and issue the Generation command. The sentence to type is K $\equiv$ M. So far, your derivation looks like Figure 5.22b. Do likewise for your third premise—that is, for K $\rightarrow$ $\neg$S—so that the three premises look like Figure 5.22c.

---

[10] The strategy of working from the bottom of the proof upward is called **top-down**; the strategy taken by working your way down from the top of the proof (i.e., from the premises to the conclusion) is known as **bottom-up**! These names emphasize the fact that in the case of a top-down strategy, one works from the *top-level goal* down to what is given—the premises (in the process one 'breaks down' goals into subgoals); in bottom-up one works from what is given toward the desired goal. To avoid possible confusion we use the term 'goal analysis method' for a top-down strategy.

[11] Alternatively, you could have typed PREMISE, moved the cursor to the Theorem Field, typed your first premise and moved to the beginning of the next line.

```
SD : BOOLE

PREMISE           1      (¬S → J) & M
■                 2
                  3
                  4
                  5
                  6
                  7
                  8
                  9
                 10
                 11
                 12
                 13
                 14
                 15
                 16
```

Figure 5.22a

The sentence you want to derive is J. This will be the final sentence of your proof. Let us guess that when the proof is complete, this sentence will occur on line 12. Because we are now going to use the goal analysis method, enter the sentence J in the Theorem Field of this line, so that your screen looks like Figure 5.22d. Since J is not yet justified, *Symlog* posts a mark in the Mark Field. (The Information Line at the top of the screen also carries a mark indicating that the derivation itself is not yet complete.) In essence, this is how the goal analysis method works: If your goal is a sentence α, find some

```
SD : BOOLE

PREMISE           1      (¬S → J) & M
PREMISE           2      K ≡ M
■                 3
                  4
                  5
                  6
                  7
                  8
                  9
                 10
                 11
                 12
                 13
                 14
                 15
                 16
```

Figure 5.22b

SD : BOOLE		
PREMISE	1	(¬S → J) & M
PREMISE	2	K ≡ M
PREMISE	3	K → ¬S
■	4	
	5	
	6	
	7	
	8	
	9	
	10	
	11	
	12	
	13	
	14	
	15	
	16	

Figure 5.22c

sentence β (there may be several of them) (1) from which you can easily obtain α and (2) which is no harder to derive than α itself. In our example, the sentence J could be derived by a single application of →E, *if* you had both ¬S and ¬S → J. What encourages this line of thinking is the fact that ¬S → J happens to be an easily derivable part of premise 1. So let us follow this approach and suppose that the two sentences you need will be obtained in lines 7 and 11, respectively. Thus, in the Justification Field for line 12, type →E 7,11 and issue the Goal Analysis command (with Shift-Tab) to let

SD : BOOLE			■
PREMISE	1	(¬S → J) & M	
PREMISE	2	K ≡ M	
PREMISE	3	K → ¬S	
	4		
	5		
	6		
	7		
	8		
	9		
	10		
	11		
■	12	J	■
	13		
	14		
	15		
	16		

Figure 5.22d

```
 ┌──────────────────────────────────────────────────────────────┐
 │ SD : BOOLE                                                  ■  │
 ├──────────────────────────────────────────────────────────────┤
 │  PREMISE              1    (¬S → J) & M                        │
 │  PREMISE              2    K ≡ M                               │
 │  PREMISE              3    K → ¬S                              │
 │                       4                                       │
 │                       5                                       │
 │                       6                                       │
 │                       7    α                               ■  │
 │                       8                                       │
 │                       9                                       │
 │                      10                                       │
 │  ■                   11    α → J                           ■  │
 │  →E  7, 11           12    J                                  │
 │                      13                                       │
 │                      14                                       │
 │                      15                                       │
 │                      16                                       │
 └──────────────────────────────────────────────────────────────┘
```

Figure 5.22e

Symlog know that J is going to come from the rule →E applied to these two lines.

Now, *Symlog* knows that J must be the consequent of some conditional sentence, $\alpha \rightarrow J$, and it also knows that the antecedent of that conditional will have to occur by itself in the other line. However, the program knows only the forms of these sentences rather than their contents, which is why it will display the metalogical sentence α in line 7 (the antecedent) and $\alpha \rightarrow J$

```
 ┌──────────────────────────────────────────────────────────────┐
 │ SD : BOOLE                                                  ■  │
 ├──────────────────────────────────────────────────────────────┤
 │  PREMISE              1    (¬S → J) & M                        │
 │  PREMISE              2    K ≡ M                               │
 │  PREMISE              3    K → ¬S                              │
 │                       4                                       │
 │                       5                                       │
 │                       6                                       │
 │                       7    α                               ■  │
 │                       8                                       │
 │                       9                                       │
 │                      10                                       │
 │  &EL  1              11    ¬S → J                             │
 │  →E  7, 11           12    J                                  │
 │                      13                                       │
 │                      14                                       │
 │                      15                                       │
 │                      16                                       │
 └──────────────────────────────────────────────────────────────┘
```

Figure 5.22f

```
┌─────────────────────────────────────────────────────────┐
│ SD : BOOLE                                            ■  │
├─────────────────────────────────────────────────────────┤
│  PREMISE              1    (¬S → J) & M                  │
│  PREMISE              2    K ≡ M                         │
│  PREMISE              3    K → ¬S                        │
│                       4                                  │
│                       5                                  │
│                       6                                  │
│  ■                    7    ¬S                         ■  │
│                       8                                  │
│                       9                                  │
│                      10                                  │
│  &EL  1              11    ¬S → J                        │
│  →E  7, 11           12    J                             │
│                      13                                  │
│                      14                                  │
│                      15                                  │
│                      16                                  │
└─────────────────────────────────────────────────────────┘
```

Figure 5.22g

in line 11 (the conditional), as you will see in Figure 5.22e. Notice that α and α → J have marks because they have not yet been justified.

   We just saw how ¬S → J could be obtained from the first premise. So, in the Justification Field for line 11, type &EL 1 and issue the Generation command (with the Tab key). This will produce the desired sentence in the Theorem Field, replacing α → J, and the mark in the Mark Field will disappear too (Figure 5.22f).

```
┌─────────────────────────────────────────────────────────┐
│ SD : BOOLE                                            ■  │
├─────────────────────────────────────────────────────────┤
│  PREMISE              1    (¬S → J) & M                  │
│  PREMISE              2    K ≡ M                         │
│  PREMISE              3    K → ¬S                        │
│                       4                                  │
│                       5                                  │
│  ■                    6    K                          ■  │
│  →E  3, 6             7    ¬S                            │
│                       8                                  │
│                       9                                  │
│                      10                                  │
│  &EL  1              11    ¬S → J                        │
│  →E  7, 11           12    J                             │
│                      13                                  │
│                      14                                  │
│                      15                                  │
│                      16                                  │
└─────────────────────────────────────────────────────────┘
```

Figure 5.22h

```
SD : BOOLE                                                    ■

PREMISE          1    (¬S → J) & M
PREMISE          2    K ≡ M
PREMISE          3    K → ¬S
                 4
&ER  1           5    M
■                6    K                                       ■
→E  3, 6         7    ¬S
                 8
                 9
                10
&EL  1          11    ¬S → J
→E  7, 11       12    J
                13
                14
                15
                16
```

Figure 5.22i

The next step is to obtain α, the antecedent of the conditional. Since we know what sentence this has to be, move your cursor to line 7, delete α and enter ¬S in its place (Figure 5.22g). ¬S has now become your immediate goal because it is a crucial link in the derivation of J. As for ¬S, you will notice that it occurs as the consequent in premise 3. Consequently, if you had K in, say, line 6, a single application of →E to lines 3 and 6 would de-

```
SD : BOOLE

PREMISE          1    (¬S → J) & M
PREMISE          2    K ≡ M
PREMISE          3    K → ¬S
                 4
&ER  1           5    M
≡E  2, 5         6    K
→E  3, 6         7    ¬S
                 8
                 9
                10
&EL  1          11    ¬S → J
→E  7, 11       12    J
                13
                14
                15
                16
```

Figure 5.22j

```
SD : BOOLE

PREMISE        1      (¬S → J) & M
PREMISE        2      K ≡ M
PREMISE        3      K → ¬S
&ER 1          4      M
≡E 2, 4        5      K
→E 3, 5        6      ¬S
&EL 1          7      ¬S → J
→E 6, 7        8      J
               9
              10
              11
              12
              13
              14
              15
              16
```

Figure 5.22k

liver what you want. Let us follow this reasoning. Type →E 3,6 in line 7 and again issue the Goal Analysis command (with Shift-Tab). *Symlog* immediately responds by placing a K in line 6. The reason it does not display an α this time is because *Symlog* is clever enough to figure out that the only possible sentence that can yield ¬S from K → ¬S by one application of →E is K. This step is shown in Figure 5.22h.

The focus is now on K. If you obtain it, your derivation will be complete. Since the second premise is K ≡ M, K could be obtained by one application of ≡E if you had M in another line (say, in line 5). But M is easy to obtain: You have only to apply &ER to the first premise, that is, to (¬S → J) & M. Thus, type &ER 1 in line 5 and issue the Generation command (with the Tab key) to make *Symlog* produce M in that line (Figure 5.22i).

All that remains is to apply ≡E to lines 2 and 5: Type ≡E 2,5 in line 6 and issue the Justification command (with the Enter key). As soon as you do, all the marks disappear, including the one at the top in the Information Line, indicating that your derivation is complete and correct. (See Figure 5.22j.)

Finally, you can easily get rid of the unwanted blank lines in the middle of your derivation. Simply place the cursor on any blank line and issue the Delete—Ctrl-Y—command. The line will be deleted and all the justifications readjusted automatically with new line numbers. Do likewise for the remaining blank lines. Once you have eliminated all blank lines, your derivation should look like the one depicted in Figure 5.22k.

Let us examine another derivation in which we put *Symlog* to work. Suppose that you are asked to derive the sentence A → [(R ∨ H) & D] from the set of premises {D ≡ ¬B, A → (¬¬R & K), ¬B}. If you wish, save your derivation BOOLE to the disk, then retrieve a new blank page from the Derivation Pad and call it WHITE. *Symlog* produces the screen displayed in Figure 5.23a.

To get your first premise, type PREMISE, and issue the Generation command; when *Symlog* asks you in the Message Line what your premise is, enter D $\equiv$ $\neg$B. Do the same for the other two premises—namely, A $\rightarrow$ ($\neg\neg$R & K) and $\neg$ B. Since you do not know at this time how many lines will be needed to derive A $\rightarrow$ [(R $\vee$ H) & D], enter this sentence on line 15 (Figure 5.23b).

Since the conclusion is a conditional, it makes sense to try to obtain it by using the rule $\rightarrow$I, that is, by assuming A in line 4 and then seeking to derive (R $\vee$ H) & D, as the last line of the subderivation, in line 14. If you succeed, your justification in line 15 for A $\rightarrow$ [(R $\vee$ H) & D] would read $\rightarrow$I 4-14. Let us adopt this strategy: In line 15, type $\rightarrow$I 4-14 and issue the Goal Analysis—Shift-Tab—command. As soon as you do, *Symlog* automatically opens a subderivation having A as its assumption and (R $\vee$ H) & D as its conclusion. This conjunction is now your immediate goal (Figure 5.23c). It makes sense to try to obtain this sentence by using &I. To do so, you need R $\vee$ H and D in two different lines—lines 10 and 13, for instance. So, in line 14, type &I 10,13 and issue the Goal Analysis command, thereby making *Symlog* produce the screen in Figure 5.23d.

These two new sentences are your immediate goals now. D is easy to obtain by using $\equiv$E on the first and third premises, respectively, that is, on D $\equiv$ $\neg$B and $\neg$B. So, in line 13, enter $\equiv$E 1,3. (See Figure 5.23e.)

The other conjunct, R $\vee$ H, could be obtained by adding H to the right of R, if you had R in, say, line 9. So, in line 10, type $\vee$IR 9, and issue the Goal Analysis command. As displayed in Figure 5.23f, R appears in line 9, which has now become your immediate goal. There is no R in sight directly obtainable from any previous line. In such cases, the best strategy may be to try to obtain the needed sentence by contradiction, in this particular case, by using $\neg$E; in other words, you could open a subderivation by assuming $\neg$R and obtaining two contradictory sentences within it. This subderivation will show that $\neg$R cannot be the case because it leads to an absurdity, and that therefore R must be the case. Let us suppose that your subderivation begins at line 5 and that the two contradictory sentences will be obtained in, say, lines 7 and 8, respectively. In line 9, type $\neg$E 5-7,5-8 and issue the Goal Analysis command. *Symlog* produces the screen depicted in Figure 5.23g.

Symlog produces α and $\neg\alpha$ inside the subderivation because it does not know what the two contradictory sentences will be. But you may already have a clue. As you can see, $\neg\neg$R appears as part of the second premise and is the contradictory of your assumption, $\neg$R. So, you can make α be $\neg$R and $\neg\alpha$ be $\neg\neg$R. The sentence $\neg$R is very easy to obtain; all you have to do is to reiterate it from line 5 to line 7. Thus, in line 7, type R 5, and issue the Generation command, which will cause *Symlog* to generate $\neg$R in line 7, thereby making α disappear. Then, go to line 8, delete $\neg\alpha$ and enter $\neg\neg$R. There will be a mark (in the Mark Field) until this sentence is properly

SD : WHITE

	1	
	2	
	3	
	4	
	5	
	6	
	7	
	8	
	9	
	10	
	11	
	12	
	13	
	14	
	15	
	16	
	17	
	18	

Figure 5.23a

SD : WHITE

PREMISE	1	$D \equiv \neg B$
PREMISE	2	$A \rightarrow (\neg\neg R \mathbin{\&} K)$
PREMISE	3	$\neg B$
	4	
	5	
	6	
	7	
	8	
	9	
	10	
	11	
	12	
	13	
	14	
	15	$A \rightarrow [(R \lor H) \mathbin{\&} D]$
	16	
	17	
	18	

Figure 5.23b

SD : WHITE   ■

PREMISE	1	$D \equiv \neg B$
PREMISE	2	$A \rightarrow (\neg \neg R \, \& \, K)$
PREMISE	3	$\neg B$
ASSUMPTION	4	A
	5	
	6	
	7	
	8	
	9	
	10	
	11	
	12	
	13	
■	14	(R v H) & D ■
→I 4-14	15	$A \rightarrow [(R \lor H) \, \& \, D]$
	16	
	17	
	18	

Figure 5.23c

SD : WHITE   ■

PREMISE	1	$D \equiv \neg B$
PREMISE	2	$A \rightarrow (\neg\neg R \, \& \, K)$
PREMISE	3	$\neg B$
ASSUMPTION	4	A
	5	
	6	
	7	
	8	
	9	
	10	R v H ■
	11	
	12	
■	13	D ■
&I 10, 13	14	(R v H) & D
→I 4-14	15	$A \rightarrow [(R \lor H) \, \& \, D]$
	16	
	17	
	18	

Figure 5.23d

SD : WHITE

PREMISE	1	D ≡ ¬B
PREMISE	2	A → (¬¬R & K)
PREMISE	3	¬B
ASSUMPTION	4	A
	5	
	6	
	7	
	8	
	9	
■	10	R v H
	11	
	12	
≡E 1, 3	13	D
&I 10, 13	14	(R v H) & D
→I 4-14	15	A → [(R v H) & D]
	16	
	17	
	18	

Figure 5.23e

SD : WHITE

PREMISE	1	D ≡ ¬B
PREMISE	2	A → (¬¬R & K)
PREMISE	3	¬B
ASSUMPTION	4	A
	5	
	6	
	7	
	8	
■	9	R
v IR 9	10	R v H
	11	
	12	
≡E 1, 3	13	D
&I 10, 13	14	(R v H) & D
→I 4-14	15	A → [(R v H) & D]
	16	
	17	
	18	

Figure 5.23f

SD : WHITE				■
PREMISE	1	D ≡ ¬B		
PREMISE	2	A → (¬¬R & K)		
PREMISE	3	¬B		
ASSUMPTION	4	A		
ASSUMPTION	5	¬R		
	6			
	7	α		■
■	8	¬α		■
¬E 5-7, 5-8	9	R		
vIR 9	10	R v H		
	11			
	12			
≡E 1, 3	13	D		
&I 10, 13	14	(R v H) & D		
→I 4-14	15	A → [(R v H) & D]		
	16			
	17			
	18			

Figure 5.23g

SD : WHITE				■
PREMISE	1	D ≡ ¬B		
PREMISE	2	A → (¬¬R & K)		
PREMISE	3	¬B		
ASSUMPTION	4	A		
ASSUMPTION	5	¬R		
	6			
R 5	7	¬R		
■	8	¬¬R		■
¬E 5-7, 5-8	9	R		
vIR 9	10	R v H		
	11			
	12			
≡E 1, 3	13	D		
&I 10, 13	14	(R v H) & D		
→I 4-14	15	A → [(R v H) & D]		
	16			
	17			
	18			

Figure 5.23h

SD : WHITE   ■

PREMISE	1	$D \equiv \neg B$
PREMISE	2	$A \rightarrow (\neg\neg R \,\&\, K)$
PREMISE	3	$\neg B$
ASSUMPTION	4	A
ASSUMPTION	5	$\neg R$
	6	
R 5	7	$\neg R$
	8	
	9	
■	10	$\neg\neg R$
$\neg$E 5-7, 5-10	11	R
vIR 11	12	R v H
	13	
	14	
$\equiv$E 1, 3	15	D
&I 12, 15	16	(R v H) & D
$\rightarrow$I 4-16	17	$A \rightarrow [(R \vee H) \,\&\, D]$
	18	

Figure 5.23i

SD : WHITE   ■

PREMISE	1	$D \equiv \neg B$
PREMISE	2	$A \rightarrow (\neg\neg R \,\&\, K)$
PREMISE	3	$\neg B$
ASSUMPTION	4	A
ASSUMPTION	5	$\neg R$
	6	
R 5	7	$\neg R$
	8	
$\rightarrow$E 2, 4	9	$\neg\neg R \,\&\, K$
■	10	$\neg\neg R$
$\neg$E 5-7, 5-10	11	R
vIR 11	12	R v H
	13	
	14	
$\equiv$E 1, 3	15	D
&I 12, 15	16	(R v H) & D
$\rightarrow$I 4-16	17	$A \rightarrow [(R \vee H) \,\&\, D]$
	18	

Figure 5.23j

SD : WHITE

PREMISE	1	D ≡ ¬B
PREMISE	2	A → (¬¬R & K)
PREMISE	3	¬B
ASSUMPTION	4	A
ASSUMPTION	5	¬R
	6	
R 5	7	¬R
	8	
→E 2, 4	9	¬¬R & K
&EL 9	10	¬¬R
¬E 5-7, 5-10	11	R
vIR 11	12	R v H
	13	
	14	
≡E 1, 3	15	D
&I 12, 15	16	(R v H) & D
→I 4-16	17	A → [(R v H) & D]
	18	

Figure 5.23k

SD : WHITE

PREMISE	1	D ≡ ¬B
PREMISE	2	A → (¬¬R & K)
PREMISE	3	¬B
ASSUMPTION	4	A
ASSUMPTION	5	¬R
R 5	6	¬R
→E 2, 4	7	¬¬R & K
&EL 7	8	¬¬R
¬E 5-6, 5-8	9	R
vIR 9	10	R v H
≡E 1, 3	11	D
&I 10, 11	12	(R v H) & D
→I 4-12	13	A → [(R v H) & D]
	14	
	15	
	16	
	17	
	18	

Figure 5.23l

justified, which you will do in a short while; in the meantime, look at Figure 5.23h.

Now, to give yourself room to obtain ¬¬R, you need some blank lines. This is easily done: With the cursor in line 8, issue the Insert—Ctrl-N—command twice, and *Symlog* will give you two extra blank lines right there. Notice that *Symlog* automatically makes the necessary adjustments in line numbering (Figure 5.23i). If you had the sentence ¬¬R & K (which is part of the second premise) in line 9, you could easily get ¬¬R by using &EL. But ¬¬R & K can be easily obtained by →E from lines 2 and 4. So, in line 9, type →E 2,4 and issue the Generation command. Your work should now match the screen in Figure 5.23j.

Finally, ¬¬R in line 10 can be justified by &EL 9. Once you have done this step, your derivation is complete. Observe that there are no marks in the Mark Field and that the one at the top in the Information Line has disappeared as well (Figure 5.23k). To get rid of the unnecessary blank lines, take the cursor to each of them and repeatedly issue the Delete command; *Symlog* removes the blank lines and renumbers the entries in the Justification Field (Figure 5.23l).

Let us move on to a final example. Suppose you are asked to show that P ≡ ¬¬P can be derived from Ø, that is, from no premises at all. As you know, to show this proof you must construct a derivation with no premises and having P ≡ ¬¬P as its last sentence. In effect, this will not be the proof of an argument, since every argument has at least one premise, but rather of a logical truth. Retrieve a new blank Derivation Pad and call it TURING. Since you do not know how long your derivation is going to be, take a guess and enter the sentence P ≡ ¬¬P in line 14, as shown in Figure 5.24a. Because the goal sentence P ≡ ¬¬P is a biconditional, this sentence could be obtained if, first, by assuming P you can obtain ¬¬P, and if, second, by assuming ¬¬P you can obtain P. Then we would be able to apply the rule ≡I. As you know from its formal definition, ≡I requires two parallel subderivations. Suppose, then, that your first subderivation is to run from line 1 to line 7 and that the second will run from line 8 to line 13. In line 14, issue the Goal Analysis command after typing ≡I 1-7,8-13. *Symlog* produces the screen displayed in Figure 5.24b.

You must now obtain ¬¬P and P in the two subderivations (respectively): These two sentences have now become the new subgoals. Suppose that you first attempt to get P in the second subderivation. Notice that you cannot reiterate P from line 1 into line 13 because line 1 is not accessible outside the first subderivation. So how can P be obtained? In cases like these, where so few sentences are available to work with, give some thought to using indirect proof. Here you can try to obtain P by opening another subderivation with ¬P in line 9 as its assumption and by obtaining inside it two contradictory sentences in, say, lines 10 and 12. So, in line 13, type ¬E 9-10,9-12 and issue the Goal Analysis command. *Symlog* responds with the screen in Figure 5.24c.

Figure 5.24a

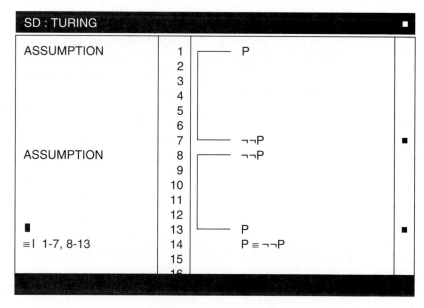

Figure 5.24b

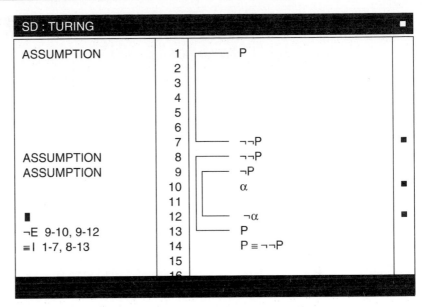

SD : TURING		
ASSUMPTION	1	P
	2	
	3	
	4	
	5	
	6	
	7	¬¬P
ASSUMPTION	8	¬¬P
ASSUMPTION	9	¬P
	10	α
	11	
	12	¬α
¬E 9-10, 9-12	13	P
≡I 1-7, 8-13	14	P ≡ ¬¬P
	15	
	16	

Figure 5.24c

It is very easy to obtain two contradictory sentences inside this new subderivation. You can simply have α be ¬P (which can be reiterated from line 9) and ¬α be ¬¬P (which can be reiterated from line 8). So, in line 12, type R 8 and issue the Generation command; and in line 10, type R 9 and reissue the Generation command; this command, as shown in Figure 5.24d, generates the two contradictory sentences inside the new subderivation.

You must now obtain ¬¬P in the first subderivation. You can proceed in an analogous manner; however, instead of using ¬E, this time you use ¬I; that is, in line 7, type ¬I 2-4,2-6 and issue the Goal Analysis command (Figure 5.24e). Once again, it is very easy to obtain two contradictory sentences inside this new subderivation: Simply reiterate P and ¬P. So, in line 6, type R 2 and issue the Generation command, and in line 4 type R 1 and reissue the same command (Figure 5.24f).

Since by assuming P (in line 1) you have arrived at ¬¬P (in line 7), and by assuming ¬¬P (in line 8) you have arrived at P (in line 13), you have justified the derivation of P ≡ ¬¬P in line 14, and your derivation is complete. Notice that all the marks have disappeared. *Symlog* is satisfied. If you wish, you can issue the Delete command on the unnecessary blank lines so that your derivation matches the one in Figure 5.24g.

In the next section we will offer a succinct list of hints and strategies for proof making and will enlist them in more challenging examples. Our advice is based on experience and is meant to supplement—not replace—the experience you yourself will gain through practice.

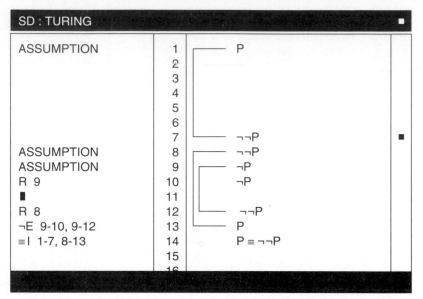

Figure 5.24d

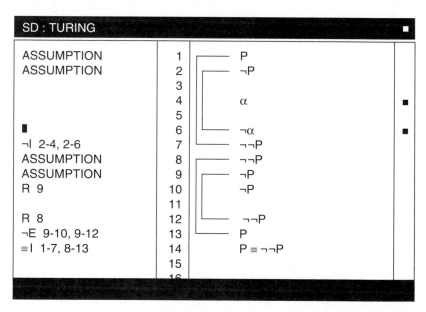

Figure 5.24e

```
SD : TURING

ASSUMPTION        1  ┌──── P
ASSUMPTION        2  │ ┌── ¬P
                  3  │ │
R 1               4  │ │   P
                  5  │ │
R 2               6  │ └── ¬P
¬I 2-4, 2-6       7  │ ──── ¬¬P
ASSUMPTION        8  │ ──── ¬¬P
ASSUMPTION        9  │ ┌── ¬P
R 9              10  │ │   ¬P
                 11  │ │
R 8              12  │ └── ¬¬P
¬E 9-10, 9-12    13  │ ──── P
≡I 1-7, 8-13     14  │    P ≡ ¬¬P
                 15
                 16
```

Figure 5.24f

```
SD : TURING

ASSUMPTION        1  ┌──── P
ASSUMPTION        2  │ ┌── ¬P
R 1               3  │ │   P
R 2               4  │ └── ¬P
¬I 2-3, 2-4       5  │ ──── ¬¬P
ASSUMPTION        6  │ ──── ¬¬P
ASSUMPTION        7  │ ┌── ¬P
R 7               8  │ │   ¬P
R 6               9  │ └── ¬¬P
¬E 7-8, 7-9      10  │ ──── P
≡I 1-5, 6-10     11  │    P ≡ ¬¬P
                 12
                 13
                 14
                 15
                 16
```

Figure 5.24g

Exercises

5.2.1 To gain more practice with rule applications, use *Symlog* to construct a derivation for the following by *using only the* Generation *command*. (This command is invoked by pressing the Tab key.) That is, at no time are you allowed to write a theorem in the Derivation Pad's Theorem Field; *work only in the* Justification Field.

$$P \to (S \,\&\, (P \equiv \neg Q))$$
$$\neg Q \equiv (R \equiv S)$$
$$[(P \,\&\, R) \lor M] \to [(P \,\&\, S) \to (T \equiv R)]$$
$$\overline{T}$$

5.2.2 Using *Symlog*, construct a derivation by *using mostly the* Goal Analysis *command*. (The command is invoked by pressing the Shift-Tab key combination.) That is, try to work, as long as you can, from the bottom of the derivation to the top.

$$P \to R$$
$$Q \to S$$
$$\overline{P \to (Q \to (R \,\&\, S))}$$

5.2.3 Using *Symlog*, construct a derivation to derive the given sentence from the given set. Try, as long as you can, to work your way up from the bottom of the derivation to the top (i.e., by using the goal analysis technique).

a. $\{(P \,\&\, Q) \to S, R \,\&\, \neg T, R \to P, \neg T \to Q\}, S$

b. $\{(P \equiv Q) \,\&\, R, R \to S, S \to P\}, Q$

c. $\{A \,\&\, B, (B \lor D) \to C, (A \,\&\, F) \to E, (B \,\&\, C) \equiv F\}, E$

d. $\{H \,\&\, (L \,\&\, F), (L \,\&\, H) \to J, K \equiv S, H \to (L \to S), J \to M\}, M \,\&\, K$

e. $\{P \to \neg R, (P \,\&\, S) \to M, \neg R \equiv S\}, P \to M$

5.2.4 Use *Symlog* to derive $(P \,\&\, Q) \equiv (R \to S)$ from $\{R, S \equiv (P \,\&\, Q)\}$.

5.2.5 Use the Create option under *Symlog*'s File menu to ask the program to generate (randomly) valid arguments whose derivations you should then attempt. When asked for the level of difficulty, select 'Easy-to-Medium.' Submit your work when done. (Note: If, after trying a few problems, you find them difficult to solve, move to the next section, where we present a powerful set of strategies for proof construction and where we also explain how *Symlog* can give you expert advice.)

5.3   Strategies for Constructing Derivations in SD

The art of derivation in SD can actually be made into a science: For a given set of premises Γ and a conclusion α, there are systematic methods which (blindly—mechanically—followed) will produce a derivation of α from Γ, if one such derivation exists. Moreover, these methods will even tell you if no such derivation exists. Our approach to SD falls on the side of art, however—the art of reasoning. We will discuss some useful *strategies* for the successful construction of derivations in SD. Our reasons for doing so are twofold: (1) These systematic methods are far from 'natural' in the sense that they lack the intuitive flavor of ordinary deductive reasoning; in contrast, the strategies we present here will help you gain more insight in the construction of derivations, mathematical proofs, and arguments in general; and (2) even if we were to introduce these systematic methods, they cannot be so readily extended to the deduction system PD to be presented later, whereas the set of strategies can.

Let us suppose that you want to derive a sentence α (your current goal) from some given set of premises (which could be empty) or from the set of sentences already obtained in your derivation. Then, to derive α, it is useful to try the following:

1. Look at the lines in the derivation which are accessible from your goal sentence α (at the beginning these are just the premises, if any), and try to determine whether α can be obtained from them, or from any of their subwffs, by the application of one of the elimination rules that does not require a subderivation: reiteration, &E, →E and ≡E. To illustrate, if P ≡ (Q → R) is accessible and your goal is R, try to get both Q → R and Q. Similarly, if [(J ≡ S)≡¬K] & M is accessible and your goal is J ≡ S, try to get both (J ≡ S) ≡ ¬K and ¬K. Clearly, this strategy cannot be applied if the goal α does not occur as a subwff in any of the accessible sentences. There are two exceptions to this subderivation-free strategy, however: (a) If you spot two readily available contradictory sentences, get your goal by ¬E; (b) If you spot a disjunction with a disjunct equal to your goal, it is sensible to apply ∨E: One of this rule's parallel subderivations will be trivial; the other gives you one extra assumption to work with (namely, the other disjunct). In most cases this strategy will bring you one step closer to completing your proof. However, in those cases in which it does not apply (e.g., α does not even occur in the accessible sentences) or in which the subgoals it requires you to derive seem harder to prove than α itself, go to step 2.

2. Your goal sentence α is either an atomic sentence (i.e., a sentence letter) or a compound sentence:

   2.1. *If α is an atomic sentence:* Reconsider step 1 again more carefully; if step 1 still seems to fail, go to step 3.

   2.2. *If α is a compound sentence:* Employ the goal analysis method according to the main connective of α. If the strategy suggested below, which depends on the main connective of α, seems to fail, go to step 3. Specifically,

2.2.1. *The main connective of α is ¬:* Here α is of the form ¬β. Apply goal analysis by using ¬I; that is, construct a sub-derivation with β as assumption and derive two contradictory sentences δ and ¬δ, which become your new goals. Although it may not be clear what δ should be, a good candidate for δ is any sentence, not necessarily atomic, whose negation appears in some accessible line. However, in many cases, as we will illustrate later, you will have to forge the contradictory sentences you are seeking. Until discharged, the assumption β is available for further work in your derivation.

2.2.2. *The main connective of α is &:* Apply the goal analysis method by using &I; that is, derive each of the conjuncts in α separately. The left and the right conjuncts of α become your new (simpler) subgoals.

2.2.3. *The main connective of α is ∨:* Consider deriving α by trying to derive either one of its disjuncts (i.e., using the goal analysis method with ∨IL or ∨IR). Which disjunct it is depends on the sentences accessible from the line where you are working. So, you should apply step 1 (to each disjunct separately) to determine which one looks more promising. Keep in mind that in many cases one cannot derive a disjunction by deriving one of its disjuncts and then applying ∨IL or ∨IR. But if it seems feasible that you can derive one of the disjuncts, make it your new (simpler) goal.

2.2.4. *The main connective of α is →:* In this case, apply goal analysis by using →I, that is, by constructing a subderivation having as assumption the antecedent of α and as conclusion its consequent (which becomes a simpler goal).

2.2.5. *The main connective of α is ≡:* Here α is of the form β≡δ. Apply the goal analysis method by using ≡I, that is, by constructing two subderivations, the first of which has β as assumption and δ as conclusion, and the second has δ as assumption and β as conclusion. The sentences β and δ, which are simpler in structure than the original goal α, become your new goals.

3. If both steps 1 and 2 seem to fail but there are disjunctions among your available sentences, try to get α by ∨E; consider each disjunction in turn, beginning with the most promising one. Your new goal is still α but now you possess one more assumption for each of ∨E's parallel subderivations. If it does not seem possible to get α this way, go to step 4.

4. If all else fails obtain α by ¬E; that is, assume ¬α and set out to derive two contradictory sentences β and ¬β, which become your new goals.

As with ¬I, it may not be clear what sentence β you should derive. A good candidate for β is any sentence, not necessarily atomic, whose negation appears in any accessible line. However, in many cases you will have to construct the contradictory sentences you are seeking.

We are now going to apply these strategies and strongly suggest you follow along with *Symlog*. Refer to Figure 5.25a (which, by the way, also illustrates how to construct more than one derivation in the Derivation Pad).[12] The purpose of the first derivation, which runs from line 1 to line 15, is to prove the logical truth $[(P \& Q) \to R] \to [P \to (Q \to R)]$. We begin by checking whether strategy step 1 applies to our goal sentence. Certainly, since there are no premises and hence no accessible lines, step 1 does not apply, so we move on to step 2. Since our goal sentence is a conditional, we use 2.2.4. Thus, in line 15 we justify the goal with →I, and we open a subderivation running from line 1 to line 14.[13] The consequent $P \to (Q \to R)$ becomes the immediate goal, while we add to our stock of available sentences the assumption $(P \& Q) \to R$. Note that since our new goal is now to derive $P \to (Q \to R)$, we apply the strategies again (i.e., we go back to step 1). Again, step 1 does not seem to apply here—our goal is not a subwff of any of the available sentences—so we move to step 2.2.4 since our goal is another conditional. Hence, we justify line 14 with →I and we open a subderivation running from lines 2 to 13; the assumption P is added to our stock of available sentences, and $Q \to R$ becomes the new goal. Again, step 1 does not seem to help in deriving $Q \to R$, and once again we go on to 2.2.4. This step gives Q as a new assumption, and R becomes the immediate goal. But, finally, in step 1, there is a simple way of obtaining R from the sentences in lines 1, 2 and 3: Form the conjunction of lines 2 and 3 and apply →E with line 1. Hence, after generating P & Q in line 5, we obtain R in line 12 by →E 1,5.

If at any point in the construction of a derivation you get stuck—you do not know what strategy to apply to reach your goal—expert help is one keypress away: With the cursor in your goal's line issue *Symlog*'s Advice command—press the function key F3.[14] Figure 5.25b shows *Symlog*'s advice when it was requested in order to prove the sentence in line 13 of Figure 5.25a.

Let us now move to a more challenging example. In the second derivation in Figure 5.25a we want to derive the sentence $K \to (J \& L)$ from the set of premises given in lines 20 to 23. We begin by using the strategy suggested

---

[12] Although this use is perfectly possible in *Symlog*, we actually recommend that you stay with one derivation per file.

[13] In *Symlog*, justify the goal with →I 1-14 and press Shift-Tab—the goal analysis command.

[14] Advice is generated by *Symlog*'s built-in theorem prover, a program which constructs natural deduction proofs the way you are being taught here. The prover effectively implements the strategies outlined above. I am indebted to Andrew McCafferty and Richard Scheines for discussions on their implementation.

SD : CAESAR

ASSUMPTION	1	(P & Q) → R
ASSUMPTION	2	P
ASSUMPTION	3	Q
	4	
&I 2, 3	5	P & Q
	6	
	7	
	8	
	9	
	10	
	11	
→E 1, 5	12	R
→I 3-12	13	Q → R
→I 2-13	14	P → (Q → R)
→I 1-14	15	[(P & Q) → R] → [P → (Q → R)]
	16	
	17	
	18	
	19	
PREMISE	20	(K & M) → J
PREMISE	21	M
PREMISE	22	L v H
PREMISE	23	H → ¬M
	24	
ASSUMPTION	25	K
	26	
&I 25, 21	27	K & M
→E 20, 27	28	J
	29	
ASSUMPTION	30	L
R 30	31	L
ASSUMPTION	32	H
ASSUMPTION	33	¬L
	34	
R 21	35	M
	36	
	37	
	38	
	39	
	40	
→E 23, 32	41	¬M
¬E 33-35, 33-41	42	L
vE 22, 30-31, 32-42	43	L
&I 28, 43	44	J & L
→I 25-44	45	K → (J & L)
	46	

Figure 5.25a

SD : CAESAR

ADVICE

Use →I to get your goal wff, Q → R.

WHY

Because none of the elimination strategies seems to apply but also because Q → R is a conditional.

REMARKS

Justifying Q → R by →I i-j involves constructing a subderivation whose assumption is the goal's antecedent, Q, and whose conclusion is the goal's consequent, R.

Figure 5.25b

SD : CAESAR

ADVICE

Use →E to get your goal wff, J.

WHY

Because J is a subwff of (K&M)→J and this sentence, but also its antecedent K&M, can be derived from what is available.

REMARKS

After justifying J by →E i,j derive the two new goals (K&M)→J and K&M.

Figure 5.25c

in step 1, but since it does not apply we move straight to 2.2.4. Having justified line 45 with →I, the sentence J & L (in line 44) becomes the new goal within the subderivation headed by K (in line 25). Since J & L is a conjunction (and step 1 fails), we shall apply 2.2.2. The goal analysis method dictates that the conjuncts J and L should become the new goals. So, after justifying J & L with &I, we start working with our first subgoal J. After inspecting the available sentences, we note that J could be easily obtained from (K & M) → J in line 20, if we had K & M, and that K & M itself is easily constructed from lines 21 and 25. So strategy step 1 succeeds here and J is derived. (We realize that since you are just learning to apply the strategies, getting J may not seem to you as easy as we claim it is. In this initial learning period you may find *Symlog*'s assistance most pedagogically useful. For instance, Figure 5.25c shows what *Symlog* has to say if asked to derive the current goal J. As you master the art of proof making you should depend less and less on *Symlog*'s advice.)

As for our second subgoal, L (in line 43), step 1 succeeds, for our goal is the left disjunct of a readily available sentence, L ∨ H. (Being L atomic, it is important to consider step 1 with care (as suggested by step 2.1) before embarking on an indirect proof, especially if there are no clear candidates for contradictory sentences in sight.) To repeat, if L is to be derived by the strategy suggested in step 1, we must concentrate on sentences with occurrences of L. The only sentence accessible from line 43 which contains an occurrence of L is the sentence L ∨ H in line 22. Since this sentence is a disjunction (with a disjunct equal to our goal), applying ∨E would mean constructing two subderivations, one having L as both assumption and conclusion and the other having H as assumption with L as conclusion. The first subderivation is trivial, and even though the second subderivation would make L the new subgoal (which is the same goal we have now), we are not going in circles because this subderivation provides a new sentence to our stock, namely, the assumption H. Thus, if we apply ∨E, we are in the same position as we were before but with one more sentence to play with, namely, the assumption H. So let us take this approach. After justifying L in line 43 with ∨E we justify line 31 with an application of reiteration—this completes the first subderivation—and then we move to line 42, our new goal. To complete the second subderivation we apply step 1, but it seems to fail. L being atomic, we reconsider step 1 more carefully, but since line 22 has been used up before, there seems to be no hope here. Step 3 fails for a similar reason—L ∨ H is the only disjunction and it has already been used up—and so we move to step 4 and try an indirect proof. We thus open a subderivation with ¬L as assumption and try to derive two contradictory sentences β and ¬β (α and ¬α, on *Symlog*'s computer screen) in, say, lines 35 and 41. What should β be? The sentence M looks promising since it appears both negated and unnegated in lines accessible from both lines 35 and 41. M can be easily obtained from line 21 by reiteration. As for ¬M, a single application of →E on lines 23 and 32 will do the job. Strategy step 1 provides the required final link, which completes the proof.

In the third example, you are asked to prove the logical truth $(A \lor B) \equiv \neg(\neg A \& \neg B)$, a derivation of which is given in Figure 5.26. Study this proof carefully in the light of the strategies given above. In lines 1 through 20 of Figure 5.27a you will find an alternative proof of the first half of this biconditional. There, the goal sentence $\neg(\neg A \& \neg B)$ is obtained by first making use of $\neg I$ instead of $\lor E$. In your own proof making, you may sometimes discover alternative solutions to the same problem. *Symlog*, however, has a preference for this second alternative: Its construction more closely follows the strategies. If asked for a hint, it would initally suggest to use $\neg I$, and when asked again to advise on the derivation of one of the contradictory sentences, A, it would then spot the left disjunct of $A \lor B$ as being the goal (in line 17) and, to stay in line with the strategies, would recommend to obtain it by $\lor E$ (Figure 5.27b).

Figure 5.27a also contains two other illustrations. The first one runs from lines 25 to 35, and the second runs from lines 38 to 45. Both derivations are variations of the same theme: to prove $P \lor \neg P$ from the empty set. Note that in both derivations, we have no other choice but to assume the negation of the goal, that is, to apply strategy step 4, since steps 1, 2.2.3 and 3 all fail (you should convince yourself that applying 2.2.3 leads to a dead end, no matter which disjunct you consider). The difficult part in using step 4 is to determine suitable contradictory sentences α and $\neg\alpha$ to derive. That is why we offer two different solutions for deriving $P \lor \neg P$. In the first derivation, the choice for α is the sentence P. Since both P and $\neg P$ appear in accessible lines within the subderivation (both in line 25), it is sensible to consider them as possible candidates. Then the goal in this first derivation becomes deriving P (in line 29) and $\neg P$ (in line 34). As for the second derivation, the choice for $\neg\alpha$ is the sentence $\neg(P \lor \neg P)$. (This is actually *Symlog*'s choice if asked for advice. See Figure 5.27c.) Note that even though our—*Symlog*'s—choice for α is the sentence $P \lor \neg P$, which is the same goal we had before, we are not going in circles since we now have available to us a new sentence we did not have before, namely, the assumption $\neg(P \lor \neg P)$. Using this approach, it becomes feasible to obtain, by applying step 2.2.3, the goal sentence $P \lor \neg P$ from either one of its disjuncts (in our example we use the left disjunct). Both approaches lead to a successful completion of the derivation. We leave it to you to add the steps needed.

The sequence of strategic steps outlined at the beginning of this section does not constitute an infallible method for constructing derivations. Much depends on experience in proof making. Thus, with reference to strategy step 2.2.3, being able to determine which disjunct 'looks more promising' when trying to derive a disjunction very much depends on the degree of expertise you have acquired by constructing derivations in SD. However, as a group, they form a useful set of rules of thumb which will allow you in many cases to achieve a successful derivation. Try to see the thread of common sense running through them. By all means, do not try to memorize these strategy steps. You will find them becoming second nature, all the same, as your experience grows.

SD : NAPOLEON

ASSUMPTION	1	A v B
	2	
ASSUMPTION	3	A
	4	
ASSUMPTION	5	¬A & ¬B
	6	
R 3	7	A
&EL 5	8	¬A
¬I 5-7, 5-8	9	¬(¬A & ¬B)
ASSUMPTION	10	B
	11	
ASSUMPTION	12	¬A & ¬B
	13	
	14	
	15	
R 10	16	B
&ER 12	17	¬B
¬I 12-16, 12-17	18	¬(¬A & ¬B)
vE 1, 3-9, 10-18	19	¬(¬A & ¬B)
ASSUMPTION	20	¬(¬A & ¬B)
	21	
ASSUMPTION	22	¬(A v B)
	23	
ASSUMPTION	24	A
	25	
	26	
	27	
vIR 24	28	A v B
R 22	29	¬(A v B)
¬I 24-28, 24-29	30	¬A
	31	
	32	
ASSUMPTION	33	B
	34	
	35	
	36	
	37	
	38	
vIL 33	39	A v B
R 22	40	¬(A v B)
¬I 33-39, 33-40	41	¬B
&I 30, 41	42	¬A & ¬B
R 20	43	¬(¬A & ¬B)
¬E 22-42, 22-43	44	A v B
≡I 1-19, 20-44	45	(A v B) ≡ ¬(¬A & ¬B)
	46	

Figure 5.26

SD : PATTON		
ASSUMPTION	1	A v B
	2	
ASSUMPTION	3	¬A & ¬B
	4	
ASSUMPTION	5	A
R 5	6	A
ASSUMPTION	7	B
	8	
ASSUMPTION	9	¬A
	10	
	11	
	12	
R 7	13	B
	14	
&ER 3	15	¬B
¬E 9-13, 9-15	16	A
vE 1, 5-6, 7-16	17	A
&EL 3	18	¬A
¬I 3-17, 3-18	19	¬(¬A & ¬B)
→I 1-19	20	(A v B) → ¬(¬A & ¬B)
	21	
	22	
	23	
	24	
ASSUMPTION	25	¬(P v ¬P)
ASSUMPTION	26	¬P
vIL 26	27	P v ¬P
R 25	28	¬(P v ¬P)
¬E 26-27, 26-28	29	P
	30	
ASSUMPTION	31	P
vIR 31	32	P v ¬P
R 25	33	¬(P v ¬P)
¬I 31-32, 31-33	34	¬P
¬E 25-29, 25-34	35	P v ¬P
	36	
	37	
ASSUMPTION	38	¬(P v ¬P)
ASSUMPTION	39	¬P
vIL 39	40	P v ¬P
R 38	41	¬(P v ¬P)
¬E 39-40, 39-41	42	P
vIR 42	43	P v ¬P
R 38	44	¬(P v ¬P)
¬E 38-43, 38-44	45	P v ¬P
	46	

Figure 5.27a

SD : PATTON   ■

ADVICE

   Use vE to get your goal wff, A.

WHY

   Because A is one of the disjuncts of A v B and also because vE
   allows you to add the other disjunct of A v B as a (free) extra
   assumption. Moreover, deriving A v B seems feasible.

REMARKS

   Justifying A by vE i, j-k, l-m first involves deriving the disjunction
   A v B and then constructing two subderivations: Assume its left
   disjunct, A, and derive A, and then assume its right disjunct, B, and
   derive A. Note that one of these subderivations is trivial.

Figure 5.27b

SD : PATTON   ■

ADVICE

   Use ¬E to get your goal wff, Pv¬P.

WHY

   Because all the other strategies seem to fail.

REMARKS

   Justifying Pv¬P by ¬E i-j, i-k involves constructing a subderivation
   with ¬(Pv¬P) as its assumption and deriving two contradictory
   sentences within the subderivation. I recommend you try to derive
   Pv¬P and ¬(Pv¬P).

Figure 5.27c

Exercises

5.3.1 Assume the following three sentences are the only ones accessible from your goal wff:

P ≡ S
R & (S → T)
¬(T ∨ ¬S)

According to the strategies, which rule should one apply first to the following (goal) sentence in an attempt to derive it from the above accessible set?

a. R	b. P → T	c. P ≡ T
d. S	e. M ∨ R	f. A
g. R & ¬T	h. (S ∨ P) → ¬S	i. ¬(S → P)

5.3.2 Repeat as in 5.3.1 for the following pairs of accessible sets and goal sentences:

a. {R & Q, S ≡ R}, S   b. {R → (K ∨ L), S & R}, K ∨ L
c. {¬B, E → C, B}, E → (C & B)   d. Ø, S → (K ∨ S)
e. {E, K, E → K}, K   f. {F & (L → H), F ≡ (H ∨ L)}, H
g. Ø, S ∨ ¬S   h. {¬K → B, C ∨ ¬K, C → B}, B
i. {P & S, K, E ≡ (S → P)}, M ∨ P   j. {R → ¬S, Q & (R ≡ P)}, ¬(P & S)

5.3.3 Use the strategies to derive, with the help of *Symlog*, the given sentence from the given set. (Ask *Symlog* for expert advice only if you truly need it. Apply a strategy by invoking the Goal Analysis command—Shift-Tab.)

a. {(P & Q) → T, (R & T) → S}, P → (Q → (R → S))
b. {¬P → R, ¬R}, P ≡ (S → P)
c. {L ≡ ¬K, K ∨ ¬L}, K
d. Ø, (¬R ∨ S) → (R → S)
e. {¬(K ∨ H)}, ¬K

5.3.4 Use *Symlog* to derive S → [(R → Q) ≡ [(R ∨ Q) → (S → Q)]] from the empty set of premises, Ø.

5.3.5 Use the Create option under *Symlog*'s File menu to ask the program to generate (randomly) valid arguments whose derivations you should then construct. When asked for the level of difficulty, select 'Easy-to-Medium.' Submit your work when done.

5.3.6 Repeat as in 5.3.5 but select 'Medium-to-Difficult.'

5.3.7 Repeat as in 5.3.5 but select 'Difficult.'

5.4 *Properties of Sentences and Sets of Sentences in SD*

In this section we introduce some formal definitions for the derivation system SD which will help give a more complete understanding of deductive systems of logic. Although we have been using all along the terms 'derivation,' and 'derivable,' we now introduce formal definitions of these terms:

> **Definition.** A **derivation in SD** is a finite sequence of sentences of SL each of which has been justified by using one of the rules of SD.

> **Definition.** Given a set Γ of sentences of SL and a sentence α of SL, α is **SD-derivable from** Γ if and only if there is a derivation in SD in which Γ is the set of premises and α is on the last line of the derivation, where this occurrence of α is not within the scope of an assumption.

If α is SD-derivable from Γ we write Γ $\vdash_{\overline{SD}}$ α (or Γ ⊢ α, for short). Figure 5.23l is an example of a derivation in SD and, line 13 being its last line, the sentence on that line is SD-derivable from the set of premises on lines 1, 2 and 3. Similarly, the sentence P ≡ ¬¬P is SD-derivable from the empty set, as Figure 5.24g shows. Sentences which are capable of being derived from a given set of premises are called theorems (of the set of premises in question). More formally,

> **Definition.** Given a set Γ of sentences of SL, a sentence α of SL is an **SD-theorem of** Γ if and only if α is SD-derivable from Γ.

To illustrate, since with the sole help of the rules of SD it is possible to derive the sentence A → D from the set {A → B, D ≡ B}, we say that A → D is an SD-theorem of {A → B, D ≡ B}. The case in which the set Γ is the empty set is of utmost importance in symbolic logic. (We will say more about this later.) For instance, since the sentence P → P can be derived from the empty set (using only the rules of SD), we say that P → P is a theorem of the empty set, Ø.[15]

> **Definition.** Two sentences α and β of SL are **SD-equivalent** if and only if {α} $\vdash_{\overline{SD}}$ β and {β} $\vdash_{\overline{SD}}$ α.

What this definition says is that two sentences of SL are SD-equivalent if and only if the first sentence can be derived from the set consisting of the second sentence, and the second sentence can be derived from the set consisting of the first one. Or in other words, α is a theorem of {β} and β is a theorem of {α}. For instance, the sentences ¬A ∨ B and A → B are SD-equivalent because ¬A ∨ B can be derived from {A → B}, and A → B can be derived from {¬A ∨ B}. The screens in Figure 5.28 show this relationship.

Inconsistency in SD is defined as

> **Definition.** A set Γ of sentences of SL is **SD-inconsistent** if and only if both α and ¬α (where α is a sentence of SL) are derivable from Γ. A set Γ of sentences of SL is **SD-consistent** if and only if it is not SD-inconsistent.

---

[15] If it is clear from the context, and to avoid overqualification, SD-theorems will be simply called theorems; we will do likewise for SD-derivability.

SD : HILBERT

PREMISE	1	A → B
	2	
ASSUMPTION	3	¬(¬A v B)
	4	
ASSUMPTION	5	A
	6	
→E 1, 5	7	B
vIL 7	8	¬A v B
R 3	9	¬(¬A v B)
¬I 5-8, 5-9	10	¬A
vIR 10	11	¬A v B
R 3	12	¬(¬A v B)
¬E 3-11, 3-12	13	¬A v B
	14	
	15	
	16	

SD : BROWER

PREMISE	1	¬A v B
	2	
ASSUMPTION	3	A
	4	
ASSUMPTION	5	¬A
	6	
ASSUMPTION	7	¬B
R 3	8	A
R 5	9	¬A
¬E 7-8, 7-9	10	B
ASSUMPTION	11	B
	12	
R 11	13	B
vE 1, 5-10, 11-13	14	B
→I 3-14	15	A → B
	16	

Figure 5.28

For example, the set {¬M → G, C & ¬M, G ≡ (R & ¬C)} is SD-inconsistent since it is possible to derive from it both the sentences C and ¬C (Figure 5.29). It is worth remarking that the contradictory sentences which must be derived to establish the SD-inconsistency of a set (these are C and ¬C in Figure 5.29) do not have to occur literally in the set at all. As an exercise, you may want to show that the set of premises of Figure 5.29 is SD-inconsistent by deriving the sentences, say, S v G and ¬(S v G).

Note that whenever Γ is SD-inconsistent, any sentence whatsoever of SL is a theorem of Γ; that is, it can be derived from Γ. To see this, let Γ be an SD-inconsistent set, and let δ be any sentence. Since Γ is by assumption

SD : PEIRCE

PREMISE	1	¬M → G
PREMISE	2	C & ¬M
PREMISE	3	G ≡ (R & ¬C)
	4	
&EL 2	5	C
&ER 2	6	¬M
→E 1, 6	7	G
≡E 3, 7	8	R & ¬C
&ER 8	9	¬C
	10	

Figure 5.29

	i	α
	j	$\neg\alpha$
ASSUMPTION	k	$\neg\delta$
R i	l	α
R j	m	$\neg\alpha$
$\neg$E k-l, k-m	n	δ

Figure 5.30

SD-inconsistent, it follows by the definition of SD-inconsistency that both α and $\neg\alpha$ (where α is a sentence of SL) can be derived from it. Thus, in a few more steps, and with the use of the rule $\neg$E, the sentence δ could be derived. This is shown in the 'metaderivation' of Figure 5.30, in which the sentence α has been derived from Γ in line i and the sentence $\neg\alpha$ in line j.[16]

The converse of this result is also true: If all the sentences of SL are theorems of Γ, then Γ is SD-inconsistent. This result is easy to see. Suppose that all sentences of SL are theorems of Γ; then, in particular, both A and $\neg$A are theorems of Γ, and clearly A and $\neg$A are of the form α and $\neg\alpha$, respectively, which means that the set Γ is SD-inconsistent. Hence, we can conclude, a set Γ of sentences of SL is SD-inconsistent if and only if its set of theorems is precisely the whole of SL. This reasoning, in turn, allows us to conclude that a set Γ is SD-*consistent* if and only if there is at least one sentence of SL that is *not* a theorem of Γ.[17]

As we have seen, any sentence of SL is derivable from an SD-inconsistent set. Intuitively, this fact shows why it is so important to avoid inconsistent sets of beliefs or opinions, for otherwise any statement could be proved from them, leading to all kinds of conclusions, from the most rational to downright absurdities. For instance, from an inconsistent set of beliefs you can show, as Bertrand Russell did, that he and the Pope were one and the same person. However, as seen earlier with truth-tables, you can make the concept of inconsistency work to your advantage. Suppose a sentence β is derivable from a (possibly empty) set Γ. Then, it is clear that if we were to add the sentence $\neg\beta$ to Γ, the newly obtained set, $\Gamma \cup \{\neg\beta\}$, would be SD-inconsistent. It is so because both β and $\neg\beta$ can be derived from it. (β can be derived from the Γ 'fragment' of $\Gamma \cup \{\neg\beta\}$, and $\neg\beta$ is easily derived from $\{\neg\beta\}$ by reiteration.) Hence, we have shown that if β is derivable from a

---

[16] Note that, strictly speaking, Figure 5.30 is not a derivation in SD since the expressions which occur in it are not sentences of SL—α and δ are foreign to SL's alphabet—but are, instead, **metasentences** or sentence variables ranging over sentences of SL. Each substitution of the variables α and δ (but also the numeric variables i through n) constitutes a specific derivation in SD. Thus, Figure 5.30 stands for an infinite collection of derivations in SD—a **metaderivation.**

[17] Proving that a sentence α *cannot* be derived from a set Γ (i.e., that there is not a derivation in SD of α from Γ) is far from clear. In a later section we will show how to solve this problem.

(possibly empty) set Γ, then $\Gamma \cup \{\neg\beta\}$ is SD-inconsistent. Let us now show the converse, namely, that if $\Gamma \cup \{\neg\beta\}$ is SD-inconsistent then β is derivable from Γ. To show that β is derivable from Γ (on the assumption that $\Gamma \cup \{\neg\beta\}$ is SD-inconsistent), construct a derivation in SD as follows: Assume $\neg\beta$ and derive a contradiction. That a contradiction can be derived can be easily seen by noting that by assuming $\neg\beta$, we merely enlarge our existing set (of premises) Γ to $\Gamma \cup \{\neg\beta\}$, which we already know to be SD-inconsistent. Our arguments have justified the following:

> **Test for Derivability.** The sentence β is derivable (in SD) from an SL set $\{\alpha_1, \alpha_2, \ldots, \alpha_n\}$—possibly empty—if and only if the test set $\{\alpha_1, \alpha_2, \ldots, \alpha_n, \neg\beta\}$ is SD-inconsistent.

For example, the sentence H can be derived from $\{\neg H \rightarrow (F \, \& \, (K \rightarrow \neg G)), (G \, \& \, K) \equiv (S \vee M), M\}$ because, as Figure 5.31 shows, the test set $\{\neg H \rightarrow (F \, \& \, (K \rightarrow \neg G)), (G \, \& \, K) \equiv S \vee M), M, \neg H\}$ is SD-inconsistent.

We come finally to define the concept of validity in SD:

> **Definition.** An argument of SL having a set Γ of premises and a sentence α as its conclusion is **SD-valid** if and only if α is an SD-theorem of Γ. An argument of SL is **SD-invalid** if and only if it is not SD-valid.

Correspondingly, an argument of SL is SD-valid if and only if its test set is SD-inconsistent.

SD : MOON		
PREMISE	1	$\neg H \rightarrow (F \, \& \, (K \rightarrow \neg G))$
PREMISE	2	$(G \, \& \, K) \equiv (S \vee M)$
PREMISE	3	M
PREMISE	4	$\neg H$
	5	
vIL 3	6	$S \vee M$
≡E 2, 6	7	G & K
&EL 7	8	G
→E 1, 4	9	$F \, \& \, (K \rightarrow \neg G)$
&ER 9	10	$K \rightarrow \neg G$
&ER 7	11	K
→E 10, 11	12	$\neg G$
	13	
	14	
	15	
	16	

Figure 5.31

Exercises

In these exercises feel free to use the Justification (Enter key), Generation (Shift key), or Goal Analysis (Shift-Tab) commands in any combination you think most appropriate to construct the needed derivations. Let *Symlog* help as you go along: Ask for its expert advice if you truly need it, but also ask *Symlog* to check individual lines in your derivation (Justification command) or the whole derivation (with Submit). You may sometimes want to simulate tests or quizzes by disabling *Symlog*'s supervising capabilities (select Interactive/Noninteractive Mode from the Services menu). Then, by using Submit, you can let *Symlog* check your work.

5.4.1   Answer true or false (but not both) to each of the following.
   a. The sentence K & M is a theorem of {P & ¬Q, P → Q}.
   b. If α is a sentence of SL, then ¬α cannot be a theorem of {α}.
   c. β is the only sentence of SL that is a theorem of {β}.
   d. If α is not a theorem of Γ then Γ is SD-consistent.
   e. All sentences of SL are theorems of {P & Q, Q → ¬P}
   f. There are infinitely many sets, Γ, of which the sentence P of SL is a theorem.
   g. If P is not a theorem of Γ then ¬P is.
   h. If α is theorem of Γ_1 and β is a theorem of Γ_2, then both α and β are theorems of $\Gamma_1 \cup \Gamma_2$.
   i. If α is theorem of Γ_1 and also a theorem of Γ_2, then α is a theorem of $\Gamma_1 \cap \Gamma_2$.
   j. $\varnothing \vdash_{SD} \neg(\neg P \,\&\, P)$.

5.4.2   Use *Symlog* to show that the given sentence is SD-derivable from the corresponding set.
   a. {((¬H ≡ J) & (S ∨ M), L → D}, (L → D) & (S ∨ M)
   b. {A & B, B → ¬M, S & R}, ¬M & R
   c. {G & D, D → R}, H → (R & G)
   d. {D → M, R ≡ (¬M & S), R}, ¬D
   e. {K ≡ (K → M), M → ¬E}, (K → ¬E) ∨ G
   f. {(A & B) → (¬M ∨ D)}, A → [B → (¬M ∨ D)]
[PR21] g. {D → ¬J, P & D, ¬P ≡ (M ∨ ¬J)}, S ≡ (M ∨ ¬J)
   h. {L ∨ Q, (Q ∨ L) → R, H}, R & H
[PR22] i. {S ≡ (B & D), B → ¬¬P, (S ∨ G) → ¬P, S}, ¬G & ¬¬B
[PR23] j. {A ∨ B, B → (D & ¬M), A ≡ G}, D ∨ G

5.4.3 Using *Symlog*, show that each sentence below is a theorem of the given set.
   a. A ∨ A, {A ∨ A}
   b. ¬¬A ≡ B, {A ≡ B}
   c. P → (Q → P), ∅
   d. M ≡ ¬¬M, ∅

[PR24] e.   A & ¬A, {K & L, L → J, A → ¬(K & L), L → (¬A → ¬J)}

[PR25] f.   R, {¬(¬E ∨ F), ¬(F → G)}

[PR26] g.   D ∨ L, {¬C ∨ ¬K, D ∨ (K ∨ L), ¬K ∨ C}

h.   ¬A → B, {A ∨ B}

[PR27] i.   (G & H) → I, {(¬H ∨ ¬J) & (D ≡ H), J ∨ (G → I)}

[PR28] j.   (F ∨ C) ∨ (¬A ∨ G), {B → (A → G), C ∨ (F ∨ B)}

[PR29] k.   (P → Q) ≡ (¬P ∨ Q), Ø

[PR30] l.   (P → Q)≡(¬Q → ¬P), Ø

[PR31] m.   ¬(P ∨ Q) ≡ (¬P & ¬Q), Ø

n.   ¬(P ∨ P) → ¬P, Ø

o.   [(P & Q) → R] → [P → (Q → R)], Ø

5.4.4   Use *Symlog* to show that the following sets are SD-inconsistent.

a. {R ≡ ¬R}

[PR32] b. {(A → B) → C, B ∨ (D ≡ M), A → ¬M, ¬C & D} [Hint: Derive C and ¬C.]

[PR33] c. {I & (G → H),(¬¬G ∨ ¬I) & K,K → (¬H ∨ ¬G)} [Hint: Derive ¬G and ¬¬G.]

[PR34] d. {F ∨ G,(¬J & H) ∨ (¬G & ¬F),(J ∨ ¬G) & (¬H ∨ J)} [Hint: Derive F and ¬F.]

e. {A → (B ∨ C),¬C & A,¬D → ¬B,¬D ≡ (G ∨ ¬C)}

f. {A ≡ ¬¬B,B → ¬M,(A ∨ B) & M}

g. {¬(S ∨ J) ≡ D,D & ¬¬M,M → ¬¬J} [Hint: Derive ¬J and ¬¬J.]

[PR35] h. {¬K → M, ¬(K ∨ M) ≡ R, R & S}

i. {(A → B) → C, ¬B → ¬A, ¬C}

[PR36] j. {H, ¬(R ∨ S) ≡ ¬H, (¬D & ¬S) & ¬R}

5.4.5 Use the test for derivability to show, using *Symlog,* that the given sentence is derivable from the corresponding set.

a. {C & D, (D & ¬N) → ¬S, Q & S}, N

[PR37] b. {¬N ∨ (F & J), (¬N ≡ L) & (F → ¬J)}, L

c. Ø, A ∨ ¬A

d. {D → M, R ≡ (¬M & S),R}, ¬D

e. {¬L ≡ (¬L → N),(N → ¬F) & F}, L

5.4.6   Use *Symlog* to show that the following arguments are SD-valid.

[PR38] a. A ∨ S

¬G → ¬S

¬¬¬G

―――――――

H ∨ A

[PR39] b. (K → J) → R

¬R ∨ D

(¬D & M) & S

―――――――

¬(K → J)

c. A ≡ B

―――――――――――――――――

[P → (Q → P)] ≡ (P ∨ ¬P)

d. $\dfrac{P \equiv \neg P}{Q}$

e. $\dfrac{P \equiv \neg P}{\neg Q}$

f. $\dfrac{S \rightarrow S}{P \equiv (P \vee P)}$

[PR40] g. $\dfrac{\begin{array}{l}(M \,\&\, \neg S) \vee (A \,\&\, G) \\ (M \,\&\, H) \equiv (\neg S \rightarrow G) \\ H \vee (M \rightarrow G)\end{array}}{G}$

[PR41] h. $\dfrac{\begin{array}{l}\neg M \,\&\, H \\ \neg S \equiv H\end{array}}{A \rightarrow [B \rightarrow \neg(S \vee M)]}$

[PR42] i. $\dfrac{\begin{array}{l}A \rightarrow B \\ \neg C \rightarrow \neg B \\ C \rightarrow D \\ \neg E \rightarrow \neg D\end{array}}{A \rightarrow E}$

[PR43] j. $\dfrac{\neg(A \,\&\, B)}{\neg A \vee \neg B}$

5.4.7   Show with *Symlog* that the sentences in each of the following pairs are SD-equivalent.

[PR44] a. $\neg(A \vee B)$ and $\neg A \,\&\, \neg B$

[PR45] b. $A \rightarrow B$ and $\neg(A \,\&\, \neg B)$

[PR46] c. $\neg(P \,\&\, \neg Q)$ and $\neg P \vee Q$

[PR47] d. $\neg(M \equiv G)$ and $\neg(M \rightarrow G) \vee \neg(G \rightarrow M)$

[PR48] e. $(R \vee S) \,\&\, \neg H$ and $\neg[(\neg R \,\&\, \neg S) \vee H]$

[PR49] f. $(A \vee P) \,\&\, (R \rightarrow A)$ and $A \vee (P \,\&\, \neg R)$

[PR50] g. $(M \equiv \neg S)$ and $(S \vee M) \,\&\, (M \rightarrow \neg S)$

[PR51] h. $(A \,\&\, B) \vee (A \,\&\, C)$ and $A \,\&\, (B \vee C)$

[PR52] i. $(A \vee B) \vee C$ and $A \vee (B \vee C)$

[PR53] j. $E \rightarrow (J \rightarrow K)$ and $(J \,\&\, \neg K) \rightarrow \neg E$

5.4.8   Translate the following statements into SL and show, using *Symlog*, that the conclusion is derivable from the premises.

a. Either Argentina or Italy will win the soccer World Cup. If Argentina wins the World Cup, then Germany will win the European Cup. But if Italy wins the World Cup, Germany will still win the European Cup. Hence, the Germans will win the European Cup. (A, I, G)

b. Almonds are increasing in price these days but not coconuts. But if bananas increase in price then the price of coconuts will increase too. From this we can conclude that, no, it is not the case that almonds increase in price just in case bananas do. (A, C, B)

    c. It is not true that both Bob and Jane are going to Spain for the holidays. Instead, it is Bob and Lucy who are. Therefore, Jane is not going to Spain for the holidays. (B, J, L)

[PR54] d. Williams is planning either not to take mathematics or to take computer science or to study biology. If he takes biology he must give up logic. Then, if he enrolls in both mathematics and logic he can do computer science as well. (M, C, B, L)

    e. If Kent and Howard were at home at the time of the crime, then Suzy was there too. However, if Suzy was there at that time, then it is not the case that Howard or Albert were. Therefore, if Kent was at home at the time of the crime, Howard wasn't. (K, H, S, A)

5.4.9 Translate the following statements into SL and show, using *Symlog*, that they form an SD-inconsistent set.

[PR55] a. A particles and B particles interact with electromagnetic radiation if and only if C particles don't. It is the case that D, E and B particles interact with electromagnetic radiation. But if either D or F particles interact with electromagnetic radiation so do both A particles and C particles. (A, B, C, D, E, F)

    b. It is not the case that it is either raining or not raining. (R)

    c. If I am hungry then I am not hungry but if I am not hungry then I am. (H)

[PR56] d. Either Albert and Bob will attend the lecture or Carol will. Peter will attend unless Albert does not go. Carol won't be able to attend the lecture; but if Albert and Peter go then either Carol will be there or Bob won't go. (A, B, C, P)

[PR57] e. Either the demand will increase and the prices will go down or the prices will go up and the demand will decrease. The demand will increase if and only if the prices go up. (D, P)

5.4.10 Translate the following arguments into SL and show with *Symlog* that they are SD-valid.

[PR58] a. Movies with violence are not good for your mental health. And neither is cheap literature and much of what is shown on television. But cheap literature is good for your mental health if either reading astrology or having your palm read is. Hence, either much of what is shown on television or reading astrology is good for your mental health only if having your palm read is. (M, C, T, A, P)

    b. No, it is not the case that there is nuclear reactor meltdown if and only if the reactor's temperature rises. The reactor's temperature is not rising. Hence, there will be a nuclear reactor meltdown. (M, T)

[PR59] c. Andrew or Bill will go to the party tonight only if it is not the case that both Caroline and Bill will go. Either Bill won't go or, if he does, so does Caroline. In conclusion, Diane will go if Bill goes. (A, B, C, D)

    d. The test results will not be satisfactory unless the students study hard. Thus, it is not true that both the test results will be satisfactory and the students don't study hard. (T, S)

[PR60] e. If the price of gold increases, that of silver will increase as well. But either the price of silver won't go up or that of gold will. Therefore, the price of gold will increase just in case that of silver increases too. (G, S)

5.4.11 Answer true or false (but not both) and explain why to each of the following.

     a. If Γ_1 and Γ_2 are SD-inconsistent so is $\Gamma_1 \cup \Gamma_2$.

     b. If Γ_1 and Γ_2 are SD-consistent so is $\Gamma_1 \cap \Gamma_2$.

     c. If Γ_1 is SD-consistent and Γ_2 is SD-inconsistent then $\Gamma_1 \cup \Gamma_2$ is SD-inconsistent.

     d. If Γ_1 is SD-consistent and Γ_2 is SD-inconsistent then $\Gamma_1 \cap \Gamma_2$ is SD-inconsistent.

5.4.12 Let Γ be a set (of sentences of SL). A sentence α in Γ is **redundant** if and only if $\Gamma - \{\alpha\} \vdash_{\overline{SD}} \alpha$, that is, if α can be derived from the remaining sentences in Γ. Given the set $\{P \mathbin{\&} Q, (Q \lor S) \rightarrow R, Q \mathbin{\&} R, \neg S\}$, show that the sentence Q & R is redundant.

5.4.13 A set Γ of sentences of SL is **SD-independent** if and only if no sentence in Γ is redundant (see exercise 5.4.12). Show that the set $\{Q \equiv (R \mathbin{\&} S), S \lor T, Q \mathbin{\&} \neg P\}$ is not **SD-independent** (i.e., that at least one sentence in it is redundant).

5.4.14 Use the Create option under *Symlog*'s File menu to ask the program to generate (randomly) SD-valid arguments whose derivations you should then construct. When asked for the level of difficulty, select 'Medium-to-Difficult.' Submit your work when done.

5.4.15 Repeat as in 5.4.14 but select 'Difficult.'

5.5   *The Rules of SD+*

In this section we introduce a supplementary set of rules for SD that is intended to shorten the steps needed for constructing derivations. After applying the same sequence of rules over and over to obtain, say, P from $\neg\neg$P, Q from $\neg\neg$Q, K $\lor$ M from $\neg\neg$(K $\lor$ M) and so on, you may already have wished for a way of combining these sequences into a single rule to obtain *in just one step* the sentence α from $\neg\neg\alpha$, for any sentence α of SL. Our objective here is to extend SD by adding some new rules to facilitate proof making. We call this enriched version of SD the derivation system SD+.

     To illustrate further the convenience of having shortcut rules on hand when constructing derivations, consider the following. Suppose you wanted to derive G & H from H & G, $\neg$P & (M $\equiv \neg\neg$T) from (M $\equiv \neg\neg$T) & $\neg$P and so on. Instead of repeating several derivation steps every time this situation is encountered, it would be convenient, for practical purposes, to be able to derive a sentence of the form $\beta \mathbin{\&} \alpha$ from a sentence of the form $\alpha \mathbin{\&} \beta$ in a single step. Similarly, derivations would be shortened if from a sentence of the form $\alpha \lor (\beta \lor \delta)$ it were possible to derive $(\alpha \lor \beta) \lor \delta$ in a single step. It is with shortcuts like these that the system SD+ is concerned. As you can see, they are in fact new derivation rules. SD+ consists of all the derivation rules of SD plus some others intended to make derivations shorter. Since

SD+ has some rules that SD lacks, they are different derivation systems. However, as we will point out several times in our discussion of SD+, the extra rules found in SD+ can all be reduced to the rules of SD. What this means is that although SD+ allows you to construct shorter derivations than SD does, any sentence which can be derived with the rules of SD+ (from a given set of premises Γ) can also be derived with the rules of SD, and vice versa. More precisely, let Γ be a set and let α be a sentence of SL. Then, α is an SD-theorem of Γ if and only if it is an SD+-theorem of Γ. Because of this fact, we say that SD and SD+ are **equally powerful**. Although in practice it is often more convenient to work with SD+ than with SD, their deductive power is the same. Later, we will construct corresponding metaproofs for the first three rules of SD+ to show that they can be reduced to rules of SD. As for the rest of the rules of SD+, we ask you to take our word that they can also be reduced to rules of SD (some of the exercises take up this problem).

As you will quickly notice, *Symlog* does not support the goal analysis method for those rules which belong specifically to SD+. The reason is that the usual approach taken in the construction of derivations with rules of SD+ (but which are not of SD) is from the premises to the conclusion, rather than the other way around.

Let us begin with the first three rules, designated by their traditional names: modus tollens, hypothetical syllogism and disjunctive syllogism.

Modus Tollens (MT)

MT i, j	i	$\alpha \to \beta$
	j	$\neg\beta$
	k	$\neg\alpha$

Modus tollens (MT) allows you to derive the sentence $\neg\alpha$ from the sentences $\alpha \to \beta$ and $\neg\beta$ (it does not matter whether $\alpha \to \beta$ or $\neg\beta$ occurs earlier in the derivation). This inferential pattern is very common. For example, it is true that if your car is out of gas, then it stalls. Let us say that your car is running along nicely. Then you can safely infer (for the moment at least) that the car is not out of gas. Figure 5.32 gives a metaproof of MT by show-

		i	$\alpha \to \beta$
		j	$\neg\beta$
ASSUMPTION		k	α
$\to$E i, k		l	β
R j		m	$\neg\beta$
$\neg$I k-l, k-m		n	$\neg\alpha$

Figure 5.32

ing how this brief pattern can be re-expressed in terms of SD rules alone. Modus tollens is thus reducible to SD.

Hypothetical Syllogism (HS)

	i	$\alpha \to \beta$
	j	$\beta \to \delta$
HS i, j	k	$\alpha \to \delta$

The hypothetical syllogism (HS) rule links a pair of conditionals which share a sentence in common (β). If β occurs both as the consequent of $\alpha \to \beta$ and as the antecedent of $\beta \to \delta$, then α materially implies δ also: They are 'hooked' together by β. The rule HS sanctions the derivation of $\alpha \to \delta$ in one move. All the same, HS is itself reducible to the rules of SD, as an inspection of Figure 5.33 will show.

Disjunctive Syllogism (DS)

The disjunctive syllogism (DS) rule takes the following two forms:

	i	$\alpha \vee \beta$			i	$\alpha \vee \beta$
	j	$\neg\alpha$			j	$\neg\beta$
DS i, j	k	β		DS i, j	k	α

This rule is met with in natural language almost as often as its cousin, modus ponens ($\to$E).[18] You will recall our earlier point that a disjunction en-

	i	$\alpha \to \beta$	
	j	$\beta \to \delta$	
ASSUMPTION	k	$\ulcorner \alpha$	
$\to$E i, k	l	β	
$\to$E j, l	m	$\llcorner \delta$	
$\to$I k-m	n	$\alpha \to \delta$	

Figure 5.33

---

[18] We call it a cousin because any sentence of the form $\alpha \vee \beta$ is logically equivalent to both $\neg\alpha \to \beta$ and $\neg\beta \to \alpha$. You may want to prove these equivalences in SD.

	i	$\alpha \vee \beta$
	j	$\neg\alpha$
ASSUMPTION	k	α
ASSUMPTION	l	$\neg\beta$
R k	m	α
R j	n	$\neg\alpha$
¬E l-m, l-n	o	β
ASSUMPTION	p	β
R p	q	β
vE i, k-o, p-q	r	β

Figure 5.34

tails neither of its disjuncts. But the rule DS requires something crucial in addition—the negation of one of the disjuncts. For example, it is true that you will either pass this course on symbolic logic or fail it; that fact, plus the fact that it is false that you will fail the course, enables you to infer confidently that you will pass. Figure 5.34 sets out the reduction of the first form of DS to the rules of SD. We suggest that you try to prove a particular case—an example—of the second form of DS, such as the derivation of A from {A ∨ B, ¬B}, by using only the rules of SD. Then, you may want to attempt to construct a metaproof showing the reducibility of its general form. Before you move on, try to justify the theorems in the derivations SDPLUS01 and SDPLUS02 on your disk by filling in the missing entries in the Justification Field.

The rules which belong specifically to SD+ fall into two different groups. Modus tollens, hypothetical syllogism and disjunctive syllogism form the first group and are deployed exactly like the rules of SD. In the second group are found what we call **rules of replacement**. What distinguishes these latter rules is that they can be applied not only to the entire sentence occupying a line of proof but also to any well-formed part (a subwff) of such a sentence. This application is possible because the replacement is carried out between sentences which are logically equivalent to each other. For example, since the two sentences P → Q and ¬P ∨ Q are logically equivalent, one of them could replace the other in a whole line of proof without changing the logical character of that proof. If ¬P ∨ Q is entailed by a set of premises, so is any sentence logically equivalent to it, such as P → Q. Equally, if R ≡ (¬P ∨ Q) is entailed, then R ≡ (P → Q) would be too. Rules of replacement, therefore, allow for the substitution of logically equivalent sentences in the course of a derivation. You will find them enormously useful. To mark out the rules of replacement distinctly, we will use a special notation. The symbol :: means that any sentence corresponding to the form on the left-hand side can be replaced by a sentence matching its counterpart form on the right-hand side, and vice versa. The example just used is an instance of implication (IM), one of the ten rules of replacement.

Commutation (CM)

$\alpha \mathbin{\&} \beta :: \beta \mathbin{\&} \alpha$
$\alpha \lor \beta :: \beta \lor \alpha$
$\alpha \equiv \beta :: \beta \equiv \alpha$

Association (AS)

$\alpha \mathbin{\&} (\beta \mathbin{\&} \delta) :: (\alpha \mathbin{\&} \beta) \mathbin{\&} \delta$
$\alpha \lor (\beta \lor \delta) :: (\alpha \lor \beta) \lor \delta$
$\alpha \equiv (\beta \equiv \delta) :: (\alpha \equiv \beta) \equiv \delta$

Implication (IM)

$\alpha \to \beta :: \neg \alpha \lor \beta$

Double Negation (DN)[19]

$\alpha :: \neg\neg\alpha$

De Morgan (DM)

$\neg(\alpha \mathbin{\&} \beta) :: \neg\alpha \lor \neg\beta$
$\neg(\alpha \lor \beta) :: \neg\alpha \mathbin{\&} \neg\beta$

Idempotence (ID)

$\alpha :: \alpha \mathbin{\&} \alpha$
$\alpha :: \alpha \lor \alpha$

Transposition (TR)

$\alpha \to \beta :: \neg\beta \to \neg\alpha$

Exportation (EX)

$\alpha \to (\beta \to \delta) :: (\alpha \mathbin{\&} \beta) \to \delta$

Distribution (DI)

$\alpha \mathbin{\&} (\beta \lor \delta) :: (\alpha \mathbin{\&} \beta) \lor (\alpha \mathbin{\&} \delta)$
$\alpha \lor (\beta \mathbin{\&} \delta) :: (\alpha \lor \beta) \mathbin{\&} (\alpha \lor \delta)$

Equivalence (EQ)

$\alpha \equiv \beta :: (\alpha \to \beta) \mathbin{\&} (\beta \to \alpha)$
$\alpha \equiv \beta :: (\alpha \mathbin{\&} \beta) \lor (\neg\alpha \mathbin{\&} \neg\beta)$

To get acquainted with these rules try the following exercises on disk: SDPLUS03 (provides practice with all the rules up to association), SDPLUS04 (up to implication), SDPLUS05 (up to De Morgan), SDPLUS06 (up to idempotence), SDPLUS07 and SDPLUS08 (up to exportation), and SDPLUS09 and SD-PLUS10 (up to equivalence). When solving the exercises you will find the Generation command useful. To see how to apply the rule of commutation, let us suppose you have entered on the screen the sentence (M ≡ E) & (¬G ∨ D) as a premise in line 1. You are now going to apply CM on the sentence in line 1 to obtain the desired sentence (¬G ∨ D) & (M ≡ E). Hence, in line 2, in the Justification Field, type CM 1, and issue the Generation command. This step will allow you to obtain the sentence you want. However, notice that CM works for & and ∨ as well as for ≡ and that in the premise in line 1 there is an &, ∨ and ≡, which means that the resulting generated sentence could be any one of the sentences (E ≡ M) & (¬G ∨ D), (¬G ∨ D) & (M ≡ E) or (M ≡ E) & (D ∨ ¬G). *Symlog* will display them one by one in the Message Line and will ask you which one you want. If you do not choose any of the different possibilities, that is, if you do not answer Y (for 'yes') to any of the choices you are offered, *Symlog* will produce the message MISAPPLICATION OF RULE.

---

[19] If you apply DN to the sentence A by using the Generation command, the only choice *Symlog* gives you is ¬¬A because this is the only sentence that can be generated out of A by one application of DN. However, if your sentence is ¬A, *Symlog* asks you first if you want ¬¬¬A; if you press N (for 'no'), *Symlog* asks you if you then want ¬¬¬A. Now, the question is why should *Symlog* ask you twice about the same sentence. The reason is that the first time *Symlog* is asking you about the sentence resulting from adding ¬¬ to the left of ¬A, whereas the second time the program is asking about the sentence resulting from adding ¬¬ between the connective ¬ and A in ¬A. Although the resulting sentence, ¬¬¬A, is, of course, the same in both cases, *Symlog*'s routine displays the two ways DN can be applied to ¬A.

SD+ : FREGE		
PREMISE	1	$(R \lor \neg M) \to \neg J$
PREMISE	2	$J \& (R \lor S)$
PREMISE	3	$(J \lor S) \to (S \& J)$
TR 1	4	$\neg\neg J \to \neg(R \lor \neg M)$
DN 4	5	$J \to \neg(R \lor \neg M)$
&EL 2	6	J
→E 5, 6	7	$\neg(R \lor \neg M)$
DM 7	8	$\neg R \& \neg\neg M$
DN 8	9	$\neg R \& M$
&ER 9	10	M
IM 3	11	$\neg(J \lor S) \lor (S \& J)$
DM 11	12	$(\neg J \& \neg S) \lor (S \& J)$
CM 12	13	$(S \& J) \lor (\neg J \& \neg S)$
CM 13	14	$(S \& J) \lor (\neg S \& \neg J)$
EQ 14	15	$S \equiv J$
≡E 6, 15	16	S
&I 16,10	17	$S \& M$
	18	

Figure 5.35

Before we start discussing strategies for proof construction in SD+, we recommend that you study the derivation in Figure 5.35, which illustrates how several of the rules of SD+ are applied. Note that several of the rules are applied not only to entire wffs but also to subwffs.

Having a larger set of rules to work with certainly expedites proof making, yet it may also appear to complicate the strategies needed to use them. We offer some advice. The basic principle to follow is this: Plan your strategy in terms of the rules of SD; if a shortcut can be found by using a rule of SD+, by all means take it. To illustrate, if your goal α is of the form $\neg\neg\beta$, it would make sense to consider using double negation if you can easily derive β. Or if α is of the form $\neg(\beta \lor \delta)$, it is wise to consider the rule De Morgan if $\neg\alpha$ and $\neg\beta$ can be easily derived. Also keep in mind that the rules of SD+ can often provide great savings because they can be applied to the subwffs of a wff, which is not true of the rules of SD. For instance, from $R \to (P \to Q)$ you can get $R \to (\neg P \lor Q)$ by one single application of implication; it is not obvious how you could derive this result by the sole use of SD rules.

Since SD+ is an extension of SD, all the formal concepts of SD, such as SD-derivability, SD-inconsistency, SD-validity and so on, naturally extend to SD+. The formal definitions of these concepts, which will not be paraphrased here, can be obtained simply by replacing the term 'SD' with 'SD+' in any of the SD definitions.

Now that we have introduced the rules, let us reconsider an important question: Why these rules and not others? Can I design a deduction system of my own and introduce any rules I please? This answer is, of course, yes.

But, given that one can arbitrarily design new deductive systems of logic, you may now be wondering what makes one system better than another. The two fundamental requirements for any set of natural deduction rules are that the set should (1) preserve truth-functional validity and (2) capture all the truth-functionally valid arguments. Derivation systems meeting these two requirements would be considered, for our purposes, equally good. That SD and SD+ are adequate in this sense is revealed in their metatheory. To this topic we now turn for a brief discussion.

Exercises

5.5.1   Answer true or false (but not both) to each of the following questions.
  a. There is a sentence which is an SD+-theorem of Γ but not an SD-theorem of Γ for some set Γ.
  b. There is a sentence which is an SD-theorem of Γ but not an SD+-theorem of Γ for some set Γ.
  c. If Γ is a set of premises then Γ has infinitely many SD+-theorems.
  d. If Γ is SD+-inconsistent, then its set of SD+-theorems is no other than SL itself.
  e. If Γ is SD+-consistent, then there is a sentence which is not an SD+-theorem of Γ.
  f. If α is a sentence of SL, then $\neg\alpha$ is not SD+-derivable from the empty set, $\varnothing$.
  g. If $\Gamma \vdash_{\text{SD+}} \alpha$, then $\Gamma \cup \{\neg\alpha\} \vdash_{\text{SD+}} \beta$, for any β.
  h. If $\neg\alpha$ is an SD+-theorem of Γ, then α is not.

5.5.2   Using *Symlog* show that the given sentence is SD+-derivable from the corresponding set.
[PR61] a. $\{(A \rightarrow \neg B) \,\&\, H, (\neg F \rightarrow \neg E) \,\&\, (A \equiv H), (\neg A \vee \neg B) \rightarrow \neg F\}, \neg E \vee G$
[PR62] b. $\{\neg I \,\&\, \neg J, [L \,\&\, (H \vee \neg G)] \,\&\, M, (G \,\&\, H) \rightarrow I\}, (K \vee \neg G) \,\&\, L$
[PR63] c. $\{(N\&H) \rightarrow (I\&\neg L), M \rightarrow (J\rightarrow I), \neg I \vee (M\&J), (J\rightarrow L) \,\&\, N\}, H \rightarrow S$
  d. $\varnothing, (A \rightarrow C) \vee A$
  e. $\{\neg(T \vee \neg M), (S \vee M) \rightarrow \neg(A \,\&\, B)\}, (A \,\&\, B) \rightarrow (D \equiv \neg A)$
  f. $\{(D \vee S) \equiv \neg\neg M\}, (M \vee \neg S) \,\&\, (\neg D \vee M)$
[PR64] g. $\{(C \rightarrow A) \,\&\, (A \rightarrow B), [(C \,\&\, A) \,\&\, B] \vee (C \vee \neg B)\}, (C \,\&\, B) \vee \neg(B \vee C)$
[PR65] h. $\{I \rightarrow (T \vee B), (T \rightarrow E) \,\&\, (T \rightarrow D), G \vee \neg D\}, (\neg B \,\&\, I) \rightarrow (G \,\&\, E)$
[PR66] i. $\{D \rightarrow G, (H \rightarrow R) \equiv M, H \rightarrow D, \neg G \vee (R \,\&\, H)\}, (M \,\&\, \neg D) \vee (G \,\&\, \neg\neg M)$
[PR67] j. $\{\neg(F \,\&\, L), (L \,\&\, K) \rightarrow F\}, (F \equiv K) \vee \neg L$

5.5.3   Show with *Symlog* that each sentence below is an SD+-theorem of the corresponding set.
  a. $C \rightarrow G, \{[\neg(A \,\&\, C) \vee D] \,\&\, \neg F, \neg(A \rightarrow D) \vee (F \,\&\, B), \neg D\}$
  b. $K, \{(C \,\&\, J) \vee (C \,\&\, A), A \rightarrow \neg(A \equiv C), (L \vee A) \,\&\, \neg L\}$
  c. $(A \,\&\, \neg B) \rightarrow C, \{\neg(A \rightarrow B) \rightarrow C\}$
[PR68] d. $[(A \equiv B) \,\&\, (B \vee M)] \,\&\, (B \vee R), \{\neg\neg A \,\&\, \neg G, A \rightarrow \neg\neg B\}$

    e. R, {¬P → Q, Q → R, ¬(P ∨ R)}

    f. A ≡ ¬¬A, Ø

    g. (S ∨ M) ≡ ¬(¬S & ¬M), Ø

    h. P → ¬(S ∨ ¬R), {¬(P & ¬Q), ¬Q ∨ R, S → ¬R}

    i. P, {(Q → R) → Q, (Q ∨ R) → P}

    j. (Q ∨ R) → ¬(Q ∨ S), {¬[(P ∨ Q) ∨ (R & S)]}

5.5.4 Using *Symlog,* show that the following sets are SD+-inconsistent.

    a. {¬[A & (C ≡ A)], (A & ¬L) ∨ (L & ¬L), (C & I) ∨ (A & C)}

    b. {A → (B ∨ C), (C ∨ B) ≡ ¬(R ∨ G), (G ∨ G) & ¬¬A}

    c. {¬¬¬K → ¬N, ¬¬E & N, E ≡ ¬(K ∨ T)}

    d. {(S → ¬S) ≡ (¬S → S)}

[PR69] e. {(A & B) ∨ (¬B & ¬A), ¬(¬A ∨ M), (M ∨ ¬B) & (A ∨ M)} [Hint: Derive B and ¬B.]

    f. {[(K ∨ M) & [[Q ≡ (¬K & ¬M)] & S]] & Q}

    g. {¬D → ¬(B → C), C ∨ (E ≡ N), (N → ¬B) & (E & ¬D)} [Hint: Derive N and ¬N.]

    h. {(H ∨ G), (K ∨ ¬I) & (¬H ∨ K), (¬K & I) ∨ ¬(H ∨ G)}

    i. {(C ∨ ¬B) → D, (B → C) & ¬D}

    j. {(H ∨ ¬D) ≡ ¬E, C → E, B & ¬D, (D ∨ C) ≡ B}

5.5.5 Use the test for derivability to show, using *Symlog,* that the given sentence is SD+-derivable from the corresponding set.

[PR70] a. {¬(¬R ∨ ¬A), D & E, ¬(E & ¬O) ∨ ¬A}, O

    b. {¬E ∨ N, S ≡ (¬N & A), ¬¬S}, ¬E

    c. {¬(O & G), (¬K ≡ M) & (¬P → Q)}, ¬(G & O) & (¬P → Q)

    d. {M ≡ (¬K → ¬M), ¬¬G → ¬K}, ¬((M & G) & ¬J)

    e. Ø, (A ≡ (B ≡ C)) ≡ ((A ≡ B) ≡ C)

5.5.6 Show with *Symlog* that the following arguments are SD+-valid.

[PR71] a. A ≡ B

       (B ∨ D) ≡ ¬[¬G & (B ≡ C)]

       ―――――――――――――――――

       [A & (B ≡ C)] → (G ∨ R)

    b. ¬A ∨ B

       C ∨ ¬B.

       ¬C ∨ D

       E ∨ ¬D

       ――――――

       ¬A ∨ E

    c. (¬T → H) & (H → ¬¬¬T)

       ¬N

       ¬¬H

       ――――――――――――――

       (B & C) → ¬(T ∨ N)

    d. ¬(O ∨ ¬I)

       ¬I → N

       ¬N ∨ ¬I

       ―――――――――――――――

       C → [D → (¬N & ¬O)]

e. $[\neg A \lor \neg(B \lor C)] \equiv (F \equiv G)$
   G & F
   ————————————————
   $\neg[(A \& B) \lor (C \& A)]$

[PR72] f. $P \to Q$
   $R \to P$
   ————————————————
   $[(P \& Q) \to P] \equiv [(P \& R) \lor (\neg R \& \neg P)]$

g. $\neg(P \equiv P)$
   ————————————————
   Q

h. $(A \& \neg G) \lor (\neg G \& S)$
   $(\neg S \lor G) \& R$
   ————————————————
   $(\neg\neg H \lor \neg\neg A) \lor \neg M$

[PR73] i. $\neg A \lor [\neg B \lor (B \& D)]$
   $\neg B \lor [(\neg D \lor A) \& (B \lor \neg D)]$
   ————————————————
   $(A \& B) \equiv (B \& D)$

j. $\neg B \to \neg A$
   $\neg C \lor \neg\neg D$
   $\neg C \to \neg\neg\neg B$
   $D \to E$
   ————————————————
   $E \lor \neg A$

5.5.7   Show with *Symlog* that the sentences in each of the following pairs are SD+-equivalent.

a. $\neg(\neg M \lor K)$ and $\neg K \& M$

b. $P \to (Q \to P)$ and $(\neg P \lor P) \lor \neg Q$

c. $\neg A \to (\neg B \lor C)$ and $(A \lor \neg B) \lor \neg\neg C$

d. $(\neg M \lor \neg\neg R) \& (\neg S \lor \neg M)$ and $M \to \neg(R \to S)$

e. $\neg(A \equiv B)$ and $(\neg\neg A \& \neg B) \lor \neg(\neg B \lor A)$

f. $(H \lor \neg K) \& (\neg\neg\neg H \lor \neg\neg K)$ and $K \equiv H$

g. $(\neg\neg M \lor R) \& (R \lor \neg\neg S)$ and $\neg(S \to \neg M) \lor R$

h. $\neg K \to \neg(G \to E)$ and $\neg(\neg E \& G) \to \neg\neg K$

i. $\neg(\neg F \lor \neg D) \to E$ and $\neg(D \to E) \to \neg F$

j. $(\neg S \& \neg A) \lor (\neg\neg K \& \neg S)$ and $\neg[S \lor \neg(A \to K)]$

5.5.8   Translate the following statements into SL and show, using *Symlog*, that the conclusion is SD+-derivable from the premises.

[PR74] a. Either David and Robert will attend the meeting scheduled next week or neither of them will because if David attends the meeting, then Albert will have a great deal to say against the company's current policy on hiring practices. Also, if Robert is not there, then Albert will be quiet. And yet, either David and Robert will attend the meeting and Albert will have a great deal to say, or either David will attend or Robert won't. (D, R, A)

b. The goverment will not fund both space exploration and the development of new strategic nuclear weapons. But if the goverment provides funding for either the development of new strategic nuclear weapons or basic research on massively parallel computer technology, then it will fund space exploration as well. It inexorably follows that there will be funding for space exploration just in case there is funding for basic research on massively parallel computer technology, or there just won't be any funding for the development of strategic nuclear weapons. (S, N, B)

[PR75] c. It is not the case that either the experiment involving human subjects will go unnoticed or that the public image of the research institution will not suffer. Although an official comission is looking into the matter, the scientists feel confident that the experiment will work. Yet, either it is not the case that both the scientists feel confident about the success of the experiment and that funding for it will stop or that the public image of the institute will not suffer. Hence, funding for the experiment will not stop. (E, P, O, S, F)

d. Many animal species will become extinct in a short period of time unless there is enough public awareness. Goverments will not do anything about it if and only if there is not enough public awareness and there is mutual support from other goverments. Goverments will not do antything about it. Hence, many species will become extinct. (E, P, G, M)

e. Lisa didn't order the coffee unless John did. If Ted didn't ask for the Coke then John didn't order the coffee. But if Ted did ask for the Coke then David did too. Moreover, Paul didn't ask for the tea only if David didn't order the Coke. Hence, either Lisa didn't order the coffee or Paul asked for the tea. (L, J, T, D, P)

5.5.9 Translate the following statements into SL and show, using *Symlog*, that they form an SD+-inconsistent set.

a. Carol will graduate in logic and pursue graduate studies in the foundations of mathematics or in complexity theory. Carol will pursue her graduate studies in the foundations of mathematics unless Sam helps her. But Sam won't help her. Carol won't do any graduate work in the foundations of mathematics or it is not the case that she will do so if and only if she graduates in logic. (L, F, C, S) [Hint: Derive $\neg(F \equiv L)$ and $F \equiv L$.]

[PR76] b. Either my computer's keyboard is working or both the printer is but not the monitor screen. If the monitor screen is not working properly then my floppy disk is damaged if and only if the disk drive is. And when the disk drive is damaged so is the printer. The floppy disk is damaged and the keyboard is not working properly. (K, P, M, F, D)

c. I'll become a lawyer and either I will specialize in computer law or run for president. I will do both; namely, I will specialize in computer law and run for president; or I will neither specialize in computer law nor run for the presidency. I will not do both, however, become a lawyer and run for the presidency. (L, S, R)

[PR77] d. It is not the case that both the expedition was a success and that it reached the Kilimanjaro if and only if it was a success. Although everybody perished in the quest the expedition was still a success.

Either the expedition reached the Kilimanjaro and the supplies didn't last or it reached the Kilimanjaro and, above all, it was a success. (S, K, P, L) [Hint: Derive ¬(K ≡ S) and K ≡ S.]

e. If it rains we go to the movies and if it doesn't rain we will still go to the movies. Either it rains or we don't go to the movies. Moreover, either it doesn't rain or we don't go to the movies. (R, M)

5.5.10 Translate the following arguments into SL and show, using *Symlog*, that they are SD+-valid.

a. If you either understand Russell's writings or not Moore's then you don't understand Frege's. But you understand Frege's writings and either Russell's or Ayer's. If you understand either Frege's or Wittgenstein's then you understand them both. Therefore, you understand both Wittgenstein's and Moore's. (R, M, F, A, T)

b. You either don't know how to solve this problem, or if you study hard, you'll know how to solve it. Hence, if you study hard, you'll know how to solve it or you won't. (S, H)

[PR78] c. It is neither the case that Peter and Mary are going to Paris nor that Robert and Silvia are. So, it is not the case that either Peter or both Peter and Silvia are going to Paris or that if Mary or Robert is then neither Mary nor Silvia is. (P, M, R, S)

[PR79] d. Einstein, Bohr and Heisenberg were great physicists. If either Schrödinger or Heisenberg was a great physicist, then not both Bohr and Einstein were. Hence, deBroglie was a great physicist if and only if Einstein was not. (E, B, H, S, D)

e. Neither squares have three sides nor triangles have four. If squares don't have three sides then triangles have four. Therefore, french fries with ketchup taste better. (S, T, F)

5.5.11 To appreciate the practical value of the new rules of SD+ which are not part of SD, use *Symlog* to derive the sentence (A ≡ B) ≡ C from {A ≡ (B ≡ C)} by (a) using the rules of SD+ and (b) using only the rules of SD [PR80].

5.5.12 Use the Create option under *Symlog*'s File menu to ask the program to generate (randomly) SD+-valid arguments whose derivations you should then construct. Submit your work when done. (You may want to solve them in SD too and compare the lengths of the SD+ proofs with their SD counterparts.)

5.6   *Metatheory of SD and SD+*

The sentence

A → B

is a sentence of SL. Since SL supplies the language for the derivation system SD, we say that A → B is a sentence *in* SD. Hence, by the same token, P & Q, (Q ∨ M) ≡ ¬S and R → ¬(S ∨ ¬P) are all sentences in SD. This fact is to be contrasted with the following statement:

P → P can be derived from ∅ in fewer than five steps.

This is not only a statement in English (with some logicalese) but also a statement *about* SD, that is, about some specific feature of the derivation system SD. Statements of this type are said to belong to the metatheory of SD. The **metatheory** of a system of logic provides a theoretical account of the system's essential properties. Among other things, the metatheory of SD tells us which sentences can be derived by using the rules of the system and which cannot, whether for instance it is a futile task attempting to derive some particular sentence from a given set of premises and so on. One of the aims of metatheory is to settle such specific matters, but there are also more general and comprehensive aims. The metatheory of SD contains two all-important results, known as the completeness theorem and the soundness theorem, which we will briefly describe.[20]

The completeness theorem says that if a set of sentences, Γ, truth-functionally entails a sentence, α, then α can be derived from Γ by means of the rules of SD. Consider for a moment what this statement means. Previous chapters have set out decision procedures for SL by which to identify cases of entailment. The completeness theorem tells us that any case of entailment—any valid argument—is also provable in SD. Similarly, any logical truth of SL is derivable from ∅ in SD. The syntactical rules of SD, then, are powerful enough to capture these familiar semantical notions (and it goes without saying that the same holds for the rules of SD+). The relationship between them is summarized in this way:

The Completeness Theorem. If $\Gamma \vDash \alpha$ then $\Gamma \vdash_{SD} \alpha$.

Now, what about the converse of this statement? Would it be possible in SD to derive some sentence α from Γ which nevertheless is not entailed by Γ? If so, the test set, $\Gamma \cup \{\neg\alpha\}$, would not be (truth-functionally) inconsistent. Or suppose that a set of derivation rules was so powerful that some pair of sentences, α and ¬α, could be derived from any given set of premises Γ, so that in effect any sentence whatever could be derived from Γ by using reductio ad absurdum. Such a set of rules would be much too complete: Nothing would be excluded. Hardly better would be a less powerful set of rules which allowed the derivation of (just) contingent sentences from the empty set. The soundness theorem of SD provides the right degree of completeness. It assures us that the rules of SD are truth-preserving, that is, that any sentence α which can be derived from a set Γ by means of those rules is truth-functionally entailed by Γ.

The Soundness Theorem. If $\Gamma \vdash_{SD} \alpha$ then $\Gamma \vDash \alpha$.

[20] It is one of the tasks of metatheory, which is not covered in this text, to establish such results.

Together, the completeness and soundness theorems establish that the formal concepts defined semantically (in terms of truth-tables) for SL coincide exactly with those defined syntactically (in terms of derivations) for SD. Thus, any set of sentences of SL which is truth-functionally consistent is SD-consistent also, and vice versa; any sentence which is SD-derivable from the empty set is logically true, and vice versa; and so on.

You can put the completeness and soundness theorems to work as follows: Suppose that you want to derive a sentence α of SL from a set Γ of premises. You know that the sentence α can be derived from Γ if and only if the argument with Γ as its set of premises and α as its conclusion is SD-valid. Since, by the completeness and soundness theorems, an argument of sentences of SL is SD-valid if and only if it is truth-functionally valid, to know whether α can be derived at all from Γ it is enough to construct a truth-table (or even better, a short truth-table or a truth-tree) to find out whether the argument is truth-functionally valid or invalid. If it turns out to be truth-functionally valid, you immediately know that it is SD-valid and that, hence, the sentence α can be derived from Γ in SD. If it turns out to be truth-functionally invalid, you know at once that the argument is SD-invalid and that α cannot be derived from Γ, so that you will not even have to bother attempting the construction of such a derivation, for it cannot be done. To illustrate, the sentence P *cannot* be derived from the set $\{P \lor Q, \neg Q \equiv P\}$ since there is a truth-value assignment—F to P and T to Q—which satisfies both $P \lor Q$ and $\neg Q \equiv P$ but not P. This fact, by the way, shows the SD-consistency of $\{P \lor Q, \neg Q \equiv P\}$. As you can see, a purely theoretical result can have great practical advantages. Of course, these metatheorems will not tell you how to construct a proof when you encounter a difficult case; the experience you gain by constructing derivations with *Symlog* will.

Exercises

5.6.1   Suppose that the $\lor$-elimination rule of SD is replaced by a new rule to eliminate disjuncts ($\lor$E') which takes the following two forms:

$\lor$E' i	i	$\alpha \lor \beta$		$\lor$E' i	i	$\alpha \lor \beta$
	j	α			j	β

a. Show that in this new derivation system thus obtained, call it SD*, every set turns out to be SD*-inconsistent.

b. Show that if we introduce in SD a rule to capture the following inference pattern

$\alpha \rightarrow \beta$
$\underline{\neg \alpha}$
$\neg \beta$

then any set Γ turns out to be SD*-inconsistent (SD* is the new system obtained by adding to SD this new rule of inference).

5.6.2   A rule $\mathfrak{R}$ in a deduction system Ω is **dispensable**, or **reducible**, if and only if any Ω-theorem of Γ is a $(\Omega - \mathfrak{R})$-theorem of Γ, where $\Omega - \mathfrak{R}$ is the deduction system Ω with the rule $\mathfrak{R}$ removed from it. (Intuitively, this definition says that any derivation that is constructed by using the rule $\mathfrak{R}$ can be constructed without it.) Show the following:

a. Reiteration is dispensable in SD

b. $\neg$-introduction is also dispensable in SD

c. If we add commutation to SD then &ER becomes dispensable.

5.6.3   (a) Show that association (for &), as it applies to entire sentences, is reducible to rules of SD (see 5.6.2). Do the same for (b) transposition, (c) exportation and (d) implication.

5.6.4   Let SD* be the new deduction system obtained by adding to SD the following new rule:

EX i	i	$\alpha \rightarrow (\beta \rightarrow \delta)$
	j	$(\alpha \, \& \, \beta) \rightarrow \delta$

Is there an SD*-theorem of Γ which is not an SD-theorem of Γ?

5.6.5   Show that if to SD we were to add the new rule (thereby obtaining the new derivation system SD*),

DS i, j	i	$\alpha \vee \beta$
	j	$\neg \alpha$
	k	β

then for any Γ, (a) if α is an SD-theorem of Γ then α is also an SD*-theorem of Γ, and (b) if α is an SD*-theorem of Γ then α is also an SD-theorem of Γ.

5.6.6   Answer true or false (but not both) to each of the following.

a. Any set which is truth-functionally consistent is also SD-consistent.

b. Any set which is SD-consistent is also truth-functionally consistent.

c. If α is a sentence of SL that is truth-functionally true then α is an SD-theorem of Γ, regardless of the sentences in Γ.

d. If Γ is SD-consistent, then all truth-functionally true sentences of SL are SD-theorems of Γ.

e. There is a set whose SD-theorems are precisely the contingent sentences of SL.

f. If there is a sentence which is not an SD+-theorem of Γ then Γ is SD+-consistent.

g. There is a set Γ which has no SD-theorems.

h. If SL is the set of SD+-theorems of Γ then Γ must be SD+-inconsistent.

i. If $\Gamma \vdash_{\overline{SD}} P \lor (R \rightarrow \neg Q)$ then $\Gamma \vdash_{\overline{SD}} P \lor (\neg R \lor \neg Q)$.

j. The rule of De Morgan is dispensable in SD+.

5.6.7 Use the soundness theorem to show (a) that the sentence R is not SD-derivable from the set $\{P \lor R, \neg Q \And P\}$—(Hint: If not $\Gamma \vDash \alpha$ then not $\Gamma \vdash_{\overline{SD}} \alpha$)—and (b) that the sentence M is not SD+-derivable from the set $\{M \equiv K, \neg K \And \neg M\}$.

5.6.8 Answer true or false (but not both) and explain why to each of the following.

a. $P \rightarrow P$ is SD-derivable from $\varnothing$ in more than five steps.

b. If $\varnothing \vDash \alpha$ then $\Gamma \vdash_{\overline{SD}} \alpha$.

c. If there is a truth-value assignment which satisfies Γ but not α, then α is not derivable from Γ.

d. Let SD* be SD+ with the rule HS removed, and let Γ be the set $\{A \rightarrow B, B \rightarrow C\}$. Then there is a sentence α such that α is SD+-derivable from Γ but is not SD*-derivable from Γ.

e. There is a derivation (in SD+) of P & Q from $\{P, Q\}$ of precisely seven steps.

f. If $\Gamma \vDash \alpha$ then $\Gamma \vdash_{\overline{SD+}} \alpha$, and if $\Gamma \vdash_{\overline{SD+}} \alpha$ then $\Gamma \vDash \alpha$.

5.6.9 Show that if the empty set, $\varnothing$, is SD-inconsistent so is every set.

5.6.10 Show that the empty set is SD-consistent.

5.6.11 SD-Popper is just like SD with a new SL connective (called Prior's *tonk*) defined by the following introduction-elimination rules: From α you can derive α *tonk* β, and from α *tonk* β you can derive β. Show that any set Γ becomes inconsistent in SD-Popper.

6

The Basic Sentences of PL

In this chapter we shall extend the language of SL to a new domain. We are going to analyze the structure of those statements which, until now, have been represented by capital letters like A, B, C, P, Q and R, the so-called simple statements. In SL, any statement which cannot be classified as one of the five compounds counts as simple; but now we are going to see that it is possible to pick out different types of structure among these simple statements and that it is logically important to do so. The name given to this extension of SL is PL (standing for 'predicate logic' or 'predicate language'). Think of PL as an enrichment of the logic that you have already learned in the preceding chapters: a formal language that shares SL's goal to provide an account of arguments measured by the standards of deductive logic, only better equipped to handle a wider range of cases. To get an idea of why this language is desirable, consider the following little argument:

Number 2 is even; therefore, at least one number is even.

Logical intuition prompts us to call this a valid argument. So it is—in PL. However, a quick check will show that in SL it is truth-functionally *in-*

valid.[1] Its validity *in PL* depends on details of statements not investigated in truth-functional logic.

Many of the ingredients of SL are carried over to PL. You will recognize at once a number of structural details, such as the five statement compounds—negations, conjunctions, disjunctions, conditionals and biconditionals—as well as familiar semantic concepts like logical truth, consistency and validity. Nevertheless, much will seem rather new, not only because of the way in which PL analyzes the simple statements of SL, but also because the tools needed for this analysis have to be introduced first. The purpose of the next few sections is to fashion tools for representing what will be called the basic statements of PL and then to use them for translating both basic and compound sentences from ordinary language into PL (and back). The final section of the chapter will discuss the semantics of PL in a way that parallels as much as possible what was presented earlier for SL. The chapter as a whole is designed as a self-contained unit which will prepare you to master predicate logic by means of *Symlog*.

6.1   Referring and Describing

SL is packed with information about statements. It tells us how to form compound statements from simple ones, how to classify compounds and determine their truth-values and how to find out whether one or more statements entail another. Yet SL says nothing about the structure of simple statements. It is designed to use simple statements rather than to analyze them. In the eyes of SL, all the following statements are reckoned as simple:

(1) Caesar was ambitious.
(2) Anne and Bob are married.
(3) Some computers are smarter than humans.
(4) All zoo animals should be liberated.

But viewed on their own, apart from SL, these statements seem very dissimilar. The first two examples name particular individuals; the other two refer to groups of things (computers and zoo animals) without mentioning any individual by name. Sentence (3) makes a claim only about some of the things which are computers, and (4) is meant to apply to every zoo animal. Are such differences logically important? An example will help show that they are.

---

[1] To see this assertion, consider the symbolization

N : number 2 is even
L : at least one number is even

Note now that a truth-value assignment which assigns T to N and F to L makes the premise of the argument T while making the conclusion F, hence rendering the argument truth-functionally invalid.

Suppose for a moment that your favorite zoo animal is Hortense the hippo, a placid, middle-aged hippopotamus who spends her day sleeping, wallowing, rubbing against her offspring and eating what looks like garbage. Her behavior never shows any restlessness, which inclines you to believe that although Hortense is confined to a pen she is quite content. Suppose, however, that you become a committed animal rights advocate who proclaims that all zoo animals should be liberated. In that case, you have a logical problem on your hands. You would have to recognize that Hortense should be liberated too, for this act is entailed by sentence (4). However, if you make an exception for Hortense, you cannot hold that all zoo animals should be liberated. It would be self-contradictory to assert both that all of them and that not all of them should be liberated. This example reminds us that simple statements in SL sometimes fail to be logically independent;[2] it also suggests the possibility of systematic connections. If (4) is true, it applies truly to any zoo animal you can name (Pete the python, Olive the ostrich, Gregor the gorilla, etc.); indeed it applies to every individual zoo animal, including those which the keepers have never named.

PL explores systematic connections like these. The job requires close attention to the form or structure of statements, beginning with those—like the four examples above—which are not truth-functional compounds. This job is best handled in separate steps that explore the different forms of statements which are basic to PL.

Atomic Statements

The first two statements listed above single out particular things: sentence (1) mentions Caesar; (2) refers to Bob and Anne. Both count in PL as atomic statements. We will take a few moments to examine their structure.

Proper names like 'Caesar' and 'Anne' are a familiar way of picking out or directing attention to individuals. The examples used so far happen to be names of people or of zoo animals, but it is easy to judge from the following examples that anything whatever could be given its own special name:

The Matterhorn
London
Haley's Comet
Panama
π
The Hope diamond
Mahler's Second Symphony
The Eiffel Tower

[2] See Chapter 3.

Although proper names play a much wider role in ordinary language (e.g., to call a person by name), PL is concerned with them only to the extent that they are used in statements to refer to individuals. When they have this role they are called **referring expressions** and the individuals are called **objects of reference**. Statements such as (1) and (2) will be called **atomic statements**.

There are many other expressions in ordinary language which play the very same role that proper names do. Here are the main types, with some illustrations:

(1) *Pronouns*. Expressions like 'he,' 'she,' 'it' and 'they' often substitute for proper names and are meant to single out the same individuals, as in the following pair of examples:

Caesar wanted to be perpetual dictator of Rome; *he* was ambitious.

Bob and Anne are married; *he* likes to stay at home playing computer games, while *she* spends a lot of time at the zoo. *They* seem happy, all the same.

Just as often, pronouns are used to refer to things which have no proper name at all or whose name is not known. You can talk about a particular tree you see during a walk and may even be able to identify what kind of tree it is, but unless you have some special need to give it a name the pronoun 'it' will do nicely.

(2) *Demonstratives*. Expressions like 'this' serve to single out an object of reference, frequently one which is on hand to be pointed out:

This is the bottle of wine which I brought but *that one* is what she brought.

Here is the spot where the assailant waited.

Will Anne attempt to liberate Hortense the hippo? *That* is a question which deeply troubled Bob.

(3) *Definite descriptions*.[3] Objects of reference can often be identified by descriptive language. For instance, suppose you are in a store that sells wristwatches and want to see a particular model that has caught your interest. You do not know its name and you cannot get close enough to single it out by pointing because there are too many others nearby. And of course the watch is behind glass, which prevents you from reaching for it. You could try describing the watch to the salesperson in enough detail that only one

---

[3] The designation 'definite description' is somewhat awkward but is used here because it has become well established in formal logic. Initially, PL assigns definite descriptions to the category of names, but later a different analysis will be suggested.

watch in the display case fits the description, such as

> I would like to see the black watch with all the dials and the red and
> yellow hands.
>
> I would like to see the watch in the second row from the front on my
> left-hand side between the two silver ones.

Definite descriptions begin with the word 'the' followed by details, such as the kind of thing in question plus the mention of enough character- istics to help distinguish it from others of the same kind.[4] The use of 'the' is meant to convey uniqueness: Only one object is meant to answer the de- scription when it is given. Definite descriptions are rarely too precise; more often, they fail to contain sufficient detail to enable the hearer to identify the intended object. That, however, is a problem of communication between speakers which does not concern us here. The definite descriptions which PL uses are always assumed to be successful.

(4) *Plural names.* Giving special names to groups of things and treating the groups themselves as objects of reference are common practices in lan- guage. Think for a moment of the names of certain geographic regions ('United States', 'Canary Islands'), teams ('Blue Jays', 'Buffalo Bills'), or- chestras, rock groups, committees, clubs and religious denominations. They are proper names of groups. No matter that the members of such groups all have their own proper names and could be referred to separately, they share a different identity in the group itself and are not distinguished from one another by the use of a plural name. Some examples follow:

> The Ethics Committee has received numerous complaints about sexual
> harassment.
>
> The Baptists are holding a big convention in town this year.
>
> The Rolling Stones will never stop.
>
> The Blue Jays and Boston are playing a doubleheader next Sunday.
>
> The Hilbert hotel chain can accomodate a denumerably infinite num-
> ber of guests.

The five categories just listed—from proper names to plural names— are intended to help you recognize when a word or phrase occurs as a refer- ring expression. Though differing in some ways, they all function in the same fashion and for this reason are classified as **names**. Whatever form they take, names are one essential component of the atomic statements of PL, but it is obvious that atomic statements must consist of more than just names. 'Caesar' by itself says nothing that is either true or false; 'Anne and Bob' is just a pairing of proper names. Atomic statements remain incom-

---

[4] Not all expressions beginning with 'the' are definite descriptions, but the task of sorting out different varieties and describing their various uses in language does not belong to formal logic. In PL, the main concern is whether any such expression is being used as a name.

plete until something is said about their objects of reference (e.g., Caesar *was ambitious*; Anne and Bob *are married*). What is said about the objects of reference forms the other major component in an atomic statement. In the terminology of logic this is called a **predicate** or **relation**. In atomic statements, predicates describe the objects of reference.

The easiest way of locating the predicate in an atomic statement is to remove the names or, better still, to replace them by a marked space or by a letter such as *N* (which stands for a name). Here are both methods applied to our two familiar examples:

_____ was ambitious.

N was ambitious.

_____ and _____ are married.

N and *N* are married.

Relations standing alone (e.g., *being ambitious*, or *being married*), like isolated names, are neither true nor false. They become atomic statements by being joined with names, with the relation or predicate acting as a kind of force that binds the names into an intelligible unit. In every atomic statement there can be just one predicate, but there may be any (finite) number of names. To illustrate, the atomic statement '2 is less than 5' contains two names, '2' and '5,' and one predicate, 'less than.' If there is just one name, as in 'Caesar was ambitious,' the predicate is called in logic a one-place predicate; if two, it is known as a two-place predicate and so on. In general, if the predicate relates *k* names it is known as a ***k*-place predicate**. The names (or 'places') can be proper names or demonstratives or any of the other sorts previously described, and they can be used more than once in a given statement. The following examples, in which names are replaced by a marked space, will help make these details clear:

John is happy.

_____ is happy. (one-place)

I would like to see the black watch with all the dials and the red and yellow hands.

I would like to see _____ . (one-place)

That is a question which deeply troubled Bob.

_____ is a question which deeply troubled Bob. (one-place)

Bob is married to the woman who liberated Hortense the hippo.

_____ is married to _____ . (two-place)

2 is less than 5.

_____ is less than _____ . (two-place)

The place where Henry's assailant was waiting has been thoroughly examined by the police forensic team.

_____ has been thoroughly examined by _____ . (two-place)

The Blue Jays beat Boston in the second game of a doubleheader.

_____ beat _____ in the second game of a doubleheader. (two-place)

The Blue Jays beat Boston in the second game of a doubleheader that took place in Fenway Park.

_____ beat _____ in the second game of a doubleheader that took place in _____ . (three-place)

Caesar loved himself more than Brutus.

_____ loved _____ more than _____ . (three-place)

I give this ring to you as a memento of Grandmother.

_____ give _____ to _____ as a memento of _____ . (four-place)

You may have noticed that the phrase 'the second game of a doubleheader that took place in Fenway Park' was treated as part of a predicate rather than as a definite description. The reason is that this phrase would apply to many games played in Fenway Park, not just a single game, whereas a successful definite description would pick out one and only one ballgame played there. Admittedly, a sharp line cannot always be drawn. For 'the police forensic team' to be successful as a definite description, it is necessary to assume that there is only one object of reference, and since examples usually omit any mention of the context of a statement, the role of such phrases may sometimes be unclear. Therefore, to avoid ambiguity, the exercises will always indicate how many 'places' belong to a given predicate.

Quantificational Statements

So far, names have been our guide for identifying things. But many sentences manage to talk about things without using any proper name (or equivalent) at all. Two such examples were given earlier:

(3) Some computers are smarter than humans.

(4) All zoo animals should be liberated.

Despite the absence of names,[5] it is easy to detect a similarity between these and the various examples containing names. Sentence (3) is about computers and human beings, (4) about zoo animals. Specifically, the former is about an indefinite number of things which are computers, though not all such things, and also about any human being,[6] whereas the latter is about every zoo animal. The referring expressions in these statements, then, are

---

[5] If you are still not convinced, because of the presence of the phrases 'computers' and 'zoo animals,' that these sentences lack names, consider 'someone is happy' or 'nobody is alive.'

[6] Note that the use of 'all' before the word 'humans' in sentence (3) is implicit. This type of case will be discussed in a moment.

'some computers,' 'humans' and 'all zoo animals.' They apply to collections or groups of things but are not plural names because their role is not to pick out individuals. Nevertheless, when these phrases have been replaced by marked spaces, what remains are predicates:

> _____ are smarter than _____ .
> _____ should be liberated.

Atomic statements could be formed from these phrases by filling in the blanks with names. In (3) and (4), however, the blanks are filled by this new type of referring expression—'some computers,' 'all humans' and 'all zoo animals'—which will be called a **quantified phrase**. Statements of this sort, which are distinct from atomic ones, will be called **quantificational statements**.

Let us look more closely at the quantified phrases in these examples. Words like 'all' and 'some' apply to groups or collections of individuals; the difference between them is obvious: One word applies to the individuals globally ('all'); the other applies only partially ('some'). The members of these groups, instead of being named, are characterized by predicates, which in turn can be 'unpacked' for later translation:

> which is a computer
> which is a human
> which is a zoo animal

In short, there are two elements at work in these quantified phrases, that is, in 'some computers' and 'all zoo animals'. One describes the members of a group ('which is a computer,' 'which is a human' and 'which is a zoo animal'), whereas the other indicates whether all of them are being referred to or only some ('everything' and 'something'). The element which does the referring is called a **quantifier**; in formal logic, quantifiers are classifed as either **universal** or **partial** (also commonly known as **existential**), corresponding to the words 'everything' and 'something.' Because the word 'thing' is not treated as a name in formal logic, such words refer to groups of things without singling anything out. However, unlike a universal quantifier, which is designed to take everything in its sweep, a partial quantifier is deliberately indefinite regarding the number of things to which it might apply. In formal logic 'something' means 'at least one thing and possibly more.' As we shall see later, the indefiniteness belonging to partial quantifiers is closely related to the truth-functional meaning of inclusive disjunction ('at least one disjunct is true and possibly both').

Here again are examples (3) and (4), now showing these further details of logical structure:

> Something which is a computer is smarter than everything which is a human.
> Everything which is a zoo animal should be liberated.

Admittedly, these renditions are clumsy in comparison with the original sentences, but the aim is not to create something beautiful or to change the way you write or speak. Formal logic resorts to 'logicalese' to help you isolate the logically important parts of simple statements, which sometimes fail to be sharply distinguished in the grammatical forms of ordinary language. However, the analysis has uncovered so many details that it might be helpful now to give a brief summary:

1. Every simple statement involves a reference to objects. Referring expressions take the form either of names or of quantified phrases. Although several varieties of names were identified—proper names, pronouns, demonstratives, definite descriptions and plural names—they can all be regarded as tags ('name tags') that single out objects. Quantified phrases—some computers, all humans, all zoo animals—refer to groups of things, either in whole or in part, without naming them, although the job of referring is performed essentially by a quantifier. (The examples above consist of a quantifier—something, everything—plus a predicate or descriptive phrase which characterizes the members of a group—is a computer, is a human, is a zoo animal.)
2. Every simple statement describes its objects of reference. In an atomic statement, the description is applied to named objects, whereas in a quantificational statement it is applied to the one or more members of a group picked out by a quantified phrase.

As a result of this analysis, the simple statements of SL are *replaced* by both atomic and quantificational statements in PL. They make up the foundation of PL and, to avoid any misleading associations with SL, will both be called **basic statements**.[7]

Suppose that a basic statement contains both names and quantified phrases, as in 'Everybody loves God.' In that case, formal logic classifies the statement as quantificational. However, for a basic statement to count as atomic, it must consist of a single k-place predicate followed by k names, and nothing else.

A few more examples will help fill out the picture of quantificational statements as well as sharpen the distinction between the two types of basic statement. First the examples, then their translation into 'logicalese':

(a) Something has worried all of Bob's friends.
(b) Everything was created by God.
(c) Everyone loves someone.
(d) Kids love chocolate.

---

[7] In PL, just as in SL, the other main class of statements are truth-functional compounds: negations, conjunctions, disjunctions and so on. Examples will be given later.

(a′) Something has worried everything which is a friend of Bob.

(b′) Everything was created by God.

(c′) Everything which is a human loves something which is a human.

(d′) Everything which is a kid loves anything which is chocolate.

Let us take the first two statements, (a) and (b), together. Notice that each begins with a quantified phrase that is unspecified: Neither incorporates a descriptive phrase to be unpacked. The first says just that something has worried Bob's friends but does not describe what that might be; the second indicates that everything without exception was created by God. These two examples show that referring expressions sometimes consist only of quantifiers, that is, that a quantifier may be the sole constituent of a quantified phrase. In contrast, the words 'everyone' and 'someone,' which occur in the third example, are specific to the extent that they apply to people rather than to things in general. This particular example contains two quantified phrases. As with names in atomic statements, there can be any finite number of such phrases in quantificational statements (e.g., everyone loves someone who loves everybody). Any basic statement with more than one quantified phrase will be called a **multiple quantification**. You will meet many instances of these later on.

The fourth example, (d), which is also an example of a multiple quantification, illustrates a regular occurrence in ordinary language: a quantified phrase which lacks an explicit quantifier. There was an earlier illustration of this in the statement 'Some computers are smarter than humans.' It is more common for a universal quantifier to be dropped than a partial one, but the very fact that both can be omitted might create ambiguity. However, this particular example (like the previous one) is not ambiguous. The statement refers to all kids and anything which is chocolate. ('Anything' is logically equivalent to 'everything' here.) But other examples are not so clear:

Kids are fond of ghost stories.

Members of the committee spoke against John.

Using explicit quantifiers would eliminate ambiguity in such cases. Since this problem relates primarily to language, however, we will not dwell on it. In PL statements there are no implicit quantifiers.

A few words should be added about the variety of quantifiers in ordinary language. 'Everything' and 'something' head two rather long lists of words, many of which (like 'everyone' and 'someone') have a descriptive element built into them. Here is a selection:

Universal: everything, all, any, anybody, every, everyone, always, anytime, everywhere, each

Partial: something, some, somebody, someone, sometime, somewhere, all but one, most, half, many, several, few, very few, at least one, only one

Notice that the difference in length between these lists results from the fact that in ordinary language, partial quantifiers cover a broad range of reference that extends from 'all but one' to 'only one.' As mentioned earlier, *the partial quantifier in formal logic has only one meaning: 'at least one.'* This choice has the advantage of being compatible with all the other meanings in the range.[8]

Exercises

6.1.1 In the following statements single out the individuals and the predicates describing and relating them.
   a. John is happy.
   b. Lucy loves Mike.
   c. The sales report did not satisfy the company's manager.
   d. 2 is between 1 and 5.
   e. 4 is even, but 5 is not since it is odd.
   f. The Steering Committee is doing a great job.
   g. The purpose of the space shuttle is to advance space exploration.
   h. The trial was a success: Lucy presented the case and Bob could not refute her.
   i. Suzy will marry Jim just in case he's in love with her.
   j. Although Robert does not like Dave he respects him anyhow.
   k. Bill enjoys studying logic.
   l. We need more funding for this research project.
   m. $1 + 2 = 3$
   n. $3 < 5$
   o. John is going to Sara's graduation.
   p. Mike is the father of Lucy and she is the mother of Andrew.
   q. I have no need for money.
   r. Canada won a gold medal at the Olympic Games.
   s. My daughter will drink the milk only if she watches 'Sesame Street.'
   t. The planning of our trip to Spain is very exciting.

6.1.2 Which of the following statements contain a definite description?
   a. I love rainy days.
   b. The Empire State Building has become a symbol of American architecture.

---

[8] Other quantifiers in ordinary language such as 'nothing,' 'no one' and 'never' contain a negative element which puts them into the class of compound statements in PL; these quantifiers will be discussed later.

    c. 2 is the smallest prime number.

    d. Symbolic logic has many applications in computer science.

    e. Everest is the tallest mountain on earth.

    f. No one deserves this prize more than you do.

    g. The computer system we just bought is causing all kinds of headaches.

    h. I live right at the intersection of St. Clair Avenue and Yonge Street.

6.1.3 Classify the following basic statements as either atomic or quantificational, and in the case of a quantificational statement, state whether it is universal or existential (i.e., partial).

    a. Paris is the capital of France.

    b. All dogs have four legs.

    c. Some people are lucky.

    d. Whales are mammals.

    e. Symbolic logic is a great intellectual achievement.

    f. Some computers are more powerful than others.

    g. $x + y = y + x$, for any two real numbers.

    h. He who hesitates is wise.

    i. The mission must be completed at any cost.

    j. There is at least one person who matters to me in this life: myself.

6.1.4 Repeat as in 6.1.3 for the following statements.

    a. John needs help.

    b. Some people seem happy.

    c. Everybody needs someone.

    d. My dog is extremely smart.

    e. There is a rational number between any other two.

    f. Canadians are proud of their country.

    g. Whoever wrote this must be mad.

    h. Every odd number is the sum of an even and an odd number.

    i. Electrons are leptons.

    j. It is colder than I thought.

6.1.5 Give three examples of each one-place, two-place and three-place predicates.

6.1.6 Give three examples of three-place predicates and two of four-place predicates.

6.2   Symbolizing Basic Statements

Portraying the structure of PL's basic statements requires four different classes of symbols: names, predicates, quantifiers and variables. This section will describe their use as well as illustrate how the symbols work together, and the next one will sum things up by listing the formation rules for PL, which cover both basic and compound sentences. The compounds formed from basic sentences involve the same five types of connectives used in SL. They will be examined in due course. For now, however, our focus continues to be on basic sentences.

Names

Although names take various forms in ordinary language, PL uses only one class of symbol for them all:

$$a, b, c, d, \ldots, t, a_1, b_1, \ldots, t_1, a_2, \ldots$$

In formal logic, these lower-case letters are called **constants**. Like the class of simple sentences in SL, constants are infinite in number (thanks to the changing subscripts) although, as you can see, the initial segment in the list ends with the letter t because the remaining lowercase letters of the alphabet have other uses. In practice, however, only a handful of these letters are used at one time in the course of either translating sentences or working in *Symlog*. You may wonder why anyone would bother to have a surplus of constants. The essential reason involves theory rather than practice. An infinite vocabulary of constants is required in PL to give an account of both the meaning and the truth conditions of quantificational statements, which are matters to be discussed in the last section of the chapter. Constants in PL are like proper names (in English) for objects, a different name being assigned to each object, *so that a list of constants can be treated as though it were the set of objects they represent.* The practice of making some word stand for a particular thing, or a group of names substitute for a group of things, is already quite familiar from ordinary language. We speak of lists of people, such as a slate of candidates or a roster of players, and lists of ingredients. What we really mean of course are lists of the *names* of such things. This practice will prove convenient for giving a preliminary account of what makes quantificational statements true or false. You will find that it sharpens the focus of reasoning about things and their properties, despite the fact that the objects ranged over by PL's quantifiers are infinite in number.

When we talk about things, we usually mean things of a certain kind, for instance, people, teams, planets, atoms or numbers. Kinds of things consist of individual things. An individual person, team or number is called an **object**. Some of these objects are infinite in number (numbers or even numbers); other groups of them are finite in size (planets in our solar system or professional baseball teams); still others could be either (planets in the universe or intelligent beings), in which case their number can be considered as indefinitely large. Formal logic refers to any collection of such objects as a **domain** or a **universe of discourse**.

The role of constants in PL is to assign a distinct name to the objects of a given domain, whether or not those objects already possess another name. Take for example the domain of all atoms. We could use the name a to stand for a single atom arbitrarily selected from this domain, b for the next atom chosen, c for the next and so on. In this domain, then, a, b and c are treated as three different individual atoms. The names are special to them, which is why constants are able to serve as surrogate objects. However, despite having an endless list of names at its disposal, PL does not stipulate that each letter be used only once and then discarded. The letter a may be reassigned to another object in a *new* context (e.g., to Anne). In other words, the names of things in PL need not be absolutely unique, like 'The Eiffel Tower,' to be effective in referring to an individual. To eliminate any ambiguity, however, PL stipulates that a constant like a must never be used to stand for two or more different individuals in the same context. From example to example (i.e., from context to context), you will see different domains of objects brought into view but the same set of names will reappear for designating one or more of their objects.

When translating a sentence into symbols, you may find it desirable to select letters that will help you recall the names they substitute for, as in the case of some earlier examples. (Note: the symbol := stands for 'means.')

> a := Anne
> b := Bob; the Blue Jays; the black watch with all the dials and the red
>   and yellow hands
> c := Caesar; he
> h := Hortense the hippo
> p := π
> t := this bottle of wine

However, the same ground rule of consistency applies here as it did in SL for using sentence letters. In a given context,[9] a lowercase letter can stand for only one object. For instance, if you let b represent the Blue Jays in the sentence 'The Blue Jays beat the Boston Red Sox in Boston,' you cannot use it there to name a different object. However, if two forms of a name refer to the same object in a sentence, the same letter must be used to reflect this fact, as the following two cases show:

> Caesar admired himself.
> The report shocked the committee more than it pleased them.

In the first example, a constant (say c) should be used for both names 'Caesar' and 'himself' since both denote the same individual, namely, Caesar. And the same holds for the two names 'the report' and 'it.'

---

[9]'Context' means the same basic sentence, compound sentence, set of sentences or argument. Chapter 9, 'Structures,' adds more precision to this concept.

Predicates

The uppercase letters which were used in SL to represent simple statements will now be converted into symbols for predicates (in PL). From now on, think of the letters

$$A, B, C, \ldots, T, A_1, B_1, \ldots, T_1, A_2, \ldots$$

as standing for the *descriptive component* of basic statements and no longer as statements (as in SL). Thus, on its own, an uppercase letter will not count as a statement in PL. They will now be called **predicate letters**.[10] Although predicate letters appear in every sort of PL statement, their use will become immediately clear if we concentrate for the moment on atomic statements.

In the last section, we saw that predicates are classified as one-place, two-place, three-place and so on, but these 'places' are not shown in the preceding list. The assignment of k places to a given uppercase letter is a matter of choice. For instance, the predicate letter A may stand for a one-place predicate in one context and a three-place predicate in another. The number of places assigned to A cannot vary in the same context; it must not occur as both a one-place and a three-place predicate. Any finite number of places is acceptable in PL, although the typical number encountered in examples and exercises is quite small. But once the places have been assigned to a predicate, where would they appear? The conventional practice in formal logic is to write the predicate directly in front of the k places assigned to it, and this practice will be adopted in PL. The resulting syntactical structure may seem unusual at first when compared with the sentences of ordinary language, but the main advantage of this practice is to show at a glance exactly how many places are attached to a given predicate.

Names and predicates join to form the **atomic sentences** of PL. The choice of an appropriate predicate letter from the alphabetical list is guided by the same consideration as for constants, namely, mnemonic convenience. Here now is a translation of some recent examples (to avoid inconsistency, we assume that each statement has a separate context):

Statement	*PL Symbolization*
Caesar was ambitious.	Ac
Anne and Bob are married.	Mab
John loves cake.	Ljc
Brutus admired himself.	Abb

---

[10] The suggestion is sometimes made that we can look on the simple statements of propositional logic as zero-place predicates of predicate logic. Our approach has been to analyze the simple statements of SL and to *replace* them by more detailed structures. Reusing the capital letters is a matter of convenience.

The Blue Jays beat the Boston Red Sox in Boston.	Bjrb
Albert is the father of Bob.	Fab
The letter shocked the producer more than the commercial pleased the viewers.	Slpci
The report shocked the committee more than it pleased them.	Srcrc
2 is less than 5.	Ltf

There is no need to introduce an artificial way of reading or expressing these symbolic statements once the meaning of the symbols has been fixed. The sentence Ac says that Caesar is ambitious, and Abb says that Brutus admired himself (remember, the contexts are different, so that both constant and predicate are free to receive another interpretation). But suppose that you meet an atomic sentence of PL whose symbols have not been interpreted, for instance, the sentence Jet. It can be read 'e and t are related by J' or 'e and t are J-related,' or it can be expressed simply by saying the letters in the order of their occurrence: 'J,e,t.' In other words, the sentence has no meaning beyond what is given by its syntactical structure, consisting of the predicate and the two constants it relates. It is an example of an *uninterpreted* atomic sentence and is as legitimate a sentence of PL as the others just listed. The strangeness of these symbolizations, in comparison with sentences in ordinary language, will soon disappear.

An important convention about these expressions should always be kept in mind. Every atomic sentence of PL involving two or more constants expresses an *ordered* relationship among its terms; that is, which particular place a constant happens to occupy in a sentence uniquely affects the meaning of the expression as a whole. Thus the two symbolic sentences Jet and Jte are different in meaning and therefore count as two different sentences, just as would these two sentences in ordinary language:

Ellen is more jittery than Tanya.
Tanya is more jittery than Ellen.

Admittedly, there are many sentences of ordinary language in which the order of terms makes no difference. In the example 'Anne and Bob are married,' the proper names can be reversed without altering the meaning of the statement itself, and this would be reflected in the fact that the sentence itself could be correctly symbolized as either Mab or Mba. However, the convention about the order of constants following a predicate is intended to apply to all symbolic sentences, regardless of whether they are interpreted. So taken by themselves, Mab and Mba will count as different sentences of PL.

These two syntactical characteristics of a predicate—the same number of places in a given context and a fixed order to those places—will also be found in quantificational statements. Before moving on, however, you should try the exercises PL01 to PL10 by using *Symlog*'s Symbolizations.

Quantifiers and Variables

Quantifiers, when they occur in a sentence, are always accompanied by a corresponding variable. **Variables**, sometimes called **individual variables**, form, with constants, the class of **terms**. Variables are symbolized by lower-case letters from the end of the alphabet:

$$u, w, x, y, z, u_1, w_1, \ldots, u_2, \ldots \,^{11}$$

Their primary role is to be attached to predicates, standing for objects in the universe of discourse and following essentially the same rules for filling places as constants do. Here are two familiar examples from the last section, translated and outfitted now with variables:[12]

_____ should be liberated.	Lx
_____ is smarter than _____ .	Sxy

Please note that these symbolic expressions (like the ones they translate) *are not sentences but predicate phrases.* Since x and y are not objects—to be more precise, names of objects—the predicates L and S are not being stated of anything. However, there is an obvious parallelism of syntactical structure between these two phrases and atomic sentences, for the variables occupy the very places that would be filled by constants, such as

Hortense the hippo should be liberated.	Lh
Hortense the hippo is smarter than Peter the python.	Shp

In the last section we described PL's two quantifiers: universal and partial. The symbols associated with them are, respectively, ∀ and ∃, but logical syntax requires that they never stand alone. ∀ and ∃ are always accompanied by a single variable, called a **quantifier variable** or **variable of quantification**, and each quantifier symbol together with its variable of quantification is always surrounded by parentheses, as the following examples show:

Universal: (∀x), (∀y), (∀z), . . .
Partial: (∃x), (∃y), (∃z), . . .

---

[11] This series does not contain the letter v because it has already been coopted as the symbol for disjunction. *Symlog* is programmed to reject the use of this letter as a variable.

[12] In making these two translations, we have followed an old tradition in formal logic of starting with x and y as the quantifier variables. Although there is no rule regarding variables whereby x must occur before y and y before z, this order is a useful one to follow when writing 1-, 2- and 3-place predicates. If more are needed, the list continues with u, w and so on.

From now on, when we speak of PL's quantifiers we will mean expressions like these. Roughly, universal quantifiers mean 'everything' and partial ones mean 'something.' The use of a different variable does not by itself alter the meaning of these quantifiers; that is, a quantifier has the same meaning regardless of whether its variable is an x or a y or any of the other possibilities. The need for different variables will become plain in a moment.

Every quantificational statement of PL begins with a quantifier. Phrases like Lx and Sxy become sentences by means of quantifiers preceding them:

PL Sentence	Translation
(∀x)Lx	Everything should be liberated.
(∃x)Lx	Something should be liberated.
(∃y)Ly	Something should be liberated.
(∃x)(∃y)Sxy	Something is smarter than another.
(∃y)(∃x)Syx	Something is smarter than another.
(∃x)(∀y)Sxy	Something is smarter than everything.[13]

These translations are meant to give a smooth and 'natural' reading to the symbols. Other forms of translation—in logicalese—have the advantage of following more closely the contours of the symbolic structures themselves. We will be looking more closely at both forms of quantificational statement—universal and partial—soon, but for now here are some examples of such translations of the first and last statements in the list:

(∀x)Lx	Everything is such that it should be liberated.
	Take anything at all, it should be liberated.
	For all x, x should be liberated.
(∃x)(∀y)Sxy	There is something which is such that it is smarter than anything at all.
	There exists something which, take anything at all, it is smarter than that thing.
	There exists at least one thing, x, such that for every y, x is smarter than y.

Notice that for the last example, which is a multiple quantification, all of the translations have one feature in common: They 'scan' the quantifiers from left to right. Notice too that variables (like constants) follow their predicates in an ordered relation. It is important that you retain this sense of left-to-right order whenever you read a multiple quantification or set out

---

[13] Notice that the second and third examples share the same translation, as do the next two, despite the use of different variables. Taken in themselves, x, y, z and so on all mean the same and one is just as good as another; when used together, their role is to help distinguish one quantifier from another and one predicate place from another.

to construct one. Just how important can be seen by comparing the following two scientific claims:

> Everything attracts something.
> Something attracts everything.

Since the first of these statements may well be true with the second being false, it is crucial for any PL translation to capture the difference in their meaning. This task is achieved by using different variables and by the fact that both quantifiers and variables have an ordered occurrence:

> $(\forall x)(\exists y)Axy$
> $(\exists x)(\forall y)Axy$

The first sentence says, 'For anything at all, x, there is something, y, which x attracts.' (Despite the 'logicalese,' this means the same as 'Everything attracts something.') The second sentence says, 'There is something, x, which attracts y, for all y' (i.e., 'Something attracts everything'). The ordered structure of each sentence clearly indicates which quantifier pertains to which variable after the two-place predicate, A. Now, given the very same context, how would you read the following sentence?

> $(\exists x)(\forall y)Ayx$

Notice how it differs from the second sentence in the above pair; it differs in the order of the variables following the predicate. This new sentence would have to mean, then, that there is at least one thing, x, which is such that everything, y, attracts it. More crisply, 'Something is attracted by everything.' Its meaning is distinct from that of the first sentence as well, although their translations may give the appearance of having the same meaning. The first and third sentences differ in the order of both the quantifiers and the variables following the predicate, and although grammatically similar they are not logically equivalent.[14]

These sentences illustrate a standing rule which applies throughout PL. In the case of a sentence, the variables which follow predicates must always have a matching quantifier variable. Symbolic strings such as $(\forall y)Lx$, $(\forall x)Ly$ and $(\exists x)(\exists y)Sxz$ conflict with this particular rule and therefore do not count *as sentences* of PL (although, as we will see later, they still count as legal expressions—well-formed formulas—of PL). When a variable (e.g., x)

---

[14] This is a case in which the use of formal logic helps to expose differences in meaning that grammar sometimes conceals. Compare the following two sentences, which have the same meaning: 'Everyone admires Helen' and 'Helen is admired by everyone.' Now compare 'Everyone admires someone' and 'Someone is admired by everyone,' and assume that the first member of this pair is true. What the second member of the pair says might still be false, nevertheless, for it makes the stronger claim that there is at least one person who is admired by all. Thus the two sentences do not mean the same. Formal syntax—in contrast with the grammar of natural language—helps to sharpen the difference.

following a predicate (e.g., Lx) has a matching variable in a quantifier, such as (∀x)Lx, it is called a **bound** variable; if it lacks a matching variable, as in (∀y)Lx, it is said to be **free.**[15] In any quantificational sentence there can be no free variables. If you glance for a moment at the three strings (∀y)Lx, (∀x)Ly and (∃x)(∃y)Sxz, you will see that each of them contains a free variable.

So far in this section, all the quantified phrases used for illustration have been of the 'everything' or 'something' variety, but you will recall from the previous section that quantifiers are often combined with descriptive words which need to be unpacked as predicates (e.g., 'some computers' or 'all zoo animals'). We must now consider how PL represents these phrases and the statements that contain them. To emphasize their different patterns of translation, we will look at the two kinds of quantificational statements— existential and universal—separately. Then, after a pause to discuss some syntactical matters, we will examine some examples which mix both types of quantifier. But now, get some practical experience by solving the exercises PL11 to PL20 by using *Symlog*'s Symbolizations.

∃-Sentences

Statements whose main logical operator is the partial quantifier, ∃, are often identified in logic as **existential sentences**, and the use of the backward 'E' as a symbol for this quantifier is traditional. This designation (which has nothing to do with a philosophical view) reflects a common way of rephrasing partial quantifications that makes their translation much easier. The following sentences would all be judged to mean the same thing in ordinary language:

> Bob is allergic to some foods.
> Some foods exist to which Bob is allergic.
> There are some foods to which Bob is allergic.

Although the claim made by these sentences is as much about Bob as about foods, the presence of a quantified phrase requires it to be counted as quantificational rather than atomic. Primarily, then, the statement is about some foods. Unpacked further and rephrased in the language of PL, the statement says that there is at least one thing which is a food, Fx, to which Bob is allergic, Abx:

> (∃x)(Fx & Abx)

which can be read,

> There is at least one thing, x, which is a food and to which Bob is allergic.

---

[15] A more precise definition of these terms will be given in the next section.

or as

> There is something, x, which is a food and to which Bob is allergic.

For simplicity's sake, the latter way of translating existential statements is to be preferred, but it should be understood that the phrase 'There is something, x' means here the same as 'There is at least one thing, x.'

As you can see from both translations, PL makes a sharp distinction between **reference** and **description**. The burden of reference is carried by the quantifier ('There is something, x'); what comes next are the predicates, which pin down or specify the meaning of x for this particular statement (x is a food, Bob is allergic to x). The predicates are joined together by a familiar SL connective, &, and the whole descriptive component of the statement is surrounded by parentheses. This pattern is typical of existential statements which (unlike the earlier examples) contain more than one predicate. Let us add another predicate to the example and symbolize it:

> There are some foods which Bob loves which he is allergic to.
> (∃x)((Fx & Lbx) & Abx)

Since there are three predicates in the descriptive component following (∃x), all of them conjoined, a further pair of parentheses is needed, in much the same manner as for an SL sentence. Nevertheless, it is important to recognize that in this example, these descriptive components, which are often called the **scope** of a quantifier, are not actually sentences. Remember that expressions such as Abx fall short of being statements because they contain at least one free variable. Consequently, the & sign of SL which surfaces in the scope of one or another quantificational statement has been assigned a *new* use, that of conjoining predicates as in Fx & Lbx. PL assigns a comparable use to the four other connectives of SL as well, so that descriptive phrases which contain free variables might take the form of a disjunction, a conditional or a negated conditional and so on. In addition, the rules for parentheses in SL apply without change to these phrases. However, this new use for the five connectives merely supplements their fundamental role of forming compound statements.

For a last example, let us replace 'Bob' with a quantifier:

> There are some foods which *some people* love which they are allergic to.

Since this sentence begins the same way as the other two, so will its translation: (∃x)(Fx & . . .) ('There are some foods, x, which . . .'). What comes next? The sentence goes on to say that 'there are some people who love x.' This introduces another quantifier phrase ('some people'), which will have to be unpacked since it contains a descriptive element, and the new quantifier will have to have a different variable attached to it. We will use y. This analysis enables us to fill in a bit more of the symbolization:

(∃x)(Fx & (∃y)(Py & Lyx) . . .)

('There is something, x, which is a food and there is something, y, which is a person and which loves x . . .'). The remainder of the statement says that 'y is allergic to x.' This predicate will complete the symbolization, but to make sure that all the variables fall within the scope of their quantifiers, further parentheses are needed to produce the finished product:

(∃x)(Fx & (∃y)((Py & Lyx) & Ayx))

The statement as a whole is made up of the following major components: an initial existential quantifier and its scope. This scope takes the form of a conjunction: On the left hand is the predicate phrase, Fx; on the right, an embedded quantified phrase, (∃y)((Py & Lyx) & Ayx), which is not a statement since it contains a free variable, x. The embedded quantifier has its own scope, which like that of the whole statement, assumes the form of a conjunction.[16]

Some existential statements are more complicated than this; others of course are less so. Nevertheless, the scope of such statements usually has the overall structure of a conjunction, a fact worth recalling when you set out to translate them. Incidentally, there are several logically equivalent renderings of this statement. One such is

(∃x)(∃y)(Fx & ((Py & Lyx) & Ayx))

This version introduces both of the quantifiers before presenting the variables they affect, and therefore, as you can see, the scope of (∃y) differs in the two renderings. (The scope of this quantifier is now the entire conjoined phrase within the parentheses.) The earlier version was emphasized to reflect a step-by-step approach to analyzing structure. As your facility grows, you may come to prefer one or another equivalent form as a model for translation. Here are some more examples which display the typical conjunctive 'signature' of existential sentences:

Someone likes logic.	(∃x)(Px & Lxl)
Some people need help.	(∃x)(Px & Nxh)
Some people need money.	(∃x)(Px & Nxm)
Some road leads to Rome.	(∃x)(Rx & Lxr)
Someone loves Suzy.	(∃x)(Px & Lxs)
Suzy loves someone.	(∃x)(Px & Lsx)
Somebody loves someone.	(∃x)(∃y)((Px & Py) & Lxy)

---

[16] Although the variables x and y are (syntactically) distinct, the objects they pick out do not have to be necessarily so: Let both x and y denote Bob, a cannibal allergic to human flesh.

Somebody who is happy loves Suzy.   (∃x)((Px & Hx) & Lxs)

Some sad person loves someone who   (∃x)(∃y) [((Px & Sx) &
is happy.

Suzy loves a lover.   (Py & Hy)) & Lxy]

Someone loves herself.   (∃x)(∃y) [(Px & Py) & (Lsx & Lxy)]

Some people are smokers.   (∃x)(Px & Lxx)

Some beer drinkers are smokers.   (∃x)(Px & Sx)

There is a number which is both   (∃x)((Px & Dxb) & Sx)
prime and even.   (∃x)(Nx & (Px & Ex))

∀-Sentences

The scope of **universal sentences** (those whose main logical operator is the universal quantifier, ∀) also carries a typical 'signature.' We will start with a basic example and then, as before, add more details.

There is an old saying, 'All roads lead to Rome.' The quantificational phrase, 'All roads,' gives a clear sign that this is a universal statement, so we can be sure the translation will have the general form (∀x)(. . .). Now for the scope of the quantifier. The descriptive parts unpack easily into 'x is a road' and 'x leads to Rome,' which can be represented as Rx and Lxr. In logicalese, then, the old saying means that 'everything, x, which is a road leads to Rome.' But how are these two descriptive components to be related? If the conjunction sign is used, as it was for existential statements, the result—(∀x)(Rx & Lxr)—will certainly fail to express what is meant. Although a legitimate sentence of PL, this is a bad translation since it says that 'everything, x, is a road which leads to Rome,' which is going a bit too far. For the statement to be true, you and I would have to be roads (leading to Rome), and so would Bob and Anne, Hortense the hippo, the Blue Jays, π, each planet and anything else there is. Obviously, the old saying meant something else. The idea it conveys is that anything which happens to be a road leads to Rome; in other words, that *if* anything, x, is a road, *then* it leads to Rome. The descriptive components are therefore related conditionally: Rx → Lxr. Here is the proper translation:

(∀x)(Rx → Lxr)

This example illustrates the typical form taken by universal statements in PL. As with the symbol & in existential statements, → carries out the further role of joining predicates. The antecedent (though not itself a sentence) contains the descriptive component of a universally quantified phrase; it specifies the objects of reference (in the present case, roads). The consequent expresses what the statement as a whole says about these objects (here, that they lead to Rome).

Now let us specify the objects of reference a bit more: 'All roads in Europe and the Middle East lead to Rome.' These additional descriptive elements are to be inserted into the antecedent, whereas the consequent remains unchanged:

$$(\forall x)[(Rx \ \& \ (Fxo \lor Fxm)) \rightarrow Lxr]$$

In logicalese, 'With regard to everything, x, if it is a road which is either found in Europe, Fxe, or found in the Middle East, Fxm, then x leads to Rome.' Note how parentheses are used here to relate smaller components to larger ones within the scope of the quantifier.

For a final step, let us add a new quantified phrase to the consequent: 'All roads in Europe and the Middle East lead to every parking lot in Rome.' What is now said about the same objects of reference (all the roads in either Europe or the Middle East) is a little more complicated and will have to be unpacked with the help of a different variable. The description asserts of everything, y, that if it is a parking lot in Rome then x leads to it. Here is the finished version. Try to read it in the way just suggested:[17]

$$(\forall x)[(Rx \ \& \ (Fxe \lor Fxm)) \rightarrow (\forall y)(Pyr \rightarrow Lxy)]$$

An equivalent rendering of the example involves placing both quantifiers at the beginning:

$$(\forall x)(\forall y)[(Rx \ \& \ (Fxe \lor Fxm)) \rightarrow (Pyr \rightarrow Lxy)]$$

This form may show the general structure of universally quantified statements even more clearly, but it should not be regarded as a simpler or better translation. The important thing is not to lose sight of the details of this linguistic structure. When translating any universal statement that contains more than one quantified phrase, keep a sharp eye out for the intended scope of each quantifier, whether it pertains to the entire scope or just to the antecedent or the consequent. Make certain too that every variable which follows a predicate falls within the scope of a preceding quantifier with a matching variable, as do these two alternative translations. In every quantified statement the main operator must be a quantifier; it is the one which begins the whole formula and within whose scope everything else in the formula falls. Here are some further examples which reflect the typical conditional signature of universally quantified sentences:

Everybody loves math.	$(\forall x)(Px \rightarrow Lxm)$
Each one of us needs help.	$(\forall x)(Px \rightarrow Nxh)$
We all need money.	$(\forall x)(Px \rightarrow Nxm)$

---

[17] Without introducing a different variable, y, but instead reusing x as in

$$(\forall x)[(Rx \ \& \ (Fxe \lor Fxm)) \rightarrow (\forall x)(Pxr \rightarrow Lxx)]$$

the consequent would have been saying the wrong thing (that all parking lots in Rome lead to themselves).

Every mark counts.	$(\forall x)(Mx \rightarrow Cx)$
Dolphins are mammals.	$(\forall x)(Dx \rightarrow Mx)$
Everybody loves Suzy.	$(\forall x)(Px \rightarrow Lxs)$
Suzy loves everybody.	$(\forall x)(Px \rightarrow Lsx)$
Everybody loves someone.	$(\forall x)[Px \rightarrow (\exists y)(Py \,\&\, Lxy)]$; or
	$(\forall x)(\exists y)[Px \rightarrow (Py \,\&\, Lxy)]$
Everybody loves everybody.	$(\forall x)[Px \rightarrow (\forall y)(Py \rightarrow Lxy)]$; or
	$(\forall x)(\forall y)[Px \rightarrow (Py \rightarrow Lxy)]$; or
	$(\forall x)(\forall y)[(Px \,\&\, Py) \rightarrow Lxy]$
Every happy person loves Suzy.	$(\forall x)((Px \,\&\, Hx) \rightarrow Lxs)$
Every sad person loves someone who is happy.	$(\forall x)[(Px \,\&\, Sx) \rightarrow (\exists y)((Py \,\&\, Hy) \,\&\, Lxy)]$
Everybody smokes.	$(\forall x)(Px \rightarrow Sx)$
Every beer drinker is a smoker.	$(\forall x)((Px \,\&\, Dxb) \rightarrow Sx)$
Every natural number has a successor.	$(\forall x)[Nx \rightarrow (\exists y)(Ny \,\&\, Sxy)]$

Before moving on, use *Symlog*'s Symbolizations to solve the exercises PL21 to PL30.

Negation and Mixed Quantification

So far, no examples have included negation. Like the four binary or dyadic connectives, $\neg$ combines in PL both with sentences and with predicate phrases containing free variables, as the following examples illustrate:

$\neg Lcc$

$(\exists x)\neg Lcx$

$\neg(\forall x)Lcx$

$(\exists x)\neg(\forall y)Lxy$

Let us relate these statements to the same context and interpret the first as saying, 'Caesar did not love himself.' The second statement then says, 'There is something which Caesar did not love'; the third, 'It is false that Caesar loved everything'; and the fourth, 'There is something, x, with regard to which it is false to say that it loved everything, y.' Even though these examples are meant to illustrate syntax, your logical intuition may have noticed other relations among them of a semantic nature. And with good reason. The first statement, $\neg Lcc$, entails the second. If Caesar did not love himself, there must be at least one thing which he did not love. Also, the second and third statements are logically equivalent, for if there is something which Caesar did not love, it cannot be true to say that he loved everything; and if it is false that he loved everything, there must be something that he did not love. We will return to semantic matters in the final section of the chapter. For the present, here are some further examples of the use of negation in PL statements (in a few cases alternative but equivalent translations are given):

Caesar loved everyone except senators.	$(\forall x)(Px \rightarrow (Lcx \equiv \neg Sx))$
Any friend of Caesar is no friend of mine.	$(\forall x)((Px \,\&\, Fxc) \rightarrow \neg Fxm)$
Caesar did not trust every senator.	$\neg(\forall x)(Sx \rightarrow Tcx)$; or
	$(\exists x)(Sx \,\&\, \neg Tcx)$
Caesar did not trust any senator.	$\neg(\exists x)(Sx \,\&\, Tcx)$; or
	$(\forall x)(Sx \rightarrow \neg Tcx)$
None of the senators who conspired against Caesar loved him.	$\neg(\exists x)((Sx \,\&\, Cxc) \,\&\, Lxc)$; or $(\forall x)((Sx \,\&\, Cxc) \rightarrow \neg Lxc)$
Only the senators did not love Caesar.	$(\forall x)(\neg Lxc \rightarrow Sx)$
Only senators and Caesar's rivals do not love him.	$(\forall x)(\neg Lxc \rightarrow (Sx \lor Rxc))$
Only the senators who did not conspire against Caesar were guiltless.	$(\forall x)(\neg Gx \rightarrow (Sx \,\&\, \neg Cxc))$

Notice the rather complicated role that the word 'only' plays in the last three statements. It is, first, a universal quantifier, and therefore the typical syntactical structure of its scope will have the form of a conditional. Further, like the phrase 'only if,' which was discussed in SL, the descriptive phrase introduced by 'only' will be inserted into the consequent of that conditional. The combined role may be more evident if we read the first and second of this group in logicalese. The first says, 'For all x, x did not love Caesar only if x was a senator.' The second says, 'For all x, x did not love Caesar only if x was either a senator or a rival of Caesar.' Why not take a moment to translate the third of these statements into logicalese?

Universes of discourse or domains are part of the 'stage machinery' which accompany quantifiers. They furnish the objects we talk about whenever we use quantifiers, whether we refer to everything or merely to something. However, the concept of a universe of discourse can also be tailored to a more definite range of objects that constitute a special domain, which can thus help reduce the number of predicates needed for translating a sentence. Take, for instance, the following sentence:

Everyone at the picnic had a delightful time.

The quantifying phrase, 'everyone,' contains a descriptive element, for the sentence is not about everything in general but only about people. The claim is that everything which is a person and which also was at the picnic had a delightful time:

$(\forall x)((Px \ \& \ Ax) \rightarrow Dx)$

However, by restricting the universe of discourse to persons, we would eliminate the need for the separate predicate, Px, and thereby simplify the translation:

$(\forall x)(Ax \rightarrow Dx)$

Notice that the stipulation of a universe of discourse (UD) is necessary. Otherwise the translation would read, 'Everything at the picnic had a delightful time,' and would refer to more than just people; it would also indicate what kind of time the ants at the picnic had, the sparrows, the bees, the flies, and so on. Consequently, whenever a quantifier is to carry a restricted sense in a particular translation, the sense must be supplied along with the predicates and terms, all of which can be conveniently listed in what will be called a **symbolization.** The symbolization for our example in its simpler translation would take the form

UD := {persons}
Ax := x was at the picnic
Dx := x had a delightful time

The first line serves merely as a guide to the reading of quantifiers in the symbolic translation. It only mentions a set of particulars; it does not introduce a PL symbol. Whether a symbolization should contain such a line is a matter of choice, however, for in place of a specific UD an extra predicate could always be substituted. If no UD is mentioned, the quantifiers in the translation will be understood to carry their normal, unrestricted sense of 'everything' and 'something.' These are the 'default' meanings of the two quantifiers.

Some further examples may be useful. The symbolization and translation for 'Everybody loves someone' would be

Symbolization	*Translation*
UD := {persons}	$(\forall x)(\exists y)Lxy$
Lxy := x loves y	

The same symbolization will do for 'There is no one who loves everybody':

$\neg(\exists x)(\forall y)Lxy$

These two renderings are quite compact.[18] Without the UD, the translations would have to include a predicate describing x as a person:

$(\forall x)[Px \rightarrow (\exists y)(Py \ \& \ Lxy)]$
$\neg(\exists x)[Px \ \& \ (\forall y)(Py \rightarrow Lxy)]$

Introducing a specific UD and thereby saving a predicate is handy for translating statements about things such as people, animals in general, numbers, atoms and planets—collections which are indefinitely large or infinite—but there is an important ground rule that limits its use. When a UD is mentioned in a symbolization, it affects the interpretation of all quantifiers in the corresponding translation. Hence, to eliminate any chance of ambiguous reference, only one UD per symbolization is allowed. This rule limits their use to statements about collections of things of a single type, but even so, specific UDs are useful for many cases of multiple quantification. You will have an opportunity to employ them later in several of the exercises.

To present some further patterns of statement which you will meet in those exercises, we now give three different groups of sentences, each with its own domain. First the sentences, then the symbolization, then the translations:

Sentences

(1) A number is even only if it is divisible by two.
(2) All and only even numbers are divisible by two.
(3) Not every prime number is odd, nor is every odd number a prime.
(4) There is no highest prime number.
(5) For every prime number there is a nonprime number higher than it.
(6) No number is higher than itself.
(7) Whenever one number is higher than another, the converse does not hold.
(8) If one number is higher than a second number and the second is higher than a third, then the first is higher than the third also.

Symbolization

UD := {numbers}
Ex := x is even
Dxy := x is divisible by y
Px := x is prime

---

[18] Take a moment to remind yourself of the fact that the places following a predicate have an ordered relationship. Reversing the order of x and y after the predicate L in these last two sentences would completely change their meaning: $(\forall x)(\exists y)Lyx$ would read, 'Everybody is loved by someone' (in other words, every single person is loved by at least one person), and $\neg(\exists x)(\forall y)Lyx$ would read, 'There is no one to whom everybody loves.'

Ox := x is odd

Hxy := x is higher than y

t := two

Translations

(1) $(\forall x)(Ex \rightarrow Dxt)$

(2) $(\forall x)(Dxt \equiv Ex)$

(3) $\neg(\forall x)(Px \rightarrow Ox) \ \& \ \neg(\forall x)(Ox \rightarrow Px)$[19]

(4) $\neg(\exists x)(Px \ \& \ (\forall y)(Py \rightarrow Hxy))$

(5) $(\forall x)(Px \rightarrow (\exists y)(\neg Py \ \& \ Hyx))$

(6) $\neg(\exists x)Hxx$

(7) $(\forall x)(\forall y)(Hxy \rightarrow \neg Hyx)$

(8) $(\forall x)(\forall y)(\forall z)((Hxy \ \& \ Hyz) \rightarrow Hxz)$

The following group of sentences is less abstract in content than the first. By now you should have enough familiarity with quantificational techniques to attempt your own translations (using the symbolization provided) before looking at ours. Why not at least have a try? You can always take a peek if you happen to get stuck, and the effort will help you become even more familiar with the techniques.

Sentences

(9) Bob and Anne and all their friends are attending the Animal Rights Ball.

(10) Everyone who attends the ball is a vegetarian unless he or she is also a hunter.

(11) Bob never danced at the ball but Anne always did, although ungracefully so.

(12) Sometimes Bob drinks dandelion wine and does silly things.

(13) If Bob eats a goldfish, Anne will be horrified and will scold him.

(14) If someone eats a goldfish, Anne will be horrified.

(15) If someone eats a goldfish, Anne will scold him.

Symbolization

UD := {persons, goldfish, wines, times, and other things}

Axy := x attends y

Cxy := x will scold y

Dxyz := x dances at y at time z

Exy := x eats y

Fxyz := x is a friend of y and z

---

[19] Notice that the two quantifiers in this statement can have the same variable because the second does not fall within the scope of the first. The statement is a truth-functional compound—a conjunction.

Gx := x is graceful

Hx := x will be horrified

Kx := x is a hunter

Lx := x is dandelion wine

Nxyz := x drinks y at time z

Ox := x is a goldfish

Px := x is a person

Qxyz := x does y at time z

Rx := x is a vegetarian

Sx := x is silly

Tx := x is a time

a := Anne

b := Bob

r := the Animal Rights Ball

Translations

(9) (Abr & Aar) & (∀x)[(Px & Fxba) → Axr]

(10) (∀x)[(Px & Axr) → (¬Kx → Rx)]

(11) ¬(∃x)(Tx & Dbrx) & ((∀x)(Tx → Darx) & ¬Ga)

(12) (∃x)(Tx & ((∃y)(Ly & Nbyx) & (∃z)(Sz & Qbzx)))

(13) (∃x)(Ox & Ebx) → (Ha & Cab)

(14) (∃x)(∃y)[(Px & Oy) & Exy] → Ha; or (∀x)(∀y)[((Px & Oy) & Exy) → Ha]

(15) (∀x)[(Px & (∃y)(Oy & Exy)) → Cax]

The last group of sentences will express in PL (not necessarily true) facts about the following diagram (the UD is the set of three nodes):

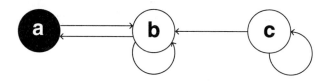

Sentences

(16) Node a is black but c is not.

(17) Node c points to node b and node a points to itself.

(18) Some nodes point to node a.

(19) Some nodes point to themselves.

(20) All black nodes point to themselves.

(21) There is a node to the left of node c which points to node a.

(22) All black nodes are to the left of node b.

(23) No black node is at the right of node c.

(24) Not all nodes are to the left of node b.

(25) No black node points to a node pointing to itself.

(26) All white nodes are to the left of all black ones.

(27) Some nodes which point to themselves point to some black nodes too.

(28) Nodes which point to nodes b and c do not point to themselves.

(29) Nodes which point to node a do not point to black nodes which point to themselves.

(30) No node points to a node which points to a black node pointing to itself.

Symbolization

UD := {node a, node b, node c}

Bx := x is black

Lxy := x is to the left of y

Pxy := x points to y

a := node a

b := node b

c := node c

Translations

(16) Ba & ¬Bc

(17) Pcb & Paa

(18) (∃x)Pxa

(19) (∃x)Pxx

(20) (∀x)(Bx → Pxx)

(21) (∃x)(Lxc & Pxa)

(22) (∀x)(Bx → Lxb)

(23) ¬(∃x)(Bx & ¬Lxc)

(24) ¬(∀x)Lxb

(25) ¬(∃x)[Bx & (∃y)(Pxy & Pyy)]

(26) (∀x)[¬Bx → (∀y)(By → Lxy)]

(27) (∃x)[Pxx & (∃y)(By & Pxy)]

(28) (∀x)[(Pxb & Pxc) → ¬Pxx]

(29) (∀x)[Pxa → ¬(∃y)((By & Pyy) & Pxy)]

(30) ¬(∃x)(∃y)[Pxy & (∃z)((Bz & Pzz) & Pyz)]

To reinforce the material introduced up to this point, you should solve the exercises PL31 to PL50 by using *Symlog*'s Symbolizations.

Identity Statements

This final section on symbolization deals with a familiar and important concept—**identity**—which was deliberately omitted from earlier examples. This concept is quite familiar to us from natural language. For instance, in the sentence 'Napoleon was in love with somebody,' what usually would be understood is that Napoleon was in love with someone *else*, that his love was directed to *another person*. Or in the sentence 'There is something in the universe which caused everything,' what is meant is that one particular thing caused every *other* thing, not that one thing caused absolutely everything, *including* itself. Such clarifications show the concept of identity to be at work. Frequently, it is combined with negation to fix the sense of words like 'else,' 'another' and 'different,' which are intended to distinguish one thing from another (i.e., to indicate their *not being identical*). Nevertheless, these two examples show that the absence of words like these certainly does not render our meaning unclear. We often resort to such words only when somebody misunderstands the meaning we intended. In formal logic, however, the situation is different. Symbolizations mean only what they say, so unless what is meant has been captured in symbols, it has not been said at all. This fact becomes evident by trying to render the two examples in the language of PL introduced thus far; symbolized (using obvious symbols), the two sentences read

(1) $(\exists x)(Px \ \& \ Lnx)$
(2) $(\exists x)(\forall y)Cxy$

But these symbolizations obviously fail to capture all the intended meaning, for there is nothing in them which indicates that the x whom Napoleon loves is a *different* person. After all, the sentence would be quite true if Napoleon happened to love no one at all except himself, yet that is not really what was meant. As for the second case, nothing shows that x is to be excluded from those things, y, which it caused. Thus, it is important to introduce a special symbol which will do for symbolizations what words like 'another' and 'different' do in natural language. The symbol to be used is I_ _, a two-termed relation, where the two spaces following I are to be filled in the usual way by some combination of terms (i.e., constants or variables).[20] For example, the sentence $(\forall x)Ixx$ symbolizes the claim that everything is identical to itself, and $(\exists x)((Px \ \& \ \neg Ixb) \ \& \ Dx)$ translates the sentence 'Someone other than Barbara drank the wine.' With the help of I, the two sentences we tried to symbolize previously can now be restated with greater precision:

(1′) $(\exists x)((Px \ \& \ \neg Ixn) \ \& \ Lnx)$
(2′) $(\exists x)(\forall y)(\neg Iyx \rightarrow Cxy)$

---

[20] Identity is often symbolized in formal logic by the mathematical symbol '='; however, to avoid associations with *numerical* mathematics we will use 'I' instead.

Please note that the order of the terms following I does not affect its meaning. Ixn, for instance, means the same as Inx.

The symbol I is sometimes described in formal logic as a **predicate constant**, signifying that its special meaning, which is to stand for the two-termed relation of identity, does not vary from one symbolization to another. Unlike F, G and P, whose meaning as predicates can change from one sentence or context to another, I will always stand for identity whenever that concept is needed (in this respect it resembles &, → or ¬). Of course, whenever identity happens not to be needed for a symbolization, I is free to represent other *n*-termed predicates, such as 'x is intelligent,' 'x is intrigued by y' and 'x is in between y and z.' In this section, however, as well as in several of the exercises, the symbol I will figure as a predicate constant.

Before continuing with more illustrations of identity, let us take a moment to consider more fully what this relation means, compared with other two-termed relations. Here are some atomic statements about Napoleon along with their symbolizations:

(3) Napoleon was in love with himself.   Lnn
(4) Napoleon was the husband of Josephine.   Hnj
(5) Napoleon was the same height as Josephine. Snj
(6) Napoleon was Bonaparte.   Inb

Notice the crucial difference between sentences (5) and (6): The former says that Napoleon and Josephine were the same size, that is, that these two people had the same measurement, whereas the latter says that Napoleon and Bonaparte were the same person. In other words, the crucial difference is that whereas sentence (5) compares *two* objects (called 'Napoleon' and 'Josephine') in terms of their height, (6) is concerned with only *one* object called by two different names. So, what this sentence says is that the person who was called 'Napoleon' is none other than (is identical with) the person called 'Bonaparte.' Now compare sentence (6) with (3). Like (6), sentence (3) concerns only one object (Napoleon), but it describes him in two different respects, first as lover and then as the thing loved. However, when Napoleon is said to be identical to Bonaparte, or indeed when Napoleon is said to be identical to himself, two different aspects of the same object are not being described. The identity statement merely indicates two different ways of referring to that object.

The need for clarity in the interpretation of identity statements forces us to distinguish between objects and the names by which we designate them. This fact should be kept in mind for all cases in which I is made to represent the relation of identity. In formalese, for example, the symbolization given earlier, (∃x)((Px & ¬Ixb) & Dx), can be read, 'Someone other than the person whose name is 'Barbara' drank the wine.' It is more natural, of course, to use the sentence originally given ('Someone other than Barbara drank the wine'), and there is no harm in doing so as long as it does not promote the idea that identity is a mysterious relation between an object and itself, an object and a variable or two variables. It is useful to remind

ourselves from time to time that an unnegated true identity sentence like
Iab concerns, numerically, a *single* object.

Let us move on to further examples in which identity is needed, beginning with some of the forms introduced in the last section:

(7) All the senators were in debt to Brutus (their colleague).
   $(\forall x)((Sx \ \& \ \neg Ixb) \to Dxb)$

(8) All the senators feared Caesar except for Brutus.
   $(\forall x)(Sx \to (Fxc \equiv \neg Ixb))$

(9) Caesar will listen to a senator, but only if that senator is Brutus.
   $(\forall x)(Sx \to (Lcx \to Ixb))$

(10) Brutus was the noblest senator of all.
   $(\forall x)((Sx \ \& \ \neg Ixb) \to Nbx)$

Two comments should be made about example (10). First, the word 'noblest' is taken in the comparative sense as a two-termed relation, Nxy, 'x is nobler than y'; with the help of the identity predicate, plus negation, this predicate means 'nobler than any other thing, x.' Words like 'oldest,' 'fastest,' 'wisest' and 'best' can be treated in a similar way. Second, the identity relation itself, which is implicit in the English sentence, is absolutely needed in the symbolization, for if it were omitted the sentence would run

$(\forall x)(Sx \to Nbx)$

which says merely that 'take anything x, if it was a senator then Brutus was nobler than it.' However, since Brutus was also a senator, if the claim happens to be true, it would follow that he was nobler than himself, which, if not plain nonsense, is just plain false. The identity predicate, I, prevents either result. In formalese, sentence (10) reads, 'Take anything, x, if it is a senator other than Brutus, then Brutus is nobler than it.' Since human beings are not older than themselves, faster than themselves or wiser or better than themselves, the identity predicate is a constant companion in symbolizations of such words.

I is indispensable for separating not only one individual (such as Brutus) from a group (his Senate colleagues) but also one individual from another, as when we want to say that Cicero and Cassius were two different senators:

(11) $(Si \ \& \ Sa) \ \& \ \neg Iia$

The same applies when no individuals have been named. Suppose, for instance, that the chief magistrate investigating the assassination of Caesar tells the Roman citizens, 'At least two senators are prime suspects.' This sentence would be symbolized as

(12) (∃x)(∃y)[((Sx & Sy) & ¬Ixy) & (Tx & Ty)]

A few days later the magistrate revises his estimate downward, telling them, 'One senator is our prime suspect'; that is, exactly one senator is currently suspected (in Caesar's assassination). The new announcement would look like this:

(13) (∃x)[(Sx & Tx) & ¬(∃y)(¬Iyx & (Sy & Ty))]

A rendering of sentence (13) in formalese may help to clarify what this symbolization means: 'There is at least one senator, x, who is a prime suspect and there is no senator, y, other than x who is a prime suspect.' In other words, 'one' means 'exactly one' here, not 'at least one' (which is the default meaning of a single existential quantifier). Using formal equivalences (with which you will become familiar in the following chapters of PL), sentence (13) can also be rendered in a way which reads, 'There is at least one senator, x, who is a prime suspect and, take anything, y, if y is a senator and a prime suspect, then it is identical to x':

(13') (∃x)[(Sx & Tx) & (∀y)((Sy & Ty) → Iyx)]

Sentences like (13) and (13') illustrate an interesting and potentially important benefit of combining the identity predicate with predicates and quantifiers: The combination enables us to refer to and describe things whether or not we happen to know their names, and indeed even when those things have no names. For instance, 'The fifty-seventh stone which was used in building the Washington Monument' is a description that refers to a single stone which has never had its own proper name and is unlikely ever to have one. Still, we can refer to it if we want to. Again, the knife which Brutus used to stab Caesar in the Senate has no known name, but the phrase just used manages well enough to refer to it. Phrases of the form '*The so-and-so*' are known in logic as **definite descriptions**. They are referring expressions which can be used instead of names; that is, the formal counterparts of definite descriptions can take the place of individual terms in our symbolizations. And here is where the distinctive structure of sentences like (13) and (13') come into play. Suppose the chief magistrate in Rome tells the reporters, 'The murder weapon was owned by Brutus.' Notice that the phrase 'the murder weapon' is a definite description. It refers to something described as a murder weapon and indicates further that this is unique, that there was only one such thing which answers to the description. Let us now symbolize the magistrate's statement, with (13') as the model since this form illustrates the standard way of rendering definite descriptions:

(14) (∃x)[(Mx & (∀y)(My → Iyx)) & Oxb]

Definite descriptions are interesting because they enable us to secure reference to an individual without the device of a name. Earlier in this chapter, our list of namelike expressions, that is, of expressions to be represented by individual terms, included definite descriptions, but that was before we saw the identity predicate at work. With I on hand, however, definite descriptions can now be removed from that list since we can analyze such phrases as existentially quantified descriptions. Should we do so, then? For practical purposes in our symbolizations, the answer is 'No: Definite descriptions stay on the list.' This decision merely reflects a convention of natural language to treat definite descriptions as functionally equivalent to names. Among other uses, definite descriptions are indispensable for making up trivia questions, such as 'What was the team that won the 1931 World Series?' Keep in mind, however, that whenever you symbolize a definite description by means of an individual term, what you mean is that there is an object corresponding to that phrase; whether the object is historically real or only fictional or in some sense abstract, you nevertheless mean that a particular object is being referred to, the object represented by the individual term. But what if there happens to exist no such object at all? What if the individual term you use represents nothing at all? Suppose, for instance (taking a famous example), the definite description is 'the present King of France.' Here is a case in which no object whatever is picked out because for many years now France has had no monarchy. So, if we select k as an individual term—a constant—for our symbolization, it would not stand for anything at all, unless we pretended it did, but then that would expose logic to the charge that its account of names conflicts with our sense of reality. As it happens, examples like 'the present King of France,' 'the round square' and 'the even number between 1 and 2' bother philosophically inclined logicians, especially those who wish to remain in contact with reality; puzzles concerning how best to interpret these descriptions led eventually to the so-called '**theory of definite descriptions**,' which resolves basically to avoid treating all such phrases as names.[21] With the help of this device of symbolization, for instance, it is possible both to affirm that the present King of France is bald and to deny that he is bald, without self-contradiction. A glance at the renderings of these two sentences will show that they *do not* have the form α and $\neg\alpha$:

(15) $(\exists x)[(Kx \mathbin{\&} (\forall y)(Ky \rightarrow Iyx)) \mathbin{\&} Bx]$

(16) $(\exists x)[(Kx \mathbin{\&} (\forall y)(Ky \rightarrow Iyx)) \mathbin{\&} \neg Bx]$

Because there is no King of France, both of these sentences would be false. This example illustrates why definite descriptions are potentially important. They allow us to assert that there is something which uniquely meets a particular description, without committing us to the existence of such an

---

[21] Bertrand Russell introduced the theory of definite descriptions in a famous essay, *On Denoting*, published in 1905.

object. Thus, logic escapes the charge of overpopulating the world with nonexistent entities.[22]

For a final illustration of the identity predicate at work, we turn to theology. Whatever our religious beliefs, it is clear that the resources of PL do not allow 'God' to be treated as a name. The reason is that whereas we can say in natural language, intelligibly enough, that God exists, our formal machinery requires at least one predicate in every well-formed sentence; but the sentence 'God exists' if 'God' is interpreted as a name has no predicate. Consequently, we shall treat this word as a predicate, using G to represent all the properties that are taken to constitute some generally recognized definition of what 'God' means (and that is as far into theology as we are going to go). Accordingly, the sentence that God exists becomes

(17) $(\exists x)Gx$

But such a symbolization will strike any monotheist (a person who holds that there is only one God) as unsatisfactory, and this objection would be justified: Sentence (17) merely says that there is at least one thing with all the properties expressed by G, but it fails to capture the special feature of the monotheist's claim. To answer the criticism, we can shape a new symbolization which treats 'God,' in effect, as a definite description:

(18) $(\exists x)[Gx \ \& \ (\forall y)(Gy \rightarrow Iyx)]$

Disputes in theology can be as complicated as in politics. Besides monotheists, there are polytheists, namely, those who believe in the existence of more than one God. However, the language of PL does not cater easily to just any expression of polytheism, for (we recall) it cannot symbolize quantifying words like 'several,' 'quite a few', and 'indefinitely many.' As a result, the polytheist who wants to speak formalese must either be fairly noncommittal, declaring, say, that there are at least two Gods, or else more precise, holding, say, that there are exactly nine of them. Here is the symbolization of a polytheist's claim that there are at least three Gods.

(19) $(\exists x)(\exists y)(\exists z)[((Gx \ \& \ Gy) \ \& \ Gz) \ \& \ ((\neg Ixy \ \& \ \neg Ixz) \ \& \ \neg Iyz)]$

At the other extreme, of course, are atheists, whose general position can be rendered as the denial of sentence (17): It is false that there exists anything with the properties expressed by G, $\neg(\exists x)Gx$. In between are the agnostics, who refuse to side with either theists or atheists. We shall mention just two sorts. Someone who denies sentence (18), that there is only one God, is equivalently (in formal terms) affirming that either there is no God at all or else there are at least two Gods. (The steps needed for this transfor-

---

[22] Another way of avoiding the problem of referential failure is to prescribe a total mapping—in the mathematical sense—between names and the members of a chosen (nonempty) domain of objects. This is the course followed in the concluding chapter of PL, 'Structures.'

mation—equivalence—will become clearer in later chapters of PL.) The denial of (18) thus expresses the view of the polytheistic agnostic, who in rejecting monotheism makes no further commitment to either atheism or polytheism. Then there is the position of the monotheistically inclined agnostic, of the person who says, 'There is *at most* one God.' It is the view that either there is no God at all, ¬(∃x)Gx, or else that there is only one God, (∃x)[Gx & (∀y)(Gy → Iyx)]. This position is formally equivalent to denying that there are at least two Gods; that is,

(20) ¬(∃x)(∃y)[(Gx & Gy) & ¬Ixy]

which in turn can be transformed into

(21) (∀x)(∀y)[(Gx & Gy) → Ixy]

    With this modest contribution of logic to theology, we conclude the discussion of the identity predicate but suggest that to become fully familiar with the ideas introduced in this section, you turn now to the exercises. Please note that these exercises are of the 'paper' variety; with the exception of the Environment Models, *Symlog* was not programmed to recognize I— equality—as a predicate constant.

Exercises

6.2.1   Symbolize the following sentences in PL.

        UD := a birthday party
        Cx := x likes cake
        Sx := x smokes
        Dx := x drinks wine
        Ixy := x is identical with y
        Lxy := x loves y
        a := Albert
        j := Jane
        m := Mary
        p := Peter
        r := Robert

    a.   Jane likes cake.
    b.   Mary drinks wine but Robert doesn't.
    c.   Peter loves Jane only if she doesn't smoke.
    d.   Either Robert likes cake or Peter drinks wine; however, Robert doesn't drink wine unless Albert smokes or Mary does.
    e.   Everybody likes cake.
    f.   Someone drinks wine.

    g. Someone loves Mary unless she is a wine drinker.

    h. No one drinks wine unless some smoker loves Peter.

    i. If Robert smokes then someone loves him. But everybody hates him if he is both a wine drinker and a smoker.

    j. If Mary loves someone then they both drink wine.

    k. Jane loves some smoker but it is not Peter.

    l. No one likes cake but Mary.

    m. Exactly one person smokes.

    n. At most one person smokes.

    o. Everybody but Robert likes cake.

    p. Some wine drinker is a cake lover.

    q. Smokers are cake lovers.

    r. Jane loves a lover.

    s. Everybody loves a lover.

    t. Smokers love wine drinkers.

6.2.2 Keeping in mind the symbolization of exercise 6.2.1, express in colloquial English the following PL sentences.

    a. $\neg$Sr & Cr   b. Ljp & Lpj   c. ($\exists$x)Lxa & $\neg$Lma

    d. ($\forall$x)(Sx $\rightarrow$ $\neg$Dx)   e. ($\forall$x)($\exists$y)(Lxy & Dy)   f. $\neg$($\exists$x)Lxa

    g. $\neg$($\exists$x)(Cx & Lxa)   h. ($\forall$x)(Sx $\rightarrow$ $\neg$($\exists$y)Lxy)   i. ($\forall$x)(Sx $\equiv$ Dx)

6.2.3 Using the symbolization of exercise 6.2.1, symbolize the following sentences in PL.

    a. Someone loves everybody.

    b. Everybody loves everybody.

    c. Everybody loves anyone who drinks wine.

    d. Anyone who is a wine drinker and a smoker loves anyone who loves Jane.

    e. Anyone who is a wine drinker and a smoker loves anyone who loves everybody.

    f. Everybody who loves Albert also loves Peter. But someone who loves Mary loves Jane as well.

    g. If someone is a smoker then not everybody loves this smoker.

    h. Exactly one person is a wine drinker.

    i. At most one person loves Mary.

    j. Exactly two people are in love with Peter.

    k. Not everybody loves anyone who loves Robert.

    l. Not everybody loves anyone who loves everybody.

    m. Everybody loves anyone who loves himself.

    n. Anyone who smokes and drinks wine is in love with someone.

    o. Smokers drink wine.

6.2.4 Symbolize the following arguments in PL.

UD := the natural numbers: 0, 1, 2, . . .

Ex := x is even

Ox := x is odd
Ixy := x is identical with y
Lxy := x is less than y
Gxy := x is greater than y
Sxy := the successor of x is y
a := 0
b := 1
t := 2

a. Zero is an even number. Therefore, it is not odd.
b. 0 is even but 1 is odd. No number is both even and odd. Hence, 0 is not equal to 1.
c. 1, besides being greater than 0, is also odd. But 2 is not odd. Hence, either 2 is greater than 0 or 1 is.
d. Some number is greater than 1 but it's not 0. Hence, an even number distinct from 0 is greater than 1.
e. 2 is not less than 0 since no number is.
f. For every number there is always a greater one. It follows that there is no largest number.
g. All numbers are even or all are odd. It follows from this that each number is either even or it is odd.
h. A number is even if and only if it is not odd, and since 2 is even it can't be odd.
i. Every number has a successor but no two numbers have the same successor. Hence, if two numbers are equal so are their predecessors.
j. No number has 0 as its successor. Thus, a successor's successor of a number can't be 0.
k. If a number is even then its successor is odd and if a number is odd then its successor is even. 0 is even. Therefore, the successor's successor of 0 is even.
l. Numbers are less than their successors. It follows that if x is less than y then x's successor is less than y's successor.

6.2.5 Given the following symbolization, express the given sentences in PL. (Note: Assume that Bob, Danny, Frank and Tom are males, and that Lucy and Suzy are females.)

UD := people
Ex := x is an engineer
Lx := x is a logician
Cx := x is a computer scientist
Bxy := x is the brother of y
Dxy := x is the daughter of y
Fxy := x is the father of y
Mxy := x is the mother of y

Sxy := x is the son of y

Pxy := x is a parent of y

Txy := x is the sister of y

Ixy := x is identical with y

b := Bob

d := Danny

f := Frank

l := Lucy

s := Suzy

t := Tom

a. Bob is the father of Lucy. But she is not the mother of either Frank or Tom.
b. Danny has no children.
c. Tom, the only computer scientist, has no brothers.
d. All of Lucy's brothers and some of her sisters are engineers. But she doesn't have a son who is an engineer.
e. Bob and Danny are sons of Frank and Suzy. They are all logicians except Danny, who is a computer scientist.
f. None of Frank's children is a logician, but a grandchild of his is.
g. Suzy is a computer scientist and so are all her children and grandchildren.
h. Lucy is the mother of Frank and Suzy is Lucy's grandmother.
i. Tom and Suzy have only two daughters.
j. Danny has no logicians among his grandchildren.
k. The sons of logicians are logicians too.
l. No logician has an engineer as a brother.
m. Suzy has two sisters who are logicians.
n. No brother of Tom is a computer scientist.
o. Logicians are computer scientists.
p. Tom has a brother and a sister; his brother is a logician but the other, his sister, is an engineer.
q. Danny's father is an engineer and so is his mother. Moreover, all of his brothers and sisters are engineers too, but Danny himself is not an engineer.
r. No logician is an engineer.
s. Some logicians are the brothers of some engineers.
t. Every engineer has a logician as a sister.

6.2.6 Symbolize in PL the following statements about real numbers.

UD := the real numbers

Ixy := x = y

Lxy := x < y

Bxyz := y is between x and z

Sxyz := x + y = z
Pxyz := xy = z
a := 0
b := 1

a. Between any two real numbers there is always another one.
b. There is no largest real number. Also, there is no smallest one.
c. x + 0 = x, for any real number x.
d. If x is a real number then 1x = x.
e. Given any two real numbers x and y, x + y = y + x.
f. If x and y are real numbers such that x ≠ 0 and y ≠ 0 then xy ≠ 0.
g. If x < y and y < z, then x < z, for any real x, y and z.
h. Given three real numbers x, y and z, where x < y and z > 0, xz < yz.
i. (x + y) + z = x + (y + z), for any real numbers x, y and z.
j. Every real number has an additive inverse. And any real number distinct from zero has a multiplicative inverse.

6.2.7 Using the same symbolization as that of exercise 6.2.6 but with the UD given by

UD := {0,1,2,3,4,5}

translate the following sentences of PL into colloquial English (allow some math symbolism). In each case, determine if what the sentence says about this subset of real numbers is true or false.

a. Saaa & Sabb   b. (∀x)Saxx   c. ¬(∃x)Pbxb
d. (∃x)(∀y)Pxyy   e. (∀x)(∃y)Pxyy   f. (∃x)(∀y)Lxy
g. (∀x)Ixx   h. (∃x)Baxb → Iab   i. (∀x)(∀y)(∃z)Bxzy

6.2.8 Give an example of a symbolization in which the sentence (∀x)(∃y)Lxy is true but (∃x)(∀y)Lxy is false.

6.2.9 Using the 'lexicon' provided, symbolize each of the following English sentences as sentences of PL.

a. There is a place in this company suitable for either George or Harry, though definitely not for both. (UD := everything; Pxy := x is a place in y; Sxy := x is suitable for y; c := this company; g := George; h := Harry)

b. Everyone who was invited to the wedding by the bride attended, except for those whom the groom had cheated. (UD := everything; Px := x is a person; Axy := x attended y; Cxy := x had cheated y; Ixyz := x was invited to attend y by z; d := the wedding; b := the bride; g := the groom)

c. Not all people who like dogs also like cats. However, I like them both. (UD := everything; Px := x is a person; Dx := x is a dog; Cx := x is a cat; Lxy := x likes y; i := I)

d. Some people always get what they aim for. (UD := everything; Px := x is a person; Tx := x is a time; Gxy := x gets y; Axy := x aims at y)

e. People don't always get what they aim for. (UD := everything; Px := x is a person; Tx := x is a time; Gxy := x gets y; Axy := x aims at y)

f. Anytime I earn some money, the government takes it away from me. (UD := everything; Tx := x is a time; Mx := x is money; Exyz := x earns y at (time) z; Rxyz := x takes y away from z; i := I; g := the government)

g. There is a time and a place for everything. (UD := everything; Txy := x is a time for y; Pxy := x is a place for y)

h. There is never a time for this. (UD := everything; Txy := x is a time for y; t := this)

i. The king listens to everyone except the experts. (UD := everything; Px := x is a person; Ex := x is an expert; Lxy := x listens to y; k := the king)

j. Philosophers understand everything except themselves. (UD := everything; Px := x is a philosopher; Dxy := x understands y)

6.2.10 Using the 'lexicon' provided, symbolize each of the following English sentences as sentences of PL.

a. Politicians blame everyone except themselves. (UD := everything; Hx := x is human; Px := x is a politician; Bxy := x blames y)

b. Politicians blame everyone except their mothers. (UD := everything; Hx := x is human; Px := x is a politician; Bxy := x blames y; Mxy := x is the mother of y)

c. Whoever likes dogs also likes cats. However, I dislike them both. (UD := everything; Px := x is a person; Dx := x is a dog; Cx := x is a cat; Lxy := x likes y; i := I)

d. Nobody likes dogs and cats except me. (UD := everything; Px := x is a person; Dx := x is a dog; Cx := x is a cat; Lxy := x likes y; i := I)

e. Bach may play for God but Mozart plays for the angels. (UD := everything; Ax := x is an angel; Pxy := x plays for y; b := Bach; m := Mozart; g := God)

f. You'll never see a picture more beautiful than this. (UD := everything; Px := x is a picture; Tx := x is a time; Bxy := x is more beautiful than y; Sxyz := x sees y at (time) z; o := you; t := this)

g. Only logicians are allowed to think. (UD := everything; Lx := x is a logician; Tx := x is allowed to think)

h. Only God can make a tree. (UD := everything; Tx := x is a tree; Mxy := x can make y; Ixy := x is identical to y; g := God)

i. Somewhere, someday, somebody will speak the truth. (UD := everything; Px := x is a place; Tx := x is a time; Hx := x is a human; Sxyuw := x speaks y at (place) u at (time) w; t := the truth)

j. Any friend of Minnesota Fats' ain't no friend of mine. (UD := everything; Fxy := x is a friend of y; m :– Minnesota Fats; i := I)

6.2.11 After adding

Dxy := x is divisible by y

to the lexicon—symbolization—of exercise 6.2.4, express the following statements in PL.

a. Even numbers are different from odd ones.
b. If a number is odd it isn't divisible by 2.
c. If a number is odd, it is not divisible by an even number.
d. All natural numbers are either greater than or equal to zero.
e. Every number is divisible by itself except zero.
f. Zero divides no number.
g. Every number is divisible by 1.
h. Every odd number is divisible by some odd number.
i. There are infinitely many even numbers.
j. Some numbers divide their successors.

6.2.12 Let the UD be the following **directed graph,** which is a set of nodes (the circles) and arcs (the arrows connecting the nodes). According to the symbolization below, express the following statements in PL.

Pxy := x points to y
p := node p
q := node q
r := node r
s := node s

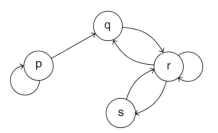

a. Node p points to node q.
b. Node s points to itself.
c. Node q points to some node.
d. Every node is pointing to node r.
e. Any node pointing to r points to s as well.
f. Nodes pointing to q point to themselves.
g. No node points to both p and s.
h. Not every node points to node s.
i. For any two nodes there's a third one both point to.
j. Node q points to a node that r points to as well.
k. All nodes point to themselves.
l. No node points to itself.
m. Node p doesn't point to any node q is pointing to.
n. No node points to a node s points to.
o. Nodes which point to themselves point to q as well.

6.2.13 Add Ixy := x = y (i.e., x is identical with y) to the symbolization of exercise 6.2.12, and then represent the following statements into PL.

a. Node s is pointing to at least one other node.
b. Only node r points to s.
c. Node p is the only node pointing to itself.
d. p and s point to totally different nodes.
e. There's only one node pointing to s.

6.2.14 Symbolize the statements a–j of exercise 9.3.5. (Note: Your job is simply to symbolize these statements; ignore any other question not related to this current chapter.)

6.3   Formation Rules of PL

In this section we introduce the rules of formation for PL, which are a bit more complicated than those given earlier for SL. The specification of PL's syntax begins by laying out its alphabet:

1. **Constant symbols:** lowercase Roman letters from a to and including t with or without positive integer numerical subscripts
2. **Variable symbols:** comprising the lowercase Roman letters u, w, x, y and z with or without positive integer numerical subscripts
3. **Predicate symbols:** capital Roman letters from A to and including T with or without positive integer numerical subscripts
4. **Truth-functional connectives:** $\neg$, &, $\vee$, $\rightarrow$ and $\equiv$
5. **Quantifier symbols:** $\forall$ and $\exists$
6. **Punctuation symbols:** (, and)

The constant and variable symbols are collectively known as the **individual terms—terms,** for short—of PL, and the truth-functional connectives with the quantifier symbols are the **logical operators** of PL. Expressions which conform to the rules given below are sometimes referred to as **well-formed formulas** (of PL), or **wffs,** for short. As with SL, we will continue to use the metalogical symbols α and β, which now are to stand for any well-formed formula of PL. For the job of specifying quantified statements we will be using also the following new metalogical symbols:

a stands for any constant whatever (a, b, c, etc.).
x stands for any variable whatever (x, y, z, etc.).
P stands for any predicate symbol whatever (A, B, C, etc.).

Here are PL's rules of formation:

1. A predicate symbol followed by k individual terms—a k-place predicate, $k \geqslant 0$—is a wff.
2. If α is a wff, then so is $\neg\alpha$.
3. If α and β are wffs, then so are $(\alpha \& \beta)$, $(\alpha \vee \beta)$, $(\alpha \rightarrow \beta)$ and $(\alpha \equiv \beta)$.
4. If α is a wff and **x** is a variable symbol, then $(\exists\mathbf{x})\alpha$ and $(\forall\mathbf{x})\alpha$ are wffs.
5. Nothing else is a wff.

Clause 1 specifies what an **atomic formula** is in PL. For example, Raxy, Kba and Lx are all atomic formulas. A **ground atomic formula**, or **atomic sentence,** is an atomic formula in which all its individual terms are constants.

For instance, Fab, Rc and Sijk are all ground atomic formulas. Clauses 2 and 3 specify PL's truth-functional compounds, which in metalogical form at least are identical to those in SL. Clause 4 describes a necessary and sufficient condition for being either sort of quantificational statement. No other string of symbols of PL counts as a wff.

The rules of formation are designed to work together whenever a formula has a complicated syntactical structure. Probably the best way of seeing how the rules do so is to apply them to a few formulas; we start with one from the last section:

$$(\exists x)(\exists y)(Fx \mathbin{\&} ((Py \mathbin{\&} Lyx) \mathbin{\&} Ayx))$$

The formula is of the form $(\exists \mathbf{x})\alpha$, with α being $(\exists y)(Fx \mathbin{\&} ((Py \mathbin{\&} Lyx) \mathbin{\&} Ayx))$, and according to clause 4 it is a wff of PL if α is. To find whether α is a wff, clause 4 needs to be reapplied since α is itself of the form $(\exists \mathbf{x})\beta$, with β being $(Fx \mathbin{\&} ((Py \mathbin{\&} Lyx) \mathbin{\&} Ayx))$. Hence, α is a wff if β is. But β is of the form $(\delta \mathbin{\&} \gamma)$, which clause 3 says is a wff if both δ and γ are; δ—Fx—clearly is (by clause 1), and it is easy to see that γ—$((Py \mathbin{\&} Lyx) \mathbin{\&} Ayx)$—is also a wff by repeated applications of clauses 3 and 1. So the original expression is a wff of PL.

Now for another example, also taken from the last section:

$$(\forall x)((Rx \mathbin{\&} (Fxe \lor Fxm)) \to (\forall y)(Pyr \to Lxy))$$

Being of the form $(\forall \mathbf{x})\alpha$, this too is subject to clause 4, so the original expression is a wff if α is. Since this expression is of the form $(\beta \to \delta)$, it will count as a wff if both β and δ do. The antecedent certainly does since it is a conjunction of one atomic formula with a disjunction of two others (clauses 3 and 1). Determining whether the consequent, δ, is a wff takes us back to clause 4; δ, of the form $(\forall \mathbf{x})\gamma$, is a wff if γ is, which it clearly is. The original expression, therefore, is a wff of PL.

Now that PL's formation rules have been introduced, a few concepts which have been previously presented in an intuitive fashion deserve a more formal definition.

> **Definition.** In a quantified wff of either form $(\exists \mathbf{x})\alpha$ or $(\forall \mathbf{x})\alpha$, the wff α is called the **scope** of the quantifier.

To illustrate, the scope of the universal quantifier in $(\forall x)((Kax \lor Lxc) \to (\exists y)(Lyx \mathbin{\&} Kxy))$ is the wff $((Kax \lor Lxc) \to (\exists y)(Lyx \mathbin{\&} Kxy))$, and the scope of the existential quantifier is the wff $(Lyx \mathbin{\&} Kxy)$.

Having formally defined the scope of a quantifier, we now introduce the definition of bound and free variables:

> **Definition.** Any occurrence of a variable that falls within the scope of a quantifier with the same variable is said to be **bound** by the quantifier in question; otherwise, the occurrence of the variable is said to be **free**.

For instance, x in $(\exists x)\neg Lcx$ is bound, but it is free in both $(\exists y)(Fcx \rightarrow Gay)$ and $(\forall z)((\exists y)Gy \equiv \neg Fxz)$. However, in $(\exists z)Fcz$ & Gzb the variable in Fcz is bound, but the one in Gzb is free—note that the scope of $(\exists z)$ only includes Fcz. To the preceding definition we should add that in a case of overlapping scopes corresponding to quantifiers sharing the same variable of quantification, the variable within the scopes is to be bound by the quantifier with the innermost scope. For example, in $(\forall x)(Lax \rightarrow (\exists x)Fxc)$, the variable in Fxc is bound by the existential quantifier, $(\exists x)$, and not by the universal quantifier, $(\forall x)$. Finally, as opposed to SL, PL makes a distinction between its wffs and its sentences.

Definition. A sentence of PL is a wff with no free variables.

Hence, by this definition, any variable in a sentence of PL must be bound by some quantifier. The following are examples of sentences of PL.

    Ga
    $\neg(\neg Ga \equiv \neg\neg Hcb)$
    $(\forall w)Hwwm$
    $(\forall z)(\exists w)\neg(Maw \rightarrow Kwzg)$
    $(P \vee \neg(\exists x)(Lxx \equiv Rxx))$

Finally, the following are not sentences of PL.

    (A)
    $A \vee \neg G$
    $(\forall w)Hww$ & Rw
    $(\forall z)Lazy$
    $(\neg(\exists w)(\forall z)((Ma \rightarrow \neg Gaw) \equiv Dcz) \vee Hw)$

The first expression is not even a formula of PL because sentence letters are not enclosed in parentheses, and because all the sentences of PL are formulas of PL, it is not a sentence of PL. The second and third expressions are not formulas of PL either because they lack the outermost set of parentheses (and even then, w would still be free in the third expression); hence, they are not sentences of PL. The fourth expression, although a formula of PL, is not a sentence of PL because the occurrence of the variable y is free. Finally, the last expression is a formula, but not also a sentence, because the third occurrence of the variable w is not bound by any quantifier (i.e., it is free).

As we did earlier for SL, we will adopt some conventions for the language PL. First, you may use square brackets in your formulas if you wish. Second, you may drop the outermost set of parentheses in the formulas of PL.[23] Thus, according to these conventions, $Ga \equiv \neg(\forall x)Ex$ and $(\forall x)[Cx \rightarrow$

---

[23] It may help to think of quantifiers and quantificational sentences as following rules of punctuation which run parallel to those for negation, $\neg$.

$\neg(\exists y)(Dy \& Nxy)]$ will be considered formulas of PL, as would $A \lor \neg G$ in the preceding list.

Already, you have probably noticed that there is a structural similarity between atomic and quantificational sentences. Take a moment to examine the following sentences, from left to right, looking only at the symbolic patterns:

Aa	$(\exists x)Ax, (\exists y)Ay, \ldots$
	$(\forall x)Ax, (\forall y)Ay, \ldots$
Laba	$(\exists x)Lxbx, (\exists y)Lyby, \ldots$
	$(\forall x)Lxbx, (\forall y)Lyby, \ldots$
Laba	$(\exists x)Laxa, (\exists y)Laya, \ldots$
	$(\forall x)Laxa, (\forall y)Laya, \ldots$
$(\exists x)Lxbx$	$(\exists y)(\exists x)Lxyx, (\exists z)(\exists x)Lxzx, \ldots$
	$(\forall y)(\exists x)Lxyx, (\forall z)(\exists x)Lxzx, \ldots$
$(\forall y)Lyby$	$(\exists x)(\forall y)Lyxy, (\exists z)(\forall y)Lyzy, \ldots$
	$(\forall x)(\forall y)Lyxy, (\forall z)(\forall y)Lyzy, \ldots$

Starting with an atomic sentence such as Laba, one can replace each of its distinct constants by a different variable and then append a matching quantifier (i.e., with matching variable) to the beginning of the sentence. By means of this syntactical routine, which is called **generalization**, the list of quantified sentences on the right-hand side could be continued indefinitely. There is no fundamental restriction on which variables to use (as long as they are different), on the class of quantifier or on the order of terms, even though the usual order of a before b and x before y and so on has been followed here in constructing each list. In short, any constant can be syntactically 'generalized' by converting it into a bound variable. The result is a quantified sentence (a multiple quantification, if the initial sentence is already quantificational). The process which yields these statements is often described in logic as **quantifying over terms**.

A comparable syntactical routine leads in the opposite direction: Strip off the initial quantifiers one after another, starting with the left-most, and replace the free variables by constants, using the same constant for each distinct variable. The procedure can be done just once or repeated until there are no more quantifiers to remove, as here:

$(\forall x)(\exists y)Sxy$	$(\exists y)Say, (\exists y)Sby, \ldots$
$(\exists y)Say$	Saa, Sab, Sac, $\ldots$
$(\exists x)(\forall y)Lyxy$	$(\forall y)Lyay, (\forall y)Lyby, \ldots$
$(\forall y)Lyby$	Laba, Lbbb, Lcbc, $\ldots$

This particular process is called **instantiation**. Removal of the left-most quantifier produces one or more free variables, all of which are then replaced by the same constant. The procedure can be carried out once or successively, and (as the examples show) the same constant can be used more than once when instantiating a quantified sentence. Carried to the limit, the process yields atomic sentences (or in general, truth-functional compounds or atomic sentences) in place of any quantified sentence. Both it and the process of generalization reveal important details of PL's syntax. Instantiation is possible only for quantified statements, that is, when the main operator is either a universal or an existential quantifier. Later, you will find both of these procedures related to *Symlog*'s rules of inference. For instance, from a general claim such as 'All zoo animals should be liberated,' one would like to be able to infer the more particular claim 'If Hortense the hippo is a zoo animal, she should be liberated.' This wish provides the motivation for the following two formal definitions of instantiation and generalization:

> **Definition.** Given a quantified sentence β of PL of the form $(\exists \mathbf{x})\alpha$ or $(\forall \mathbf{x})\alpha$, an **instantiation**, or an **instance**, $\alpha(\mathbf{a}/\mathbf{x})$ of β is whatever sentence results from applying the following syntactical transformation to β:
> 1. Drop the quantifier—either $(\exists \mathbf{x})$ or $(\forall \mathbf{x})$—that is the main logical operator of β. (Note that at this point $\mathbf{x}$ may become free in α.)
> 2. Replace *each* occurrence of the free variable $\mathbf{x}$ in α, if any, with corresponding occurrences of the constant $\mathbf{a}$.

For instance, the sentences

Kg
Fa & (∃y)Gya
(∃y)Gcyc
La → (∃z)Kz

are, respectively, instantiations of the four sentences

(∀x)Kx
(∀w)(Fw & (∃y)Gyw)
(∃x)(∃y)Gxyx
(∀z)(Lz → (∃z)Kz)

where x has been substituted by g, w by a, x by c and z by a in the first, second, third and fourth sentences, respectively. Note that instantiation applies only to quantified sentences. For instance, the sentence Fa & (∀y)Gya cannot itself be instantiated to obtain, say, Fa & Gba since it is a conjunction. The reverse of instantiation is generalization. More formally,

> **Definition.** Given a sentence α of PL, a **universal generalization** of α is whatever sentence $(\forall \mathbf{x})\alpha(\mathbf{x}/\mathbf{a})$ results from applying the following syntactical transformation to α:
> 1. Replace *each* occurrence of the constant $\mathbf{a}$ in α with corresponding occurrences of the variable $\mathbf{x}$ but only if $\mathbf{x}$ becomes free.

2. Prefix the resulting formula with a universal quantifier (having **x** as its variable of quantification) as the main logical operator.[24]

Similarly,

> **Definition.** Given a sentence α of PL, an **existential generalization** of α is whatever sentence $(\exists\textbf{x})\alpha(\textbf{x}/\textbf{a})$ results from applying the following syntactical transformation to α:
>
> 1. Replace *some or all* occurrences of the constant **a** in α with corresponding occurrences of the variable **x** but only if **x** becomes free.
> 2. Prefix the resulting formula with an existential quantifier (having **x** as its variable of quantification) as its main logical operator.

Keep in mind that no occurrence of the constant **a** may be substituted by the variable **x** if **x** is to become bound by a quantifier already in α. Some examples will help to illustrate this point. The sentence Fa gives $(\forall x)Fx$ and $(\forall y)Fy$ as two possible universal generalizations and $(\exists x)Fx$ and $(\exists z)Fz$ as two possible existential generalizations. Similarly,

$$Fab \rightarrow \neg Ga$$

gives

$(\forall x)(Fxb \rightarrow \neg Gx)$
$(\forall z)(Fzb \rightarrow \neg Gz)$
$(\forall x)(Fax \rightarrow \neg Ga)$
and so on

as universal generalizations, and

$(\exists x)(Fxb \rightarrow \neg Ga)$
$(\exists x)(Fab \rightarrow \neg Gx)$
$(\exists x)(Fxb \rightarrow \neg Gx)$

as the set of all existential generalizations where x replaces a. However, note that although

$$(\exists x)[Faxb \rightarrow \neg(\forall x)(Hx \equiv Gab)]$$

is a valid existential generalization of

$$Faab \rightarrow \neg(\forall x)(Hx \equiv Gab)$$

---

[24] Although admittedly more pathetic, the move from Fa to $(\forall x)Fa$ is formally correct. Here, we are replacing each occurrence of the constant, say, b in Fa by x. Since b does not occur in Fa there is nothing to replace, and prefixing the resulting formula after the 'replacement' (still Fa) with $(\forall x)$ gives $(\forall x)Fa$. Similar considerations apply to the definitions of instantiation and existential generalization.

the sentences

$$(\exists x)[Faxb \rightarrow \neg(\forall x)(Hx \equiv Gxb)]$$
$$(\exists x)Faxb \rightarrow \neg(\forall x)(Hx \equiv Gab)$$

are not since, in the first sentence, the variable x in Gxb became bound by a quantifier already in the original sentence, namely, $(\forall x)$. As for the second sentence, the existential quantifier $(\exists x)$ did not become the main logical operator ($\rightarrow$ is). It is important to understand the definitions given above because they play an important role in the chapters in which we introduce the derivation systems PD and PD+; these syntactic transformations of instantiation and generalization provide the framework for four new rules of inference (of the same name). To this end, we provide several exercises at the end of this section.

Before we conclude this section, there is one matter which deserves a brief discussion. It can be framed as a question: Since quantified sentences can be easily produced from either atomic ones or from truth-functional compounds by means of generalization, why should they be regarded as a distinct type of basic sentence? The reason lies not with syntax, which has been the recent focus, but with semantics; it concerns the truth-conditions of quantified statements. A fuller account of these will be given later, but some indication of what is involved can be sketched now through an example. As far as their structure is concerned, the following two statements are very similar, both in words and symbols:

Every food is either solid or liquid $(\forall x)(Fx \rightarrow (Sx \vee Lx))$
Every integer is either odd or even $(\forall x)(Ix \rightarrow (Ox \vee Ex))$

Where they differ in a logically important way, however, is in their respective universes of discourse.[25] The foods of the world are many, though not infinite, but there is no end to the number of integers. Suppose you attended a fantastically comprehensive International Food Fair in which all the foods of the world were gathered and labeled before your very eyes. Then you would be in an excellent position to find out whether it is true that every food is either solid or liquid (by some agreed standard of what these two words mean). The first statement would 'cash out' in the form of a large series of instantiations, such as Fa $\rightarrow$ (Sa $\vee$ La), Fb $\rightarrow$ (Sb $\vee$ Lb), where a is the label given to the first food in the catalog, b to the second and so on; and although there would be a staggering number of statements like this one, the process of checking each of them would be the same: Each conditional statement would be true according to the familiar truth-functional rules of SL. Moreover, if all of these instantiations were found to be true, the first quantified statement itself would also be true.

As long as its universe of discourse is finite, any universal quantification can be regarded as an abbreviation for a finitely long conjunction of

[25] See section 6.2 for a brief discussion of the concept of a universe of discourse.

instantial sentences: In principle, the conjunction could always be written in place of the quantification. But whenever the universe of discourse is infinite, as with the second sentence, it would be impossible to make this substitution. The list of instantial constants would never be exhausted, and a conjunction with infinitely many conjuncts is not a sentence of either SL or PL. The same holds for any statement whose universe of discourse is indefinitely large. In such cases, universal quantifications cannot be treated as abbreviations.

Formal logic includes no routine for checking whether a universe of discourse is finite, indefinitely large or infinite. Instead, it assumes that every quantificational statement (existential and universal alike) has an infinite domain. Such a policy seems generous, perhaps even excessive. A sentence such as 'All of Henry VIII's wives lived in fear' hardly requires such a domain (six is enough). However, any excess here is only on the side of names. Henry's six wives would each receive at least one name, allowing six different instantiations to be conjoined, and by testing the conjunction we could find out whether the original (universally quantified) statement is true. Of course, an infinite number of redundant names would remain, but that is far preferable to a situation in which failure to provide enough names causes some things to be named ambiguously or never even named at all, which would directly affect what we mean by the truth-conditions of a quantified statement. So the policy adopted by logic is generous and more prudent than excessive, and also it avoids the need for any sort of empirical survey of the actual size of classes. In checking on whether some universal statement is true, we realize that we might run out of objects but never out of names. This is the underlying reason why atomic sentences and quantificational sentences have been treated as two different types, despite their close syntactical relations.

Exercises

6.3.1 According to PL's formation rules, which of the following are well-formed formulas?

    a. Fab   b. $(\neg Hab \rightarrow Gc)$ c. $((\forall x)Gxa)$

    d. $\neg(\exists x)Kxy$ e. Bxyy   f. $(\exists x \forall y)Lxy$

    g. $(\neg \forall x)Fxx$ h. $(\exists x)(Bax \rightarrow Lab)$ i. $(\forall x)(\forall y)(\exists z)Bxzy$

6.3.2 Single out the bound and free variables in each of the following wffs.

    a. $(\forall x)Fxy$ b. $(\forall z)Kxy$ c. $(\forall x)(Gxz \rightarrow Lyb)$

    d. $(\forall x)Gxz \vee Lyx$ e. $(\exists x)(\forall y)Lyx$ f. $(\forall x)(Bxy \rightarrow (\exists y)Lxy)$

6.3.3 Which of the following are sentences (as opposed to merely wffs)?

    a. Fab   b. Kxac   c. $(\exists x)(Gxa \rightarrow Lxx)$

    d. $(\exists y)Gye \vee Lyx$ e. $(\exists x)Fy \vee (\exists y)Fx$ f. $(\forall z)(Baz \rightarrow (\forall y)Lzy)$

6.3.4 Which of the following sentences are of the form $\neg \alpha \rightarrow \beta$?

    a. $\neg Fa \rightarrow Gc$ b. $\neg(Fa \rightarrow Gc)$ c. $Fa \rightarrow \neg Gc$

    d. $\neg Fa \rightarrow \neg Gc$ e. $\neg(\exists x)Fx \rightarrow Gc$ f. $\neg(\forall x)Fx \rightarrow \neg(\exists y)Gy$

6.3.5 Which of the following sentences are of the form $(\forall \mathbf{x})\alpha$?

a. $(\forall x)(Fx \rightarrow Fa)$ b. $(\forall x)Fx \mathbin{\&} Fa$ c. $(\forall y)(Gy \rightarrow (\exists z)Fzy)$

d. $(\forall x)\neg(\exists y)Lxy$ e. $(\exists y)\neg(\forall x)Lxy$ f. $\neg\neg(\forall x)(Fx \rightarrow Gb)$

6.3.6 (For the mathematically inclined student) Let α and β be formulas of PL and let **R** be a k-ary predicate symbol, $k \geqslant 0$. Define (inductively) the set Free(γ) of free variables of a formula γ of PL as

1. Free($\mathbf{R}t_1 \ldots t_k$) = $\{t_i : t_i$ is a variable$\}$
2. Free($\neg\alpha$) = Free(α)
3. Free($(\alpha\ \theta\ \beta)$) = Free(α) $\cup$ Free(β), where θ is &, $\vee$, $\rightarrow$ or $\equiv$
4. Free($(\Theta\mathbf{x})\alpha$) = Free(α) $-$ $\{\mathbf{x}\}$, where Θ is $\exists$ or $\forall$

Show that Free($(Fxay \vee (\neg Gxa \rightarrow (\forall z)Hzwb))$) = $\{x,y,w\}$. Illustrate with a few examples that Free(α) = $\varnothing$, where α is a sentence of PL.

6.3.7 (For the mathematically inclined student) Let α and β be formulas of PL and let **R** be a k-ary predicate symbol, $k \geqslant 0$. Define (inductively) the set SubWffs(γ) of all the (sub)formulas in a formula γ of PL as

1. SubWffs($\mathbf{R}t_1 \ldots t_k$) = $\{\mathbf{R}t_1 \ldots t_k\}$
2. Subwffs($\neg\alpha$) = $\{\neg\alpha\}$ $\cup$ SubWffs(α)
3. SubWffs($(\alpha\ \theta\ \beta)$) = $\{(\alpha\ \theta\ \beta)\}$ $\cup$ SubWffs(α) $\cup$ SubWffs(β), where θ is &, $\vee$, $\rightarrow$ or $\equiv$
4. SubWffs($(\Theta\mathbf{x})\alpha$) = $\{(\Theta\mathbf{x})\alpha\}$ $\cup$ SubWffs(α), where Θ is $\exists$ or $\forall$

Define the **size** of a wff α of PL, denoted by Size(α), as the number of subwffs it has. Determine SubWffs(α) and Size(α) for the following wffs:

a. $\neg Fab$

b. $Gabc \rightarrow \neg(Fa \mathbin{\&} Hm)$

c. $(\forall x)Fx \equiv \neg\neg Fa$

d. $(\exists x)(\forall y)\neg Fxy \mathbin{\&} (\forall y)\neg Fxy$

e. $\neg(\forall x)Fxx \vee \neg(\exists x)Fxx$

6.3.8 For each of the following quantified sentences give the instantiation associated with the substitution a/x (i.e., where the constant a is to replace the variable x).

a. $(\forall x)Fx$ b. $(\forall x)(Fcx \mathbin{\&} Fbx)$ c. $(\forall x)(\exists y)(Fx \mathbin{\&} Kyx)$

d. $(\forall x)\neg(\exists y)Lxy$ e. $(\exists x)Gx \rightarrow Fa$ f. $(\exists x)(Gx \rightarrow (\exists x)Fxc)$

g. $(\exists x)Lxc$ h. $(\exists x)(Kxx \vee Fbxc)$ i. $(\forall x)(Sx \equiv (\exists x)Kxx)$

j. $(\forall x)((\exists x)Sx \equiv (\exists y)Kxy)$ k. $(\forall x)(\forall y)Sxyx$ l. $\neg(\forall x)Fxb$

6.3.9 For each of the following sentences give the universal generalization associated with the substitution y/c (i.e., where the variable y is to replace the constant c).

a. Fcc b. $Fabc$ c. $\neg Fc \equiv Rbca$

d. $(\exists x)Lcx$ e. $(\exists y)Kyc \rightarrow Fc$ f. $(\exists x)Kxc \rightarrow Fc$

6.3.10 For each of the sentences of exercise 6.3.9 give *all* the possible existential generalizations associated with the substitution y/c (i.e., where the variable y is to replace the constant c).

6.4   *The Semantics of PL: An Overview*

For atomic sentences and truth-functional compounds, questions of truth and falsity are decided by the same standards and rules found in SL. An atomic sentence is true or false on a given truth-value assignment if it is assigned this truth-value, that is, it is assigned either a ⊤ or an ⊦ on that assignment. A sentence of the form ¬α is true on a given assignment if and only if α itself is false on that assignment. A sentence of the form α & β is true on a given truth-value assignment iff each of the components, α and β, is true on that assignment—and so on for the other three binary connectives.[26] Consequently, even if the immediate component of a truth-functional compound happens to be a quantificational sentence, as in ¬Fab & (∀x)Gx, we can see how its own truth-value would affect that of the compound itself. For instance, if a quantificational sentence α happens to be false on a given assignment, any conditional sentence with α as the antecedent would have to be true on that assignment, and any conjunction with α as one of the two conjuncts would have to be false on the same assignment.

However, the truth-conditions for quantificational sentences themselves—(∃x)α and (∀x)α—are more elaborate to state. One reason is that although they are compounds of a sort, they do not have components in the way that a truth-functional compound of SL does. An SL compound can always be analyzed into its immediate components (its disjuncts, for example, or its antecedent and consequent), and if any of these also are compounds the process of analyzing them can be carried down to the level of atomic sentences, where it ends. In any case, these atomic sentences can always be readily identified within the structure of an SL compound. They constitute an explicit part of that structure. However, you recall that the explicit components of a quantified sentence are not sentences at all but only phrases, which typically contain at least one free variable. The instances of a quantified sentence, which we will need here in our informal account of the semantics of quantified sentences, are therefore not really its components; they are not part of its *explicit* structure but have to be generated from it by the mechanical process of instantiation. Another reason why quantified sentences require a more elaborate account stems from our discussion at the end of the last section. The quantified sentences of PL are assumed to range over domains which are either infinite or indefinitely large. As a result, we could never replace a quantified sentence by a truth-functional compound of its instances, except when that sentence clearly applies to a known, limited domain, as the wives of Henry VIII. Since the business of formal logic does not involve investigating the actual size of finite classes, we will take it for granted that no quantified sentence can be reduced to a truth-functional compounding of its instances.

The consequence of this assumption may not be immediately apparent. An SL sentence's components are always finite in number and the same

---

[26] If you need to review them, look back at the definitions given in Chapter 2.

holds for its atomic components. But in the case of a quantified sentence, the number of its instances and hence of its atomic instances will be infinite. A finite number of atomic components becomes the basis for calculating a finite number of logically possible truth-value assignments in SL. For any number, n, of atomic sentences, there are 2^n possible assignments. For a quantified sentence, however, since the number of atomic instances is infinite, there are uncountably many such assignments. Therefore, the truth-conditions for quantified sentences can only be described but they cannot in any literal sense be listed. A further consequence of this fact is that the truth-table method of SL becomes inoperative in PL wherever quantified sentences are involved, whether these sentences occur alone or as part of a truth-functional compound. As you will see in the next chapter, however, PL puts the method of truth-trees to good use.

We have not reached an impasse in the account of quantificational truth. The descriptions of truth-conditions can be detailed and precise, and they will make clear what any quantificational sentence aims to say. Take, for instance, any universal sentence of the form $(\forall x)\alpha$, say, $(\forall x)Txb$. If a sentence of this form is true, then *all* of its instances must be true. If

> Everything troubles Bob.

is true, then whatever constant **a** you take, say, c, it must be the case that Bob is troubled by c; that is, if $(\forall x)Txb$ is true then T**ab** (e.g., Tcb) holds for any constant **a**, and vice versa. It would be impossible to mention all the things there are, but if the sentence is true it must be true in the case of each of these things that it troubles Bob. Each sentence which is an instance of $(\forall x)Txb$ must be true. Otherwise, this universal sentence would be false. In other words, if there is even one thing which fails to trouble Bob, $(\forall x)Txb$ would be false. Suppose that in fact Bob is quite pleased with the quality of McDonald's cheeseburgers—their quality troubles him not in the least. Then the universal sentence would be false. Take another example we met earlier, that all roads lead to Rome: $(\forall x)(Rx \rightarrow Lxr)$. This sentence will be true if but only if each of its instances, Ra $\rightarrow$ Lar, Rb $\rightarrow$ Lbr, Rc $\rightarrow$ Lcr, ... is true, for an indefinite number of constants. Suppose that you come upon a road which you name a_{237} and which you discover does not in any sense lead to Rome, simply because this road is unconnected with any road at all. The instance, $Ra_{237} \rightarrow La_{237}r$, would then be false since its antecedent and consequent, respectively, would be true and false. And so too would be the universal sentence itself.

Accordingly, we can say of any such sentence,

Definition. $(\forall \mathbf{x})\alpha$ is true iff $\alpha(\mathbf{a}/\mathbf{x})$ is true for every constant **a**.

In truth-functional terms, the instances of a universal sentence $(\forall \mathbf{x})\alpha$, on which its truth depends, would form an infinite conjunction:

$\alpha(a/\mathbf{x})$ & $\alpha(b/\mathbf{x})$ & $\alpha(c/\mathbf{x})$ & ...

The conjunction would be true, and hence $(\forall \mathbf{x})\alpha$ itself, if and only if each of its conjuncts is true. If one happened to be false, so would the conjunction. However, since this conjunction has an infinite (or indefinitely extended) number of conjuncts, it is a sentence of neither SL nor PL, and is therefore not a wff. Sometimes an instance, $\alpha(\mathbf{a/x})$, of a universal might also be a universal, as in the case of this sentence: $(\forall \mathbf{x})(\forall \mathbf{y})A\mathbf{x}\mathbf{y}$. Here, the sentence is true if each instance, $(\forall \mathbf{y})A\mathbf{a}\mathbf{y}$, is true. And each of these instances—that is, for a chosen constant **a**—will be in turn true iff all of its instances are true as well. In other words, a doubly universally quantified sentence is true if all the instances of all its instances are true. The instances would make use of the same terms, as the following fragmentary list suggests:

Sentence	Its instances
$(\forall x)(\forall y)Axy$	$(\forall y)Aay, (\forall y)Aby, (\forall y)Acy, (\forall y)Ady, \ldots$
$(\forall y)Aay$	$Aaa, Aab, Aac, Aad, \ldots$
$(\forall y)Aby$	$Aba, Abb, Abc, Abd, \ldots$
$(\forall y)Acy$	$Aca, Acb, Acc, Acd, \ldots$

Where necessary, a process of multiple instantiations will ultimately yield a set of atomic sentences. These are no other than the ground atomic subformulas of the given quantificational sentence. By means of necessarily incomplete lists we can always describe what these ground atomic subformulas are, and it is to these that the truth or falsity of quantificational sentences is anchored. Looking at the previous example, $(\forall x)(\forall y)Axy$ is true if and only if the atomic sentences $Aaa, Aab, Aac, \ldots, Aba, Abb, Abc, \ldots, Aca, Acb, Acc, \ldots$ are all true. As another example, $(\forall x)\neg(Fx \rightarrow Gx)$ is true iff the instances $\neg(Fa \rightarrow Ga), \neg(Fb \rightarrow Gb), \neg(Fc \rightarrow Gc), \ldots$ are all true, i.e., iff $Fa \rightarrow Ga, Fb \rightarrow Gb, Fc \rightarrow Gc, \ldots$ are all false, i.e., iff $Fa, Fb, Fc, \ldots$ are all true and $Ga, Gb, Gc, \ldots$ are all false.

Now let us change the focus to sentences of the form $(\exists \mathbf{x})\alpha$. Unlike universal sentences, the truth of a partial quantification does not require that each of its instances be true. It is sufficient that one such instance be true (recall their translation in logicalese, which begins 'There is at least one thing, x, which . . .'). Here, to illustrate, is another former example,

Bob is allergic to some foods.

which in symbols is

$(\exists x)(Fx \ \& \ Abx)$

This sentence says that there is at least one food to which Bob is allergic. For it to be true, Bob need not have an allergy to every food. The sentence would be true if *some* instance or other were true for some constant, **a**. If Bob were allergic to tofu, for instance, or oat bran potato chips or hominy or even goldfish (assuming he indulges in goldfish every so often, such as at the annual Animal Rights Ball), the sentence would be true. However, it would be false if there were no instance of this sentence which is true. Accordingly, we can say of any such sentence,

> **Definition.** A sentence of the form $(\exists \mathbf{x})\alpha$ is true iff $\alpha(\mathbf{a}/\mathbf{x})$ is true for some constant $\mathbf{a}$.

If it were possible to express a partial quantification $(\exists \mathbf{x})\alpha$ as a truth-functional compound of its instances, it would have this form:

$$\alpha(a/\mathbf{x}) \vee \alpha(b/\mathbf{x}) \vee \alpha(c/\mathbf{x}) \vee \ldots$$

The disjunction would be true, and so would the quantification itself, if and only if at least one of the disjuncts is true; otherwise, as in the case of any disjunction, it would be false.

You will recall from the last section that instantiation and generalization are complementary syntactical routines. The one proceeds from a quantified sentence to the level of its instances; the other produces a quantificational compound from any of its instances. Instantiation replaces a variable with a constant; generalization is the reverse process of replacing a constant by a variable and quantifying over it. These relations provide a framework for interpreting questions of truth-value. Compare the following similarities and differences:

(1) A universal sentence is true iff all of its instances are true.
(2) A partial sentence is false iff all of its instances are false.
(3) A universal sentence is false iff at least one instance is false.
(4) A partial sentence is true iff at least one instance is true.

The list shows that the semantic relations of universal and partial quantifications are complementary also. This being the case, the known or assumed truth-value of any given sentence which contains a constant has a bearing on the truth-value of any sentence obtained from it by the process of generalization. An example will help bring out the point. Consider the following atomic sentence (whose symbolization in PL is given to its right):

> This magnet attracts that piece of iron.   Amp

First let us assume that Amp is true. Then the following four sentences would also be true (by clause 4):

  (i) $(\exists x)Axp$
 (ii) $(\exists x)Amx$
(iii) $(\exists y)(\exists x)Axy$
(iv) $(\exists y)(\exists x)Ayx$[27]

---

[27] Sentences (iii) and (iv) are logically equivalent.

Also, the truth of Amp would be compatible with the truth of the corresponding universal sentences: (∀x)Axp, (∀x)Amx, (∀y)(∀x)Axy and (∀y)(∀x)Ayx. This is the case because Amp would be numbered among the infinitely many ground atomic subformulas of each of these sentences and its truth would be a necessary condition for their truth, though certainly not a sufficient one. Now let us assume that Amp is false. Then these same four universal sentences would each have to be false (by clause 3) since at least one of their ground atomic subformula instances would be false.[28]

Changing direction, we will now follow other lines of inference, starting with a fresh pair of sentences. Suppose the sentence (∃x)(Ax & Bx) is false; then (by clause 2) each of its instances would be false. These would take the form of conjunctions of the ground atomic subformulas Aa and Ba, Ab and Bb, Ac and Bc and so on. Thus the assumption that (∃x)(Ax & Bx) is false implies that there is some truth-value assignment to the ground atomic subformulas of (∃x)(Ax & Bx) on which each instance, and hence the sentence itself, is false. In fact there are several such assignments to the infinite number of these subformulas: false to Aa, Ab, Ac, . . . and true to Ba, Bb, Bc, . . . ; false to all the ground atomic subformulas Aa, Ab, Ac, . . . and Ba, Bb, Bc, . . . ; or false to just Ba, Bb, Bc, . . . ; and so on. Suppose instead that this existential sentence, (∃x)(Ax & Bx), is true; then it can be inferred (clause 4) that at least one of its instances is true, although it would be impossible to infer which sentence that is. If this seems odd, recall a previous example. If all you are told is that Bob is allergic to some foods, it would be impossible from that information alone to infer which food (or foods) that might be. You would know only that at least one disjunct is true in the endless disjunction that expresses the truth conditions of (∃x)(Ax & Bx). What you would know, then, is that the statement 'Every A fails to be B' is false; in symbols, ¬(∀x)(Ax → ¬Bx).

Similarly, if the universal sentence (∀x)(Fx → Gx) is true on some truth-value assignment to its ground atomic subformulas, then (clause 1) all of its instances, Fa → Ga, Fb → Gb, Fc → Gc, . . . are true. And there are several possible assignments which would fulfill the requirement. However, if this universal sentence is false, it is certain that at least one of its instances is false (clause 3), though once again it is impossible to deduce that instance on the basis of this fact alone. You could infer only that there is at least one thing, x, which is F but not G, or in symbols, (∃x)(Fx & ¬Gx).

The last two examples make use of two logical equivalences which play a useful role in PL. We represent them schematically:

$$(\forall \mathbf{x})\alpha \equiv \neg(\exists \mathbf{x})\neg\alpha$$
$$(\exists \mathbf{x})\alpha \equiv \neg(\forall \mathbf{x})\neg\alpha$$

To say that a sentence which has the form (∀**x**)α is logically equivalent to one whose form is ¬(∃**x**)¬α means that these sentences would have the

---

[28] Amp is an instance of only the first two sentences in each group, but it is a ground instance of all four.

same truth-value on every logically possible assignment of truth-values to their ground atomic subformulas. For instance, $(\forall x)(Fx \rightarrow Gx)$ and its equivalent $\neg(\exists x)\neg(Fx \rightarrow Gx)$ would be true or false on all and only the same truth-value assignments to their ground atomic subformulas, Fa, Fb, Fc, . . . , Ga, Gb, Gc, . . . and so on. You should satisfy yourself that this is so by referring to the four clauses listed above.[29]

A sentence is **quantificationally**, or **logically, true** if and only if it is true on every possible truth-value assignment to its ground atomic subformulas. In the case of a universally quantified sentence, therefore, each of its instances would have to be true, not on just one but on every truth-value assignment to the ground atomic components of that instance. (These assignments would constitute a subset of all those that are logically possible for the quantificational sentence itself.) In other words, each instance would have to be itself a logical truth. The following sentence is logically true:

$$(\forall x)(Bx \rightarrow (\exists y)By)$$

To see that it is so, take any instance of it (we will use the constant a as a representative):

$$Ba \rightarrow (\exists y)By$$

Since this sentence has the form of a truth-functional compound, we can readily apply the technique of indirect proof used in SL to show that it is logically true: We assume that there is some truth-value assignment on which the sentence is false:

Ba → (∃y)By
 T F   F

On this assignment, as you can see, the truth-values of the immediate components follow by truth-functional definition. Since the consequent is false, so too must be each of its instances (clause 2). But numbered among these instances is Ba, which must be true on this assignment, and thus we have run into a contradiction. The fact that Ba is true on this assignment is sufficient to make $(\exists y)By$ true, and yet it follows from the original assumption that this quantificational sentence is false. Consequently, the assumption itself must be rejected. The conditional sentence is therefore logically true, and the fact that it has served as a representative instance of $(\forall x)(Bx \rightarrow (\exists y)By)$ shows that the universal sentence itself is a logical truth, for what was found in the case of the substitution of a for x, a/x, would hold for any chosen substitution, b/x, c/x, d/x and so on.

---

[29] A highly intuitive example to convince you of the truth of the previous two logical equivalences is the following: 'Everybody is happy'—$(\forall x)Hx$—says the same as 'No one is sad'—$\neg(\exists x)\neg Hx$—and 'Someone is happy'—$(\exists x)Hx$—says the same as 'Not everybody is sad'—$\neg(\forall x)\neg Hx$.

With the definition of logical truth on hand, two related concepts fall easily into place. A sentence α is **quantificationally**, or **logically**, **false** if and only if it is false on every possible truth-value assignment to its ground atomic subformulas, for an existential α, each instance of α would itself be logically false. More simply, α is logically false iff $\neg\alpha$ is logically true. A sentence α is **quantificationally indeterminate** (or **contingent**) if and only if α is neither logically true nor logically false. The majority of sentences which have appeared in this section are contingent: It would be possible to describe a truth-value assignment on which any such sentence is true as well as one on which it is false.

The full apparatus of semantical concepts introduced for SL can now be rolled out for quantificational logic:

Entailment.   A sentence α or a set of sentences, $\{\alpha_1, \alpha_2, \ldots, \alpha_n\}$, **quantificationally entails** a given sentence, β, iff the conditional analogue corresponding to these sentences, $(\alpha_1 \,\&\, \alpha_2 \,\&\, \ldots \,\&\, \alpha_n) \to \beta$ is a logical truth. (See also the test set below.) As in SL, if a set Γ entails β then we write $\Gamma \vDash \beta$.

Validity.   An argument of the form,

α_1
α_2
.
.
.
α_n
$\overline{\beta}$

is **quantificationally valid** iff the set of its premises, $\{\alpha_1, \alpha_2, \ldots, \alpha_n\}$, entails the conclusion, β.

Consistency.   A set of sentences $\{\alpha_1, \alpha_2, \ldots, \alpha_n\}$ is **quantificationally consistent** iff there is a truth-value assignment to the ground atomic subformulas of the members of the set on which they (i.e., the members of the set) are all true. A set is **inconsistent** iff there is no such assignment. Relatedly, a sentence α, or a set of sentences $\{\alpha_1, \alpha_2, \ldots, \alpha_n\}$, entails a given sentence, β, iff the test set corresponding to these sentences, $\{\alpha_1, \alpha_2, \ldots, \alpha_n, \neg\beta\}$ is inconsistent; similarly, an argument is valid iff the test set made up of its premises plus the denial of its conclusion is inconsistent.

It is worth pointing out that every case of entailment and every case of validity found in SL remains so when suitably translated into the symbolism of PL. Thus, for instance, an argument of the form,

$$\frac{\begin{array}{c} \alpha \rightarrow \beta \\ \neg \beta \end{array}}{\neg \alpha}$$

remains valid in PL. However, there are many arguments that are valid in PL which, as symbolized in SL, are invalid. Here is an example:

> Every book worth reading is worth reading well.
> This book is worth reading.
> _____
> This book is worth reading well.

Here are the symbolizations of the argument in SL and in PL (in the latter, we assume the set of books as the universe of discourse):

In SL   *In PL*

P	(∀x)(Rx → Lx)
Q	Rt
R	Lt

Clearly, the SL form of this argument is invalid (as P and Q can be made true and R false). But its analogue in PL is easily shown to be valid. Let us take a moment to prove this. The key move is the instantiation of the first premise. If we assume that both premises are true, each instance of (∀x)(Rx → Lx) is true and, in particular, Rt → Lt is true. But since we have assumed Rt to be true it follows that Lt must be true too. Hence, if the premises are true then the conclusion cannot be false and, by definition, the argument is valid.

Although the semantical apparatus of PL is now in place, there remains much detail to be filled in regarding techniques of proving logical truth, validity and the like. The structure of individual sentences, as well as of arguments themselves, is often more complicated than is evident from the last example. The semantic route which leads from quantifications to ground atomic subformulas must sometimes proceed through several stages of instantiation and decomposition, just as the route of generalization sometimes requires repeated steps before one arrives at what is needed. But if you will keep in mind the picture of the relationships sketched in this section, you are sure not to lose your way. The techniques of truth-trees and derivations are well designed to carry you through those stages. It goes without saying that this book is worth reading—after all, how could any logic book fail to be? We are certain you will continue to find in the following chapters that *Symlog*'s tools make this book that much easier to read well.

A more sophisticated account of the semantics of PL will be found in Chapter 9, 'Structures.' Both the preceding account and the one in Chapter 9 are compatible with the presentation of truth-trees for PL and with PL's derivation system, PD.

Exercises

6.4.1   For each of the sentences a, b and c of exercise 6.3.8 give its ground atomic subformulas.

6.4.2   Assign the truth-value T to each of Fa, Fb, Fc and so on and the truth-value F to the remaining atomic sentences of PL. Under this truth-value assignment, what is the truth-value of the following sentences?

a. Fa ∨ Rab   b. Raa → Fc   c. (∀x)Fx → Kca

d. (∃x)(∃y)Gxy   e. (∃x)Bx → Fe   f. (∀x)(¬Fx → Lxc)

g. (∀x)Kxy   h. Fa → (∃y)Gy   i. (∀x)Fx & ¬(∃x)Kx

6.4.3   Consider the truth-value assignment which assigns T to each of Faa, Fab, Fac and so on and the truth-value F to the remaining atomic sentences of PL. Under this truth-value assignment, what is the truth-value of the following sentences?

a. Fab ≡ Fba   b. (∃x)(Fxa ≡ Fax)   c. (∃x)(Fxb ≡ Fbx)

d. (∀x)(∃y)Fxy   e. (∃x)(∀y)Fxy   f. (∀x)(∃y)Fyx

6.4.4   Give a truth-value assignment under which each sentence in the set {La & ¬Kb, (∃x)Kx, (∀x)¬Hx} comes out T.

6.4.5   Give a truth-value assignment under which the sentence (∀x)(∃y)Fxy comes out T but (∃x)(∀y)Fxy comes out F.

6.4.6   Show that the argument whose set of premises is the set {(∀x)Fx} and whose conclusion is the sentence Fa is quantificationally valid.

6.4.7   Show that the argument whose (only) premise is the sentence (∀x)¬Fx and whose conclusion is the sentence ¬(∃x)Fx is quantificationally valid.

6.4.8   Show that the following argument is quantificationally valid in PL.

Albert is rich.
If someone is rich then Mary is happy.

Someone is happy.

6.4.9   Show that the set {(∀x)(¬Fx & Gbx), (∃x)Fx} is quantificationally inconsistent.

6.4.10 Why is this argument truth-functionally invalid (in SL) but quantificationally valid (in PL)?

All even numbers are divisible by 2.
16 is an even number.

16 is divisible by 2.

6.4.11 Which of the following arguments are valid and which are invalid?

a. (∀x)(Fx → Gx)
   Fa & (∃x)Hxx

   (∃x)Gx

b. (∀x)¬Fx

   ¬(∃x)Fx

c. $\dfrac{\neg(\forall x)Fx}{(\exists x)\neg Fx}$

d. $\dfrac{(\exists x)\neg Fx}{\neg(\forall x)Fx}$

e. $\dfrac{(\forall x)Fx \vee (\forall x)Gx}{(\forall x)(Fx \vee Gx)}$

f. $\dfrac{(\forall x)(Fx \vee Gx)}{(\forall x)Fx \vee (\forall x)Gx}$

g. $\dfrac{\neg(\forall x)\neg Fx}{(\exists x)\neg Fx}$

h. $\dfrac{(\exists x)Fx \rightarrow Ga}{(\forall x)(Fx \rightarrow Ga)}$

i. $\dfrac{Fa \rightarrow (\exists x)Gx}{(\forall x)(Fa \rightarrow Gx)}$

j. $\dfrac{Fa \rightarrow (\forall x)Gx}{(\forall x)(Fa \rightarrow Gx)}$

6.4.12 Answer true or false (but not both) to each of the following questions. (Note: The conventions which relax the syntax of PL are allowed.)

a. A universe of discourse can be infinite in size.

b. The main logical operator of $(\forall x)(\exists y)Fxy \vee \neg(\forall z)Gza$ is $\vee$.

c. If a sentence of PL has exactly two quantifiers then their scopes must intersect.

d. If a quantified sentence of PL has exactly two quantifiers then their scopes must intersect.

e. There is a sentence of PL with exactly three free variables.

f. $(\forall x)Fx \rightarrow \neg(\forall y)Hyy$ is a quantified sentence of PL.

g. PL has infinitely many variables.

h. z is an individual term of PL.

i. $(\forall x)(P \,\&\, Q)$ is a formula of PL.

j. All the sentences of SL are sentences of PL.

k. Some well-formed formulas of PL are well-formed formulas of SL.

l. $\neg((\exists x)Ax \equiv \neg(\forall y)(Bxy \vee \neg Ay))$ is a sentence of PL.

m. $Fa \vee (\exists x)Gxx$ is an instantiation of $(\forall x)(Fx \vee (\exists x)Gxx)$.

n. $(\forall x)Fx \rightarrow Gc$ is a universal generalization of $Fa \rightarrow Gc$.

o. $(\exists z)(Abz \,\&\, (\forall z)Hzb)$ is an existential generalization of $Aba \,\&\, (\forall z)Hab$.

6.4.13 Show that if $\Gamma \models \alpha$ and $\Gamma \models \neg\alpha$ then Γ is quantificationally inconsistent.

7

PL Truth-Trees

The quantificational concepts sketched in the last chapter run parallel to those of SL. Yet there is a crucial difference between these two systems of logic which directly affects the possibility of carrying out a complete analysis of quantificational sentences, a difference which not even *Symlog* could minimize. As we saw, PL's quantified sentences range over infinite domains, and their truth (or falsity) may depend on the truth-values of an infinite number of instances. However, it would be impossible to upgrade the truth-table method of SL for cases involving an infinite number of truth-value assignments because the task of constructing the matrix of assignments to atomic subformulas would never be completed to enable row-by-row testing to begin. Infinite domains thus offer a new challenge to mechanical methods of testing in logic. The purpose of this chapter is to adapt the truth-tree method to cope with this fact.

The overall aim of the truth-tree method, as it applies to PL, remains the same as in SL. The concepts of consistency and inconsistency furnish the basis for defining the now familiar range of semantical properties which extends from logical truth to validity. The method allows the systematic decomposition of a set of sentences into the atomic subformulas of its members, and as a result of this process each branch of the emerging truth-tree either closes or remains open. A set having a tree with all 'dead' branches is declared an inconsistent set of sentences, just as in SL. Similarly, a tree having at least one 'living' branch, and to which no further atomic subformulas are to be added, corresponds to a consistent set. As is only to be expected, however, there are different varieties of living—open—branches in PL, some of which are *infinitely long* and therefore incapable of being represented. The truth-tree method makes it possible to recognize *some* of these varieties of open branches and, in most cases, affords a simple way of demonstrating the consistency of the sets to which they belong.

7.1 *The Decomposition Rules*

Since SL and PL share the same truth-functional connectives, all the decomposition rules introduced in Chapter 4 for determining consistency can be extended in a natural way to deal with sets of PL sentences. Of course, a few additional rules will be needed for the decomposition of quantificational sentences (and their negations). But before introducing these, and for the sake of a quick review, let us see how *Symlog* applies the older rules of the truth-tree method to the new context of PL. As an example, we show that the set {(∀x)Fx → ¬¬Gb, ¬(Hab & Gb), Hab & (∀x)Fx} is quantificationally inconsistent and that the set {¬(¬Ea & Ob), Ob & Lba} is quantificationally consistent. The resulting trees for these sets can be seen in Figure 7.1a and Figure 7.1b, respectively. Take a moment to study them.

All the branches in the PL truth-tree in Figure 7.1a have been closed. Thus it is impossible for all the sentences in {(∀x)Fx → ¬¬Gb, ¬(Hab & Gb), Hab & (∀x)Fx} to be true together, and hence this set is inconsistent. However, the fact that the tree in Figure 7.1b has one completed open branch is enough to establish the consistency of {¬(¬Ea & Ob), Ob & Lba}. The branch contains no pair of self-contradictory sentences and no sentences remain to be decomposed on it. Indeed, for the set shown in Figure 7.1b, a truth-value assignment can be easily found on which both members of the set, ¬(¬Ea & Ob) and Ob & Lba, are true. The routine to follow for this example is exactly the same as for **SL**: To every (ground) atomic sentence which appears on the completed open branch assign the truth-value T, to every atomic sentence which occurs negated on that branch assign an F and to any atomic sentence not occurring on the branch at all assign either a T or an F. Thus, the sentences Ea, Ob and Lba at the bottom of the tree each receive a T, and the two conjunctions which make up the original set are thereby certain to be true. In this particular case, no atomic sentences remain negated on the open branch, so that the truth-value F is not assigned, and no atomic sentences belonging to the set are missing from the branch itself. You will find more complicated examples in the exercises, where such details arise. But first you will need to know something about the assignment of truth-values when an open branch contains one or more quantificational sentences. As you recall, these come in two basic forms, universal and existential: (∀x)α and (∃x)α. For truth-trees, it is necessary to include their negations as well: ¬(∀x)α and ¬(∃x)α.

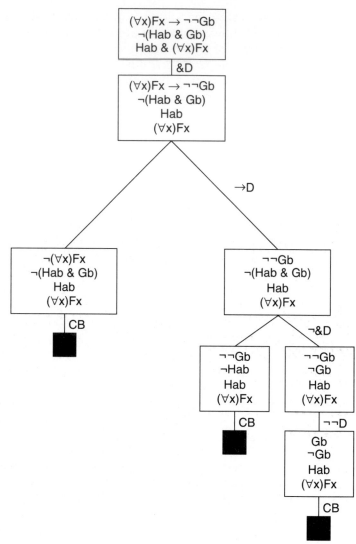

Figure 7.1a

In view of the discussion in the last chapter, you can appreciate why the task of determining the truth-values of quantificational sentences of these four kinds is a complicated business. The truth or falsity of such sentences depends on that of their instances, which are infinite in number. Whereas the truth of an existential sentence depends on just one of its instances being true, a universal sentence is true if and only if *every* one of its instances is true; however, it would be plainly impossible to show all these instances on any open branch. Intuitively, if a PL set is consistent and a universal sentence is one of its members, then any nonclosing branch stemming from it will likewise be consistent. Yet since the branch is infinite, there is no sense in 'retrieving' a truth-value assignment to its members. A

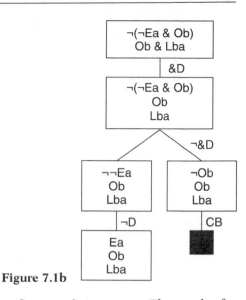

Figure 7.1b

similar contrast holds for negated quantificational sentences: The truth of a negated universal entails the falsehood of the universal sentence itself and hence the falsehood of at least one of its instances, whereas the truth of a negated existential entails the falsehood of the existential sentence itself and thus the falsehood of all of its instances. Here, too, it would be impossible to complete the list of all the instances on which the falsehood of that existential sentence depends. Thus, any open branch containing a universal or negated existential (and which remains open after instantiating the sentence) is potentially infinite in length, and a tree with at least one open branch of this kind is potentially infinite in size. How, then, is it possible to grow truth-trees in PL, when they might require an endless amount of space? More to the point: If a tree is potentially infinite, what would justify our declaring the set of sentences from which it springs to be consistent, when it is impossible to list all the instances of any sentence on whose truth the set's consistency depends? The answer is to be found by adopting a few simple procedures (called **ground rules**) which accompany the rules for decomposing quantificational sentences.

   To construct PL truth-trees you may use any of the SL rules, such as those illustrated in the preceding examples. All the old rules are now officially redesignated as 'tree rules for PL,' and to this list we will now add another four decomposition rules, one for each type of quantificational sentence and its respective negation mentioned above, all to be presented in the framework of *Symlog*. However, the four new rules differ from those imported from SL in an interesting way which you should keep in mind. Unlike conjunctions, conditionals and the other truth-functional compounds, quantificational sentences do not decompose literally into subcomponents for the simple reason that the *instances* of a quantified sentence are not components at all. (The number of instances such a sentence has is infinite, but a symbolic string containing an infinite number of components would not count as a wff of either SL or PL.) Therefore, the process of decomposing a quantified sentence will be the familiar routine of instantiating that sentence, that is, of removing the left-most quantifier and immediately replacing its newly freed variable occurrences by some one constant throughout the scope of the quantifier. Once the rules for sentences of the form $(\forall \mathbf{x})\alpha$ and $(\exists \mathbf{x})\alpha$ have been set out, it will be a simple matter to handle their negated counterparts. Let us now proceed with these rules.

∀-Decomposition (∀D)

In this diagram, the upper box represents an open branch containing a universal quantification, and the lower box contains the same sentence plus one of its instances. You will get this result whenever you apply the decomposition rule ∀D in *Symlog:* The universal sentence will not disappear from the lower box but remains with its instance. This feature of the rule merely reflects a deeper semantical fact, that a sentence of the form $(\forall \mathbf{x})\alpha$ is true if and only if all of its instances, $\alpha(a/\mathbf{x})$, $\alpha(b/\mathbf{x})$, $\alpha(c/\mathbf{x})$, $\alpha(d/\mathbf{x})$, . . . are true, so on any open branch the universal sentence remains available for further instantiations. Whether a given branch closes or fails to close may well depend on the instantial constant being used. Suppose, for instance, that a branch contains the two sentences $(\forall x)Fx$ and $\neg Fb$. By applying ∀D, you could of course instantiate the universal by means of the constant, a, and the branch would remain open. The same consequence would follow if c, d, e, . . . were used as instantial constants. However, using b as the instantial constant would produce a contradictory pair of sentences, thus making it possible to close the branch at once with CB. To ensure, then, that the 'right' instantiation is made on an open branch—that is, one that will help produce a closed branch if the branch is one that does close—you should be prepared to apply ∀D as many times as there are different constants on the open branch. In other words, you may have to instantiate the universal sentence for all the different constants which occur on the branch. If three constants (say, a, b and c) are found in the sentences on the branch, then be prepared to instantiate the universal three times by using a, b and c as the instantial constants. (If no constant at all appears on the branch, simply instantiate the universal for an arbitrary constant, say, a.) However, there is clearly no point to instantiating the universal sentence by means of constants which fail to occur at all on the branch. Remember: An infinite number of instances is possible, so it is important to avoid taking unnecessary steps that would not affect the closing of a branch. The advice just given can be summarized in the following pair of ground rules:

Ground Rule 1. For a given universal sentence on an open branch, be prepared to apply ∀D successively: It may be necessary to instantiate the sentence for *all* the different constants occurring on that branch to help produce its closing.

Ground Rule 2. When applying ∀D on an open branch, instantiate the universal sentence for *only* those constants that occur on that branch; if no constant occurs, let a be the instantial constant.

Figure 7.2 illustrates the use of ∀D and both of these ground rules. Because each branch eventually closes, the initial set of sentences is declared inconsistent. Note that ground rule 1 does not require that every constant occurring on an open branch be used as an instantial constant if the branch is to close eventually. Sometimes (as in this example) it is possible to anticipate what particular instantiation will ensure a branch's closure. However, in more complicated cases, especially when instantiating a universal sentence yields a new sentence to which an SL type of rule applies, it may not be immediately evident which instantial constant among several should be

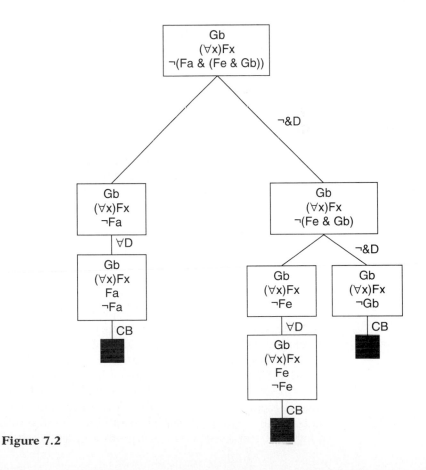

Figure 7.2

used and in what order. In such cases, it is prudent to instantiate first the universal sentence for every constant on the open branch. That way, one is sure that no instantiation that might lead to the branch closing is omitted. And for the sake of keeping order in the whole process of instantiating several quantificational sentences, it makes sense to select instantial constants in an alphabetical order, that is, choosing a first, b next, then c, then d and so on, for as many constants as are needed on a given branch. Sometimes a set being tested will already contain constants that have been selected for mnemonic reasons (such as j or m), and in such cases ground rules 1 and 2 should take precedence over alphabetical order. But when a set being tested contains no constants whatever, then you have a choice, and we recommend that you select instantial constants in an alphabetical order.

∃-Decomposition (∃D)

Restriction: The constant a must be foreign to the branch.

A constant is said to be foreign to a branch of sentences when it is not to be found in any member of that branch. Since only finitely many constants can ever occur on any given branch, there will always be a constant foreign to it. The reason for this restriction concerns a basic fact about existential sentences: They do not entail any of their instances. Whenever an existential sentence is true, it follows that some one of its instances is true, but not that *this* instance—as opposed to *that* instance—is true. In this respect, an existential differs entirely from a universal sentence, which entails each of its instances. An example will make things clearer. Let us say that I am thinking of a number greater than 10, that is (in logicalese), there is a number of which I am thinking and which is greater than 10. Symbolized (the UD being the set of natural numbers), this sentence becomes

(∃x)(Tix & Gxt)

Since the sentence is true, some instance of it, $\alpha(\mathbf{a}/x)$, must be true concerning a specific number of which two things hold: I am thinking of that particular number and it is greater than 10. But precisely what number is it? The answer can be learned from me but is certainly not to be obtained from the sentence itself. The sentence has an infinite number of instances, yet in this particular case only one of them is true. (In general, more than one instance of an existential sentence might be true, but that possibility is excluded here.) How then are we to instantiate this sentence? We cannot do so by means of a constant already occurring on whatever branch the sentence is located. Let us suppose that other sentences on the branch contain the constants a, b and c which stand for, say, the numbers 18, 11 and 37. Although all three numbers are greater than 10, it could easily be the case that I am not thinking of any of them. That is, it is possible for all the sentences Tia, Tib and Tic to be false whereas our original sentence is true. Yet (to repeat), since the sentence is true, one of its instances must be. Intuitively, if {(∃x)Fx} is consistent, so is *some set* containing one of its instances {Fa}. This is where a foreign constant enters the picture. We select a constant not previously used on the branch, and for convenience we choose the alphabetically next constant: d. Here, d stands for the number greater than 10 of which I have been thinking, whatever one that happens to be. It is, in effect, the constant whose use to instantiate x satisfies the desired truth-condition for our original sentence, (∃x)(Tix & Gxt). Unlike a constant such as a, b or c, d represents a particular number which cannot be further identified on the basis of this sentence: Describing d merely as the number of which I am thinking expresses all the semantical content which we can squeeze from the sentence. Nevertheless, d is a genuine constant, and what is more important, it enables us to produce a legitimate decomposition of the sentence.

Those, then, are the semantical considerations which lie behind the rule ∃D and which account for the restriction, but once you have understood them it is not necessary to call them to mind every time you use the rule. *Symlog* makes it easy to apply ∃D. When you have to instantiate an existential sentence, simply check the branch to which it belongs and choose a constant that is foreign to it, if possible the alphabetically next constant foreign to the list. Note that once instantiated, an existential sentence disappears from the resulting branch because the truth of such a sentence depends on the truth of at least one instance. The truth of a single instance is not only necessary but sufficient for the truth of the corresponding existential sentence, and the new sentence containing the foreign constant represents just that instance. Figure 7.3 shows the rule ∃D at work.

In this example, the original set is declared consistent because there is at least one completed open branch (in fact, both branches are completed open). Suppose, however, that you had been doing this example on your

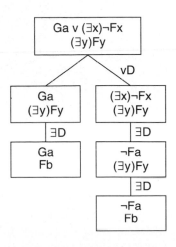

Figure 7.3

TRUTH-TREE : BETH   ■

Figure 7.4   ■■■ INSTANTIATING CONSTANT MUST BE FOREIGN TO THE BRANCH

own, using *Symlog*, but had forgotten the restriction on constants. Let us say that when you came to the lower branch on the right consisting of {¬Fa, (∃y)Fy}, you applied the rule ∃D, using a (again!) as your instantial constant. That would be a mistake, and *Symlog* would tell you so. In such cases, the program will serve up an error message—see Figure 7.4—and prevent the branch from being closed.

When doing truth-trees, you will often face branches containing both sorts of quantified sentences, and probably a few truth-functional compounds besides. Keep the following ground rule in mind as a practical guide:

Ground Rule 3. Decompose sentences in the following order throughout the process of decomposition, until no further rules can be applied: (1) truth-functional compounds, before (2) existential sentences, before (3) universal sentences.

This ground rule is meant to be applied recursively, that is, the first step takes precedence over the second and the second over the third, whenever the situation arises in the course of applying PL's rules. Let us suppose you encounter a branch of sentences containing each of the three types. Begin with the truth-functional compounds (i.e., apply the old rules imported from SL); then move on to the existential sentences (observing the restriction on constants). The result of applying ∃D may yield an instance which has the form of a truth-functional compound, in which case go back to the previous step and decompose it. The reason for decomposing existentials before universals will now be obvious from the previous discussion. Universal sentences never disappear from an open branch but remain available for

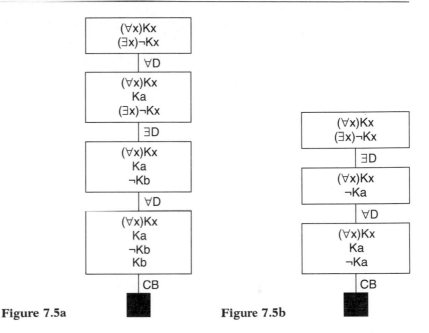

Figure 7.5a   Figure 7.5b

reinstantiation. So, bring in whatever constants are required by using ∃D; then instantiate the universal sentences for just those terms by means of ∀D. If ∀D were used first, a new constant would thereby appear which might have to be used in the instantiation of other universals but which could not be used in the instantiation of any existential. A tree which grows in this manner would not be unacceptable, just bigger than necessary (the violation of this ground rule would not vitiate the whole process, just make it more tedious). We will give you a comparison in Figures 7.5a and 7.5b. Compare the sizes of the two trees, which stem from the same set of sentences. Note how the premature application of ∀D in 7.5a to obtain Ka, besides delaying the whole process, contributes nothing toward the closing of the branch (in this case the tree itself).

¬∃-Decomposition (¬∃D) and ¬∀-Decomposition (¬∀D)

The following two sentence forms are logical equivalences:

$$\neg(\exists \mathbf{x})\alpha \equiv (\forall \mathbf{x})\neg\alpha$$
$$\neg(\forall \mathbf{x})\alpha \equiv (\exists \mathbf{x})\neg\alpha$$

Please take a moment to examine them. They indicate that a negated existential is logically equivalent to a universal, and a negated universal is logically equivalent to an existential. Because of these equivalences, the tree method is able to look on (singly) negated quantifications as special cases to which the rules of ∀-decomposition and ∃-decomposition already apply.

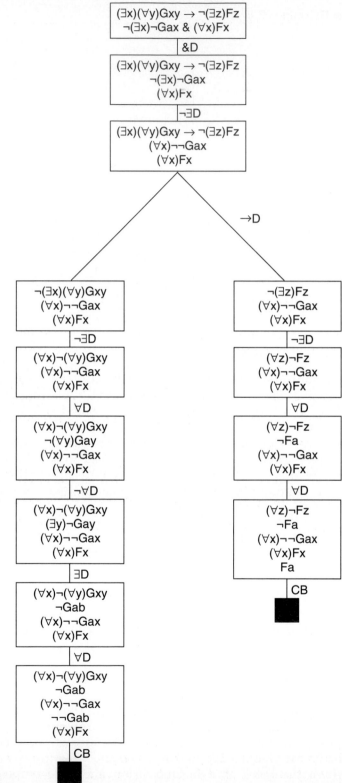

Figure 7.6

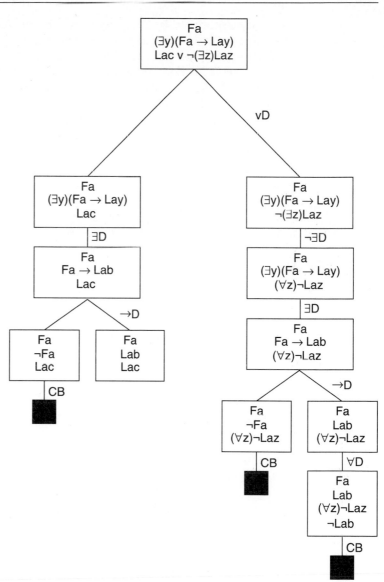

Figure 7.7

However, in the interest of formality, we are going to set out a further pair of rules which explictly cover the case of negated quantifiers:

Essentially, applying either of these new rules transforms a negated quantification into a logically equivalent quantified sentence. Your next move, of course, could be to apply either ∃D or ∀D to the resulting sentence. Figure 7.6 illustrates the use of the new rules combined with the previous ones. The original set proves to be inconsistent.

Now for a fuller example of a consistent set: {Fa, (∃y)(Fa → Lay), Lac ∨ ¬(∃z)Laz}. (See Figure 7.7.) Once a completed open branch was found, there was no need to close the other branches on the tree; this was done just for the sake of illustration.[1] And from that open branch it is possible to retrieve a truth-value assignment on which the original set of sentences is shown to be consistent. Assign the truth-value T to the atomic sentences on that branch: Fa, Lab and Lac. To gain more practice in the method of truth-trees, you should now turn to exercises PLTREE01 through PLTREE05 on your disk. Remember that the method involves not only the rules for handling the four types of quantificational sentence but also the three ground rules, which contribute a sense of order in the deployment of those rules.

Exercises

At some point, when solving some of the following exercises with *Symlog*, you may want to use the Submit option so that *Symlog* can check your work. *Symlog* will let you know whether more work should be done on the tree.

7.1.1 Answer true or false (but not both) and explain why to each of the following.

    a. {(∀x)Fx} is consistent if and only if {Fa} is consistent.

    b. {(∀x)Fx} is consistent if and only if {(∀x)Fx, Fa} is consistent.

    c. By applying ∀D to the set {Hbc, (∀x)Fx} you can obtain {Hbc, Fa}.

    d. {(∃x)Fx} is consistent if and only if {Fa} is consistent.

    e. By applying ∃D to the set {(∃x)Fx, Gca} you can obtain {Fa, Gca}.

7.1.2 Using *Symlog*, construct truth-trees to determine whether the following sets are quantificationally consistent or inconsistent.

    a. {(∀x)(Ax → Ba), (∃x)Ax & Cbee, Cbee → ¬Ba}

[PR81] b. {(∀x)(Bx ∨ Cx), ¬Ba, (∃x)¬Cx}

    c. {(∃x)(Gxa → Axb), ¬(∀x)¬Axc, Gbc ∨ ¬(∃x)Gbx}

[PR82] d. {(∀x)Gxx, (∃y)(Ay → Cy), ¬(∃x)(∃y)Gyx ∨ ¬¬(∀z)(¬Cz & Az)}

    e. {(¬La ∨ Hb) → (∃x)(Hx ∨ Lx), ¬(∃y)(Ly ∨ Hy), ¬La}

    f. {(∃x)Gx → (∀x)(Hx ∨ (∃y)Jyx), (∀y)Gy & (∀z)(¬Hza ∨ Gc), ¬(∃x)Gx}

    g. {(∃x)Bax → Sb, ¬(∀y)(Bay → Sb)}

[PR83] h. {(∃x)Fx, ¬(∃y)Gay, Gab → Fa, (∀y)(Fy ≡ Gay), (∃x)(∃y)Gyx ≡ ¬Fb}

---

[1] Incidentally, this tree would have ended up shorter if the second member of the set (the existential sentence) had been decomposed first instead of the third member (the disjunction)—in other words, if ground rule 3 had not been followed in making the first step. That is why, we have referred to ground rule 3 as a 'practical guide.' Despite exceptions, such as in this case, it is indeed a reliable guide to follow in trying to reach the goal of a completed tree, and we shall refer to it again in section 7.3.

7.1.3 Use *Symlog* to determine which of the following sets are satisfiable (i.e., consistent), and when the set is satisfiable, recover a truth-value assignment which satisfies it.

   a. {Ga, (∃x)Fx, ¬Fb}
   b. {Fa, ¬(∃x)Fx & Gc}
   c. {(∃x)(∃y)(Bxy → Fx), (∃z)¬Fz, Bab}
   d. {(∃x)Bx → Ca, ¬(Ba → (∃y)Cy)}
   e. {Ra ≡ (∃x)¬Rx}

7.1.4 Use the Create option under *Symlog*'s File menu to ask the program to generate (randomly) PL sets of sentences, whose truth-trees you should then construct to determine whether they are (quantificationally) consistent or inconsistent.

7.2   *The Tree Method and Semantical Properties in PL*

As in SL, the tree method provides a means for exhibiting the inconsistency of an inconsistent set of sentences in PL. The two fundamental theorems (which we shall not prove) are these:

> **The Completeness Theorem.** If a PL set is quantificationally inconsistent, then it has a closed truth-tree.

> **The Soundness Theorem.** If a truth-tree for a PL set is closed, then the set is quantificationally inconsistent.

The former theorem assures us that no inconsistent set of PL sentences is beyond the reach of the tree method. The latter assures us that whenever we have a closed tree on our hands we can declare the set from which it stems to be inconsistent. Notice that the two definitions mention *a* closed tree rather than *the* closed tree for an inconsistent set. The reason is that not all truth-trees for an inconsistent set of PL sentences may be shown to close, though at least one can be shown to close. The issue relates to a feature of the decomposition rule ∀D, which was mentioned in a previous section, namely, that a universal sentence on an open branch is always available for further instantiations. However, by using the three ground rules which accompany the rules, you are sure to bring an inconsistent PL set to the point of closing.

As you recall, the concept of inconsistency provides the basis for defining other important semantical notions. We begin with entailment.

> **Entailment.** A PL set {$\alpha_1, \alpha_2, \ldots, \alpha_n$} **quantificationally entails** a sentence β if and only if the test set {$\alpha_1, \alpha_2, \ldots, \alpha_n, \neg\beta$} has a closed tree.

> **Validity.** An argument of PL is **valid** if and only if the set of its

premises quantificationally entails its conclusion, that is, iff the test set for the argument is quantificationally inconsistent.

Consider the following argument whose translation into PL is given to its right (Hx stands for 'x is happy'):

Not everybody is happy	$\neg(\forall x)Hx$
Someone is not happy	$(\exists x)\neg Hx$

That this argument is valid can be determined by first constructing its test set and then testing for inconsistency. Thus, we first form the test set $\{\neg(\forall x)Hx, \neg(\exists x)\neg Hx\}$ and we then check if it has a closed truth-tree. As the tree in Figure 7.8 shows this test can be done in just two steps. Try now to solve the disk exercises PLTREE06 to PLTREE09, which bear on these semantical notions.

Another semantical property which can be expressed directly in terms of inconsistency is that of logical falsehood:

> **Theorem.** A sentence α of PL is **quantificationally false** if and only if the set $\{\alpha\}$ has a closed tree.

Since a sentence is quantificationally true if and only if its negation is quantificationally false, an account of logical truth in PL is easily obtained:

> **Theorem.** A sentence α of PL is **quantificationally true** if and only if the set $\{\neg\alpha\}$ has a closed tree.

Finally, two sentences α and β are quantificationally equivalent if and only if $\alpha \equiv \beta$ is quantificationally true. Hence,

> **Theorem.** Two sentences α and β of PL are **quantificationally equivalent** if and only if $\{\neg(\alpha \equiv \beta)\}$ has a closed tree.

To become more familiar with the interrelation of these concepts, select exercises PLTREE10 to PLTREE15 on your disk.

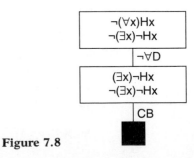

Figure 7.8

Exercises

7.2.1 Construct with *Symlog* a truth-tree, using the test for entailment to determine whether each of the following is true or false (i.e., whether the given set quantificationally entails the corresponding sentence).

  a. {(∀x)(∀y)Rxy} ⊨ Rab

  b. {(∀x)(Mx & Lx)} ⊨ (∀x)Mx & (∀x)Lx

[PR84] c. {¬(∃x)Fx → ¬(∃y)(∃z)¬Gyz, La → ¬(∃x)Fx, (∀z)Lz} ⊨ Gbc

[PR85] d. {(∀x)(∀y) [¬(Dx & Ey) ∨ (Fx & Gy)], (∃z)Dz ≡ (∃x)Ex, ¬(∃x)(Dx & Ex)} ⊨ (∀z) (¬Ez ∨ Gz)

  e. {(∃x)(∀y)Rxy} ⊨ (∀y)(∃x)Ryx

7.2.2 Use *Symlog* to determine whether the following arguments are quantificationally valid or invalid.

  a. (∀x)((∃y)Gy ∨ Ax)
     (∀u)¬Gu
     ─────────────
     Ac

[PR86] b. (∃x)((∃y)Rxy → Fa)
        ─────────────────
        (∀x)(∃y)Rxy → Fa

  c. ¬(∃x)¬Tx
     (∀x)Rxb
     Tc → ¬(∃x)Sx
     ─────────────
     Jab

[PR87] d. (∀x)(∀y)(Ax → By)
        (∀x)(∀y)(By → Ax)
        ─────────────────
        (∀x)(∀y)(Ax ≡ By)

  e. Rab
     ─────────────────
     (∃x)Rxb & (∃x)Rax

[PR88] f. ¬(∀x)Kx
        (∀z)(Jz ∨ Kz)
        ─────────────────
        (∃x)(¬Lxa ∨ Jx)

  g. (∀x)Hax
     (∀y)Ky
     ─────────────────
     ¬(∃x)(∃y)¬(Kx ∨ Hay)

[PR89] h. (∀x)(Kx → Jax)
        (∀x)(∀y)[Jxy ∨ ¬(Jay & Jxa)]
        ¬(∀x)(¬Kx ∨ ¬Jxa)
        ─────────────────────────
        ¬(∀x)[¬Kx ∨ (∀y)(Ky & ¬Jxy)]

  i. (∀x)Kx
     ¬(∃x)Fx ∨ (∀x)Gx
     ─────────────
     (∃x)Gx

j. $(\forall z)[\neg Lz \lor (Mz \to Nz)]$

   $(\forall z)[\neg(Lz \mathbin{\&} Mz) \lor Nz]$

7.2.3 Symbolize the following arguments into PL and determine, using *Symlog*'s truth-trees, whether they are quantificationally valid or invalid.

   a. No one is happy unless Albert is. But Albert isn't happy at all. Hence, everybody is sad. (Hx)

[PR90] b. Someone loves everybody but surely isn't John. Yet, everybody loves him and there is no one he hates. Therefore, everybody hates someone. (Lxy)

   c. If Paul is rich, someone is rich. Yet, if Paul is rich, someone isn't. Thus, Paul isn't rich. (Rx)

   d. If, on the one hand, Diane likes logic, someone likes logic. On the other hand, if Diane doesn't like logic, someone still does. It follows that someone likes logic. (Lx)

[PR91] e. All roads lead to Rome. The Don Valley Parkway is either a road or it doesn't lead anywhere. But the Don Valley Parkway leads to Richmond Hill. Hence, the Don Valley Parkway leads to Rome. (Rx, Lxy)

7.2.4 Use *Symlog* to construct a truth-tree for each sentence to show that it is quantificationally true.

[PR92] a. $(P \to (\exists x)Fx) \equiv (\exists x)(P \to Fx)$

   b. $(P \to (\forall x)Fx) \equiv (\forall x)(P \to Fx)$

   c. $(\exists x)(Fx \lor \neg Fx)$

   d. $(\exists x)Gx \lor (\forall x)\neg Gx$

   e. $(\exists x)(Fx \lor Gx) \equiv ((\exists x)Fx \lor (\exists x)Gx)$

7.2.5 Use *Symlog* to construct a truth-tree for each sentence to show that it is quantificationally false.

   a. $(\exists x)(Fx \mathbin{\&} \neg Fx)$

   b. $\neg(\forall x)(Fx \lor \neg Fx)$

   c. $\neg[\neg(\exists x)Gx \equiv (\forall x)\neg Gx]$

   d. $(Fa \mathbin{\&} \neg Gb) \lor (Fa \to Gb)$

   e. $(\forall x)\neg(\exists y)Rxay \mathbin{\&} (\exists u)(\exists z)Ruaz$

7.2.6 Construct appropriate truth-trees with *Symlog* to show that the sentences in each of the following pairs are quantificationally equivalent.

   a. $(\exists x)(Fx \lor Gx)$ and $(\exists x)Fx \lor (\exists x)Gx$

   b. $(\forall x)(Fx \lor P)$ and $(\forall x)Fx \lor P$

   c. $(\exists x)(Fx \mathbin{\&} P)$ and $(\exists x)Fx \mathbin{\&} P$

   d. $(\forall x)(Fx \mathbin{\&} Gx)$ and $(\forall x)Fx \mathbin{\&} (\forall x)Gx$

   e. $(\exists x)(Fx \to P)$ and $(\forall x)Fx \to P$

   f. $(\exists x)(P \to Fx)$ and $P \to (\exists x)Fx$

[PR93] g. $(\forall x)(Fx \to P)$ and $(\exists x)Fx \to P$

   h. $(\forall x)(P \to Fx)$ and $P \to (\forall x)Fx$

7.2.7 Use the Create option under *Symlog's* File menu to ask the program to generate (randomly) PL sentences, whose truth-trees you should then construct to determine their quantificational status (e.g., quantificationally true, false or indeterminate).[2]

7.3   *The Problem of Infinite Branches*

To this point, the three ground rules for the tree method of PL have played a role which is more utilitarian than theoretical. Serving as a kind of procedural checklist, these ground rules have helped you gain experience in constructing trees. The time has come to look at them from the theoretical side. Let us begin by reflecting on the recent results of applying the tree method (the rules of decomposition plus the three ground rules). The method proves to be an effective procedure whenever a set of PL sentences is inconsistent. The procedure is also effective whenever a consistent set is found to have at least one completed open branch from whose atomic sentences can be retrieved a truth-value assignment which establishes the consistency of that branch, in the manner familiar from SL trees. That situation was encountered in several of our examples. An open branch consisting of nothing but noncontradicting literals[3] counts as a completed open branch, whether the sentences were obtained from truth-functional compounds or from existential sentences (or negated universals), and a tree with even one such branch would count as a completed (open) tree. But what is to be done when each of the open branches contains at least one universal sentence? As we recognized earlier, none of these branches could contain all the instances of a universal, so it becomes literally impossible to retrieve a truth-value assignment from any of them that would establish consistency for the branch (and hence for the original set). If we did not resort to the ground rules, a branch with a universal sentence would go on and on, as illustrated in Figure 7.9.

However, by applying ground rules 1 and 2 we would have reached a point of discovering the futility of further instantiations of the universal sentence on the open branch. This point would have been reached after the sentence had been instantiated for all and only the constants occurring on the branch. Clearly, no *further* instance of $(\forall x)Ex$ would be inconsistent with—contradict—any of the negated atomic sentences on the branch ($\neg Lba$ here). It makes sense to halt the process, and although we cannot retrieve a truth-value assignment from the branch we can nevertheless *describe* one. Assign to the infinite instances of $(\forall x)Ex$ the very same truth-value, T, retrievable from either of the two instances (Ea, Eb) on the open branch. As-

---

[2] Paralleling SL, a sentence is quantificationally indeterminate iff it is neither quantificationally true nor quantificationally false. More about these sentences in the following section.

[3] Recall that a **literal** is a ground atomic sentence or the negation of a ground atomic sentence. Fa, $\neg$Rab and Ljc are all examples of literals.

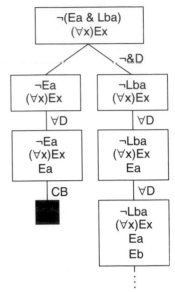

Figure 7.9

sign F to the sentence Lba. In this way, we can characterize a truth-value assignment on which the branch, and thus the original set, are shown to be consistent. Such a branch may therefore count as a completed open branch, and the tree from which it was grown a completed open tree.

When can we declare a halt and proceed to calculate a truth-value assignment for a consistent set? Essentially, when the tree method has left us with an open branch containing a universal sentence and there are no other rules to be applied, as called for by the method. So, there are no truth-functional compounds on the branch waiting to be decomposed and no existentials, and each universal sentence has been instantiated according to ground rules 1 and 2. Note the implicit requirement of ground rule 2, that a universal sentence be instantiated at least once on the branch. Without such a requirement, a branch might be declared consistent which is in fact not so, as can be seen in the simple case illustrated in Figure 7.10. The branch consisting of this single universal cannot be declared consistent on the ground that there seems nothing to do; there is. The instantiation of the sentence leads to the closing of the branch. To summarize, a branch will thus be considered **completed open** when

1. No more rules can be applied to it. (This situation happens precisely when each sentence on the branch is a literal not contradicting any other literal on the branch—the criterion for consistent SL sets.)
2. Or, the only rule that can be applied is ∀D, but for each universally quantified sentence $(\forall \mathbf{x})\alpha$ on the branch, the following two conditions are met: (a) there is already an instance—any instance—$\alpha(\mathbf{a/x})$ of $(\forall \mathbf{x})\alpha$ on the branch, and (b) for each constant **a** present in the branch, the instance $\alpha(\mathbf{a/x})$ of $(\forall \mathbf{x})\alpha$ is on the branch.

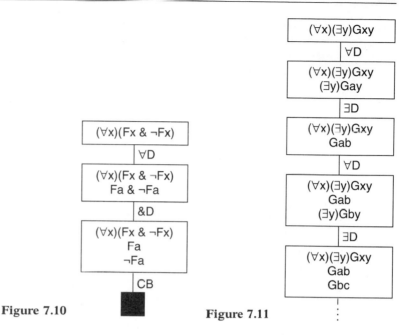

Figure 7.10

Figure 7.11

In such a way, it might seem, we can put the awkward problem of determining consistency behind us and declare the tree method effective for every consistent set of PL sentences. Either the tree for a particular set closes (in which case the set is inconsistent), or the tree does not close (so the set is consistent). An open tree will be finite if at least one of its open branches is finite (as declared by clause 1), or else it will be infinite but terminating (as declared by clause 2). The problem of determining consistency will not go away, however. Consider with care the tree in Figure 7.11.

Ground rule 3 advises you to instantiate existentials before universals (to take step 2 before taking step 3—see the description of the ground rule in section 7.1). Although this advice is sound, it presupposes that you have a choice about which kind of instantiation—existential or universal—to make first, which is not the case here. The only step you can take is step 3 (replace a for x, a/x), the immediate result of which is to generate an existential sentence. Now indeed you have a choice, and you proceed to instantiate the existential by means of a foreign constant (b/y), and since this step introduces a new constant, you are obliged by ground rule 1 to reinstantiate the universal (with b/x). Consequently, a new existential sentence is produced, to which step 3 applies; but when you have instantiated this sentence (with c/y), a new constant has appeared, which has to be covered in turn by a fresh universal instantiation. Where does this process stop? It does not. You are caught in an unending cycle of instantiations. The problem is not that ground rule 3 has to be patched up, for the problem would recur in other cases which, like this one, would force the routine of instantiations to loop back on itself endlessly. A branch of this kind is open but nonterminating, and a tree with only nonterminating branches counts as a strictly infinite or nonterminating tree. In such cases, the original set of sentences is consistent yet cannot be declared so by means of a routine. That is, a truth-value assignment showing the consistency of a set of sentences can be neither retrieved nor calculated on the basis of the tree method.

Sometimes a truth-value assignment might be found, as in the tree in Figure 7.11: Assign the truth-value T to the atomic sentences Gab, Gbc, Gcd and so on and, say, the truth-value F to every other atomic sentence, such as Gaa, Gbb and so on. On this assignment, the sentence (∀x)(∃y)Gxy comes out true, and the original set consisting of this sentence alone is therefore declared to be consistent. But assignments like this one are obtained by experiment, *not by a mechanical method*. And it is this fact which is most striking. In truth-functional logic, tree testing provides a **decision method** for consistency. Given any SL set of sentences, the tree method determines in a *systematic* way whether the given set is consistent or inconsistent.[4] If inconsistent, we know that all of the branches will close in a finite number of steps or applications of the decomposition rules; but if consistent, then we know that at least one branch will remain open and be complete, after finitely many steps. Not so for PL. The tree method described above is *not* a decision procedure for determining the consistency status of a set of PL sentences. If a given set is inconsistent, then—thanks to the completeness theorem—there is a guarantee that a tree obtained according to the method will eventually close. But for consistent sets *in general* there is no absolute guarantee that the method will deliver a concrete result when dealing with nonterminating branches. Therefore, the fact that a particular set—branch—has failed to close, after a finite number of steps have been traversed and sentences remain to be decomposed, would not conclusively indicate that the tree for the set was sure to remain open. In other words, the tree method fails to determine the consistency of some sets whose trees have nothing but nonterminating (infinite) branches. You may suppose that this wrinkle only shows a defect in the tree method as presented and that we should now return to the drawing board for improvement. However, patch-ups designed to cope with sets like the one seen in Figure 7.11 would break down in the face of more complicated cases. In fact, the problem we face is not a correctable one. In 1936, the American logician Alonzo Church demonstrated that *there cannot be a decision method in predicate logic for determining consistency.*[5] Undeniably, this was a milestone in the history of logic.

While appreciating this fact about PL, it is important that you not lose your practical bearings. Church's proof does not cut down the tree method but merely enlightens us about its limitations, and there remain innumerable consistent sets of PL sentences for which the method is adequate, such

---

[4] The same can be said of the truth-table method.

[5] The term 'method' has a very specific meaning in logic. Intuitively, it means 'mechanical method,' that is, a deterministic, finite sequence of instructions. A precise formulation of this concept would require the introduction of one out of many alternative formalisms (e.g., Turing machines, recursive function theory, etc.), but this topic is beyond the scope of this text.

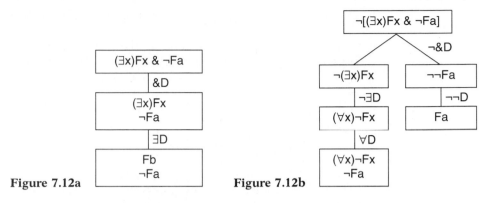

Figure 7.12a

Figure 7.12b

as those found in the exercises. Remember, too, how the concept of inconsistency was employed in the last section for defining semantical notions like entailment, validity and logical truth. The tree method may not decide the *invalidity* of an argument in certain cases; but if an argument is valid, you are assured that it is provably so by the method.

Because of the existence of strictly infinite trees, we chose to delay giving an account of indeterminacy for a sentence of PL, that is, for a sentence which is neither logically true nor logically false. Presenting this notion in terms of these other notions would only have disguised what is sometimes involved when a tree for a set of sentences remains open. Here is the account now:

> **Theorem.** A sentence α of PL is **quantificationally indeterminate** if and only if neither $\{\neg\alpha\}$ nor $\{\alpha\}$ has a closed tree.

The conjunction $(\exists x)Fx \,\&\, \neg Fa$ is found to be contingent by the construction of the two trees in Figures 7.12a and 7.12b.

Speaking of exercises, why not turn now to problems PLTREE16 through PLTREE23 on your disk?

Exercises

7.3.1 Answer true or false (but not both) to each of the following.

a. If Γ is a quantificationally inconsistent set then all its associated truth-trees are closed.

b. If one of the truth-trees of Γ is closed then Γ is a quantificationally inconsistent set.

c. If a set is quantificationally consistent then one of its truth-trees has at least one completed open branch.

d. If one of the truth-trees of Γ has a nonterminating (open) branch then Γ cannot be a quantificationally inconsistent set.

e. If one of the truth-trees of Γ is closed then Γ cannot be a quantificationally consistent set.

f. If α is quantificationally true then one of the truth-trees of $\{\neg\alpha\}$ does not close.

g. Any set with a quantificationally false sentence as one of its members must have, among its truth-trees, one which is closed.

h. If α is quantificationally indeterminate then one of the truth-trees of $\{\alpha\}$ is completed open.

i. If α is quantificationally indeterminate then one of the truth-trees of $\{\neg\alpha\}$ is completed open.

j. If one of the truth-trees of $\{\alpha\}$ is completed open and one of the truth-trees of $\{\neg\alpha\}$ is also completed open then α is quantificationally indeterminate.

7.3.2 Construct truth-trees with *Symlog* to determine which of the following sentences are satisfiable, and when the sentence is satisfiable, give a truth-value assignment which satisfies it.

a. $(\exists x)Bx \rightarrow Ba$

b. $(\forall x)Fx \& (\exists x)\neg Fx$

c. $[(\forall x)Ax \& (\exists y)(By \rightarrow \neg Ac)] \& (\exists x)(Cx \& Bx)$

d. $Ba \rightarrow (\exists x)Bx$

e. $(\exists z)(Hz \& Kz) \& [(Ka \rightarrow Jb) \equiv (Jb \rightarrow Kc)]$

7.3.3 Use *Symlog* to construct appropriate truth-trees for each sentence to show that it is quantificationally indeterminate.

a. $(\exists x)Fx \& (\exists x)\neg Fx$

b. $(\forall x)(\forall y)Mxy \& [\neg Mab \vee (\exists z)Rz]$

c. $[(\forall x)Gx \vee (\forall x)\neg Gx] \equiv [(\exists x)Gx \vee (\exists x)\neg Gx]$

d. $Fa \rightarrow (\exists x)\neg Fx$

e. $(Rab \rightarrow (\exists x)Lxb) \equiv ((\exists x)Lxb \rightarrow Rab)$

7.3.4 Determine, by constructing truth-trees with *Symlog*, whether each of the following sentences is quantificationally true, quantificationally false or quantificationally indeterminate.

a. $Fa \& \neg(\exists x)Fx$

b. $(\exists x)Rx \& (\forall x)\neg Rx$

c. $(\exists x)(\exists y)(Rxy \vee \neg Rxy)$

[PR94] d. $(\forall x)(\neg Rax \vee Rbb) \rightarrow [(\forall x)(\exists y)Rxy \rightarrow (\exists x)Rxx]$

e. $(\exists x)(\exists y)(Rxy \equiv Rxy)$

f. $(\forall x)Kx \& (\neg Ka \vee \neg Kb)$

g. $(\forall x)(\forall y)Bxy \vee \neg(\exists x)\neg(\forall z)Bxz$

h. $\neg(\forall x)Kx \& Ka$

i. $(\exists x)Rx \& (\neg Ra \vee \neg(\forall x)Rx)$

j. $(Fa \rightarrow (\exists x)Fx) \vee ((\exists x)Fx \rightarrow Fa)$

k. $(Kab \equiv (\exists x)Gxb) \equiv \neg((\exists x)Gxb \rightarrow Kab)$

[PR95] l. $\neg[((\forall x)Hx \rightarrow Ja) \equiv ((\exists y)\neg Hy \vee Ja)]$

m. $[(\forall x)Fx \& (Fa \rightarrow Gb)] \rightarrow (\exists x)Gx$

n. $[\neg(\exists x)Ax \& Ab] \vee [(\exists x)Ax \vee \neg(\forall x)Ax]$

o. $\neg Rab \equiv (Rab \equiv \neg(\exists x)(\exists y)Rxy)$

7.3.5 Explain why the truth-tree method fails to reveal the consistency of the set $\{(\forall x)\neg(\forall y)Rxy\}$.

7.3.6 Give an example of (a) a consistent set all of whose truth-trees are composed solely of nonterminating branches and (b) a consistent set all of whose truth-trees are composed solely of completed open branches.

7.3.7 Use the Create option under *Symlog*'s File menu to ask the program to generate (randomly) PL sets of sentences, whose truth-trees you should then construct to determine whether they are (quantificationally) consistent or inconsistent.

7.3.8 Use the Create option under *Symlog*'s File menu to ask the program to generate (randomly) PL sentences, whose truth-trees you should then construct to determine their quantificational status (e.g., quantificationally true, false or indeterminate).

8

Natural Deduction in Predicate Logic

In this chapter we will enrich PL with a set of derivation rules to enable the construction of valid arguments and the proof of logical truths. This development not only parallels what was done earlier in our study of SL but also builds directly on that work. PL's derivation system absorbs the rules of SD and then adds four new rules of its own. All of SD's derivation rules are to be promoted to rules of **PD** (as the new system is called), the only difference being, of course, that these rules now apply exclusively to sentences of PL. This new derivation system will be our focus in the current chapter, and the pattern of study to be followed will be familiar to you from SD. We will introduce and illustrate the four new rules, then give you plenty of opportunity through exercises at the back of the section—as well as on disk—to 'embed' them firmly in that portion of your subconscious which is devoted to proofmaking. In section 8.5, the system PD will be enlarged by bringing in the rules of SD+, together with a few other '+-type' rules, to facilitate the construction of longer proofs.

8.1 *The Derivation System PD*

As mentioned, the system PD includes all the rules of SD, understood to apply to the sentences of PL. To illustrate the point and to reacquaint you with some of these rules, here are two derivations (Figures 8.1 and 8.2)

PD : FRAENKEL

PREMISE	1	$(\forall x)Dxa \rightarrow [((\exists y)Fy \equiv Gb) \& (\forall w)Mw]$
PREMISE	2	$Gb \& (\forall x)Dxa$
&ER 2	3	$(\forall x)Dxa$
→E 1, 3	4	$((\exists y)Fy \equiv Gb) \& (\forall w)Mw$
&EL 4	5	$(\exists y)Fy \equiv Gb$
&EL 2	6	Gb
≡E 5, 6	7	$(\exists y)Fy$
	8	
	9	
	10	
	11	
	12	
	13	
	14	
	15	
	16	

Figure 8.1

PD : ZERMELO

PREMISE	1	$Ga \equiv (M \rightarrow Bc)$
PREMISE	2	$(\exists w)Abwc \rightarrow Ga$
PREMISE	3	$M \& (\exists w)Abwc$
ASSUMPTION	4	$(\exists x)Hgx$
&ER 3	5	$(\exists w)Abwc$
→E 2, 5	6	Ga
&EL 3	7	M
≡E 1, 6	8	$M \rightarrow Bc$
→E 7, 8	9	Bc
→I 4-9	10	$(\exists x)Hgx \rightarrow Bc$
vIR 10	11	$((\exists x)Hgx \rightarrow Bc) \vee (\forall y)Kyd$
	12	
	13	
	14	
	15	
	16	

Figure 8.2

which we invite you to follow with the help of *Symlog*.[1] Once you have completed them, you should continue by doing problems PD01 and PD02, which are stored on your disk, and then submit them to the program to be checked.

You may have guessed already that the four new rules of PD pertain to quantified sentences: To deal with them, the derivation system requires an

---

[1] The procedure is to invoke the OPTIONS menu and then select Derivation System PD You may want to review quickly the section 'Derivation Pad Commands' in Appendix C.

introduction rule and an elimination rule for PL's two quantifiers. Like SD's rules, they are rules of natural deduction; that is, they have a basis in the deductive reasoning of natural language (to the extent that such reasoning is deductive). Two of them are especially easy to grasp. Suppose, for instance, that all artists are self-centered; then Rembrandt was self-centered, and so was Picasso. Or suppose that Hulk Hogan can defeat anyone in a wrestling match; then it is certain that he could beat me in a wrestling match. The deductive inference in both cases takes a claim about *every member* of a class and applies it to a *particular member* of that same class. The first rule to be described sanctions this procedure. It allows the instantiation of universal quantifications. The next rule moves in the opposite direction. Suppose that Socrates is bald; then there is at least one thing which is bald. Or suppose that Socrates is a liar; then there must be at least one liar. Again, since 41 is a prime number greater than 37, it follows that there is at least one prime number greater than 37. Here the deductive reasoning proceeds from a sentence containing an *individual constant* to an *existential quantification* of that sentence. Clearly, the relation between the first and the second sentence is one of entailment. This second rule licenses this sort of inference. In a moment we shall present both rules briefly, with further examples. Following these are the remaining two rules, which require a slightly fuller commentary.

∀-Elimination (∀E)

	i	$(\forall \mathbf{x})\alpha$
∀E **a/x** i	j	$\alpha(\mathbf{a/x})$

The rule ∀-elimination (∀E) allows you to derive any instance you choose from a universally quantified sentence. In other words, from a PL sentence like

$(\forall y)Py$

which occurs in the course of a proof you could correctly infer any of its instances, say,

Pn

The reason is that if P is a property of everything, y, then it must be a property of n (as well as of a, b, c, d, . . .). If it is true that every river is polluted, the Nile River must be polluted; and the same holds for the Mississippi, the Ganges, the Seine and so on. In other words, if all the elements in the uni-

```
PD : FITCH

PREMISE              1    (∀x)Fx ≡ Ma
PREMISE              2    (∃x)Gxx & ((∀y)Dyya & Ma)
&ER  2               3    (∀y)Dyya & Ma
&EL  3               4    (∀y)Dyya
∀E  b/y  4           5    Dbba
&ER  3               6    Ma
≡E  1, 6             7    (∀x)Fx
∀E  m/x  7           8    Fm
&I  5, 8             9    Dbba & Fm
                    10
```

Figure 8.3

verse of discourse have a certain property, then each of them in particular has such property. The rule ∀-elimination is also known as the rule of **universal instantiation** because from a universal assertion, an instance of it can be inferred. That is, $\alpha(\mathbf{a/x})$ is an instance of $(\forall \mathbf{x})\alpha$. The expression **a/x** (called a **substitution**) indicates that when the rule ∀-elimination is applied to the universally quantified sentence $(\forall \mathbf{x})\alpha$, the constant **a** is to replace all the free occurrences of the variable **x** that fall within the scope, α, of the universal quantifier being eliminated. (The **a** is in boldface because it is meant to stand for any constant of PL: a, b, c, ... The **x** is in boldface because it is meant to stand for any variable of PL: u, w, x, y, . . .).[2] The screen depicted in Figure 8.3 displays a derivation in PD in which the rule ∀-elimination is used. Make sure that when you use this rule you apply it to a universally quantified sentence. Otherwise, *Symlog* will warn you of such an error, as illustrated in Figure 8.4.

Try now to solve all the Learn Exercises from PD03 to PD08 on disk, where you are asked to fill in some missing entries in both the Justification and Theorem fields or to derive a conclusion from a given set of premises. Once an exercise is solved, let *Symlog* check your answer.

∃-Introduction (∃I)

```
              i    α
∃I x/a i      j    (∃x)α(x/a)
```

Note: Partial substitution is allowed.

---

[2] At this point you should review the definition of instantiation in section 6.3. While you are at it, also review the ones for universal and existential generalization. You will need them fairly soon.

```
PD : FITCH                                                        ■

PREMISE            1       (∀x)Fx → Mb
∀E a/x 1 ■         2       Fa → Mb                                ■
                   3
                   4
                   5
                   6
                   7
                   8
                   9
                  10
                  11
                  12
                  13
                  14
                  15
                  16
■■■ LINE BEING APPEALED TO IS NOT UNIVERSALLY QUANTIFIED
```

Figure 8.4

The rule ∃-introduction (∃I) is a rule for constructing existential quantifications. Typically, the rule applies to any sentence containing an individual constant; the resulting sentence is clearly entailed. ∃I merely formalizes a rule of inference with which we are quite familiar in natural language. Suppose you see that a friend has just been injured: You could make an emergency call to report that *someone* has just been injured. Or again, you hear that Gloria is going to be a mother: Mg. It follows at once (using ∃I and letting our UD consist of persons) that someone is going to be a mother: (∃x)Mx. Applying this rule to a sentence containing a constant combines the two-step process of replacing at least one of the occurrences of the constant (with variable) and then prefixing an existential quantifier to the resulting wff, as shown in the diagram—the formal definition—of the rule. The expression **x/a**, in the context of this rule, means that the variable **x** replaces *one or more* occurrences of the constant **a** in the sentence α, to obtain the existentially quantified sentence $(\exists \mathbf{x})\alpha(\mathbf{x/a})$. The resulting sentence $(\exists \mathbf{x})\alpha(\mathbf{x/a})$ is known as an **existential generalization** of α. The note in the diagram indicates that ∃-introduction allows partial substitution. To illustrate, consider the sentence 'Socrates is in love with himself':

Lss

∃-introduction allows you to derive any one of the three sentences

(∃x)Lxs   (∃x)Lsx   (∃x)Lxx.

Deductively speaking, this process makes sense. For if Socrates loves himself, then each of the following sentences would be true:

At least one person loves Socrates.

Socrates loves someone.

Someone loves himself.

Note that to obtain the sentence $(\exists y)(\exists x)Lxy$—'Someone loves somebody'— from $(\exists x)Lxs$ requires a *separate* application of $\exists I$.

Figure 8.5 illustrates the use of $\exists$-introduction. Figure 8.6 illustrates a misapplication of the $\exists$-introduction rule. The error consists in applying $\exists I$ to a (proper) subwff of a wff. Since this move is not legal and the resulting sentence is not an existentially quantified sentence, *Symlog* objects. The Learn Exercises PD09 to PD14 on disk illustrate the use of this rule. As usual, let *Symlog* check your work once it is completed.

PD : GENTZEN

PREMISE	1	$Fma \rightarrow Sd$
PREMISE	2	$Mab \;\&\; ((\forall x)Fxa \equiv \neg Rg)$
PREMISE	3	$\neg Rg \;\&\; A$
&EL 3	4	$\neg Rg$
&ER 2	5	$(\forall x)Fxa \equiv \neg Rg$
$\equiv$E 4, 5	6	$(\forall x)Fxa$
$\forall$E m/x 6	7	Fma
$\rightarrow$E 1, 7	8	Sd
$\exists$I w/d 8	9	$(\exists w)Sw$
	10	

Figure 8.5

PD : GENTZEN   ■

PREMISE	1	$Fa \rightarrow Gc$
$\exists$I x/a 1■	2	$(\exists x)Fx \rightarrow Gc$ ■
	3	
	4	
	5	
	6	
	7	
	8	
	9	
	10	
	11	
	12	
	13	
	14	
	15	
	16	

■■■ CURRENT LINE IS NOT AN EXISTENTIALLY QUANTIFIED WFF

Figure 8.6

∀-Introduction (∀I)

∀I **x/a** i	i	α
	j	$(\forall\textbf{x})\alpha(\textbf{x/a})$

Restrictions: 1. **a** must not occur in a premise or undischarged assumption.
2. **a** must not occur in $(\forall\textbf{x})\alpha(\textbf{x/a})$.

The ∀-introduction rule (∀I)—also known as the rule of **universal generalization**—says that from a particular sentence you can infer a sentence having a universal quantifier as its main logical operator. At first sight, this type of move seems illegitimate. It is counterintuitive to deduce a sentence about *all* of a class on the basis of a sentence about just one of its members. For instance, from a particular true sentence like

Hilbert is a mathematician.

you cannot simply generalize and obtain the sentence

Everybody is a mathematician.

Similarly, from the particular sentence

Ottawa is in Canada.

you cannot generalize and conclude

Everything is in Canada.

Therefore, certain restrictions apply to this rule, as noted in the diagram, and by obeying them no invalid inference will result. However, let us take a moment to consider what makes ∀I a legitimate rule of deductive inference in the first place. Suppose a mathematician wants to prove that in every triangle the sum of the angles is 180°. The mathematician will begin by taking a triangle—any triangle—as the starting point. There is nothing special about *this* particular triangle; it is simply *a* triangle. In the course of the proof, the mathematician does not make use of the particular properties of this particular triangle. That is, there is no appeal to the size of the triangle or to whether it is a right triangle or whether it is drawn with chalk or ink. In other words, any other triangle whatsoever would have served equally well for the purposes of the proof. Thus, once the proof is worked out for this triangle, the mathematician is entitled to assert that the sum of the angles of *any* triangle equals 180°. The result is a generalization from a **representative instance.**

The legitimacy of ∀I is based on the fact that our generalizations use representative instances. We restrict ourselves to 'indeterminate' individuals rather than to specific ones. Constants which appear in premises or undischarged assumptions cannot be counted as (names of) representative individuals since the sentences in which they occur are assuming—saying—something specific about them that, in general, may not be the case about all individuals. This matter is covered by the first restriction mentioned in the diagram for ∀I. It preserves our logical intuition that you cannot logically infer a general sentence from a single, nonrepresentative, instance.

From a premise (or assumption) that Socrates is a philosopher—Ps—it cannot be deduced that everybody is a philosopher—(∀x)Px. But if the constant s does not appear in a premise or undischarged assumption, the sentence in which it does appear is a legitimate candidate for generalization. *Symlog* will enforce this restriction, as Figure 8.7 shows. In an effort to obtain (∃y)Hy by ≡E, the sentence (∀x)Px is incorrectly derived in line 3.

In contrast with ∃I, the rule ∀I does not allow for partial generalizations. Nor would we want it to since (for instance) from the fact that Socrates is as tall as Socrates it does not follow that everybody is as tall as Socrates. Here the second restriction is violated because although one occurrence of the constant s is replaced with the variable x, there is still another occurrence of s in the universally quantified sentence which was not replaced. Assuming s does not occur in any premise or undischarged as-

PD : CURRY			■
PREMISE	1	Ps	
PREMISE	2	(∀x)Px ≡ (∃y)Hy	
∀I x/s 1■	3	(∀x)Px	■
	4		
	5		
	6		
	7		
	8		
	9		
	10		
	11		
	12		
	13		
	14		
	15		
	16		
■■■ CONSTANT OCCURS IN PREMISE OR UNDISCHARGED ASSUMPTION			

Figure 8.7

sumption,

   Tss

would then generalize to

   (∀x)Txx

by one application of ∀-introduction. One could argue that this restriction is redundant because, after all, the definition of the syntactic transformation of (universal) generalization—see section 6.3—requires that *both* ocurrences of the constant s in Tss be replaced by x. But this second restriction is designed to handle cases in which certain quantifiers fall within the scope of others. For instance, according to section 6.3, the universal generalization of (∃x)Tsx → Ls, when x is the generalizing variable, is (∀x)[(∃x)Tsx → Lx]. The second restriction of the ∀-introduction rule, however, prevents the latter sentence from being inferred from the former because in fact it is not entailed (you may want to show a case in which the former is true and the latter is false).[3] This is the role of the rule's restrictions, namely, to block some generalizations (which although syntactically correct, are inferentially invalid). Figure 8.8 illustrates the use of the rule ∀-introduction. Note that in line 10 we can apply the rule ∀I to generalize Sba to (∀x)Sxa since the constant b does not occur in any premise or in any undischarged assumption

PD : CURRY		
PREMISE	1	(∀w)Bw & Hm
PREMISE	2	Bg → ¬(∃x)(∃y)¬Sxy
ASSUMPTION	3	┌ ¬Sba
∃I y/a 3	4	(∃y)¬Sby
∃I x/b 4	5	(∃x)(∃y)¬Sxy
&EL 1	6	(∀w)Bw
∀E g/w 6	7	Bg
→E 2, 7	8	└ ¬(∃x)(∃y)¬Sxy
¬E 3-5, 3-8	9	Sba
∀I x/b 9	10	(∀x)Sxa
∀I y/a 10	11	(∀y)(∀x)Sxy
	12	
	13	
	14	
	15	
	16	

Figure 8.8

[3] Here is one: If we read (∃x)Tsx → Ls as 'If Sandy is tutoring someone she will be late for the party tonight,' then (∀x)[(∃x)Tsx → Lx] effectively says, 'If Sandy is tutoring someone then everybody will be late for the party tonight'. The invalid move is clear.

(b is in line 3 but the assumption was discharged in line 8). A similar argument applies to line 11, where ∀I is applied again to obtain (∀y)(∀x)Sxy from (∀x)Sxa.

You should now, with the help of *Symlog*, solve and submit the on-disk exercises PD15 to PD21, which illustrate the workings of ∀I.

∃-Elimination (∃E)

	i	(∃**x**)α
ASSUMPTION	j	⌐ α(**a**/**x**)
	k	⌊ β
∃E **a**/**x** i, j-k	l	β

Restrictions: 1. **a** must not occur in a premise or undischarged assumption.
2. **a** must not occur in (∃**x**)α.
3. **a** must not occur in β.

Like the previous three rules, ∃-elimination (∃E) is embedded in the reasoning of natural language. Suppose a detective has been called to the scene of a crime. The initial facts are few: A person has been murdered; someone (at least one) is the murderer. Such facts do not point to the murderer—it will be the goal of the investigation to find the culprit. Meanwhile, it is possible to do some deductive speculation. Let us call the murderer m, the detective proposes. Since the victim was male and there are clear signs of a struggle, it is evident that the assailant was also male (the detective relies on a generalization that in cases like this, the attacker is male). Further, the victim was shot, but the gun is nowhere to be found; also, although his car is not in the garage, the police now have a clear description of it from a neighbor. All this information enables the detective to issue an all-points bulletin to look for a man, possibly armed, driving, say, a white 1938 Cord convertible.

Who is m? It is the murderer, the person the police want to arrest. His name, m, is an indeterminate name, a term of convenience. The detective knows that there is at least one such person because *someone* has committed this murder. Notice that from this fact alone, (∃x)Cx, it is impossible to deduce that Tom (the victim's brother) has committed this murder or that it is Dick (his son) or Harry (his business partner). The same holds for any other person we could identify by name. That is why the reasoning described above begins with an *assumption and a name stipulated for convenience.* Notice too that the all-points bulletin does not mention anyone by name, including m.

This example illustrates reasoning like that sanctioned by the rule ∃E, including the three restrictions attached to the rule. The rule is also known as **existential instantiation.** When we apply ∃E to an existential sentence, we make an assumption consisting of an instance of that sentence, and the instantiating constant selected is an 'indeterminate' constant for it has not already occurred either in a premise or undischarged assumption or in the existential sentence itself (see restrictions 1 and 2). Our reasoning then proceeds under this assumption in a subordinate derivation. This subderivation is eventually terminated by a sentence, β, to which the instantiating constant is foreign (restriction 3).

The three restrictions are crucial to $\exists$E. If some people are liars and Socrates is a person, it cannot be deduced that Socrates is a liar. The need for the first restriction is as evident here as it is for $\forall$-introduction: The instantiating constant cannot therefore be s but must be a constant which is foreign to all premises and undischarged assumptions in the derivation. Moving on, suppose that you have derived the sentence

$(\exists x)Hxg$

Suppose that you now assume an instance of that sentence, using g as your constant (violating the second restriction). Your assumption $\alpha(\mathbf{a/x})$, that is, $\alpha(g/x)$, is then the sentence

Hgg

Then you apply the rule of $\exists$-introduction to obtain

$(\exists x)Hxx$

This is the sentence β. Finally, you infer β outside the subderivation to conclude the main derivation. That is, you finally obtain

$(\exists x)Hxx$

An interpretation will make clear why this move is incorrect. You can interpret the original sentence as

Something is heavier than gold.

Clearly, from here it does not follow that

Something is heavier than itself.

Symlog, as shown in Figure 8.9, immediately detects a violation of this restriction, where the constant g has been wrongly selected for the assumption of line 6 when instantiating the existentially quantified sentence in line 5.

Consider now an example in which the third restriction is violated. Suppose that you have derived the sentence

$(\exists x)Mx$

```
┌─────────────────────────────────────────────────────────────┐
│ PD : FITCH                                                  ■ │
├─────────────────────────────────────────────────────────────┤
│ PREMISE              1    (∃x)(∃y)Gxy ≡ (∃x)Hxg              │
│ PREMISE              2    Gab                                │
│ ∃I  y/b  2           3    (∃y)Gay                            │
│ ∃I  x/a  3           4    (∃x)(∃y)Gxy                        │
│ ≡E  1, 4             5    (∃x)Hxg                            │
│ ASSUMPTION           6    ┌ Hgg                              │
│                      7    │                                  │
│                      8    │                                  │
│ ∃I  x/g  6           9    └ (∃x)Hxx                          │
│ ∃E  g/x  5, 6-9 ■    10   (∃x)Hxx                          ■ │
│                      11                                      │
│                      12                                      │
│                      13                                      │
│                      14                                      │
│                      15                                      │
│                      16                                      │
├─────────────────────────────────────────────────────────────┤
│ ■■■ CONSTANT OCCURS IN EXISTENTIAL WFF BEING INSTANTIATED    │
└─────────────────────────────────────────────────────────────┘
```

Figure 8.9

Then, using the constant s, you assume—as your assumption $\alpha(\mathbf{a/x})$, that is, $\alpha(\text{s/x})$—the sentence

    Ms

Then you obtain the sentence β merely by reiterating your assumption. That is, β is

    Ms

And, finally, you take β outside the subderivation under the main derivation, thus violating the third restriction.

To see where the problem is, let the sentence

    (∃x)Mx

mean

    Someone is a mathematician.

From here you cannot *conclude* that Socrates is a mathematician if you have *assumed* this already. (Figure 8.10).

Now that we have seen the need for ∃E's restrictions, let us look at the reasoning behind this rule from a different angle. Think of an existential sentence as a generalized disjunction: To say that someone is a mathematician is to say that either Hilbert is a mathematician or Noether is a mathe-

PD : FITCH   ■

PREMISE	1	$(\forall x)(\forall y)Fxy$
PREMISE	2	$(\exists x)Mx \equiv Fab$
$\forall E$ a/x 1	3	$(\forall y)Fay$
$\forall E$ b/y 3	4	Fab
$\equiv E$ 2, 4	5	$(\exists x)Mx$
ASSUMPTION	6	⌐ Ms
	7	
	8	
R 6	9	∟ Ms
$\exists E$ s/x 5, 6-9 ■	10	Ms ■
	11	
	12	
	13	
	14	
	15	
	16	

Figure 8.10   ■■■ CONSTANT OCCURS IN SUBDERIVATION'S CONCLUSION

matician or Shakespeare is or. . . . Now, recall that the ∨-elimination rule involves the construction of two subderivations, one for each disjunct. Since ∃ is a 'short-hand disjunction,' it is not surprising that its elimination rule should involve subderivations, one per disjunct. However, since the universe of discourse covered by ∃ may be infinite in size, we would face the possibility of an infinite disjunction—requiring the construction of infin-

PD : CANTOR

PREMISE	1	$\neg Sabn \rightarrow Bcb$
PREMISE	2	$(\forall x)(\forall y)(\forall w)\neg Swxy$
PREMISE	3	$(\forall x)(\forall y)[Byx \equiv (Dg \vee Mf)]$
$\forall E$ b/x 2	4	$(\forall y)(\forall w)\neg Swby$
$\forall E$ n/y 4	5	$(\forall w)\neg Swbn$
$\forall E$ a/w 5	6	$\neg Sabn$
$\rightarrow E$ 1, 6	7	Bcb
$\exists I$ y/c 7	8	$(\exists y)Byb$
$\exists I$ x/b 8	9	$(\exists x)(\exists y)Byx$
ASSUMPTION	10	⌐ $(\exists y)Bys$
ASSUMPTION	11	⌐ Bhs
$\forall E$ s/x 3	12	│ $(\forall y)[Bys \equiv (Dg \vee Mf)]$
$\forall E$ h/y 12	13	│ $Bhs \equiv (Dg \vee Mf)$
$\equiv E$ 11, 13	14	∟ $Dg \vee Mf$
$\exists E$ h/y 10, 11-14	15	∟ $Dg \vee Mf$
$\exists E$ s/x 9, 10-15	16	$Dg \vee Mf$
	17	
	18	

Figure 8.11

itely many subderivations. But the rule ∃-elimination avoids this problem. Its single subderivation stands for any one of indefinitely many subderivations (corresponding to ∃'s implicit disjuncts), *as long as the individual mentioned in its assumption is an indeterminate or representative individual.* The derivation depicted in Figure 8.11 further illustrates the use of ∃-elimination.

To finish this section, we suggest you try the on-disk exercises PD22 to PD26, which illustrate the use of the ∃E rule. As usual, let *Symlog* check your work.

Exercises

8.1.1 By now you should have solved *all* of the PD Learn Exercises, PD01 to PD26, on your disk. In case you have not done so, now is the time to do it.

8.1.2 Assume that $(\forall x)Fabxa$ and $(\forall x)Max \rightarrow Bc$ are the only premises in a derivation. Which of the following sentences can be derived from these premises by a *single* application of one of the quantifier rules? (State also which rule is being used.)

a. Fabca	b. Mab → Bc	c. (∀y)[(∀x)Max → By]
d. (∃z)(∀x)Fzbxz	e. (∃z)(∀x)Fzbxa	f. (∃y)[(∀x)Max → By]
g. Fabba	h. (∃x)(∀x)Faxxa	i. (∃x)[(∀x)Mxx → Bc]

8.1.3 The following derivation has four errors. Find them.

PD : ERRORS			
PREMISE	1	(∃z)(∀x)Gxz ≡ Hc	■
PREMISE	2	(∀x)Hx → (∃z)Bz	■
PREMISE	3	(∀x)(Fx → (∀y)Gxy) & (∃x)Fx	■
&ER 3	4	(∃x)Fx	■
ASSUMPTION	5	⌐ Fa	■
&EL 3	6	(∀x)(Fx → (∀y)Gxy)	■
∀E a/x 6	7	Fa → (∀y)Gay	■
→E 5, 7	8	(∀y)Gay	■
∀E b/y 8	9	⌊ Gab	■
∃E a/x 4, 5-9	10	Gab	■
∀I x/a 10	11	(∀x)Gxb	■
∃I z/b 11	12	(∃z)(∀x)Gxz	■
≡E 1, 12	13	Hc	■
∀E c/x 2	14	Hc → (∃z)Bz	■
→E 13, 14	15	(∃z)Bz	■
∃E c/z 15	16	Bc	■
∀I y/c 16	17	(∀y)By	■
	18		

8.1.4 Use *Symlog* to derive the given sentence from the given set of premises.

    a. {Fs ≡ ¬Her, ¬Her & Ga, Fs → (∀w)Mwws}, Mhhs

    b. {(∀w)(Mw → ¬Ga), Mb, (Mb & ¬Ga) → ¬Ha}, (∃w)¬Hw

    c. {(∃x)Mxx & Sq, (∀w)(Mww ≡ Fd)}, Fd

    d. {(∀x)(∀y)(∃z)(Gax ≡ Byz)}, (∀z)(∃x)(Gaz ≡ Bzx)

    e. {(∀x)(Mx → Bc)}, (∃z)Mz → Bc

8.2 Constructing Derivations in PD

Selecting Derivation System PD from *Symlog*'s Environment menu enables you to construct derivations in PD. Remember that, as it was for SD and SD+, the Derivation Pad offers a host of commands of which the Justification, Generation and Goal Analysis commands are especially useful. As in SD, there is also expert advice from *Symlog* for proof construction in PD. We will now provide two detailed examples showing how to construct derivations in PD; we suggest that you follow along with your computer.

To begin, we show how the sentence ¬(∃x)¬(Bax ∨ Dx) can be derived from the premise (∀x)(Bax ∨ Dx). For this work, your derivation must begin with (∀x)(Bax ∨ Dx) and end with ¬(∃x)¬(Bax ∨ Dx). (See the screen in Figure 8.12a.)

Since you do not know how long the complete derivation will be, you guess and enter the goal sentence on line 16. Perhaps this sentence can be obtained by using ¬-introduction. So after entering the proper justification

PD : SKOLEM		■
PREMISE	1	(∀x)(Bax v Dx)
	2	
	3	
	4	
	5	
	6	
	7	
	8	
	9	
	10	
	11	
	12	
	13	
	14	
	15	
■	16	¬(∃x)¬(Bax v Dx) ■
	17	
	18	

Figure 8.12a

in the Justification Field, you can invoke the Goal Analysis command (with Shift-Tab). The two contradictory sentences you will attempt to obtain are $(\forall x)(Bax \lor Dx)$—which is the premise on line 1—and $\neg(\forall x)(Bax \lor Dx)$. The sentence on line 1 can simply be reiterated on line 15. Your immediate goal, then, is to obtain $\neg(\forall x)(Bax \lor Dx)$. (See Figure 8.12b.)

Now, the assumption on line 2—that is, the sentence $(\exists x)\neg(Bax \lor Dx)$—is an existentially quantified sentence. It is a rule of thumb that whenever you have an existentially quantified sentence in a premise or undischarged assumption (or anywhere in the derivation, for that matter), you should use $\exists$-elimination to obtain your immediate goal. Let us follow this advice to obtain the sentence $\neg(\forall x)(Bax \lor Dx)$ on line 14. To put $(\exists x)\neg(Bax \lor Dx)$ to work, we will want to instantiate it. Recall, however, that the first two restrictions accompanying the rule $\exists$E prevent the use of any constant occurring in the premise on line 1, or in the existential sentence itself, as an instantiating constant. These restrictions exclude a, but any other constant will do, for instance, c. Enter $\exists$E c/x 2, 3-13 as the justification for the sentence on line 14, and then invoke the Goal Analysis command once again. (See Figure 8.12c.)

As you can see, the instance of $(\exists x)\neg(Bax \lor Dx)$ now appears on line 3, and the sentence $\neg(\forall x)(Bax \lor Dx)$ comes at the foot of the subderivation on line 13. This sentence is your immediate goal now. To obtain it, you can apply the rule $\neg$-introduction again. Since on line 3 you have the sentence $\neg(Bac \lor Dc)$, you will try to get $Bac \lor Dc$ and $\neg(Bac \lor Dc)$ as your two contradictory sentences inside the new subderivation to be opened. (Notice that at this point, we are applying tactics familiar from proofs in SD.) In the Justification Field for line 13 type $\neg$I 4-11, 4-12 as the justification for

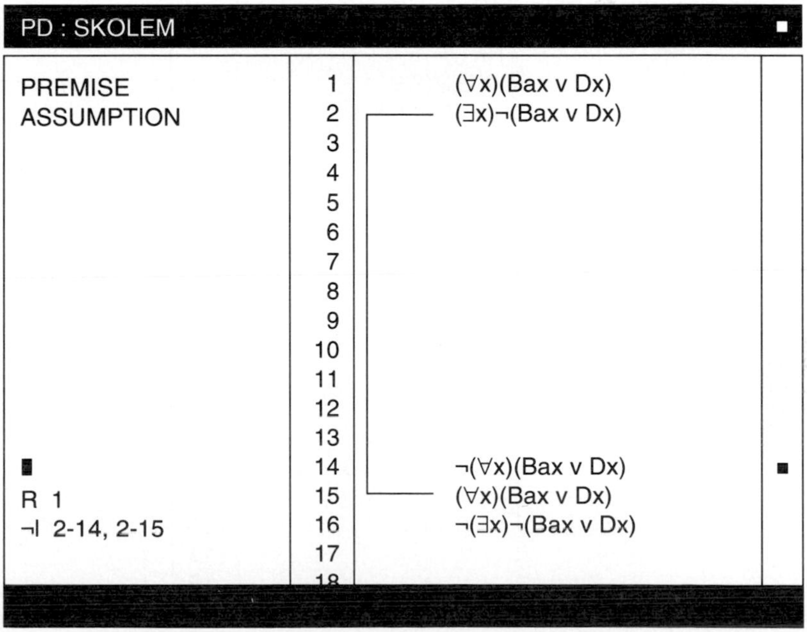

Figure 8.12b

PD : SKOLEM

PREMISE	1	(∀x)(Bax v Dx)
ASSUMPTION	2	(∃x)¬(Bax v Dx)
ASSUMPTION	3	¬(Bac v Dc)
	4	
	5	
	6	
	7	
	8	
	9	
	10	
	11	
	12	
■	13	¬(∀x)(Bax v Dx)
∃E c/x 2, 3-13	14	¬(∀x)(Bax v Dx)
R 1	15	(∀x)(Bax v Dx)
¬I 2-14, 2-15	16	¬(∃x)¬(Bax v Dx)
	17	
	18	

Figure 8.12c

PD : SKOLEM

PREMISE	1	(∀x)(Bax v Dx)
ASSUMPTION	2	(∃x)¬(Bax v Dx)
ASSUMPTION	3	¬(Bac v Dc)
ASSUMPTION	4	(∀x)(Bax v Dx)
	5	
	6	
	7	
	8	
	9	
	10	
■	11	Bac v Dc
R 3	12	¬(Bac v Dc)
¬I 4-11, 4-12	13	¬(∀x)(Bax v Dx)
∃E c/x 2, 3-13	14	¬(∀x)(Bax v Dx)
R 1	15	(∀x)(Bax v Dx)
¬I 2-14, 2-15	16	¬(∃x)¬(Bax v Dx)
	17	
	18	

Figure 8.12d

```
PD : SKOLEM

PREMISE              1           (∀x)(Bax v Dx)
ASSUMPTION           2           (∃x)¬(Bax v Dx)
ASSUMPTION           3           ¬(Bac v Dc)
ASSUMPTION           4           (∀x)(Bax v Dx)
                     5
                     6
                     7
                     8
                     9
                     10
∀E c/x  4            11          Bac v Dc
R 3                  12          ¬(Bac v Dc)
¬I 4-11, 4-12        13          ¬(∀x)(Bax v Dx)
∃E c/x  2, 3-13      14          ¬(∀x)(Bax v Dx)
R 1                  15          (∀x)(Bax v Dx)
¬I 2-14, 2-15        16          ¬(∃x)¬(Bax v Dx)
                     17
                     18
```

Figure 8.12e

```
PD : SKOLEM

PREMISE              1           (∀x)(Bax v Dx)
ASSUMPTION           2           (∃x)¬(Bax v Dx)
ASSUMPTION           3           ¬(Bac v Dc)
ASSUMPTION           4           (∀x)(Bax v Dx)
∀E c/x  1            5           Bac v Dc
R 3                  6           ¬(Bac v Dc)
¬I 4-5, 4-6          7           ¬(∀x)(Bax v Dx)
∃E c/x  2, 3-7       8           ¬(∀x)(Bax v Dx)
R 1                  9           (∀x)(Bax v Dx)
¬I 2-8, 2-9          10          ¬(∃x)¬(Bax v Dx)
                     11
                     12
                     13
                     14
                     15
                     16
                     17
                     18
```

Figure 8.12f

¬(∀x)(Bax ∨ Dx), and invoke the Goal Analysis command. Next, reiterate the sentence on line 3 to line 12 by typing R 3 and then use the Generation—Tab— command to get ¬(Bac ∨ Dc) (as well as to get rid of ¬α). Then type the sentence Bac ∨ Dc on line 11: This is now your immediate goal. (See Figure 8.12d.)

Obtaining Bac ∨ Dc is easy. You can instantiate the universal sentence on line 4, using c to replace the variable x. That is, enter ∀E c/x 4 as the justification of Bac ∨ Dc on line 11. Note that there are no marks in the Mark Field or in the Information Line at the top. Figure 8.12e shows your completed derivation.

Finally, you may want to get rid of the extra blank lines. Move the cursor to line 5 and delete the blank lines until your derivation looks like the one in Figure 8.12f. If you wish, you can submit your derivation for *Symlog* to check.

Let us go on to a second example. Suppose that you are asked to construct a derivation of the sentence (∃x)(Dax ∨ Sx) from the set of premises {(∃x)Mx → (∃w)(Daw ∨ Sw), (∀x)(∀y)¬Kyx, (∀y)My ≡ ¬Keh}. Figure 8.13a shows the problem set out in the usual way. Since the main logical operator of the sentence to be derived is an existential quantifier, it seems at first sight that this sentence should be obtained by applying ∃-introduction to a sentence like, say, Dar ∨ Sr. Notice though that the sentence (∃x)(Dax ∨ Sx) has the same form as the consequent of the first premise; that is, it has the same form as (∃w)(Daw ∨ Sw). The only difference between these two is that in the former the variable of quantification is x, whereas in the latter it is w. To change a variable in such a case is easy, as you will see. Of course, you must first ob-

PD : HINTIKKA			■
PREMISE	1	∙(∃x)Mx → (∃w)(Daw v Sw)	
PREMISE	2	(∀x)(∀y)¬Kyx	
PREMISE	3	(∀y)My ≡ ¬Keh	
	4		
	5		
	6		
	7		
	8		
	9		
	10		
	11		
	12		
	13		
	14		
■	15	(∃x)(Dax v Sx)	■
	16		
	17		
	18		

Figure 8.13a

tain (∃w)(Daw ∨ Sw), and since this is an existentially quantified sentence, you will try to obtain (∃x)(Dax ∨ Sx) by applying ∃-elimination to (∃w)(Daw ∨ Sw). Remember, if you are going to work with an existentially quantified sentence in a derivation, you will probably have to apply this rule. Therefore, suppose you type ∃E b/w 11, 12-14 as the justification for (∃x)(Dax ∨ Sx) on line 15 and then invoke the Goal Analysis command. *Symlog* automatically places (∃w)α on line 11, opens a subderivation with the assumption α(b/w) on line 12 and places the sentence (∃x)(Dax ∨ Sx) at the foot of the subderivation on line 14. *Symlog* inserts (∃w)α because it does not know to what sentence you arc going to apply ∃-elimination. *Symlog* uses the variable w in (∃w)α because you said in the justification for (∃x)(Dax ∨ Sx) that the variable w was to be replaced with the constant b. This choice complies with the restrictions imposed on ∃-elimination. (Note that the constants a, e and h appear in the premises.) (See Figure 8.13b.)

The sentence you want on line 11 is (∃w)(Daw ∨ Sw). So, suppose you enter it there. Then the assumption on line 12 must be Dab ∨ Sb because you said in the justification on line 15 that the constant b is to replace the variable w in whatever sentence you would have on line 11, and Dab ∨ Sb is an instance of (∃w)(Daw ∨ Sw). Once this step is done, you must obtain two sentences: the sentence (∃x)(Dax ∨ Sx) on line 14, and the sentence (∃w)(Daw ∨ Sw) on line 11. (See Figure 8.13c.)

Let us first take care of the sentence (∃x)(Dax ∨ Sx) on line 14. This sentence is easy to obtain by applying ∃-introduction to the assumption Dab ∨ Sb on line 12 by replacing the constant b with the variable x. Thus,

---

PD : HINTIKKA   ■

PREMISE	1	(∃x)Mx → (∃w)(Daw v Sw)
PREMISE	2	(∀x)(∀y)¬Kyx
PREMISE	3	(∀y)My ≡ ¬Keh
	4	
	5	
	6	
	7	
	8	
	9	
	10	
	11	(∃w)α ■
ASSUMPTION	12	┌─ α(b/w)
	13	│
■	14	└─ (∃x)(Dax v Sx) ■
∃E b/w 11, 12-14	15	(∃x)(Dax v Sx)
	16	
	17	
	18	

Figure 8.13b

```
PD : HINTIKKA                                                      ■

PREMISE                1      (∃x)Mx → (∃w)(Daw v Sw)
PREMISE                2      (∀x)(∀y)¬Kyx
PREMISE                3      (∀y)My ≡ ¬Keh
                       4
                       5
                       6
                       7
                       8
                       9
                      10
                      11      (∃w)(Daw v Sw)                        ■
ASSUMPTION            12   ┌─ Dab v Sb
                      13   │
■                     14   └─ (∃x)(Dax v Sx)                       ■
∃E b/w 11, 12-14      15      (∃x)(Dax v Sx)
                      16
                      17
                      18
```

Figure 8.13c

∃I x/b 12 justifies the sentence (∃x)(Dax ∨ Sx) on line 14. This step is illustrated in Figure 8.13d.

Now you need to justify the sentence (∃w)(Daw ∨ Sw) on line 11. This sentence is the consequent of the first premise; so if you had (∃x)Mx on, say, line 10, one application of →-elimination would be enough. The justification to be typed on line 11 therefore is →E 1,10. By invoking the Goal Analysis command you make *Symlog* produce (∃x)Mx on line 10, which now becomes your immediate goal (Figure 8.13e).

Since the sentence (∃x)Mx is an existentially quantified sentence, it makes sense to try to get it by using ∃-introduction on a sentence like, say, Mg, which could be placed on line 9. So in the Justification Field of line 10, suppose you type ∃I x/g 9, followed by the Goal Analysis command. *Symlog* produces the sentence Mg on line 9, which becomes your immediate goal (Figure 8.13f). As for Mg, it could be obtained in the following way. The left side of the biconditional on line 3 (the third premise) is (∀y)My. If you obtained this sentence on, say, line 8, one application of ∀-elimination would yield Mg. So to justify line 9, type ∀E g/y 8, and again use the Goal Analysis command. *Symlog* produces (∀y)My on line 8, which is the sentence you must worry about now. This step is illustrated in Figure 8.13g.

The sentence (∀y)My could be obtained if you had ¬Keh on, say, line 7, by applying ≡-elimination to the sentences on lines 3 and 7. Thus, the justification for (∀y)My on line 8 is ≡ E 3,7. Once the Goal Analysis command is issued, *Symlog* produces ¬Keh on line 7, your new immediate goal (Figure 8.13h).

```
┌──────────────────────────────────────────────────────────────────┐
│ PD : HINTIKKA                                                    ■ │
├──────────────────────────────────────────────────────────────────┤
│  PREMISE                    1         (∃x)Mx → (∃w)(Daw v Sw)      │
│  PREMISE                    2         (∀x)(∀y)¬Kyx                 │
│  PREMISE                    3         (∀y)My ≡ ¬Keh                │
│                             4                                      │
│                             5                                      │
│                             6                                      │
│                             7                                      │
│                             8                                      │
│                             9                                      │
│                            10                                      │
│  ■                         11         (∃w)(Daw v Sw)            ■  │
│  ASSUMPTION                12    ┌─    Dab v Sb                    │
│                            13    │                                 │
│  ∃I  x/b  12               14    └─    (∃x)(Dax v Sx)              │
│  ∃E  b/w  11, 12-14        15         (∃x)(Dax v Sx)              │
│                            16                                      │
│                            17                                      │
│                            18                                      │
└──────────────────────────────────────────────────────────────────┘
```

Figure 8.13d

```
┌──────────────────────────────────────────────────────────────────┐
│ PD : HINTIKKA                                                    ■ │
├──────────────────────────────────────────────────────────────────┤
│  PREMISE                    1         (∃x)Mx → (∃w)(Daw v Sw)      │
│  PREMISE                    2         (∀x)(∀y)¬Kyx                 │
│  PREMISE                    3         (∀y)My ≡ ¬Keh                │
│                             4                                      │
│                             5                                      │
│                             6                                      │
│                             7                                      │
│                             8                                      │
│                             9                                      │
│  ■                         10         (∃x)Mx                    ■  │
│  →E  1, 10                 11         (∃w)(Daw v Sw)               │
│  ASSUMPTION                12    ┌─    Dab v Sb                    │
│                            13    │                                 │
│  ∃I  x/b  12               14    └─    (∃x)(Dax v Sx)              │
│  ∃E  b/w  11, 12-14        15         (∃x)(Dax v Sx)              │
│                            16                                      │
│                            17                                      │
│                            18                                      │
└──────────────────────────────────────────────────────────────────┘
```

Figure 8.13e

PD : HINTIKKA   ■

PREMISE	1	(∃x)Mx → (∃w)(Daw v Sw)
PREMISE	2	(∀x)(∀y)¬Kyx
PREMISE	3	(∀y)My ≡ ¬Keh
	4	
	5	
	6	
	7	
	8	
■	9	Mg ■
∃I x/g 9	10	(∃x)Mx
→E 1, 10	11	(∃w)(Daw v Sw)
ASSUMPTION	12	⌐ Dab v Sb
	13	
∃I x/b 12	14	└ (∃x)(Dax v Sx)
∃E b/w 11, 12-14	15	(∃x)(Dax v Sx)
	16	
	17	
	18	

Figure 8.13f

PD : HINTIKKA   ■

PREMISE	1	(∃x)Mx → (∃w)(Daw v Sw)
PREMISE	2	(∀x)(∀y)¬Kyx
PREMISE	3	(∀y)My ≡ ¬Keh
	4	
	5	
	6	
	7	
■	8	(∀y)My ■
∀E g/y 8	9	Mg
∃I x/g 9	10	(∃x)Mx
→E 1, 10	11	(∃w)(Daw v Sw)
ASSUMPTION	12	⌐ Dab v Sb
	13	
∃I x/b 12	14	└ (∃x)(Dax v Sx)
∃E b/w 11, 12-14	15	(∃x)(Dax v Sx)
	16	
	17	
	18	

Figure 8.13g

PD : HINTIKKA ◼

PREMISE	1	(∃x)Mx → (∃w)(Daw v Sw)
PREMISE	2	(∀x)(∀y)¬Kyx
PREMISE	3	(∀y)My ≡ ¬Keh
	4	
	5	
	6	
◼	7	¬Keh ◼
≡E 3, 7	8	(∀y)My
∀E g/y 8	9	Mg
∃I x/g 9	10	(∃x)Mx
→E 1, 10	11	(∃w)(Daw v Sw)
ASSUMPTION	12	Dab v Sb
	13	
∃I x/b 12	14	(∃x)(Dax v Sx)
∃E b/w 11, 12-14	15	(∃x)(Dax v Sx)
	16	
	17	
	18	

Figure 8.13h

PD : HINTIKKA ◼

PREMISE	1	(∃x)Mx → (∃w)(Daw v Sw)
PREMISE	2	(∀x)(∀y)¬Kyx
PREMISE	3	(∀y)My ≡ ¬Keh
	4	
	5	
∀E h/x 2	6	(∀y)¬Kyh
◼	7	¬Keh ◼
≡E 3, 7	8	(∀y)My
∀E g/y 8	9	Mg
∃I x/g 9	10	(∃x)Mx
→E 1, 10	11	(∃w)(Daw v Sw)
ASSUMPTION	12	Dab v Sb
	13	
∃I x/b 12	14	(∃x)(Dax v Sx)
∃E b/w 11, 12-14	15	(∃x)(Dax v Sx)
	16	
	17	
	18	

Figure 8.13i

PD : HINTIKKA

PREMISE	1	$(\exists x)Mx \rightarrow (\exists w)(Daw \lor Sw)$
PREMISE	2	$(\forall x)(\forall y)\neg Kyx$
PREMISE	3	$(\forall y)My \equiv \neg Keh$
	4	
	5	
$\forall$E h/x 2	6	$(\forall y)\neg Kyh$
$\forall$E e/y 6	7	$\neg Keh$
$\equiv$E 3, 7	8	$(\forall y)My$
$\forall$E g/y 8	9	Mg
$\exists$I x/g 9	10	$(\exists x)Mx$
$\rightarrow$E 1, 10	11	$(\exists w)(Daw \lor Sw)$
ASSUMPTION	12	$Dab \lor Sb$
	13	
$\exists$I x/b 12	14	$(\exists x)(Dax \lor Sx)$
$\exists$E b/w 11, 12-14	15	$(\exists x)(Dax \lor Sx)$
	16	
	17	
	18	

Figure 8.13j

An application of the rule $\forall$-elimination to $(\forall x)(\forall y)\neg Kyx$ on line 2 (the second premise) would obviously yield the sentence $(\forall y)\neg Kyh$, where the constant h replaces the variable x; and another application of $\forall$-elimination to this new sentence would yield $\neg Keh$, where e replaces the variable y. Thus, in the Justification Field for line 6, type $\forall$E h/x 2 and issue the Generation command to produce the sentence $(\forall y)\neg Kyh$. (See Figure 8.13i.) Similarly, the sentence on line 7 can be justified with $\forall$E e/y 6. (See Figure 8.13j.)

You may want to get rid of the unnecessary blank lines and, to double-check (using Submit), have *Symlog* evaluate the completed proof.

Exercises

8.2.1 To gain more practice with rule applications, use *Symlog* to construct a derivation for the following by *using only the Generation command*. That is, at no time are you allowed to write a theorem in the Derivation Pad's Theorem Field; work only in the Justification Field.

$(\forall x)(Fxe \rightarrow Gxa)$
$(\forall y)(\forall x)(Fxy \equiv (\exists z)Hazx)$
$(\forall x)Hxcc$
———————
$(\exists y)(\exists z)Gyz$

8.2.2 Using *Symlog*, construct a derivation by *using mostly the Goal Analysis command*. That is, try to work as long as you can from the bottom of the derivation to the top.

$$\frac{(Gaa \ \& \ (\forall z)Fz) \equiv Haa}{(\forall x)Fx \rightarrow [(\forall y)(\forall z)Gyz \rightarrow (Fa \ \& \ (\exists x)Hxa)]}$$

8.2.3 Using *Symlog*, construct a derivation to derive the given sentence from the given set. Try as long as you can to work your way up from the bottom of the derivation to the top.

    a. $\{(\forall z)Fz, Ha\}, ((\forall x)Fx \rightarrow Ga) \rightarrow (\exists x)(Hx \ \& \ Gx)$

    b. $\varnothing, (\forall x)(Fx \ \& \ Gx) \equiv (\forall z)(Gz \ \& \ Fz)$

    c. $\varnothing, \neg(\exists x)\neg Fx \rightarrow (\forall x)Fx$

    d. $\{(\forall x)(Hx \equiv Ga)\}, (\forall x)Fx \rightarrow [((\exists x)Fx \rightarrow Ha) \rightarrow Ga]$

    e. $\varnothing, (\exists x)Fx \equiv (\exists y)Fy$

8.2.4 Assume that the UD is the set of all people. Although rather counterintuitive, it is true that there is a person such that if he is a fool then everybody is! This fact can be shown by deriving the sentence $(\exists x)(Fx \rightarrow (\forall x)Fx)$ from no premises. Since the proof in PD of this sentence is rather difficult, here you are asked to derive the equivalent sentence $(\exists x)(\neg Fx \lor (\forall x)Fx)$. Hint: Do it by reductio ad absurdum; the contradictory sentences are $(\forall x)Fx$ and $\neg(\forall x)Fx$.

8.2.5 Use the Create option under *Symlog*'s File menu to ask the program to generate (randomly) quantificationally valid arguments, whose derivations you should then attempt. When asked for the level of difficulty, select 'Easy-to-Medium.' Submit your work when done. (Note: If, after trying a few problems, you find them difficult to solve, go to the next section, where we present a powerful set of strategies for proof construction in PD and where we also explain how *Symlog* can give you expert advice.)

8.3   Strategies for Constructing Derivations in PD

We now give a set of strategies which you will find extremely useful for constructing derivations in PD. Some of the strategies suggested closely resemble those introduced earlier for the construction of derivations in SD. This is not surprising since many PL sentences have a truth-functional connective as main operator. The remaining strategies take account of quantified sentences and of the restrictions which must be recalled whenever two of the four new rules are used.

    Let us suppose that your aim is to derive a goal sentence α from some given set of sentences. (At the beginning, this will be the set of premises, which could possibly be empty.) To obtain α, it is useful to try the following:

    1. Look at the lines in the derivation which are accessible from your goal sentence α, and try to determine if α can be obtained from them by a single application of an elimination rule involving no subderivations: reiteration, &E, →E, ≡ E and ∀E. To illustrate, if $(\exists x)Kx \equiv (Gb \rightarrow (\forall x)Fx)$ is available and your goal is Fa, try to get $(\forall x)Fx$; to get this sentence get

both Gb → (∀x)Fx and Gb. As the example illustrates, engage in this strategy if the goal α occurs as a subwff, or is an instance of a subwff, of any of the accessible sentences. There are three exceptions to this subderivation-free strategy, however: (a) If you spot two easily derivable contradictory sentences, get your goal by ¬E; (b) If you spot a disjunction with a disjunct which is equal to your goal or from which your goal is easily derivable by ∃I or ∀E, it is sensible to apply ∨E: One of this rule's parallel subderivations will be rather trivial, the other gives you one extra assumption to work with (namely, the other disjunct); (c) If there are existentially quantified sentences available, be prepared to use ∃E but recall the restrictions associated with this rule; in most proofs, you will find that it pays to apply ∃E at an early stage. (As an illustration, read the text explaining how to go from Figure 8.12b to Figure 8.12c in the first example above.)

Supposing both types of universally and existentially quantified sentences occur among the available sentences and you want to instantiate them to obtain α, then give priority to the rule ∃E. In the case of universally quantified sentences, if you decide to use ∀-elimination, choose your constant wisely. That is, select as your constant of instantiation one that already occurs in a premise or previously derived sentence, for such instances are more likely to prove useful in applying a derivation rule imported from SD. (If no constant has occurred but you want to use ∀E, select a.) If there does not seem to be a simple way of obtaining α, go to step 2 below.

2. Your goal sentence α is either an atomic sentence (i.e., a k-ary predicate symbol followed by k constants, $k \geq 0$) or a compound sentence. According to whichever is the case, do:

   2.1. *α is an atomic sentence:* It is advisable that you reconsider step 1 again more carefully. If step 1 still seems to fail, go to step 3 below.

   2.2. *α is a compound sentence:* Apply the goal analysis method according to the main logical operator of α. If the moves suggested below seem to fail, proceed to step 3.

      2.2.1. *The main logical operator of α is* ¬: Here, α is of the form ¬β. Apply goal analysis by using ¬I; that is, construct a subderivation with β as assumption and derive (as your new goals) two contradictory sentences, δ and ¬δ. Unfortunately, it may not be clear what δ should be, but a good candidate for δ is any sentence, not necessarily atomic, whose negation appears (or is an instance of a universal sentence which appears) in any accessible line. However, in many cases you will have to manufacture the contradictory sentences you are seeking. In any event, this procedure adds a new sentence to your stock, namely, the assumption β. It is worth mentioning that if the sentence α is of the special form $\neg(\forall x)\beta$, then before attempting $\neg I$ you should first try $\exists E$ (assuming that you have, or that you can obtain, a suitable sentence with an existential quantifier to eliminate). As an illustration of this last suggestion, see the approach taken to go from Figure 8.12b to Figure 8.12c, where $\neg(\forall x)\beta$ is the sentence $\neg(\forall x)(Bax \lor Dx)$.

2.2.2. *The main logical operator of α is &:* Apply the goal analysis method by using &I; that is, derive each of the conjuncts in α separately. The left and the right conjuncts of α become your new (simpler) subgoals.

2.2.3. *The main logical operator of α is $\lor$:* You should first consider deriving α by trying to derive either of its disjuncts (i.e., by using the goal method with $\lor$IL or $\lor$IR). Which disjunct you should worry about depends on the sentences accessible from the line you are working. So you should apply step 1 above (on each disjunct separately) to determine which disjunct looks more promising. Keep in mind that in many cases one cannot derive a disjunction by deriving one of its disjuncts. Hence, this approach works only occasionally.

2.2.4. *The main logical operator of α is $\rightarrow$:* In this case apply the goal analysis method by using $\rightarrow$I, that is, by constructing a subderivation having as assumption the antecedent of α and as conclusion its consequent (which becomes a simpler goal).

2.2.5. *The main logical operator of α is $\equiv$:* Here, α is of the form $\beta \equiv \delta$. Apply the goal analysis method by using $\equiv$I, that is, by constructing two subderivations, the first of which has β as assumption and δ as conclusion, the second subderivation having δ as assumption and β as conclusion. The sentences β and δ, which are simpler than the original goal α, become your new goals.

2.2.6. *The main logical operator of α is $\exists$:* Here, α is of the form $(\exists x)\beta$. Basically there are two approaches you can take. The first approach is similar to that used when the main logical operator of α is $\lor$ (in 2.2.3). The idea is to consider deriving an instance $\beta(a/x)$ of α and then obtaining α in one single step by $\exists$I. The similarity between this approach and the one taken in 2.2.3 stems from the fact that $\exists$ is a generalized form of $\lor$. But just as in 2.2.3, where it may not be clear what disjunct to try, here it may not be apparent what instance $\beta(a/x)$ of α you should derive. In any event, as in 2.2.3, this approach seems to work only occasionally. The second approach, as illustrated in one of the preceeding examples (see the text explaining the steps to go from Figure 8.13a to Figure 8.13b), is to apply $\exists E$ to obtain the sentence α you are after (even though α is an existentially quantified sentence itself). Of course, here we assume you have (or can easily obtain) a suitable existentially quantified sentence among your accessible lines that you can use in the deployment of ∃E.

2.2.7. *The main logical operator of α is ∀:* Here, α is of the form $(\forall \mathbf{x})\beta$. The advisable course of action is to apply the goal analysis method by deriving first an instance $\beta(\mathbf{a}/\mathbf{x})$ of α and then obtaining α by a single application of ∀I. As with ∃E, choose your constant carefully, making sure you do not violate any of the restrictions associated with this rule.

3. If both steps 1 and 2 seem to fail but there are disjunctions or existentially quantified sentences among your available sentences, try to get α by ∨E or ∃E; consider each disjunction or existential sentence in turn, beginning with the most promising one. Your new goal is still α, but now you posses the assumption(s) for the subderivation(s) associated with ∃E or ∨E. If it does not seem possible to get α in this way, go to step 4.

4. If all else fails, then as a last resort plan to use ¬E to derive α, that is, assume ¬α and derive two contradictory sentences, δ and ¬δ. The main problem here is that it may not be clear what sentence δ you should derive. A good candidate for δ is any sentence, not necessarily atomic, whose negation appears (or is an instance of a universal sentence which appears) in any accessible line. However, in some cases you will have to manufacture the contradictory sentences you are seeking. But at least you have a new sentence in your stock to work with, namely, the assumption ¬α.

To see these strategies for PD in action, reread the commentary on constructing the two sample derivations of the preceeding section or, at least, study carefully the completed derivations in Figure 8.12e and Figure 8.13j.

We are now going to apply the strategies to a further two derivations. You are invited to follow along with *Symlog*. We will start with the problem set out in Figure 8.14, in which & is the main logical operator of our goal sentence. Hence, applying the goal analysis method, we try to derive both conjuncts on lines 15 and 29, concentrating on line 15 first. Since line 1 is an existentially quantified sentence, we give it priority (the same strategy will be used in deriving line 29). The constant a will do for the instantiation because it does not violate any of the restrictions of ∃E: It does not occur in any premise (lines 1, 2 and 3) or undischarged assumption (none) or in the sentence we want to instantiate (line 1) or in the theorem we want to prove (line 15). So after assuming Fa, line 14 becomes the new goal. It is worth remarking that even though our current goal is the same as before, we are not going in circles since a new sentence has been added (namely, the assump-

PD : CLAUSEWITZ

PREMISE	1	$(\exists x)Fx$
PREMISE	2	$(\forall y)(Fy \rightarrow (\forall z)Gzy)$
PREMISE	3	$(\forall u)(\forall w)(Guw \equiv Hwu)$
	4	
ASSUMPTION	5	Fa
$\forall$E a/y 2	6	$Fa \rightarrow (\forall z)Gza$
$\rightarrow$E 5, 6	7	$(\forall z)Gza$
	8	
	9	
	10	
	11	
$\forall$E b/z 7	12	Gba
$\exists$I y/a 12	13	$(\exists y)Gby$
$\forall$I x/b 13	14	$(\forall x)(\exists y)Gxy$
$\exists$E a/x 1, 5-14	15	$(\forall x)(\exists y)Gxy$
	16	
ASSUMPTION	17	Fa
$\forall$E a/y 2	18	$Fa \rightarrow (\forall z)Gza$
$\rightarrow$E 17, 18	19	$(\forall z)Gza$
$\forall$E b/z 19	20	Gba
$\forall$E b/u 3	21	$(\forall w)(Gbw \equiv Hwb)$
$\forall$E a/w 21	22	$Gba \equiv Hab$
	23	
	24	
	25	
$\equiv$E 20, 22	26	Hab
$\forall$I y/b 26	27	$(\forall y)Hay$
$\exists$I x/a 27	28	$(\exists x)(\forall y)Hxy$
$\exists$E a/x 1, 17-28	29	$(\exists x)(\forall y)Hxy$
&I 15, 29	30	$(\forall x)(\exists y)Gxy$ & $(\exists x)(\forall y)Hxy$
	31	

Figure 8.14

tion Fa) to our stock of available sentences. Now, since the current goal is a universally quantified sentence and we have given priority to the only existentially quantified sentence (line 1), we should apply the strategy described above in 2.2.7. Here, any constant of instantiation would do as long as it is not a (which occurs in line 5—an undischarged assumption). However, in the interest of keeping an eye on constants, we suggest that you select the alphabetically first constant which meets the restrictions set by $\forall$I and $\exists$E. In the present case, we choose b as the constant in line 13, which becomes the new goal. Since this is an existentially quantified sentence, applying $\exists$I (the first approach suggested in 2.2.6) seems a reasonable move (before using $\neg$E, as recommended by strategic step 4). But what constant should we choose? For the moment, let us denote this constant by the symbol **c** (**c**, in boldface, is a variable ranging over constants). The only place where the sentence Gbc can be obtained from is either line 2 or line 3 (they are the only accessible lines with this predicate). We can rule out line 3 because to obtain Gbc from it we would need Hcb (and one application of ≡E), but no other sentence containing the predicate H is in sight. Thus, we are left with line 2. Since we are planning to derive Gbc by (a) a suitable instantiation of line 2, (b) applying →E by using line 5, and (c) instantiating the resulting sentence, you can see now that the constant c we are seeking is a. The reason for choosing a as the constant in line 12 is ultimately linked to the fact that it appears in line 5. Thus, after applying ∀E a/y 2 to obtain line 6 and →E 5,6 to obtain line 7, Gba is obtained from 7 by universal instantiation. This completes the first subderivation.

As for the second subderivation, we shall repeat the move made in the previous subderivation by existentially instantiating line 1. So after assuming Fa in line 17, line 28 becomes the new goal. (Note that a is a proper choice for an instantiating constant because it occurs in no previous premise or *undischarged* assumption.) The current goal on line 28 is an existentially quantified sentence which we can try to obtain by deriving an instance of it on line 27. (∀y)Hay is a *suitable* instance of (∃x)(∀y)Hxy since there are no restrictions attached to the rule ∃I; it is also a *desirable* instance, for the constant a is already in use (in Fa). (∀y)Hay itself, being a universal sentence, might be derived from Hab (whose constant, b, would meet the restrictions for this rule). Let us then make Hab our new goal sentence (line 26). How to obtain it? Consider what sentences are accessible at this point: the three premises (the first of which, already put to work, we do not expect to use again) plus the assumption on line 17. On these three sentences we must focus our efforts. Study them carefully, keeping in mind the goal sentence Hab, which we want them to yield. By applying ∀E twice over to premise 3 (b/u and a/w), we can easily derive Gba ≡ Hab. What we need next is Gba in order to apply ≡E. And this sentence is easy to get: Apply ∀E a/y to premise 2, which gives Fa → (∀z)Gza, and the rest you ought to be able to plot out on your own. Why not do so before comparing your work to the finished proof in Figure 8.14?

As you have now seen, constructing derivations in PD is a more complex affair than in SD. When constructing a derivation where there are several quantified sentences, some of which may be multiply quantified, do not instantiate them blindly but keep an eye on the possible uses of the instantiated sentences you obtain by applying the quantifier elimination rules. Examine the *patterns* of constants and variables, comparing what you need with what you are able to get. And never let the restrictions on ∀I and ∃E drift from sight.

In the second example (Figure 8.15), the goal is a universally quantified sentence. Making now a familiar move, we give priority to the existential sentence on line 2, instantiating it (line 6) as the assumption of the subderivation that has line 29 as its conclusion. Then as suggested by strategy 2.2.7, we make line 28 the new goal, where b is the alphabetically first appropriate constant to select. Line 28 has → as its main logical opera-

PD : NELSON			
PREMISE	1	$(\forall x)(Fx \rightarrow Gx)$	
PREMISE	2	$(\exists x)(\forall y)(Fy \rightarrow Hxy)$	
PREMISE	3	$(\forall w)(\forall z)(Hwz \equiv Kzw)$	
PREMISE	4	$(\forall x)(\forall u)(Hxu \rightarrow (Gu \rightarrow Gx))$	
	5		
ASSUMPTION	6	$(\forall y)(Fy \rightarrow Hay)$	
	7		
ASSUMPTION	8	Fb	
$\forall$E a/x 4	9	$(\forall u)(Hau \rightarrow (Gu \rightarrow Ga))$	
$\forall$E b/y 6	10	$Fb \rightarrow Hab$	
$\rightarrow$E 8, 10	11	Hab	
$\forall$E b/u 9	12	$Hab \rightarrow (Gb \rightarrow Ga)$	
$\rightarrow$E 11, 12	13	$Gb \rightarrow Ga$	
$\forall$E b/x 1	14	$Fb \rightarrow Gb$	
$\rightarrow$E 8, 14	15	Gb	
$\rightarrow$E 13, 15	16	Ga	
	17		
$\forall$E b/y 6	18	$Fb \rightarrow Hab$	
$\rightarrow$E 8, 18	19	Hab	
$\forall$E a/w 3	20	$(\forall z)(Haz \equiv Kza)$	
$\forall$E b/w 20	21	$Hab \equiv Kba$	
$\equiv$E 19, 21	22	Kba	
	23		
	24		
	25		
&I 16, 22	26	Ga & Kba	
$\exists$I y/a 26	27	$(\exists y)(Gy \& Kby)$	
$\rightarrow$I 8-27	28	$Fb \rightarrow (\exists y)(Gy \& Kby)$	
$\forall$I x/b 28	29	$(\forall x)(Fx \rightarrow (\exists y)(Gy \& Kxy))$	
$\exists$E a/x 2, 6-29	30	$(\forall x)(Fx \rightarrow (\exists y)(Gy \& Kxy))$	
	31		

Figure 8.15

tor, so we assume its antecedent Fb and try to derive its consequent $(\exists y)(Gy \& Kby)$ by $\exists$I, applying strategy 2.2.6. These are the main steps of this derivation. Filling in the details makes a good exercise. Along the way, ask yourself what makes the choice of a as constant in Ga & Kba (line 26) a good one. (Hint: Look at line 6.)

As with proof construction in **SD**, expert advice from *Symlog* is just one key away: With the screen cursor on the line containing your goal sentence, press the Advice key. After looking at the goal and after analyzing all the available information, *Symlog* will recommend a strategy—'the most logical thing to do next'—pointing to a solution of the problem at hand (see Figure 8.16).

PD : NELSON

ADVICE

Use ∀I to get your goal wff, (∀x)(Fx→(∃y)(Gy&Kxy)).

WHY

Because none of the elimination strategies seems to apply but also because (∀x)(Fx→(∃y)(Gy&Kxy)) is a universal sentence.

REMARKS

After justifying (∀x)(Fx→(∃y)(Gy&Kxy)) by ∀I x/b i, derive one of its instances. I recommend you try Fb→(∃y)(Gy&Kby) as the instance. Note, in particular, how the constant chosen, b, respects the restrictions of ∀I.

Figure 8.16

Exercises

8.3.1 Assume the following three sentences are accessible:

(∀x)Fx
(∃x)Gx
(∀z)Fz → ¬Fa

According to the strategies, which rule should you apply first to the following (goal) sentence in an attempt to derive it from the above accessible set?

a. Fc   b. Fa → (∃x)Kx   c. (∀y)Fy
d. Fa & Fb   e. (∃x)(Fx ∨ Gx)   f. Ga
g. (∃y)Gy   h. ¬(∀z)¬Fz   i. ¬Fa

8.3.2 Use the strategies to derive, with the help of *Symlog*, the given sentence from the given set. (Remark: Recall that in *Symlog*, the strategies can be conveniently applied by using the Goal Analysis command.)

a. {(∃x)(Fx & Hx) → Ga}, (∀x)Fx → ((∀x)Hx → (∃x)Gx)
b. {(∃x)(∃y)Fxy → (∀x)Hxx}, (∀x)[(∀y)Fxy → (∃x)Hxx]
c. {(∃x)Fx, (∀x)(Fx → (∃y)Hxy), (∃x)(∃y)Hxy ≡ (∀x)(∀y)Kxy}, (∃x)(Fx & (∃y)Kxy)
d. {(∀x)(∀y)(Fx ∨ Gy), (∃x)(Fx → Kx), (∃x)(Gx → Hx)}, (∃x)(Kx ∨ Hx)
e. ∅, Fa → [((∃x)Fx → (∀x)Kx) ≡ (∀y)Ky]
f. {(∀x)(Hx → Kx)}, (∀x) [Hx → (Kx & (∃y)Hy)]

g. $\{(\exists x)Hx \rightarrow (\forall x)Kx\}, (\forall x)(\neg Kx \rightarrow \neg Hx)$

h. $\{(\forall x)(\neg Fx \vee Gx), (\forall x)(\neg Hx \vee \neg Gx)\}, (\forall x)(Hx \rightarrow \neg Fx)$

i. $\{(\exists x)Fx\}, (\exists z)Gz \rightarrow ((\exists x)Gx \ \& \ (\exists z)Fz)$

j. $\{(\exists x)[(\exists y)Fy \rightarrow (Gx \vee \neg Fx)]\}, (\forall y)Fy \rightarrow (\exists x)Gx$

8.3.3 Derive $(\exists x)(Fx \rightarrow (\forall x)Fx)$ from no premises. Hint: Assume the negation of the conclusion and use $(\forall x)Fx$ and $\neg(\forall x)Fx$ as contradictory sentences.

8.3.4 Use the Create option under *Symlog*'s File menu to ask the program to generate (randomly) quantificationally valid arguments, whose derivations you should then construct. When asked for the level of difficulty, select 'Easy-to-Medium.' Submit your work when done.

8.3.5 Repeat as in 8.3.4 but select 'Medium-to-Difficult.'

8.3.6 Repeat as in 8.3.4 but select 'Difficult.'

8.4 *Properties of Sentences and Sets of Sentences in PD*

This section offers a formal characterization of the system PD as well as definitions, from the perspective of PD, of some basic metalogical concepts of PL.

> **Definition.** A **derivation in PD** is a finite sequence of sentences of PL, each of which has been justified by using one of the rules of PD.

> **Definition.** Given a set Γ of sentences of PL and a sentence α of PL, α is **PD-derivable from** Γ if and only if there is a derivation in PD in which Γ is the set of premises and α is on the last line of the derivation, where this occurrence of α is not within the scope of an assumption.

If α is PD-derivable from Γ, then we write $\Gamma \vdash_{\overline{PD}} \alpha$ (or $\Gamma \vdash \alpha$, for short). Figure 8.15 illustrates such a derivation in PD, the premises being lines 1 through 4 and the sentence on line 30 corresponding to α.

> **Definition.** Given a set Γ of sentences of PL, a sentence α of PL is a **PD-theorem of** Γ if and only if α is PD-derivable from Γ.

Referring once again to Figure 8.15, we see that the sentence on line 30 is a PD-theorem of Γ where Γ is the set of premises on lines 1, 2, 3 and 4. If Γ is the empty set, $\emptyset$, then the PD-theorems of $\emptyset$—known as the **theorems of logic**—are precisely those sentences which are quantificationally true (i.e., the logical truths). Figure 8.17 shows that the sentence $(\forall x)(Fx \vee \neg Fx)$ is a theorem of logic[4] (as you can see, no premises are required for its derivation).

---

[4] As we did with SD, if it is clear from the context and to avoid overqualification, PD-theorems will be simply called theorems; we will do likewise for PD-derivability.

```
 PD : CHURCH

 ASSUMPTION          1    ┌───── ¬(Fa v ¬Fa)
                     2    │
 ASSUMPTION          3    │ ┌─── ¬Fa
                     4    │ │
 vIL  3              5    │ │    Fa v ¬Fa
                     6    │ │
 R  1                7    │ └─── ¬(Fa v ¬Fa)
 ¬E  3-5, 3-7        8    │      Fa
 vIR  8              9    │      Fa v ¬Fa
 R  1                10   │ └─── ¬(Fa v ¬Fa)
 ¬E  1-9, 1-10       11   │      Fa v ¬Fa
 ∀I x/a  11          12   │      (∀x)(Fx v ¬Fx)
                     13
                     14
                     15
                     16
```

Figure 8.17

Definition. Two sentences α and β of PL are **PD-equivalent** if and only if $\{\alpha\} \vdash_{PD} \beta$ and $\{\beta\} \vdash_{PD} \alpha$.

Figure 8.18 shows that the sentences $\neg(\forall x)Fx$ and $(\exists x)\neg Fx$ are PD-equivalent.

Definition. A set Γ of sentences of PL is **PD-inconsistent** if and only if both α and $\neg\alpha$ (where α is a sentence of PL) are derivable from Γ. A set Γ of sentences of PL is **PD-consistent** if and only if it is not PD-inconsistent.

In other words, Γ is PD-inconsistent if and only if there is a sentence α such that both $\Gamma \vdash_{PD} \alpha$ and $\Gamma \vdash_{PD} \neg\alpha$. The set $\{(\exists x)Fx \rightarrow \neg Ga, (\forall x)(\forall y)(Hyx \& Gy), (\exists y)Hay \equiv Fb\}$ is PD-inconsistent, since both Ga and $\neg$Ga can be derived from it (Figure 8.19).

Test for Derivability. The sentence β is derivable (in PD) from a PL set $\{\alpha_1, \alpha_2, \ldots, \alpha_n\}$—possibly empty—if and only if the test set $\{\alpha_1, \alpha_2, \ldots, \alpha_n, \neg\beta\}$ is PD-inconsistent.

As an exercise, you may want to show that $\{(\forall x)(Fx \rightarrow Gx), Fa\} \vdash_{PD} Ga$ by showing that the test set $\{(\forall x)(Fx \rightarrow Gx), Fa, \neg Ga\}$ is PD-inconsistent.

Definition. An argument of PL having a set Γ of premises and a sentence α as its conclusion is **PD-valid** if and only if α is a PD-theorem of Γ. An argument of PL is **PD-invalid** if and only if it is not PD-valid.

PD : GODEL		
PREMISE	1	¬(∀x)Fx
	2	
ASSUMPTION	3	┌── ¬(∃x)¬Fx
	4	
ASSUMPTION	5	┌── ¬Fa
	6	
	7	
∃I x/a 5	8	(∃x)¬Fx
R 3	9	└── ¬(∃x)¬Fx
¬E 5-8, 5-9	10	Fa
	11	
∀I x/a 10	12	(∀x)Fx
R 1	13	└── ¬(∀x)Fx
¬E 3-12, 3-13	14	(∃x)¬Fx
	15	
	16	

PD : HILBERT		
PREMISE	1	(∃x)¬Fx
	2	
ASSUMPTION	3	┌── ¬Fa
	4	
ASSUMPTION	5	┌── (∀x)Fx
	6	
	7	
∀E a/x 5	8	Fa
R 3	9	└── ¬Fa
¬I 5-8, 5-9	10	¬(∀x)Fx
∃E a/x 1, 3-10	11	¬(∀x)Fx
	12	
	13	
	14	
	15	
	16	

Figure 8.18

PD : HERBRAND			
PREMISE	1	(∃x)Fx → ¬Ga	
PREMISE	2	(∀x)(∀y)(Hyx & Gy)	
PREMISE	3	(∃y)Hay ≡ Fb	
	4		
∀E b/x 2	5	(∀y)(Hyb & Gy)	
∀E a/y 5	6	Hab & Ga	
&EL 6	7	Hab	
∃I y/b 7	8	(∃y)Hay	
≡E 3, 8	9	Fb	
∃I x/b 9	10	(∃x)Fx	
→E 1, 10	11	¬Ga	
&ER 6	12	Ga	
	13		
	14		
	15		
	16		

Figure 8.19

Consider the PL symbolization of the following argument:

Not everybody is French.

Someone is not French.

That the argument is PD-valid is shown by deriving the conclusion, $(\exists x)\neg Fx$, from the set of premises, $\{\neg(\forall x)Fx\}$. In fact, this was done in the derivation GODEL in Figure 8.18. By the way, the derivation HILBERT (also in Figure 8.18) shows that the converse argument

$(\exists x)\neg Fx$

$\neg(\forall x)Fx$

is also PD-valid.

Exercises

In the exercises that follow, feel free to use the Justification (Enter key), Generation (Tab) or Goal Analysis (Shift-Tab) commands in any combination you think most appropriate to construct the needed derivations. Let *Symlog* check all your work by submitting your derivations once they are completed. You may also want to simulate tests by disabling *Symlog*'s supervising capabilities (select Interactive/Noninteractive Mode from the Services menu). Then, by using Submit, you can let *Symlog* check your work.

8.4.1   Answer true or false (but not both) to each of the following.
   a. The sentence $(\exists x)Gx$ is a theorem of $\{(\forall x)Fx, \neg Fa\}$.
   b. If α is a theorem of Γ then $\neg\alpha$ is not a theorem of Γ.
   c. $\neg\alpha$ is not a theorem of $\{\alpha\}$.
   d. If α is not a theorem of Γ then Γ is PD-consistent.
   e. There is a sentence of PL which is not a theorem of $\{(\forall x)Hx \,\&\, Fa, Fa \equiv \neg Hb\}$.
   f. If $\Gamma \vdash_{PD} \alpha \rightarrow \beta$ then $\Gamma \cup \{\alpha\} \vdash_{PD} \beta$.
   g. If $\Gamma \vdash_{PD} \alpha \vee \beta$ then $\Gamma \vdash_{PD} \alpha$ or $\Gamma \vdash_{PD} \beta$.
   h. If α is a theorem of Γ_1 and β is a theorem of Γ_2 then both α and β are theorems of $\Gamma_1 \cup \Gamma_2$.
   i. If α is a theorem of Γ_1 and also a theorem of Γ_2 then α is a theorem of $\Gamma_1 \cap \Gamma_2$.
   j. $\varnothing \vdash_{PD} ((\forall x)Fx \vee (\forall x)Gx) \rightarrow (\forall x)(Fx \vee Gx)$.

8.4.2   Using *Symlog*, show that the given sentence is PD-derivable from the corresponding set.
   a. $\{(\exists x)Kx \rightarrow La\}$, $(\forall x)(Kx \rightarrow La)$
[PR96] b. $\{(\forall x)(\neg Bx \vee (\exists y)Cy)\}$, $(\exists x)Bx \rightarrow (\exists y)Cy$
   c. $\{(\exists x)(Hx \vee Ka), (\forall x)(Kx \rightarrow Gx)\}$, $(\exists x)(Ga \vee Hx)$

[PR97] d. {¬(∃x)Bx ∨ (∀x)Cx, ¬(∃x)¬Bx}, ¬(∀x)¬Cx

e. {(∀x)(Fx ∨ Gx)}, (∀x)¬Fx → (∃x)Gx

8.4.3   Using *Symlog* show that each sentence is a theorem of the given set.

a. (∀x)(∀y)(Gxy ≡ Gyx), ∅

b. (∃x)Fx, {(∃y)Fy}

[PR98] c. (∃x)¬(∃w)Jwx ≡ (∃w)¬(∃x)Jxw, ∅

d. (∀x)(∃w)Fwx → (∃x)Fxa, ∅

e. (∃x)Gx & (∃y)Hy, {(∃w)(Gw & Hw)}

f. (∀w)Gw → (∀w)Mw, {(∀w)(Gw → Mw)}

g. (∃x)(Bx ∨ Cx), {(∃x)Bx ∨ (∃x)Cx}

h. (∀x)(Gx ∨ Fx), {(∀x)(Fx ∨ Gx)}

[PR99] i. (∃x)Fx → Ga, {(∀x)(∀y)Hxy → Ga, (∀x)(∀y)(Hxy ≡ (∃y)Fy)}

[PR100] j. (∃z)Gz, {(∀x)[(Gx ∨ ¬(∃x)Hbax) & Hbax]}

8.4.4   Show with *Symlog* that the following sets are PD-inconsistent.

a. {¬(∃x)Fx, (∀x)Fx}

[PR101] b. {(∀x)Gx ≡ ¬Hb, ¬(∃y)Gy ∨ Sa, ¬Sa & ¬Hb}

c. {(∀x)(Hx → Kf), (∃x)Hx & Bacc, Bacc → ¬Kf}

[PR102] d. {(∃w)Sw, (∀y)¬Sy}

[PR103] e. {(∀x)¬(∃y)Baxy, (∃w)(∃y)Bawy} [Hint: Derive P & ¬P.]

[PR104] f. {(∀x)(¬Kxdg ∨ ¬Dx), (∃x)Dx, (∀y)Kydg} [Hint: Derive P & ¬P.]

g. {(∀x)(∀y)(Mxy ≡ ¬Mxy)}

h. {(∃x)(Fx & ¬Fx)}

[PR105] i. {(∀x)Hx & ((∃x)Gx → ¬Ha), (∀x)(Fx → ¬Hx), (∀x)(Fx ∨ Gx)}

j. {(∀x)Gx, (∃x)Hx → ¬Gb, (∃x)(Fx & Hx)}

8.4.5   Use the test for derivability to show, using *Symlog,* that the given sentence is derivable from the corresponding set.

a. {(∀x)(Fx & Gx), Gb → Hc}, Hc

[PR106] b. {¬(∃x)¬Gx ∨ ¬Fa, ¬Gb → Fa}, Gb

[PR107] c. {(¬Ka ∨ Gb) → (∃x)(Gx ∨ Kx), ¬(∃x)(Kx ∨ Gx)}, Ka

d. ∅, (∀x)(Fx ≡ Fx)

e. ∅ + , Fa ∨ ¬Fa

8.4.6   Show with *Symlog* that the following arguments are PD-valid.

a. (∀x)(∀y)(∀w)(Hxyw → (∀z)Mz)
(∀z)Mz → (∃x)Bxg
───────────────────────
Habc → (∃x)Bxg

[PR108] b. (∃x)(∃y)Gxy
──────────────
¬(∀x)(∀y)¬Gxy

c. (∀x)Hx & (∀w)Gaw
────────────────────
(∀x)(∀w)(Gaw & Hx)

d. ¬(∃z)¬Pzfh
──────────────
(∀z)Pzfh

[PR109] e. $\dfrac{\neg(\forall y)\neg(\text{Bay} \equiv \neg\text{Gy})}{(\exists w)(\neg\text{Gw} \equiv \text{Baw})}$

[PR110] f. $(\forall x)(\neg\text{Px} \to \text{Qx})$
            $(\exists y)\neg\text{Qy}$
            $\overline{(\exists x)(\text{Px} \vee \neg\text{Rxc})}$

[PR111] g. $(\forall x)(\forall y)[(\text{Pay \& Pxa}) \to \text{Pxy}]$
            $(\exists z)(\text{Rz \& Pza})$
            $(\forall x)(\text{Rx} \to \text{Pax})$
            $\overline{(\exists x)[(\exists z)(\text{Rz} \to \text{Pxz}) \text{ \& Rx}]}$

         h. $\dfrac{(\forall x)(\text{Kx} \to (\text{Lx} \to \text{Mx}))}{(\forall x)((\text{Kx \& Lx}) \to \text{Mx})}$

[PR112] i. $(\forall x)(\text{Ax} \to \text{Bx})$
            $(\forall x)(\forall z)[(\text{Ax \& Bz}) \to (\text{Cx \& Dz})]$
            $(\exists x)\text{Ax} \equiv (\exists y)\text{By}$
            $\overline{(\forall x)(\text{Bx} \to \text{Dx})}$

[PR113] j. $(\exists x)\text{Fx} \to (\forall x)(\text{Gx} \vee (\exists y)\text{Hyx})$
            $(\forall x)\text{Fx \& } (\forall x)(\neg\text{Hxa} \vee \text{Gc})$
            $\overline{(\exists x)\text{Gx}}$

8.4.7   Use *Symlog* to show that the sentences in each of the following pairs
        are PD-equivalent.

        a. $(\exists w)\text{Maw} \to \text{Sh}$ and $(\forall w)(\text{Maw} \to \text{Sh})$

[PR114] b. $\neg(\exists x)\neg\text{Fx}$ and $(\forall x)\text{Fx}$

[PR115] c. $(\exists x)\text{Fx}$ and $\neg(\forall x)\neg\text{Fx}$

[PR116] d. $(\exists x)(\text{Bx} \vee \text{Nx})$ and $\neg(\forall y)(\neg\text{Ny \& } \neg\text{By})$

        e. $(\exists w)\text{Mw} \to \text{Mg}$ and $(\exists w)\text{Mw} \equiv \text{Mg}$

[PR117] f. $\neg(\exists w)\text{Gaw} \vee \text{Ga}$ and $\text{Ga} \vee (\forall z)\neg\text{Gaz}$

        g. $(\forall x)(\text{Bx \& Cx})$ and $(\forall x)\text{Bx \& } (\forall x)\text{Cx}$

        h. $(\forall x)(\text{P} \to \text{Fx})$ and $\text{P} \to (\forall x)\text{Fx}$

[PR118] i. $(\forall x)\text{Hx} \to (\exists w)\text{Dw}$ and $(\forall w)\neg\text{Dw} \to (\exists z)\neg\text{Hz}$

[PR119] j. $(\exists x)\neg\text{Fx}$ and $\neg(\forall x)\text{Fx}$

8.4.8   Translate the following statements into PL and show with *Symlog*
        that the conclusion is derivable from the premises.

        a. Someone is sad. Therefore, not everybody is happy. (Hx)

        b. Horses are mammals, and since all mammals are insects, it fol-
            lows that all horses are insects. (Hx, Mx, Ix)

        c. Since there is someone who loves everybody, someone loves me.
            (Lxy)

[PR120] d. Everybody loves lovers. Bob loves Jane. Hence, Bob loves himself. (Lxy)

e. Horses are mammals but no mammal is an insect. Hence, no horse is an insect. (Hx, Mx, Ix)

f. If anyone is loyal to the king so is the queen. But the queen is loyal to him only if he is loyal to everybody. So, someone is loyal to the king only if he is loyal to her. (Lxy)

[PR121] g. If there are pions or lambda particles in this bubble chamber then there is hydrogen too. Moreover, all hydrogen in this chamber is ionized. Since, as revealed by new experiments, there are pions in the chamber, it follows that there is an ion as well. (Px, Lx, Hx, Ix)

h. Since there is at least one mammal which is not a horse, not all mammals can be horses. (Mx, Hx)

i. If anyone goes out with Lucy tonight, Mike will get very jealous. Either Albert or Paul will go out with Lucy tonight if someone is already going out with Suzy. Since Albert is going out with Suzy, someone is bound to get very jealous. (Oxy, Jx)

j. Anybody who enjoys abstract thinking enjoys symbolic logic. At least one person enjoys abstract thinking or playing cards. Thus, not everyone dislikes symbolic logic and playing cards. (Exy)

8.4.9 Translate the following statements into PL and show, with the assistance of *Symlog*, that they form a PD-inconsistent set.

[PR122] a. If a number is between two numbers then this number is greater than the first but the second is greater than it. There is a number between two numbers, *a* and *b*, such that it is neither greater than *a* nor *b* is greater than it. (Bxyz, Gxy) [Hint: Derive P & ¬P.]

b. A set is normal if and only if it is not a member of itself. There is a normal set all whose members are precisely the normal sets. (Nx, Mxy) [Hint: Derive P & ¬P.]

[PR123] c. A set is normal if and only if it is not a member of itself. There is a nonnormal set all whose members are precisely the normal sets. (Nx, Mxy) [Hint: Derive P & ¬P.]

[PR124] d. Multiples of natural numbers are natural numbers. Two is a natural number. There is a number which is a multiple of a multiple of two and which is not a natural number. (Mxy, Nx) [Hint: Derive P & ¬P.]

e. The sum of a number with the identity element gives us the same number. A number is the inverse of a second number if and only if their sum is the identity element. No number is its own inverse. (Sxyz, Ixy)

8.4.10 Translate the following arguments into PL and show, with *Symlog*, that they are PD-valid.

a. No one is rich. Thus, everybody is poor. (Rx)

b. Someone loves everybody but not everybody loves someone. Hence, someone loves himself and someone does not love himself. (Lxy)

[PR125] c. No one will get rich although the price of silver is not higher than that of gold. Still, if Bill invests in silver someone will get rich. Thus, it is not the case that either everybody will invest in silver or that the price of silver is higher than that of gold. (Rx, Hxy, Ixy.)

     d. People who get fat are happy people, and no matter what Alice eats she'll get fat. However, if she doesn't eat anything then she won't get fat. Therefore, Alice will eat something if and only if both she gets fat and she's happy. (Fx, Hx, Exy)

     e. People who smoke have a high chance of getting cancer and so does anyone working with radioactive materials. Since at least one person either smokes or handles radioactive material, someone has a high chance of getting cancer. (Sx, Cx, Rx)

8.4.11 Use the Create option under *Symlog*'s File menu to ask the program to generate (randomly) PD-valid arguments, whose derivations you should then construct. When asked for the level of difficulty, select 'Medium-to-Difficult.' Submit your work when done.

8.4.12 Repeat as in 8.4.11 but select 'Difficult.'

8.5   *The Rules of PD+*

Essentially, the system PD+ is to PD what SD+ was to SD, a supplementary set of shortcut rules designed to reduce the number of steps needed to complete a derivation. Rules of the '+' variety are introduced only for the sake of efficiency; they are not basic, for any derivation done with them could be completed without their help. PD+ has these distinguishable components: (1) all the rules of PD; (2) the '+'-rules of SD+, now rechristened and understood to hold for PL sentences; and (3) a '+'-rule which applies to universal and existential quantifiers. Before we introduce this new rule, take a moment to review the old '+'-rules of SD+ in section 5.5. Then we suggest that you renew your familiarity with them by trying the exercises PDPLUS01 and PDPLUS02 on your disk. *Symlog* will let you know if your derivations contain any mistakes. After that, you are ready to meet the one and only new rule of PD+.

Quantifier Negation (QN)

$$\neg(\exists \mathbf{x})\alpha :: (\forall \mathbf{x})\neg\alpha$$
$$\neg(\forall \mathbf{x})\alpha :: (\exists \mathbf{x})\neg\alpha$$

Note that quantifier negation (QN) is a replacement rule. That is, it can be applied to parts of sentences as well as to entire sentences. (Recall that the symbol :: means that the wff on one side can be replaced by the wff on the opposite side.) Sentences which conform to either of these two patterns are equivalent. In other words,

$$\emptyset \vdash_{\overline{PD}} \neg(\exists \mathbf{x})\alpha \equiv (\forall \mathbf{x})\neg\alpha$$

and

$$\varnothing \vdash_{\overline{PD}} \neg(\forall\mathbf{x})\alpha \equiv (\exists\mathbf{x})\neg\alpha$$

These equivalences—and the transformations incorporated into QN—are abundantly familiar to us from natural language. For example, if none of the students passed the quiz, we know at once that all of them failed, that is, did not pass (the first type of QN pattern). If it is false that all of them passed, we know that at least one (possibly several, maybe all) did not pass (the second pattern of QN). But let us balance things with another example. If all the professor's questions were unfair, not one of them was fair (first pattern); if some of the questions were unclear, it cannot be that all of them were clear (second pattern). So common are such transformations that we do not even think of ourselves as making inferences with them: We count them at once as meaning the same, as saying the same thing. (This is the characteristic too of many of the equivalences imported from SD+.) The examples just given are of whole sentences. Here is one of a partial replacement:

> If the professor gives another sneak quiz with those unclear questions, none of the students will stay in the course.

This sentence is equivalent to

> If the professor gives another sneak quiz with those unclear questions, all of the students will drop the course.

Figures 8.20 and 8.21 illustrate the use of QN.

As with some of the rules of SD+, the rule of quantifier negation can be applied to subwffs as well as to entire wffs of PL. When you use *Symlog* to apply this rule, using the Generation command, the program displays in the Message Line, one by one, the possible alternative sentences that can be derived. You must then choose just one of them; otherwise *Symlog* displays the message MISAPPLICATION OF RULE in the Error Line. To illustrate, if you have the sentence $(\forall x)\neg(\exists y)Bxy$ on a line and you apply QN by using the Generation command, *Symlog* will produce the two possible alternatives $(\forall x)(\forall y)\neg Bxy$ and $\neg(\exists x)(\exists y)Bxy$. Similarly, for the sentence $\neg(\forall x)\neg(\exists y)Bxy$, the alternatives $(\exists x)\neg\neg(\exists y)Bxy$, $\neg(\forall x)(\forall y)\neg Bxy$ and $\neg\neg(\exists x)(\exists y)Bxy$ are displayed. What four sentences can be obtained from $\neg\neg(\forall x)\neg(\exists y)\neg Bxy$ by the application of QN? Check your answer against *Symlog*'s. Use the opportunity to solve the on-disk Learn Exercises PDPLUS03, PDPLUS04 and PDPLUS05, which illustrate the use of the QN rule.

As you probably recall, *Symlog*'s Goal Analysis command is not programmed to work with the rules of the '+' type. The reason is that the typical strategy for constructing derivations which make full use of these rules is to work downward from the top, rather than upward from the ultimate

PD+ : CARNAP		
PREMISE	1	$(\exists x)(Dax \rightarrow Gbx) \,\&\, (\forall w)Mw$
&EL 1	2	$(\exists x)(Dax \rightarrow Gbx)$
IM 2	3	$(\exists x)(\neg Dax \lor Gbx)$
CM 3	4	$(\exists x)(Gbx \lor \neg Dax)$
DN 4	5	$(\exists x)(\neg\neg Gbx \lor \neg Dax)$
DM 5	6	$(\exists x)\neg(\neg Gbx \,\&\, Dax)$
QN 6	7	$\neg(\forall x)(\neg Gbx \,\&\, Dax)$
	8	
	9	
	10	
	11	
	12	
	13	
	14	
	15	
	16	

Figure 8.20

goal sentence. Remember, PD+ derivations are shorter because of an enlarged set of rules, which means that there are more rules to manipulate; thus you will have to discover through practice what combination of strategies seems more suitable. We encourage you to study the derivation in Figure 8.22, which illustrates the combined strategies of PD+. Keep in mind that many '+'-rules apply to subwffs as well as to whole wffs.

As deductive systems, PD and PD+ are *equally powerful*. If α is PD-derivable from a set Γ ($\Gamma \vdash_{PD} \alpha$), it is PD+-derivable (from Γ) as well ($\Gamma \vdash_{PD+} \alpha$),

PD+ : LEIBNIZ		
PREMISE	1	$(\forall x)(\forall y)(Kax \lor \neg Dyx)$
PREMISE	2	$(\exists w)\neg Pwa \,\&\, Dga$
$\forall$E a/x 1	3	$(\forall y)(Kaa \lor \neg Dya)$
$\forall$E g/y 3	4	$Kaa \lor \neg Dga$
&ER 2	5	Dga
DN 5	6	$\neg\neg Dga$
DS 4, 6	7	Kaa
$\exists$I x/a 7	8	$(\exists x)Kxa$
$\exists$I y/a 8	9	$(\exists y)(\exists x)Kxy$
DN 9	10	$\neg\neg(\exists y)(\exists x)Kxy$
QN 10	11	$\neg(\forall y)\neg(\exists x)Kxy$
QN 11	12	$\neg(\forall y)(\forall x)\neg Kxy$
	13	
	14	
	15	
	16	

Figure 8.21

PD+ : KASPAROV		
PREMISE	1	$\neg(\forall x)(\forall y)(\neg Gx \, \& \, Fy) \equiv \neg(\exists x)(\exists y)Hxy$
	2	
ASSUMPTION	3	$(\exists x)(\forall y)(Fx \rightarrow Gy)$
	4	
ASSUMPTION	5	$(\forall y)(Fa \rightarrow Gy)$
	6	
ASSUMPTION	7	$(\forall y)(\forall x)Hyx$
	8	
$\forall$E a/y 7	9	$(\forall x)Hax$
$\forall$E b/x 9	10	Hab
$\exists$I y/b 10	11	$(\exists y)Hay$
$\exists$I x/a 11	12	$(\exists x)(\exists y)Hxy$
	13	
	14	
$\forall$E b/y 5	15	$Fa \rightarrow Gb$
IM 15	16	$\neg Fa \lor Gb$
CM 16	17	$Gb \lor \neg Fa$
DN 17	18	$\neg\neg Gb \lor \neg Fa$
DM 18	19	$\neg(\neg Gb \, \& \, Fa)$
$\exists$I y/a 19	20	$(\exists y)\neg(\neg Gb \, \& \, Fy)$
$\exists$I x/b 20	21	$(\exists x)(\exists y)\neg(\neg Gx \, \& \, Fy)$
QN 21	22	$(\exists x)\neg(\forall y)(\neg Gx \, \& \, Fy)$
QN 22	23	$\neg(\forall x)(\forall y)(\neg Gx \, \& \, Fy)$
$\equiv$E 1, 23	24	$\neg(\exists x)(\exists y)Hxy$
	25	
$\neg$I 7-12, 7-24	26	$\neg(\forall y)(\forall x)Hyx$
	27	
$\exists$E a/x 3, 5-26	28	$\neg(\forall y)(\forall x)Hyx$
	29	
$\rightarrow$I 3-28	30	$(\exists x)(\forall y)(Fx \rightarrow Gy) \rightarrow \neg(\forall y)(\forall x)Hyx$
	31	

Figure 8.22

for the simple reason that the rules of the former are incorporated into the latter. Proof of the converse, that if $\Gamma \vdash_{\overline{PD+}} \alpha$ then $\Gamma \vdash_{\overline{PD}} \alpha$, is a greater challenge. The obvious route to follow would be to show that QN (as well as the other '+' type rules) is indeed a derivative rule in the sense that whatever sentences are derived with its help could be obtained without it. Such would be the objective of a 'metaproof'—a proof about proofs. Part of what it involves is shown in Figure 8.23, where a schematic proof of one form of QN (as it applies to whole sentences) is given with metalogical symbols.[5]

In the same way, the three remaining forms of QN can be established (you should satisfy yourself that this is the case). Please note, however, that a full metalogical proof of QN would have to take into account its role as a

---

[5] The restrictions involved in the use of $\forall$I (line n) are assumed to be met.

	i	$\neg(\exists\mathbf{x})\alpha$
ASSUMPTION	j	$\alpha(\mathbf{a}/\mathbf{x})$
$\exists$I **x/a** j	k	$(\exists\mathbf{x})\alpha$
R i	l	$\neg(\exists\mathbf{x})\alpha$
$\neg$I j-k, j-l	m	$\neg\alpha(\mathbf{a}/\mathbf{x})$
$\forall$I **x/a** m	n	$(\forall\mathbf{x})\neg\alpha$

Figure 8.23

replacement rule for parts of PL sentences rather than for just whole sentences, but we will not continue here along this line. Instead we want to call attention to a general result, that the metalogical theorems described for PD in the next section hold equally for PD+.

Exercises

8.5.1   Answer true or false (but not both) to each of the following.

a. The sentence Fa & ¬Fa is a (PD+) theorem of {(∀x)Gx, ¬Gb}.

b. Any derivation in PD is also a derivation in PD+.

c. If Γ is PD+-consistent, then there is a sentence which is not PD+-derivable from Γ.

d. Any derivation in PD+ is also a derivation in PD.

e. If α is a sentence of PL, then Ø $\vdash_{\overline{\text{PD+}}} \alpha$ or Ø $\vdash_{\overline{\text{PD+}}} \neg\alpha$.

f. If α is PD+-derivable from the empty set, then it is PD+-derivable from any set.

g. If Ø is PD+-inconsistent so is every set.

h. If Γ ∪ {α} is PD+-inconsistent then Γ $\vdash_{\overline{\text{PD+}}} \alpha$.

i. Γ $\vdash_{\overline{\text{PD+}}} \alpha$ if Γ ∪ {¬α} is PD+-inconsistent.

j. Γ $\vdash_{\overline{\text{PD+}}} \alpha$ if Γ $\vdash_{\overline{\text{PD+}}} \alpha \lor \beta$ and Γ ∪ {β} is PD+-inconsistent.

8.5.2.   Show, using *Symlog*, that the given sentence is PD+-derivable from the corresponding set.

a. {(∀x)(∀y)(Bx ≡ My)}, (∀x)¬(∃y)[¬(Bx → My) ∨ ¬(My → Bx)]

b. {¬(∃w)(¬Baw ∨ Dbw)}, ¬Dbh & Bah

[PR126] c. {(∀x)[(Gx ∨ ¬(∃y)Hyax) & Hbax]}, (∃w)Gw

d. {(∀x)Mx}, ¬(∃w)¬¬¬Mw

[PR127] e. {(∀x)Hxx, (∃w)(Aw → Cw)}, (∃x)(∃w)Hwx & ¬(∀w)(¬Cw & Aw)

8.5.3   Use *Symlog* to show that each sentence given below is a PD+-theorem of the corresponding set.

a. (∀x)¬Jx ≡ ¬(∃y)Jy, Ø

b. ¬(∃z)Lz → ¬Le, Ø

[PR128] c. ¬(∃x)(∃w)Rxw ≡ ¬(∃w)(∃x)Rwx, Ø

d. (∃w)[(Haw ∨ ¬Gwb) ∨ ¬Ew], {¬(∀w)¬[¬(Ew & Gwb) ∨ Haw]}

e. ¬Ma, {(∀w)Bw & Gb, ¬(∃x)(Bx & Mx)}

8.5.4   Use *Symlog* to show that the following sets are PD+-inconsistent.

[PR129] a. {(∀w)Nw, (∃x)¬Nx}

[PR130] b. {¬(∃z)(Saz ∨ ¬Mz), ¬(∀y)(My & ¬Say)}

[PR131] c. {¬(∃z)(Gzb → Azc) & ¬(∀w)(¬Awc & Gwb)}

[PR132] d. {Lm → ¬(∃x)Rmx, (∀w)(∀x)(Rwx & Lw) & Sam}

      e. {(∃x)(∃y)(∃w)Dxywacc, (∀y)(∀z)¬(∃w)Dyzwacc}

8.5.5   Use the test for derivability to show, with the assistance of *Symlog*, that the given sentence is PD+-derivable from the corresponding set.

      a. {(∀w)Fw, ¬Fa ∨ Nb}, Nb

[PR133] b. {Ma → Kc, (∃y)Ky ≡ Sa}, ¬(∀x)(Mx & ¬Sx)

[PR134] c. Ø, ¬(∀x)Fx ≡ (∃x)¬Fx

[PR135] d. {¬(∃w)(∃x)(¬Cwx ∨ ¬Nw)}, ¬(∃z)Caz ∨ ¬Na

[PR136] e. Ø, (∀x)(Fx ≡ Fx)

8.5.6   Show, using *Symlog*, that the following arguments are PD+-valid.

      a. (∃x)[¬Kx & (Dx → ¬Gax)]

      ――――――――――――――

      ¬(∀x)[(Gax & Dx) ∨ Kx]

[PR137] b. (∃x)Rx

      (∀y)(Ry ≡ Say)

      ――――――――――

      (∃w)Saw

      c. (∃w)Fw → Id

      ――――――――

      (∀z)(Fz → Id)

[PR138] d. (∀x)(¬(∃y)Gy → Bx)

      (∀w)¬Gw

      ――――――――――――

      Bm

[PR139] e. ¬(∃z)Rz → (∀x)(∀w)Hxw

      (Sd → (∀x)¬Rx) & (∀x)Sx

      ――――――――――――――

      ¬¬Hmc

8.5.7   Show with *Symlog* that the sentences in each of the following pairs are PD+-equivalent.

[PR140] a. (∃x)(Fx ∨ P) and (∃x)Fx ∨ P

[PR141] b. (∀x)Fx → P and (∃x)(Fx → P)

[PR142] c. P → (∃x)Fx and (∃x)(P → Fx)

[PR143] d. (∀x)Fx ∨ P and (∀x)(Fx ∨ P)

8.5.8   Translate the following statements into PL and show, using *Symlog*, that the conclusion is derivable (in PD+) from the premises.

[PR144] a. Not all the windows in the house are open but all the doors are. Hence, some windows are closed but there is no door which is closed. (Nx, Ox, Dx)

[PR145] b. God loves anybody who loves someone. But he also loves anyone who doesn't love anybody. Hence, God loves you. (Lxy)

[PR146] c. Some soldiers like some of their generals but some don't. Thus, although not all soldiers like all their generals not all dislike them. (Sxy, Lxy, Gx) [Note: Prove each conjunct in the conclusion separately since the conclusion is too large to fit in *Symlog*'s Theorem Field.]

[PR147] d. If we detect a pair of atomic particles, where one is negatively charged or the other has a mass larger than that of a proton, then any particle in this bubble chamber is an E-particle. But if all are E-particles, any pair of particles that we will detect will not interact with each other. There is a particle, heavier than a proton, that we can detect. Unfortunately, from this it follows that if a proton interacts with itself then we will not be able to detect it. (Dx, Nx, Lxy, Ex, Ixy)

[PR148] e. Anyone who loves Dracula does not love himself. Dracula loves anyone not loved by Frankenstein and, moreover, Dracula does not love Frankenstein. Hence, Frankenstein does not love Dracula. (Lxy)

8.5.9 A pigeon can only be in one and only one hole, and a hole can contain one and only one pigeon. Intuitively, this statement should be in contradiction with the sentence 'There are three pigeons in two holes.' Here, you will show this contradiction formally. Let Pxy stand for 'Pigeon x is in hole y.' Also, let p, q, and r be the names for the three pigeons, and let a and b be the names for the two holes. Translate into PL, *without using any quantifiers*: 'A pigeon is in at least one hole. No hole has more than one pigeon in it.' Show that the resulting PL set is PD+-inconsistent. (Note: If you don't use quantifiers, the set has about nine sentences.) [PR149]

8.5.10 To appreciate the practical value of the new rules of PD+ which are not part of PD, use *Symlog* to derive the sentence (∀x)¬Fx → (∃y)¬Gy from the set {(∀y)Gy → (∃x)Fx} by (a) using the rules of PD+ (which can be done in fewer than five steps) and (b) using only the rules of PD. [PR150]

8.5.11 Show that the second, third and fourth forms of quantifier negation (as they apply to entire sentences of PL) are reducible to rules of PD.

8.5.12 Show that in PD+ the rule of ∀-elimination is dispensable.

8.5.13 Show that in PD+ the rule of ∃-introduction is dispensable.

8.5.14 Show that if the empty set, Ø, is PD-inconsistent, so is every set.

8.5.15 Let PD* be the new deduction system obtained by adding to PD a new rule, CV, whose purpose is to change the variable of quantification. The rule takes two forms:

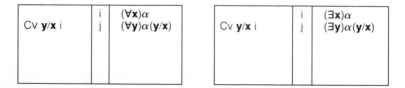

Restriction (to both forms): The variable **y** does not occur in α.

For instance, by using this rule, the sentence (∀y)(Hy → (∃w)(Faw → Gy)) can be obtained from (∀x)(Hx → (∃w)(Faw → Gx)) in one single step. Show that for any Γ, (a) if α is PD-derivable from Γ, then α is also PD*-derivable from Γ, and (b) if α is PD*-derivable from Γ, then it is also PD-derivable from Γ.

8.5.16 A set Γ of sentences is **PD+-independent** iff no sentence in Γ is PD+-derivable from the rest. Show that the set {Fga, (∃y)(∃x)Hxy, (∀x)(∀y)(Hxy ∨ ¬Fyx)} is *not* PD+-independent.

8.6 *Metatheory of PD and PD+*

In this section we will briefly state the most important metatheoretical results of PD and PD+. The proof of these results is beyond the scope of this book, and you are referred to some of the references in the Bibliography for detailed accounts. Paralleling sentential logic, the chief results of metatheory for PD (and PD+) involve the concepts of completeness and soundness.

The Completeness Theorem. If Γ ⊨ α then Γ ⊢$_{PD}$ α.

That is, if a set Γ quantificationally entails a sentence α, then α can be derived from Γ by using the rules of PD. Thus, a notion central to all logic, that one sentence 'follows from' another (more generally, that a conclusion 'follows from' the premises of an argument) can be captured by a set of formal rules.

The soundness theorem is the converse of the completeness theorem. In essence, it states that the rules of PD are truth-preserving.

The Soundness Theorem. If Γ ⊢$_{PD}$ α then Γ ⊨ α.

That is, any sentence α which is derivable from a set Γ by using the rules of PD is quantificationally entailed by Γ. Thus, whenever all of the PL sentences of Γ are true, the soundness theorem assures us that α will also be true (or in the language of Chapter 9, 'Structures,' any interpretation that satisfies Γ satisfies α as well).

These two results show that certain semantical concepts of PL, in particular quantificational validity and inconsistency, have proof-theoretic analogues in PD (PD-validity and PD-inconsistency). As a result, techniques described in earlier chapters can be used to establish these proof-theoretic properties, and vice versa. For instance, you can show that a set of sentences, Γ, is PD-inconsistemt by deriving from it a contradictory pair of sentences, α and ¬α. Alternatively, you can construct a truth-tree for the set and see that its branches all close. But what of the property of PD-consistency? If we assume that Γ is consistent, how is it possible to show that α and ¬α *cannot* be derived from that set? Here we confront a problem discussed earlier in connection with the truth-tree method in PL.[6] Unlike

---

[6] Section 7.3.

SL, PL lacks a mechanical procedure for deciding the consistency of sets and the closely related semantical notions of invalidity and indeterminacy. Similarly, the rules of PD cannot be manipulated to prove for every imaginable case that a set is PD-*consistent* or an argument PD-*invalid*. This matter is of great significance in metatheory, yet it must be balanced by the fact that we are often able to devise a truth-value assignment (or an interpretation) to the atomic subformulas of a set which establishes quantificational consistency for that set. (Recall the many examples and exercises from Chapter 7 that had decisive outcomes.) The completeness theorem assures us that any set which is found by such means to be quantificationally consistent is PD-consistent as well. It also follows from the completeness and soundness theorems that a sentence α of PL is a theorem of the empty set, that is, $\varnothing \vdash_{\overline{PD}} \alpha$, if and only if α is quantificationally true.

Exercises

8.6.1 Answer true or false (but not both) to each of the following.
  a. $\varnothing \vdash_{\overline{PD}} \alpha$, for any α.
  b. If α is a sentence of PL that is quantificationally true, then α is PD+-derivable from $\varnothing$.
  c. If Γ is PD-consistent then it is quantificationally consistent.
  d. If $\varnothing \vdash_{\overline{PD+}} \alpha$, then some truth-tree for $\{\neg\alpha\}$ closes.
  e. All quantificationally true sentences of PL are PD-theorems of Γ, regardless of what Γ is.
  f. If Γ is PD-consistent then one of its truth-trees has a completed open branch.
  g. There is a set Γ such that no quantificationally true sentence is PD-derivable from it.
  h. If the set $\Gamma \cup \{\neg\alpha\}$ has a closed truth-tree then there is a derivation in PD of α from Γ.
  i. If all the truth-value assignments (or interpretations) which satisfy Γ also satisfy α then there is a derivation in PD of α from Γ.
  j. If all the truth-value assignments (or interpretations) which satisfy α also satisfy Γ then there is a derivation in PD of α from Γ.

8.6.2 Use the soundness theorem to show that the sentence Fa cannot be derived from the set {Fa ∨ Ga, ¬Gb & Fb}. (Hint: If not $\Gamma \models \alpha$, then not $\Gamma \vdash \alpha$.)

8.6.3 Show that the set {Fa} is PD-consistent. (Hint: See exercise 8.6.2.)

8.6.4 Given a set Γ, **the theory of Γ**, Theory(Γ), is the set of all theorems derivable from Γ, that is, Theory(Γ) = {α : $\Gamma \vdash \alpha$}. Determine Theory($\varnothing$) and Theory({($\forall$x)Fx, ¬Fa}).

8.6.5 Given the definition of a theory of exercise 8.6.4 and given two sets Γ_1 and Γ_2, Theory(Γ_1) is a **subtheory** of Theory(Γ_2) iff Theory(Γ_1) is a subset of Theory(Γ_2). Show that the theory of {Fb ∨ Hc, ($\exists$x)($\exists$y)Gxy, ($\exists$x)Fx} is a subtheory of that of {Gab, ($\forall$x)(Fx & ¬Kx)}.

Structures

This chapter is more theoretical than practical. Our purpose is not to introduce yet another technique of showing inconsistency or of proving the logical truth, validity and so on of PL sentences and arguments. Rather, it is to furnish a fuller and more precise account of the semantics of predicate logic. The explanation of this cluster of notions, as given in section 6.4, is sometimes called a '**substitutional**' account: The truth of universal and existential sentences is explained in terms of the truth of their infinitely many instances, each instance being obtained in the familiar manner by removing the initial quantifier and replacing the newly freed variables by the same constant. The substitutional account works simply and efficiently, yet it depends on the noteworthy assumption that the set of constants {a, b, c, . . .}, on which we draw to designate the objects of any infinite domain, is precisely coextensive with that domain. In other words, we have assumed that whatever objects are referred to in a given *quantificational* sentence could be designated in one or more of the infinitely many instances obtainable through the process of instantiation and that no object which we wanted to designate would be omitted. This assumption is legitimate in a vast number of cases, including the many examples which have been mentioned or examined in the preceding chapters. Nevertheless, there are times when the assumption breaks down, as in the following case. Consider the sequence of *true* atomic sentences which begins, '1 is an odd number,' '3 is an odd number,' '5 is an odd number,' . . . ; this sequence is infinite, of course, since there are infinitely many odd numbers. To this group we add one further sentence, which is also true: 'Not all numbers are odd.' Now let us assign the constants a to 1, b to 3, c to 5 and so on, for the set of infinitely many constants, and have the predicate Ox stand for 'x is odd.' Next, having formed the infinite set of sentences, {Oa, Ob, Oc, . . . , ¬(∀x)Ox}, we can ask whether or not this set is consistent. It seems that it should be since the original sentences are all true. Yet by the substitutional account, the set turns out to be inconsistent. A reductio-style proof shows why. If the set is consistent, all of its members must be true on some truth-value assignment. Accordingly, we assume the set to be consistent and therefore assign the truth-value ⊤ to Oa, Ob, Oc and so on, as well as to ¬(∀x)Ox. It follows that the universal sentence, (∀x)Ox, must be false and hence that at least one of its instances must also be false. But all of the instances of (∀x)Ox belong to the set and they are all true, by assumption. There is no constant which has not been paired with an odd number. So the set is plainly inconsistent—on the substitutional account.

In the light of this and similar problematic examples, a more detailed account of truth and related notions is needed which will not only handle such difficulties but also be fully applicable to earlier examples that come within the scope of the substitutional account. Such is the aim of the present chapter. Before digging into it, however, you will find it useful to read (or review) the material related to sets given in Appendix D. This appendix will introduce you to some basic concepts which we presuppose in what will be called an 'interpretational' account of the quantifiers. To assist you in mastering this material, the chapter has been written in a way that will introduce you rather quickly to the *Symlog* environment called Models. Most of the examples will be worked out as though the program were active on your computer, so you may want to duplicate on your screen what you will see in the text. The examples will help you focus on the essentials of the interpretational account. At the end of the chapter you will find a revised set of definitions of the central semantical notions of PL set out in terms of this new account.

9.1   Interpretations

In previous discussions of PL, we have kept in mind that a compound sentence α is neither true (⊤) nor false (F) on its own; rather, it is true or false on a given truth-value assignment to its ground atomic subformulas. Similarly, an atomic sentence is true (or false) depending on what truth-value is assigned to it. But what determines these truth-value assignments themselves? Essentially, such assignments depend on what are called **interpretations.** An interpretation consists of a coordination—a 'match-up'—between objects constituting a given domain and the symbols (the constants and predicates) which are used in sentences to identify and describe these objects. In general, whether a particular sentence is true or not will depend on the particular interpretation it is given, and the choice of what interpretation to give the sentence is something over which we have control. The whole procedure of constructing an interpretation is closely related to what were earlier called symbolizations. The formal features of this concept will be given in a moment, but first it is better to consider a few examples informally.

Suppose, on the one hand, you wish to find an interpretation for the atomic sentence Ea on which it says something true, that is, on which this sentence would be assigned the truth-value T. There are many possibilities. For instance, let the domain (the UD) be the set of natural numbers, the predicate Ex mean 'x is even' and the constant a stand for the number 2. Then, under this interpretation, Ea symbolizes the true statement that 2 is even. Or let the UD be countries, Ex mean 'x is in Europe' and a stand for Austria. Then Ea states that Austria is in Europe, which is another true statement. On the other hand, you can make Ea express a false statement on the following interpretation: Let the UD again be the set of natural numbers, Ex mean 'x is odd' and a stand for the number 6. Moving on, let us find an interpretation on which the quantified sentence (∀x)(Ex ∨ Ox) has the value T. Here is one that does the job: UD, the natural numbers; Ex, 'x is even'; Ox, 'x is odd.' On this interpretation the sentence reads, 'Every natural number is either even or odd,' which is true. On the same interpretation, the existential sentence, (∃x)(Ex & Ox), would make a false claim, for it says that there is at least one natural number that is both even and odd. For a final example, let us compare the next two sentences,

(1) (∀x)(∃y)Sxye

(2) (∃y)(∀x)Sxye

on the following interpretation: UD, the integers, that is, the set $\{. . . , -2, -1, 0, 1, 2, . . .\}$; Sxyz, 'The sum of x and y is z'; e, the number 0. On this interpretation, sentence (1) reads,

For any given integer there is an integer such that their sum is zero.

This statement, incidentally, is true since for any given integer, n, there is another integer, namely, $-n$, such that their sum is zero. In contrast, what (2) says is false:

There is at least one integer such that the sum of any integer with it is zero.

A sentence, then, says something true or false *relative to an interpretation* which fixes the sense of its symbols. This emphasis allows a sharp distinction to be made between sentences and statements. Strictly speaking, because a sentence is just a string of symbols, it is not the string itself which is true or false but rather the statement which the sentence makes. A statement always presupposes the existence of an interpretation. Statements, not sentences, are the bearers of truth and falsity. However, for convenience, we shall sometimes indicate that a given sentence is true (or false) or that it 'takes on' the truth-value T (or F). What this means in a compressed way is that the sentence in question makes a true (or false) statement on a particular interpretation.

When constructing interpretations, we associate the objects of a UD not only with the symbols for constants but also with the symbols for predicates. The conventional practice in formal logic is to identify predicates with their so-called **extensions.** In recent examples, though we did not stop to point it out, the predicate 'x is odd' was associated with the numbers 1, 3, 5 and so on, which form an infinite set, whereas the predicate 'x is even' was associated with the infinite set {2, 4, 6, . . .}. Similarly, on suitable interpretations, the predicate 'x is green' could be assigned to all the things which are green, 'x is a doctor' with all the people who are doctors, and in general 'x is Φ' with the (possibly infinite) set of things which are Φ. In the case of predicates having two or more places, the sets of things which are their extensions are represented in a manner which, although precise, will seem unfamiliar at first. In a typical interpretation, the extension of the two-place predicate 'x is the mother of y' would be a set of *pairs* of things, specifically all those pairs of things which meet the following criterion: the first member of the pair is a mother and the second is her child. The extension of 'x is a child of y' would be the set containing just those pairs of things fulfilling the requirement that for any given pair, the first member is an offspring of the second member. The typical extension of the three-place predicate 'x steals y from z,' on a given interpretation, would be the set of all *trios* or *triples* such that, for each member of the set, the first member of the trio is a thief, the second the thing stolen by that thief and the third the victim of the theft. In general, using the language of set theory, the extension of the k-place predicate Φ for a given interpretation is the set of just those k-tuples whose components partake in the relation Φ. A trio is called a 3-tuple, a quintet is called a 5-tuple, and a pair a 2-tuple. The extension of a one-termed predicate for a given interpretation is a set of objects drawn from the UD selected for that interpretation. The objects constituting such a set are sometimes referred to as elements, as are the individuals making up a given 2-tuple, a given 3-tuple and so on. A tuple is always a specific ordering of its elements, which are members of the UD, the order proceeding from left to right. For the sake of regularity, the extension of a one-termed predicate is sometimes characterized as a set of 1-tuples. We will not follow this route here, however, and we will identify a 1-tuple with an element or object of a UD.

The time has come to capture some of these ideas in a more succinct way, using the language of set theory. To specify an interpretation in PL, we need (1) linguistic symbols, (2) things for which these symbols stand, and (3) a set of rules for associating symbols with things. The symbols needed are of course the familiar ones of PL, together with the grammatical rules for writing well-formed formulas. We must now characterize (2) and (3) in more detail.

The things which are identified and described in an interpretation constitute what we shall call a structure. A structure is a world of objects and possibly also of sets of tuples (of objects). The objects may be anything we care to speak about—numbers, neutrinos, logicians and so on—and they may form relations of whatever size we care to describe.

> **Definition.** A **structure,** $\mathfrak{A}$, consists of
> 1. A nonempty set of **individuals** or **elements,** which together constitute a **universe of discourse** (UD), also called a **domain.**
> 2. One or more **relations** defined on this universe.[1]

An example of a structure is the set of natural numbers, being the individuals which constitute a UD, and the infinitely many pairs (2-tuples) which constitute the relations of 'equality' and of 'being less than,' which hold between the individuals in this universe. (There are no 3-tuples or relations of higher order in this particular example.) Euclidean space is another example of a structure. Its UD consists of points, lines and planes; coincidence and parallelism are some of its relations. We will now consider the rules which coordinate symbols with things:

> **Definition.** For a given structure $\mathfrak{A}$, an **interpretation function** (or simply an **interpretation**) assigns
> 1. To each constant symbol of PL, an individual belonging to the UD of $\mathfrak{A}$.
> 2. To each k-ary predicate symbol of PL ($k \geq 1$), a set of k-tuples consisting of individuals belonging to the UD of $\mathfrak{A}$.[2]

The symbol := is already quite familiar from previous chapters and will play a comparable role in the formal account of interpretations. We will use this symbol to stand, specifically, for the (metalogical) relation of assigning to symbols things, that is, of giving symbols a specific meaning for a given interpretation, as for the structure of natural numbers just mentioned:[3]

---

[1] Formally speaking, a structure need not have relations defined on its universe. However, all the structures being discussed here will contain at least one relation.

[2] In section 6.3 we suggested that atomic sentences of SL could be construed as zero-place predicates. Following this suggestion, the interpretation function could be extended to include these atomic sentences by allowing the extension of a zero-place predicate to be either the empty set or the singleton set containing the empty tuple, ().

[3] To avoid deploying another symbol when specifying the UD with *Symlog*, the symbol := will also be used for this purpose. *This usage, however, is purely a matter of convenience and it is not part of the definition of the interpretation function.* (Note that 'UD' is not even a legal syntactic element of PL.)

UD := {0, 1, 2, 3, . . .}
Lxy := {(0,1),(0,2),(0,3), . . . , (1,2),(1,3),(1,4), . . . , (2,3),(2,4),(2,5), . . .}
Ixy := {(0,0),(1,1),(2,2), . . .}
a := 2
b := 17

The symbol := will then stand for an entire interpretation function itself. On the other hand, when the structure symbol $\mathfrak{A}$ is combined with another symbol of PL, such as a predicate or a constant, the resulting expression will stand for the extension assigned to that predicate or the object assigned to that constant. Thus, $a^{\mathfrak{A}}$ is the object assigned to the symbol a in the previous interpretation, namely, 2, and $L^{\mathfrak{A}}$ is the set of pairs assigned on the same interpretation to the two-place predicate symbol, L. These expressions enable us to speak of the objects or the sets of tuples of a structure, in contrast to the symbols matched up with them.

To save space in writing interpretations, we will often abbreviate the reference to whatever set (of tuples) is associated with a given predicate. So for the predicates Lxy and Ixy in the preceding case, one could alternatively write

Lxy := {(x,y) : x < y}
Ixy := {(x,y) : x = y}

The first of these reads, 'Lxy is interpreted as the set of all 2-tuples of natural numbers such that, for each 2-tuple, the first number is less than the second.' Try now to read the second formulation for Ixy in a similar way.

As another example, here is how a second interpretation looks:

UD := {0, 1, 2, 3, . . .}
Ex := {0, 2, 4, 6, . . .}
Ox := {1, 3, 5, 7, . . .}
Ixy := {(x,y) : x = y}
Sxyz := {(x,y,z) : x + y = z}
a := 1
b := 5
c := 5

The constant symbol a is interpreted here as the natural number 1, which is an element of the UD. Two different constant symbols, b and c, are interpreted as the same element, the number 5. (Please note: An element of the UD may have two or more different names, but no constant symbol may be interpreted as more than one element; also, in this example, no constant symbol could be interpreted as the rational number 1/2 since this number does not belong to the designated UD.) As for the predicate symbols in this interpretation, Ex is being interpreted as a set of 1-tuples (elements) of the

UD, and the same holds for Ox. Ixy is being interpreted as a set of 2-tuples, each of whose components is a member of the UD. Similarly, Sxyz is interpreted as a set of 3-tuples of UD's elements. Note that a tuple such as (2,4) cannot fall within the extension of Sxyz because it is not a 3-tuple. The interpretation specifies that only 3-tuples drawn from the UD constitute the extension of this predicate. However, its extension would not include every possible 3-tuple from the domain—it would exclude (1,2,1), for instance, since the sum of the first two components is not identical to the third component.

By now it should be fairly clear that, for instance, the sentence Sabb has the truth-value F (under the preceding interpretation) since what it says, namely, that $1 + 5 = 5$, is false of the structure of natural numbers. The following question now arises: Given a wff with *free variables* such as Sabx (whose reading here is $1 + 5 = x$), what should its truth-value be? The answer is, of course, 'it depends on the value of x.' If we *assign* the value 6 to the variable x, this assignment will *satisfy* this equation. On the other hand, if 12 is assigned to x, the equation will not be satisfied. Once an interpretation has been fixed there is still freedom in the assignment of values—elements of the UD—to the variables. This motivates the following definition:

> **Definition.** Given an interpretation and its associated structure, an **assignment function** assigns elements of the UD of the structure to the variables of PL.

Assignment functions will be denoted by the symbol α. As we did before with constants and predicate symbols, $x^{\mathfrak{A}}$ will be no other than that element of the UD of the structure $\mathfrak{A}$ assigned to x by α. For instance, if α assigns 5 to x and 3 to y then $x^{\mathfrak{A}}$ and $y^{\mathfrak{A}}$ are precisely 5 and 3, respectively. Note that although x and y are *linguistic* entities—variables of PL—$x^{\mathfrak{A}}$ and $y^{\mathfrak{A}}$ are not; they are components of the structure.[4]

One clear difference between the substitutional and interpretational accounts has begun to emerge. The interpretational account places equal stress on things and symbols, and more important, it preserves the difference between them. Unlike the substitutional account, it avoids treating the symbols themselves as *virtual* objects, an approach which is essential if problems like the one mentioned at the beginning of this chapter are to be dealt with successfully. *On the interpretational account, the values of variables such as x and y are identified as objects of a given UD rather than as constants standing for such objects.* Roughly speaking, this—interpretational—account holds that a universal statement like $(\forall x)Fx$ is true of a structure[5] if

---

[4] When using *Symlog* to construct interpretations, you will find that the program disallows the assignment of individuals of a UD to the variables of PL; *Symlog* performs this task automatically as the need arises.

[5] We will use the phrase 'true of a structure' as short form of the more precise statement 'true of the structure associated with an interpretation.' Moreover, as every interpretation is associated with a specific structure, we will use both terms interchangeably (unless the context demands it otherwise).

and only if every individual of the UD has the property F; more precisely, every individual of the UD is found in the extension assigned by the interpretation to the symbol F, $F^{\mathfrak{A}}$. Note how this description contrasts with the one given formerly in the substitutional account, according to which $(\forall x)Fx$ is held to be true if and only if the instance $F(\textbf{c}/x)$ is true for every constant **c**. The association of x and y with objects in a domain is especially relevant to the interpretational account of quantified sentences, and this is the main reason why we have introduced the definition of an assignment function.

To prepare for the account of truth in **PL**, to be given in the next section, we must introduce one final detail in the interpretational apparatus, called a variant of α. For any given assignment, α, a variant of α would be any assignment which differs from α at most with respect to the object which is assigned to one of its variables. For instance, with regard to the assignment α (where the UD of $\mathfrak{A}$ is the set of natural numbers) such that

$$x^{\mathfrak{A}} = 0$$
$$y^{\mathfrak{A}} = 1$$
$$z^{\mathfrak{A}} = 2$$

and so on

the following assignments count as variants of α:

$\alpha(3/x^{\mathfrak{A}})$	$\alpha(12/x^{\mathfrak{A}})$	$\alpha(0/y^{\mathfrak{A}})$
$x^{\mathfrak{A}} = 3$	$x^{\mathfrak{A}} = 12$	$x^{\mathfrak{A}} = 0$
$y^{\mathfrak{A}} = 1$	$y^{\mathfrak{A}} = 1$	$y^{\mathfrak{A}} = 0$
$z^{\mathfrak{A}} = 2$	$z^{\mathfrak{A}} = 2$	$z^{\mathfrak{A}} = 2$
and so on	and so on	and so on

These variants of α differ only with regard to the assignment of objects to just one variable, in each case a different member of the UD being reassigned. In general, assignment variants change the assignment of no more than one variable.[6] Since the change of assignment concerns the variable x in the first two variants and y in the third, we can distinguish between them by calling the first two x-variants of α and the third a y-variant. As long as a particular structure has an infinite domain, the number of assignment variants of α would be infinite. The concept of a variant of α will have a direct bearing on how to construe the truth of universal and existential sentences. $(\forall x)Fx$ is true of a structure if and only if Fx is satisfied by each of the assignment x-variants of α. That is, no matter what object of the domain is assigned to x, that assignment will satisfy Fx. (Recall that the interpretation of predicates as sets of tuples remains constant for all of α's variants.) Here

---

[6] The qualifying phrases 'at most' and 'no more than,' which are used in the text, allow for the limiting case that any assignment may be considered as an assignment variant of itself. This detail simplifies the definition of truth for existential and universal statements, to be given in the next section.

now is a definition of this concept:

> **Definition.** Let $\mathfrak{A}$ be a structure with a universe of discourse UD; let **x** be a variable symbol with $\mathbf{x}^{\mathfrak{A}}$ the element of UD assigned by α to **x**; let σ be an arbitrarily chosen element belonging to UD. Then, an **x-variant** of α, $\alpha(\sigma/\mathbf{x}^{\mathfrak{A}})$, is any assignment function identical to α except that σ replaces $\mathbf{x}^{\mathfrak{A}}$ as the element assigned to the variable **x**.

Exercises

9.1.1 Answer true or false (but not both) to each of the following.

a. A structure can have a UD with no individuals.

b. If in an interpretation the UD is the set of real numbers, then a := π is allowed.

c. If in an interpretation the UD is the set of natural numbers, then c := $1/2$ is allowed.

d. In an interpretation, Fx can be interpreted as the whole UD.

e. There is some interpretation where it is legal to say Lxy := {0,2,3,5}.

f. A k-place predicate is interpreted as a set of k-tuples of elements of the UD.

g. Two different constants (of PL) can be interpreted as the same individual of the UD.

h. If $x^{\mathfrak{A}} = 3$ in α then $x^{\mathfrak{A}} = 5$ in $\alpha(5/x^{\mathfrak{A}})$.

i. If $x^{\mathfrak{A}} = 5$ and $z^{\mathfrak{A}} = 8$ in α then $x^{\mathfrak{A}} = 8$ in $\alpha(z^{\mathfrak{A}}/x^{\mathfrak{A}})$.

j. If $x^{\mathfrak{A}} = \sigma$ in α then $\alpha(\sigma/x^{\mathfrak{A}})$ is the same as α.

9.1.2 Let $\mathfrak{A}$ be the structure of the number system you use in your daily life to count, make payments and so on. Answer the following.

a. What is its underlying UD?

b. Give three relations in $\mathfrak{A}$.

c. Give a three-place relation in $\mathfrak{A}$.

d. Give a relation not in $\mathfrak{A}$.

9.1.3 Let $\mathfrak{A}$ be a structure whose UD is the set of natural numbers, $\{0, 1, 2, \ldots\}$. Construct an interpretation, :=, that allows you to name the relations 'being less than,' 'being equal to' and 'being a multiple of' as well as the numbers 0 and 1 by selecting suitable predicates and constants of PL.

9.1.4 Let α be an assignment such that $x^{\mathfrak{A}} = 2$ and $y^{\mathfrak{A}} = 0$. Give (a) $\alpha(1/x^{\mathfrak{A}})$, (b) $\alpha(4/x^{\mathfrak{A}})$ and (c) $\alpha(2/y^{\mathfrak{A}})$. Let α' be $\alpha(5/x^{\mathfrak{A}})$. What are (d) $\alpha'(0/x^{\mathfrak{A}})$ and (e) $\alpha'(3/y^{\mathfrak{A}})$? Are these two assignments x- or y-variants of α?

9.1.5 Let α be an assignment and let $\mathfrak{A}$ be a structure with universe of discourse UD whose cardinality is n (i.e., the number of elements in the UD is n). How many x-variants of α are there? List them if UD := $\{0,1,2\}$ and α is such that $x^{\mathfrak{A}} = 2$ and $y^{\mathfrak{A}} = 1$.

9.1.6 Given an assignment α, a **y-x-variant** of α, denoted by $\alpha(\sigma_1/\mathbf{x}^{\mathfrak{A}})(\sigma_2/\mathbf{y}^{\mathfrak{A}})$, is a **y**-variant of an **x**-variant of α. Given the assignment of exercise

9.1.4, specify (a) its y-x-variant $\alpha(3/x^{\mathfrak{A}})(4/y^{\mathfrak{A}})$ and (b) its x-x-variant $\alpha(5/x^{\mathfrak{A}})(1/x^{\mathfrak{A}})$. Also, (c) is the **x-x**-variant $\alpha(\sigma_1/x^{\mathfrak{A}})(\sigma_2/x^{\mathfrak{A}})$ the same as the **x**-variant $\alpha(\sigma_1/x^{\mathfrak{A}})$ or is it equal to the **x**-variant $\alpha(\sigma_2/x^{\mathfrak{A}})$ or neither?

9.1.7 Let α be an assignment and let $\mathfrak{A}$ be a structure with universe of discourse UD whose cardinality is n (i.e., the number of elements in the UD is n). How many y-x-variants of α are there?

9.1.8 Let $\mathfrak{A}$ be a structure with {0, 1, 2} as its UD. Let α_1 and α_2 be assignments such that, respectively, $x^{\mathfrak{A}} = 2$ and $y^{\mathfrak{A}} = 1$, and $x^{\mathfrak{A}} = 1$ and $y^{\mathfrak{A}} = 0$.

a. Which y-x-variant of α_1 is equal to α_2?

b. Which y-x-variant of α_2 is equal to α_1?

9.2   The Satisfaction Relation

All the details are now in place for giving an interpretational account of the semantics of PL. Instead of describing a particular sentence, α, of PL as being true or false on a truth-value assignment, the new account characterizes α as true or false of a structure (under a given interpretation). Before the concept of truth is defined, however, we must define first the closely related concept of satisfaction. The following definition of this concept, due to Alfred Tarski, is subdivided in a way which corresponds to the different sorts of well-formed formulas (wffs) to be found in PL.[7]

> **Definition.** Let $\mathfrak{A}$ be the structure associated with an interpretation and let α be an assignment function. If α is a wff of PL, then α **satisfies** α in $\mathfrak{A}$, written as $\mathfrak{A} \vDash_\alpha \alpha$, if and only if
>
> 1. If α is of the form $\mathbf{R}t_1 \ldots t_k$, where $\mathbf{R}$ is a k-ary predicate symbol and $t_1, \ldots, t_k$ are individual terms ($k \geqslant 1$), then $\mathfrak{A} \vDash_\alpha \mathbf{R}t_1 \ldots t_k$ if and only if $(t_1^{\mathfrak{A}}, \ldots, t_k^{\mathfrak{A}}) \in \mathbf{R}^{\mathfrak{A}}$.
> 2. If α is of the form $\neg\beta$, then $\mathfrak{A} \vDash_\alpha \neg\beta$ if and only if it is not the case that $\mathfrak{A} \vDash_\alpha \beta$.
> 3. If α is of the form $\beta \mathbin{\&} \delta$, $\beta \vee \delta$, $\beta \to \delta$ or $\beta \equiv \delta$, then
>
> $$\mathfrak{A} \vDash_\alpha \beta \mathbin{\&} \delta \text{ iff } \mathfrak{A} \vDash_\alpha \beta \text{ and } \mathfrak{A} \vDash_\alpha \delta$$
> $$\mathfrak{A} \vDash_\alpha \beta \vee \delta \text{ iff } \mathfrak{A} \vDash_\alpha \beta \text{ or } \mathfrak{A} \vDash_\alpha \delta$$
> $$\mathfrak{A} \vDash_\alpha \beta \to \delta \text{ iff either not } \mathfrak{A} \vDash_\alpha \beta \text{ or } \mathfrak{A} \vDash_\alpha \delta$$
> $$\mathfrak{A} \vDash_\alpha \beta \equiv \delta \text{ iff } \mathfrak{A} \vDash_\alpha \beta \text{ if and only if } \mathfrak{A} \vDash_\alpha \delta$$
>
> 4. If α is of the form $(\exists x)\beta$, then $\mathfrak{A} \vDash_\alpha (\exists x)\beta$ if and only if there is an element σ in the UD such that $\mathfrak{A} \vDash_{\alpha(\sigma/x^{\mathfrak{A}})}\beta$
> 5. If α is of the form $(\forall x)\beta$, then $\mathfrak{A} \vDash_\alpha (\forall x)\beta$ if and only if, for each element σ in the UD, $\mathfrak{A} \vDash_{\alpha(\sigma/x^{\mathfrak{A}})}\beta$.

[7] The specification was given in section 6.3.

A few remarks about this definition are in order. Recall that if **t** is a term—constant or variable—then $t^{\mathfrak{A}}$ is that element of the UD which the assignment function (if **t** is a variable) or the interpretation function (if **t** is a constant) assigns to **t**, and likewise for a predicate symbol **R**. Thus, what clause 1 says is that $Rt_1 \ldots t_k$ is satisfied by α in $\mathfrak{A}$ if and only if the tuple of domain elements $(t_1^{\mathfrak{A}}, \ldots, t_k^{\mathfrak{A}})$ is in the extension of **R**, $R^{\mathfrak{A}}$, or in more informal words, if the elements $t_1^{\mathfrak{A}} \ldots t_k^{\mathfrak{A}}$ partake in the relation $R^{\mathfrak{A}}$.[8] Clauses 2 and 3 should be straightforward as they are the standard definitions of the truth-functional connectives. On the other hand, clauses 4 and 5 deal with quantified wffs. Clause 4 says that an assignment α satisfies an existential wff, $(\exists x)\beta$, iff there is an x-variant of α, that is, an assignment of a value to x, which satisfies β. Similarly, clause 5 says that α satisfies $(\forall x)\beta$ iff all assignments to x (i.e., all of α's x-variants) satisfy β.

Now for a few examples to help make this definition more familiar. Consider the following interpretation over $\mathfrak{A}$:

UD := {0, 1, 2, 3, . . .}
Ex := {0, 2, 4, . . .}
Ixy := {(0,0), (1,1), (2,2), . . .}
Lxy := {(x,y) : x < y}
a := 1
b := 5
c := 12

On this interpretation, does the assignment α which assigns 2 to x satisfy the wff Lxb—is it the case that $\mathfrak{A} \models_\alpha Lxb$? On intuitive grounds the answer is, of course, yes: We are asking if the assignment of 2 to x satisfies the statement 'x is less than 5.' More formally, the wff conforms to clause 1 of the definition, and thus this particular α satisfies Lxb (in the structure $\mathfrak{A}$) if and only if the tuple $(x^{\mathfrak{A}}, b^{\mathfrak{A}})$ belongs to the extension of L, in other words, if and only if the tuple $(2,5) \in \{(x,y) : x < y\}$, as indeed it does. Hence, $\mathfrak{A} \models_\alpha Lxb$. However, the wff Iax is not satisfied by this assignment since the tuple $(a^{\mathfrak{A}}, x^{\mathfrak{A}})$, that is, (1,2), does not belong to the extension of I. So, $\mathfrak{A} \not\models_\alpha Iax$. What about the wff Ex & $\neg$Icb? Clause 3 of the definition applies here: That is, $\mathfrak{A} \models_\alpha Ex \& \neg Icb$ if and only if $\mathfrak{A} \models_\alpha Ex$ and $\mathfrak{A} \models_\alpha \neg Icb$. Clearly, $\mathfrak{A} \models_\alpha Ex$ since $x^{\mathfrak{A}} \in E^{\mathfrak{A}}$; as for $\neg$Icb, we have to turn to clause 2. $\mathfrak{A} \models_\alpha \neg Icb$ if and only if it is not the case that $\mathfrak{A} \models_\alpha Icb$. In fact, α does not satisfy Icb because (12,5) does not belong to the extension of I (i.e., 12 $\neq$ 5), and therefore α satisfies $\neg$Icb. Consequently, $\mathfrak{A} \models_\alpha Ex \& \neg Icb$.

Let us move on to quantified expressions. Although it is obvious that α satisfies the existential sentence, $(\exists x)Ex$ ('There is at least one natural number which is even'), since the extension of the predicate E is not empty, let

---

[8] As hinted before, the preceding definition of satisfaction could be extended to include the atomic sentences of SL—zero-place predicates—by allowing k (in clause 1) take the value 0.

us apply clause 4 in detail. $\mathfrak{A} \models_\alpha (\exists x)Ex$ if and only if there is at least one x-variant of α which satisfies Ex. And there is at least one such x-variant: Assign the number 42 (which is an element of the UD) to x, making the x-variant be $\alpha(42/x^\mathfrak{A})$. Since this particular σ, namely, the number 42, is a member of $E^\mathfrak{A}$, we have $\mathfrak{A} \models_{\alpha(42/x^\mathfrak{A})} Ex$ and, hence, $\mathfrak{A} \models_\alpha (\exists x)Ex$. There are infinitely many such x-variants of this particular α, although not every x-variant of α would qualify. For instance, choosing the number 37 as the σ would not do the job. Now, how about the universal quantification, $(\forall x)Ixx$ ('Every number is identical to itself')?[9] According to clause 5, $\mathfrak{A} \models_\alpha (\forall x)Ixx$ if and only if Ixx is satisfied by every x-variant of α. In other words, for each element, σ, of the UD, $\mathfrak{A} \models_{\alpha(\sigma/x^\mathfrak{A})} Ixx$. It is easy to see that every member of the UD can be found paired with itself in tuples belonging to the extension of Ixx. Hence, $\mathfrak{A} \models_\alpha (\forall x)Ixx$.

In regard to the preceding examples and, more generally, to our presentation of the intrepretational acount, we remind you that we are making use of the fact that the satisfaction of a wff is not affected by the meaning that the interpretation or assignment functions may assign to symbols not occurring in the wff. Moreover, the satisfaction of a *sentence* by an assignment α is independent of the specific assignments that α makes to the variables of PL, *including those variables which occur in the sentence*. This result follows from the fact that sentences have no free variables and, hence, are immune to their assigned values. In other words, if an assignment satisfies a sentence α in $\mathfrak{A}$, then *all* assignments satisfy α in $\mathfrak{A}$.

> **Definition.** Let $\mathfrak{A}$ be the structure associated with an interpretation and let α be an assignment function. A sentence α of PL is **true** of $\mathfrak{A}$ (or α **holds** in $\mathfrak{A}$) iff $\mathfrak{A} \models_\alpha \alpha$ for all α.[10]

If α is true of $\mathfrak{A}$ then, by the definition, α is satisfied by all assignments α in $\mathfrak{A}$ and, without fear of falling into ambiguity, we can drop the subscript in $\models_\alpha$ and simply write $\mathfrak{A} \models \alpha$. Moreover, if the context makes it clear, we will simply say 'α is true' (as opposed to 'α is true *of* $\mathfrak{A}$'). In formal logic, a sentence α which is true of some structure $\mathfrak{A}$ is said to have a model; $\mathfrak{A}$ is a **model** of α—hence, the name for *Symlog*'s Models environment—and $\mathfrak{A}$ is said to **satisfy** α or that α is **satisfiable**. A sentence α is false of a structure, of course, if and only if α is not true of it. This will be symbolized as: $\mathfrak{A} \not\models \alpha$.

You can now anticipate how the interpretational account will deal

---

[9] Pondering the meaning of this sentence for a moment, you will discover that it is a curiosity. How could any number fail to be identical to itself? Indeed, how could anything whatever fail to be the same as itself? The sentence expresses one of the so-called laws of identity, and presupposing a careful specification of what the identity predicate means, it would be classified as a logical truth. However, the rules which enable the identity predicate to be used in quantificational logic have not been included in our treatment of PL (but see the epilogue, 'Further Developments in Predicate Logic.')

[10] This definition can easily be extended to wffs in general: A wff is true of $\mathfrak{A}$ iff it is satisfied by all assignments. We do not lose generality by restricting to sentences as it can be shown that a wff α with free variables $x_1, x_2, \ldots, x_k$ is true of $\mathfrak{A}$ iff its **universal closure** $(\forall x_1)(\forall x_2) \ldots (\forall x_k)\alpha$, and which is a sentence, is true of $\mathfrak{A}$.

with the problem mentioned at the outset of this chapter concerning the infinite set, $\{$Oa, Ob, Oc, . . . , $\neg(\forall x)$Ox$\}$. Intuitively, we wanted to declare this set consistent, only we found that we could not do so in terms of the substitutional account. We will return to this matter in sections 9.4 and 9.5, where we will enlarge the interpretational account by specifying further semantic concepts such as logical truth, consistency and entailment. In the next section, however, we want to put the essentials of this account to work, using *Symlog*. In that way, we will be able to call on *Symlog* for illustrating these further concepts.

Exercises

9.2.1 Answer true or false (but not both) to each of the following.

    a. If $\mathfrak{A} \models_\alpha \alpha$ then $\mathfrak{A} \models_\alpha \alpha \vee \beta$.

    b. If $\mathfrak{A} \not\models_\alpha \alpha$ then $\mathfrak{A} \models_\alpha \neg\alpha$.

    c. If $\mathfrak{A} \models \alpha \vee \beta$ then $\mathfrak{A} \models \alpha$ or $\mathfrak{A} \models \beta$, where α and β are *wffs*.

    d. If $\mathfrak{A} \models \alpha \vee \beta$ then $\mathfrak{A} \models \alpha$ or $\mathfrak{A} \models \beta$, where α and β are *sentences*.

    e. $\mathfrak{A} \models_{\alpha(2/x^{\mathfrak{A}})}$ Ex iff $2 \in$ E$^{\mathfrak{A}}$.

    f. If Hx := $\{2,3\}$ in an interpretation over $\mathfrak{A}$ and α is such that $y^{\mathfrak{A}} = 3$ then $\mathfrak{A} \models_\alpha$ Hy.

    g. If Lxy := $\{(1,5), (2,4), (2,2)\}$ and a := 1 in an interpretation over $\mathfrak{A}$ then $\mathfrak{A} \models$ Laa.

    h. If Bx := $\{3, 6\}$, a := 0 and c := 6 in an interpretation over $\mathfrak{A}$ then $\mathfrak{A} \models$ Ba $\vee$ Bc.

    i. If Bx := $\{3, 6\}$ in an interpretation over $\mathfrak{A}$ and α is such that $z^{\mathfrak{A}} = 1$ then $\mathfrak{A} \models_{\alpha(3/z^{\mathfrak{A}})}$ Bz.

    j. If Bx := $\{3, 6\}$ in an interpretation over $\mathfrak{A}$ and α is such that $z^{\mathfrak{A}} = 6$ then $\mathfrak{A} \models_{\alpha(z^{\mathfrak{A}}/x^{\mathfrak{A}})}$ Bx.

    k. If α is a sentence then, for any α, $\mathfrak{A} \models_\alpha \alpha$ iff $\mathfrak{A} \models \alpha$.

    l. $(\exists x)$Gx is false of $\mathfrak{A}$ iff G$^{\mathfrak{A}} = \emptyset$.

    m. $(\forall x)$Fx is true of $\mathfrak{A}$ iff F$^{\mathfrak{A}}$ is the UD of $\mathfrak{A}$.

    n. Let x be the only free variable in α. Then, $\mathfrak{A} \models \alpha$ iff $\mathfrak{A} \models_\alpha (\forall x)\alpha$.

    o. If $\mathfrak{A} \models_\alpha$ Fx then $\mathfrak{A} \models_{\alpha(x^{\mathfrak{A}}/z^{\mathfrak{A}})}$ Fz.

9.2.2 Let $\mathfrak{A}$ be the structure associated with the interpretation given by

    UD := $\{0, 1, 2, 3, 4, 5\}$

    Ex := $\{0, 2, 4\}$

    Ox := $\{1, 3, 5\}$

    Bxy := $\{(3,1), (1,5), (3,2), (2,0), (0,1), (4,0), (5,1)\}$

    Lxy := $\{(x,y) : x$ is less than $y\}$

    Ixy := $\{(x,y) : x = y\}$

    a := 0

    b := 1

    c := 3

Which of the following are true of $\mathfrak{A}$?

a. Ea   b. ¬Eb   c. Lbb
d. Lab ∨ lab   e. (∃x)Bcx   f. (∃x)(Lxx ∨ ¬Ixx)
g. (∀x)(Lxx → ¬Lxx)   h. (∀x)(∃y)Bxy   i. (∃x)(∀y)Bxy
j. (∀x)(Lxc → (∃y)Byx)   k. (∀x)(Bbc → Ox)   l. (∃x)(∃y)(Bxy & Byx)

9.2.3 Given the following three interpretations (tagged with their corresponding structures),

$\mathfrak{A}_1$	$\mathfrak{A}_2$	$\mathfrak{A}_3$
UD := {0, 1, 2, 3, . . .}	UD := {0, 3, 5, 7, 10}	UD := {0, 1, 2}
Ex := {0, 2, 4, . . .}	Ex := {0, 5, 10}	Ex := {0, 2}
Lxy := {(x,y) : x < y}	Lxy := {(x,y) : x ⩽ y}	Lxy := {(x,y) : x ⩽ 2}
a := 0	a := 7	a := 2
b := 2	b := 3	b := 2

a. Give a sentence which is true of $\mathfrak{A}_1$.
b. Give one which is true of both $\mathfrak{A}_2$ and $\mathfrak{A}_3$.
c. Give one which is true of $\mathfrak{A}_2$ but not of $\mathfrak{A}_3$.
d. Give one which is true of all $\mathfrak{A}_1$, $\mathfrak{A}_2$ and $\mathfrak{A}_3$.
e. Which of the structures is a model of (∀x)Lxa?

9.2.4 For each of the sentences below give a model.

a. Fa   f. (∃x)(Lax & Lxa)
b. ¬Fb & Laa   g. Lab & (∀x)(Lax → Lxa)
c. ¬(Fa & Fb)   h. (∀x)(∃y)Bxy
d. Lab & (Lab → Lba)   i. (∃x)(∀y)Bxy
e. (∃x)Bx   j. (Lac & Lcc) & (∀x)(Lxc → (∃y)Byx)

9.2.5 (a) Give an example of an interpretation in which all the instances of (∀x)Ex are true of the interpretation's associated structure, yet (∀x)Ex is itself false of it; (b) give another example of an interpretation in which, although (∃x)Ex is true of the structure, all its instances are false of it.

9.3   Constructing Interpretations

In this section you are going to construct interpretations and their associated structures with the help of *Symlog*'s Models environment. You will be able to test whether some given sentences are satisfied by the structures which you provide. To access this environment, select the Options menu, and from the Environment option, select Models. After telling *Symlog* that you want a new file, it will ask for its name. You can either supply the name of your file now or simply press Enter. In any case, in a few seconds you should see the screen depicted in Figure 9.1.

Figure 9.1

The little dot, called the Models **prompt** or *Symlog* prompt, tells you that *Symlog* is ready to work. Our first example of a structure, which we will denote by $\mathfrak{A}$, has as UD the subset {0, 1, 2, 3, 4, 5} of natural numbers. To tell *Symlog* that this is your UD, simply type (no need to type the dot prompt, which is already on the screen)

. UD := {0,1,2,3,4,5}

and then press Enter, at which point *Symlog* displays

ok

to confirm that it has accepted the set {0, 1, 2, 3, 4, 5} as a valid UD for your interpretation's structure. To interpret Ex as the set {0, 2, 4} of even numbers of the UD and Ox as the set {1, 3, 5} of odd numbers, simply type (again, pressing Enter after each interpretation)

. Ex := {0,2,4}
ok
. Ox := {1,3,5}
ok

Finally, let us interpret the constant a as 0 and b as 1. Enter

```
. a := 0
ok
. b := 1
ok
.
```

If you have followed the steps up to this point, your screen should look like the one depicted in Figure 9.2.

Now that you have specified your interpretation, you can start evaluating the truth-value of sentences of PL. For instance, if you type

```
. Ea
```

Symlog replies with

```
TRUE
```

That response means that the sentence Ea is true of the structure 𝔄 of your interpretation; that is, 𝔄 ⊨ Ea. Obviously, ¬Ea should be false of 𝔄. To check, enter

```
. ¬Ea
```

```
MODEL :

. UD := {0,1,2,3,4,5}
ok
. Ex := {0,2,4}
ok
. Ox := {1,3,5}
ok
. a := 0
ok
. b := 1
ok
. ■
```

Figure 9.2

at which point *Symlog* promptly replies with

   FALSE

since $\mathfrak{A} \not\models \neg Ea$. This is, in a nutshell, how the Models environment of *Symlog* works: After you specify an interpretation, *Symlog* will evaluate the truth-value (under the interpretation) of the sentences that you enter.

Let us now move to more interesting sentences. You may ask, Is there an even number in the UD? You can find the answer to this question by evaluating the truth-value of the sentence $(\exists x)Ex$. Again, if you enter

   . $(\exists x)Ex$

Symlog will respond with TRUE since the extension of E, $E^{\mathfrak{A}}$, is not empty. You may also ask, Is every element in the UD either even or odd? Is there any element which is both even and odd? To find out, simply evaluate the truth-value of the sentence $(\forall x)(Ex \lor Ox)$ and that of $(\exists x)(Ex \& Ox)$:

   . $(\forall x)(Ex \lor Ox)$
   TRUE
   . $(\exists x)(Ex \& Ox)$
   FALSE

   .

By now your UD and your interpretations have gone off the screen. At any time you can list your UD with the command

   . list UD

Try it. Similarly,

   . list constants

will list all your constants and their corresponding interpretations. The command

   . list predicates

will list all your predicates and their interpretations. If you want to check your UD, constants, predicates and their corresponding interpretations (i.e., all of them) you can type

   . list all

Finally, the command

   . clear

will clear your screen (not your interpretation!).[11] Incidentally, at any time you can change or add a new interpretation for any of your symbols of PL by entering the new desired interpretation (or by using the command edit, as in edit E, to change $E^{\mathfrak{A}}$).

Now, let us introduce an interpretation for the predicate Ixy (x is equal to y). Since Ixy is a 2-ary (binary) predicate it must be interpreted as a set of 2-tuples (whose components are individuals of the UD). Moreover, in this set, the first component of any tuple must equal its second component. Carefully type

   . Ixy := {(0,0),(1,1),(2,2),(3,3),(4,4),(5,5)}

This expression will define 'equality' in your UD. You can now ask, Does $\mathfrak{A}$ $\models$ Iaa, $\mathfrak{A}$ $\models$ $\neg\neg$Iaa, $\mathfrak{A}$ $\models$ Iab and $\mathfrak{A}$ $\models$ ($\forall$x)Ixx? Try to think about the answers first; then you can check them with *Symlog*.

Let us introduce an interpretation for Lxy.[12] We want Lxy to denote the 'less than' relation. Note that the extension of Lxy should be the set of all those 2-tuples—'less than' is a binary relation—whose first component is less than the second component. That is, $L^{\mathfrak{A}}$ is

$$\{(0,1), (0,2), \ldots, (0,5), (1,2), (1,3), \ldots, (1,5), (2,3), \ldots, (3,5), (4,5)\}$$

Given the finiteness of your UD, the extension of Lxy is certainly a finite set but with enough elements to discourage anyone from typing it. Thus, in *Symlog*, you are allowed to type the following instead:

   . Lxy := x < y

which you can *read* as

   Lxy := x is less than y

and which is closer to the symbolizations you have done before. Again, once you have interpreted Lxy, try to work out the truth-values of the following

---

[11] As you can see, *Symlog*'s Models environment accepts not only sentences of PL but also some extralinguistic operators such as list all and clear to make your work easier. **ML**—for model-theoretic logic—is what we call the new language which results from adding to PL these extralinguistic operators. ML has the capability of interpreting formal symbols of PL in terms of set-theoretic entities. The complete syntax of ML is given in Appendix C, under 'BNF Syntax of ML.'

[12] Formally speaking, we should just say L. We will use a form like Lxy, however, to make explicit a predicate's arity as well as the intended order of its places.

sentences before you check your answers with *Symlog:*

> Lab
> Lab → ¬lab
> (∃x)Lxx
> (∃x)(∃y)¬Lxy.

List your UD (with list UD) and consider the following: Is there an element in the UD less than all elements? In other words, is the sentence (∃x)(∀y)Lxy true of 𝔄? Think about this question for a moment; then evaluate the truth-value of (∃x)(∀y)Lxy by using *Symlog.* Your screen should display

> . (∃x)(∀y)Lxy
> FALSE

You may be surprised by this answer. Isn't 0 less than all the elements in the UD? No, 0 is not less than itself! (A judicious use of the equality predicate will allow you to express the intended fact. Why not try this symbolization now?) As one final example, let us introduce an interpretation for the 3-ary predicate Sxyz (the sum of x and y is z). Note that the extension of this predicate is the set of all those 3-tuples whose third component is the sum of the other two components. Typical elements in this set are the 3-tuples (0,0,0), (1,2,3) and (2,3,5). Again, there is no need to type the set in its entirety with *Symlog.* Just enter

> . Sxyz := x + y = z

as a formal notation for

> Sxyz := the sum of x and y is z

By the way, you could have typed instead

> Sxyz := z = x + y

or even

> Sxyz := y+1 = 1−(x−z)

all of which would have given you the same extension for the predicate in all three cases (even though the English wording of the predicate would have been different in all three cases). Now that the predicate Sxyz (+, for short) has been interpreted, let us find out whether the UD contains a particular element, called an identity element, with regard to this predicate. If x is a member of the UD, then x counts as an **identity element** with regard to + if and only if, for every member y of the UD, x + y = y. In other words, we want to learn whether there is a number belonging to the UD which, when added to any member of the same UD, leaves that member the same. This question amounts to asking whether the sentence (∃x)(∀y)Sxyy is true of 𝔄; let us have *Symlog* give the answer:

    . (∃x)(∀y)Sxyy
    TRUE

    .

So there is indeed such an element in the six-member domain of this interpretation. Which one is it? Looking back at the UD, you will discover that there seems to be only one possibility: 0, which we had defined as the element associated with the individual term a. Not surprisingly, then, *Symlog* will evaluate the following sentence as TRUE:

    . (∀x)Saxx

In fact, there is *only one* candidate from the UD which meets the test for being an identity element with regard to +, as you will find by having *Symlog* now evaluate the following:

    . (∃x)(∀y)[Sxyy & (∀z)(Szyy → Izx)]
    TRUE

    .

Although true of 𝔄, the sentence is a bit complicated, so let us unpack it. Notice how this sentence combines the two distinct claims: it says (1) that there is at least one element, x, which, added to any element, y, yields the very same element, y, and (2) that if any element z leaves y the same when it is added to y, that element z is identical to (=) x itself. More compactly, what the sentence says is that there is *one and only one* element which, when added to y, yields y itself. There is an important difference between this sentence and the one which immediately preceded it. On the one hand, the former sentence, (∀x)Saxx, is about 0 as an identity element but leaves as an open question whether there are other members of the UD which meet the test. On the other hand, whereas the latter sentence declares that there is one and only one element that meets the test of being the identity element, it does not mention which element that is. Sentences like the latter, which inform you that there is one and only one thing of a certain kind without identifying that thing by name, are called, as we saw in Chapter 6, **definite descriptions**. In fact, though neither sentence tells you, 0 is the only member of this UD which added to any number (including itself) leaves that number unaltered.[13]

As a final example for this interpretation, you are going to check if the UD is closed under addition. The domain is **closed** with regard to addition if and only if the sum of any two elements of the domain also belongs to that domain. For our current domain, this is not the case since *Symlog* evaluates

$$. \ (\forall x)(\forall y)(\exists z)Sxyz$$

as FALSE.[14]

Before moving to the next example you may want to save your work. Then, you can either retrieve a new blank pad or you can simply type

. new

which will clear the current interpretation. In our second example of an interpretation, the underlying structure is a **directed graph**—see Figure 9.3 which is a set of nodes (the circles) and arcs (the arrows connecting the nodes).

Here, the UD is the set of nodes in the graph. We also need a binary predicate, Cxy, to be interpreted as 'x is connected to y'—a relation in the structure of the interpretation. Note that the extension of Cxy is a set of 2-tuples whose components are individuals of the UD, namely, nodes. A tuple

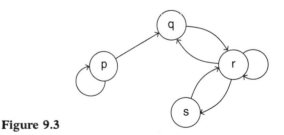

Figure 9.3

---

[13] Please note that the *identity element* of this UD (with regard to +) is not the same thing as the *identity predicate*, symbolized as Ixy in this interpretation, and sometimes symbolized also by the more familiar symbol =. In the present interpretation, an identity element is a single object of the domain, whereas the identity predicate, Ixy, is defined in terms of its extension: the 2-tuples (x, y) of elements of the domain such that x = y.

[14] One may argue that this expression evaluates to FALSE by pointing to a pair of elements in the UD, say 3 and 4, whose sum, 7, is not in the UD. Although intuitively satisfying, this way of reasoning is formally incorrect since, given that 7 is not a member of the UD, one cannot even speak of it. The correct way to argue is to say that there is at least one pair of elements in the UD, x and y, for which there is no element z such that the triple (x,y,z) is a member of the extension of S. *Symlog* is actually programmed to reason informally by implementing what we call the **background world assumption**: It assumes the existence of a (background) universe underlying the UD, where out-of-UD-bounds computations can take place. This feature was implemented to make it computationally more efficient and to prevent you from having to explicitly state in excruciating detail the extension of some of the predicates being interpreted.

(x,y) is in the extension of Cxy if and only if x is connected to y (through an arc). Finally, we will name every node by supplying a constant for it. Enter[15]

```
. UD := {p,q,r,s}
ok
. Cxy := {(p,p),(p,q),(q,r),(r,q),(r,r),(r,s),(s,r)}
ok
. p := p
ok
. q := q
ok
. r := r
ok
. s := s
ok
.
```

Note that, for instance, the tuple (q,r) of nodes is in the extension of Cxy since node q is connected to node r (through an arc) in the graph. Also, do not be confused by the constant symbols and the individuals of the UD they denote. Here, we could have chosen constants such as a, b, c and d to name the nodes in the graph, but constants p, q, r and s seem more appropriate since they will easily remind us of what nodes they stand for. Now, make a PL translation of each of the following claims about the graph; however, first try to determine whether each claim is true before getting *Symlog* to answer.

(1) Node p is connected to node q.
(2) There is a node connected to itself.
(3) Node r is connected to all nodes (including itself).
(4) If a node is connected to node q then it is connected to node s too.
(5) Not every node is connected to itself.

Possible translations are

```
. Cpq
TRUE
. (∃x)Cxx
TRUE
```

[15] This interpretation is on your disk under the name MODEL01.

. (∀x)Crx

FALSE

. (∀x)(Cxq → Cxs)

FALSE

. ¬(∀x)Cxx

TRUE

.

For the following examples you need to introduce equality. First enter

. Ixy := x=y

ok

.

and then try to answer the following:

(6) All nodes, with the exception of node p, are connected to node r.
(7) If there is a node which is connected to some node (possibly the same) then all nodes are connected to themselves.
(8) Every node is connected to some node which is not connected to itself.
(9) There are at least two distinct nodes, each connected to itself.
(10) There is a node such that any node connected to it connects to itself.

Possible, but not unique, answers to the above are

. (∀x)(¬Ixp ≡ Cxr)

TRUE

. (∃x)(∃y)Cxy → (∀x)Cxx

FALSE

. (∀x)(∃y)(Cxy & ¬Cyy)

FALSE

. (∃x)(∃y)[(Cxx & Cyy) & ¬Ixy]

TRUE

. (∃x)(∀y)(Cyx → Cyy)

TRUE

.

As a final illustration, let us check if the 'connectivity' relation is **reflexive**. A relation R (on a set S) is **reflexive** if and only if each element in S is R-related to itself. Hence, $C^{\mathfrak{A}}$ is reflexive if and only if the sentence (∀x)Cxx is T of $\mathfrak{A}$. Let us verify this statement.

. (∀x)Cxx
FALSE

.

So the 'connectivity' relation in the structure of this interpretation is not reflexive. Similarly, you can check for the relation of symmetry. A relation R (on a set S) is **symmetric** if and only if for any elements x and y in S, if x is R-related to y, then y is R-related to x. To find out if $C^{\mathfrak{A}}$ is symmetric enter

. (∀x)(∀y)(Cxy → Cyx)
FALSE

.

Therefore, $C^{\mathfrak{A}}$, in the intepretation, is not symmetric either. Finally, you can check it for transitivity. A relation R (on a set S) is **transitive** if and only if for any elements x, y and z in S, if x is R-related to y and y is R-related to z, then x is R-related to z. But again, $C^{\mathfrak{A}}$ is not transitive since

. (∀x)(∀y)(∀z)[(Cxy & Cyz) → Cxz]
FALSE

.

You may want to save your work before trying the following exercise: Let your UD be the graph of Figure 9.3 with node p removed (as well as its incoming and outgoing arcs). Then reinterpret Cxy accordingly (i.e., no tuple in the extension of $C^{\mathfrak{A}}$ should contain the node p since p is not an individual of the UD anymore). Is the newly obtained $C^{\mathfrak{A}}$ reflexive, symmetric or transitive? How would you modify $C^{\mathfrak{A}}$ (by adding or removing arrows in the graph) so that it becomes an **equivalence relation** (i.e., a relation which is reflexive, symmetric and transitive)?

Before we move on to further examples, something should be said concerning the efficiency of *Symlog* at evaluating the truth-value of a sentence under a given interpretation. By now you have probably noticed that some sentences take longer to evaluate than others. For instance, suppose that the UD has 10 elements. Then, if the sentence α takes some specific amount of time to evaluate, a sentence of the form $(\forall x)\alpha$, will take about 10 times longer, and $(\forall x)(\forall y)\alpha$ about 100 times longer.[16] The moral is, Beware of multiple quantified sentences.

Also, you may have noticed that *Symlog* evaluates some sentences to the **undefined symbol** ⊥, usually because some of the symbols in your sentence are still uninterpreted. Undefined evaluations may also arise when *Symlog* is interpreting your sentence, but in the process of doing so, a rule

---

[16] This is a worst-case (time complexity) result.

which defines the underlying structure of the interpretation is violated. *Symlog* makes sure that every single component (which is a wff) of your sentence strictly adheres to Tarski's definition of the satisfaction relation (e.g., it is not undefined) before attempting to compute the truth-value for the entire sentence.

For our final example, we will create an interpretation based on an imaginary birthday party. The individuals of this domain are precisely the partygoers, let us say John, David, Mary, Suzy and Peter. There are also some relations: 'x likes music,' 'x smokes,' 'x is dancing with y' and finally, 'x loves y.' Let us begin by entering the UD in Symlog as[17]

```
. UD := {John,David,Mary,Suzy,Peter}
ok

  .
```

Next, we let the one-place predicate Mx stand for the relation 'x likes music.' Note that the extension of the predicate Mx has as members individuals of the UD. Moreover, the elements in the extension of Mx will be precisely those people who, we will decree, like music (say, David, Mary, Suzy and Peter). The interpretation of Mx is specified by entering

```
. Mx := {David,Mary,Suzy,Peter}
ok

  .
```

We let the one-place predicate Sx stand for 'x smokes.' Again, the members of the extension of Sx are those individuals in the UD who (we will stipulate) smoke. So, enter

```
. Sx := {John,Mary,Suzy}
ok

  .
```

In the party there are two couples dancing: David with Suzy and Mary with Peter. The relation 'x is dancing with y' deserves some special care. The extension of Dxy will have 2-tuples (whose components are individuals of the UD) as elements. The tuple (x,y) is in the extension of Dxy if and only if x is dancing with y. Thus, the extension of Dxy has the 2-tuple (David,Suzy) since David is dancing with Suzy. But note that by our knowledge of the world, x is dancing with y if and only if y is dancing with x. Hence, the extension of Dxy has to contain the 2-tuple (Suzy,David) as well. Similar considerations apply to the other dancing couple. All this said, enter the inter-

---

[17] This interpretation is on your disk under the name MODEL02.

pretation of Dxy as

. Dxy := {(David,Suzy),(Suzy,David),(Mary,Peter),(Peter,Mary)}
ok
.

Let Lxy stand for 'x loves y.' Again, the members of the extension of Lxy are
2-tuples of individuals of the UD. Note that 'x loves y' does not necessarily
imply that 'y loves x,' so the considerations mentioned above for dancing do
not apply here. Let us then decree those 2-tuples of individuals x and y such
that x loves y:

. Lxy := {(John,Mary),(David,Suzy),(Suzy,John),(Suzy,Peter),(Suzy,David)}
ok
.

Finally, we use constants of PL to stand for some individuals in the UD.
Enter

. d := David
ok
. j := John
ok
. m := Mary
ok
. s := Suzy
ok
.

Our interpretation is complete. To master your understanding of interpretations (and of translations too) there are several things you could try at
this point. For instance, you can look at the structure underlying the interpretation and come up with facts which are to be expressed with sentences
of PL (this is an important aspect in the formalization and axiomatization
of concepts). Then, with *Symlog,* you can evaluate the truth-value of the sentence of PL you have translated and see if it reflects the actual structure. Another thing you could try is the following: When a structure is sufficiently
large or complex, such as this one, it does not take long to forget facts about
it. You can use PL, with the help of *Symlog,* to rediscover what those facts
are (or even better, you can ask a friend to create a structure for you to explore and discover). In any case, you probably no longer remember who
likes music or who is in love with whom in the structure we have just given.
So, you can use PL as the language of your investigations to find out who is
dancing with whom, what smokers also like music or if Suzy is dancing

with a smoker who is in love with her. Also, in a variation of this exercise, you can make up sentences of PL and then try to see if the structure 𝔄 is a model for them. Or finally, if a sentence is not satisfied by 𝔄, how would you modify 𝔄—the birthday party—so that it becomes a model for the sentence? By letting *Symlog* evaluate your sentences, you can find out whether your own answers are correct. Let us actually take up some of these suggestions by working on the examples that follow.

We begin by asking, Does John smoke? To find out, enter

```
. Sj
TRUE
```

Also, to find out if David is dancing with Suzy and to see whether John and Mary's love is mutual, enter

```
. Dds
TRUE
. Ljm & Lmj
FALSE
```

Now, is Suzy in love with John and dancing with him? If not, is she dancing with someone she loves? Is it David?

```
. Lsj & Dsj
FALSE
. (∃x)(Lsx & Dsx)
TRUE
. Lsd & Dsd
TRUE
```

To find out if there are two people dancing who are not both in love with each other, enter

```
. (∃x)(∃y)(Dxy & ¬(Lxy & Lyx))
TRUE
```

Try to determine the truth-value of the following sentences before evaluating your answers with *Symlog:*

(1) Everybody likes music.

(2) No one smokes.

(3) Every person who likes music is dancing.

(4) A smoker is dancing with Suzy.

(5) Mary is dancing with someone who doesn't like music.

Possible answers, and their corresponding truth-values, are

. (∀x)Mx

FALSE

. ¬(∃x)Sx

FALSE

. (∀x)(Mx → (∃y)Dxy)

TRUE

. (∃x)(Sx & Dxs)

FALSE

. (∃x)(Dmx & ¬Mx)

FALSE

.

For the following you will need equality. Thus, first enter

. Ixy := x=y

ok

.

and then try

(6) David is dancing with someone who loves him.

(7) Mary is dancing with someone she doesn't love.

(8) All smokers like music.

(9) All smokers, except John, like music.

(10) There is someone who likes music but doesn't smoke.

(11) John is in love with someone but this person is dancing with someone else.

(12) There is only one person who doesn't like music.

Possible translations, and their corresponding truth-values, are

. (∃x)(Ddx & Lxd)

TRUE

. (∃x)(Dmx & ¬Lmx)

TRUE

. (∀x)(Sx → Mx)

FALSE

. (∀x)[(Sx & ¬Ixj) → Mx]

TRUE

. (∃x)(Mx & ¬Sx)

TRUE

. (∃x)[Ljx & (∃y)(Dxy & ¬Iyj)]

TRUE

. (∃x)[¬Mx & (∀y)(¬My → Iyx)]

TRUE

.

In the following examples we test if a given sentence of PL is satisfied by the structure 𝔄, that is, if 𝔄 is a model of the sentence. Try to work out the truth-value of each sentence by using the definition of the satisfaction relation (in section 9.2) before evaluating its truth-value with *Symlog*.

Sm

Lsj

Lds & Mj

(∀x)Sx

¬Sj & (∃x)Mx

(∀x)(∃y)(Dxy → Sy)

(∀x)(∀y)(Dxy ≡ Dyx)

Exercises

9.3.1   In this exercise you are going to work with *Symlog* to study an interpretation whose structure 𝔄 is a directed graph. (The interpretation provided below is stored on your disk under the name MODEL03.)

UD := {a,b,c,d,e}

Cxy := {(a,b),(a,c),(a,d),(b,b),(b,c),(c,c),(d,a),(d,d)}

Ixy := x = y

a := a

b := b

c := c

d := d

(At this point you may find useful to draw a diagram—the directed graph—of the structure. To do so, inspect both the UD and the extension of Cxy, C𝔄). (i) In this first part of the exercise, determine whether 𝔄 satisfies the following sentences before you let *Symlog* check your answers:

a. Cbb

f. (∀x)Cxx

b. Cba ∨ Cab

g. (∀x)(∃y)Cxy

c. Cab → Cba

h. (∃x)(∀y)Cxy

d. Cba → Cab

i. (∃x)(∃y)[¬Ixy & (Cxy & Cyx)]

e. (∃x)Ccx

j. (∀x)[Cxx → (∃y)(¬Ixy & Cxy)]

(ii) In this second part, first translate each of the following sentences into PL and then determine its truth-value in 𝔄 by using the definition of the satisfaction relation; then check if your truth-value agrees with *Symlog's*.

a. Every node is connected to a (possibly the same) node.

b. Every node is connected to another, distinct, node.

c. No node is connected to itself and to node c as well.

d. Any node connected to itself is connected also to either node c or to node a.

e. There is a node connected to b which is also connected to c, besides node a.

f. The connectivity relation in this graph is reflexive.

g. The connectivity relation in this graph is symmetric.

h. The connectivity relation in this graph is transitive.

9.3.2   Redefine the connectivity relation, C𝔄, of exercise 9.3.1 as

Cxy := {(a,b),(a,c),(b,b),(b,c),(c,b),(c,c)}

(a) Is C𝔄 transitive? Check your answer with *Symlog*. (b) Which of the sentences (a through j) in the first part of exercise 9.3.1 are satisfied by this new structure?

9.3.3   In this exercise you are going to work with *Symlog* to study an interpretation whose structure is a group of students and their final marks in mathematics and philosophy, given in the following table:

Student	Mathematics	Philosophy
John	68	75
Diane	38	50
Mike	70	42
Lucy	92	86

The UD will be the set of all the students and their marks. We also need to interpret a few predicates and constants of PL as entities in the structure. Below we provide a few predicates and constants and their intended interpretations in English. Begin by replacing the English wording of the intepretations by their formal counterparts, that is, their extensions. Once you have done so, check your answer by retrieving the structure MODEL04 from your disk.

PL symbol   Intended interpretation

Mxy	Student x has got mark y in mathematics.
Pxy	Student x has got mark y in philosophy.
Ixy	x is equal to y.
Gxy	x is greater than y.
j	John
d	Diane
m	Mike
l	Lucy
p	the passing mark (i.e., 50)

Now, translate the following sentences into PL and then determine their truth-value in 𝔄 by using the definition of the satisfaction relation. Check if your truth-values agree with *Symlog*'s.

a. John's mark in math is higher than 50.

b. Mike's mark in philosophy is higher than Lucy's.

c. Mike's mark in math is higher than his mark in philosophy.

d. Everybody has passed philosophy.

e. Someone has failed math but is not John.

f. Lucy has got the highest mark in philosophy.

g. Not everybody has passed math.

h. At least two students have got a 50 in philosophy and Mike is one of them.

i. No one has got a mark in math lower than Diane's.

j. All the students have failed both mathematics and philosophy.

9.3.4   Add suitable predicates and constants (and their corresponding extensions) to the interpretation of exercise 9.3.3 so that the sentence 'Mike's average mark (in math and philosophy) is higher than 50' can be expressed in PL. (There is no need to evaluate the truth-value of this sentence with *Symlog* since this process may take the program a while to complete.)

9.3.5   The Blocks World, depicted below, consists of a few colored, three-dimensional polyhedra—cubes and pyramids—arranged in a spatial configuration:

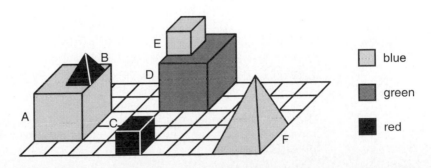

The UD is the set {A, B, C, D, E, F} of cubes and pyramids. Begin by providing the extensions to all the predicates given below. Check your answer by retrieving the structure MODEL05 from your disk.

PL symbol	Intended interpretation
Cx	x is a cube.
Px	x is a pyramid.
Bx	x is blue.
Gx	x is green.
Rx	x is red.
Sx	x is small.
Lxy	x is to the left of y.
Txy	x is on top of y.
Ixy	x is equal to y.

Now, translate each of the following sentences into PL and then determine its truth-value in the Blocks World by using the definition of the satisfaction relation. Check if your truth-values agree with *Symlog*'s.

a. There is a blue cube on top of a green one.
b. No small cube supports a pyramid.
c. There is a green pyramid to the left of a large blue cube.
d. All small cubes are either blue or red.
e. There is only one red cube.
f. All large pyramids are standing on the floor.
g. There is a small pyramid to the left of a cube, where this cube has a cube on top of it.
h. Cubes are the only figures supporting others.
i. No small cube supports a figure.
j. All the figures to the left of a red cube are either blue cubes or green pyramids.

9.3.6 Use the definition of the satisfaction relation to determine the truth-value of the following sentences under the interpretation for the Blocks World of exercise 9.3.5. Check if your answers agree with *Symlog*'s.

a. $Cc \mathbin{\&} Rc$
b. $(\exists x)(Px \mathbin{\&} Gx)$
c. $(\forall x)(Cx \rightarrow Sx)$
d. $(\forall x)(Px \rightarrow (Rx \lor Bx))$
e. $(\exists x)(Bx \mathbin{\&} \neg Bx)$
f. $(\exists x)(\exists y)((Cx \mathbin{\&} Py) \mathbin{\&} Lxy)$
g. $(\exists x)(\exists y)((Px \mathbin{\&} Cy) \mathbin{\&} Tyx)$
h. $(\forall x)[(\exists y)Tyx \rightarrow Cx]$
i. $(\exists x)[(Px \mathbin{\&} Bx) \mathbin{\&} \neg(\exists y)Tyx]$
j. $(\exists x)(\exists y)(\exists z)(Lxy \mathbin{\&} Lyz)$

9.3.7 The structure associated with the interpretation in this exercise is a personnel data base. The data for each employee is given in the following table:

Employee	Department	Rank	Rate
Han	MKT	Sr	9
Katz	MKT	Jr	10
Sun	ACC	Jr	8
Imlay	ENG	Sr	24

(i) The UD is the set of all the employees, departments, employee ranks (junior or senior) and rates (i.e., hourly wages). Note that the table *relates* elements of the UD, and thus it is a four-place relation, which we will denote by the predicate Pxyzu. This predicate is to be interpreted as 'Employee x in department y with rank z has a rate of u dollars/hour.' Give the extension of Pxyzu. Check your answer by retrieving the structure MODEL06 from your disk. After inspecting it, translate into PL, and by using the definition of the satisfaction relation, determine the truth-value of the following:

a. Katz is working in the marketing department.
b. Someone in engineering is making more than $10/hr.
c. All seniors in engineering make more than $10/hr.
d. Katz is a senior employee working in the marketing department.
e. Imlay is a junior engineer making less than $10/hr.

(ii) As you may have noticed, the above translations involve excessive quantification. To avoid this, we will replace the four-place predicate Pxyzu by new unary and binary predicates. These are given below with their intended interpretations, which you are to replace by their extension. Once you have done so, check your answer by retrieving the structure MODEL07 from your disk.

PL symbol   Intended interpretation

Mx	Employee x works in the marketing department.
Ax	Employee x works in the accounting department.
Ex	Employee x works in the engineering department.
Jx	x is a junior employee.
Sx	x is a senior employee.
Rxy	Employee x has a rate of y dollars/hr.

Now, translate the sentences a through e above into PL by using this new interpretation, and determine their truth-value.

9.3.8   The following facts are known about David's birthday party:

John is dancing with Sue, Lucy is dancing with Bill and Al is dancing with Mary. Sue, John, Bill and Mary like music. Sue and Bill are both in love with each other, John is in love with Mary but Mary is in love with David.

What is the UD? Interpret the predicates Mx (x likes music), Lxy (x loves y), and Dxy (x is dancing with y) by giving their extensions. Also, interpret Ixy (x is identical with y). Finally, name Bill, Mary and John as b, m and j, respectively. Check your answers by retrieving the file MODEL08 from your disk. Then, symbolize into PL and find the truth-value of the following:

a. Every music lover is dancing.
b. Mary is dancing with someone who doesn't like music.
c. Everybody likes music but no one is dancing.
d. At least two people are in love with Bill.
e. Mary is dancing with someone who loves her.
f. John loves someone who is dancing with someone else.
g. There is a music lover dancing with someone who is in love with Bill.
h. John loves someone who loves somebody who is not dancing with anyone.

9.3.9   Given the structure

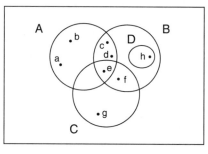

begin by constructing an appropriate interpretation, that is, one that will allow you to translate into PL the set-theoretic sentences given below. (Hint: If S is a set, let Sx stand for $x \in S$—'x belongs to S.') Check your answer by retrieving the structure MODEL09 from your disk. Then translate into PL the following set-theoretic sentences and evaluate their truth-value (under your interpretation). Compare your truth-values against *Symlog*'s.

a. $A = \emptyset$ b. $C \neq \emptyset$ and $A \cap B = \emptyset$ c. $A = B$
d. $A^c = C$ e. $A \cup B = B \cup A$ f. $C \cup D = A^c \cup \{e\}$

9.3.10 Consider the following properties of a relation R (defined on a UD):

Nonreflexivity: $\neg(\forall x)Rxx$
Nonsymmetry: $\neg(\forall x)(\forall y)(Rxy \rightarrow Ryx)$
Nontransitivity: $\neg(\forall x)(\forall y)(\forall z)[(Rxy \ \& \ Ryz) \rightarrow Rxz]$

Given the UD $\{a,b,c,d\}$, determine which of the above properties are possessed by the following relations. Verify your answer against *Symlog*'s.

Cxy := {(a,b),(a,c),(b,b),(c,b)}
Dxy := {(a,a),(a,c),(b,b),(b,c),(c,a),(c,b),(c,c),(d,d)}
Exy := {(a,a),(a,b),(a,c),(b,b),(b,c),(c,b),(c,c),(d,d)}

9.3.11 Consider the following properties of a relation R (defined on a UD):

Irreflexivity:	$(\forall x)\neg Rxx$
Asymmetry:	$(\forall x)(\forall y)(Rxy \rightarrow \neg Ryx)$
Antisymmetry:	$(\forall x)(\forall y)[(Rxy \ \& \ Ryx) \rightarrow x=y]$
Intransitivity:	$(\forall x)(\forall y)(\forall z)[(Rxy \ \& \ Ryz) \rightarrow \neg Rxz]$

Given the UD {a,b,c,d}, determine which of the above properties are possessed by the following relations. Verify your answer against *Symlog*'s.

Fxy := {(a,b),(a,c),(b,b),(c,b)}
Gxy := {(a,c),(b,c),(c,a),(c,b)}
Hxy := {(a,b),(c,a),(d,c)}

9.3.12 Consider the following properties of a relation R (defined on a UD):

Connectedness:	$(\forall x)(\forall y)(\forall z)[(Rxy \ \& \ Rxz) \rightarrow (Ryz \lor Rzy)]$
Convergence:	$(\forall x)(\forall y)(\forall z)[(Rxy \ \& \ Rxz) \rightarrow (\exists u)(Ryu \ \& \ Rzu)]$

We define two relations, J and K, on a UD {a,b,c,d} as represented in the following two diagrams. Specify their extensions and determine which of the above properties are possessed by these two relations. Verify your answer against *Symlog*'s.

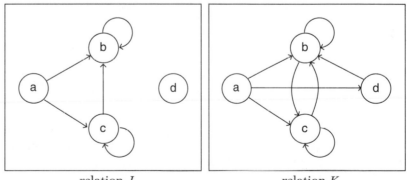

relation J relation K

9.3.13 Give a model for each of the sentences below. Let *Symlog* assist you in your search.

a. $Fa \ \& \ [(\exists x)Gx \ \& \ \neg Ga]$

b. $(\forall x)Kx \ \& \ (\forall x)(Kx \rightarrow \neg Lx)$

    c. (Ba & (∃x)Cx) & (∀x)(Bx ≡ ¬Cx)

    d. (∀x)Hx & (∀x)(Hx → (∃y)Lxy)

    e. [(∀x)(∃y)Rxy & (∀x)(∃y)¬Rxy] & ¬(∃x)(∀y)Rxy

9.3.14 Give a model with at least three individuals for each of the sentences of exercise 9.3.13. Verify your answer with *Symlog*.

9.3.15 Give a model which satisfies both sentences (∀x)(∃y)Rxy and (∀x)(∀y)(Rxy → ¬Ryx). Verify your answer with *Symlog*.

9.3.16 Give a model which satisfies both sentences (∀x)Rxx and (∀x)(∀y)(Rxy → (∃z)(Ryz & ¬Ixz). The predicate Ixy should be interpreted as equality. Verify your answer with *Symlog*.

9.4   *Formal Properties of Sentences of PL*

In the last section of Chapter 6 we introduced several quantificational concepts—quantificational truth, consistency and so on—in an intuitive way. They will now be placed in a more formal setting. We will discuss first the semantical properties of sentences and then, in the next section, those of sets of sentences and arguments.

We begin by reminding you that a sentence α of PL is **satisfiable** if and only if there is at least one model for it, that is, a structure $\mathfrak{A}$ (with its corresponding interpretation) in which α is true. The details of this definition relating to different types of sentences are to be found in section 9.2. To illustrate, the sentence Sabc is satisfiable. The following is a model for it:

    UD := {x : x is a natural number}

    Sxyz := {(x,y,z) : x + y = z}

    a := 2

    b := 3

    c := 5

Note that the sentence Sabc is true of this structure, $\mathfrak{A}$, since $(a^{\mathfrak{A}}, b^{\mathfrak{A}}, c^{\mathfrak{A}}) \in S^{\mathfrak{A}}$; that is, $(2,3,5) \in \{(x,y,z) : x + y = z\}$. (Recall that in *Symlog*, $\mathfrak{A} \models$ Sabc if and only if Sabc evaluates to TRUE.)

Some sentences are satisfied by all structures.

Definition. A sentence α of PL is **quantificationally true** if and only if it is satisfied by every structure.

That is, for any structure $\mathfrak{A}$, $\mathfrak{A} \models \alpha$ (every structure is a model of α). In other words, α is true of any structure (associated with any interpretation). For instance, the sentence Fa∨¬Fa is quantificationally true. To show this fact we argue as follows: Choose any interpretation with associated structure $\mathfrak{A}$. Then, either $\mathfrak{A} \models$ Fa or $\mathfrak{A} \not\models$ Fa. If $\mathfrak{A} \models$ Fa then $\mathfrak{A} \models$ Fa∨¬Fa, by clause 3 in the definition of the satisfaction relation. However, if $\mathfrak{A} \nvDash$ Fa then $\mathfrak{A} \vDash \neg$Fa, and by clause 3 of that definition, $\mathfrak{A} \vDash$ Fa$\vee\neg$Fa. Hence, Fa$\vee\neg$Fa is quantificationally true. The sentence $(\forall x)(Fx \equiv Fx)$ is also quantificationally true since for any choice of an individual σ in the UD, $\mathfrak{A} \vDash_{a(\sigma/x^{\mathfrak{A}})}$ Fx $\equiv$ Fx.

Conversely, some sentences have no models.

> **Definition.** A sentence α of PL is **quantificationally false** if and only if it is satisfied by no structure.

That is, for any interpretation with associated structure $\mathfrak{A}$, $\mathfrak{A} \nvDash \alpha$ (α has no models). The sentence Gab & $\neg$Gab is quantificationally false since no structure satisfies both conjuncts. Try to give examples of quantificationally false sentences and *illustrate* this property by constructing interpretations with *Symlog*. Any structure you define will fail to satisfy a quantificationally false sentence.

Before continuing our discussion we would like to stop here to give a word of caution. If you have a sentence α which is not satisfied by any structure you have cared to define so far, it does not mean that the sentence is quantificationally false. There could well be a structure which satisfies α but which you have not found yet, either because it may be very difficult to find or maybe because you just gave up. So keep in mind that even after trying, say, 1 trillion structures with *Symlog* in each of which α turns out to be FALSE, it does not follow that α is quantificationally false (although it would follow, after only one of these structures, that α is not quantificationally true). Even if you try all the structures you could possibly construct with *Symlog* and α comes out FALSE in each of them, α could still fail to be quantificationally false. The point to keep in mind here is that *Symlog*'s Models environment evaluates a given sentence relative to a given structure which you *yourself* provide. The program will not construct structures on its own, much less provide the set of all possible structures as background for evaluating a given sentence. Thus, the Models environment offers a means for illustrating and checking sentences against a given structure, but it does not constitute a step-by-step method of proof. We will return to this point at the end of the chapter.

As you know, there are sentences which are satisfied by some structures but not by others. So, we have:

> **Definition.** A sentence α of PL is **quantificationally indeterminate** if and only if there is at least one structure which satisfies α and there is at least one structure which does not.

That is, there are structures $\mathfrak{A}_1$ and $\mathfrak{A}_2$ such that $\mathfrak{A}_1 \vDash \alpha$ and $\mathfrak{A}_2 \nvDash \alpha$. In other words, $\mathfrak{A}_1$ is a model of α but $\mathfrak{A}_2$ is not. The sentence $(\forall x)(\exists y)$Lyx is quantificationally indeterminate. To show this fact, we give two structures

$\mathfrak{A}_1$ and $\mathfrak{A}_2$ such that $\mathfrak{A}_1 \models (\forall x)(\exists y)Lyx$ and $\mathfrak{A}_2 \not\models (\forall x)(\exists y)Lyx$:

$\mathfrak{A}_1$	$\mathfrak{A}_2$
UD := $\{\ldots, -2, -1, 0, 1, 2, \ldots\}$	UD := $\{0, 1, 2, \ldots\}$
Lxy := x < y	Lxy := x < y

In $\mathfrak{A}_1$, the sentence $(\forall x)(\exists y)Lyx$ says that for any *integer* there is always a smaller one, which is true. The same sentence, in $\mathfrak{A}_2$, says that for any *natural number* there is always a smaller one, which is false (there is no natural number less than 0). Hence, $(\forall x)(\exists y)Lyx$ is quantificationally indeterminate. As an exercise, construct two other interpretations, using *Symlog*, which show that this sentence is quantificationally indeterminate. Is its negation, namely, $\neg(\forall x)(\exists y)Lyx$, also quantificationally indeterminate?

Finally, there are sentences which have precisely the same models.

> **Definition.** Two sentences α and β of PL are **quantificationally equivalent** if and only if every structure which satisfies (fails to satisfy) one of the sentences also satisfies (fails to satisfy) the other.

That is, for any $\mathfrak{A}$, $\mathfrak{A} \models \alpha$ if and only if $\mathfrak{A} \models \beta$. It is left as an exercise to show that the sentences Fa $\rightarrow$ Gab and $\neg$Fa $\vee$ Gab are quantificationally equivalent. Illustrate—which, again, is not the same as proving—this fact by constructing several interpretations in *Symlog*. Note that any structure which you construct and which satisfies Fa $\rightarrow$ Gab will satisfy $\neg$Fa $\vee$ Gab as well (and vice versa), and any structure which falsifies Fa $\rightarrow$ Gab will falsify $\neg$Fa $\vee$ Gab (and vice versa).

Exercises

9.4.1 Answer true or false (but not both) to each of the following.

   a. Any satisfiable sentence has at least one model.
   b. If α is quantificationally true then any structure whatsoever satisfies it.
   c. The sentence Fa & $\neg$Gb has a model.
   d. The negation of any quantificationally indeterminate sentence has at least one model.
   e. If α has a model, $\alpha \rightarrow \beta$ must have a model as well.
   f. If the sentences α and β are satisfiable, so is the sentence α & β.
   g. If the sentence α & β has a model, then α has a model and β has a model.
   h. If the sentence α & β has no model, then α has no model and β has no model.
   i. $(\exists y)(Fy \rightarrow (\forall x)Fx)$ is quantificationally true.
   j. Any model of $(\forall x)Fx \vee (\forall x)Gx$ is also a model of $(\forall x)(Fx \vee Gx)$.

9.4.2 Construct a few structures, using *Symlog*, to illustrate (which is not the same as proving) that the following sentences are quantificationally true.

a. Fa ∨ ¬Fa

b. (∀x)(Hx ≡ Hx)

c. ¬(∀x)Gx ≡ (∃x)¬Gx

d. (∃x)(∀y)Lxy ≡ ¬(∀x)(∃y)¬Lxy

e. [(∀x)Bx → Ba] & [Ba → (∃x)Bx]

9.4.3 Construct a few structures, using *Symlog*, to illustrate (which is not the same as proving) that the following sentences are quantificationally false.

a. Fa & ¬Fa

b. (∃x)¬(Fx ≡ Fx)

c. ¬[[(∃x)Fx → Gb] ≡ (∀x)(Fx → Gb)]

d. (∀x)Fx & ¬Fa

e. ¬[(∀x)(∃y)Lxy ≡ (∀y)(∃x)Lyx]

9.4.4 Construct appropriate structures, using *Symlog*, to show that the following sentences are quantificationally indeterminate.

a. Fa

b. ¬Fa

c. (∀x)Fx → Gb

d. (∃x)(∀y)Lxy

e. [(Sab & Scd) & ¬Iab] & (∀x)(∃y)Sxy

9.4.5 Two sentences, α and β, are **quantificationally independent** if and only if there are structures, $\mathfrak{A}_1$ and $\mathfrak{A}_2$, such that (i) $\mathfrak{A}_1 \models \alpha$ and $\mathfrak{A}_1 \not\models \beta$ and (ii) $\mathfrak{A}_2 \not\models \alpha$ and $\mathfrak{A}_2 \models \beta$. Show that (a) Fa ∨ Gb and ¬Fa ∨ Gb are quantificationally independent and (b) Fa ∨ Gb and ¬Fa & Gb are not quantificationally independent.

9.4.6 With the help of *Symlog*, construct a model for the sentence Na & (∀x)[Nx → (∃y)(Sxy & Ny)] whose UD has at least four individuals.

9.5   *Properties of Sets of Sentences and Arguments*

Let us now extend the definition of the satisfaction relation to sets of sentences:

> **Definition.** A structure $\mathfrak{A}$ **satisfies** a set Γ of sentences of PL if and only if $\mathfrak{A}$ satisfies every sentence in Γ.

If a structure $\mathfrak{A}$ satisfies a set Γ, we say that $\mathfrak{A}$ is a **model** of Γ and write $\mathfrak{A} \models$ Γ and $\mathfrak{A} \not\models$ Γ otherwise. Consider the set Γ = {(∀x)Sxax, (∀x)Pxaa, Pbbb}. You can check, as an exercise, that the following structure satisfies the set; that is, it satisfies each sentence in Γ:

UD := {0, 1}
Sxyz := {(x,y,z) : x + y = z}
Pxyz := {(x,y,z) : xy = z}
a := 0
b := 1

Once you have concluded that $\mathfrak{A} \models \Gamma$ by finding that $\mathfrak{A} \models (\forall x)Sxax$, $\mathfrak{A} \models$ ($\forall x$)Pxaa and $\mathfrak{A} \models$ Pbbb, go on, as an exercise, to construct another model of α.

> **Definition.** A set Γ of sentences of PL is **quantificationally consistent**— or simply **consistent** or **satisfiable**—if and only if Γ has at least one model.

> **Definition.** A set Γ of sentences of PL is **quantificationally inconsistent**—or simply **inconsistent** or **nonsatisfiable**—if and only if Γ has no models.

Just as in the case of single sentences, finding a structure which satisfies a given set of sentences may not be an easy task. Thus, answering the question 'Is this set of sentences satisfiable?' or equivalently, 'Does this set of sentences have a model?' may be very difficult to answer.

Quantificational entailment is a relation between a set Γ of sentences of PL and a sentence α of PL.

> **Definition.** A set Γ of sentences of PL **quantificationally entails**—or simply **entails**—a sentence α of PL if and only if there is no structure which satisfies Γ and does not satisfy α.

If Γ quantificationally entails α, we write $\Gamma \models \alpha$; if it does not, we write $\Gamma \not\models \alpha$. So by the definition above, Γ quantificationally entails α if and only if there is no structure $\mathfrak{A}$ such that $\mathfrak{A} \models \Gamma$ and $\mathfrak{A} \not\models \alpha$. That is, there is no structure which is a model of Γ but which fails to be a model of α. Please note that the expression $\Gamma \models \alpha$ does not mean that the set Γ satisfies the sentence α. Only structures (or assignments) can sensibly be said to satisfy sentences or sets of sentences. What $\Gamma \models \alpha$ expresses, in a compressed way, is that any model of Γ is also a model of α. Some examples will help consolidate this point. For instance, since {($\forall x$)Fx, $\neg$Fa $\vee$ Gab} quantificationally entails the sentence ($\exists x$)($\exists y$)Gxy, any model of the set that you construct with *Symlog* will also be a model of the sentence. Then, show with the help of *Symlog* that {($\exists x$)Fx} *does not* quantificationally entail Fa.

> **Definition.** An **argument of sentences of PL** consists of a set Γ of sen-

tences of PL, the **premises**, and a sentence α of PL, the **conclusion**, which is presented as following from the set of premises.

Definition. An argument of sentences of PL is **quantificationally valid**—or simply **valid**—if and only if its set of premises entails the conclusion.

For instance, the following argument expressed in English

Every man is mortal. Plato is a man. Therefore, Plato is mortal.

can be symbolized in PL as

UD := people
Mx := x is a man
Tx := x is mortal
p := Plato

$(\forall x)(Mx \rightarrow Tx)$
Mp
_____

Tp

To test this argument for validity, we write

$\{(\forall x)(Mx \rightarrow Tx), Mp\}, Tp$

where the sentences $(\forall x)(Mx \rightarrow Tx)$ and Mp are the premises and Tp is the conclusion. This is a quantificationally valid argument, as you will surmise by constructing several interpretations in *Symlog*. For each one, you should note that if all the premises, that is, the sentences $(\forall x)(Mx \rightarrow Tx)$ and Mp, are satisfied, so is the conclusion, Tp. While you are at it, examine the following argument for *invalidity* (i.e., produce a structure which is a model of the set of premises but not of the conclusion—a 'countermodel'):

$(\forall x)Sbxx$
$Sbcc \rightarrow \neg Pccc$
_____

Pccc

We mentioned previously that the Models environment in *Symlog* does not constitute a formal procedure—mechanical method—for deciding such matters as logical falsity. It serves to illustrate the semantic definitions just given but is not designed to apply them in the manner of a decision procedure. The interpretational account can indeed be taken further than we have, but it falls outside our scope to examine it in more detail. However, we want at least to point out what would be involved.

For the substitutional account of PL, the tree method of Chapter 7 is as effective a method as it is possible to have.[18] Yet this method could not begin to handle the example about odd numbers encountered at the beginning of the present chapter. For one thing, the set of sentences which was described, {Oa, Ob, Oc, . . . , ¬(∀x)Ox}, is an infinite set, whereas *Symlog's* tree method is limited to finite ones. For another (as we saw), this infinite set exhausts our (infinite supply) of names: a, b, c, . . . are all assigned to odd numbers, leaving nothing behind as the name of an even number. Of course, we *know* that not all numbers are odd and thus have good reason to *say* that there is at least one number which is not odd; only—strange though it may seem—having run out of constants, we are prevented from formulating an atomic sentence which designates an even individual number. The example shows that we are up against the limits of the substitutional method. Informally, however, it should now be easy to see why the set of sentences could be declared consistent on the interpretational account. Here is a model for it. As before, let the UD of 𝔄 be {0, 1, 2, 3, . . .}; let a, b, c, . . . be interpreted as the (infinitely many) odd numbers of this domain; and interpret the predicate Ox as the set {1, 3, 5, . . .} of odd numbers. Clearly, 𝔄 satisfies each of the instances Oa, Ob, Oc, . . . but it also satisfies ¬(∀x)Ox since there is an assignment to x which fails to satisfy Ox (e.g., the one which assigns 4 to x). So the set is consistent on the interpretational account.

This example and similar ones make it evident that the tree method (which was presented in terms of the substitutional account) needs to be adapted to cope with infinite sets. Also, the familiar semantical concepts of consistency and entailment will have to be adjusted to this more complicated world we have briefly encountered, in which it sometimes happens that the correlation between the objects of a domain and the names used to designate them is not one to one. The interpretational account would become the basis for this fuller account, but that is another story.

Exercises

9.5.1 Construct appropriate structures, using *Symlog,* to show that the following sets are satisfiable.

a. {Fa & Gb, Fa → ¬(∀x)Gx}

b. {Fa & Fb, (∀x)(Fx → Gx), (∃x)[Gx & (∀y)(Gy → Iyb)]}

c. {(∃x)Fx, (∃x)Gx, (∀x)(Fx ≡ ¬Gx), (∀x)(∀y)((Fx & Gy) → Hxy)}

d. {(∃x)(∀y)Syxy, (∃x)(∀y)Pyxy, (∃x)(∀y)Pyxx}

e. {(∀x)Cxx, (∀x)(∃y)¬Cxy}

9.5.2 Give a model for the set {(∀x)Sxex, (∀x)(∃y)Sxye} whose UD has at least two elements.

9.5.3 A set of sentences Γ of PL is **quantificationally independent** if and only if for each sentence α ∈ Γ there is a structure 𝔄 such that 𝔄 ⊨ Γ − {α}

---

[18] See the discussion of this point in section 7.3.

but $\mathfrak{A} \nvDash \alpha$. Show that the set of exercise 9.5.2 is quantificationally independent.

9.5.4 Construct a few structures, using *Symlog*, to *conjecture* the (quantificational) validity of the following arguments.

a. Fa & Gab

   Gab → Ha

   ─────────

   Ha

b. (∀x)Fx

   ─────

   Fa

c. Gb & (∀x)(∀y)Hxy

   Hca ≡ Fb

   ──────────

   (∃x)Fx

d. (∀x)(Ax → (Bx & Gxa))

   Ac

   Gca ≡ Dcb

   ───────────

   (∃x)Dxb

e. (∀x)(∀y)Cxy

   ────────

   (∀y)(∀x)Cyx

9.5.5 *Prove* that the arguments a, b and c of exercise 9.5.4 are quantificationally valid.

9.5.6 Construct appropriate structures, using *Symlog*, to *prove* that the following arguments are quantificationally invalid.

a. Fb

   Fa → Fb

   ────────

   Fa

b. Fa ∨ Gab

   ────────

   Fa

c. Fa → Gb

   ────────

   (∃x)Fx → Gb

d. Lab

   Lab → Ga

   ────────

   (∀x)Gx

e. (∀x)(∃y)Lxy

   ────────

   (∃x)(∀y)Lxy

Epilogue

Further Developments in Predicate Logic

Since we hope that by now you have acquired a taste for logic, we want to give you some idea of what lies ahead. The formal logic presented in this book, often referred to as classical or standard symbolic logic, was presented in two major waves: sentential logic and predicate logic. Recall for a moment why we found it desirable to move beyond the arguments of SL to examine sentences in finer detail. It was because our logical intuition helps us recognize logical truths and valid arguments, which the tools of SL were not designed to handle. Common sense tells us clearly that if the Toronto Blue Jays won the World Series, then they surely won something. In PL, this conditional sentence is easily shown to be logically true, though not in SL, whose symbolism fails to capture enough of the logical content of the sentence. So we fashioned a new set of tools—constants, predicates, variables, and quantifiers—to accompany those of SL and then we adapted SL's methods of deduction—from SD to PD—to test against our logical intuitions. However, the process of augmenting our logic toolbox does not seem to reach an end. The same intuitions that demanded the move from SL to PL tell us that there is further logical content that even our PL symbolism fails to capture. We brushed up against this fact in Chapter 6 in the brief discussion of the concepts of identity and definite descriptions. The use of a special symbol to express identity (a predicate constant) enables us to capture sentences such as 'The Toronto Blue Jays are the American League team that played in the 1992 World Series,' and 'The American League team that played in the 1992 World Series won that series.' Logical intuition tells us clearly that these two sentences entail the further sentence 'The Toronto Blue Jays won the Series'; however, none of the rules that were introduced for PL's deductive system, PD, can establish that fact. (You may want to assure yourself that this is the case.) Let us take just a moment, then, to see how the formal system of PD might be enriched to handle derivations involving identity. What is needed are rules that will articulate what is meant by the identity relation, that is, rules enabling us to manage sets of statements containing this relation. Traditionally, the so-called **law of identity** expressed part of this recognized meaning. In quantificational terms (and using the familiar symbol for identity introduced in Chapter 9), this law can be written as a universal quantification:

$$(\forall x)(x = x)$$

That is, take anything x you will, that thing is the same as itself, or more simply, everything is identical to itself. This sentence expresses a logical truth. Thus, each of its instances, $a = a$, $b = b$, $c = c$ and so on is itself logically true, and its negation $\neg(a = a)$, $\neg(b = b)$, $\neg(c = c)$ and so on is logically false—false in any situation. Note that atomic identity sentences in which the *same* individual constant is repeated, such as $a = a$, form an exception to the semantical account of atomic sentences given in both SL and PL: Atomic identity sentences of this sort are always true; all other atomic sentences are contingent, including atomic identity sentences made up of two *different* atomic constants, such as $a = b$, $a = c$, $c = b$ and so on. In any given case, whether something called a is none other than the thing called b depends on facts, not on syntactic form. It happens to be a fact that the French emperor known as 'Napoleon' also bore the name 'Bonaparte' (so the sentence $n = b$ is true). It is false, though, that 'Napoleon's spouse' refers to the person known as 'Marie Antoinette' (which therefore makes the sentence $s = m$ false). Now, assuming that it is true that, say, $a = b$, we can engage another logical intuition about identity: Any claim that applies to a will be equally expressible as a claim about b. For example, given that Napoleon lost the Battle of Waterloo, it must be the case that Bonaparte lost the Battle of Waterloo. Napoleon and Bonaparte are not two different people: 'They' are really one and the same person; we are simply using two names for the same individual. Whenever $t_1 = t_2$, then, the legitimate substitution of t_1 in sentences about t_2 (and vice versa) constitutes another important part of the meaning of the identity relation.

To develop derivations involving identity sentences, a new pair of deduction rules is needed. The law of identity stands in the background of the identity introduction rule, which says that at any point within a derivation an atomic identity sentence containing the same individual constant may be introduced. The elimination rule for identity is a license for substituting one constant—name—for another in any sentence during the course of a derivation, given an existing (unnegated) atomic identity sentence containing two individual constants. Here are both rules in schematic form:

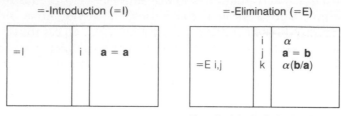

Note: Partial substitution is allowed.

With these two rules added to PD, you could now show in a formal way that the Toronto Blue Jays won the World Series.

A further enrichment of PL's symbolism can be obtained by adding what are known as **functional terms**. Just as predicate symbols denote relations, function symbols denote operations or functional relations, such as *plus*, *times*, or *successor*—expressions that are particularly useful to have on hand when the UD being described consists of numbers. A functional term combines a k-ary function symbol, f, with k terms $t_1, t_2, \ldots , t_k$, the result being an expression of the form $ft_1t_2 \ldots t_k$. This expression compresses a distinct but complicated meaning: $ft_1t_2 \ldots t_k$ refers to that particular object that is the value—result—of applying the function denoted by f to the objects denoted by $t_1, t_2, \ldots , t_k$. For instance, if f is interpreted as the *times* function, and the constants a and b are interpreted as the numbers 2 and 3, respectively, the functional term fab denotes 6. By importing common arithmetical symbols and using them in the same manner as =, various general truths about numbers can be easily stated:

$(\forall x)(\forall y)(x + y = y + x)$

$(\forall x)(\forall y)(\forall z)[(x < y \ \& \ y < z) \rightarrow x < z]$

$(\forall x)(\forall y)[x < y \rightarrow (\exists z)(x + z = y)]$

It is worth remarking that the addition of functional terms to **PL** yields a system of logic whose descriptive power is essentially equivalent to the fully relational notation used in this text. Nevertheless, they are of obviously great convenience for managing claims and proofs about mathematical matters.[1] Functional terms could also be employed as definite descriptions. For instance, let f denote the function of being the famous teacher of an individual; then fa could denote the person who was the famous teacher of Alexander the Great, and fe could denote the famous teacher of Eloise. This method will work as long as the individual in question (Alexander, Eloise) did indeed have a famous teacher (Aristotle, Abelard), but it becomes problematic when such a mentor does not exist, as happens in the

---

[1] Functions also play an important role outside mathematical contexts: 'The father of,' 'the husband of' or 'the tax of a purchase' are everyday uses of the concept of a function.

case of "the teacher of Socrates." (We are assuming that Socrates was born smart!) In such cases, the analysis of definite descriptions described in Chapter 6 would come into play.

A dramatic increase in PL's expressive power would come from extending the quantificational domain (i.e., the UD) beyond individuals to include also their properties and relations as members themselves. Such a move would comport quite well with other logical intuitions, for in natural language we often refer to properties and relations as though they were a type of object. For example, we say not only that each person has a right to life but also that the right to life (i.e., having a right to life) is inalienable; or we might describe a group of bank robberies as having some common features (i.e., there are some properties that all the bank robberies in question share); or we might affirm that Mario has everything it takes to be a professional organist (i.e., we affirm that Mario has all the required properties). In other words, since we have the resources in natural language to quantify over properties and relations and to build arguments dealing with them, PL's rules of quantification (with appropriate changes in symbolism) could be easily adapted to cover these areas of discourse as well.

Here is a nice illustration of the utility of doing so, and an altogether fitting one. Some three centuries ago, the philosopher Leibniz (whom we spoke of in the Introduction) formulated a famous criterion of identity, known ever since as the principle of the **identity of indiscernibles**. This principle can be symbolized by using an enriched PL symbolism:

$$(\forall x)(\forall y)[(x = y) \equiv (\forall X)(Xx \equiv Xy)]$$

In this notation, x and y are the familiar *individual variables*, and X is assigned the role of being a *predicate variable* (i.e., as ranging over properties of individuals). Leibniz's formula states that any individuals x and y are identical if and only if they share precisely the same properties (every property of x is a property of y and conversely). Leibniz's principle, which many philosophers and logicians have taken to be a self-evident truth, stands in the background of the elimination rule for identity presented previously. Extending its domain of quantification to include properties and relations would qualify PL as a **second-order** system of logic. It would become a third-order system if further modified to enable reference to the properties of properties, and there is no theoretical limit to this progression. The extension of logic into higher-order realms is needed to formalize the more abstract concepts dealt with in some branches of logic itself and in mathematics. As presented in this text, PL is a first-order system of formal logic since the only variables it has are those quantifying over individuals.

Moving in another direction, we want to mention something about alternative semantical interpretations. Standard logic, including the extensions mentioned above, depends on the noteworthy assumption that every statement is either true or false. **Three-valued logic** assigns any of three values to a given statement: true, false and indeterminate. Is there really a middle truth-value between being true and false? Aristotle once reasoned that statements referring to events in the future ought not to be considered either true or false. In that sense, then, 'The sea battle tomorrow will be a victory' is neither true nor false, for the battle has not yet been fought and its outcome is not yet determined. Another way of making this point is to give an epistemic interpretation to the three values, contrasting them in this manner: known to be true, known to be false and not known. Such an interpretation is associated with what is called an **intuitionist** view of formal logic, and it is one that deeply affects the assessment of statements and arguments. For example, a statement from SL such as $P \lor \neg P$ would no longer count as a truth-functional truth in a three-valued logic (given a suitable definition of the two logical operators $\neg$ and $\lor$), since if both P and $\neg P$ were not known, then neither would be their disjunction, so the statement would fail to be always true (i.e., known).

Other interpretations of the three values are also possible. There are **many-valued logics** that increase the number of "truth"-values to four, five or even infinitely many. In each case, these logics require a suitable definition of the familiar logical connectives by means of "truth"-tables. In the case of an infinitely many-valued logic, for instance, a statement α could take as a value any real number, $v(\alpha)$, in the real closed interval [0,1], and the values of the logical connectives could be set in the following way: $\neg \alpha$'s value could be defined as $1 - v(\alpha)$, a conjunction's value as the smaller of the two values assigned to its conjuncts, a disjunction's as the larger of its disjuncts' values. So, for example, if the values of P and Q are 0.25 and 0.65, respectively, then the value of $\neg(P \ \& \ (Q \lor P))$ would be 0.75. Note that by restricting the set of values to the interval's two end points, 0 and 1, these three definitions match those of the familiar two-valued model of standard logic (letting 0 be false and 1 be true). Many-valued logics have been successfully used in logical theory to show the independence of the axioms of formal systems. They have also found important practical applications in the field of electrical engineering.

In our presentation of PL, the notions of necessity and possibility were 'cashed out' in terms of the results of assigning truth-values to sentences. Suppose that α is a conditional sentence. Then it is possible for α to be true (i.e., α is satisfiable) if and only if there is at least one truth-value assignment to its atomic components on which α bears the truth-value true. But if it is impossible for α to be false, its antecedent entails its consequent: This is what would be meant by calling α necessarily true. However, when it comes to representing the two sentences 'God possibly exists' and 'God necessarily exists', there is no symbol at hand in PL to capture the obvious difference between them. Our logical intuitions recognize that there is a difference even if it is unclear what that difference is. What our intuitions have responded to is said to be the *modal character* of these two sentences. In a modal sentence, either necessity or possibility forms part of the sentence's meaning. Standard logic ignores the modal character of sentences, though it is clearly evident in such sentences as the following:

A square must have four sides.

Anne and Bob may have gotten lost at the zoo.

One cannot be both a professional logician and a professional soccer player.

Modal logic is the prime example of a *nonstandard* logic. To represent the modal character of sentences like those just given, modal logic introduces a special pair of non-truth-functional operators, one for possibility (◇), the other for necessity (□), which it combines with sentences like those of either SL or PL. To illustrate the use of these operators, here are two samples using the syntax of PL (with identity):

Dalí may have painted this canvas but it is impossible for him to have painted it and not painted it.

◇Pdc & ¬◇(Pdc & ¬Pdc)

Necessarily, if two things are equal to a third, they are equal to each other.

□(∀x)(∀y)(∀z)[(x = z & y = z) → x = y]

That modal operators cannot be regarded as truth-functional is evident from a brief reflection. On the one hand, if it is *possible* that P is true, it may or may not be the case that P *is* true. If P *is* true, on the other hand, it may or may not be the case that P is *necessarily* true. Various systems of deductive modal logic have been elaborated in this century. Modal logic has also provided a particularly rich territory for philosophical logic. (Some references are given in the bibliography.) Modal logic itself, however, does not advance any philosophical theses about different types of necessity or possibility (logical as opposed to physical impossibility, for instance) or about whether the world contains such things as necessary facts. All the same, our logical intuition recognizes more than just these two modal properties. Common sense tells us that there is also a great difference between saying that a square must have four sides and that a judge must be impartial. The word *must* is used here in two different senses; in the latter sense, it means 'ought to be' or 'is obliged to be.' The formal analysis of expressions such as these belongs to what is called **deontic logic.**

So far in this survey, we have moved in a horizontal direction by considering ways of expanding the coverage of PL, but from time to time in earlier chapters we paused for some condensed discussion of metalogical questions about, for example, the soundness and completeness of SL and PL. **Metalogic** involves a kind of vertical movement, rising to survey an entire domain of logic in order to analyze and compare the rules used there and to characterize the formal features of that domain and its limits. In the early years of this century modern logic was presented in the form of an axiomatic system, rather like a system of geometry with its axioms, definitions and theorems. Understandably, therefore, the first major contributions to metalogic concentrated on axiomatic systems, but even so, several of the discoveries in metalogic are certain to be permanently recognized for their importance in the history of logic. For example, Kurt Gödel and Alonzo Church, two logicians who made important contributions to logic, established in separate but equally rigorous ways that there are inherent limitations in the capacity of a formal system of predicate logic to determine, for any given sentence, whether or not it is a member of the class of logical truths. Their work concerns what is known as the decision problem. Later on, with the development of natural deduction systems, new species of analysis and description evolved in metalogic, even though the change in emphasis from axiomatics to natural deduction did not essentially alter the results reached by Gödel and Church. A deeper understanding of SL, PL and comparable systems of logic—indeed, of the nature of formal logic itself—can be gained through the study of metalogic, and we therefore wholeheartedly recommend it.

Before ending, we want to call your attention to an exciting prospect for the logician: the use of computers as a tool of analysis and development. Just picture yourself, as a logician, facing the daunting task of having to check for the consistency of a set of sentences numbering in the thousands (a not unusual situation confronting people who work in the field of logic programming); or of wanting to test whether some sentence of PL is satisfied by a certain mathematical structure involving a domain of, say, 50 elements (see Chapter 9); or of wishing to investigate alternative definitions for the conditional connective in a 4-valued logic (a task that requires examining 4,294,967,296 16-row truth-tables); or of merely having to complete a 2,500-line derivation in all its excruciating detail. Such challenges may not exceed the ability of an extraordinarily patient human being who is armed with a pen and much paper, but they are well beyond the limit of time most people would be willing to spend on them. It is in situations like these that computers have already proven themselves to be invaluable research tools. People working in the field of **automated reasoning** have taken up the task of creating computer programs with powerful deductive capabilities and whose job is to assist the researcher in tasks like those just outlined. Much of the effort these days is focused on the design of automated theorem provers—systems that assist the researcher in the interactive construction of formal proofs (very much like the derivations you have done in this text with *Symlog*). In some of these computer systems, humans dictate the overall strategy used to attack a problem while the system is relegated to the task of filling in the details or, even, to explore alternative paths to the problem's solution. Some other systems are more ambitious in scope: Their goal is to automate fully the entire reasoning task.

These last remarks are not meant to be another plug for *Symlog*, which we are sure you have enjoyed using. Without doubt, *Symlog* will extend its scope in the future to include some of the areas of logic that we have described in the past few pages, but that is not now the point. The point, rather, is that *Symlog* is just the beginning.

APPENDIX A

Installing Symlog

If you own a PC and want to install *Symlog* in it, then read this appendix; else, skip the entire appendix.

The following sections describe the minimum system requirements to run *Symlog*, the contents of the *Symlog* distribution disk, directions on securing a copy of the program, installing it and starting it up, as well as advice about certain problems you may encounter in this process. (Instructions to install *Symlog* on a local area network (LAN) can be found in the Instructor's Manual and Guide.) When installing *Symlog* in your PC it is assumed that you have a minimal background of DOS; if not, ask a friend to help you with the installation. *Please read the information in this appendix carefully: If you do, then you will find it easy to install Symlog by yourself, without having to trouble your course instructor or others.*

A.1 System Requirements

The computer system required to run *Symlog* is

IBM-PC or compatible (from humble 8088s to the most powerful PCs).

At least 256K of free RAM. In this minimal configuration, however, you will not be able to take advantage of the Proof Advisor (*Symlog*'s built-in expert system which provides advice when doing proofs). Also, the Models environment (which allows you to explore the formal semantics of predicate logic) will be short in memory, but just about everything else will be unaffected. To be able to invoke the Proof Advisor you need at least 420K of free RAM.

One 360K floppy disk drive, although a hard disk is strongly recommended.[1]

Monochrome or color monitor. No graphics required. *Symlog* supports the IBM text monochrome and color (CGA) cards, Hercules monochrome and color cards, EGA, VGA, and cards which are 100% compatible with any of these.

Just about any printer. To take advantage of *Symlog*'s High Quality print option (available through any of the options in the Print pull-down menu), your printer must support the so-called extended ASCII charac-

---

[1] If you do not have a hard disk but your system has enough memory to create a RAM disk you may want to try setting up one (see your DOS manual on how to do this).

ter set. If your printer does not support this extended character set, then you can always print your work using *Symlog*'s Draft mode.

DOS 3.0 or higher. *Symlog* also runs, as a DOS session, under Microsoft's Windows and IBM's OS/2.

If you are a course instructor, you should know that *Symlog* has built-in network capabilities; that is, it also runs off file servers in DOS-based networks such as Novell's Netware. In such a network environment, *Symlog* supports an unlimited number of users and its performance does not essentially degrade as more users are added to the network. In other words, it is perfectly feasible to have, say, 50 network users working on *Symlog* simultaneously.

A.2   *Securing Your Copy of Symlog*

This text comes with *Symlog*—the software—in one 3.5″ 720K disk and it is ready to be installed in your PC's hard disk. If your PC does not have a 3.5″ disk drive (but it has a 5.25″ drive instead) or your PC does not have a hard disk, then do one of the following:

If your PC has a hard disk (but no 3.5″ disk drive):

1. With the help of a friend who has a PC with both drive formats (3.5″ and 5.25″), simply copy the contents of the *Symlog* 3.5″ disk to a 5.25″ disk;[2] or

2. Your instructor will let you know within the first week of class (or so) how to get a copy of *Symlog* on a 5.25″ disk from one of the campus machines; or

3. Fill out the disk request card that you will find included in this book and mail it to Prentice Hall *right away*. Prentice Hall will mail to you a copy of *Symlog* on a 5.25″ disk.

If your PC lacks a hard disk: See the section 'Installing *Symlog*' below.

The *Symlog* disk comes with one single file on it: EXTRACT.EXE. The file is designed to self-decompress into 42 system files and 407 exercises. Here is a list of these files, as well as a short description of their functionality. (Files marked with an asterisk (*) come into use when *Symlog* is used on a computer network.)

System Files:

| SYMLOG.EXE | *Symlog*'s start-up file. |
| LOGIC.COM | This is the core of the program: the system manager. |

---

[2] You can make a copy of the *Symlog* software for your personal use—as stated in the *Symlog* license agreement—as long as you have purchased a copy of the *Symlog* textbook; else, copying the software constitutes a violation of copyright laws.

LOGIC.000-021	This contains all the logic modules and system facilities.
VSITRES.EXE	The user interface manager.
REMOVE.EXE	The user interface manager's unloader.
EXPERT.COM	*Symlog*'s built-in (proof construction) expert system.
EXPERT.000-005	Auxiliary expert system files.
SYMLOG.BKT	The Logic Booklet (on-line help file).
SYMLOG.GDE	The Reference Guide (on-line help file).
SYMLOG.BOX*	The Mailbox (a text file).
SYMLOG.NWS*	The Newsletter (a text file).
SYMLOG.BIB*	The Bibliography (a text file).
SYMLOG.REP	The Progress Report. (Note: If this file is missing, *Symlog* will create one at the right time.)
SYMLOG.ADV	A temporary text file used by EXPERT.COM. (Note: If this file is missing, *Symlog* will create one at the right time.)
VIDEO.EXE	An installation utility for non-standard video boards/displays.
SYMLOG.CNF	A configuration file. (Note: This file only exists when created with the VIDEO.EXE utility; most systems will not need it.)
FLOPPY.BAT	A utility to install *Symlog* on only-floppy drive systems (i.e., those which lack a hard disk). It can also be used to make a copy of the *Symlog* 3.5″ disk (which comes bundled with the textbook) to a 5.25″ disk.
SYMLOG.FLP	A batch file—it gets renamed to SYMLOG.BAT—used when starting-up *Symlog* on only-floppy drive systems (i.e., those which lack a hard disk).
README	A text file containing last-minute information about *Symlog*. You can read this file with a text editor or wordprocessor, or by simply entering the command type readme at the DOS prompt (and pressing Ctrl-S if the screen scrolls too fast).

Exercises:

Learn Exercises	A collection of files whose names correspond to topics introduced in the text. There should be 257 exercises, classified in ten groups: SL (English-to-Sentential Logic translations), TABLE (truth-tables), SLTREE (SL truth-trees), SD (derivations in SD), SDPLUS (derivations in SD+), PL (English-to-Predicate Logic translations), PLTREE (PL truth-trees), PD (derivations in PD), PDPLUS (derivations in PD+), and MODEL (semantics of PL).

PR Exercises   A collection of 150 files, named PR001 to PR150. As
                      you solve these (and successfully submit them with
                      the Submit menu option) *Symlog* will automatically
                      update your Progress Report. These exercises are a se-
                      lection from the most challenging end-of-section
                      exercises in the text: PR001-PR010 (English-to-Senten-
                      tial Logic translations), PR011-PR015 (truth-tables),
                      PR016-PR020 (SL truth-trees), PR021-PR060 (deriva-
                      tions in SD), PR061-PR080 (derivations in SD+),
                      PR081-PR095 (PL truth-trees), PR096-PR125 (deriva-
                      tions in PD), and PR126-PR150 (derivations in PD+).

A.3 Installing Symlog

We recommend that you first make a backup of your *Symlog* disk and that
you use the backup during installation. Store the original disk in a safe
place. That way, files can be easily restored if damaged. Instructions to install *Symlog* for different computer configurations now follow; but first, a
tip on performance: *Symlog* makes frequent disk access; so, if your PC has a
hard disk, install the program on it (as opposed to running it from a floppy
disk).

PCs With a Hard Disk

As mentioned previously, the *Symlog* disk comes with one single file on it:
EXTRACT.EXE. Copy this file to a directory in your hard disk (e.g., C:\SYMLOG),
and then execute it by typing EXTRACT. The following is worth calling to
your attention:

1. If the directory in which you want to install *Symlog* (e.g., C:\SYMLOG)
   has a previous version of the program, make sure the directory is
   empty.
2. The file EXTRACT will self-decompress into 449 files (42 system files and
   407 exercises). After decompression, you can delete EXTRACT.EXE from
   the hard disk as it is no longer needed.[3]
3. You will need about 1MB of free disk space to install *Symlog* (1.23MB
   to be more precise; only 900K once EXTRACT.EXE has been deleted).
4. The installation takes about 5 minutes.

---

[3] The *Symlog* distribution files were compressed with the file compression utility LHA version
2.13, Copyright (c) Haruyasu Yoshizaki, 1988-1991.

PCs Without a Hard Disk

If your home PC lacks a hard disk then we strongly recommend that you work with Symlog in the computer installations provided by your school. As *Symlog* makes frequent disk access, it will prove more efficient to work from a hard disk than from your floppy-based PC. However, if you need or still want to run *Symlog* from a floppy disk you can certainly do so but you should also keep in mind that, depending on the number and type of floppy drives that your PC has, you may not be able to use certain features of the program. For instance, PCs with a high-density floppy drive will be able to do anything a hard disk based machine would—use *Symlog* to its full power—albeit certain things will be done slower, but users of machines with only one 360K drive will not be able to invoke some facilities such as *Symlog*'s proof expert system or retrieve any of the disk exercises (however, *Symlog*'s exercise random generator can still be invoked and, of course, exercises can always be keyed in from the text). Here we tabulate the restrictions that apply, depending on the number and type of floppy drives:

System Configuration	*Restrictions*
Only one 360K disk drive	(1) You will not be able to access the exercises stored on disk (you can, however, key them in yourself); (2) you will not be able to invoke *Symlog*'s expert system (which provides advice when doing proofs); (3) *Symlog* will not be able to keep track of your Progress Report (not a problem if not required by your instructor); (4) you will not be able to take the System Tour (an on-screen introduction to *Symlog*).
Only one 720K disk drive	You will not be able to access all the exercises stored on disk but only those that will fit in the floppy disk.
Two 360K disk drives	(1) You will not be able to invoke *Symlog*'s expert system (which provides advice when doing proofs); (2) *Symlog* will not be able to keep track of your Progress Report (not a problem if not required by your instructor); (3) you will not be able to take the System Tour (an on-screen introduction to *Symlog*).
Two 720K disk drives	No restrictions.
Both 360K and 720K disk drives	No restrictions.
A high-density disk drive	No restrictions.

You can install *Symlog* on any one of three different floppy disk formats: 5.25″ 360K disks (you will need four disks), 3.5″ 720K disks (you will need two disks), and 1.2MB or 1.44MB high-density disks (only one disk is needed). (Note: If your PC has both 360K and 720K disk drives then install *Symlog* twice, once per each disk format; use the 720K drive to start-up *Symlog* and the 360K drive to retrieve the disk exercises.) Before starting the installation process make sure that the floppy disks are both formatted and empty. (Note: Your disks should *not* be formatted as DOS system—'bootable'—disks as this consumes precious disk space.) You should also label them (Disk 1, Disk 2, etc.). To install *Symlog* on your floppies, do one of the following:

1. With the help of a friend who has a PC with a hard disk (where *Symlog* has already been installed) and a floppy drive like the one in your PC, enter the command FLOPPY and follow its intructions;[4] or
2. Your instructor will let you know within the first week of class (or so) how to install *Symlog* on floppy disks using one of the campus machines.

Installing *Symlog* on a Network or Computer Lab

If you are a technical support professional in need of installing *Symlog* on a network or computer lab where the *Symlog* files will be shared, then see the Instructor's Manual and Guide.

A.4   *Starting-Up Symlog*

Symlog is activated by entering symlog at the DOS prompt. Please keep in mind that when *Symlog* is run from a floppy drive the disk *cannot* be removed from the disk drive.

Starting-Up *Symlog* from a Hard Disk

1. Start-up your system with DOS.
2. Make the directory in the hard-disk where *Symlog* resides the default directory. Then, enter symlog.

Starting-Up *Symlog* from a High-Density Disk Drive

1. Start-up your system with DOS.

---

[4] You can make a copy of the *Symlog* software for your personal use—as stated in the *Symlog* license agreement—as long as you have purchased a copy of the *Symlog* textbook; else, copying the software constitutes a violation of copyright laws.

2. With the *Symlog* disk in the high-density drive, enter symlog. Do not remove this disk from the disk drive.

Starting-Up *Symlog* from a 360K Disk Drive

1. Start-up your system with DOS.
2. With *Symlog's* Disk 1 (or whatever disk contains the file SYMLOG.EXE) in the 360K drive, enter symlog.
3. When you see *Symlog's* Entry Point replace Disk 1 with Disk 2 (or whatever disk contains the file LOGIC.005). Do not remove this disk from the disk drive.
4. If your PC has a second disk drive then place in it any *Symlog* disk containing exercises and access them by invoking the menu option Access under File (see Chapter 1 in the text for details). Enter B:\SYMLOG (or A:\SYMLOG) when the program asks for the 'data directory.' If *Symlog* says that the data directory does not exist or if you do not see any exercises listed on the screen when selecting a *Symlog* environment (e.g., Truth-Tables) then try other *Symlog* disk.

Starting-Up *Symlog* from a 720K Disk Drive

1. Start-up your system with DOS.
2. With *Symlog's* Disk 1 (or whatever disk contains the file SYMLOG.EXE) in the 720K drive, enter symlog. Do not remove this disk from the disk drive.
3. If your PC has a second disk drive then place in it any *Symlog* disk containing exercises and access them by invoking the menu option Access under File (see Chapter 1 in the text for details). Enter B:\SYMLOG (or A:\SYMLOG) when the program asks for the 'data directory.' If Symlog says that the data directory does not exist or if you do not see any exercises listed on the screen when selecting a *Symlog* environment (e.g., Truth-Tables) then try other *Symlog* disk.

Starting-Up *Symlog* from a Network or Computer Lab

Your course instructor should provide you with a handout with instructions on how to access the network where *Symlog* resides and how to activate the program.

Starting-Up *Symlog* from a RAM Disk

1. Start-up your system with DOS.
2. Create a RAM disk (see your DOS manual).

3. Copy the following *Symlog* system files to the RAM disk: SYMLOG.EXE, VSITRES.EXE, LOGIC.COM, all the files LOGIC.000-021, and REMOVE.EXE. (Optionally, you may want to copy as well other files such as SYMLOG.BKT, SYMLOG.GDE, and all the EXPERT files if you want *Symlog* to provide on-line help and expert assistance while you work.)

4. Make the RAM disk the default disk. Then, enter symlog.

5. Access the exercises by invoking the menu option Access under File (see Chapter 1 in the text for details). Enter C:\SYMLOG (or A:\SYMLOG or B:\SYMLOG) when the program asks for the 'data directory.' If *Symlog* says that the data directory does not exist or if you do not see any exercises listed on the screen when selecting a *Symlog* environment (e.g., Truth-Tables) then try other *Symlog* disk.

Starting-Up *Symlog* in Windows or OS/2

To invoke *Symlog* within Windows or OS/2 simply locate its icon (you may have to open some folders for this) and double-click on it; *Symlog* should promptly show up on the screen. Alternatively, you can open a DOS session within Windows or OS/2 and, after moving to the directory where *Symlog* is located, enter symlog.

A.5   Other Issues

Here we provide some suggestions in case you run into some problems when running *Symlog*.

The VIDEO.EXE Utility

The VIDEO utility should be used if *Symlog's* text color defaults do not display properly on your computer screen.

When *Symlog* is invoked it automatically tries to determine the video display configuration of the PC in which it is run. Based on this information *Symlog* then selects a suitable foreground/background color combination (or its monochrome counterpart) for the text to be displayed on the screen. In the unlikely event that *Symlog* does not display properly in your PC's screen (or if you cannot stand its default color selection) the VIDEO utility may solve the problem. With this utility you can explicitly specify the kind of video display adaptor/screen monitor that your PC has (mono/mono, color/mono, or color/color). The utility also allows you to cycle through all the possible foreground/background text color combinations until you find one that works with your system. You can independently assign different foreground/background color combinations to *Symlog's* text editors, menus and error messages, warning messages, the Entry Point screen, and its opening logo screen. Your selections are saved in a configuration file—SYMLOG.CNF—that *Symlog* will read at start-up time. (If you are a network supervisor in need of creating different configuration files for different workstations see the Instructor's Manual and Guide for more details.)

Finally, if you run *Symlog* from a floppy disk make sure that the SYMLOG.CNF configuration file is on the same disk as LOGIC.COM.

Questions & Answers

Here we list a number of problems, and their *possible* solutions, that you may encounter when using *Symlog* in your PC[5].

Problem	The *Symlog* disk that comes with the book is a 3.5″ disk but my PC has only 5.25″ disks drives. What do I do?
Solution	Read the section 'Installing *Symlog*' in this appendix.
Problem	*Symlog* comes as a single file that must be decompressed in a hard disk, but my PC lacks a hard disk. What do I do?
Solution	Read the section 'Securing Your Copy of *Symlog*' in this appendix.
Problem	I am trying to install *Symlog* on floppy disks using the FLOPPY utility but, when doing so, it displays the message 'Insufficient disk space.'
Solution	Your floppy disks are either not empty or they were formatted with the DOS system on them (and which uses precious disk space). Empty your disks or reformat them again without placing the DOS system on them (i.e., use the format DOS command as opposed to format/s). Also, some floppy disks claim to be high-density but they can only store about 800K; treat them as if they were 720K disks.
Problem	When I run *Symlog* it stops unexpectedly.
Solution	*Symlog*'s error handler has caught an unrecoverable internal error. Here are some possibilities: (1) The default directory from which *Symlog* is invoked is not the directory where the *Symlog* files are. Move to the directory where *Symlog* is located and then invoke the program again; or (2) if you run *Symlog* from a floppy disk, do not remove the *Symlog* disk from the disk drive; or (3) one of the system files LOGIC.000 to LOGIC.010 or LOGIC.012 to LOGIC.021 is missing. Get it back from the distribution disk; or (4) *Symlog* interferes with a memory resident utility. Remove it; or (5) your system is low in memory. Get more or use another PC.
Problem	When I run *Symlog* the screen remains blank with a flashing cursor in the upper left corner.
Solution	*Symlog* is running all right but, for some reason, its user in-

---

[5] Technical note: When we say below that your PC may be low in memory we mean that it has less than 640K of RAM. Adding more RAM beyond 1MB does not help, as DOS itself cannot recognize the extra memory.

terface manager is not active (this could have happened if, by accident, the file logic.com was activated prior to entering symlog). Restart your PC and run *Symlog* again by typing symlog.

Problem   I run *Symlog* as explained above; yet, the screen is still blank.

Solution   Assuming that your screen monitor is on, there are two possible reasons for this: (1) you may have some memory resident utilities (TSRs) in your system which interfere with *Symlog*. Remove them; or (2) your PC has a video display board wholly incompatible with *Symlog* (an unlikely event). Use another PC.

Problem   The textual information that *Symlog* displays on the screen is hard to read: It seems blurred, it has a strange 3-D effect, and/or some characters can barely be distinguished from their background.

Solution   Use *Symlog*'s VIDEO.EXE utility, as explained in the section 'The VIDEO.EXE Utility' in this appendix.

Problem   *Symlog* is running fine but when I retrieve files (with Retrieve under the File menu) *Symlog* does not list on the screen any of the exercises recommended in the text. Where are they?

Solution   They are probably on a different disk or DOS directory: Carefully read about the Access option in Chapter 1, '*Symlog*'s Tools.' If you are running *Symlog* from a floppy disk then you should read again the section 'Installing *Symlog*' which lists some restrictions (related to accessing files) that may apply to your PC. If you are running *Symlog* from your school's network then ask your lecturer for instructions.

Problem   When I retrieve exercises from the disk *Symlog* actually retrieves new—blank—exercises. Why?

Solution   If this happens to you repeatedly with several exercises it is because the files have been improperly set as *read-only* when installing *Symlog*. Let the network lab supervisor (or your lecturer) be aware of the situation right away.

Problem   I have a PC with only one floppy disk drive and the start-up instructions tell me that I cannot remove the disk from the drive. How can I then retrieve the disk exercises?

Solution   If yours is a 360K drive then you can't. If it is a 720K drive then try first to place as many exercises as will fit on the floppy disk from which *Symlog* is run. (As you only have one drive, the copying must be done on another machine with two drives.)

Problem   When doing problems with *Symlog* I don't get the logic connectives (¬, &, etc.) on the screen; instead I see 'foreign' characters (such as é, ü, ç, etc.).

Solution   (1) Your system has a memory resident utility which remaps the standard ASCII alphabet (a probable situation in a PC being used for foreign languages). Remove the utility before calling *Symlog*; or (2) your system has a different—foreign—keyboard driver (e.g., european-type keyboard driver). See your DOS manual on how to start-up your system with an american-type keyboard driver; or (3) your system has a special-purpose ROM character chip. Replace it or use another PC.

Problem   I am trying to select items from the menus but the cursor—arrow—keys don't seem to respond.

Solution   You have accidentally pressed the key NumLock (which deactivates the cursor keys and activates the numeric key pad). Press NumLock again.

Problem   When getting a hardcopy of my work the printer prints 'funny' characters.

Solution   The printer does not support *Symlog*'s High Quality printing mode; print using Draft mode instead. In this mode some logic symbols will print differently as they appear on the screen: ~ for ¬, > for →, = for ≡, E for ∃ and A for ∀. However, if in the unlikely event that derivation or truth-table horizontal and vertical lines still get printed as strange symbols, as numbers or as letters *even in Draft print mode* try this: Print your work to a disk (as opposed to a printer) using the option To Disk in the Print menu. Then, quit *Symlog*, invoke your favourite wordprocessor, retrieve the 'printed' files into it and, finally, print them—this time to a real printer—using your wordprocessor commands. More easily, work on your home PC but print with your school's printer.

Problem   I tell *Symlog* to print my work but nothing comes out on my PC's printer.

Solution   Check if your printer is on-line. If when on-line no printout is forthcoming then check the port it is connected to (at the back of your PC). By default, *Symlog* sends its print jobs to your PC's first parallel port (LPT1). If, on the one hand, yours is a parallel-type printer connected to your PC's second parallel port (LPT2) then either connect the printer's cable to LPT1 or invoke *Symlog* with the command symlog /p which tells it to send print jobs to LPT2. If, on the other hand, your printer is a serial-type printer (i.e., it is connected to COM1, COM2, etc.) then use the DOS command

mode to redirect the output from the parallel port to the se-
rial port—see your DOS manual for details. If all fails, work
on your home PC but print with your school's printer.

Problem   When I ask for advice, the Proof Advisor can't be activated.

Solution   If, on the one hand, *Symlog* displays a message saying that
it *cannot find* the Proof Advisor then it is probably because
you are running *Symlog* from a 360K floppy drive, in which
case the Proof Advisor is not available—it does not fit in the
disk. If, on the other hand, *Symlog* displays a message saying that the Proof Advisor *cannot be loaded* then your system
is probably low in memory and you may need to free up
some RAM (e.g., by removing memory resident utilitites),
get more RAM or use another PC.

Problem   I get frequent 'out of resources' or 'out of memory condition' messages. Why?

Solution   Your system is probably low in memory. This is especially
true if the messages occur when submitting symbolizations
in SL or when invoking the Proof Advisor when doing derivations in SD/SD+. Get more or use another PC with more
RAM. However, if those messages appear *only* when doing
complex symbolizations in PL or, especially, when invoking
the Proof Advisor when doing derivations in PD/PD+ then do
not be too concerned about it: There are deep reasons—
both metalogical and technical—for those messages which
cannot be briefly stated here.

Problem   I have enjoyed learning symbolic logic with *Symlog*. How
can I get new upgrades of the software?

Solution   Purchase a copy of a newer edition of the textbook,
whenever it becomes available.

Problem   I believe I have detected a problem in the software, or I
have thought up a feature which could nicely improve
Symlog. How can I report it?

Solution   Tell your instructor about it or, better still, write directly
to:

SYMLOG PROJECT
Att: Frederic D. Portoraro
Department of Philosophy
University of Toronto
215 Huron Street, 9th floor
Toronto, Ontario M5S 1A1
Canada

Your Computer System

Since you are going to be learning symbolic logic with the help of a computer but may know very little about computers in general, we want to offer some basic information that you will find helpful before beginning to read Chapter 1, '*Symlog*'s Tools.' This information concerns your computer; the routines that will soon become second nature as you progress with *Symlog*; and the keyboard, which will be your communication link with *Symlog*.

B.1 Your Computer System

Computers are electronic machines with very few moving parts which move 'packets' of electronic signals at lightning speed. The signals are mainly of two different sorts: (1) electronic data, information which has been 'fed' to the computer, and (2) instructions, which direct the computer to perform operations on the data. The instructions given to a computer fall into two different classes. The first consists of instructions bundled together into a comprehensive series of steps and routines which are intended to make the computer perform a certain kind of activity, such as the processing of numbers or words. These bundles of instructions are called **programs**, and they are often referred to as **software** to distinguish them from the various physical components of a computer (the **hardware**). The other sort of instructions are given by the person who uses a particular program to carry out a particular task, for instance, comparing the monthly mortgage charges for a 15-year or 20-year period or inserting a new paragraph in an essay between two already written. *Symlog* is a program of symbolic logic. You cannot use it to figure out your mortgage payments or write a term paper, but you can learn to evaluate and construct arguments. The program will transform your computer into a personal assistant for learning logic.

Think of programs as highly specialized servants who are ready to carry out a vast number of instructions on your behalf. Programs stand midway between you, the user, and your computer. You tell the program what to do, and at once the program tells the computer what to do and then brings back the results to you, often in a fraction of a second. A program is a multilingual servant, too. It recognizes the commands that you give and then translates them into language which the computer will understand; fortunately, the user is not required to learn any of the technical languages which computers (and the experts who write programs for them) understand. *Symlog* itself was written in a particular computer language, but to work with the program you will not have to know this language or learn anything about computer programming. When you type instructions to *Symlog* from the keyboard, the program directs the computer to reproduce those instructions on your screen in a legible manner so that you can see what you have typed and proceed to act on the results and, because of this feature, computer programs are called interactive. However, one important difference between programs and servants should never be forgotten. Unlike a 'good servant,' a computer program will not try to guess what you are trying to tell it or helpfully anticipate your every move. You have to tell a program precisely what you want, otherwise it will either do nothing at all or respond that the command is incorrect. The commands you give must be the kind it was programmed to accept. *Symlog* was designed to make it easy to learn and use its commands, and you will soon find them becoming second nature (some of *Symlog*'s commands are no other than the rules of logic themselves).

Computer programs are stored in the form of code recorded on a physical medium called a disk. Your computer is sure to have a slot for holding a removable **floppy disk;** it may also have a built-in '**hard**' or '**fixed**' disk as well. These disks can store not only programs but also the data created by the user with the help of those programs. A disk functions somewhat like an audio- or videocassette. It can be recorded on and recorded over; the contents of one disk can be copied to another; the contents can also be erased, in whole or in part. A disk's programs or data are read by the computer and stored in its main memory (called **RAM,** for random access memory), where it can be accessed with great speed. New data which a user creates by means of a program are also stored in RAM. It is most important to understand that a computer's main—RAM—memory is temporary. When the computer is switched off, whatever was stored in RAM disappears, whatever filled its memory vanishes, so that unless a copy of these new data was recorded on disk before power was turned off, they no longer exist. Therefore it is essential that any data which you wish to save be recorded on disk. In this way, the data can be retrieved later on (read into RAM) when needed, and subsequent changes can then be rerecorded for further use. The early chapters of *Symlog* mention time and again the importance of saving your work, so you will have plenty of opportunity to acquire this indispensable habit.

Data created while you are using a program are stored in units of information called **files.** (Programs themselves are also stored in files.) The routines of copying files, transferring them and recopying or erasing them, which *Symlog* uses, conform to a convention established for the large family of personal computers known as IBM compatibles. This convention is set by DOS, which stands for disk operating system. **DOS** is itself a piece of software, a master program designed to monitor and direct the flow of signals from one part of the computer to another, keep track of its memory, group sets of files into **directories** and manage file-handling routines including the printing of files. The DOS program is read by the computer when it is switched on and automatically loaded into its memory (the process called **booting**) before any specific programs are loaded. Thus, *Symlog*'s routines regarding files are in fact those of DOS itself (and if you are already familiar with either DOS or another program conforming to this standard, you will already be familiar with them). It is worthwhile to mention two of these routines here. For a floppy disk (of either the 5.25" or 3.5" size) to be recorded on for the first time, it must be **formatted** as a DOS-type disk. Details about this procedure will be found in your DOS manual. For a file to be stored, DOS requires that it be given a unique name, that is, a name not shared with any other file in the same directory on the disk. The name of a file must consist of alphanumeric characters only (letters or numbers, in any combination); it must have at least one character but not more than eight. DOS file names may also carry an optional component called an **extension,** which is made up of a dot ('.') plus up to three additional alphanumeric characters. *Symlog* adds its own extensions to file names in order to keep track of them. The rest of the name is up to you. However, *Symlog* will tell you if a name you have selected is unacceptable (it may be a name already in use, it may be too long or it may have nonalphanumeric characters). In the early chapters, particular file names will be suggested so that you can become quickly familiar with this feature of DOS. *Symlog* will also make it easy for you to see a list of your own data files as well as of those files which contain logic exercises. The program also makes it easy for you to store, copy and retrieve files. These matters are explained in '*Symlog*'s Tools.'

The computer on which you will be operating *Symlog* will be either self-contained or part of a network. A **computer network** is a set of several personal computers linked together in a way which allows one of them, often called a **server,** to act as a storehouse of programs that can be summoned by the other computers. A server makes it possible to communicate information (including messages) across the network and also provides access to printers, so that you can take away a 'hard copy' of any of your files. Some networks are large and sophisticated. If you are operating *Symlog* on a network, the person in charge will explain how to 'log in' to the network, access *Symlog*, format floppy disks, save and copy data on them and print files.

B.2   Your Keyboard

When you operate a computer program you *look* at a screen and *handle* a keyboard. By typing on the keyboard you enter data and commands into the computer's memory; on the screen you will see what you have typed and the results of your commands. Once your computer has been started, but before you summon a specific program such as *Symlog*, you are likely to see two things on your screen, a prompt and a cursor. The **prompt** is a marker which indicates to the user that the computer's operating system (DOS) stands ready to accept a DOS command. Prompts can take various forms, such as A>, C:>, or F:\>, depending on how your computer has been configured and whether it is part of a network. Immediately to the right of the prompt is the **cursor,** taking the form of a bright, flashing square or straight line. The cursor marks the exact spot on the screen where whatever you type at the keyboard will begin to appear. The cursor advances from left to right as you type. Once you have loaded *Symlog* into memory (by typing the required command at the DOS prompt), the prompt will disappear but the cursor will remain to locate your position on the screen. Now let us see what you can do with the keyboard.

Figure B.1 depicts a standard keyboard of an IBM personal computer. As you can see, some of the keys have their names indicated as they are referred to in this text. Your keyboard may look slightly different: It may have 12, as opposed to just 10, function keys across the top, and the Arrow keys may be located in a separate area by themselves. In any case, your computer keyboard resembles very much the standard keyboard of a typewriter. For instance, the **Space Bar** is used to type blank spaces between words. Characters appear in uppercase or in lowercase, depending on whether any of the **Shift** keys is pressed at the time of typing or not. If the key **Caps Lock** is pressed, it activates the capital letters in the keyboard until it is pressed again. Having Caps Lock activated makes any letters you type appear as capital letters in your screen. Notice, however, that this feature applies just to the letters in the keyboard; even if Caps Lock has been pressed so that capital letters are obtained when typing, if you want to get in your screen an opening parenthesis, say, you still have to press one of the Shift keys at the time of typing the key containing number 9 and the opening parenthesis. In other words, Caps Lock acts on capitalization of the letters but not on the uppercase of all the keys in the keyboard. Also, if Caps Lock is down and you press one of the Shift keys at the time of typing letter M, what you get on the screen is a lowercase m; that is, Caps Lock reverses the function of the Shift keys. In this text, whenever we ask you to press, say, Shift-C, what we mean is that you type letter C *while you are holding down* one of the Shift keys.

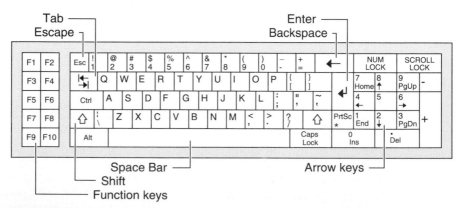

Figure B.1

When you use *Symlog* you will notice that whenever you are typing, there is a blinking light telling you where you are on the screen at that moment. As you know from the previous section, this blinking light is the cursor. In general, the cursor can be moved about the screen freely by using the **Left, Right, Up** and **Down Arrow** keys. Each time the Left or the Right Arrow key is pressed, the cursor moves one character to the left or to the right, respectively. Each time the Up or the Down Arrow is pressed, the cursor moves one line up or down, respectively. The arrow keys are also used to select the different options being offered by the so-called OPTIONS menu.

We all make typing mistakes that need to be corrected. If you type by mistake, say, PROOFF, and you want to get rid of the last F, all you have to do is position the cursor on the character right after the unwanted F and then press the **Backspace** key once: The cursor moves to the left over the unwanted F and makes it disappear, so that on the screen you end up with PROOF. That is, the Backspace key deletes the character immediately to the left of the cursor. Another way of correcting the same mistake is by using the **Del** key. This key deletes the character on which the cursor is located; thus, if you want to get rid of the second F in PROOF, all you have to do is place the cursor on the unwanted character and then press Del once. That is, the Del key deletes the character at the cursor's current position.

Generally speaking, the **Enter** key is used to let a program know that a certain command is to be executed. For instance, if *Symlog* asks you what name you wish to give one of your files, and you type PROOF1, you still have to press the Enter key before *Symlog* acknowledges the name. In *Symlog*, as you will later see, the Enter key is also used to *evaluate* what you type (i.e., *Symlog* checks whether what you type is right or wrong in the given context).

The **Ins** key acts as a switch; when Ins is activated, whatever you type is inserted into existing text; when Ins is pressed again, it is deactivated, and whatever you type overwrites existing text.

When working with *Symlog*, the **Tab** key differs from that of a standard typewriter; its function will be explained later in the text.

Ctrl and **Alt** are keys that change the behavior of other keys in the keyboard. For instance, typing E by itself will produce a letter E on the screen, but pressing Ctrl-E (i.e., typing E while holding down the Ctrl key) will, under some circumstances, erase some of the contents of your screen completely.

Finally, the keys labeled **F1** to **F10** (F1 to F12 in many keyboards) are called **function keys.** In *Symlog*, pressing F1 will invoke the OPTIONS menu; use the **Esc** key to close a pull-down menu. (Do not worry, you will be reminded of this feature later. The OPTIONS menu, as is explained in Chapter 1, allows you to have access to the features available in *Symlog*.) To minimize memorization, pressing F2 will make *Symlog* display on the screen a list of all the commands available to you (in the current context). F3 is a rather powerful key: If pressed at a difficult spot (or at any time for that matter) when you are engaged in the construction of a logic proof, *Symlog* will provide expert advice about how to proceed. Also, in symbolic logic we use some special symbols that are not present in the standard keyboard. You can obtain these symbols on your screen by using some of the function keys, as shown in the following table. (Alternatively, some of the symbols can also be obtained by pressing other keys in the keyboard which resemble the logic symbols they generate; these keys are also given in the table.[1]) You will learn later what these symbols are used for in symbolic logic.

Function Key	Alternative Key	Logic Symbol
F4	˜ (tilde)	¬
F5	& (and)	&
F6	v (lowercase *v*)	∨
F7	> (greater than)	→
F8	= (equal)	≡
F9	None	∃
F10	None	∀

(Note: Because of hardware restrictions, the existential quantifier symbol, ∃, and the universal quantifier symbol, ∀, will be displayed on the screen as Σ and Π, respectively.)

The **Num Lock** key changes the status of the Arrow keys in the pad on the right side of the keyboard; this pad, instead of acting as an Arrow key pad to move the cursor, becomes a numeric key pad. Thus, if when you press one of the Arrow keys you get on the screen a number instead of a cursor movement, press the Num Lock key once and try again.

If you are not familiar with the keyboard, we suggest you study it with some attention because you need to know it well when you work with *Symlog*. When you are in the middle of a proof in symbolic logic the last thing you want to worry about is where to find the opening parenthesis or a Shift key; thus, get to know where the keys are located on the keyboard.

---

[1] Some of these alternative keys are not available in the Models environment of *Symlog* since there they represent their respective standard arithmetic functions and relations.

Symlog Commands

Here we present a collection of all the commands required to operate *Symlog* successfully. All the commands are given first with a brief explanation of their intended purpose. Following is an entire list of all the commands which you can use as a quick reference guide. Since this guide is something you will refer to quite frequently, we have compiled a list of all these commands in the so-called Reference Guide (under the Help pull-down menu), which can be readily accessed while you work with *Symlog* (pressing the function key F2 will also achieve access.) Some of the commands may appear rather idiosyncratic (e.g., Ctrl-N to insert a line); they actually follow some well-established conventions set by popular PC software packages.

C.1 Special Keys

F1   Pressing F1 from almost anywhere in *Symlog* will invoke the OPTIONS menu.

F2   Pressing F2 will make *Symlog* display on the screen a list of all the commands available to you (in the current context).

F3   Press F3 to ask *Symlog* to provide expert advice on how to proceed in the construction of a proof.

F4, F5, F6, F7, F8, F9, and F10   The function keys F4 through F10 stand F5, for the logic symbols ¬ (tilde), & (ampersand), ∨ (wedge), → (horseshoe), ≡ (triple-bar), ∃ (existential quantifier) and ∀ (universal quantifier), respectively. Alternatively, some of these and logic symbols can also be obtained by pressing other keys in the keyboard which resemble the logic symbols they generate. The following table summarizes this information:

Function key	Alternative key	Logic symbol
F4	~ (tilde)	¬
F5	& (and)	&
F6	v (lowercase *v*)	∨
F7	> (greater than)	→
F8	= (equal)	≡
F9	None	∃
F10	None	∀

Some of these alternative keys are not available in the Models environment of *Symlog* since there they represent their respective standard arithmetic functions and relations. Also, because of hardware restrictions, the existential quantifier symbol, $\exists$, and the universal quantifier symbol, $\forall$, are actually displayed on the screen as Σ and Π, respectively.

C.2 OPTIONS Menu Commands

Up Arrow, Down Arrow	The Up and Down Arrow keys are used to make a selection from one of the pull-down menus in the OPTIONS menu: Use the Up Arrow or the Down Arrow to position the cursor in the desired selection, and press Enter to activate it. For instance, if you have in view the Environment pull-down menu, and if the blinking cursor is in the selection Models, pressing the Down Arrow key moves the cursor one selection down to Truth-Tables. If you now press Enter, you will activate the Truth-Tables environment.
Left Arrow, Right Arrow	The Left and Right Arrow keys are used to select an option from *Symlog*'s OPTIONS menu. Press the Right Arrow or the Left Arrow to highlight the desired option and to open its corresponding pull-down menu. For instance, if you have in view the Environment pull-down menu, pressing the Right Arrow key will make *Symlog* open the File pull-down menu (i.e., the menu to its right).
Enter	Press the Enter key to make your selection, that is, to activate that feature of *Symlog* you are selecting in the menu.
Esc	The Esc key will hide the OPTIONS menu, except when pressed from the Entry Point.

C.3 Note Pad Commands

Up Arrow, Down Arrow	The Up and Down Arrow keys allow you to move the cursor from one row in the Note Pad to the next.
Left Arrow, Right Arrow	The Left and Right Arrow keys allow you to move the cursor to the left and to the right, respectively.
PgUp	Pressing PgUp will place the cursor at the top of the pad.
PgDn	Pressing PgDn will place the cursor at the bottom of the pad.
Home	Pressing Home will place the cursor at the beginning of the line the cursor is on.
End	Pressing End will place the cursor at the end of the line the cursor is on.
Del	Pressing Del will delete the character the cursor is on.
Backspace	Use Backspace to backspace and delete the character at the left of the cursor.
Ctrl-Y	Issue the Ctrl-Y command to delete a line.

Ins	The Ins key is used to toggle the text insert feature on and off. If active, whatever you type is inserted into existing text; when deactivated, whatever you type overwrites existing text.
Ctrl-N	Issue the Ctrl-N command to insert a blank line.
Enter	Press Enter to move to the beginning of the next line (it is just a carriage return, as in a typewriter).
Esc	Pressing the Esc key hides the Note Pad.

C.4   Symbolization Pad Commands

Up Arrow, Down Arrow	The Up and Down Arrow keys allow you to scroll up and down the PREVIOUS and CURRENT symbolization stages (i.e., they bring you, respectively, one step farther from or closer to the answer of the exercise being solved).
Left Arrow, Right Arrow	The Left and Right Arrow keys allow you to move the cursor to the left and to the right, respectively, in the ANSWER section of the screen.
Home	Pressing Home will place the cursor at the beginning (i.e., at the far left) of the ANSWER section.
End	Pressing End will place the cursor at the end of the expression you are typing in the ANSWER section.
Del	Pressing Del will delete the character the cursor is on.
Backspace	Use the Backspace key to backspace and delete the character at the left of the cursor.
Ins	The Ins key is used to toggle the text insert feature on and off. If active, whatever you type is inserted into existing text; when deactivated, whatever you type overwrites existing text.
Ctrl-R	Issue the Ctrl-R command (immediately followed by the Enter key) to retrieve the next exercise—symbolization—from the disk.
Enter	Press Enter to submit your answer.

C.5   Truth-Table Pad Commands

Up Arrow, Down Arrow	The Up and Down Arrow keys allow you to move the cursor from one row in the truth-table to the next.
Left Arrow, Right Arrow	The Left and Right Arrow keys allow you to move the cursor from one column in the truth-table to the next.
PgUp	Pressing PgUp will place the cursor at the top of the pad.
PgDn	Pressing PgDn will place the cursor at the bottom of the pad.
Home	Pressing Home will place the cursor at the beginning (i.e., at the far left) of the field in the pad the cursor is in.

End	Pressing End will place the cursor at the right of the last entry in the row the cursor is on.
Ctrl-S	The Ctrl-S command will place the cursor in the Sentence Field in the pad. Issue this command anytime you want to edit (i.e., change) the sentence or set of sentences for which you are going to construct a truth-table.
Del	Pressing Del will delete the character the cursor is on.
Backspace	Use Backspace to backspace and delete the character at the left of the cursor.
Ctrl-Y	Issue the Ctrl-Y command to delete a row in your truth-table.
Ctrl-E	The Ctrl-E command erases a field—section—in the pad, that is, erases part or all of a truth-table. When you issue this command, *Symlog* asks which field in the pad you want to erase.
Ins	Ins is used to toggle the text insert feature on and off. If active, whatever you type is inserted into existing text; when deactivated, whatever you type overwrites existing text.
Ctrl-N	Issue the Ctrl-N command to insert a blank row in your truth-table.
Ctrl-R	Issue the Ctrl-R command (immediately followed by the Enter key) to retrieve the next exercise—truth-table— from the disk.
Enter	Enter is the Justification command. If this key is pressed when the cursor is in the Sentence Field, *Symlog* accepts whatever you have typed in this field (it is hoped, a sentence or a set of sentences) if it is syntactically correct. However, if the Enter key is pressed when you are constructing a truth-table, *Symlog* checks for correctness in the cell in the truth-table the cursor is on.
Tab	Tab is the Generation command. This command will prompt *Symlog* to generate a truth-value in the current truth-table cell, if possible.
Shift-Tab	Shift-Tab is the Goal Analysis command. This command will prompt *Symlog* to apply the so-called goal analysis method to the current truth-table cell, if possible. This command is especially useful when constructing shortened truth-tables, where you can 'branch' your truth-table rows.
Ctrl-C	The Ctrl-C command is the same as the Enter (Justification) and Tab (Generation) commands, but instead of appplying to a single truth-table cell, it acts on an entire column of the truth-table. When this command is issued *Symlog* asks if you want either (1) to check the entire column in the truth-table or (2) to generate an entire column of truth-values in the truth-table. This command is especially useful when you already know how to construct truth-tables and you are attacking a more sophisticated problem (which requires the construction of a truth-table) in which you want *Symlog* to generate quickly entire columns in a truth-table to save you from doing routine work.

C.6   Truth-Tree Pad Commands

Up Arrow,
Down Arrow

The Up and Down Arrow keys allow you to move the cursor from one row in the Truth-Tree Pad—when entering the set of sentences to be analyzed—to the next. In a branch, they allow you to move from sentence to sentence. They act similarly in the pop-up window with the truth-tree decomposition rules.

Left Arrow,
Right Arrow

In the Truth-Tree Pad—when entering the set of sentences to be analyzed—the Left and Right Arrow keys allow you to move the cursor to the left and to the right, respectively. When constructing a truth-tree, they allow you to jump from branch to branch in the tree.

PgUp

Pressing PgUp will place the cursor at the top of the pad.

PgDn

Pressing PgDn will place the cursor at the bottom of the pad.

Home

Pressing Home will place the cursor at the beginning of the line the cursor is on.

End

Pressing End will place the cursor at the end of the line the cursor is on.

Del

Pressing Del will delete the character the cursor is on.

Backspace

Use Backspace to backspace and delete the character at the left of the cursor.

Ctrl-Y

Issue the Ctrl-Y command to delete a line.

Ins

Ins is used to toggle the text insert feature on and off. If active, whatever you type is inserted into existing text; when deactivated, whatever you type overwrites existing text.

Ctrl-N

Issue the Ctrl-N command to insert a blank line.

Ctrl-T

Issue the Ctrl-T command to begin constructing the truth-tree, after you have entered all your sentences in the pad.

Ctrl-R

Issue the Ctrl-R command (immediately followed by the Enter key) to retrieve the next exercise—truth-tree—from the disk.

Enter

In the pad, press Enter to move to the beginning of the next line (it is just a carriage return, as in a typewriter). In a branch, pressing this key allows you to choose a sentence to which a decomposition rule will be applied. *Symlog* will pop up a window with all the decomposition rules. Pressing the Enter key on a rule selects it; *Symlog* will then apply the rule if possible. For instance, if you select a conditional sentence, say, $P \rightarrow Q$, in a branch and apply the $\rightarrow$D rule to it, *Symlog* will automatically replace the current branch with two new branches, the first of which will contain $\neg P$ and the other Q (plus, of course, the remaining sentences in the original branch).

C.7   Derivation Pad Commands

Up Arrow,
Down Arrow

The Up and Down Arrow keys allow you to move the cursor from one line in the derivation to the next.

Left Arrow, Right Arrow	The Left and Right Arrow keys allow you to move the cursor to the left and to the right, respectively, in a derivation line.
PgUp	Pressing PgUp will move the cursor 20 lines up in the derivation.
PgDn	Pressing PgDn will move the cursor 20 lines down in the derivation.
Home	Pressing Home will place the cursor at the beginning (i.e., at the far left) of the previous field (Justification or Theorem Field) in the Derivation Pad.
End	Pressing End will place the cursor at the beginning (i.e., at the far left) of the next field (Justification or Theorem Field) in the Derivation Pad.
Del	Pressing Del will delete the character the cursor is on.
Backspace	Use Backspace to backspace and delete the character at the left of the cursor.
Ctrl-Y	Issue the Ctrl-Y command to delete a line in your derivation. All sentences in the derivation which appeal to the line being deleted will be marked invalid, and an error message will be associated with each offending line as a reminder. Also, *Symlog* will automatically renumber all the justifications in the derivation, if needed, so that their corresponding theorems appeal to the appropriate lines after the line has been deleted.
Ctrl-K	The Ctrl-K command kills (i.e., erases) an entire *subderivation*. All sentences in the derivation which appeal to the subderivation just killed or to any sentence in it will be marked invalid, and an error message will be associated with each offending line as a reminder. (Note: *Symlog* will not need to renumber all the justifications in the derivation—as with Ctrl-Y or Ctrl-N—since there is no line compression.)
Ctrl-E	The Ctrl-E command erases all the contents of the Derivation Pad.
Ins	Ins is used to toggle the text insert feature on and off. If active, whatever you type is inserted into existing text; when deactivated, whatever you type overwrites existing text.
Ctrl-N	Issue the Ctrl-N command to insert a blank line in your derivation. *Symlog* will automatically renumber all the justifications in the derivation, if needed, so that their corresponding theorems appeal to the appropriate lines after the line has been inserted.
Ctrl-D	Issue the Ctrl-D command to open a new *subderivation*. After opening the subderivation, *Symlog* will ask for its assumption (which you are free not to enter). Also, *Symlog* will automatically renumber all the justifications in the derivation, if needed, so that their corresponding theorems appeal to the appropriate lines after the subderivation has been opened. More commonly, subderivations can also be opened by entering the rule ASSUMPTION in the Justification Field and issuing the Generation command (by pressing the Tab key).
Ctrl-R	Issue the Ctrl-R command (immediately followed by the Enter key) to retrieve the next exercise—derivation—from the disk.
Enter	Enter is the Justification command. When this key is pressed *Symlog* checks your derivation line for correctness. If the sentence in the line is

properly justified, it is unmarked (i.e., flagged as properly derived). Otherwise it is marked invalid, and an appropriate error message is associated with the line.

Tab

Tab is the Generation command. This command will prompt *Symlog* to generate a sentence in the current derivation line according to the rule of logic you want to apply. For instance, if in lines 2 and 5 you have the sentences P and P → (Q ∨ ¬S), respectively, and if in the current line you enter the rule application →E 2,5, then (after you press Tab) *Symlog* will place in the current line the sentence Q ∨ ¬S. Once you learn the effect of a rule of logic, this command is a great type-saving device.

Shift-Tab

Shift-Tab is the Goal Analysis command. This command will prompt *Symlog* to apply the so-called goal analysis method to the current derivation line, if possible. For instance, if the current line has the sentence P → Q, and in the Justification Field you enter the rule application →I 2,10, then (after you press Shift-Tab) *Symlog* will open a subderivation running from lines 2 to 10 having P as assumption and Q as conclusion; the sentence P → Q is unmarked (i.e., flagged as properly derived), the assumption P is automatically justified by the rule ASSUMPTION and the cursor is placed on the line containing Q, which becomes your new goal. Like the Generation command, this is also a great type-saving device. As most derivations (in SD and PD) are more effectively constructed by moving from the bottom of the derivation toward the top, it pays to become familiar with this command.

F3

If at any point in the construction of a derivation you get stuck—you do not know what strategy to apply to reach your goal—expert help is one keypress away: With the cursor on your goal's line issue *Symlog*'s Advice command by pressing the F3 key. After analyzing your (partially completed) work, *Symlog* will suggest 'the most logical thing to do next.' Advice is generated by *Symlog*'s built-in theorem prover, a program which constructs natural deduction proofs in the way you are being taught here. The prover effectively implements the proof construction strategies outlined in the chapters on deduction in propositional (SD) and predicate logic (PD).

Shift-F3

Press the Shift-F3 combination to *redisplay* the advice recently generated—with F3—by *Symlog*.

C.8   Model Pad Commands

Left Arrow, Right Arrow

The Left and Right Arrow keys allow you to move the cursor to the left and to the right, respectively, in the edit line.

Home

Pressing Home will place the cursor at the beginning of the edit line.

End

Pressing End will place the cursor at the end of the edit line.

Del

Pressing Del will delete the character the cursor is on.

Backspace   Use Backspace to backspace and delete the character at the left of the
              cursor.

Ins   Ins is used to toggle the text insert feature on and off. If active, what-
              ever you type is inserted into existing text; when deactivated, whatever
              you type overwrites existing text.

Clear   This command, if *typed* at the Models—dot—prompt, is used to clear the
              pad (i.e., the screen). It does not clear your interpretations!

Edit   *Type* edit at the Models—dot—prompt to change an interpretation. For
              instance, by entering edit F, *Symlog* will display on the screen the cur-
              rent interpretation of the predicate F, if any, for you to edit. When you
              are done with your changes press Enter.

List   *Type* list at the Models—dot—prompt to see your interpretations. For in-
              stance, list UD displays the universe of discourse, and list predicates dis-
              plays the interpretations attached to your predicate symbols. A useful
              form of list is list all, which lists the UD and all your interpretations.

New   This command, when *typed* at the Models—dot—prompt, destroys all
              your interpretations and the underlying structure.

Ctrl-R   Issue the Ctrl-R command (immediately followed by the Enter key) to re-
              trieve the next exercise—model—from the disk.

Enter   Press Enter at the end of your query; *Symlog* will then evaluate it. If
              your query is a command (such as list all or new) *Symlog* will execute it;
              if it is a wff, *Symlog* will attempt to determine if the structure you have
              defined is a model for it.

C.9 BNF Syntax of ML

When constructing structures in the Models environment you communicate
with *Symlog* by using the language ML (for model-theoretic logic). ML is actually the language PL of first-order (relational) predicate logic, as given in
this text, extended with a few operators, which among other things, allow
you to specify the interpretations (and their associated structures) you may
have in mind. The precise syntax of ML is given below, using the Backus-
Naur formalism. The following metasyntactical conventions are used:

⟨...⟩	a class of symbols
⟨...⟩*	zero or more occurrences of ⟨...⟩
{...}+	one or more occurrences of elements in {...}
(⟨...⟩,...,⟨...⟩)	a tuple of zero or more ⟨...⟩'s
{⟨...⟩,...,⟨...⟩}	a set of zero or more ⟨...⟩'s
|	or
::=	defined as

To illustrate, the first **production** (i.e., definition) below says that a *constant* is either the letter a or b or . . . or t. Similarly, the fourth production states that a *term* is either a *constant* or a *variable*. Note that one of the things a *wff* can be is a *predicate* followed by zero or more *terms*. These definitions should all be familiar; they are no other than PL's formation rules.

As also given by the syntax of ML, a *number* is a sequence of one or more digits, and a *string* is a sequence of one or more letters. A *setOfObjects* is a set of zero or more *objects*, where an *object* is either a *number* or a *string*. And so on. Note how the ML syntax rules, as given below, declare valid expressions like UD := {fred, montse, bianca} and Sxyz := x+y=z but they rule out Fx := 3 or a := {(2, 3), (4, 6)} as nonsensical. And now for the syntax:

⟨constant⟩	::=	a | b | . . . | t
⟨variable⟩	::=	u | w | . . . | z
⟨predicate⟩	::=	A | B | . . . | T
⟨term⟩	::=	⟨constant⟩ | ⟨variable⟩
⟨wff⟩	::=	⟨predicate⟩⟨term⟩* |
		¬⟨wff⟩ |
		(⟨wff⟩&⟨wff⟩) |
		(⟨wff⟩∨⟨wff⟩) |
		(⟨wff⟩→⟨wff⟩) |
		(⟨wff⟩≡⟨wff⟩) |
		(∃⟨variable⟩)⟨wff⟩ |
		(∀⟨variable⟩)⟨wff⟩
⟨number⟩	::=	{0 | 1 | . . . | 9}+
⟨string⟩	::=	{a | b | . . . | z | A | B | . . . | Z}+
⟨truthValue⟩	::=	TRUE | FALSE
⟨object⟩	::=	⟨number⟩ | ⟨string⟩
⟨tuple⟩	::=	(⟨object⟩, . . . , ⟨object⟩)
⟨setOfObjects⟩	::=	{⟨object⟩, . . . , ⟨object⟩}
⟨setOfTuples⟩	::=	{⟨tuple⟩, . . . , ⟨tuple⟩}
⟨setTheoreticTerm⟩	::=	⟨number⟩ |
		⟨variable⟩ |
		(⟨setTheoreticTerm⟩+⟨setTheoreticTerm⟩) |
		(⟨setTheoreticTerm⟩−⟨setTheoreticTerm⟩) |
		(⟨setTheoreticTerm⟩*⟨setTheoreticTerm⟩) |[1]
		(⟨setTheoreticTerm⟩/⟨setTheoreticTerm⟩)
⟨setTheoreticWff⟩	::=	⟨truthValue⟩ |
		(⟨setTheoreticTerm⟩=⟨setTheoreticTerm⟩) |
		(⟨setTheoreticTerm⟩<⟨setTheoreticTerm⟩) |
		(⟨setTheoreticTerm⟩>⟨setTheoreticTerm⟩) |

[1] Here '*' is the multiplication symbol (not the grammar symbol standing for '0 or more occurrences').

$\neg\langle$setTheoreticWff$\rangle$ |
$(\langle$setTheoreticWff$\rangle\&\langle$setTheoreticWff$\rangle)$ |
$(\langle$setTheoreticWff$\rangle\vee\langle$setTheoreticWff$\rangle)$ |

$\langle$interpretation$\rangle$	$::=$	UD $:= \langle$setOfObjects$\rangle$
		$\langle$constant$\rangle := \langle$object$\rangle$
		$\langle$predicate$\rangle\langle$variable$\rangle^* := \langle$setOfObjects$\rangle$
		$\langle$predicate$\rangle\langle$variable$\rangle^* := \langle$setOfTuples$\rangle$
		$\langle$predicate$\rangle\langle$variable$\rangle^* := \langle$setTheoreticWff$\rangle$
$\langle$command$\rangle$	$::=$	$\langle$interpretation$\rangle$
		clear
		edit $\langle$constant$\rangle$
		edit $\langle$predicate$\rangle$
		list UD
		list constants
		list predicates
		list all
		new
		F1
		F2
$\langle$query$\rangle$	$::=$	$\langle$wff$\rangle$
		$\langle$command$\rangle$

C.10   Summary of Symlog Commands

We now give a concise summary of all *Symlog* commands. Remember that this summary of commands is accessible to you while you work with *Symlog* through the Reference Guide under Help or by simply pressing F2.

1. SPECIAL KEYS

F1	Call OPTIONS menu
F2	Display commands
F3	Advice (for proofs)
F4, ~	$\neg$ (tilde)
F5, &	& (ampersand)
F6, v	$\vee$ (wedge)
F7, >	$\rightarrow$ (horseshoe)
F8, =	$\equiv$ (triple-bar)
F9	$\exists$ (existential quantifier; actually displayed as Σ)
F10	$\forall$ (universal quantifier; actually displayed as Π)

2. OPTIONS MENU COMMANDS

Up Arrow	Highlight option (up)
Down Arrow	Highlight option (down)
Left Arrow	Open menu on the left
Right Arrow	Open menu on the right
Enter	Select option
Esc	Exit OPTIONS menu

3. NOTE PAD COMMANDS

Cursor Movement Commands:

Up Arrow	Line up
Down Arrow	Line down
Left Arrow	Character left
Right Arrow	Character right
PgUp	Top of pad
PgDn	Bottom of pad
Home	Beginning of line
End	End of line
Enter	Carriage return

Insert and Delete Commands:

Del	Delete character
Backspace	Backspace and delete
Ctrl-Y	Delete line
Ins	Toggle text insert mode on/off
Ctrl-N	Insert line
Esc	Hide pad

4. SYMBOLIZATION PAD COMMANDS

Cursor/Stage Movement Commands:

Up Arrow	Previous stage
Down Arrow	Next stage
Left Arrow	Character left
Right Arrow	Character right
Home	Beginning of line
End	End of line

Insert and Delete Commands:

Del	Delete character
Backspace	Backspace and delete
Ins	Toggle text insert mode on/off
Ctrl-R	Retrieve next exercise

Evaluate Commands:

Enter	Submit answer

5. TRUTH-TABLE PAD COMMANDS

Cursor Movement Commands:

Up Arrow	Row up
Down Arrow	Row down
Left Arrow	Column left
Right Arrow	Column right
PgUp	Top of pad
PgDn	Bottom of pad
Home	Beginning of field
End	End of field
Ctrl-S	To sentence field

Insert and Delete Commands:

Del	Delete character
Backspace	Backspace and delete
Ctrl-Y	Delete row
Ctrl-E	Erase field (erase part or all of truth-table)
Ins	Toggle text insert mode on/off
Ctrl-N	Insert row
Ctrl-R	Retrieve next exercise

Evaluate Commands:

Enter	Justify truth-value in current truth-table cell
Tab	Generate truth-value in current truth-table cell
Shift-Tab	Apply goal analysis method to current truth-table cell
Ctrl-C	Evaluate or generate entire column in truth-table

6. TRUTH-TREE PAD COMMANDS

Cursor Movement Commands:

Up Arrow	Line up, in pad
	Sentence up, in a branch
	Rule up, in rule window
Down Arrow	Line down, in pad
	Sentence down, in a branch
	Rule down, in rule window
Left Arrow	Character left, in pad
	Move across branches, in tree
Right Arrow	Character right, in pad
	Move across branches, in tree
PgUp	Top of pad
PgDn	Bottom of pad
Home	Beginning of line
End	End of line
Enter	Carriage return, in pad
	Choose sentence, in a branch
	Select rule, in rule window
Ctrl-T	Begin constructing truth-tree

Insert and Delete Commands:

Del	Delete character
Backspace	Backspace and delete
Ctrl-Y	Delete line
Ins	Toggle text insert mode on/off
Ctrl-N	Insert line
Ctrl-R	Retrieve next exercise

7. DERIVATION PAD COMMANDS

Cursor Movement Commands:

Up Arrow	Line up
Down Arrow	Line down
Left Arrow	Character left
Right Arrow	Character right
PgUp	Page up
PgDn	Page down

Home	To previous field
End	To next field

Insert and Delete Commands:

Del	Delete character
Backspace	Backspace and delete
Ctrl-Y	Delete line
Ctrl-K	Kill subderivation
Ctrl-E	Erase all
Ins	Toggle text insert mode on/off
Ctrl-N	Insert line
Ctrl-D	Open subderivation
Ctrl-R	Retrieve next exercise

Advice Commands:

F3	Ask for expert advice
Shift-F3	Redisplay expert advice

Evaluate Commands:

Enter	Justify sentence in current line
Tab	Generate theorem in current line
Shift-Tab	Apply goal analysis method to sentence in current line

8. MODEL PAD COMMANDS

Cursor Movement Commands:

Left Arrow	Character left
Right Arrow	Character right
Home	To beginning of edit line
End	To end of edit line

Insert and Delete Commands:

Del	Delete character
Backspace	Backspace and delete
Ins	Toggle text insert mode on/off
clear	Clear pad
edit	Edit interpretations

list all	List interpretations
new	Destroy interpretations
Ctrl-R	Retrieve next exercise

Evaluate Commands:

Enter	Evaluate query (command or wff)

APPENDIX D
Elementary Set Theory

The purpose of this appendix is to introduce some basic concepts of set theory which are required for the reading of this text, in particular for the chapter on the formal semantics of PL, that is, the chapter on structures. Even though these basic set-theoretic concepts are introduced here in an informal way, please understand that set theory has a rigorous axiomatic foundation. We first introduce sets and operations defined on sets; then we explain what tuples are and how to construct some specific sets of tuples, namely, relations.

D.1 Sets

Intuitively, a **set** is a collection of objects. For instance, a group of people is a set; so is a flock of birds and so are all the birds' feathers. Similarly, the infinitely many real numbers greater than 0 but less than 1 also form a set. Sets are usually denoted by Roman or Greek capital letters, subscripted if so desired. Roman lowercase letters are regularly used to denote the objects in the set. We say that an object is a **member** or an **element** of a set if and only if it **belongs** to the set. For example, 2 is a member of the set of natural numbers less than 5. If we let the letter S denote this set, then the fact that 2 is a member of S can be written as

$2 \in S$

Also, the fact that 15 is not a member of S can be expressed as

$15 \notin S$

It is sometimes possible, and often very convenient, to show what the elements of a set are by listing the elements—separated by commas—between braces, as in the following example:

$S = \{0, 1, 2, 3, 4\}$

When listing the elements of a set, the order in which they occur is not important. Furthermore, a set does not change if you list one of its elements more than once inside the braces. For instance, the following three lists

$$\{0, 1, 2, 3, 4\}, \{2, 1, 3, 4, 0\} \text{ and } \{1, 3, 2, 0, 4, 4, 1\}$$

all represent the same set. In set theory, two sets are counted as equal if and only if they have the same elements. Sets can be represented in an abbreviated form. For example,

$$\{0, 1, 2, \ldots, 10\}$$

lists the set of natural numbers between 0 and 10 (inclusive). Here the abbreviation is useful though not essential; in the case of infinite sets, however, the use of dots in the list is necessary, as in the following representation of the infinite set of natural numbers:

$$\{0, 1, 2, \ldots\}$$

Another useful device for specifying a set is by indicating the property that any object must satisfy to belong to the set. For example, letting x stand for any natural number and $\mathbb{N}$ stand for the entire set of natural numbers, the following set

$$\{x : x \in \mathbb{N} \text{ and } x < 10\}$$

is the set of all those objects x such that x is a natural number less than 10. Letting x range over any real number at all,

$$\{x : 0 \leq x \text{ and } x \leq 1\}$$

is the set of all those real numbers which are greater than or equal to zero but less than or equal to one. This is the set of real numbers in the interval [0,1].

There is one set which has no elements—the **empty set,** denoted by $\emptyset$. For instance, the set of all those real numbers greater than 1 and less than -1 is empty (since no real number is greater than 1 and less than -1). Sets can have other sets as members. For instance, the set

$$\{2, \{1, 2\}, 5\}$$

has three members, namely, the number 2, the set $\{1, 2\}$ and the number 5. Do not confuse the set $\{1\}$ with the set $\{\{1\}\}$. Whereas the former has as its only element the number 1, the latter has (as its sole member) the set $\{1\}$. As another example, the empty set $\emptyset$ has no members, but the set $\{\emptyset\}$ has one member: the empty set.

There are sets whose elements are all members of another set. This fact is important enough to deserve a definition in its own right.

Definition. A set A is a **subset** of a set B (or A is **contained** in B), denoted by $A \subseteq B$, if and only if all the elements in A are also in B.

By this definition, the set $\{b, e\}$ is a subset of the set $\{a, b, c, e, f\}$, since every element in $\{b, e\}$, namely, b and e, is in $\{a, b, c, e, f\}$. Similarly, the set of even natural numbers is a subset of the set of natural numbers—$\{2, 4, 6, \ldots\} \subseteq \{x : x \in \mathbb{N}\}$—and the natural numbers is a subset of the real numbers. Note that the empty set is a subset of any set and that any set is a subset of itself.

A **universe of discourse, UD,** is a domain—set—of elements which enable various subsets to be formed. In our previous examples, the UD is the set of (real) numbers. Some of its subsets include the natural numbers, the real numbers between 0 and 1, the even numbers less than 20 and so on. The elements of each of these subsets are drawn from the UD itself.

D.2   Operations on Sets

Sets can be combined to produce new sets by means of set-theoretic operations.

Definition. The **intersection** of two sets A and B, denoted by $A \cap B$, is the set of those elements which are in both A and B.

For instance,

$$\{2, 3, 4, 6, 11\} \cap \{1, 3, 5, 6\} = \{3, 6\}$$

and

$$\{0, 2, 4, 6, \ldots\} \cap \{1, 3, 5, 7, \ldots\} = \varnothing$$

Note that in this last example, the intersection is empty since no natural number is both even and odd. Also, for any set A, $A \cap A = A$ and $A \cap \varnothing = \varnothing$.

Definition. The **union** of two sets A and B, denoted by $A \cup B$, is the set of those elements which are in either A or B.

In effect, this operation combines the members of two sets. If we let $A = \{0, 2, 4\}$ and $B = \{1, 6\}$ then $A \cup B = \{0, 2, 4, 1, 6\}$. Similarly, if $A = \{a, b, c\}$ and $B = \{b, d, a\}$ then $A \cup B = \{a, b, c, d\}$. Also note that for any set A, $A \cup A = A$ and $A \cup \varnothing = A$.

Definition. The **difference** or **relative complement** of two sets A and B, denoted by $A - B$, is the set of those elements which are in A but not in B.

Let the UD be the set $\{a, b, c, d, e, f, g, h, i\}$ and let A, B and C be the following subsets: $A = \{a, b, e, g\}$, $B = \{a, e, f, h\}$ and $C = \{a, b, e, f, h, i\}$. Then, $A - B = \{b, g\}$, $B - C = \emptyset$ and $(C - A) - B = \{i\}$. Also, $\{a, b, c\} - \{c\} = \{a, b\}$ and $\{a, b, c\} - \{a, c\} = \{b\}$. For any set A, one can show that $A - A = \emptyset$, $A - \emptyset = A$ and $\emptyset - A = \emptyset$. For any subset A of the UD, the difference $UD - A$ is called the **complement** of A and is denoted by A^c. Note that in this specific example where A is the set $\{a, b, e, g\}$, A^c is the set $\{c, d, f, h, i\}$. In general, for any UD and any of its subsets A, it is true that $A \cap A^c = \emptyset$ and $A \cup A^c = UD$.

Definition. The **power set** of a set A, denoted by $\mathcal{P}(A)$, is the set of all the subsets of A.

Note that the elements of the power set of A, $\mathcal{P}(A)$, are sets (more specifically, subsets of A). In general, if A has n elements, then $\mathcal{P}(A)$ has 2^n elements. For instance, if $A = \{a, b\}$ then $\mathcal{P}(A)$ has as elements the sets $\emptyset$, $\{a\}$, $\{b\}$, and $\{a, b\}$. Similarly, if $B = \{a, b, c\}$ then $\mathcal{P}(B)$ is

$$\{\emptyset, \{a\}, \{b\}, \{c\}, \{a, b\}, \{a, c\}, \{b, c\}, \{a, b, c\}\}$$

The empty set, $\emptyset$, is a member of $\mathcal{P}(A)$ because it is a subset of A. As for the remaining elements of $\mathcal{P}(A)$, they are constructed by taking the elements one at a time, then combining them two at a time, then three at a time—all the way up to n. Finally, note that $\mathcal{P}(\emptyset) = \{\emptyset\}$.

D.3   Relations

The order of the elements in any set is irrelevant. When it is desirable to put one element into first place, another into second and so on, we speak of sequences or tuples.

Definition. A **tuple** is an *ordered* collection of objects (called the **components** of the tuple).

Tuples are denoted by listing their components—separated by commas—between parentheses. Hence, examples of tuples are (3,1,9), (h,e,l,l,o), (Paul,PHL245,B+) and (Mary,25,logician). Note that since order is important, the tuple (3,1,9) is not the same as the tuple (1,3,9). The **arity** of a tuple is the number of components it has. Thus, the tuple (Mary,25,logician) has arity 3 and (a,a) has arity 2. Tuples with arity k, that is, tuples with k components, are called **k-tuples**. As examples, (T,o,r,o,n,t,o) is a 7-tuple and (4) is a 1-tuple. For the sake of notational simplicity, we will identify 1-tuples with their components. For instance, the 1-tuple (5) will be identified with the number 5 itself. You can also construct sets so that some of their members are tuples. The set

{2, Ø, (32,45,6), 75, (James,21), {Ø}}

has among its elements two tuples: the 3-tuple (32,45,6) and the 2-tuple
(James,21). However, for the purposes of the chapter on structures, we are
especially interested in sets whose elements are all tuples of the same arity;
that is, they are all k-tuples, for some k. For instance, the set of natural
numbers

{0, 1, 2, . . .}

is a set whose members are all 1-tuples, and so is the set of even numbers

{0, 2, 4, . . .}

However, if we are interested in students and their ages, the set

{(Paul,17), (Sue,26), (Mark,29), (Mary,25)}

has 2-tuples as members (and only 2-tuples).

We are interested in sets whose members are all k-tuples because we
are going to use this idea to identify properties and relations in general with
those sets. For example, assuming that the UD is the set of natural numbers,
we can identify 'evenness' with the set of 1-tuples

{0, 2, 4, . . .}

That is, a given natural number x is even if and only if $x \in \{0, 2, 4, \ldots\}$.
Similarly, 'oddness' is identified with the set of 1-tuples

{1, 3, 5, . . .}

Note that the members of the sets are 1-tuples because 'evenness' and 'oddness' are unary relations (i.e., properties). By the same token, 'equality,' being a binary relation, is identified with the set of 2-tuples given by

{(0,0), (1,1), (2,2), (3,3), . . .}

that is, that set of 2-tuples (x,y) where the first component, x, is equal to the
second component, y.

This set could also be expressed as

$\{(x,y) : x = y\}$

Similarly, the 'less than' relation is given by

$$\{(x,y) : x < y\}$$

which also is a set of 2-tuples since 'less than' is a binary relation. Finally, the ternary relation 'sum' is given by

$$\{(0,0,0), (0,1,1), \ldots, (2,3,5), \ldots, (6,8,14), \ldots\}$$

or simply as

$$\{(x,y,z) : x + y = z\}$$

that is, the set of 3-tuples (x,y,z) such that the third component z is equal to the sum of the other two components x and y. By means of this approach, properties and relations are associated with what is called their extensions. An **extension** for a given predicate is the set of elements (for a unary predicate such as 'even'), pair of elements (for a binary predicate such as 'less than') and so on which defines that predicate.

Sets of k-tuples are obtained by the operation of forming the cross-product.

Definition. The **cross-product** of k sets $A_1, \ldots, A_k$, denoted by $A_1 \times \ldots \times A_k$, is the set of k-tuples $\{(x_1, \ldots, x_k) : x_i \in A_i\}$.

What this definition states is that given, say, the two sets A_1 and A_2, their cross-product, $A_1 \times A_2$, is the set of all those 2-tuples (x_1, x_2) whose components, x_1 and x_2, are drawn from A_1 and A_2 (respectively) to form each 2-tuple. As an example, if we let $A_1 = \{a, b\}$ and $A_2 = \{c, d\}$ then

$$A_1 \times A_2 = \{(a,c), (a,d), (b,c), (b,d)\}$$

If $A_3 = \{c\}$ then

$$A_2 \times A_3 = \{(c,c), (d,c)\}$$

and

$$A_1 \times A_2 \times A_3 = \{(a,c,c), (a,d,c), (b,c,c), (b,d,c)\}$$

Note that in general, $A_1 \times A_2 \neq A_2 \times A_1$. However, the equality holds wherever a single set, A, is used to form a cross-product of itself. In such cases, the cross-product $A \times A \times \ldots \times A$ (k times) is written A^k. For instance, if $A = \{a, b\}$, then

$$A^1 = A = \{a, b\}$$
$$A^2 = A \times A = \{(a,a), (a,b), (b,a), (b,b)\}$$
$$A^3 = A \times A \times A$$

$$= \{(a,a,a), (a,a,b), (a,b,a), (a,b,b), (b,a,a), (b,a,b), (b,b,a), (b,b,b)\}$$

.
.
.

By stipulation, $A^0 = \emptyset$. Hence,

$$A^3 = A \times A^2 = A \times A \times A^1 = A \times A \times A \times A^0 = A \times A \times A \times \emptyset$$
$$= A \times A \times A$$

Thus, A^2, being the cross-product of itself taken twice, is a set of pairs. The elements of this set are all the possible 2-tuples which can be formed from the elements of A. Similarly, the elements of A^3 are all the possible triples—3-tuples—which can be formed from the elements of A. And so on. But recall that we have identified binary relations with sets of 2-tuples—their so-called extensions—, ternary relations with sets of 3-tuples, and so on. This discussion leads to our final definition.

Definition. Given a set S, a **k-ary relation on S** is a subset of S^k.

For instance, if the UD is the set $\{0, 1, 2, 3, 4\}$ then UD^2 consists of all the 25 2-tuples—pairs—which can be formed with the 5 elements in the UD. This collection of 2-tuples will include (0,0), (1,1), (2,2), (3,3) and (4,4). That is, the set $\{(0,0), (1,1), (2,2), (3,3), (4,4)\}$ is a subset of UD^2. Since this set is no other than the extension of the binary relation 'equality,' we can see that 'equality' is a subset of UD^2.

Answers to Selected Exercises

Chapter 2: Sentences and Truth-Tables

2.1.1 b, c, e, f, i, j, k, m and o.

2.2.1 b, c, d, g, i and j.

2.2.3 a. Peter is the only person (thing) that eats apples.
c. Peter eats nothing but apples.
e. Peter eats apples.
They all make different claims.

2.2.5 a and d; b and h; c and e; f and j; g and i.

2.3.1 a. simple;   c. conditional;   e. biconditional;   g. conjunction;   i. negation;
k. negation

2.3.2 a. J; T
c. L → M; T
e. M ≡ (J & L); F
g. ¬P & ¬L; F
i. ¬¬¬L; T
k. ¬(L → M); F

2.3.3 a. ¬A
c. ¬(A & B)
e. ¬A ∨ C
g. ¬B → (¬C & ¬A)
i. C → ¬B

2.3.4 a. false;   c. true;   e. false;   g. false;   i. true

2.3.5 a. true;   c. true;   e. true;   g. true;   i. true

2.3.6 a. (C ∨ F) & ¬I
c. ¬((C ∨ F) ∨ I)
e. C → ¬(I ∨ F)
g. (¬S → ¬I) & (¬I → ¬S)
i. F

2.3.7 a. F;   c. T;   e. T

2.3.8 a. F;   c. T;   e. T

2.3.9 a. S → P
c. ¬T & S
e. ¬P ≡ ¬S
g. ((T & D) & S) → P
i. (S & (T ∨ D)) → P

2.3.10 a. ¬A → T
c. (B & C) → (¬T & ¬P)
e. ((A & B) & C) → ¬P
g. (¬B & ¬C) ∨ A

    i. (¬C & ¬T) → (A & P)

    k. ¬A → (¬B & ¬C)

    m.(T & ¬P) → ((¬A & ¬C) ∨ (B & C))

    o. (A & C) → (¬P ∨ T)

    q. ((A ∨ B) ∨ C) → ¬P

    s. P → T

2.4.1 a, c, d, h and i.

2.4.2 The main connective is boxed in:

    a. A → ¬B

    c. ¬(P → Q) ¬

    e. ¬A ≡ (¬B → ¬C)

    g. [¬(¬M ≡ K) ≡ J] & [(L ∨ ¬H) → J]

    i. ¬(¬K & (D → M)) ≡ ¬((D → M) → ¬K)

2.4.3 b, d, e, h and i.

2.4.4 a. true;   c. false;   e. true;   g. true;   i. true;   k. true;   m. true;
    o. true

2.4.5 a. 2; ¬P, and P

    c. 7; ((P ≡ ¬¬Q) ∨ R), P ≡ ¬¬Q, P, ¬¬Q, ¬Q, Q, and R

    e. 8; ¬(¬(A → B) → ¬(A ∨ B)), ¬(A → B) → ¬(A ∨ B), ¬(A → B), A → B, A, B, ¬(A ∨ B), and
    A ∨ B

2.5.1

    TRUTH-TABLE : EX251A

	PQ	¬P ∨ ¬(Q & ¬P)
1	TT	F T T T T F F T
2	TF	F T T T F F F T
3	FT	T F T F T T T F
4	FF	T F T T F F T F

No (more) errors

    TRUTH-TABLE : EX251C

	HM	(H → M) → (¬H ∨ M)
1	T T	T T T T F T T T
2	T F	T F F T F T F F
3	F T	F T T T T F T T
4	F F	F T F T T F T F

No (more) errors

TRUTH-TABLE : EX251E

	AB	¬((A → B) ≡ (¬B → ¬A))
1	TT	F T T T T F T T F T
2	TF	F T F F T T F F F T
3	FT	F F T T T F T T T F
4	FF	F F T F T T F T T F

No (more) errors

TRUTH-TABLE : EX251G

	PQRS	¬(¬P ≡ (Q ∨ ¬R)) → ¬S
1	TTTT	T FT F T T FT F FT
2	TTTF	T FT F T T FT T TF
3	TTFT	T FT F T T TF F FT
4	TTFF	T FT F T T TF T TF
5	TFTT	F FT T F F FT T FT
6	TFTF	F FT T F F FT T TF
7	TFFT	T FT F F T TF F FT
8	TFFF	T FT F F T TF T TF
9	FTTT	F TF T T T FT T FT
10	FTTF	F TF T T T FT T TF
11	FTFT	F TF T T T TF T FT
12	FTFF	F TF T T T TF T TF
13	FFTT	T TF F F F FT F FT
14	FFTF	T TF F F F FT T TF
15	FFFT	F TF T F T TF T FT
16	FFFF	F TF T F T TF T TF

No (more) errors

TRUTH-TABLE : EX251I

	PQ	¬[(P & (P → Q)) → Q]
1	TT	F T T T T T T T
2	TF	F T F T F F T F
3	FT	F F F F T T T T
4	FF	F F F F T F T F

No (more) errors

2.6.1 a. yes;   c. yes;   e. yes

2.6.2 a. nonsatisfiable
   c. satisfiable; (T,F), (F,T) and (F,F)
   e. satisfiable; (T,T,T), (T,T,F), (T,F,F) and (F,T,T)

2.6.3   a. truth-functionally false

TRUTH-TABLE : EX263A

	GM	(G ≡ M) ≡ ¬(M ≡ G)
1	T T	T T T F F T T T
2	T F	T F F F T F F T
3	F T	F F T F T T F F
4	F F	F T F F F F T F

No (more) errors

c. truth-functionally indeterminate

TRUTH-TABLE : EX263C

	BDM	(M & B) → D
1	T T T	T T T T T
2	T T F	F F T T T
3	T F T	T T T F F
4	T F F	F F T T F
5	F T T	T F F T T
6	F T F	F F F T T
7	F F T	T F F T F
8	F F F	F F F T F

No (more) errors

e. truth-functionally true

TRUTH-TABLE : EX263E

	AM	(A → M) → (¬A ∨ M)
1	T T	T T T T F T T T
2	T F	T F F T F T F F
3	F T	F T T T T F T T
4	F F	F T F T T F T F

No (more) errors

g. truth-functionally indeterminate

TRUTH-TABLE : EX263G

	AH	$(A \vee H) \rightarrow \neg(A \vee H)$
1	TT	T T T F F T T T
2	TF	T T F F F T T F
3	FT	F T T F F F T T
4	FF	F F F T T F F F

No (more) errors

i. truth-functionally false

TRUTH-TABLE : EX263I

	A	$A \,\&\, \neg A$
1	T	T F F T
2	F	F F T F

No (more) errors

k. truth-functionally indeterminate

TRUTH-TABLE : EX263K

	DGH	$\neg G \rightarrow (H \equiv D)$
1	TTT	F T T T T T
2	TTF	F T T F F T
3	TFT	T F T T T T
4	TFF	T F F F F T
5	FTT	F T T T F F
6	FTF	F T T F T F
7	FFT	T F F T F F
8	FFF	T F T F T F

No (more) errors

m. truth-functionally indeterminate

TRUTH-TABLE : EX263M

	ABJM	(A ∨ B) ≡ ¬(M ≡ ¬J)
1	TTTT	T T T T T T F FT
2	TTTF	T T T F F F T FT
3	TTFT	T T T F F T T TF
4	TTFF	T T T T T F F TF
5	TFTT	T T F T T T F FT
6	TFTF	T T F F F F T FT
7	TFFT	T T F F F T T TF
8	TFFF	T T F T T F F TF
9	FTTT	F T T T T T F FT
10	FTTF	F T T F F F T FT
11	FTFT	F T T F F T T TF
12	FTFF	F T T T T F F TF
13	FFTT	F F F F T T F FT
14	FFTF	F F F T F F T FT
15	FFFT	F F F T F T T TF
16	FFFF	F F F F T F F TF

No (more) errors

o. truth-functionally true

TRUTH-TABLE : EX263O

	GM	(M & (M → G)) → (G & M)
1	T T	T T T T T T T T T
2	T F	F F F T T T T F F
3	F T	T F T F F T F F T
4	F F	F F F T F T F F F

No (more) errors

2.6.4 For each exercise, both sentences should have identical columns under their respective main connectives.

TRUTH-TABLE : EX264A

	P	P ∨ P, P & P
1	T	T T T T T T
2	F	F F F F F F

No (more) errors

TRUTH-TABLE : EX264C

	JK	¬(¬J & K) , J ∨ ¬K
1	TT	T FT FT T T FT
2	TF	T FT FF T T TF
3	FT	F TF TT F F FT
4	ΓΓ	T TF FF F T TF

No (more) errors

TRUTH-TABLE : EX264E

	EFG	(E ∨ F) & ¬G , ¬[¬(¬E & ¬F) → G]
1	TTT	T T T F FT F T FTF FT T T
2	TTF	T T T T TF T T FTF FT F F
3	TFT	T T F F FT F T FTF TF T T
4	TFF	T T F T TF T T FTF TF F F
5	FTT	F T T F FT F T TFF FT T T
6	FTF	F T T T TF T T TFF FT F F
7	FFT	F F F F FT F F TFT TF T T
8	FFF	F F F F TF F F TFT TF T F

No (more) errors

TRUTH-TABLE : EX264G

	BCE	(C ≡ ¬(B ∨ ¬E)) , (C → (¬B & E)) & ((B ∨ ¬E) ∨ C)
1	TTT	T F F T T FT T F FTFT F T T FT T T
2	TTF	T F F T T TF T F FTFF F T T TF T T
3	TFT	F T F T T FT F T FTFT T T T FT T F
4	TFF	F T F T T TF F T FTFF T T T TF T F
5	FTT	T T T F F FT T T TFTT T F F FT T T
6	FTF	T F F F T TF T F TFFF F F T TF T T
7	FFT	F F T F F FT F T TFTT F F F FT F F
8	FF.F	F T F F T TF F T TFFF T F T TF T F

No (more) errors

TRUTH-TABLE : EX264I

	LPQ	P ≡ ¬P , ¬(L ∨ ¬L) ∨ (Q & ¬Q)
1	TTT	T F FT F T T FT F T F FT
2	TTF	T F FT F T T FT F F F TF
3	TFT	F F TF F T T FT F T F FT
4	TFF	F F TF F T T FT F F F TF
5	FTT	T F FT F F T TF F T F FT
6	FTF	T F FT F F T TF F F F TF
7	FFT	F F TF F F T TF F T F FT
8	FFF	F F TF F F T TF F F F TF

No (more) errors

2.6.5   a. True. If α is truth-functionally true then any truth-value assignment satisfies α. Since any truth-value assignment which satisfies α falsifies $\neg\alpha$, no truth-value assignment satisfies $\neg\alpha$, and by definition, $\neg\alpha$ is truth-functionally false.

       c. True. If α and β are truth-functionally false then any truth-value assignment falsifies them both and, by the definition of &, falsifies α & β as well. Hence, the conjunction of α and β, α & β, is also truth-functionally false.

       e. True. If α and β are truth-functionally equivalent then any truth-value assignment which satisfies α satisfies β too and, by the definition of $\equiv$, satisfies $\alpha \equiv \beta$ as well. Similarly, any truth-value assignment which falsifies α falsifies β too and, again by the definition of $\equiv$, satisfies $\alpha \equiv \beta$. Hence, any truth-value assignment, whether it satisfies α (and β) or not, satifies $\alpha \equiv \beta$, and by definition, $\alpha \equiv \beta$ is truth-functionally true.

2.7.1   For each exercise, assume there is a truth-value assignment which falsifies the sentence (i.e., place an F under the sentence's main connective), and by backward truth-table construction, derive a contradiction from this assumption.

2.7.2   For each exercise, assume there is a truth-value assignment which satisfies the sentence (i.e., place a T under the sentence's main connective), and by backward truth-table construction, derive a contradiction from this assumption.

2.7.3   For each exercise, use backward truth-table construction to produce a truth-value assignment which satisfies the sentence and another which falsifies it. That is, the assumption that the sentence is T (or F) should not lead to a contradiction but to the desired satisfying (falsifying) truth-value assignment.

2.7.4   To test if a pair of sentences, α and β, are truth-functionally equivalent, simply test if $\alpha \equiv \beta$ is truth-functionally true. That is, for each exercise, take the pair of sentences and form their biconditional; then assume there is a truth-value assignment which falsifies it (i.e., place an F under $\equiv$), and by backward truth-table construction, derive a contradiction from this assumption.

2.7.5 $(\alpha \vee \beta) \vee \delta$ and $\alpha \vee (\beta \vee \delta)$ are truth-functionally equivalent iff $[(\alpha \vee \beta) \vee \delta] \equiv [\alpha \vee (\beta \vee \delta)]$ is truth-functionally true; similarly for & and $\equiv$.

TRUTH-TABLE : EX275

	ABD	[(A∨B)∨D] ≡ [A∨(B∨D)] ,	[(A&B)&D] ≡ [A&(B&D)] ,	[(A≡B)≡D] ≡ [A≡(B≡D)]
1	TTT	TTT TT T TT TTT	TTT TT T TT TTT	TTT TT T TT TTT
2	TTF	TTT TF T TT TTF	TTT FF T TF TFF	TTT FF T TF TF F
3	TFT	TTF TT T TT FTT	TFF FT T TF FFT	TFF FT T TF FFT
4	TFF	TTF TF T TT FFF	TFF FF I IF FFF	TFF TF T TT FTF
5	FTT	FTT TT T FT TTT	FFT FT T FF TTT	FFT FT T FF TTT
6	FTF	FTT TF T FT TTF	FFT FF T FF TFF	FFT TF T FT TFF
7	FFT	FFF TT T FT FTT	FFF FT T FF FFT	FTF TT T FT FFT
8	FFF	FFF FF T FF FFF	FFF FF T FF FFF	FTF FF T FF FTF

No (more) errors

2.8.1 a. 8 ($=2^3$);   c. 32 ($=2^5$);   e. 2 ($=2^1$)

2.8.3 1,090 years.

Chapter 3: *Translating and Analyzing Arguments*

3.1.1 a. conjunction;   c. simple;   e. conditional;   g. disjunction

3.1.2 a. ¬T → ¬B
       c. J → ¬H
       e. (A → T) & (¬A → ¬T), or more simply, A ≡ T
       g. (T & B) ∨ ((T & ¬B) ∨ (¬T & B)), or more simply, T ∨ B

3.1.3 a. J → ¬H   c. (K & ¬Q) → (J → L)
       e. T → D   g. S → M

3.1.4 a. ¬(A → B)   c. (C → A) & ¬(A → C)
       e. C → C   g. A → (¬B & ¬C)

3.1.5 a. true;   c. false;   e. false;   g. false

3.1.7 a. (S & ¬T) & ¬L   c. S → (¬L ∨ ¬T)
       e. (¬T & F) & ¬L   g. F → ¬T
       i. [(S & ¬T) → ¬F] & [(¬S & ¬T) → F]   k. [(T ∨ ¬T) → ¬C] & (C → ¬F)
       m. (¬S & ¬T) & (L & ¬F)   o. (((¬S & ¬T) & ¬L) & ¬F) & ¬C

3.2.1 a. so   c. None
       e. that's why   g. in view of the fact that

3.2.2 a. This passage contains no argument.
       c. *Premises*: Since I met Sheila I've begun to wear clean shirts. Since I met Sheila I've even started to lose interest in my male bonding seminars. If I can earn some money from magazine subscriptions then I can take her to that vegetarian dinner she keeps talking about. I just sent her two roses.
       Conclusion: I'm a fool for love. (Note: The sentence 'It all points to just one thing' has the role in this passage of an inference indicator.)

3.2.3 a. (P ∨ L) ∨ R   c. T → (M & B)
          ¬P   B & ¬M
          ¬L   —————————
          —————   ¬T
          R

e. H → S   g. (H → S) & (S → ¬H)
   S → ¬H   G → ¬H
   ─────   ¬S ∨ H
   ¬H   ──────────────────
                     G → ¬H

3.2.4 a. true;   c. false;   e. true;   g. true

3.2.5 a. R → ¬K   c. K ≡ ¬Q
          B → ¬D   J → K
          ──────   ──────────
          ¬K & ¬D   ¬J → (¬K & Q)
          ──────
          B ∨ R

       e. (K & ¬Q) → (J → L)   g. L & ¬L
          ¬K → Q   ──────
          ¬Q   G
          ──────────────────
          ¬(J & ¬L)

3.3.1 a. yes;   c. no;   e. no

3.3.2 a. nonsatisfiable
       c. satisfiable; (T,F) and (F,T)
       e. satisfiable; (T,T,T), (T,T,F), (T,F,T), (T,F,F) and (F,T,F).

3.3.3 a. inconsistent

       TRUTH-TABLE : EX333A

	R	R ≡ ¬R
1	T	T F FT
2	F	F F TF

       (No (more) errors

c. inconsistent

TRUTH-TABLE : EX333C

	FGHJ	F ∨ G , (¬J & H) ∨ (¬G & ¬F) , (J ∨ ¬G) & (¬H ∨ J)
1	TTTT	TT T FTFT F F IF FI TT FT T FTTT
2	TTTF	TT T TFTT T FTF FT FF FT F FTFF
3	TTFT	TT T FTFF F FTF FT TT FT T TFTT
4	TTFF	TT T TFFF F FTF FT FF FT F TF IF
5	TFTT	TT F FTFT F TFF FT TT TF T FTTT
6	TFTF	TT F TFTT T TFF FT FT TF F FTFF
7	TFFT	TT F FTFF F TFF FT TT TF T TFTT
8	TFFF	TT F TFFF F TFF FT FT TF T TFTF
9	FTTT	FT T FTFT F FTF TF TT FT T ГТТТ
10	FTTF	FT T TFTT T FTF TF FF FT F FTFF
11	FTFT	FT T FTFF F FTF TF TT FT T TFTT
12	FTFF	FT T TFFF F FTF TF FF FT F TFTF
13	FFTT	FF F FTFT T TFT TF TT TF T FTTT
14	FFTF	FF F TFTT T TFT TF FT TF F FTFF
15	FFFT	FF F FTFF T TFT TF TT TF T TFTT
16	FFFF	FF F TFFF T TFT TF FT TF T TFTF

No (more) errors

e. inconsistent

TRUTH-TABLE : EX333E

	DJMS	¬(S ∨ J) ≡ D , D & ¬¬M , M → ¬¬J
1	TTTT	F TTT FT TT TFT T T TFT
2	TTTF	F FTT FT TT TFT T T TFT
3	TTFT	F TTT FT TF FTF F T TFT
4	TTFF	F FTT FT TF FTF F T TFT
5	TFTT	F TTF FT TT TFT T F FTF
6	TFTF	T FFF TT TT TFT T F FTF
7	TFFT	F TTF FT TF FTF F T FTF
8	TFFF	T FFF TT TF FTF F T FTF
9	FTTT	F TTT TF FF TFT T T TFT
10	FTTF	F FTT TF FF TFT T T TFT
11	FTFT	F TTT TF FF FTF F T TFT
12	FTFF	F FTT TF FF FTF F T TFT
13	FFTT	F TTF TF FF TFT T F FTF
14	FFTF	T FFF FF FF TFT T F FTF
15	FFFT	T TTF TF FF FTF F T FTF
16	FFFF	T FFF FF FF FTF F T FTF

No (more) errors

g. consistent (tva 4 satisfies all the sentences in the set)

TRUTH-TABLE : EX333G

	ABC	(A → B) → C , ¬B ∨ ¬A , ¬C							
1	TTT	T T T	T	T	FT F	FT		FT
2	TTF	T T T	F	F	FT F	FT		TF
3	TFT	T F F	T	T	TF T	FT		FT
4	TFF	T F F	T	F	TF T	FT		TF
5	FTT	F T T	T	T	FT T	TF		FT
6	FTF	F T T	F	F	FT T	TF		TF
7	FFT	F T F	T	T	TF T	TF		FT
8	FFF	F T F	F	F	TF T	TF		TF

No (more) errors

3.3.4   a. False. For instance, {P → P} is truth-functionally consistent but {¬(P → P)} is not.

       c. True. No truth-value assignment satisfies all the sentences in {α, β} if no truth-value assignment satisfies all the sentences in {α} (or in {β}, for that matter).

       e. True. Since no truth-value assignment satisfies a truth-functionally false sentence, no truth-value assignment can satisfy all the sentences in a set which contains it.

3.4.1   a. True.

TRUTH-TABLE : EX341A

	DGHR	G & D , D → R , H → (R & G)									
1	TTTT	T T T	T T T	T T	T T T		
2	TTTF	T T T	T F F	T F	F F T		
3	TTFT	T T T	T T T	F T	T T T		
4	TTFF	T T T	T F F	F T	F F T		
5	TFTT	F F T	T T T	T F	T F F		
6	TFTF	F F T	T F F	T F	F F F		
7	TFFT	F F T	T T T	F T	T F F		
8	TFFF	F F T	T F F	F T	F F F		
9	FTTT	T F F	F T T	T T	T T T		
10	FTTF	T F F	F T F	T F	F F T		
11	FTFT	T F F	F T T	F T	T T T		
12	FTFF	T F F	F T F	F T	F F T		
13	FFTT	F F F	F T T	T F	T F F		
14	FFTF	F F F	F T F	T F	F F F		
15	FFFT	F F F	F T T	F T	T F F		
16	FFFF	F F F	F T F	F T	F F F		

No (more) errors

c. True

TRUTH-TABLE : EX341C

	EGKM	K ≡ (K → M) , M → ¬E , (K → ¬E) ∨ G
1	TTTT	T T T T T T F FT T F FT T T
2	TTTF	T F T F F F T FT T F FT T T
3	TTFT	F F F T T T F FT F T FT T T
4	TTFF	F F F T F F T FI F T FT T T
5	TFTT	T T T T T T F FT T F FT F F
6	TFTF	T F T F F F T FT T F FT F F
7	TFFT	F F F T T T F FT F T FT T F
8	TFFF	F F F T F F T FT F T FT T F
9	FTTT	T T T T T T T TF T T TF T T
10	FTTF	T F T F F F T TF T T TF T T
11	FTFT	F F F T T T T TF F T TF T T
12	FTFF	F F F T F F T TF F T TF T T
13	FFTT	T T T T T T T TF T T TF T F
14	FFTF	T F T F F F T TF T T TF T F
15	FFFT	F F F T T T T TF F T TF T F
16	FFFF	F F F T F F T TF F T TF T F

No (more) errors

e. False (Note that, for instance, tva 8 satisfies the set but not R & H)

TRUTH-TABLE : EX341E

	HLQR	L ∨ ¬Q , (Q ∨ L) → R , H , R & H
1	TTTT	T T FT T T T T T T T T T
2	TTTF	T T FT T T T F F T F F T
3	TTFT	T T TF F T T T T T T T T
4	TTFF	T T TF F T T F F T F F T
5	TFTT	F F FT T T F T T T T T T
6	TFTF	F F FT T T F F F T F F T
7	TFFT	F T TF F F T T T T T T T
8	TFFF	F T TF F F F T F T F F T
9	FTTT	T I FT T T T T T F T F F
10	FTTF	T T FT T T T F F F F F F
11	FTFT	T T TF F T T T T F T F F
12	FTFF	T T TF F T T F F F F F F
13	FFTT	F F FT T T F T T F T F F
14	FFTF	F F FT T T F F F F F F F
15	FFFT	F I TF F F T T T F T F F
16	FFFF	F T TF F F T F F F F F F

No (more) errors

3.4.2 **a.** True, since the test set {G & D, D → R, ¬(H → (R & G))} is inconsistent

TRUTH-TABLE : EX342A

	DGHR	G & D , D → R , ¬(H → (R & G))
1	TTTT	T T T T T T F T T T T T
2	TTTF	T T T T F F T T F F F T
3	TTFT	T T T T T T F F T T T T
4	TTFF	T T T T F F F F T F F T
5	TFTT	F F T T T T T T F T F F
6	TFTF	F F T T F F T T F F F F
7	TFFT	F F T T T T F F T T F F
8	TFFF	F F T T F F F F T F F F
9	FTTT	T F F F T T F T T T T T
10	FTTF	T F F F T F T T F F F T
11	FTFT	T F F F T T F F T T T T
12	FTFF	T F F F T F F F T F F T
13	FFTT	F F F F T T T T F T F F
14	FFTF	F F F F T F T T F F F F
15	FFFT	F F F F T T F F T T F F
16	FFFF	F F F F T F F F T F F F

No (more) errors

c. True, since the test set {K ≡ (K → M), M → ¬E, ¬((K → ¬E) ∨ G)} is inconsistent

TRUTH-TABLE : EX342C

	EGKM	K ≡ (K → M) , M → ¬E , ¬((K → ¬E)∨G)
1	TTTT	T T T T T T F F T F T F F T T T
2	TTTF	T F T F F F T F T F T F F T T T
3	TTFT	F F F T T T F F T F F T F T T T
4	TTFF	F F F T F F T F T F F T F T T T
5	TFTT	T T T T T T F F T T T F F T F F
6	TFTF	T F T F F F T F T T T F F T F F
7	TFFT	F F F T T T F F T F F T F T T F
8	TFFF	F F F T F F T F T F F T F T T F
9	FTTT	T T T I T T T T F F T T T F T T
10	FTTF	T F T F F F T T F F T T T F T T
11	FTFT	F F F T T T T T F F F T T F T T
12	FTFF	F F F T F F T T F F F T T F T T
13	FFTT	T T T T T T T T F F T T T F T F
14	FFTF	T F T F F F T T F F T T T F T F
15	FFFT	F F F T T T T T F F F T T F T F
16	FFFF	F F F T F F T T F F F T T F T F

No (more) errors

e. False, since the test set {L ∨ ¬Q, (Q ∨ L) → R, H, ¬(R & H)} is consistent

TRUTH-TABLE : EX342E

```
        HLQR    HLQR    L ∨ ¬Q , (Q ∨ L) → R , H , ¬(R & H)
  1 |   TTTT    TT FT    T T T  T T  T   F T T T
  2 |   TTTF    TT FT    T T T  F F  T   T F F T
  3 |   TTFT    TT TF    F T T  T T  T   F T T T
  4 |   TTFF    TT TF    F T T  F F  T   T F F T
  5 |   TFTT    FF FT    T T F  T T  T   F T T T
  6 |   TFTF    FF FT    T T F  F F  T   T F F T
  7 |   TFFT    FT TF    F F F  T T  T   F T T T
  8 |   TFFF    FT TF    F F F  T F  T   T F F T
  9 |   FTTT    TT FT    T T T  T T  F   T T F F
 10 |   FTTF    TT FT    T T T  F F  F   T F F F
 11 |   FTFT    TT TF    F T T  T T  F   T T F F
 12 |   FTFF    TT TF    F T T  F F  F   T F F F
 13 |   FFTT    FF FT    T T F  T T  F   T T F F
 14 |   FFTF    FF FT    T T F  F F  F   T F F F
 15 |   FFFT    FT TF    F F F  T T  F   T T F F
 16 |   FFFF    FT TF    F F F  T F  F   T F F F
```

No (more) errors

3.4.3   a. inconsistent;   c. inconsistent;   e. consistent

3.4.4   a. valid

TRUTH-TABLE : EX344A

```
        GHKS    K ∨ S , ¬G → ¬S , ¬¬¬G , H ∨ K
  1 |   TTTT    T T T   F T T   F T   F T F T   T T T
  2 |   TTTF    T T F   F T T   F T   F T F T   T T T
  3 |   TTFT    F T T   F T T   F T   F T F T   T T F
  4 |   TTFF    F F F   F T T   T F   F T F T   T T F
  5 |   TFTT    T T T   F T T   F T   F T F T   F T T
  6 |   TFTF    T T F   F T T   T F   F T F T   F T T
  7 |   TFFT    F T T   F T T   F T   F T F T   F F F
  8 |   TFFF    F F F   F T T   T F   F T F T   F F F
  9 |   FTTT    T T T   T F F   F T   T F T F   T T T
 10 |   FTTF    T T F   T F T   T F   T F T F   T T T
 11 |   FTFT    F T T   T F F   F T   T F T F   T T F
 12 |   FTFF    F F F   T F T   T F   T F T F   T T F
 13 |   FFTT    T T T   T F F   F T   T F T F   F T T
 14 |   FFTF    T T F   T F T   T F   T F T F   F T T
 15 |   FFFT    F T T   T F F   F T   T F T F   F F F
 16 |   FFFF    F F F   T F T   T F   T F T F   F F F
```

No (more) errors

c. valid

TRUTH-TABLE : EX344C

	PQ	$P \equiv \neg P$, Q
1	TT	T F F T T
2	TF	T F F T F
3	FT	F F T F T
4	FF	F F T F F

No (more) errors

e. valid

TRUTH-TABLE : EX344E

	PQ	$P \rightarrow Q$, $\neg Q$, $\neg P$
1	TT	T T T F T F T
2	TF	T F F T F F T
3	FT	F T T F T T F
4	FF	F T F T F T F

No (more) errors

3.4.5   a. B → S
         (P & ¬T) → B
         P & ¬B
         ――――――
         ¬S   Invalid, since the test set is consistent.

TRUTH-TABLE : EX345A

```
        BPST |  B → S , (P & ¬T) → B , P & ¬B , ¬¬S
  1     TTTT |  T T T   T F FT   T T T F FT   T F T
  2     TTTF |  T T T   T T TF   T T T F FT   T F T
  3     TTFT |  T F F   T F FT   T T T F FT   F T F
  4     TTFF |  T F F   T T TF   T T T F FT   F T F
  5     TFTT |  T T T   F F FT   T T F F FT   T F T
  6     TFTF |  T T T   F F TF   T T F F FT   T F T
  7     TFFT |  T F F   F F FT   T T F F FT   F T F
  8     TFFF |  T F F   F F TF   T T F F FT   F T F
  9     FTTT |  F T T   T F FT   T F T T TF   T F T
 10     FTTF |  F T T   T T TF   F F T T TF   T F T
 11     FTFT |  F T F   T F FT   T F T T TF   F T F
 12     FTFF |  F T F   T T TF   F F T T TF   F T F
 13     FFTT |  F T T   F F FT   T F F F TF   T F T
 14     FFTF |  F T T   F F TF   T F F F TF   T F T
 15     FFFT |  F T F   F F FT   T F F F TF   F T F
 16     FFFF |  F T F   F F TF   T F F F TF   F T F
```

No (more) errors

c. $(R \to M) \& (\neg R \to M)$
   $\neg M$
   _____
   B   Valid, since the test set is inconsistent.

TRUTH-TABLE : EX345C

```
        BMR |  (R → M) & (¬R → M) , ¬M , ¬B
  1     TTT |  T T T  T FT T T   F T   F T
  2     TTF |  F T T  T TF T T   F T   F T
  3     TFT |  T F F  F FT T F   T F   F T
  4     TFF |  F T F  F TF F F   T F   F T
  5     FTT |  T T T  T FT T T   F T   T F
  6     FTF |  F T T  T TF T T   F T   T F
  7     FFT |  T F F  F FT T F   T F   T F
  8     FFF |  F T F  F TF F F   T F   T F
```

No (more) errors

e. $\dfrac{\neg(H \to R) \ \& \ \neg(R \to H)}{(H \ \& \ \neg R) \ \& \ (R \ \& \ \neg H)}$ Valid, since the test set is inconsistent.

TRUTH-TABLE : EX345E

		HR	$\neg(H \to R) \ \& \ \neg(R \to H)$, $\neg[(H \ \& \ \neg R) \ \& \ (R \ \& \ \neg H)]$
	1	TT	F T T T F F T T T T T F FT F T F FT
	2	TF	T T F F F F F T T T T T TF F F F FT
	3	FT	F F T T F T T F F T F F FT F T T T F
	4	FF	F F T F F F F T F T F F TF F F F TF

No (more) errors

3.4.6   a. valid;   c. valid;   e. valid;   g. valid

3.4.7   a. invalid (since the test set is consistent)

TRUTH-TABLE : EX347A

		BDKR	$R \to \neg K$, $B \to \neg D$, $\neg K \ \& \ \neg D$, $\neg(B \lor R)$
	1	TTTT	T F FT T F FT FT F FT F TTT
	2	TTTF	F T FT T F FT FT F FT F TTF
	3	TTFT	T T TF T F FT TF F FT F TTT
	4	TTFF	F T TF T F FT TF F FT F TTF
	5	TFTT	T F FT T T TF FT F TF F TTT
	6	TFTF	F T FT T T TF FT F TF F TTF
	7	TFFT	T T TF T T TF TF T TF F TTT
	8	TFFF	F T TF T T TF TF T TF F TTF
	9	FTTT	T F FT F T FT FT F FT F FTT
	10	FTTF	F T FT F T FT FT F FT T FFF
	11	FTFT	T T TF F T FT TF F FT F FTT
	12	FTFF	F T TF F T FT TF F FT T FFF
	13	FFTT	T F FT F T TF FT F TF F FTT
	14	FFTF	F T FT F T TF FT F TF T FFF
	15	FFFT	T T TF F T TF TF T TF F FTT
	16	FFFF	F T TF F T TF T FT TF T FFF

No (more) errors

c. invalid (since the test set is consistent)

TRUTH-TABLE : EX347C

	JKQ	K ≡ ¬Q , J → K , ¬[¬J → (¬K & Q)]
1	TTT	T F F T T T T F F T T F T F T
2	TTF	T T T F T T T F F T T F T F F
3	TFT	F T F T T F F F F T T T F T T
4	TFF	F F T F T F F F F T T T F F F
5	FTT	T F F T F T T T T F F F T F T
6	FTF	T T T F F T T T T F F F T F F
7	FFT	F T F T F T F F T F T T F T T
8	FFF	F F T F F T F T T F F T F F F

No (more) errors

e. valid (since the test set is inconsistent)

TRUTH-TABLE : EX347E

	JKLQ	(K & ¬Q) → (J → L) , ¬K → Q , ¬Q , ¬¬(J & ¬L)
1	TTTT	T F F T T T T T F T T T F T F T T F F T
2	TTTF	T T T F T T T T F T T F T F F T T F F T
3	TTFT	T F F T T T F F F T T T F T T F T T T F
4	TTFF	T T T F F T F F F T T F T F T F T T T F
5	TFTT	F F F T T T T T T F T T F T F T T F F T
6	TFTF	F F T F T T T T T F F F T F F T T F F T
7	TFFT	F F F T T T F F T F T T F T T F T T T F
8	TFFF	F F T F T T F F T F F F T F T T T T T F
9	FTTT	T F F T T F T T F T T T F T F T F F F T
10	FTTF	T T T F T F T T F T T F T F F T F F F T
11	FTFT	T F F T T F T F F T T T F T F T F F F T
12	FTFF	T T T F T F T F F T T F T F F T F F F T
13	FFTT	F F F T T F T T T F T T F T F T F F F T
14	FFTF	F F T F T F T T T F F F T F F T F F F T
15	FFFT	F F F T T F T F T F T T F T F T F F F T
16	FFFF	F F T F T F T F T F F F T F F T F F T F

No (more) errors

g. valid (since the test set is inconsistent)

TRUTH-TABLE : EX347G

	GL	L & ¬L , ¬G
1	T T	T F F T F T
2	T F	F F T F F T
3	F T	T F F T T F
4	F F	F F T F T F

No (more) errors

3.4.8   a. True. If α is truth-functionally true then any truth-value assignment satisfies α and, consequently, falsifies $\neg\alpha$. Hence, no truth-value assignment satisfies $\{\neg\alpha\}$, and by definition, $\{\neg\alpha\}$ is truth-functionally inconsistent.

c. False. If $\{\alpha\}$ and $\{\beta\}$ are truth-functionally inconsistent then both α and β are truth-functionally false. But any two truth-functionally false sentences are truth-functionally equivalent, and hence, $\alpha \equiv \beta$ is truth-functionally true. It clearly follows that $\{\alpha \equiv \beta\}$ is truth-functionally consistent.

e. True. If α is truth-functionally true then $\neg\alpha$ is truth-functionally false, and for any set Γ, $\Gamma \cup \{\neg\alpha\}$ must be truth-functionally inconsistent. Hence, by the test of entailment, Γ truth-functionally entails α.

3.4.9   a. $(T,F,T,T) \models \{P \rightarrow R, \neg R \vee S\}$ and $(T,F,T,T) \not\models P \& Q$
$(T,T,F,T) \models \{P \& Q, \neg R \vee S\}$ and $(T,T,F,T) \not\models P \rightarrow R$
$(T,T,T,F) \models \{P \& Q, P \rightarrow R\}$ and $(T,T,T,F) \not\models \neg R \vee S$

b. Let α be a member of Γ. If α is truth-functionally true then no truth-value assignment τ is such that $\tau \models \Gamma - \{\alpha\}$ and $\tau \not\models \alpha$ since, to begin with, no truth-value assignment τ is such that $\tau \not\models \alpha$ (by the definition of truth-functional truth).

3.4.11 Assume Γ is (truth-functionally) consistent and let τ be a truth-value assignment which satisfies Γ. Then, since either α or $\neg\alpha$ is true under τ, we have that either $\tau \models \Gamma \cup \{\alpha\}$ or $\tau \models \Gamma \cup \{\neg\alpha\}$; that is, either $\Gamma \cup \{\alpha\}$ or $\Gamma \cup \{\neg\alpha\}$ is consistent. But in either case this is in contradiction with the fact that $\Gamma \models \alpha$ and $\Gamma \models \neg\alpha$ since by the test for entailment, both $\Gamma \cup \{\alpha\}$ and $\Gamma \cup \{\neg\alpha\}$ are inconsistent.

3.5.1   a. $\neg(\neg A \vee \neg B) \vee \neg(A \vee B)$ c. $\neg(\neg P \vee Q) \vee P$

3.5.3   a.

α β	$\alpha \mid \beta$
T T	F
T F	T
F T	T
F F	T

b. $\alpha \mid \alpha, (\alpha \mid \beta) \mid (\alpha \mid \beta)$, and $(\alpha \mid \alpha) \mid (\beta \mid \beta)$

Chapter 4: SL Truth-Trees

4.3.1   a. true;   c. true;   e. false

4.3.2   a. consistent;   c. inconsistent;   e. consistent;   g. inconsistent

4.4.1   For each exercise, we form the test set (the premises plus the negation of the conclusion) which we test for inconsistency: If its truth-tree closes, it is inconsistent (and hence entailment holds); else it is consistent (and entailment fails).

a. true;   c. true;   e. true

4.4.2 For each exercise, we form the test set (the premises plus the negation of the conclusion) which we test for inconsistency: If its truth-tree closes, it is inconsistent (and hence the argument is valid); else it is consistent (and the argument is invalid).
a. invalid;   c. valid;   e. valid;   g. valid;   i. invalid

4.4.3 Repeat as in 4.4.2, after symbolizing each argument into SL.

a. M → B
   ¬B
   ─────
   ¬M   Valid

c. ¬(C & M)
   M → (P ∨ L)
   ¬P
   ─────
   M ∨ L   Invalid

e. (L & M) → C
   ¬C ∨ P
   ¬P
   ─────
   ¬L & ¬M   Invalid

4.4.4 Repeat as in 4.4.2, after symbolizing each argument into SL.
a. valid;   c. valid;   e. valid;   g. valid

4.4.5 Repeat as in 4.4.2, after symbolizing each argument into SL.
a. invalid;   c. invalid;   e. valid;   g. valid

4.4.6 a. true;   c. true;   e. true;   g. true;   i. true

4.4.7 A sentence α is truth-functionally true if and only if the truth-tree for the set $\{\neg\alpha\}$ is closed. Hence, for each sentence α in exercises a through e, your truth-tree for the set $\{\neg\alpha\}$ should close.

4.4.8 A sentence α is truth-functionally false if and only if the truth-tree for the set $\{\alpha\}$ is closed. Hence, for each sentence α in exercises a through e, your truth-tree for the set $\{\alpha\}$ should close.

4.4.9 A sentence α is truth-functionally indeterminate if and only if the truth-tree for the set $\{\alpha\}$ is (completed) open and the one for $\{\neg\alpha\}$ is also (completed) open. Hence, for each sentence α in exercises a through e, your truth-trees for $\{\alpha\}$ and $\{\neg\alpha\}$ should each have at least one completed open branch.

4.4.10 a. nonsatisfiable   c. satisfiable; (F,T,F)
       e. satisfiable; (F,F)

4.4.11 a. truth-functionally false   c. truth-functionally true
       e. truth-functionally indeterminate   g. truth-functionally true
       i. truth-functionally indeterminate   k. truth-functionally false
       m. truth-functionally false   o. truth-functionally false

4.4.12 Two sentences α and β are truth-functionally equivalent if and only if the truth-tree for the set $\{\neg(\alpha \equiv \beta)\}$ is closed. Hence, for the sentences α and β in each exercise a through e, your truth-tree for the set $\{\neg(\alpha \equiv \beta)\}$ should close.

4.4.13 a. satisfiable; (T,F,T)   c. satisfiable; (T,T,F)
       e. nonsatisfiable

4.4.15 For instance, the set {P ∨ ¬P} is clearly consistent. However, by using the newly introduced ∨-decomposition rule, it is easy to see that its truth-tree closes.

4.4.17 $\alpha \downarrow \beta$ is truth-functionally equivalent to $\neg(\alpha \lor \beta)$. Hence, the $\downarrow$-decomposition rule, $\downarrow$D, is the same as the ¬∨D rule.

Chapter 5: Natural Deduction in Propositional Logic

5.1.2   The errors are in lines 6, 9 and 14. Line 6 is mistaken because by using →E one cannot get α from α → β and β. Line 9 is erroneous because the application of ¬E requires the construction of a subderivation; the correct statement of the rule application, which is ¬E i-j,i-k, indicates this requirement. Also, S cannot be derived from ¬¬S *in one single step* (there is no rule for that). Finally, line 14 introduces an especially serious error: T, which is in line 6, is not accessible from line 14 since the scope of the subderivation ends at line 11.

5.1.3

SD : EX513

PREMISE	1	M ≡ (J ∨ N)
PREMISE	2	(L ≡ M) & (J ∨ K)
PREMISE	3	(L & H) ≡ (K ∨ H)
&ER 2	4	J ∨ K
ASSUMPTION	5	J
∨IR 5	6	J ∨ N
≡E 1,6	7	M
&EL 2	8	L ≡ M
≡E 7,8	9	L
ASSUMPTION	10	K
∨IR 10	11	K ∨ H
≡E 3,11	12	L & H
&EL 12	13	L
∨E 4,5-9,10-13	14	L
&EL 2	15	L ≡ M
≡E 14,15	16	M

No (more) errors

5.1.4

SD : EX514A

PREMISE	1	(A & B) & C
PREMISE	2	B → D
PREMISE	3	(A ∨ M) → F
&EL 1	4	A & B
&ER 4	5	B
→ E 2,5	6	D
&EL 4	7	A
∨IR 7	8	A ∨ M
→E 3,8	9	F
&I 6,9	10	D & F

No (more) errors

SD : EX514C

PREMISE	1	A ∨ B
PREMISE	2	(C ∨ B) ≡ D
PREMISE	3	A ≡ D
ASSUMPTION	4	A
≡E 3,4	5	D
ASSUMPTION	6	B
∨IL 6	7	C ∨ B
≡E 2,7	8	D
∨E 1,4-5,6-8	9	D

No (more) errors

SD : EX514E

PREMISE	1	P → Q
PREMISE	2	¬M → (P & ¬Q)
ASSUMPTION	3	¬M
→E 2,3	4	P & ¬Q
&EL 4	5	P
→E 1,5	6	Q
&ER 4	7	¬Q
¬E 3-6,3-7	8	M

No (more) errors

5.2.1

SD . EX521

PREMISE	1	P
PREMISE	2	P → (S & (P ≡ ¬Q))
PREMISE	3	¬Q ≡ (R ≡ S)
PREMISE	4	((P & R) ∨ M) → ((P & S) → (T ≡ R))
→E 1,2	5	S & (P ≡ ¬Q)
&ER 5	6	P ≡ ¬Q
≡E 1,6	7	¬Q
≡E 3,7	8	R ≡ S
&EL 5	9	S
≡E 8,9	10	R
&I 1,10	11	P & R
∨IR 11	12	(P & R) ∨ M
→E 4,12	13	(P & S) → (T ≡ R)
&I 1,9	14	P & S
→E 13,14	15	T ≡ R
≡E 10,15	16	T

No (more) errors

5.2.3

SD : EX523A

PREMISE	1	(P & Q) → S
PREMISE	2	R & ¬T
PREMISE	3	R → P
PREMISE	4	¬T → Q
&EL 2	5	R
→E 3,5	6	P
&ER 2	7	¬T
→E 4,7	8	Q
&I 6,8	9	P & Q
→E 1,9	10	S

No (more) errors

SD : EX523C

PREMISE	1	A & B
PREMISE	2	(B ∨ D) → C
PREMISE	3	(A & F) → E
PREMISE	4	(B & C) ≡ F
&EL 1	5	A
&ER 1	6	B
∨IR 6	7	B ∨ D
→E 2,7	8	C
&I 6,8	9	B & C
≡E 4,9	10	F
&I 5,10	11	A & F
→E 3,11	12	E

No (more) errors

SD : EX523E

PREMISE	1	P → ¬R
PREMISE	2	(P & S) → M
PREMISE	3	¬R ≡ S
ASSUMPTION	4	⌐ P
→E 1,4	5	¬R
≡E 3,5	6	S
&I 4,6	7	P & S
→E 2,7	8	⌐ M
→I 4-8	9	P → M

No (more) errors

5.3.1   a. &EL;   c. ≡I;   e. ∨IL;   g. &I;   i. ¬I

5.3.2   a. ≡E;   c. ¬E;   e. R;   g. ¬E;   i. ∨IL

5.3.3

SD : EX533A

PREMISE	1	$(P \& Q) \to T$
PREMISE	2	$(R \& T) \to S$
ASSUMPTION	3	P
ASSUMPTION	4	Q
ASSUMPTION	5	R
&I 3,4	6	P & Q
→E 1,6	7	T
&I 5,7	8	R & T
→E 2,8	9	S
→I 5-9	10	$R \to S$
→I 4-10	11	$Q \to (R \to S)$
→I 3-11	12	$P \to (Q \to (R \to S))$

No (more) errors

SD : EX533C

PREMISE	1	$L \equiv \neg K$
PREMISE	2	$K \vee \neg L$
ASSUMPTION	3	K
R 3	4	K
ASSUMPTION	5	$\neg L$
ASSUMPTION	6	$\neg K$
≡E 1,6	7	L
R 5	8	$\neg L$
¬E 6-7,6-8	9	K
∨E 2,3-4,5-9	10	K

No (more) errors

SD : EX533E

PREMISE	1	$\neg(K \vee H)$
ASSUMPTION	2	K
∨IR 2	3	$K \vee H$
R 1	4	$\neg(K \vee H)$
¬I 2-3,2-4	5	$\neg K$

No (more) errors

5.4.1   a. true;   c. false;   e. true;   g. false;   i. false

5.4.2

SD : EX542A

PREMISE	1	$(\neg H \equiv J) \& (S \vee M)$
PREMISE	2	$L \to D$
&ER 1	3	$S \vee M$
&I 2,3	4	$(L \to D) \& (S \vee M)$

No (more) errors

SD : EX542C

PREMISE	1	G & D
PREMISE	2	D → R
ASSUMPTION	3	⎡ H
&ER 1	4	│ D
→E 2,4	5	│ R
&EL 1	6	│ G
&I 5,6	7	⎣ R & G
→I 3-7	8	H → (R & G)

No (more) errors

SD : EX542E

PREMISE	1	K ≡ (K → M)
PREMISE	2	M → ¬E
ASSUMPTION	3	⎡ K
≡E 1,3	4	│ K → M
→E 3,4	5	│ M
→E 2,5	6	⎣ ¬E
→I 3-6	7	K → ¬E
∨IR 7	8	(K → ¬E) ∨ G

No (more) errors

SD : EX542G

PREMISE	1	D → ¬J
PREMISE	2	P & D
PREMISE	3	¬P ≡ (M ∨ ¬J)
ASSUMPTION	4	⎡ S
&ER 2	5	│ D
→E 1,5	6	│ ¬J
∨IL 6	7	⎣ M ∨ ¬J
ASSUMPTION	8	⎡ M ∨ ¬J
ASSUMPTION	9	⎡ ¬S
&EL 2	10	│ P
≡E 3,8	11	⎣ ¬P
¬E 9-10,9-11	12	⎣ S
≡I 4-7,8-12	13	S ≡ (M ∨ ¬J)

No (more) errors

SD : EX542I

PREMISE	1	$S \equiv (B \, \& \, D)$
PREMISE	2	$B \to \neg\neg P$
PREMISE	3	$(S \vee G) \to \neg P$
PREMISE	4	S
ASSUMPTION	5	G
$\vee$IR 4	6	$S \vee G$
$\to$E 3,6	7	$\neg P$
$\equiv$E 1,4	8	$B \, \& \, D$
&EL 8	9	B
$\to$E 2,9	10	$\neg\neg P$
$\neg$I 5-7,5-10	11	$\neg G$
ASSUMPTION	12	$\neg B$
$\equiv$E 1,4	13	$B \, \& \, D$
&EL 13	14	B
R 12	15	$\neg B$
$\neg$I 12-14,12-15	16	$\neg\neg B$
&I 11,16	17	$\neg G \, \& \, \neg\neg B$

No (more) errors

5.4.3

SD : EX543A

PREMISE	1	$A \vee A$
R 1	2	$A \vee A$

No (more) errors

SD : EX543C

ASSUMPTION	1	P
ASSUMPTION	2	Q
R 1	3	P
$\to$I 2-3	4	$Q \to P$
$\to$I 1-4	5	$P \to (Q \to P)$

No (more) errors

SD : EX543E

PREMISE	1	K & L
PREMISE	2	L → J
PREMISE	3	A → ¬(K & L)
PREMISE	4	L → (¬A → ¬J)
ASSUMPTION	5	┌─ ¬A
&ER 1	6	L
→E 2,6	7	J
→E 4,6	8	¬A → ¬J
→E 5,8	9	└─ ¬J
¬E 5-7,5-9	10	A
ASSUMPTION	11	┌─ A
R 1	12	K & L
→E 3,11	13	└─ ¬(K & L)
¬I 11-12,11-13	14	¬A
&I 10,14	15	A & ¬A

No (more) errors

SD : EX543G

PREMISE	1	¬C ∨ ¬K
PREMISE	2	D ∨ (K ∨ L)
PREMISE	3	¬K ∨ C
ASSUMPTION	4	┌─ D
∨IR 4	5	└─ D ∨ L
ASSUMPTION	6	┌─ K ∨ L
ASSUMPTION	7	┌─ K
ASSUMPTION	8	┌─ ¬C
ASSUMPTION	9	┌─ ¬K
ASSUMPTION	10	┌─ ¬(D ∨ L)
R 7	11	K
R 9	12	¬K
¬E 10-11,10-12	13	D ∨ L
ASSUMPTION	14	C
ASSUMPTION	15	┌─ ¬(D ∨ L)
R 14	16	C
R 8	17	└─ ¬C
¬E 15-16,15-17	18	D ∨ L
∨E 3,9-13,14-18	19	D ∨ L
ASSUMPTION	20	┌─ ¬K
ASSUMPTION	21	┌─ ¬(D ∨ L)
R 7	22	K
R 20	23	└─ ¬K
¬E 21-22,21-23	24	D ∨ L
∨E 1,8-19,20-24	25	D ∨ L
ASSUMPTION	26	┌─ L
∨IL 26	27	└─ D ∨ L
∨E 6,7-25,26-27	28	D ∨ L
∨E 2,4-5,6-28	29	D ∨ L

No (more) errors

SD : EX543I

PREMISE	1	(¬H ∨ ¬J) & (D ≡ H)
PREMISE	2	J ∨ (G → I)
ASSUMPTION	3	G & H
&EL 3	4	G
ASSUMPTION	5	J
ASSUMPTION	6	¬(G → I)
R 5	7	J
&EL 1	8	¬H ∨ ¬J
ASSUMPTION	9	¬H
ASSUMPTION	10	J
&ER 3	11	H
R 9	12	¬H
¬I 10-11,10-12	13	¬J
ASSUMPTION	14	¬J
R 14	15	¬J
∨E 8,9-13,14-15	16	¬J
¬E 6-7,6-16	17	G → I
ASSUMPTION	18	G → I
R 18	19	G → I
∨E 2,5-17,18-19	20	G → I
→E 4, 20	21	I
→I 3-21	22	(G & H) → I

No (more) errors

SD : EX543K

ASSUMPTION	1	P → Q
ASSUMPTION	2	¬(¬P ∨ Q)
ASSUMPTION	3	P
→E 1,3	4	Q
∨IL 4	5	¬P ∨ Q
R 2	6	¬(¬P ∨ Q)
¬I 3-5,3-6	7	¬P
∨IR 7	8	¬P ∨ Q
R 2	9	¬(¬P ∨ Q)
¬E 2-8,2-9	10	¬P ∨ Q
ASSUMPTION	11	¬P ∨ Q
ASSUMPTION	12	P
ASSUMPTION	13	¬P
ASSUMPTION	14	¬Q
R 12	15	P
R 13	16	¬P
¬E 14-15,14-16	17	Q
ASSUMPTION	18	Q
R 18	19	Q
∨E 11,13-17,18-19	20	Q
→I 12-20	21	P → Q
≡I 1-10,11-21	22	(P → Q) ≡ (¬P ∨ Q)

No (more) errors

SD : EX543M

ASSUMPTION	1	¬(P ∨ Q)
ASSUMPTION	2	P
∨IR 2	3	P ∨ Q
R 1	4	¬(P ∨ Q)
¬I 2-3,2-4	5	¬P
ASSUMPTION	6	Q
∨IL 6	7	P ∨ Q
R 1	8	¬(P ∨ Q)
¬I 6-7,6-8	9	¬Q
&I 5,9	10	¬P & ¬Q
ASSUMPTION	11	¬P & ¬Q
ASSUMPTION	12	P ∨ Q
ASSUMPTION	13	P
R 13	14	P
ASSUMPTION	15	Q
ASSUMPTION	16	¬P
R 15	17	Q
&ER 11	18	¬Q
¬E 16-17,16-18	19	P
∨E 12,13-14,15-19	20	P
&EL 11	21	¬P
¬I 12-20,12-21	22	¬(P ∨ Q)
≡I 1-10,11-22	23	¬(P ∨ Q) ≡ (¬P & ¬Q)

No (more) errors

SD : EX543O

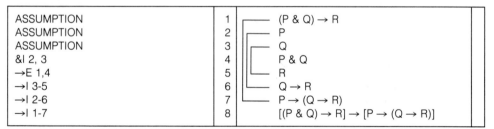

ASSUMPTION	1	(P & Q) → R
ASSUMPTION	2	P
ASSUMPTION	3	Q
&I 2, 3	4	P & Q
→E 1,4	5	R
→I 3-5	6	Q → R
→I 2-6	7	P → (Q → R)
→I 1-7	8	[(P & Q) → R] → [P → (Q → R)]

No (more) errors

5.4.4

SD : EX544A

PREMISE	1	R ≡ ¬R
ASSUMPTION	2	¬R
≡E 1,2	3	R
R 2	4	¬R
¬E 2-3,2-4	5	R
ASSUMPTION	6	R
R 6	7	R
≡E 1,6	8	¬R
¬I 6-7,6-8	9	¬R
&I 5,9	10	R & ¬R

No (more) errors

SD : EX544C

PREMISE	1	I & (G → H)
PREMISE	2	(¬¬G ∨ ¬I) & K
PREMISE	3	K → (¬H ∨ ¬G)
&ER 2	4	K
→E 3, 4	5	¬H ∨ ¬G
ASSUMPTION	6	¬H
ASSUMPTION	7	G
&ER 1	8	G → H
→E 7, 8	9	H
R 6	10	¬H
¬I 7-9, 7-10	11	¬G
ASSUMPTION	12	¬G
R 12	13	¬G
∨E 5,6-11,12-13	14	¬G
&EL 2	15	¬¬G ∨ ¬I
ASSUMPTION	16	¬¬G
R 16	17	¬¬G
ASSUMPTION	18	¬I
ASSUMPTION	19	¬G
&EL 1	20	I
R 18	21	¬I
¬I 19-20,19-21	22	¬¬G
∨E 15,16-17,18-22	23	¬¬G

No (more) errors

SD : EX544E

PREMISE	1	$A \rightarrow (B \vee C)$
PREMISE	2	$\neg C \,\&\, A$
PREMISE	3	$\neg D \rightarrow \neg B$
PREMISE	4	$\neg D \equiv (G \vee \neg C)$
&ER 2	5	A
→E 1,5	6	$B \vee C$
&EL 2	7	$\neg C$
∨IL 7	8	$G \vee \neg C$
≡E 4,8	9	$\neg D$
→E 3,9	10	$\neg B$
ASSUMPTION	11	B
ASSUMPTION	12	$\neg C$
R 11	13	B
R 10	14	$\neg B$
¬E 12-13,12-14	15	C
ASSUMPTION	16	C
R 16	17	C
∨E 6,11-15,16-17	18	C

No (more) errors

SD : EX544G

PREMISE	1	$\neg(S \vee J) \equiv D$
PREMISE	2	$D \,\&\, \neg\neg M$
PREMISE	3	$M \rightarrow \neg\neg J$
ASSUMPTION	4	J
∨IL 4	5	$S \vee J$
&EL 2	6	D
≡E 1,6	7	$\neg(S \vee J)$
¬I 4-5,4-7	8	$\neg J$
ASSUMPTION	9	$\neg M$
R 9	10	$\neg M$
& ER 2	11	$\neg\neg M$
¬E 9-10,9-11	12	M
→E 3,12	13	$\neg\neg J$

No (more) errors

SD : EX544I

PREMISE	1	$(A \rightarrow B) \rightarrow C$
PREMISE	2	$\neg B \rightarrow \neg A$
PREMISE	3	$\neg C$
ASSUMPTION	4	A
ASSUMPTION	5	$\neg B$
R 4	6	A
→E 2,5	7	$\neg A$
¬E 5-6,5-7	8	B
→I 4-8	9	$A \rightarrow B$
→E 1,9	10	C
R 3	11	$\neg C$

No (more) errors

5.4.5

SD : EX545A

PREMISE	1	C & D
PREMISE	2	(D & ¬N) → ¬S
PREMISE	3	Q & S
PREMISE	4	¬N
&ER 3	5	S
&ER 1	6	D
&I 6,4	7	D & ¬N
→E 2,7	8	¬S

No (more) errors

SD : EX545C

PREMISE	1	¬(A ∨ ¬A)
ASSUMPTION	2	┌ ¬A
∨IL 2	3	│ A ∨ ¬A
R 1	4	└ ¬(A ∨ ¬A)
¬E 2-3,2-4	5	┌ A
ASSUMPTION	6	│ A
∨IR 6	7	│ A ∨ ¬A
R 1	8	└ ¬(A ∨ ¬A)
¬I 6-7,6-8	9	¬A

No (more) errors

SD : EX545E

PREMISE	1	¬L ≡ (¬L → N)
PREMISE	2	(N → ¬F) & F
PREMISE	3	¬L
≡E 1,3	4	¬L → N
→E 3,4	5	N
&EL 2	6	N → ¬F
→E 5,6	7	¬F
&ER 2	8	F

No (more) errors

5.4.6

SD : EX546A

PREMISE	1	A ∨ S
PREMISE	2	¬G → ¬S
PREMISE	3	¬¬¬G
ASSUMPTION	4	A
R 4	5	A
ASSUMPTION	6	S
ASSUMPTION	7	¬A
R 6	8	S
ASSUMPTION	9	¬¬G
R 9	10	¬¬G
R 3	11	¬¬¬G
¬E 9-10,9-11	12	¬G
→E 2,12	13	¬S
¬E 7-8,7-13	14	A
∨E 1,4-5,6-14	15	A
∨IL 15	16	H ∨ A

No (more) errors

SD : EX546C

PREMISE	1	A ≡ B
ASSUMPTION	2	P → (Q → P)
ASSUMPTION	3	¬(P ∨ ¬P)
ASSUMPTION	4	¬P
∨IL 4	5	P ∨ ¬P
R 3	6	¬(P ∨ ¬P)
¬E 4-5,4-6	7	P
∨IR 7	8	P ∨ ¬P
R 3	9	¬(P ∨ ¬P)
¬E 3-8,3-9	10	P ∨ ¬P
ASSUMPTION	11	P ∨ ¬P
ASSUMPTION	12	P
ASSUMPTION	13	Q
R 12	14	P
→I 13-14	15	Q → P
→I 12-15	16	P → (Q → P)
≡I 2-10,11-16	17	[P → (Q → P)] ≡ (P ∨ ¬P)

No (more) errors

SD : EX546E

PREMISE	1	$P \equiv \neg P$
ASSUMPTION	2	Q
ASSUMPTION	3	$\neg P$
$\equiv$E 1,3	4	P
R 3	5	$\neg P$
$\neg$E 3-4,3-5	6	P
ASSUMPTION	7	P
R 7	8	P
$\equiv$E 1,7	9	$\neg P$
$\neg$I 7-8,7-9	10	$\neg P$
$\neg$I 2-6,2-10	11	$\neg Q$

No (more) errors

SD : EX546G

PREMISE	1	$(M \,\&\, \neg S) \lor (A \,\&\, G)$
PREMISE	2	$(M \,\&\, H) \equiv (\neg S \rightarrow G)$
PREMISE	3	$H \lor (M \rightarrow G)$
ASSUMPTION	4	$M \,\&\, \neg S$
ASSUMPTION	5	H
&EL 4	6	M
&I 6,5	7	$M \,\&\, H$
$\equiv$E 2,7	8	$\neg S \rightarrow G$
&ER 4	9	$\neg S$
$\rightarrow$E 8,9	10	G
ASSUMPTION	11	$M \rightarrow G$
&EL 4	12	M
$\rightarrow$E 11,12	13	G
$\lor$E 3,5-10,11-13	14	G
ASSUMPTION	15	$A \,\&\, G$
&ER 15	16	G
$\lor$E 1,4-14,15-16	17	G

No (more) errors

SD : EX546I

PREMISE	1	$A \rightarrow B$
PREMISE	2	$\neg C \rightarrow \neg B$
PREMISE	3	$C \rightarrow D$
PREMISE	4	$\neg E \rightarrow \neg D$
ASSUMPTION	5	A
ASSUMPTION	6	$\neg E$
ASSUMPTION	7	$\neg C$
$\rightarrow$E 1,5	8	B
$\rightarrow$E 2,7	9	$\neg B$
$\neg$E 7-8,7-9	10	C
$\rightarrow$E 3,10	11	D
$\rightarrow$E 4,6	12	$\neg D$
$\neg$E 6-11,6-12	13	E
$\rightarrow$I 5-13	14	$A \rightarrow E$

No (more) errors

5.4.7

SD : EX547A

PREMISE	1	¬(A ∨ B)
ASSUMPTION	2	B
∨IL 2	3	A ∨ B
R 1	4	¬(A ∨ B)
¬I 2-3, 2-4	5	¬B
ASSUMPTION	6	A
∨IR 6	7	A ∨ B
R 1	8	¬(A ∨ B)
¬I 6-7,6-8	9	¬A
&I 9,5	10	¬A & ¬B
	11	
	12	
	13	
PREMISE	14	¬A & ¬B
ASSUMPTION	15	A ∨ B
ASSUMPTION	16	A
R 16	17	A
ASSUMPTION	18	B
ASSUMPTION	19	¬A
R 18	20	B
&ER 14	21	¬B
¬E 19-20,19-21	22	A
∨E 15,16-17,18-22	23	A
&EL 14	24	¬A
¬I 15-23,15-24	25	¬(A ∨ B)

No (more) errors

SD : EX547C

PREMISE	1	¬(P & ¬Q)
ASSUMPTION	2	¬(¬P ∨ Q)
ASSUMPTION	3	Q
∨IL 3	4	¬P ∨ Q
R 2	5	¬(¬P ∨ Q)
¬I 3-4,3-5	6	¬Q
ASSUMPTION	7	¬P
∨IR 7	8	¬P ∨ Q
R 2	9	¬(¬P ∨ Q)
¬E 7-8,7-9	10	P
&I 10,6	11	P & ¬Q
R 1	12	¬(P & ¬Q)
¬E 2-11,2-12	13	¬P ∨ Q
	14	
	15	
	16	
PREMISE	17	¬P ∨ Q
ASSUMPTION	18	P & ¬Q
ASSUMPTION	19	¬P
ASSUMPTION	20	¬Q
&EL 18	21	P
R 19	22	¬P
¬E 20-21,20-22	23	Q
ASSUMPTION	24	Q
R 24	25	Q
∨E 17,19-23,24-25	26	Q
&ER 18	27	¬Q
¬I 18-26,18-27	28	¬(P & ¬Q)

No (more) errors

SD : EX547E

PREMISE	1	$(R \lor S)\ \&\ \neg H$
ASSUMPTION	2	$(\neg R\ \&\ \neg S) \lor H$
ASSUMPTION	3	$\neg R\ \&\ \neg S$
&EL 1	4	$R \lor S$
ASSUMPTION	5	R
ASSUMPTION	6	$\neg H$
R 5	7	R
&EL 3	8	$\neg R$
$\neg$E 6-7,6-8	9	H
ASSUMPTION	10	S
ASSUMPTION	11	$\neg H$
R 10	12	S
&ER 3	13	$\neg S$
$\neg$E 11-12,11-13	14	H
$\lor$E 4,5-9,10-14	15	H
ASSUMPTION	16	H
R 16	17	H
$\lor$E 2,3-15,16-17	18	H
&ER 1	19	$\neg H$
$\neg$I 2-18,2-19	20	$\neg((\neg R\ \&\ \neg S) \lor H)$
	21	
	22	
	23	
PREMISE	24	$\neg((\neg R\ \&\ \neg S) \lor H)$
ASSUMPTION	25	$\neg(R \lor S)$
ASSUMPTION	26	R
$\lor$IR 26	27	$R \lor S$
R 25	28	$\neg(R \lor S)$
$\neg$I 26-27,26-28	29	$\neg R$
ASSUMPTION	30	S
$\lor$IL 30	31	$R \lor S$
R 25	32	$\neg(R \lor S)$
$\neg$I 30-31,30-32	33	$\neg S$
&I 29,33	34	$\neg R\ \&\ \neg S$
$\lor$IR 34	35	$(\neg R\ \&\ \neg S) \lor H$
R 24	36	$\neg((\neg R\ \&\ \neg S) \lor H)$
$\neg$E 25-35,25-36	37	$R \lor S$
ASSUMPTION	38	H
$\lor$IL 38	39	$(\neg R\ \&\ \neg S) \lor H$
R 24	40	$\neg((\neg R\ \&\ \neg S) \lor H)$
$\neg$I 38-39,38-40	41	$\neg H$
&I 37,41	42	$(R \lor S)\ \&\ \neg H$

No (more) errors

SD : EX547G

PREMISE	1	M ≡ ¬S
ASSUMPTION	2	¬(S ∨ M)
ASSUMPTION	3	¬S
≡E 1,3	4	M
∨IL 4	5	S ∨ M
R 2	6	¬(S ∨ M)
¬E 3-5,3-6	7	S
∨IR /	8	S ∨ M
R 2	9	¬(S ∨ M)
¬E 2-8,2-9	10	S ∨ M
ASSUMPTION	11	M
≡E 1,11	12	¬S
→I 11-12	13	M → ¬S
&I 10,13	14	(S ∨ M) & (M → ¬S)
	15	
	16	
PREMISE	17	(S ∨ M) & (M → ¬S)
ASSUMPTION	18	M
&ER 17	19	M → ¬S
→E 18,19	20	¬S
ASSUMPTION	21	¬S
&EL 17	22	S ∨ M
ASSUMPTION	23	S
ASSUMPTION	24	¬M
R 23	25	S
R 21	26	¬S
¬E 24-25,24-26	27	M
ASSUMPTION	28	M
R 28	29	M
∨E 22,23-27,28-29	30	M
≡I 18-20,21-30	31	M ≡ ¬S

No (more) errors

SD : EX547I

PREMISE	1	$(A \vee B) \vee C$
ASSUMPTION	2	$A \vee B$
ASSUMPTION	3	A
$\vee$IR 3	4	$A \vee (B \vee C)$
ASSUMPTION	5	B
$\vee$IR 5	6	$B \vee C$
$\vee$IL 6	7	$A \vee (B \vee C)$
$\vee$E 2,3-4,5-7	8	$A \vee (B \vee C)$
ASSUMPTION	9	C
$\vee$IL 9	10	$B \vee C$
$\vee$IL 10	11	$A \vee (B \vee C)$
$\vee$E 1,2-8,9-11	12	$A \vee (B \vee C)$
	13	
	14	
	15	
PREMISE	16	$A \vee (B \vee C)$
ASSUMPTION	17	A
$\vee$IR 17	18	$A \vee B$
$\vee$IR 18	19	$(A \vee B) \vee C$
ASSUMPTION	20	$B \vee C$
ASSUMPTION	21	B
$\vee$IL 21	22	$A \vee B$
$\vee$IR 22	23	$(A \vee B) \vee C$
ASSUMPTION	24	C
$\vee$IL 24	25	$(A \vee B) \vee C$
$\vee$E 20,21-23,24-25	26	$(A \vee B) \vee C$
$\vee$E 16,17-19,20-26	27	$(A \vee B) \vee C$

No (more) errors

5.4.8

SD : EX548A

PREMISE	1	$A \vee I$
PREMISE	2	$A \rightarrow G$
PREMISE	3	$I \rightarrow G$
ASSUMPTION	4	A
$\rightarrow$E 2,4	5	G
ASSUMPTION	6	I
$\rightarrow$E 3,6	7	G
$\vee$E 1,4-5,6-7	8	G

No(more) errors

SD : EX548C

PREMISE	1	¬(B & J)
PREMISE	2	B & L
ASSUMPTION	3	⌐ J
&EL 2	4	B
&I 4,3	5	B & J
R 1	6	⌐ ¬(B & J)
¬I 3-5,3-6	7	¬J

No (more) errors

SD : EX548E

PREMISE	1	(K & H) → S
PREMISE	2	S → ¬(H ∨ A)
ASSUMPTION	3	⌐ K
ASSUMPTION	4	⌐ H
∨IR 4	5	H ∨ A
&I 3,4	6	K & H
→E 1,6	7	S
→E 2,7	8	¬(H ∨ A)
¬I 4-5,4-8	9	¬H
→I 3-9	10	K → ¬H

No (more) errors

5.4.9   In each exercise we derive a pair of contradictory sentences.

SD : EX549A

PREMISE	1	(A & B) ≡ ¬C
PREMISE	2	(D & E) & B
PREMISE	3	(D ∨ F) → (A & C)
&EL 2	4	D & E
&EL 4	5	D
∨IR 5	6	D ∨ F
→E 3,6	7	A & C
&ER 7	8	C
&EL 7	9	A
&ER 2	10	B
&I 9,10	11	A & B
≡E 1,11	12	¬C

No (more) errors

SD : EX549C

PREMISE	1	(H → ¬H) & (¬H → H)
ASSUMPTION	2	¬H
&ER 1	3	¬H → H
→E 2,3	4	H
R 2	5	¬H
¬E 2-4,2-5	6	H
ASSUMPTION	7	H
R 7	8	H
&EL 1	9	H → ¬H
→ E 7,9	10	¬H
¬I 7-8,7-10	11	¬H

No (more) errors

SD : EX549E

PREMISE	1	(D & ¬P) ∨ (P & ¬D)
PREMISE	2	D ≡ P
ASSUMPTION	3	D & ¬P
ASSUMPTION	4	¬(P & ¬P)
&EL 3	5	D
≡E 2,5	6	P
&ER 3	7	¬P
¬E 4-6,4-7	8	P & ¬P
ASSUMPTION	9	P & ¬D
ASSUMPTION	10	¬(P & ¬P)
&EL 9	11	P
≡E 2,11	12	D
&ER 9	13	¬D
¬E 10-12,10-13	14	P & ¬P
∨E 1,3-8,9-14	15	P & ¬P
&EL 15	16	P
&ER 15	17	¬P

No (more) errors

5.4.10

SD : EX5410A

PREMISE	1	$\neg M$
PREMISE	2	$\neg C \,\&\, \neg T$
PREMISE	3	$(A \vee P) \to C$
ASSUMPTION	4	$T \vee A$
ASSUMPTION	5	T
ASSUMPTION	6	$\neg P$
R 5	7	T
&ER 2	8	$\neg T$
$\neg$E 6-7,6-8	9	P
ASSUMPTION	10	A
ASSUMPTION	11	$\neg P$
$\vee$IR 10	12	$A \vee P$
$\to$E 3,12	13	C
&EL 2	14	$\neg C$
$\neg$E 11-13,11-14	15	P
$\vee$E 4,5-9,10-15	16	P
$\to$I 4-16	17	$(T \vee A) \to P$

No (more) errors

SD : EX5410C

PREMISE	1	$(A \vee B) \to \neg(C \,\&\, B)$
PREMISE	2	$\neg B \vee (B \to C)$
ASSUMPTION	3	B
ASSUMPTION	4	$\neg B$
ASSUMPTION	5	$\neg D$
R 3	6	B
R 4	7	$\neg B$
$\neg$E 5-6,5-7	8	D
ASSUMPTION	9	$B \to C$
ASSUMPTION	10	$\neg D$
$\to$E 3,9	11	C
&I 11,3	12	$C \,\&\, B$
$\vee$IL 3	13	$A \vee B$
$\to$E 1,13	14	$\neg(C \,\&\, B)$
$\neg$E 10-12,10-14	15	D
$\vee$E 2,4-8,9-15	16	D
$\to$I 3-16	17	$B \to D$

No (more) errors

SD : EX5410E

PREMISE	1		$G \rightarrow S$
PREMISE	2		$\neg S \vee G$
ASSUMPTION	3		G
$\rightarrow$E 1,3	4		S
ASSUMPTION	5		S
ASSUMPTION	6		$\neg S$
ASSUMPTION	7		$\neg G$
R 5	8		S
R 6	9		$\neg S$
$\neg$E 7-8,7-9	10		G
ASSUMPTION	11		G
R 11	12		G
$\vee$E 2,6-10,11-12	13		G
$\equiv$I 3-4,5-13	14		$G \equiv S$

No (more) errors

5.4.11 a. True. Since Γ_1 is SD-inconsistent, a sentence, α, and its negation, $\neg\alpha$, can be derived from Γ_1. It is clear that α and $\neg\alpha$ are also derivable from $\Gamma_1 \cup \Gamma_2$, regardless of what Γ_2 is. Hence, $\Gamma_1 \cup \Gamma_2$ is also SD-inconsistent.

c. True. As pointed out above, the union of an SD-inconsistent set with any other set—whether SD-consistent or not—is also SD-inconsistent.

5.4.13 $S \vee T$ can be derived from the other sentences in the set, as shown below.

SD : EX5413

PREMISE	1	$Q \equiv (R \& S)$
PREMISE	2	$Q \& \neg P$
&EL 2	3	Q
$\equiv$E 1,3	4	R & S
&ER 4	5	S
$\vee$IR 5	6	$S \vee T$

No (more) errors

5.5.1 a. False;   c. True;   e. True;   g. True

5.5.2

SD+: EX552A

PREMISE	1	(A → ¬B) & H
PREMISE	2	(¬F → ¬E) & (A ≡ H)
PREMISE	3	(¬A ∨ ¬B) → ¬F
ASSUMPTION	4	E
&EL 2	5	¬F → ¬E
TR 5	6	¬¬E → ¬¬F
DN 6	7	E → ¬¬F
DN 7	8	E → F
→E 4,8	9	F
&ER 2	10	A ≡ H
&ER 1	11	H
≡E 10,11	12	A
&EL 1	13	A → ¬B
→E 12,13	14	¬B
∨IL 14	15	¬A ∨ ¬B
→E 3,15	16	¬F
¬I 4-9,4-16	17	¬E
∨IR 17	18	¬E ∨ G

No (more) errors

SD+ : EX552C

PREMISE	1	(N & H) → (I & ¬L)
PREMISE	2	M → (J → I)
PREMISE	3	¬I ∨ (M & J)
PREMISE	4	(J → L) & N
ASSUMPTION	5	H
ASSUMPTION	6	¬S
&ER 4	7	N
&I 7,5	8	N & H
→E 1,8	9	I & ¬L
&EL 9	10	I
ASSUMPTION	11	¬I
R 11	12	¬I
ASSUMPTION	13	M & J
ASSUMPTION	14	I
IM 3	15	I → (M & J)
→E 14,15	16	M & J
&ER 16	17	J
&EL 4	18	J → L
→E 17,18	19	L
→E 1,8	20	I & ¬L
&ER 20	21	¬L
¬I 14-19,14-21	22	¬I
∨E 3,11-12,13-22	23	¬I
¬E 6-10,6-23	24	S
→I 5-24	25	H → S

No (more) errors

SD+ : EX552E

PREMISE	1	¬(T ∨ ¬M)
PREMISE	2	(S ∨ M) → ¬(A & B)
ASSUMPTION	3	A & B
ASSUMPTION	4	¬(D ≡ ¬A)
R 3	5	A & B
DM 1	6	¬T & ¬¬M
&ER 6	7	¬¬M
DN 7	8	M
∨IL 8	9	S ∨ M
→E 2,9	10	¬(A & B)
¬E 4-5,4-10	11	D ≡ ¬A
→I 3-11	12	(A & B) → (D ≡ ¬A)

No (more) errors

SD+ : EX552G

PREMISE	1	(C → A) & (A → B)
PREMISE	2	((C & A) & B) ∨ (C ∨ ¬B)
ASSUMPTION	3	(C & A) & B
&ER 3	4	B
&EL 3	5	C & A
&EL 5	6	C
&I 6,4	7	C & B
∨IR 7	8	(C & B) ∨ ¬(B ∨ C)
ASSUMPTION	9	C ∨ ¬B
ASSUMPTION	10	C
&EL 1	11	C → A
→E 10,11	12	A
&ER 1	13	A → B
→E 12,13	14	B
&I 10,14	15	C & B
∨IR 15	16	(C & B) ∨ ¬(B ∨ C)
ASSUMPTION	17	¬B
&EL 1	18	C → A
&ER 1	19	A → B
HS 18,19	20	C → B
MT 17,20	21	¬C
&I 17,21	22	¬B & ¬C
DM 22	23	¬(B ∨ C)
∨IL 23	24	(C & B) ∨ ¬(B ∨ C)
∨E 9,10-16,17-24	25	(C & B) ∨ ¬(B ∨ C)
∨E 2,3-8,9-25	26	(C & B) ∨ ¬(B ∨ C)

No (more) errors

SD+ : EX552I

PREMISE	1	D → G	
PREMISE	2	(H → R) ≡ M	
PREMISE	3	H → D	
PREMISE	4	¬G ∨ (R & H)	
ASSUMPTION	5	¬G	
MT 1,5	6	¬D	
MT 3,6	7	¬H	
∨IR 7	8	¬H ∨ R	
IM 8	9	H → R	
≡E 2,9	10	M	
&I 10,6	11	M & ¬D	
∨IR 11	12	(M & ¬D) ∨ (G & ¬¬M)	
ASSUMPTION	13	R & H	
&ER 13	14	H	
IIS 1,3	15	H → G	
→E 14,15	16	G	
&EL 13	17	R	
∨IL 17	18	¬H ∨ R	
IM 18	19	H → R	
≡E 2,19	20	M	
DN 20	21	¬¬M	
&I 16,21	22	G & ¬¬M	
∨IL 22	23	(M & ¬D) ∨ (G & ¬¬M)	
∨E 4,5-12,13-23	24	(M & ¬D) ∨ (G & ¬¬M)	

No (more) errors

5.5.3

SD+ : EX553A

PREMISE	1	[¬(A & C) ∨ D] & ¬F	
PREMISE	2	¬(A → D) ∨ (F & B)	
PREMISE	3	¬D	
ASSUMPTION	4	C	
ASSUMPTION	5	¬G	
&EL 1	6	¬(A & C) ∨ D	
DS 3,6	7	¬(A & C)	
DM 7	8	¬A ∨ ¬C	
DN 4	9	¬¬C	
DS 8,9	10	¬A	
∨IR 10	11	¬A ∨ D	
IM 11	12	A → D	
DN 12	13	¬¬(A → D)	
DS 2,13	14	F & B	
&EL 14	15	F	
&ER 1	16	¬F	
¬E 5-15,5-16	17	G	
→I 4-17	18	C → G	

No (more) errors

SD+ : EX553C

PREMISE	1	$\neg(A \rightarrow B) \rightarrow C$
ASSUMPTION	2	$A \& \neg B$
IM 1	3	$\neg(\neg A \vee B) \rightarrow C$
DM 3	4	$(\neg\neg A \& \neg B) \rightarrow C$
DN 4	5	$(A \& \neg B) \rightarrow C$
$\rightarrow$E 2,5	6	C
$\rightarrow$I 2-6	7	$(A \& \neg B) \rightarrow C$

No (more) errors

SD+ : EX553E

PREMISE	1	$\neg P \rightarrow Q$
PREMISE	2	$Q \rightarrow R$
PREMISE	3	$\neg(P \vee R)$
DM 3	4	$\neg P \& \neg R$
&EL 4	5	$\neg P$
$\rightarrow$E 1,5	6	Q
$\rightarrow$E 2,6	7	R

No (more) errors

SD+ : EX553G

ASSUMPTION	1	$S \vee M$
DN 1	2	$\neg\neg(S \vee M)$
DM 2	3	$\neg(\neg S \& \neg M)$
ASSUMPTION	4	$\neg(\neg S \& \neg M)$
DM 4	5	$\neg\neg(S \vee M)$
DN 5	6	$S \vee M$
$\equiv$I 1-3,4-6	7	$(S \vee M) \equiv \neg(\neg S \& \neg M)$

No (more) errors

SD+ : EX553I

PREMISE	1	$(Q \rightarrow R) \rightarrow Q$
PREMISE	2	$(Q \vee R) \rightarrow P$
IM 2	3	$\neg(Q \vee R) \vee P$
ASSUMPTION	4	$\neg(Q \vee R)$
DM 4	5	$\neg Q \& \neg R$
&EL 5	6	$\neg Q$
$\vee$IR 6	7	$\neg Q \vee R$
IM 7	8	$Q \rightarrow R$
$\rightarrow$E 1,8	9	Q
$\vee$IR 9	10	$Q \vee R$
$\rightarrow$E 2,10	11	P
ASSUMPTION	12	P
R 12	13	P
$\vee$E 3,4-11,12-13	14	P

No (more) errors

5.5.4   For each exercise derive a pair of contradictory sentences.

SD+ : EX554A

PREMISE	1	$\neg(A \;\&\; (C \equiv A))$
PREMISE	2	$(A \;\&\; \neg L) \lor (L \;\&\; \neg L)$
PREMISE	3	$(C \;\&\; I) \lor (A \;\&\; C)$
CM 2	4	$(\neg L \;\&\; A) \lor (L \;\&\; \neg L)$
CM 4	5	$(\neg L \;\&\; A) \lor (\neg L \;\&\; L)$
DI 5	6	$\neg L \;\&\; (A \lor L)$
&EL 6	7	$\neg L$
&ER 6	8	$A \lor L$
DS 7,8	9	A
CM 3	10	$(C \;\&\; I) \lor (C \;\&\; A)$
DI 10	11	$C \;\&\; (I \lor A)$
&EL 11	12	C
&I 12,9	13	$C \;\&\; A$
∨IR 13	14	$(C \;\&\; A) \lor (\neg C \;\&\; \neg A)$
EQ 14	15	$C \equiv A$
&I 9,15	16	$A \;\&\; (C \equiv A)$
R 1	17	$\neg(A \;\&\; (C \equiv A))$

No (more) errors

SD+ : EX554C

PREMISE	1	$\neg\neg\neg K \rightarrow \neg N$
PREMISE	2	$\neg\neg E \;\&\; N$
PREMISE	3	$E \equiv \neg(K \lor T)$
DN 2	4	$E \;\&\; N$
&EL 4	5	E
≡E 3,5	6	$\neg(K \lor T)$
&ER 2	7	N
DN 7	8	$\neg\neg N$
MT 1,8	9	$\neg\neg\neg\neg K$
DN 9	10	$\neg\neg K$
DN 10	11	K
∨IR 11	12	$K \lor T$

No (more) errors

SD+ : EX554E

PREMISE	1	(A & B) ∨ (¬B & ¬A)
PREMISE	2	¬(¬A ∨ M)
PREMISE	3	(M ∨ ¬B) & (A ∨ M)
CM 1	4	(A & B) ∨ (¬A & ¬B)
EQ 4	5	A ≡ B
DM 2	6	¬¬A & ¬M
DN 6	7	A & ¬M
&EL 7	8	A
≡E 5,8	9	B
&ER 7	10	¬M
CM 3	11	(M ∨ ¬B) & (M ∨ A)
DI 11	12	M ∨ (¬B & A)
DS 10,12	13	¬B & A
&EL 13	14	¬B

No (more) errors

SD : EX554G

PREMISE	1	¬D → ¬(B → C)
PREMISE	2	C ∨ (E ≡ N)
PREMISE	3	(N → ¬B) & (E & ¬D)
&ER 3	4	E & ¬D
&ER 4	5	¬D
→E 1,5	6	¬(B → C)
IM 6	7	¬(¬B ∨ C)
DM 7	8	¬¬B & ¬C
&ER 8	9	¬C
DS 2,9	10	E ≡ N
&EL 4	11	E
≡E 10,11	12	N
&EL 3	13	N → ¬B
TR 13	14	¬¬B → ¬N
&EL 8	15	¬¬B
→E 14,15	16	¬N

No (more) errors

SD : EX554I

PREMISE	1	(C ∨ ¬B) → D
PREMISE	2	(B → C) & ¬D
&EL 2	3	B → C
IM 3	4	¬B ∨ C
CM 4	5	C ∨ ¬B
→E 1,5	6	D
&ER 2	7	¬D

No (more) errors

5.5.5   For each exercise derive a pair of contradictory sentences from the test set.

SD+ : EX555A

PREMISE	1	$\neg(\neg R \vee \neg A)$
PREMISE	2	D & E
PREMISE	3	$\neg(E \& \neg O) \vee \neg A$
PREMISE	4	$\neg O$
DM 1	5	$\neg\neg R \& \neg\neg A$
&ER 5	6	$\neg\neg A$
DS 3,6	7	$\neg(E \& \neg O)$
DM 7	8	$\neg E \vee \neg\neg O$
&ER 2	9	E
DN 9	10	$\neg\neg E$
DN 8	11	$\neg E \vee O$
DS 10,11	12	O
R 4	13	$\neg O$

No (more) errors

SD+ : EX555C

PREMISE	1	$\neg(O \& G)$
PREMISE	2	$(\neg K \equiv M) \& (\neg P \to Q)$
PREMISE	3	$\neg[\neg(G \& O) \& (\neg P \to Q)]$
CM 1	4	$\neg(G \& O)$
&ER 2	5	$\neg P \to Q$
&I 4,5	6	$\neg(G \& O) \& (\neg P \to Q)$
R 3	7	$\neg(\neg(G \& O) \& (\neg P \to Q))$

No (more) errors

SD+ : EX555E

PREMISE	1	$\neg((A \equiv (B \equiv C)) \equiv ((A \equiv B) \equiv C))$
ASSUMPTION	2	$A \equiv (B \equiv C)$
AS 2	3	$(A \equiv B) \equiv C$
ASSUMPTION	4	$(A \equiv B) \equiv C$
AS 4	5	$A \equiv (B \equiv C)$
$\equiv$I 2-3,4-5	6	$(A \equiv (B \equiv C)) \equiv ((A \equiv B) \equiv C)$
R 1	7	$\neg((A \equiv (B \equiv C)) \equiv ((A \equiv B) \equiv C))$

No (more) errors

5.5.6

SD+ : EX 556A

PREMISE	1	A ≡ B
PREMISE	2	(B ∨ D) ≡ ¬[¬G & (B ≡ C)]
ASSUMPTION	3	⌐ A & (B ≡ C)
&EL 3	4	A
≡E 1,4	5	B
∨IR 5	6	B ∨ D
≡E 2,6	7	¬(¬G & (B ≡ C))
DM 7	8	¬¬G ∨ ¬(B ≡ C)
&ER 3	9	B ≡ C
DN 9	10	¬¬(B ≡ C)
DS 8,10	11	¬¬G
DN 11	12	G
∨IR 12	13	⌐ G ∨ R
→I 3-13	14	[A & (B ≡ C)] → (G ∨ R)

No (more) errors

SD+ : EX556C

PREMISE	1	(¬T → H) & (H → ¬¬¬T)
PREMISE	2	¬N
PREMISE	3	¬¬H
ASSUMPTION	4	⌐ B & C
&ER 1	5	H → ¬¬¬T
DN 3	6	H
→E 5,6	7	¬¬¬T
DN 7	8	¬T
&I 8,2	9	¬T & ¬N
DM 9	10	⌐ ¬(T ∨ N)
→I 4-10	11	(B & C) → ¬(T∨N)

No (more) errors

SD+ : EX556E

PREMISE	1	(¬A ∨ ¬(B ∨ C)) ≡ (F ≡ G)
PREMISE	2	G & F
∨IR 2	3	(G & F) ∨ (¬G & ¬F)
EQ 3	4	G ≡ F
CM 4	5	F ≡ G
≡E 1,5	6	¬A ∨ ¬(B ∨ C)
DM 6	7	¬(A & (B ∨ C))
DI 7	8	¬((A & B) ∨ (A & C))
CM 8	9	¬[(A & B) ∨ (C & A)]

No (more) errors

SD+ : EX556G

PREMISE	1	$\neg(P \equiv P)$
ASSUMPTION	2	$\neg Q$
EQ 1	3	$\neg((P \& P) \vee (\neg P \& \neg P))$
ID 3	4	$\neg(P \vee (\neg P \& \neg P))$
ID 4	5	$\neg(P \vee \neg P)$
DM 5	6	$\neg P \& \neg\neg P$
&EL 6	7	$\neg P$
&ER 6	8	$\neg\neg P$
$\neg$E 2-7,2-8	9	Q

No (more) errors

SD+ : EX556I

PREMISE	1	$\neg A \vee [\neg B \vee (B \& D)]$
PREMISE	2	$\neg B \vee [(\neg D \vee A) \& (B \vee \neg D)]$
ASSUMPTION	3	$A \& B$
&EL 3	4	A
DN 4	5	$\neg\neg A$
DS 1,5	6	$\neg B \vee (B \& D)$
&ER 3	7	B
DN 7	8	$\neg\neg B$
DS 6,8	9	$B \& D$
ASSUMPTION	10	$B \& D$
CM 2	11	$\neg B \vee ((\neg D \vee A) \& (\neg D \vee B))$
DI 11	12	$\neg B \vee (\neg D \vee (A \& B))$
&EL 10	13	B
DN 13	14	$\neg\neg B$
DS 12,14	15	$\neg D \vee (A \& B)$
&ER 10	16	D
DN 16	17	$\neg\neg D$
DS 15,17	18	$A \& B$
$\equiv$I 3-9,10-18	19	$(A \& B) \equiv (B \& D)$

No (more) errors

5.5.7

SD+ : EX557A

PREMISE	1	$\neg(\neg M \vee K)$
DM 1	2	$\neg\neg M \& \neg K$
DN 2	3	$M \& \neg K$
CM 3	4	$\neg K \& M$
	5	
	6	
	7	
PREMISE	8	$\neg K \& M$
CM 8	9	$M \& \neg K$
DN 9	10	$\neg\neg M \& \neg K$
DM 10	11	$\neg(\neg M \vee K)$

No (more) errors

SD+ : EX557C

PREMISE	1	¬A → (¬B ∨ C)
IM 1	2	¬¬A ∨ (¬B ∨ C)
DN 2	3	A ∨ (¬B ∨ C)
AS 3	4	(A ∨ ¬B) ∨ C
DN 4	5	(A ∨ ¬B) ∨ ¬¬C
	6	
	7	
	8	
PREMISE	9	(A ∨ ¬B) ∨ ¬¬C
DN 5	10	(A ∨ ¬B) ∨ C
AS 10	11	A ∨ (¬B ∨ C)
DN 11	12	¬¬A ∨ (¬B ∨ C)
IM 12	13	¬A → (¬B ∨ C)

No (more) errors

SD+ : EX557E

PREMISE	1	¬(A ≡ B)
EQ 1	2	¬((A → B) & (B → A))
DM 2	3	¬(A → B) ∨ ¬(B → A)
IM 3	4	¬(¬A ∨ B) ∨ ¬(B → A)
IM 4	5	¬(¬A ∨ B) ∨ ¬(¬B ∨ A)
DM 5	6	(¬¬A & ¬B) ∨ ¬(¬B ∨ A)
	7	
	8	
	9	
PREMISE	10	(¬¬A & ¬B) ∨ ¬(¬B ∨ A)
DM 10	11	¬(¬A ∨ B) ∨ ¬(¬B ∨ A)
IM 11	12	¬(¬A ∨ B) ∨ ¬(B → A)
IM 12	13	¬(A → B) ∨ ¬(B → A)
DM 13	14	¬((A → B) & (B → A))
EQ 14	15	¬(A ≡ B)

No (more) errors

SD+ : EX557G

PREMISE	1	(¬¬M ∨ R) & (R ∨ ¬¬¬S)
CM1	2	(R ∨ ¬¬M) & (R ∨ ¬¬¬S)
DI 2	3	R ∨ (¬¬M & ¬¬S)
CM 3	4	(¬¬M & ¬¬S) ∨ R
DM 4	5	¬(¬M ∨ ¬S) ∨ R
CM 5	6	¬(¬S ∨ ¬M) ∨ R
IM 6	7	¬(S → ¬M) ∨ R
	8	
	9	
	10	
PREMISE	11	¬(S → ¬M) ∨ R
IM 11	12	¬(¬S ∨ ¬M) ∨ R
CM 12	13	¬(¬M ∨ ¬S) ∨ R
DM 13	14	(¬¬M & ¬¬S) ∨ R
CM 14	15	R ∨ (¬¬M & ¬¬S)
DI 15	16	(R ∨ ¬¬M) & (R ∨ ¬¬¬S)
CM 16	17	(¬¬M ∨ R) & (R ∨ ¬¬¬S)

No (more) errors

SD+ : EX557I

PREMISE	1	¬(¬F ∨ ¬D) → E
IM 1	2	¬¬(¬F ∨ ¬D) ∨ E
DN 2	3	(¬F ∨ ¬D) ∨ E
AS 3	4	¬F ∨ (¬D ∨ E)
CM 4	5	(¬D ∨ E) ∨ ¬F
IM 5	6	(D → E) ∨ ¬F
DN 6	7	¬¬(D → E) ∨ ¬F
IM 7	8	¬(D → E) → ¬F
	9	
	10	
	11	
PREMISE	12	¬(D → E) → ¬F
IM 12	13	¬¬(D → E) ∨ ¬F
DN 13	14	(D → E) ∨ ¬F
IM 14	15	(¬D ∨ E) ∨ ¬F
CM 15	16	¬F ∨ (¬D ∨ E)
AS 16	17	(¬F ∨ ¬D) ∨ E
DN 17	18	¬¬(¬F ∨ ¬D) ∨ E
IM 18	19	¬(¬F ∨ ¬D) → E

No (more) errors

5.5.8

SD+ : EX558A

PREMISE	1	D → A
PREMISE	2	¬R → ¬A
PREMISE	3	((D & R) & A) ∨ (D ∨ ¬R)
ASSUMPTION	4	(D & R) & A
&EL 4	5	D & R
∨IR 5	6	(D & R) ∨ ¬(D ∨ R)
ASSUMPTION	7	D ∨ ¬R
ASSUMPTION	8	D
→E 1,8	9	A
TR 2	10	¬¬A → ¬¬R
DN 10	11	A → ¬¬R
→E 9,11	12	¬¬R
DN 12	13	R
&I 8,13	14	D & R
∨IR 14	15	(D & R) ∨ ¬(D ∨ R)
ASSUMPTION	16	¬R
→E 2,16	17	¬A
MT 1,17	18	¬D
&I 18,16	19	¬D & ¬R
DM 19	20	¬(D ∨ R)
∨IL 20	21	(D & R) ∨ ¬(D ∨ R)
∨E 7,8-15,16-21	22	(D & R) ∨ ¬(D ∨ R)
∨E 3,4-6,7-22	23	(D & R) ∨ ¬(D ∨ R)

No (more) errors

SD+ : EX558C

PREMISE	1	¬(¬E ∨ ¬P)
PREMISE	2	O & S
PREMISE	3	¬(S & F) ∨ ¬P
ASSUMPTION	4	¬(S & F)
DM 4	5	¬S ∨ ¬F
ASSUMPTION	6	¬S
ASSUMPTION	7	F
&ER 2	8	S
R 6	9	¬S
¬I 7-8,7-9	10	¬F
ASSUMPTION	11	¬F
R 11	12	¬F
∨E 5,6-10,11-12	13	¬F
ASSUMPTION	14	¬P
ASSUMPTION	15	F
DM 1	16	¬¬E & ¬¬P
&ER 16	17	¬¬P
DN 17	18	P
R 14	19	¬P
¬I 15-18,15-19	20	¬F
∨E 3,4-13,14-20	21	¬F

No (more) errors

SD+ : EX558E

PREMISE	1	¬L ∨ J
PREMISE	2	¬T → ¬J
PREMISE	3	T → D
PREMISE	4	¬P → ¬D
IM 1	5	L → J
TR 2	6	¬¬J → ¬¬T
DN 6	7	J → ¬¬T
DN 7	8	J → T
TR 4	9	¬¬D → ¬¬P
DN 9	10	D → ¬¬P
DN 10	11	D → P
HS 5,8	12	L → T
HS 12,3	13	L → D
HS 13,11	14	L → P
IM 14	15	¬L ∨ P

No (more) errors

5.5.9   For each exercise derive a pair of contradictory sentences.

SD+ : EX559A

PREMISE	1	L & (F ∨ C)
PREMISE	2	F ∨ S
PREMISE	3	¬S
PREMISE	4	¬F ∨ ¬(F ≡ L)
DS 2,3	5	F
DN 5	6	¬¬F
DS 4,6	7	¬(F ≡ L)
ASSUMPTION	8	F
&EL 1	9	L
ASSUMPTION	10	L
R 5	11	F
≡I 8-9,10-11	12	F ≡ L

No (more) errors

SD+ : EX559C

PREMISE	1	L & (S ∨ R)
PREMISE	2	(S & R) ∨ ¬(S ∨ R)
PREMISE	3	¬(L & R)
DM 3	4	¬L ∨ ¬R
&EL 1	5	L
DN 5	6	¬¬L
DS 4,6	7	¬R
&ER 1	8	S ∨ R
DN 8	9	¬¬(S ∨ R)
DS 2,9	10	S & R
&ER 10	11	R

No (more) errors

SD+ : EX559E

PREMISE	1	$(R \rightarrow M)$ & $(\neg R \rightarrow M)$
PREMISE	2	$R \lor \neg M$
PREMISE	3	$\neg R \lor \neg M$
ASSUMPTION	4	$\neg R$
&ER 1	5	$\neg R \rightarrow M$
$\rightarrow$E 4,5	6	M
DS 2,4	7	$\neg M$
$\neg$E 4-6,4-7	8	R
ASSUMPTION	9	R
&EL 1	10	$R \rightarrow M$
$\rightarrow$E 9,10	11	M
DN 9	12	$\neg\neg R$
DS 3,12	13	$\neg M$
$\neg$I 9-11,9-13	14	$\neg R$

No (more) errors

5.5.10

SD+ : EX5510A

PREMISE	1	$(R \lor \neg M) \rightarrow \neg F$
PREMISE	2	F & $(R \lor A)$
PREMISE	3	$(F \lor T) \rightarrow (F$ & $T)$
&EL 2	4	F
$\lor$IR 4	5	$F \lor T$
$\rightarrow$E 3,5	6	F & T
&ER 6	7	T
ASSUMPTION	8	$\neg M$
R 4	9	F
$\lor$IL 8	10	$R \lor \neg M$
$\rightarrow$E 1,10	11	$\neg F$
$\neg$E 8-9,8-11	12	M
&I 7,12	13	T & M

No (more) errors

SD+ : EX5510C

PREMISE	1	¬((P & M) ∨ (R & S))
DM 1	2	¬(P & M) & ¬(R & S)
&EL 2	3	¬(P & M)
DM 3	4	¬P ∨ ¬M
ASSUMPTION	5	¬P
∨IR 5	6	¬P ∨ ¬S
DM 6	7	¬(P & S)
&I 5,7	8	¬P & ¬(P & S)
DM 8	9	¬(P ∨ (P & S))
∨IR 9	10	¬(P ∨ (P & S)) ∨ ((M ∨ R) → ¬(M ∨ S))
ASSUMPTION	11	¬M
ASSUMPTION	12	M ∨ R
&ER 2	13	¬(R & S)
DM 13	14	¬R ∨ ¬S
ASSUMPTION	15	¬R
ASSUMPTION	16	S
DS 12,15	17	M
R 11	18	¬M
¬I 16-17,16-18	19	¬S
ASSUMPTION	20	¬S
R 20	21	¬S
∨E 14,15-19,20-21	22	¬S
&I 11,22	23	¬M & ¬S
DM 23	24	¬(M ∨ S)
→I 12-24	25	(M ∨ R) → ¬(M ∨ S)
∨IL 25	26	¬(P ∨ (P & S)) ∨ ((M ∨ R) → ¬(M ∨ S))
∨E 4,5-10,11-26	27	¬(P ∨ (P & S)) ∨ ((M ∨ R) → ¬(M ∨ S))

No (more) errors

SD+ : EX5510E

PREMISE	1	¬(S ∨ T)
PREMISE	2	¬S → T
ASSUMPTION	3	¬F
DM 1	4	¬S & ¬T
&EL 4	5	¬S
→E 2,5	6	T
&ER 4	7	¬T
¬E 3-6,3-7	8	F

No (more) errors

5.5.11 In SD+ this derivation takes a mere two steps by using association. The derivation in SD is far longer—31 steps—and more involved.

SD+ : EX5511

PREMISE	1	A ≡ (B ≡ C)
AS 1	2	(A ≡ B) ≡ C
	3	
	4	
	5	
PREMISE	6	A ≡ (B ≡ C)
ASSUMPTION	7	A ≡ B
ASSUMPTION	8	¬C
ASSUMPTION	9	B
≡E 7,9	10	A
≡E 6,10	11	B ≡ C
≡E 11,9	12	C
ASSUMPTION	13	C
ASSUMPTION	14	¬B
R 13	15	C
R 8	16	¬C
¬E 14-15,14-16	17	B
≡I 9-12,13-17	18	B ≡ C
≡E 6,18	19	A
≡E 7,19	20	B
≡E 18,20	21	C
R 8	22	¬C
¬E 8-21,8-22	23	C
ASSUMPTION	24	C
ASSUMPTION	25	A
≡E 6,25	26	B ≡ C
≡E 26,24	27	B
ASSUMPTION	28	B
ASSUMPTION	29	B
R 24	30	C
ASSUMPTION	31	C
R 28	32	B
≡I 29-30,31-32	33	B ≡ C
≡E 6,33	34	A
≡I 25-27,28-34	35	A ≡ B
≡I 7-23,24-35	36	(A ≡ B) ≡ C

No (more) errors

5.6.1 a. We should first remark that we cannot use SD's metatheory in answering this question for it may not apply to SD* (e. g., the soundness theorem does not hold for SD*). We argue, instead, as follows: Since the sentence P∨¬P can be derived from the empty set, it can clearly be derived from any set Γ. By applying ∨E' on this sentence, both P and ¬P can be derived. Hence, Γ is SD*-inconsistent.

5.6.2 a. Any use of reiteration (of a sentence α) in a derivation can be replaced by the following two steps: Derive α & α by &I and then α by &EL.
c. The step of obtaining β from α & β by &ER can always be replaced by these two steps: Apply CM to α & β to obtain β & α, and then apply &EL to obtain β.

5.6.3   a. By 'proof surgery.' Any line in a derivation using &-association, appealing to an entire sentence α & $(\beta$ & $\delta)$ to obtain $(\alpha$ & $\beta)$ & δ, can be replaced by the following sequence of lines:

	i	
	i	α & $(\beta$ & $\delta)$
&EL i	i+1	α
&ER i	i+2	β & δ
&EL i+2	i+3	β
&ER i+3	i+4	δ
&I i+1, i+3	i+5	α & β
&I i+5, i+4	i+6	$(\alpha$ & $\beta)$ & δ

Showing how to derive α & $(\beta$ & $\delta)$ from $(\alpha$ & $\beta)$ & δ is very similar to the above, and we leave it to the reader.

c. Again, use 'proof surgery.' That is, any line in a derivation using exportation, appealing to an entire sentence $\alpha \to (\beta \to \delta)$ to obtain $(\alpha$ & $\beta) \to \delta$, can be replaced by the following sequence of lines:

	i	
	i	$\alpha \to (\beta \to \delta)$
ASSUMPTION	i+1	α & β
&EL i+1	i+2	α
→E i, i+2	i+3	$\beta \to \delta$
&ER i+1	i+4	β
→E i+3, i+4	i+5	δ
→I i+1 − i+5	i+6	$(\alpha$ & $\beta) \to \delta$

If exportation is applied in the other direction then use the following:

	i	
	i	$(\alpha$ & $\beta) \to \delta$
ASSUMPTION	i+1	α
ASSUMPTION	i+2	β
&I i+1, i+2	i+3	α & β
→E i, i+3	i+4	δ
→I i+2 − i+4	i+5	$\beta \to \delta$
→I i+1 − i+5	i+6	$\alpha \to (\beta \to \delta)$

5.6.5   (a) Since all the rules of SD are rules of SD*, any SD-theorem of Γ is also an SD*-theorem of Γ; (b) this new rule is shown to be reducible to those of SD by the metaproof of Figure 5.34. Hence, any SD*-theorem of Γ is also an SD-theorem of Γ.

5.6.6   a. true;   c. true;   e. false;   g. false;   i. true

5.6.7   (a) By (the contrapositive of) the soundness theorem, if the set $\{P \lor R, \neg Q \,\&\, P\}$ does not truth-functionally entail the sentence R then R is not SD-derivable from $\{P \lor R, \neg Q \,\&\, P\}$. Hence, to show that R cannot be derived from the given set show by a truth-table or a truth-tree that the test set $\{P \lor R, \neg Q \,\&\, P, \neg R\}$ is truth-functionally consistent. More easily, give a truth-value assignment which satisfies the set $\{P \lor R, \neg Q \,\&\, P\}$ but not R. (b) Same argument as in (a).

5.6.8   a. True. To prove P → P (from the empty set) assume P and then reiterate it. The proof is three lines long.
c. True. If there is truth-value assignment which satisfies Γ but not α then Γ does not entail α, $\Gamma \nvDash \alpha$. By the soundness theorem, it follows that α is not derivable from Γ.
e. True. P & Q can be obtained by &I in one single step. The premises, P and Q, and the

conclusion, P & Q, take three lines. The remaining steps—lines 3 to 6—can be 'filled in' by, say, reiterating P four times.

5.6.9   If Ø is SD-inconsistent then two contradictory sentences, α and $\neg\alpha$, can be derived from it. But then, α and $\neg\alpha$ can be derived from any set Γ by simply ignoring the sentences in Γ.

5.6.11 P ∨ ¬P is SD-Popper-derivable from the empty set and, hence, from any set. Then, by the new rules, we can derive (P ∨ ¬P) *tonk* P but also (P ∨ ¬P) *tonk* ¬P, and from these, each P and ¬P immediately follows.

Chapter 6: The Basic Sentences of PL

6.1.1   a. John; _____ is happy
c. The sales report, the company's manager; _____ satisfies _____
e. 4, 5; _____ is even, _____ is odd
g. The purpose of the space shuttle, space exploration; _____ advances _____
i. Suzy, Jim; _____ will marry _____, _____ is in love with _____
k. Bill, logic; _____ enjoys studying _____
m. 1, 2, 3; _____ plus _____ equals _____
o. John, Sara's graduation; _____ is going to _____
q. I, money; _____ needs _____
s. My daughter, milk, 'Sesame Street'; _____ drinks _____, _____ watches _____

6.1.3   a. atomic;   c. existential;   e. atomic;   g. universal;   i. atomic

6.1.4   a. atomic;   c. universal;   e. existential;   g. universal;   i. universal

6.1.5   one-place: _____ is happy; _____ is tall; _____ is blue

two-place: _____ is larger than _____; _____ sits on top of _____; _____ is the father of _____

three-place: _____ exchanges _____ for _____; the sum of _____ and _____ is _____; _____ buys _____ for the amount of _____

6.2.1   Here we provide, besides a solution, different stages in the formalization process of the statement.
a. Cj
c. Peter loves Jane → ¬Jane smokes.
    Lpj → ¬Sj
e. For each x, x likes cake.
    (∀x)Cx
g. There is x, x loves Mary ∨ Mary drinks wine.
    (∃x)Lxm ∨ Dm
i. (Robert smokes → there is a person who loves Robert) & every person does not love Robert if (Robert drinks wine & Robert smokes).
    (Robert smokes → there is x, x loves Robert) & [(Robert drinks wine & Robert smokes) → for every x, ¬x loves Robert].
    [Sr → (∃x)Lxr] & [(Dr & Sr) → (∀x)¬Lxr]
k. There is x, Jane loves x and x smokes and x is not Peter.
    (∃x)[(Ljx & Sx) & ¬Ixp]
m. Some x smokes and for any y, if y smokes then y is x.
    (∃x)[Sx & (∀y)(Sy → Iyx)]
o. Robert does not like cake and for any x, if x is not Robert then x likes cake.
    ¬Cr & (∀x)(¬Ixr → Cx); or (∀x)(Cx ≡ ¬Ixr)
q. For any x, if x smokes then x likes cake.
    (∀x)(Sx → Cx)

s. Everybody loves some x who loves some y.
    For each z, there is x and y, z loves x & x loves y.
    (∀z)(∃x)(∃y)(Lzx & Lxy)

6.2.2   a. Robert doesn't smoke but he likes cake.
        c. Someone is in love with Albert but it is not Mary.
        e. Everybody loves a wine drinker.
        g. No one who likes cake loves Albert.
        i. Those who smoke are precisely those who drink wine.

6.2.3   Here we provide, besides a solution, different stages in the formalization process of the statement.
        a. There is a person who loves everybody.
            There is x who for each y, x loves y.
            (∃x)(∀y)Lxy
        c. Each person x loves any person y, if y drinks wine.
            (∀x)(∀y)(Dy → Lxy)
        e. For any person x, if x drinks wine and x smokes then for any y, x loves y if y loves all z.
            Any x, (x drinks wine & x smokes) → [for any y, (for all z, y loves z) → x loves y].
            (∀x)[(Dx & Sx) → (∀y)((∀z)Lyz → Lxy)]
        g. For any person, if that person is a smoker then not everybody loves this person.
            For any x, x smokes → ¬all y are such that y loves x.
            (∀x)(Sx → ¬(∀y)Lyx)
        i. Exactly one person loves Mary or no person loves Mary.
            (There is at least one person x who loves Mary, and any person y who loves Mary must be identical with x) ∨ ¬(someone loves Mary).
            (There is x, x loves Mary & for any y, y loves Mary → y is identical with x) ∨ ¬there is x, x loves Mary.
            (∃x)[Lxm & (∀y)(Lym → Iyx)] ∨ ¬(∃x)Lxm
        k. ¬everybody loves anyone who loves Robert.
            ¬(every person x loves any person y if y loves Robert).
            ¬(for every person x and any y, x loves y if y loves Robert).
            ¬(for every x and every y, y loves Robert → x loves y).
            ¬(∀x)(∀y)(Lyr → Lxy)
        m. Every person x loves any person y if y loves y.
            For every person x and every y, x loves y if y loves y.
            For every x, for every y, y loves y → x loves y.
            (∀x)(∀y)(Lyy → Lxy)
        o. Any smoker drinks wine.
            For any person, if this person smokes then this person drinks wine.
            For any x, x smokes → x drinks wine.
            (∀x)(Sx → Dx)

6.2.4   a. Ea
            ———
            ¬Oa

        c. Gba & Ob
            ———
            ¬Ot
            —————
            Gta ∨ Gba

        e. ¬(∃x)Lxa
            —————
            ¬Lta

        g. (∀x)Ex ∨ (∀x)Ox
            —————————
            (∀x)(Ex ∨ Ox)

        i. (∀x)(∃y)Sxy
            (∀x)(∀y)[¬Ixy → ¬(∃z)(Sxz & Syz)]
            ————————————————
            (∀x)(∀y)[Ixy → (∀z)(Szx ≡ Szy)]

        k. (∀x)(∃y)[Sxy & (Ex → Oy)]
            (∀x)(∃y)[Sxy & (Ox → Ey)]
            Ea
            ————————————
            (∃x)(∃y)[(Sax & Sxy) & Ey]

6.2.5 a. Fbl & ($\neg$Mlf $\lor$ $\neg$Mlt)

       c. [Ct & ($\forall$x)(Cx $\rightarrow$ Ixt)] & $\neg$($\exists$y)Byt

       e. [(Sbf & Sbs) & (Sdf & Sds)] & [(((Lb & Lf) & Ls) & $\neg$Ld) & Cd]

       g. Cs & ($\forall$x)(Msx $\rightarrow$ Cx) & ($\forall$x)[($\exists$y)(Msy & (Fyx $\lor$ Myx)) $\rightarrow$ Cx]

       i. ($\exists$x)($\exists$y)[[$\neg$Ixy & ((Dxt & Dxs) & (Dyt & Dys))] & ($\forall$z)((Dzt & Dzs) $\rightarrow$ (Izx $\lor$ Izy))]

       k. ($\forall$x)($\forall$y)[(Sxy & Ly) $\rightarrow$ Lx]

      m. ($\exists$x)($\exists$y)[($\neg$Ixy & (Txs & Tys)) & (Lx & Ly)]

       o. ($\forall$x)(Lx $\rightarrow$ Cx)

       q. ($\exists$x)($\exists$y)[($\neg$Ixy & (Fxd & Myd)) & (Ex & Ey)] & [($\forall$x)[(Bxd $\lor$ Txd)) $\rightarrow$ Ex] & $\neg$Ed]

       s. ($\exists$x)($\exists$y)[(Lx & Ey) & Bxy]

6.2.6 a. ($\forall$x)($\forall$y)($\exists$z)Bxzy

       c. ($\forall$x)Sxax

       e. ($\forall$x)($\forall$y)($\forall$z)($\forall$u)[(Sxyz & Syxu) $\rightarrow$ Izu]

       g. ($\forall$x)($\forall$y)($\forall$z)[(Lxy & Lyz) $\rightarrow$ Lxz]

       i. ($\forall$x)($\forall$y)($\forall$z)($\forall$u)($\forall$w)($\forall w_1$)($\forall w_2$)[((Sxyu & Suzw$_1$) & (Syzw & Sxww$_2$)) $\rightarrow$ Iw$_1$w$_2$)]

6.2.7 a. $0 + 0 = 0$ and $0 + 1 = 1$ (True)

       c. There is no number x such that 1x = 1. (False)

       e. For each number x there is a number y such that xy = y. (True)

       g. Every number is identical to itself. (True)

       i. Between any two numbers there is always some number. (False)

6.2.9 Here we provide, besides a solution, different stages in the formalization process of the statement.

       a. There is x, x is a place in this company & (x is suitable for George $\lor$ x is suitable for Harry) & $\neg$(x is suitable for George & x is suitable for Harry).
($\exists$x)[Pxc & ((Sxg $\lor$ Sxh) & $\neg$(Sxg & Sxh))]

       c. $\neg$all people who like dogs also like cats & I like them both.
$\neg$(for each x, if x is a person then (x likes dogs $\rightarrow$ x likes cats)) & (I like dogs & I like cats).
$\neg$(for each x, Px $\rightarrow$ [for each y, (y is a dog $\rightarrow$ x likes y) $\rightarrow$ for each y, (y is a cat $\rightarrow$ x likes y)] & (for each y, y is a dog $\rightarrow$ I like y & for each y, y is a cat $\rightarrow$ I like y).
$\neg$($\forall$x)[Px $\rightarrow$ [($\forall$y)(Dy $\rightarrow$ Lxy) $\rightarrow$ ($\forall$y)(Cy $\rightarrow$ Lxy)]] & [($\forall$y)(Dy $\rightarrow$ Liy) & ($\forall$y)(Cy $\rightarrow$ Liy)]

       e. For any x, if x is a person then $\neg$(x always gets whatever she aims for).
($\forall$x)[Px $\rightarrow$ $\neg$(for any time y and any thing z, if x aims at z then x gets z)].
($\forall$x)[Px $\rightarrow$ $\neg$($\forall$y)($\forall$z)((Ty & Axz) $\rightarrow$ Gxz)]

       g. For any thing x, there is y and z such that y is a time for x and z is a place for x.
($\forall$x)($\exists$y)($\exists$z)(Tyx & Pzx)

       i. For any x, if x is a person then the king listens to x if and only if x is not an expert.
($\forall$x)[Px $\rightarrow$ (Lkx $\equiv$ $\neg$Ex)]

6.2.10 Here we provide, besides a solution, different stages in the formalization process of the statement.

       a. For any x, if x is a politician then x blames everyone who is not a politician and x does not blame politicians.
For any x, if x is a politician then for any y, if y is human then x blames y if and only if y is not a politician.
($\forall$x)[Px $\rightarrow$ ($\forall$y)(Hy $\rightarrow$ (Bxy $\equiv$ $\neg$Py))]

       c. For each x, if x is a person then (x likes dogs $\rightarrow$ x likes cats) & ($\neg$I like dogs & $\neg$I like cats).
For each x, Px $\rightarrow$ [for each y, (y is a dog $\rightarrow$ x likes y) $\rightarrow$ for each y, (y is a cat $\rightarrow$ x likes y)] & (for each y, y is a dog $\rightarrow$ $\neg$I like y & for each y, y is a cat $\rightarrow$ $\neg$I like y).
($\forall$x)[Px $\rightarrow$ [($\forall$y)(Dy $\rightarrow$ Lxy) $\rightarrow$ ($\forall$y)(Cy $\rightarrow$ Lxy)]] & [($\forall$y)(Dy $\rightarrow$ $\neg$Liy) & ($\forall$y)(Cy $\rightarrow$ $\neg$Liy)]

       e. Bach plays for God and for any x, if x is an angel then Mozart plays for x.
Pbg & ($\forall$x)(Ax $\rightarrow$ Pmx)

       g. If x is not a logician then x is not allowed to think.
If x is allowed to think then x is a logician.
($\forall$x)(Tx $\rightarrow$ Lx)

    i. There is a place x, a time y and some human z such that z will speak the truth at place x at time y.

       (∃x)(∃y)(∃z)[((Px & Ty) & Hz) & Sztxy]

6.2.11 a. (∀x)(Ex ≡ ¬Ox)   c. (∀x)[Ox → ¬(∃y)(Ey & Dxy)]
          e. (∀x)(Dxx ≡ ¬Ixa)   g. (∀x)Dxb
          i. (∀x)[Ex → (∃y)(Ey & Gyx)]

6.2.12 a. Ppq   c. (∃x)Pqx
          e. (∀x)(Pxr → Pxs)   g. ¬(∃x)(Pxp & Pxs)
          i. (∀x)(∀y)(∃z)(Pxz & Pyz)   k. (∀x)Pxx
          m. (∀x)(Pqx → ¬Ppx); or ¬(∃x)(Ppx & Pqx)   o. (∀x)(Pxx → Pxq)

6.2.13 a. (∃x)(Psx & ¬Ixs)   c. Ppp & (∀x)(Pxx → Ixp)
          e. (∃x)[Pxs & (∀y)(Pys → Iyx)]

6.2.14 Check answers for 9.3.5.

6.3.1 a, b, d, e, h and i.

6.3.2 a. x (bound); y (free)   c. x (bound); z, y (free)
         e. x, y (bound)

6.3.3 a, c and f.

6.3.5 a, c and d.

6.3.7 a. {¬Fab,Fab}, 2
         c. {(∀x)Fx ≡ ¬¬Fa, (∀x)Fx, Fx, ¬¬Fa, ¬Fa, Fa}, 6
         e. {¬(∀x)Fxx ∨ ¬(∃x)Fxx, ¬(∀x)Fxx, (∀x)Fxx, Fxx, ¬(∃x)Fxx, (∃x)Fxx}, 6

6.3.8 a. Fa   c. (∃y)(Fa & Kya)
         e. Not a quantified sentence   g. Lac
         i. Sa ≡ (∃x)Kxx   k. (∀y)Saya

6.3.9 a. (∀y)Fyy   c. (∀y)(¬Fy ≡ Rbya)
         e. (∀y)((∃y)Kyc → Fy)

6.3.10 a. (∃y)Fyc, (∃y)Fcy, and (∃y)Fyy
         c. (∃y)(¬Fy ≡ Rbca), (∃y)(¬Fc ≡ Rbya), and (∃y)(¬Fy ≡ Rbya)
         e. (∃y)((∃y)Kyc → Fy)

6.4.1 a. Fa, Fb, Fc, . . .
         c. Fa, Kaa, Kba, . . . , Fb, Kab, Kbb, . . .

6.4.2 a. T;   c. F;   e. T;   g. F;   i. T

6.4.3 a. F;   c. T;   e. T

6.4.5 The following will do: Assign T to each Fab, Fbc, Fcd, . . . and F to the remaining atomic sentences of PL.

6.4.7 An argument is quantificationally valid if and only if it is not possible for the premises to be true and the conclusion false. Assume (∀x)¬Fx is true. Hence, so is each of its instances: ¬Fa, ¬Fb, ¬Fc and so on. Thus, Fa, Fb, Fc and so on are all false and, consequently, so is (∃x)Fx. Hence, ¬(∃x)Fx is true. Therefore, under the assumption that (∀x)¬Fx is true, ¬(∃x)Fx cannot be false and the validity of the argument is established.

6.4.9 Assume not; that is, assume the set is consistent. Then, there is a truth-value assignment which satisfies each sentence in the set. Since (∀x)(¬Fx & Gbx) is true, so is each of its instances: ¬Fa & Gba, ¬Fb & Gbb and so on. But given that they are all conjunctions, each conjunct ¬Fa, Gba, ¬Fb, Gbb and so on must be true. And since each of ¬Fa, ¬Fb and so on is true, each of Fa, Fb and so on must be false. It is then clear that (∃x)Fx cannot be true. But this statement contradicts our original assumption that the set is consistent. Hence, the set is quantificationally inconsistent.

6.4.11 a. valid;   c. valid;   e. valid;   g. invalid;   i. invalid

6.4.12 a. true;   c. false;   e. false;   g. true;   i. true;   k. true;   m. true;
       o. false

6.4.13 Assume Γ is (quantificationally) consistent and let τ be a truth-value assignment which
       satisfies Γ. Then, since either α or $\neg\alpha$ is true under τ, we have that either $\tau \models \Gamma \cup \{\alpha\}$ or
       $\tau \models \Gamma \cup \{\neg\alpha\}$; that is, either $\Gamma \cup \{\alpha\}$ or $\Gamma \cup \{\neg\alpha\}$ is consistent. But in either case this is
       in contradiction with the fact that $\Gamma \models \alpha$ and $\Gamma \models \neg\alpha$ since by the test for entailment,
       both $\Gamma \cup \{\alpha\}$ and $\Gamma \cup \{\neg\alpha\}$ are inconsistent.

Chapter 7: PL Truth-Trees

7.1.1 a. False. Although it is the case that if (∀x)Fx is T then so is Fa, its converse is clearly not
          true.
       c. False. The sentence (∀x)Fx must be kept after applying the ∀D rule. The resulting set—
          branch—should be {Hbc, (∀x)Fx, Fa}.
       e. False. The constant of instantiation, a here, must be foreign to the branch.

7.1.2 a. inconsistent;   c. consistent;   e. inconsistent;   g. inconsistent

7.1.3 a. satisfiable. Let Ga, Fc and Fb be T, T and F, respectively.
       c. satisfiable. Let Bde, Fc and Bab be F, F and T, respectively.
       e. satisfiable. Let Ra and Rb be T and F, respectively.

7.2.1 For each exercise, we form the test set (the premises plus the negation of the conclusion)
       which we test for inconsistency: If one of its truth-trees closes, it is inconsistent (and
       hence entailment holds); else it is consistent (and entailment fails).
       a. true;   c. true;   e. false

7.2.2 For each exercise, we form the test set (the premises plus the negation of the conclusion)
       which we test for inconsistency: If one of its truth-trees closes, it is inconsistent (and
       hence the argument is valid); else it is consistent (and the argument is invalid).
       a. valid;   c. invalid;   e. valid;   g. valid;   i. invalid

7.2.3 Repeat as in 7.2.2, after symbolizing each argument into PL.
       a. ¬(∃x)Hx ∨ Ha
          ¬Ha
          ———————————
          (∀x)¬Hx   Valid
       c. Rp → (∃x)Rx
          Rp → (∃x)¬Rx
          ———————————
          ¬Rp   Invalid
       e. (∀x)(Rx → Lxr)
          Rp ∨ ¬(∃x)Lpx
          Lph
          ———————————
          Lpr   Valid

7.2.4 For each sentence, α, in a given exercise, any truth-tree you construct with *Symlog* for
       $\{\neg\alpha\}$ should close.

7.2.5 For each sentence, α, in a given exercise, any truth-tree you construct with *Symlog* for $\{\alpha\}$
       should close.

7.2.6 For the sentences α and β in a given exercise, any truth-tree you construct with *Symlog*
       for $\{\neg(\alpha \equiv \beta)\}$ should close.

7.3.1 a. false;   c. false;   e. true;   g. true;   i. true

7.3.2 a. satisfiable. Let Ba be T.
       c. satisfiable. Let Aa, Ab, Ba, Bb and Cb be T, T, F, T and T, respectively; also, let any other
          instance of (∀x)Ax be T.
       e. satisfiable. Let Hd, Kd, Ka and Jb be T, T, F and F, respectively.

7.3.3 You can guarantee that each sentence α is quantificationally indeterminate by constructing truth-trees with *Symlog* for $\{\alpha\}$ and $\{\neg\alpha\}$ where each tree has at least one completed open branch. (The sentences have been carefully chosen to satisfy this property.)

7.3.4 a. quantificationally false
c. quantificationally true
e. quantificationally true
g. quantificationally indeterminate
i. quantificationally indeterminate
k. quantificationally indeterminate
m. quantificationally true
o. quantificationally indeterminate

7.3.5 Because it gets into an endless regress: $(\forall x)\neg(\forall y)Rxy$, $\neg(\forall y)Ray$, $(\exists y)\neg Ray$, $\neg Rab$, $\neg(\forall y)Rby$, $(\exists y)\neg Rby$, $\neg Rbc$ and so on.

Chapter 8: Natural Deduction in Predicate Logic

8.1.2 a. Yes, by $\forall E$ c/x
c. No (restriction 1 of $\forall I$ is violated)
e. Yes, by $\exists I$ z/a
g. Yes, by $\forall E$ a/x
i. No, x in the replacement x/a was captured by the wrong quantifier

8.1.3 The errors are in lines 10, 14, 16 and 17. Line 10 violates the third restriction of $\exists E$. Line 14 is mistaken because it is derived by using $\forall E$ on line 2, but line 2 is not a universally quantified sentence (it is a conditional). Line 16 is a blatant misapplication of $\exists E$; this rule requires a subderivation. Finally, line 17 violates the first restriction of $\forall I$.

8.1.4

PD : EX814A

PREMISE	1	Fs $\equiv$ $\neg$Her
PREMISE	2	$\neg$Her & Ga
PREMISE	3	Fs $\rightarrow$($\forall$w)Mwws
&EL 2	4	$\neg$Her
$\equiv$E 1,4	5	Fs
$\rightarrow$E 3,5	6	($\forall$w)Mwws
$\forall$E h/w 6	7	Mhhs

No (more) errors

PD : EX814C

PREMISE	1	($\exists$x)Mxx & Sq
PREMISE	2	($\forall$w)(Mww $\equiv$ Fd)
&EL 1	3	($\exists$x)Mxx
ASSUMPTION	4	Maa
$\forall$E a/w 2	5	Maa $\equiv$ Fd
$\equiv$E 4,5	6	Fd
$\exists$E a/x 3,4-6	7	Fd

No (more) errors

PD : EX814E

PREMISE	1	(∀x)(Mx → Bc)
ASSUMPTION	2	(∃z)Mz
ASSUMPTION	3	Ma
∀E a/x 1	4	Ma → Bc
→E 3,4	5	Bc
∃E a/z 2,3-5	6	Bc
→I 2-6	7	(∃z)Mz → Bc

No (more) errors

8.2.1

PD : EX821

PREMISE	1	(∀x)(Fxe → Gxa)
PREMISE	2	(∀y)(∀x)(Fxy ≡ (∃z)Hazx)
PREMISE	3	(∀x)Hxcc
∀E e/y 2	4	(∀x)(Fxe ≡ (∃z)Hazx)
∀E c/x 4	5	Fce ≡ (∃z)Hazc
∀E a/x 3	6	Hacc
∃I z/c 6	7	(∃z)Hazc
≡E 5,7	8	Fce
∀E c/x 1	9	Fce → Gca
→E 8,9	10	Gca
∃I z/a 10	11	(∃z)Gcz
∃I y/c 11	12	(∃y)(∃z)Gyz

No (more) errors

8.2.3

PD : EX823A

PREMISE	1	(∀z)Fz
PREMISE	2	Ha
ASSUMPTION	3	(∀x)Fx → Ga
∀E b/z 1	4	Fb
∀I x/b 4	5	(∀x)Fx
→E 3,5	6	Ga
&I 2,6	7	Ha & Ga
∃I x/a 7	8	(∃x)(Hx & Gx)
→I 3-8	9	((∀x)Fx → Ga) → (∃x)(Hx & Gx)

No (more) errors

PD : EX823C

ASSUMPTION	1	¬(∃x)¬Fx
ASSUMPTION	2	¬Fa
∃I x/a 2	3	(∃x)¬Fx
R 1	4	¬(∃x)¬Fx
¬E 2-3,2-4	5	Fa
∀I x/a 5	6	(∀x)Fx
→I 1-6	7	¬(∃x)¬Fx → (∀x)Fx

No (more) errors

PD : EX823E

ASSUMPTION	1	(∃x)Fx
ASSUMPTION	2	Fa
∃I y/a 2	3	(∃y)Fy
∃E a/x 1,2-3	4	(∃y)Fy
ASSUMPTION	5	(∃y)Fy
ASSUMPTION	6	Fa
∃I x/a 6	7	(∃x)Fx
∃E a/y 5,6-7	8	(∃x)Fx
≡I 1-4,5-8	9	(∃x)Fx ≡ (∃y)Fy

No (more) errors

8.3.1 a. ∀E c/x; c. ∀I y/b; e. ∃I x/a; g. ∃E b/x; i. →E

8.3.2

PD : EX832A

PREMISE	1	(∃x)(Fx & Hx) → Ga
ASSUMPTION	2	(∀x)Fx
ASSUMPTION	3	(∀x)Hx
∀E a/x 2	4	Fa
∀E a/x 3	5	Ha
&I 4,5	6	Fa & Ha
∃I x/a 6	7	(∃x)(Fx & Hx)
→E 1,7	8	Ga
∃I x/a 8	9	(∃x)Gx
→I 3-9	10	(∀x)Hx → (∃x)Gx
→I 2-10	11	(∀x)Fx → ((∀x)Hx → (∃x)Gx)

No (more) errors

PD : EX832C

PREMISE	1	(∃x)Fx
PREMISE	2	(∀x)(Fx → (∃y)Hxy)
PREMISE	3	(∃x)(∃y)Hxy ≡ (∀x)(∀y)Kxy
ASSUMPTION	4	Fa
∀E a/x 2	5	Fa → (∃y)Hay
→E 4,5	6	(∃y)Hay
∃I x/a 6	7	(∃x)(∃y)Hxy
≡E 3,7	8	(∀x)(∀y)Kxy
∀E a/x 8	9	(∀y)Kay
∀E b/y 9	10	Kab
∃I y/b 10	11	(∃y)Kay
&I 4,11	12	Fa & (∃y)Kay
∃I x/a 12	13	(∃x)(Fx & (∃y)Kxy)
∃E a/x 1,4-13	14	(∃x)(Fx & (∃y)Kxy)

No (more) errors

PD : EX832E

ASSUMPTION	1	Fa
ASSUMPTION	2	(∃x)Fx → (∀x)Kx
∃I x/a 1	3	(∃x)Fx
→E 2,3	4	(∀x)Kx
∀E b/x 4	5	Kb
∀I y/b 5	6	(∀y)Ky
ASSUMPTION	7	(∀y)Ky
ASSUMPTION	8	(∃x)Fx
∀E b/y 7	9	Kb
∀I x/b 9	10	(∀x)Kx
→I 8-10	11	(∃x)Fx → (∀x)Kx
≡I 2-6,7-11	12	((∃x)Fx → (∀x)Kx) ≡ (∀y)Ky
→I 1-12	13	Fa → [((∃x)Fx → (∀x)Kx) ≡ (∀y)Ky]

No (more) errors

PD : EX832G

PREMISE	1	(∃x)Hx → (∀x)Kx
ASSUMPTION	2	¬Ka
ASSUMPTION	3	Ha
∃I x/a 3	4	(∃x)Hx
→E 1,4	5	(∀x)Kx
∀E a/x 5	6	Ka
R 2	7	¬Ka
¬I 3-6,3-7	8	¬Ha
→I 2-8	9	¬Ka → ¬Ha
∀I x/a 9	10	(∀x)(¬Kx → ¬Hx)

No (more) errors

PD : EX832I

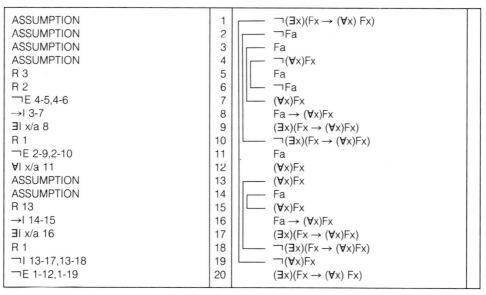

PREMISE	1	(∃x)Fx
ASSUMPTION	2	Fa
ASSUMPTION	3	(∃z)Gz
ASSUMPTION	4	Gb
∃I x/b 4	5	(∃x)Gx
∃I z/a 2	6	(∃z)Fz
&I 5, 6	7	(∃x)Gx & (∃z)Fz
∃E b/z 3,4-7	8	(∃x)Gx & (∃z)Fz
→I 3-8	9	(∃z)Gz → ((∃x)Gx & (∃z)Fz)
∃E a/x 1,2-9	10	(∃z)Gz → ((∃x)Gx & (∃z)Fz)

No (more) errors

8.3.3

PD : EX833

ASSUMPTION	1	¬(∃x)(Fx → (∀x) Fx)
ASSUMPTION	2	¬Fa
ASSUMPTION	3	Fa
ASSUMPTION	4	¬(∀x)Fx
R 3	5	Fa
R 2	6	¬Fa
¬E 4-5,4-6	7	(∀x)Fx
→I 3-7	8	Fa → (∀x)Fx
∃I x/a 8	9	(∃x)(Fx → (∀x)Fx)
R 1	10	¬(∃x)(Fx → (∀x)Fx)
¬E 2-9,2-10	11	Fa
∀I x/a 11	12	(∀x)Fx
ASSUMPTION	13	(∀x)Fx
ASSUMPTION	14	Fa
R 13	15	(∀x)Fx
→I 14-15	16	Fa → (∀x)Fx
∃I x/a 16	17	(∃x)(Fx → (∀x)Fx)
R 1	18	¬(∃x)(Fx → (∀x)Fx)
¬I 13-17,13-18	19	¬(∀x)Fx
¬E 1-12,1-19	20	(∃x)(Fx → (∀x) Fx)

No (more) errors

8.4.1   a. true;   c. false;   e. false;   g. false;   i. false
8.4.2

PD : EX842A

PREMISE	1	(∃x)Kx → La
ASSUMPTION	2	Kb
∃I x/b 2	3	(∃x)Kx
→E 1,3	4	La
→I 2-4	5	Kb → La
∀I x/b 5	6	(∀x)(Kx → La)

No (more) errors

PD : EX842C

PREMISE	1	$(\exists x)(Hx \vee Ka)$
PREMISE	2	$(\forall x)(Kx \rightarrow Gx)$
ASSUMPTION	3	$Hb \vee Ka$
ASSUMPTION	4	Hb
$\vee$IL 4	5	$Ga \vee Hb$
$\exists$I x/b 5	6	$(\exists x)(Ga \vee Hx)$
ASSUMPTION	7	Ka
$\forall$E a/x 2	8	$Ka \rightarrow Ga$
$\rightarrow$E 7,8	9	Ga
$\vee$IR 9	10	$Ga \vee Hb$
$\exists$I x/b 10	11	$(\exists x)(Ga \vee Hx)$
$\vee$E 3,4-6,7-11	12	$(\exists x)(Ga \vee Hx)$
$\exists$E b/x 1,3-12	13	$(\exists x)(Ga \vee Hx)$

No (more) errors

PD : EX842E

PREMISE	1	$(\forall x)(Fx \vee Gx)$
ASSUMPTION	2	$(\forall x)\neg Fx$
$\forall$E a/x 1	3	$Fa \vee Ga$
ASSUMPTION	4	Fa
ASSUMPTION	5	$\neg(\exists x)Gx$
R 4	6	Fa
$\forall$E a/x 2	7	$\neg Fa$
$\neg$E 5-6,5-7	8	$(\exists x)Gx$
ASSUMPTION	9	Ga
$\exists$I x/a 9	10	$(\exists x)Gx$
$\vee$E 3,4-8,9-10	11	$(\exists x)Gx$
$\rightarrow$I 2-11	12	$(\forall x)\neg Fx \rightarrow (\exists x)Gx$

No (more) errors

8.4.3

PD : EX843A

ASSUMPTION	1	Gab
R 1	2	Gab
ASSUMPTION	3	Gab
R 3	4	Gab
$\equiv$I 1-2,3-4	5	$Gab \equiv Gab$
$\forall$I y/b 5	6	$(\forall y)(Gay \equiv Gay)$
$\forall$I x/a 6	7	$(\forall x)(\forall y)(Gxy \equiv Gxy)$

No (more) errors

PD : EX843C

ASSUMPTION	1	$(\exists x)\neg(\exists w)Jwx$
ASSUMPTION	2	$\neg(\exists w)Jwa$
ASSUMPTION	3	$(\exists x)Jxa$
ASSUMPTION	4	Jba
$\exists$I w/b 4	5	$(\exists w)Jwa$
$\exists$E b/x 3,4-5	6	$(\exists w)Jwa$
R 2	7	$\neg(\exists w)Jwa$
$\neg$I 3-6,3-7	8	$\neg(\exists x)Jxa$
$\exists$I w/a 8	9	$(\exists w)\neg(\exists x)Jxw$
$\exists$E a/x 1,2-9	10	$(\exists w)\neg(\exists x)Jxw$
ASSUMPTION	11	$(\exists w)\neg(\exists x)Jxw$
ASSUMPTION	12	$\neg(\exists x)Jxa$
ASSUMPTION	13	$(\exists w)Jwa$
ASSUMPTION	14	Jba
	15	
$\exists$I x/b 14	16	$(\exists x)Jxa$
$\exists$E b/w 13,14-16	17	$(\exists x)Jxa$
R 12	18	$\neg(\exists x)Jxa$
$\neg$I 13-17,13-18	19	$\neg(\exists w)Jwa$
$\exists$I x/a 19	20	$(\exists x)\neg(\exists w)Jwx$
$\exists$E a/w 11,12-20	21	$(\exists x)\neg(\exists w)Jwx$
$\equiv$I 1-10,11-21	22	$(\exists x)\neg(\exists w)Jwx \equiv (\exists w)\neg(\exists x)Jxw$

No (more) errors

PD : EX843E

PREMISE	1	$(\exists w)(Gw \,\&\, Hw)$
ASSUMPTION	2	$Ga \,\&\, Ha$
&EL 2	3	Ga
$\exists$I x/a 3	4	$(\exists x)Gx$
&ER 2	5	Ha
$\exists$I y/a 5	6	$(\exists y)Hy$
&I 4,6	7	$(\exists x)Gx \,\&\, (\exists y)Hy$
$\exists$E a/w 1,2-7	8	$(\exists x)Gx \,\&\, (\exists y)Hy$

No (more) errors

PD : EX843G

PREMISE	1	$(\exists x)Bx \vee (\exists x)Cx$
ASSUMPTION	2	$(\exists x)Bx$
ASSUMPTION	3	Ba
$\vee$IR 3	4	$Ba \vee Ca$
$\exists$I x/a 4	5	$(\exists x)(Bx \vee Cx)$
$\exists$E a/x 2,3-5	6	$(\exists x)(Bx \vee Cx)$
ASSUMPTION	7	$(\exists x)Cx$
ASSUMPTION	8	Ca
$\vee$IL 8	9	$Ba \vee Ca$
$\exists$I x/a 9	10	$(\exists x)(Bx \vee Cx)$
$\exists$E a/x 7,8-10	11	$(\exists x)(Bx \vee Cx)$
$\vee$E 1,2-6,7-11	12	$(\exists x)(Bx \vee Cx)$

No (more) errors

PD : EX843I

PREMISE	1	$(\forall x)(\forall y)Hxy \rightarrow Ga$
PREMISE	2	$(\forall x)(\forall y)(Hxy \equiv (\exists y)Fy)$
ASSUMPTION	3	$(\exists x)Fx$
ASSUMPTION	4	Fb
$\forall$E c/x 2	5	$(\forall y)(Hcy \equiv (\exists y)Fy)$
$\forall$E d/y 5	6	$Hcd \equiv (\exists y)Fy$
$\exists$I y/b 4	7	$(\exists y)Fy$
$\equiv$E 6,7	8	Hcd
$\forall$I y/d 8	9	$(\forall y)Hcy$
$\forall$I x/c 9	10	$(\forall x)(\forall y)Hxy$
$\exists$E b/x 3,4-10	11	$(\forall x)(\forall y)Hxy$
$\rightarrow$E 1,11	12	Ga
$\rightarrow$I 3-12	13	$(\exists x)Fx \rightarrow Ga$

No (more) errors

8.4.4

PD : EX844A

PREMISE	1	$\neg(\exists x)Fx$
PREMISE	2	$(\forall x)Fx$
$\forall$E a/x 2	3	Fa
$\exists$I x/a 3	4	$(\exists x)Fx$
R 1	5	$\neg(\exists x)Fx$

No (more) errors

PD : EX844C

PREMISE	1	$(\forall x)(Hx \rightarrow Kf)$
PREMISE	2	$(\exists x)Hx \ \& \ Bacc$
PREMISE	3	$Bacc \rightarrow \neg Kf$
&EL 2	4	$(\exists x)Hx$
ASSUMPTION	5	Hb
$\forall$E b/x 1	6	$Hb \rightarrow Kf$
$\rightarrow$E 5,6	7	Kf
$\exists$E b/x 4,5-7	8	Kf
&ER 2	9	Bacc
$\rightarrow$E 3,9	10	$Bacc \rightarrow \neg Kf$

No (more) errors

PD : EX844E

PREMISE	1	(∀x)¬(∃y)Baxy
PREMISE	2	(∃w)(∃y)Bawy
ASSUMPTION	3	(∃y)Baby
ASSUMPTION	4	¬(P & ¬P)
R 3	5	(∃y)Baby
∀E b/x 1	6	¬(∃y)Baby
¬E 4-5,4-6	7	P & ¬P
∃E b/w 2,3-7	8	P & ¬P
&EL 8	9	P
&ER 8	10	¬P

No (more) errors

PD : EX844G

PREMISE	1	(∀x)(∀y)(Mxy ≡ ¬Mxy)
∀E a/x 1	2	(∀y)(May ≡ ¬May)
∀E b/y 2	3	Mab ≡ ¬Mab
ASSUMPTION	4	¬Mab
≡E 3,4	5	Mab
R 4	6	¬Mab
¬E 4-5,4-6	7	Mab
≡E 3,7	8	¬Mab

No (more) errors

PD : EX844I

PREMISE	1	(∀x)Hx & ((∃x)Gx → ¬Ha)
PREMISE	2	(∀x)(Fx → ¬Hx)
PREMISE	3	(∀x)(Fx ∨ Gx)
&EL 1	4	(∀x)Hx
∀E a/x 4	5	Ha
∀E a/x 3	6	Fa ∨ Ga
ASSUMPTION	7	Fa
ASSUMPTION	8	¬(∃x)Gx
R 5	9	Ha
∀E a/x 2	10	Fa → ¬Ha
→E 7,10	11	¬Ha
¬E 8-9,8-11	12	(∃x)Gx
ASSUMPTION	13	Ga
∃I x/a 13	14	(∃x)Gx
∨E 6,7-12,13-14	15	(∃x)Gx
&ER 1	16	(∃x)Gx → ¬Ha
→E 15,16	17	¬Ha

No (more) errors

8.4.5

PD : EX845A

PREMISE	1	(∀x)(Fx & Gx)
PREMISE	2	Gb → Hc
PREMISE	3	¬Hc
∀E b/x 1	4	Fb & Gb
&ER 4	5	Gb
→E 2,5	6	Hc
R 3	7	¬Hc

No (more) errors

PD : EX845C

PREMISE	1	(¬Ka ∨ Gb) → (∃x)(Gx ∨ Kx)
PREMISE	2	¬(∃x)(Kx ∨ Gx)
PREMISE	3	¬Ka
∨IR 3	4	¬Ka ∨ Gb
→E 1,4	5	(∃x)(Gx ∨ Kx)
ASSUMPTION	6	Gc ∨ Kc
ASSUMPTION	7	Gc
∨IL 7	8	Kc ∨ Gc
∃I x/c 8	9	(∃x)(Kx ∨ Gx)
ASSUMPTION	10	Kc
∨IR 10	11	Kc ∨ Gc
∃I x/c 11	12	(∃x)(Kx ∨ Gx)
∨E 6,7-9,10-12	13	(∃x)(Kx ∨ Gx)
∃E c/x 5,6-13	14	(∃x)(Kx ∨ Gx)

No (more) errors

PD : EX845E

PREMISE	1	¬(Fa ∨ ¬Fa)
ASSUMPTION	2	¬Fa
∨IL2	3	Fa ∨ ¬Fa
R 1	4	¬(Fa ∨ ¬Fa)
¬E 2-3,2-4	5	Fa
∨IR 5	6	Fa ∨ ¬Fa
R 1	7	¬(Fa ∨ ¬Fa)

No (more) errors

8.4.6

PD : EX846A

PREMISE	1	$(\forall x)(\forall y)(\forall w)(Hxyw \to (\forall z)Mz)$
PREMISE	2	$(\forall z)Mz \to (\exists x)Bxg$
ASSUMPTION	3	⌐ Habc
$\forall E$ a/x1	4	$(\forall y)(\forall w)(Hayw \to (\forall z)Mz)$
$\forall E$ b/y 4	5	$(\forall w)(Habw \to (\forall z)Mz)$
$\forall E$ c/w 5	6	$Habc \to (\forall z)Mz$
$\to$E 3,6	7	$(\forall z)Mz$
$\to$E 2,7	8	⌐ $(\exists x)Bxg$
$\to$I 3-8	9	$Habc \to (\exists x)Bxg$

No (more) errors

PD : EX846C

PREMISE	1	$(\forall x)Hx$ & $(\forall w)Gaw$
&EL 1	2	$(\forall x)Hx$
$\forall E$ b/x 2	3	Hb
&ER 1	4	$(\forall w)Gaw$
$\forall E$ c/w 4	5	Gac
&I 5,3	6	Gac & Hb
$\forall I$ w/c 6	7	$(\forall w)(Gaw$ & $Hb)$
$\forall I$ x/b 7	8	$(\forall x)(\forall w)(Gaw$ & $Hx)$

No (more) errors

PD : EX846E

PREMISE	1	$\neg(\forall y)\neg(Bay \equiv \neg Gy)$
ASSUMPTION	2	$\neg(\exists w)(\neg Gw \equiv Baw)$
ASSUMPTION	3	$Bab \equiv \neg Gb$
ASSUMPTION	4	$\neg Gb$
$\equiv$E 3,4	5	Bab
ASSUMPTION	6	Bab
$\equiv$E 3,6	7	$\neg Gb$
$\equiv$I 4-5,6-7	8	$\neg Gb \equiv Bab$
$\exists I$ w/b 8	9	$(\exists w)(\neg Gw \equiv Baw)$
R 2	10	$\neg(\exists w)(\neg Gw \equiv Baw)$
$\neg$I 3-9,3-10	11	$\neg(Bab \equiv \neg Gb)$
$\forall I$ y/b 11	12	$(\forall y)\neg(Bay \equiv \neg Gy)$
R 1	13	$\neg(\forall y)\neg(Bay \equiv \neg Gy)$
$\neg$E 2-12,2-13	14	$(\exists w)(\neg Gw \equiv Baw)$

No (more) errors

PD : EX846G

PREMISE	1	$(\forall x)(\forall y)[(\text{Pay \& Pxa}) \to \text{Pxy}]$
PREMISE	2	$(\exists z)(\text{Rz \& Pza})$
PREMISE	3	$(\forall x)(\text{Rx} \to \text{Pax})$
ASSUMPTION	4	Rb & Pba
∀E b/x 1	5	$(\forall y)((\text{Pay \& Pba}) \to \text{Pby})$
∀E b/y 5	6	$(\text{Pab \& Pba}) \to \text{Pbb}$
∀E b/x 3	7	$\text{Rb} \to \text{Pab}$
&EL 4	8	Rb
→E 7,8	9	Pab
&ER 4	10	Pba
&I 9,10	11	Pab & Pba
→E 6,11	12	Pbb
ASSUMPTION	13	Rb
R 12	14	Pbb
→I 13-14	15	$\text{Rb} \to \text{Pbb}$
∃I z/b 15	16	$(\exists z)(\text{Rz} \to \text{Pbz})$
&EL 4	17	Rb
&I 16,17	18	$(\exists z)(\text{Rz} \to \text{Pbz}) \ \& \ \text{Rb}$
∃I x/b 18	19	$(\exists x)((\exists z)(\text{Rz} \to \text{Pxz}) \ \& \ \text{Rx})$
∃E b/z 2,4-19	20	$(\exists x)((\exists z)(\text{Rz} \to \text{Pxz}) \ \& \ \text{Rx})$

No (more) errors

PD : EX846I

PREMISE	1	$(\forall x)(\text{Ax} \to \text{Bx})$
PREMISE	2	$(\forall x)(\forall z)[(\text{Ax \& Bz}) \to (\text{Cx \& Dz})]$
PREMISE	3	$(\exists x)\text{Ax} \equiv (\exists y)\text{By}$
ASSUMPTION	4	Ba
∃I y/a 4	5	$(\exists y)\text{By}$
≡E 3,5	6	$(\exists x)\text{Ax}$
ASSUMPTION	7	Ab
∀E b/x 2	8	$(\forall z)((\text{Ab \& Bz}) \to (\text{Cb \& Dz}))$
∀E a/z 8	9	$(\text{Ab \& Ba}) \to (\text{Cb \& Da})$
&I 7,4	10	Ab & Ba
→E 9,10	11	Cb & Da
&ER 11	12	Da
∃E b/x 6,7-12	13	Da
→I 4-13	14	$\text{Ba} \to \text{Da}$
∀I x/a 14	15	$(\forall x)(\text{Bx} \to \text{Dx})$

No (more) errors

8.4.7

PD : EX847A

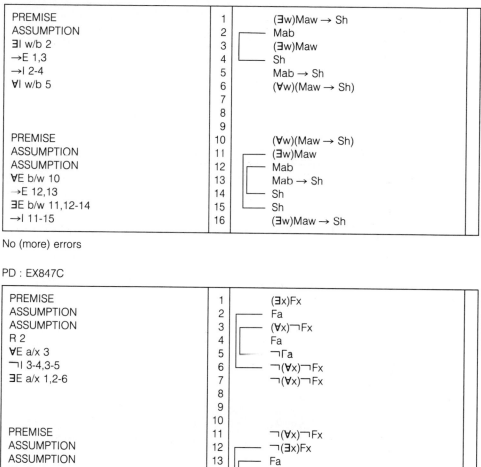

PREMISE	1	$(\exists w)Maw \rightarrow Sh$
ASSUMPTION	2	Mab
$\exists$I w/b 2	3	$(\exists w)Maw$
$\rightarrow$E 1,3	4	Sh
$\rightarrow$I 2-4	5	$Mab \rightarrow Sh$
$\forall$I w/b 5	6	$(\forall w)(Maw \rightarrow Sh)$
	7	
	8	
	9	
PREMISE	10	$(\forall w)(Maw \rightarrow Sh)$
ASSUMPTION	11	$(\exists w)Maw$
ASSUMPTION	12	Mab
$\forall$E b/w 10	13	$Mab \rightarrow Sh$
$\rightarrow$E 12,13	14	Sh
$\exists$E b/w 11,12-14	15	Sh
$\rightarrow$I 11-15	16	$(\exists w)Maw \rightarrow Sh$

No (more) errors

PD : EX847C

PREMISE	1	$(\exists x)Fx$
ASSUMPTION	2	Fa
ASSUMPTION	3	$(\forall x)\neg Fx$
R 2	4	Fa
$\forall$E a/x 3	5	$\neg Fa$
$\neg$I 3-4,3-5	6	$\neg(\forall x)\neg Fx$
$\exists$E a/x 1,2-6	7	$\neg(\forall x)\neg Fx$
	8	
	9	
	10	
PREMISE	11	$\neg(\forall x)\neg Fx$
ASSUMPTION	12	$\neg(\exists x)Fx$
ASSUMPTION	13	Fa
$\exists$I x/a 13	14	$(\exists x)Fx$
R 12	15	$\neg(\exists x)Fx$
$\neg$I 13-14,13-15	16	$\neg Fa$
$\forall$I x/a 16	17	$(\forall x)\neg Fx$
R 11	18	$\neg(\forall x)\neg Fx$
$\neg$E 12-17,12-18	19	$(\exists x)Fx$

No (more) errors

PD : EX847E

PREMISE	1	(∃w)Mw → Mg
ASSUMPTION	2	(∃w)Mw
→E 1,2	3	Mg
ASSUMPTION	4	Mg
∃I w/g 4	5	(∃w)Mw
≡I 2-3,4-5	6	(∃w)Mw ≡ Mg
	7	
	8	
	9	
PREMISE	10	(∃w)Mw ≡ Mg
ASSUMPTION	11	(∃w)Mw
≡E 10,11	12	Mg
→I 11-12	13	(∃w)Mw → Mg

No (more) errors

PD : EX847G

PREMISE	1	(∀x)(Bx & Cx)
∀E a/x 1	2	Ba & Ca
&EL2	3	Ba
∀I x/a 3	4	(∀x)Bx
&ER 2	5	Ca
∀I x/a 5	6	(∀x)Cx
&I 4,6	7	(∀x)Bx & (∀x)Cx
	8	
	9	
	10	
PREMISE	11	(∀x)Bx & (∀x)Cx
&EL 11	12	(∀)Bx
∀E a/x 12	13	Ba
&ER 11	14	(∀x)Cx
∀E a/x 14	15	Ca
&I 13,15	16	Ba & Ca
∀I x/a 16	17	(∀x)(Bx & Cx)

No (more) errors

PD : EX847I

PREMISE	1	$(\forall x)Hx \rightarrow (\exists w)Dw$
ASSUMPTION	2	$(\forall w)\neg Dw$
ASSUMPTION	3	$\neg(\exists z)\neg Hz$
ASSUMPTION	4	$\neg Ha$
$\exists I$ z/a 4	5	$(\exists z)\neg Hz$
R 3	6	$\neg(\exists z)\neg Hz$
$\neg E$ 4-5,4-6	7	Ha
$\forall I$ x/a 7	8	$(\forall x)Hx$
$\rightarrow E$ 1,8	9	$(\exists w)Dw$
ASSUMPTION	10	Db
ASSUMPTION	11	Ha
R 10	12	Db
$\forall E$ b/w 2	13	$\neg Db$
$\neg I$ 11-12,11-13	14	$\neg Ha$
$\exists E$ b/w 9,10-14	15	$\neg Ha$
$\neg E$ 3-7,3-15	16	$(\exists z)\neg Hz$
$\rightarrow I$ 2-16	17	$(\forall w)\neg Dw \rightarrow (\exists z)\neg Hz$
	18	
	19	
	20	
PREMISE	21	$(\forall w)\neg Dw \rightarrow (\exists z)\neg Hz$
ASSUMPTION	22	$(\forall x)Hx$
ASSUMPTION	23	$\neg(\exists w)Dw$
ASSUMPTION	24	Da
$\exists I$ w/a 24	25	$(\exists w)Dw$
R 23	26	$\neg(\exists w)Dw$
$\neg I$ 24-25,24-26	27	$\neg Da$
$\forall I$ w/a 27	28	$(\forall w)\neg Dw$
$\rightarrow E$ 21,28	29	$(\exists z)\neg Hz$
ASSUMPTION	30	$\neg Hb$
ASSUMPTION	31	$\neg Da$
$\forall E$ b/x 22	32	Hb
R 30	33	$\neg Hb$
$\neg E$ 31-32,31-33	34	Da
$\exists E$ b/z 29,30-34	35	Da
$\neg E$ 23-27,23-35	36	$(\exists w)Dw$
$\rightarrow I$ 22-36	37	$(\forall x)Hx \rightarrow (\exists w)Dw$

No (more) errors

8.4.8

PD : EX848A

PREMISE	1	$(\exists x)\neg Hx$
ASSUMPTION	2	$\neg Ha$
ASSUMPTION	3	$(\forall x)Hx$
$\forall E$ a/x 3	4	Ha
R 2	5	$\neg Ha$
$\neg I$ 3-4,3-5	6	$\neg(\forall x)Hx$
$\exists E$ a/x 1,2-6	7	$\neg(\forall x)Hx$

No (more) errors

PD : EX848C

PREMISE	1	(∃x)(∀y)Lxy
ASSUMPTION	2	(∀y)Lgy
∀E m/y 2	3	Lgm
∃I x/g 3	4	(∃x)Lxm
∃E g/x 1,2-4	5	(∃x)Lxm

No (more) errors

PD : EX848E

PREMISE	1	(∀x)(Hx → Mx) & ¬(∃x)(Mx & Ix)
ASSUMPTION	2	(∃x)(Hx & Ix)
ASSUMPTION	3	Ha & Ia
&EL 1	4	(∀x)(Hx → Mx)
∀E a/x 4	5	Ha → Ma
&EL 3	6	Ha
→E 5,6	7	Ma
&ER 3	8	Ia
&I 7,8	9	Ma & Ia
∃I x/a 9	10	(∃x)(Mx & Ix)
∃E a/x 2,3-10	11	(∃x)(Mx & Ix)
&ER 1	12	¬(∃x)(Mx & Ix)
¬I 2-11,2-12	13	¬(∃x)(Hx & Ix)

No (more) errors

PD : EX848G

PREMISE	1	(∃x)(Px ∨ Lx) → (∃x)Hx
PREMISE	2	(∀x)(Hx → Ix)
PREMISE	3	(∃x)Px
ASSUMPTION	4	Pa
∨IR 4	5	Pa ∨ La
∃I x/a 5	6	(∃x)(Px ∨ Lx)
→E 1,6	7	(∃x)Hx
ASSUMPTION	8	Hb
∀E b/x 2	9	Hb → Ib
→E 8,9	10	Ib
∃I x/b 10	11	(∃x)Ix
∃E b/x 7,8-11	12	(∃x)Ix
∃E a/x 3,4-12	13	(∃x)Ix

No (more) errors

PD : EX848I

PREMISE	1	$(\exists x)Oxl \rightarrow Jm$
PREMISE	2	$(\exists x)Oxs \rightarrow (Oal \lor Opl)$
PREMISE	3	Oas
$\exists I\ x/a\ 3$	4	$(\exists x)Oxs$
$\rightarrow E\ 2,4$	5	$Oal \lor Opl$
ASSUMPTION	6	Oal
$\exists I\ x/a\ 6$	7	$(\exists x)Oxl$
$\rightarrow E\ 1,7$	8	Jm
$\exists I\ x/m\ 8$	9	$(\exists x)Jx$
ASSUMPTION	10	Opl
$\exists I\ x/p\ 10$	11	$(\exists x)Oxl$
$\rightarrow E\ 1,11$	12	Jm
$\exists I\ x/m\ 12$	13	$(\exists x)Jx$
$\lor E\ 5,6\text{-}9,10\text{-}13$	14	$(\exists x)Jx$

No (more) errors

8.4.9

PD : EX849A

PREMISE	1	$(\forall x)(\forall y)(\forall z)[Bxyz \rightarrow (Gxy\ \&\ Gzx)]$
PREMISE	2	$(\exists x)(Bxab\ \&\ \neg(Gxa \lor Gbx))$
ASSUMPTION	3	$Bcab\ \&\ \neg(Gca \lor Gbc)$
ASSUMPTION	4	$\neg(P\ \&\ \neg P)$
$\forall E\ c/x\ 1$	5	$(\forall y)(\forall z)(Bcyz \rightarrow (Gcy\ \&\ Gzc))$
$\forall E\ a/y\ 5$	6	$(\forall z)(Bcaz \rightarrow (Gca\ \&\ Gzc))$
$\forall E\ b/z\ 6$	7	$Bcab \rightarrow (Gca\ \&\ Gbc)$
$\&EL\ 3$	8	$Bcab$
$\rightarrow E\ 7,8$	9	$Gca\ \&\ Gbc$
$\&EL\ 9$	10	Gca
$\lor IR\ 10$	11	$Gca \lor Gbc$
$\&ER\ 3$	12	$\neg(Gca \lor Gbc)$
$\neg E\ 4\text{-}11,4\text{-}12$	13	$P\ \&\ \neg P$
$\exists E\ c/x\ 2,3\text{-}13$	14	$P\ \&\ \neg P$
$\&EL\ 14$	15	P
$\&ER\ 14$	16	$\neg P$

No (more) errors

PD : EX849C

PREMISE	1	(∀x)(Nx ≡ ¬Mxx)
PREMISE	2	(∃x)(¬Nx & (∀y)(Myx ≡ Ny))
ASSUMPTION	3	¬Na & (∀y)(Mya ≡ Ny)
ASSUMPTION	4	¬(P & ¬P)
∀E a/x 1	5	Na ≡ ¬Maa
ASSUMPTION	6	¬Maa
≡E 5,6	7	Na
&EL 3	8	¬Na
¬E 6-7,6-8	9	Maa
ASSUMPTION	10	Maa
&ER 3	11	(∀y)(Mya ≡ Ny)
∀E a/y 11	12	Maa ≡ Na
≡E 10,12	13	Na
&EL 3	14	¬Na
¬I 10-13,10-14	15	¬Maa
¬E 4-9,4-15	16	P & ¬P
∃E a/x 2,3-16	17	P & ¬P
&EL 17	18	P
&ER 17	19	¬P

No (more) errors

PD : EX849E

PREMISE	1	(∀x)Sxex
PREMISE	2	(∀x)(∀y)(Ixy ≡ Sxye)
PREMISE	3	¬(∃x)Ixx
∀E e/x 1	4	Seee
∀E e/x 2	5	(∀y)(Iey ≡ Seye)
∀E e/y 5	6	Iee ≡ Seee
≡E 4,6	7	Iee
∃I x/e 7	8	(∃x)Ixx
R 3	9	¬(∃x)Ixx

No (more) errors

8.4.10

PD : EX8410A

PREMISE	1	¬(∃x)Rx
ASSUMPTION	2	Ra
∃I x/a 2	3	(∃x)Rx
R 1	4	¬(∃x)Rx
¬I 2-3,2-4	5	¬Ra
∀I x/a 5	6	(∀x)¬Rx

No (more) errors

PD : EX8410C

PREMISE	1	¬(∃x)Rx & ¬Hsg
PREMISE	2	Ibs → (∃x)Rx
ASSUMPTION	3	(∀x)Ixs ∨ Hsg
ASSUMPTION	4	(∀x)Ixs
∀E b/x 4	5	Ibs
→E 2,5	6	(∃x)Rx
ASSUMPTION	7	Hsg
ASSUMPTION	8	¬(∃x)Rx
R 7	9	Hsg
&ER 1	10	¬Hsg
¬E 8-9,8-10	11	(∃x)Rx
∨E 3,4-6,7-11	12	(∃x)Rx
&EL 1	13	¬(∃x)Rx
¬I 3-12,3-13	14	¬[(∀x)Ixs ∨ Hsg]

No (more) errors

PD : EX8410E

PREMISE	1	(∀x)(Sx → Cx) & (∀x)(Rx → Cx)
PREMISE	2	(∃x)(Sx ∨ Rx)
ASSUMPTION	3	Sa ∨ Ra
ASSUMPTION	4	Sa
&EL 1	5	(∀x)(Sx → Cx)
∀E a/x 5	6	Sa → Ca
→E 4,6	7	Ca
ASSUMPTION	8	Ra
&ER 1	9	(∀x)(Rx → Cx)
∀E a/x 9	10	Ra → Ca
→E 8,10	11	Ca
∨E 3,4-7,8-11	12	Ca
∃I x/a 12	13	(∃x)Cx
∃E a/x 2,3-13	14	(∃x)Cx

No (more) errors

8.5.1   a. true;   c. true;   e. false;   g. true;   i. true

8.5.2

PD+ : EX852A

PREMISE	1	(∀x)(∀y)(Bx≡My)
EQ 1	2	(∀x)(∀y)((Bx → My) & (My → Bx))
DN 2	3	(∀x)¬¬(∀y)((Bx → My) & (My → Bx))
QN 3	4	(∀x)¬(∃y)¬((Bx → My) & (My → Bx))
DM 4	5	(∀x)¬(∃y)(¬(Bx → My) ∨ ¬(My → Bx))

No (more) errors

PD+ : EX852C

PREMISE	1	(∀x)[(Gx ∨ ¬(∃y)Hyax) & Hbax]
∀E o/x 1	2	(Gc ∨ ¬(∃y)Hyac) & Hbac
&EL 2	3	Gc ∨ ¬(∃y)Hyac
ASSUMPTION	4	Gc
∃I w/c 4	5	(∃w)Gw
ASSUMPTION	6	¬(∃y)Hyac
ASSUMPTION	7	¬(∃w)Gw
&ER 2	8	Hbac
QN 6	9	(∀y)¬Hyac
∀E b/y 9	10	¬Hbac
¬E 7-8,7-10	11	(∃w)Gw
∨E 3,4-5,6-11	12	(∃w)Gw

No (more) errors

PD+ : EX852E

PREMISE	1	(∀x)Hxx
PREMISE	2	(∃w)(Aw → Cw)
∀E a/x 1	3	Haa
∃I w/a 3	4	(∃w)Hwa
∃I x/a 4	5	(∃x)(∃w)Hwx
IM 2	6	(∃w)(¬Aw ∨ Cw)
DN 6	7	(∃w)(¬Aw ∨ ¬¬Cw)
DM 7	8	(∃w)¬(Aw & ¬Cw)
QN 8	9	¬(∀w)(Aw & ¬Cw)
CM 9	10	¬(∀w)(¬Cw & Aw)
&I 5,10	11	(∃x)(∃w)Hwx & ¬(∀w)(¬Cw & Aw)

No (more) errors

8.5.3

PD+ : EX853A

ASSUMPTION	1	(∀x)¬Jx
∀E a/x 1	2	¬Ja
∀I y/a 2	3	(∀y)¬Jy
QN 3	4	¬(∃y)Jy
ASSUMPTION	5	¬(∃y)Jy
QN 5	6	(∀y)¬Jy
∀E a/y 6	7	¬Ja
∀I x/a 7	8	(∀x)¬Jx
≡I 1-4,5-8	9	(∀x)¬Jx ≡ ¬(∃y)Jy

No (more) errors

PD+ : EX853C

ASSUMPTION	1	¬(∃x)(∃w)Rxw
QN 1	2	(∀x)¬(∃w)Rxw
QN 2	3	(∀x)(∀w)¬Rxw
∀E a/x 3	4	(∀w)¬Raw
∀E b/w 4	5	¬Rab
∀I x/b 5	6	(∀x)¬Rax
∀I w/a 6	7	(∀w)(∀x)¬Rwx
QN 7	8	(∀w)¬(∃x)Rwx
QN 8	9	¬(∃w)(∃x)Rwx
ASSUMPTION	10	¬(∃w)(∃x)Rwx
QN 10	11	(∀w)¬(∃x)Rwx
QN 11	12	(∀w)(∀x)¬Rwx
∀E a/w 12	13	(∀x)¬Rax
∀E b/x 13	14	¬Rab
∀I w/b 14	15	(∀w)¬Raw
∀I x/a 15	16	(∀x)(∀w)¬Rxw
QN 16	17	(∀x)¬(∃x)Rxw
QN 17	18	¬(∃x)(∃w)Rxw
≡I 1-9,10-18	19	¬(∃x)(∃w)Rxw ≡ ¬(∃w)(∃x)Rwx

No (more) errors

PD+ : EX853E

PREMISE	1	(∀w) Bw & Gb
PREMISE	2	¬(∃x)(Bx & Mx)
QN 2	3	(∀x)¬(Bx & Mx)
∀E a/x 3	4	¬(Ba & Ma)
DM 4	5	¬Ba ∨ ¬Ma
&EL 1	6	(∀w)Bw
∀E a/w 6	7	Ba
DN 7	8	¬¬Ba
DS 5,8	9	¬Ma

No (more) errors

8.5.4

PD+ : EX854A

PREMISE	1	(∀w)Nw
PREMISE	2	(∃x)¬Nx
DN 1	3	(∀w)¬¬Nw
∀E a/w 3	4	¬¬Na
∀I x/a 4	5	(∀x)¬¬Nx
QN 5	6	¬(∃x)¬Nx
R 2	7	(∃x)¬Nx

No (more) errors

PD+ : EX854C

PREMISE	1	$\neg(\exists z)(Gzb \rightarrow Azc) \,\&\, \neg(\forall w)(\neg Awc \,\&\, Gwb)$
&EL 1	2	$\neg(\exists z)(Gzb \rightarrow Azc)$
QN 2	3	$(\forall z)\neg(Gzb \rightarrow Azc)$
IM 3	4	$(\forall z)\neg(\neg Gzb \lor Azc)$
DM 4	5	$(\forall z)(\neg\neg Gzb \,\&\, \neg Azc)$
DN 5	6	$(\forall z)(Gzb \,\&\, \neg Azc)$
CM 6	7	$(\forall z)(\neg Azc \,\&\, Gzb)$
$\forall$E a/z 7	8	$\neg Aac \,\&\, Gab$
$\forall$I w/a 8	9	$(\forall w)(\neg Awc \,\&\, Gwb)$
&ER 1	10	$\neg(\forall w)(\neg Awc \,\&\, Gwb)$

No (more) errors

PD+ : EX854E

PREMISE	1	$(\exists x)(\exists y)(\exists w)Dxywacc$
PREMISE	2	$(\forall y)(\forall z)\neg(\exists w)Dyzwacc$
$\forall$E b/y 2	3	$(\forall z)\neg(\exists w)Dbzwacc$
$\forall$E d/z 3	4	$\neg(\exists w)Dbdwacc$
$\forall$I y/d 4	5	$(\forall y)\neg(\exists w)Dbywacc$
$\forall$I x/b 5	6	$(\forall x)(\forall y)\neg(\exists w)Dxywacc$
QN 6	7	$(\forall x)\neg(\exists y)(\exists w)Dxywacc$
QN 7	8	$\neg(\exists x)(\exists y)(\exists w)Dxywacc$
R 1	9	$(\exists x)(\exists y)(\exists w)Dxywacc$

No (more) errors

8.5.5

PD+ : EX855A

PREMISE	1	$(\forall w)Fw$
PREMISE	2	$\neg Fa \lor Nb$
PREMISE	3	$\neg Nb$
$\forall$E a/w 1	4	Fa
DS 2,3	5	$\neg Fa$

No (more) errors

PD+ : EX855C

PREMISE	1	$\neg[\neg(\forall x)Fx \equiv (\exists x)\neg Fx]$
EQ 1	2	$\neg((\neg(\forall x)Fx \,\&\, (\exists x)\neg Fx) \lor (\neg\neg(\forall x)Fx \,\&\, \neg(\exists x)\neg Fx))$
DM 2	3	$\neg(\neg(\forall x)Fx \,\&\, (\exists x)\neg Fx) \,\&\, \neg(\neg\neg(\forall x)Fx \,\&\, \neg(\exists x)\neg Fx)$
&EL 3	4	$\neg(\neg(\forall x)Fx \,\&\, (\exists x)\neg Fx)$
QN 4	5	$\neg((\exists x)\neg Fx \,\&\, (\exists x)\neg Fx)$
ID 5	6	$\neg(\exists x)\neg Fx$
QN 6	7	$\neg\neg(\forall x)Fx$
&ER 3	8	$\neg(\neg\neg(\forall x)Fx \,\&\, \neg(\exists x)\neg Fx)$
QN 8	9	$\neg(\neg\neg(\forall x)Fx \,\&\, \neg\neg(\forall x)Fx)$
ID 9	10	$\neg\neg\neg(\forall x)Fx$

No (more) errors

PD+ : EX855E

PREMISE	1	¬(∀x)(Fx ≡ Fx)
ASSUMPTION	2	Fa
R 2	3	Fa
ASSUMPTION	4	Fa
R 4	5	Fa
≡I 2-3,4-5	6	Fa ≡ Fa
∀I x/a 6	7	(∀x)(Fx ≡ Fx)
R 1	8	¬(∀x)(Fx ≡ Fx)

No (more) errors

8.5.6

PD+ : EX856A

PREMISE	1	(∃x)[¬Kx & (Dx → ¬Gax)]
IM 1	2	(∃x)(¬Kx & (¬Dx ∨ ¬Gax))
CM 2	3	(∃x)((¬Dx ∨ ¬Gax) & ¬Kx)
CM 3	4	(∃x)((¬Gax ∨ ¬Dx) & ¬Kx)
DM 4	5	(∃x)(¬(Gax & Dx) & ¬Kx)
DM 5	6	(∃x)¬((Gax & Dx) ∨ Kx)
QN 6	7	¬(∀x)((Gax & Dx) ∨ Kx)

No (more) errors

PD+ : EX856C

PREMISE	I	(∃w)Fw → Id
ASSUMPTION	2	Fa
∃I w/a 2	3	(∃w)Fw
→E 1,3	4	Id
→I 2-4	5	Fa → Id
∀I z/a 5	6	(∀z)(Fz → Id)

No (more) errors

PD+ : EX856E

PREMISE	1	¬(∃z)Rz → (∀x)(∀w)Hxw
PREMISE	2	(Sd → (∀x)¬Rx) & (∀x)Sx
&ER 2	3	(∀x)Sx
∀E d/x 3	4	Sd
&EL 2	5	Sd → (∀x)¬Rx
→E 4,5	6	(∀x)¬Rx
∀E a/x 6	7	¬Ra
∀I z/a 7	8	(∀z)¬Rz
QN 8	9	¬(∃z)Rz
→E 1,9	10	(∀x)(∀w)Hxw
∀E m/x 10	11	(∀w)Hmw
∀E c/w 11	12	Hmc
DN 12	13	¬¬Hmc

No (more) errors

8.5.7

PD+ : EX857A

PREMISE	1	(∃x)(Fx ∨ P)
ASSUMPTION	2	Fa ∨ P
ASSUMPTION	3	Fa
∃I x/a 3	4	(∃x)Fx
∨IR 4	5	(∃x)Fx ∨ P
ASSUMPTION	6	P
∨IL 6	7	(∃x)Fx ∨ P
∨E 2,3-5,6-7	8	(∃x)Fx ∨ P
∃E a/x 1,2-8	9	(∃x)Fx ∨ P
	10	
	11	
	12	
PREMISE	13	(∃x)Fx ∨ P
ASSUMPTION	14	(∃x)Fx
ASSUMPTION	15	Fa
∨IR 15	16	Fa ∨ P
∃I x/a 16	17	(∃x)(Fx ∨ P)
∃E a/x 14,15-17	18	(∃x)(Fx ∨ P)
ASSUMPTION	19	P
∨IL 19	20	Fa ∨ P
∃I x/a 20	21	(∃x)(Fx ∨ P)
∨E 13,14-18,19-21	22	(∃x)(Fx ∨ P)

No (more) errors

PD+ : EX857C

PREMISE	1	P → (∃x)Fx
IM 1	2	¬P ∨ (∃x)Fx
ASSUMPTION	3	¬P
ASSUMPTION	4	¬(∃x)(P → Fx)
∨IR 3	5	¬P ∨ Fa
IM 5	6	P → Fa
∃I x/a 6	7	(∃x)(P → Fx)
R 4	8	¬(∃x)(P → Fx)
¬E 4-7,4-8	9	(∃x)(P → Fx)
ASSUMPTION	10	(∃x)Fx
ASSUMPTION	11	Fa
∨IL 11	12	¬P ∨ Fa
IM 12	13	P → Fa
∃I x/a 13	14	(∃x)(P → Fx)
∃E a/x 10,11-14	15	(∃x)(P → Fx)
∨E 2,3-9,10-15	16	(∃x)(P → Fx)
	17	
	18	
	19	
PREMISE	20	(∃x)(P → Fx)
ASSUMPTION	21	P
ASSUMPTION	22	P → Fa
→E 21,22	23	Fa
∃I x/a 23	24	(∃x)Fx
∃E a/x 20,22-24	25	(∃x)Fx
→I 21-25	26	P → (∃x)Fx

No (more) errors

8.5.8

PD+ : EX858A

PREMISE	1	¬(∀x)(Nx → Ox) & (∀x)(Dx → Ox)
IM 1	2	¬(∀x)(¬Nx ∨ Ox) & (∀x)(Dx → Ox)
DN 2	3	¬(∀x)(¬Nx ∨ ¬¬Ox) & (∀x)(Dx → Ox)
DM 3	4	¬(∀x)¬(Nx & ¬Ox) & (∀x)(Dx → Ox)
QN 4	5	¬¬(∃x)(Nx & ¬Ox) & (∀x)(Dx → Ox)
DN 5	6	(∃x)(Nx & ¬Ox) & (∀x)(Dx → Ox)
IM 6	7	(∃x)(Nx & ¬Ox) & (∀x)(¬Dx ∨ Ox)
DN 7	8	(∃x)(Nx & ¬Ox) & (∀x)(¬Dx ∨ ¬¬Ox)
DM 8	9	(∃x)(Nx & ¬Ox) & (∀x)¬(Dx & ¬Ox)
QN 9	10	(∃x)(Nx & ¬Ox) & ¬(∃x)(Dx & ¬Ox)

No (more) errors

PD+ : EX858C

PREMISE	1	(∃x)(∃y)[(Gy & Sxy) & Lxy]
PREMISE	2	(∃x)(∃y)[(Gy & Sxy) & ¬Lxy]
	3	
DN 2	4	¬¬(∃x)(∃y)((Gy & Sxy) & ¬Lxy)
QN 4	5	¬(∀x)¬(∃y)((Gy & Sxy) & ¬Lxy)
QN 5	6	¬(∀x)(∀y)¬((Gy & Sxy) & ¬Lxy)
DM 6	7	¬(∀x)(∀y)(¬(Gy & Sxy) ∨ ¬¬Lxy)
DN 7	8	¬(∀x)(∀y)(¬(Gy & Sxy) ∨ Lxy)
IM 8	9	¬(∀x)(∀y)((Gy & Sxy) → Lxy)
	10	
DN 1	11	¬¬(∃x)(∃y)((Gy & Sxy) & Lxy)
QN 11	12	¬(∀x)¬(∃y)((Gy & Sxy) & Lxy)
QN 12	13	¬(∀x)(∀y)¬((Gy & Sxy) & Lxy)
DM 13	14	¬(∀x)(∀y)(¬(Gy & Sxy) ∨ ¬Lxy)
IM 14	15	¬(∀x)(∀y)((Gy & Sxy) → ¬Lxy)

No (more) errors

PD+ : EX858E

PREMISE	1	(∀x)(Lxd → ¬Lxx)
PREMISE	2	(∀x)(¬Lfx → Ldx) & ¬Ldf
&EL 2	3	(∀x)(¬Lfx → Ldx)
∀E f/x 3	4	¬Lff → Ldf
IM 4	5	¬¬Lff ∨ Ldf
&ER 2	6	¬Ldf
DS 5,6	7	¬¬Lff
∀E f/x 1	8	Lfd → ¬Lff
IM 8	9	¬Lfd ∨ ¬Lff
DS 7,9	10	¬Lfd

No (more) errors

8.5.9

PD+ : EX859

PREMISE	1	Ppa ∨ Ppb
PREMISE	2	Pqa ∨ Pqb
PREMISE	3	Pra ∨ Prb
PREMISE	4	Ppa → (¬Pqa & ¬Pra)
PREMISE	5	Pqa → (¬Ppa & ¬Pra)
PREMISE	6	Pra → (¬Ppa & ¬Pqa)
PREMISE	7	Ppb → (¬Pqb & ¬Prb)
PREMISE	8	Pqb → (¬Ppb & ¬Prb)
PREMISE	9	Prb → (¬Ppb & ¬Pqb)
ASSUMPTION	10	¬Ppa
DS 1,10	11	Ppb
→E 11,7	12	¬Pqb & ¬Prb
&EL 12	13	¬Pqb
DS 2,13	14	Pqa
→E 5,14	15	¬Ppa & ¬Pra
&ER 15	16	¬Pra
DS 3,16	17	Prb
&ER 12	18	¬Prb
¬E 10-17,10-18	19	Ppa
ASSUMPTION	20	Ppa
→E 4,20	21	¬Pqa & ¬Pra
&EL 21	22	¬Pqa
DS 2,22	23	Pqb
→E 8,23	24	¬Ppb & ¬Prb
&ER 24	25	¬Prb
DS 3,25	26	Pra
&ER 21	27	¬Pra
¬I 20-26,20-27	28	¬Ppa

No (more) errors

8.5.11 Here we solve this exercise for the fourth form only. The other remaining forms can be obtained in a similar way. In solving this exercise, it is a good idea to try to prove first a special case (of the dispensability of QN) and then generalize it. For instance, to show that $\neg(\forall \mathbf{x})\alpha$ can be obtained from $(\exists \mathbf{x})\neg\alpha$, you may want to show first that $\neg(\forall x)Fx$ is obtainable from $(\exists x)\neg Fx$. Below we give the general result, where in line j we assume that **a** satisfies the restrictions of the ∃E rule:

	i	$(\exists \mathbf{x})\neg\alpha$
ASSUMPTION	j	$\neg\alpha(\mathbf{a}/\mathbf{x})$
ASSUMPTION	k	$(\forall \mathbf{x})\alpha$
∀E **a/x** k	l	$\alpha(\mathbf{a}/\mathbf{x})$
R j	m	$\neg\alpha(\mathbf{a}/\mathbf{x})$
¬I k-l, k-m	n	$\neg(\forall \mathbf{x})\alpha$
∃E **a/x** i, j-n	o	$\neg(\forall \mathbf{x})\alpha$

8.5.13

ASSUMPTION	i	$\alpha(\mathbf{a/x})$
	j	$\neg(\exists\mathbf{x})\alpha$
R i	k	$\alpha(\mathbf{a/x})$
QN j	l	$(\forall\mathbf{x})\neg\alpha$
$\forall$E $\mathbf{a/x}$ l	m	$\neg\alpha(\mathbf{a/x})$
$\neg$E j-k, j-m	n	$(\exists\mathbf{x})\alpha$

8.5.15 a. Since all the rules of PD are rules of PD*, any derivation in PD is also a derivation in PD*. Hence, trivially, if $\Gamma \vDash_{PD} \alpha$ then $\Gamma \vDash_{PD^*} \alpha$, for any Γ and α.
b. To show the converse, that is, that if $\Gamma \vDash_{PD^*} \alpha$ then $\Gamma \vDash_{PD} \alpha$ (for any Γ and α), we show that the rule CV of PD* is reducible to rules of PD. The following two metaproofs show this reduction for the two forms of CV. (Applications of $\forall$I and $\exists$E respect their corresponding restrictions.)

8.6.1 a. false; c. true; e. true; g. false; i. true

8.6.3 It is enough to give a sentence which is not derivable from {Fa}. We claim that Gb is one such sentence since {Fa} does not quantificationally entail Gb, as the truth-value assignment which assigns T to Fa and F to Gb readily shows. Hence, by the soundness theorem, Ga is not derivable from {Fa} and this set is PD-consistent.

8.6.5 Just show that each member in {Fb ∨ Hc, (∃x)(∃y)Gxy, (∃x)Fx} is derivable from {Gab, (∀x)(Fx & ¬Kx)}.

Chapter 9: Structures

9.1.1 a. false; c. false; e. false; g. true; i. true

9.1.2 a. Essentially, the set of real numbers
c. Betweenness

9.1.3 UD := {0,1,2, . . .}
Lxy := {(x,y) : x < y}
Ixy := {(x,y) : x = y}
Mxy := {(x,y) : there is a z such that x = zy}
a := 0
b := 1

9.1.4 a. $\alpha(1/x^{\mathfrak{A}})$ is just like α except that $x^{\mathfrak{A}} = 1$.
c. $\alpha(2/y^{\mathfrak{A}})$ is just like α except that $y^{\mathfrak{A}} = 2$.
e. $\alpha'(3/y^{\mathfrak{A}})$ is just like α except that $x^{\mathfrak{A}} = 5$ and $y^{\mathfrak{A}} = 3$; no.

9.1.5 n, one per each element of the UD.
$\alpha(0/x^{\mathfrak{A}})$, which is just like α except that $x^{\mathfrak{A}} = 0$.
$\alpha(1/x^{\mathfrak{A}})$, which is just like α except that $x^{\mathfrak{A}} = 1$.
$\alpha(2/x^{\mathfrak{A}})$, which is just like α except that $x^{\mathfrak{A}} = 2$.

9.1.6   a. $\alpha(3/x^{\mathfrak{A}})(4/y^{\mathfrak{A}})$ is just like α (of exercise 9.1.4) except that $x^{\mathfrak{A}} = 3$ and $y^{\mathfrak{A}} = 4$.
c. $\alpha(\sigma_1/\mathbf{x}^{\mathfrak{A}})(\sigma_2/\mathbf{x}^{\mathfrak{A}}) = \alpha(\sigma_2/\mathbf{x}^{\mathfrak{A}})$.

9.1.7 n^2, n assignments to y per each assignment to x

9.1.8   a. $\alpha_1(1/x^{\mathfrak{A}})(0/y^{\mathfrak{A}})$

9.2.1   a. true;   c. false;   e. true;   g. false;   i. true;   k. true;   m. true;
o. true

9.2.2   a. yes;   c. no;   e. yes;   g. yes;   i. no;   k. yes

9.2.3   a. Ea;   c. ¬Eb;   e. $\mathfrak{A}_3$

9.2.4   a. UD := {0}, Fx := {0}, a := 0
c. UD :− {0,1}, Fx := {1}, a := 0, b := 1
e. UD := {0}, Bx := {0}
g. UD := {0}, Lxy := {(0,0)}, a := 0, b := 0
i. UD := {0,1,2}, Bxy := {(1,0),(1,1),(1,2)}

9.2.5   a. Let the UD be the set of natural numbers {0, 1, 2, 3, . . .}. Interpret the constants a, b,
c and so on as the numbers 0, 2, 4 and so on and let the extension of E be the set of
even numbers {0, 2, 4, . . .}. On this interpretation, each instance—Ea, Eb, Ec and so
on—of (∀x)Ex is true of the structure. However, the x-variant in which the number 1 is
assigned to x does not satisfy Ex. Hence, (∀x)Ex is false of the structure.

9.3.1   (i) a. TRUE;   c. FALSE;   e. TRUE;   g. FALSE;   i. TRUE
(ii) a. (∀x)(∃y)Cxy; FALSE
c. ¬(∃x)(Cxx & Cxc); FALSE
e. (∃x)((Cxb & Cxc) & ¬Ixa); TRUE
g. (∀x)(∀y)(Cxy → Cyx); FALSE

9.3.2   (a) yes;   (b) a. yes;   c. no;   e. yes;   g. no;   i. yes

9.3.3   UD   := {John,Diane,Mike,Lucy,68,38,70,92,75,50,42,86}
Gxy   := x > y
Ixy   := x = y
Mxy   := {(John,68),(Diane,38),(Mike,70),(Lucy,92)}
Pxy   := {(John,75),(Diane,50),(Mike,42),(Lucy,86)}
d   := Diane
j   := John
l   := Lucy
m   := Mike
p   := 50

a. (∃x)(Mjx & Gxp); TRUE
c. (∃x)(∃y)((Mmx & Pmy) & Gxy); TRUE
e. (∃x)(∃y)[((Mxy & ¬(Iyp ∨ Gyp)) & ¬Ixj]; TRUE
g. ¬(∀x)(∃y)(Mxy & (Iyp ∨ Gyp)); TRUE
i. ¬(∃x)(∃y)(∃z)[(Mxy & Mdz) & ¬(Iyz ∨ Gyz)]; TRUE

9.3.5   UD := {A,B,C,D,E,F}
Bx   := {A,E,F}
Cx   := {A,C,D,E}
Gx   := {D}
Ixy   := x = y
Lxy   := {(A,C),(A,D),(A,E),(A,F),(B,C),(B,D),(B,E),(B,F),(C,F),(D,F),(E,F)}
Px   := {B,F}
Rx   := {B,C}
Sx   := {B,C,E}
Txy   := {(B,A),(E,D)}
c   := C

a. (∃x)(∃y)[((Cx & Bx) & (Cy & Gy)) & Txy]; TRUE
c. (∃x)(∃y)[((Px & Gx) & ((Cy & ¬Sy) & By)) & Lxy]; FALSE
e. (∃x)[(Cx & Rx) & (∀y)((Cy & Ry) → Iyx)]; TRUE
g. (∃x)(∃y)(∃z)[((Px & Sx) & (Cy & Cz)) & (Lxy & Tzy)]; TRUE
i. ¬(∃x)(∃y)[(Cx & Sx) & Tyx]; TRUE

9.3.6   a. TRUE;   c. FALSE;   e. FALSE;   g. FALSE;   i. TRUE

9.3.7   (i)   {(Han,MKT,Sr,9),(Katz,MKT,Jr,10),(Sun,ACC,Jr,8),(Imlay,ENG,Sr,24)}
        a. (∃x)(∃y)Pkmxy; TRUE
        c. (∀x)(∀y)(Pxesy → Gyt); TRUE
        e. (∃x)(Piejx & ¬(Ixt ∨ Gxt)); FALSE
        (ii) Ax := {Sun}
              Ex := {Imlay}
              Jx := {Katz,Sun}
              Mx := {Han,Katz}
              Rxy := {(Han,9),(Katz,10),(Sun,8),(Imlay,24)}
              Sx := {Han,Imlay}
        a. Mk; TRUE
        c. (∀x)(∀y)[((Ex & Sx) & Rxy) → Gyt)]; TRUE
        e. (Ji & Ei) & (∃x)[Rix & ¬(Ixt ∨ Gxt)]; FALSE

9.3.8   UD := {John, Sue, Lucy, Bill, Al, Mary, David}
        Dxy := {(John,Sue),(Sue,John),(Lucy,Bill),(Bill,Lucy),(Al,Mary),(Mary,Al)}
        Ixy := x = y
        Lxy := {(Sue,Bill),(Bill,Sue),(John,Mary),(Mary,David)}
        Mx := {Sue,John,Bill,Mary}
        b   := Bill
        j   := John
        m   := Mary

        a. (∀x)(Mx → (∃y)Dxy); TRUE
        c. (∀x)Mx & ¬(∃x)(∃y)Dxy; FALSE
        e. (∃x)(Dmx & Lxm); FALSE
        g. (∃x)[Mx & (∃y)(Dxy & Lyb)]; TRUE

9.3.9   UD := {a,b,c,d,e,f,g,h}
        Ax := {a,b,c,d,e}
        Bx := {c,d,e,f,h}
        Cx := {e,f,g}
        Dx := {h}

        a. ¬(∃x)Ax; FALSE
        c. (∀x)(Ax ≡ Bx); FALSE
        e. (∀x)[(Ax ∨ Bx) ≡ (Bx ∨ Ax)]; TRUE

9.3.11

	Irreflexivity	Asymmetry	Antisymmetry	Intransitivity
F$^{\mathfrak{A}}$:	No	No	Yes	No
G$^{\mathfrak{A}}$:	Yes	No	No	Yes
H$^{\mathfrak{A}}$:	Yes	Yes	Yes	Yes

9.3.13 a. UD := {0,1}
            Fx := {0}
            Gx := {1}
            a := 0

  c. UD := {0,1}
     Bx := {0}
     Cx := {1}
     a := 0
  e. UD := {0,1}
     Rxy := {(0,1),(1,0)}

9.3.14 a. UD := {0,1,2}
           Fx := {0}
           Gx := {1}
           a := 0
        c. UD := {0,1,2}
           Bx := {0}
           Cx := {1,2}
           a := 0
        e. UD := {0,1,2}
           Rxy := {(0,1),(1,0),(2,1)}

9.3.15   UD := {0,1,2}
          Rxy := {(0,1),(1,2),(2,0)}

9.4.1   a. true;   c. true;   e. false;   g. true;   i. true

9.4.2   For each sentence, any structure you construct with *Symlog* satisfies it; that is, *Symlog* evaluates the sentence to TRUE.

9.4.3   For each sentence, any structure you construct with *Symlog* falsifies it; that is, *Symlog* evaluates the sentence to FALSE.

9.4.4   For each sentence, construct at least two structures $\mathfrak{A}_1$ and $\mathfrak{A}_2$, where $\mathfrak{A}_1 \models \alpha$ and $\mathfrak{A}_2 \not\models \alpha$. That is, under $\mathfrak{A}_1$, *Symlog* should evaluate α to TRUE, and under $\mathfrak{A}_2$, it should evaluate α to FALSE. Here are some possible solutions:
   a. $\mathfrak{A}_1$: UD := {0,1}, Fx := {0}, a := 0
      $\mathfrak{A}_2$: UD := {0,1}, Fx := {0}, a := 1
   c. $\mathfrak{A}_1$: UD := {0,1}, Fx := {0,1}, Gx := {0}, b := 0
      $\mathfrak{A}_2$: UD := {0,1}, Fx := {0,1}, Gx := {0}, b := 1
   e. $\mathfrak{A}_1$: UD := {0,1}, Sxy := x+y = 1, Ixy := x=y, a := 0, b := 1, c := 0, d := 1
      $\mathfrak{A}_2$: UD := {0,1}, Sxy := x+y = 1, Ixy := x=y, a := 0, b := 0, c := 0, d := 1

9.4.5   a. The following two structures show this relationship:
           $\mathfrak{A}_1$: UD := {0,1}, Fx := {0}, Gx := {1}, a := 0, b := 0
           $\mathfrak{A}_2$: UD := {0,1}, Fx := {0}, Gx := {1}, a := 1, b := 0

9.5.1   For each set, the structure you construct with *Symlog* should satisfy each sentence in the set. That is, *Symlog* should evaluate each sentence in the set to TRUE. Here are some possible solutions:
   a. UD := {0,1,2}, Fx := {0,2}, Gx := {0,1}, a := 0, b := 1
   c. UD := {0,1,2,3,4}, Fx := {0,2}, Gx := {1,3}, Hxy := {(0,3),(1,4),(3,1)}
   e. UD := {0,1,2}, Cxy := {(0,0),(1,0),(1,1),(2,2)}

9.5.3   Let
           $\mathfrak{A}_1$: UD := {0,1}, Sxyz := {(0,0,1),(1,1,1)}, e := 1
           $\mathfrak{A}_2$: UD := {0,1}, Sxyz := x + y = z, e := 0
        Since (1) $\mathfrak{A}_1 \models \{(\forall x)(\exists y)Sxye\}$ but $\mathfrak{A}_1 \not\models (\forall x)Sxex$, and (2) $\mathfrak{A}_2 \models \{(\forall x)Sxex\}$ but $\mathfrak{A}_2 \not\models (\forall x)(\exists y)Sxye$, the set is quantificationally independent.

9.5.4   For each argument, any structure you construct with *Symlog* which satisfies the premises also satisfies the conclusion. That is, *Symlog* never evaluates the premises to TRUE and the conclusion to FALSE.

9.5.5   a. Assume that there is a structure $\mathfrak{A}$ such that $\mathfrak{A} \models \{Fa \,\&\, Gab, Gab \rightarrow Ha\}$. We show that

$\mathfrak{A} \models$ Ha as well. Since $\mathfrak{A} \models$ {Fa & Gab, Gab → Ha}, we then find that $\mathfrak{A} \models$ Fa & Gab and $\mathfrak{A} \models$ Gab → Ha. From $\mathfrak{A} \models$ Fa & Gab, it follows that $\mathfrak{A} \models$ Gab which, together with $\mathfrak{A} \models$ Gab → Ha, implies that $\mathfrak{A} \models$ Ha.

c. Assume that there is a structure $\mathfrak{A}$ such that $\mathfrak{A} \models$ {Gb & (∀x)(∀y)Hxy, Hca ≡ Fb}. Then, $\mathfrak{A} \models$ Gb & (∀x)(∀y)Hxy and $\mathfrak{A} \models$ Hca ≡ Fb. From $\mathfrak{A} \models$ Gb & (∀x)(∀y)Hxy it follows that $\mathfrak{A} \models$ (∀x)(∀y)Hxy, and by applying twice clause 5 in the definition of the satisfaction relation, it follows that any pair of elements of the UD is a member of the extension of H, $H^{\mathfrak{A}}$. In particular, that pair whose first and second components are the elements with names c and a, respectively, is a member of $H^{\mathfrak{A}}$. Thus, $\mathfrak{A} \models$ Hca. But since $\mathfrak{A} \models$ Hca ≡ Fb, we find that $\mathfrak{A} \models$ Fb. Clearly, there is an element, namely, the one with b as its name, and an assignment α, where $\mathfrak{A} \models_{\alpha(b^{\mathfrak{A}}/x^{\mathfrak{A}})}$ Fx. Therefore, by clause 4 in the definition of the satisfaction relation, $\mathfrak{A} \models_{\alpha}$ (∃x)Fx. But since (∃x)Fx is a sentence, by definition it follows that $\mathfrak{A} \models$ (∃x)Fx.

9.5.6 For each argument, construct at least one structure where *Symlog* evaluates the premises to TRUE and the conclusion to FALSE. Here are possible solutions:

a. UD := {Jim,Lucy,Bob}, Fx := {Jim,Bob}, a := Lucy, b := Jim

c. UD := {0,1}, Fx := {1}, Gx := {0}, a := 0, b := 1

e. UD := {0,1}, Lxy := {(0,1),(1,0)}

Bibliography

The following is a selection of books which complements and extends the material presented in this text. Without pretending to rank these texts, we have, within each category, listed them in increasing order of difficulty and specialization, from the introductory to the more technical.

Extensions of Standard Logic

FITCH, F. B. *Symbolic Logic: An Introduction*. Ronald, 1952. This is the original source (and which elaborates on the work of Gentzen and Jaśkowski) for the method of subordinate proofs presented in the *Symlog* text. We also recommend it for its similar treatment of modality, identity, general relations, and classes.

RESCHER, N. *Many-Valued Logic*. McGraw-Hill, 1969. A very good introduction to systems of many-valued logic.

BONEVAC, D. *Deduction*. Mayfield Publishing, 1987. Although the proof format in this text is slightly different from that of *Symlog*, its last chapters (9 to 12) provide a good introduction, in the spirit of natural deduction, to the topics of necessity, counterfactuals, the logic of obligation and modality.

HUGHES, G. E., and CRESWELL, M. J. *An Introduction to Modal Logic*. Methuen, 1972. A very comprehensive presentation of axiomatic systems of modal logic. (The book also provides a brief appendix on the rules of these systems from the point of view of natural deduction.) Their *A Companion to Modal Logic* (Methuen, 1984), which provides semantical characterizations of modal systems, is also highly recommended.

Logic and Natural Language

SALMON, M. H. *Introduction to Logic and Critical Thinking*. Harcourt Brace Jovanovich, 1984. Provides a broad account of both deductive and inductive reasoning with examples of such arguments in natural language. Among other topics, this text discusses the nature and types of arguments in ordinary language, deductive and inductive arguments, fallacies, causal arguments, confirmation of hypotheses, categorical syllogisms with Venn diagrams, validity in sentential and predicate logic and the nature of definitions.

GAMUT, L. T. F. *Logic, Language and Meaning (Volume 2: Intensional Logic and Logical Grammar)*. The University of Chicago Press, 1991. A very readable and clearly written presentation of intensional logic and logical grammar. Provides a treatment of intensional semantics and various intensional logics (modal propositional logic, modal predicate logic, tense logic); an introduction to type theory, lambda-abstraction and categorial syntax; intensional type logic and Montague Grammar; the theory of generalized quantifiers, flexible categorial grammar and discourse representation theory.

PARTEE, B. H., TER MEULEN, A., and WALL, R. E. *Mathematical Methods in Linguistics*. Kluwer Academic Press, 1990. Provides a basic mathematical background for the study of mathematical linguistics. Topics include elementary set theory (basic concepts, relations, infinities); logic and formal systems (sentential and predicate logic, axiomatization); algebra (operational structures, lattices, Boolean and Heyting algebras); English as a formal language (compositionality, λ-abstraction, generalized quantifiers, intensionality); formal languages, grammars and automata.

MARTIN, J. N. *Elements of Formal Semantics*. Academic Press, 1987. A rather formal introduction to logic for mathematically oriented students of language.

Logic and Related Fields

BARWISE, J., and ETCHEMENDY, J. *The Language of First-Order Logic*. Center for the Study of Language and Information (CSLI), Stanford University, 1990. We recommend this text as a companion to *Symlog*'s Chapter 6 ('The Basic Sentences of PL') and, especially, Chapter 9 ('Structures'). This text comes with *Tarski's World*, a computer program similar to *Symlog*'s Models, which is designed to let you explore the semantics of first-order sentences. Albeit less general than *Symlog*'s Models, *Tarski's World* has a very nice graphical interface which allows you to manipulate three-dimensional polyhedra, making it quite enjoyable to use. Both the text and the software provide plenty of examples and exercises which illustrate the concepts being discussed. There are versions of *Tarski's World* for both the Macintosh and the IBM-PC running *Windows*.

HAMILTON, A. G. *Numbers, Sets and Axioms*. Cambridge University Press, 1982. A good nontechnical text on axiomatic set theory.

STOLL, R. R. *Set Theory and Logic*. Dover, 1961. An accessible presentation of logic and the foundations of mathematics: set theory, the construction of the real number system, algebraic theories and a brief excursion into metamathematics. Strongly recommended as an introduction to the material covered by more technical texts.

SUPPES, P. *Axiomatic Set Theory*. Dover, 1972. An excellent formal introduction to axiomatic set theory. A historical introduction and a technical presentation of the general developments of axiomatic set theory is followed by a discussion of relations and functions, equipollence, finite sets and cardinal numbers, finite ordinals and denumerable sets, rational numbers and real numbers, transfinite induction and ordinal arithmetic, as well as a special treatment of the axiom of choice and equivalent formulations. This text is the basis for Suppes' EX-CHECK/VALID system but also for future extensions of *Symlog* already in the works.

REEVES, S., and CLARKE, M. *Logic for Computer Science*. Addison-Wesley, 1990. Intended for students of computer science, this text illustrates several applications of symbolic logic in computer science: program verification (first-order logic), reasoning about distributed and concurrent systems (modal and temporal logics), program specification (intuitionistic logic), logic programming (Horn clause logic) and theorem proving. Recommended as an overview and brief introduction to the material covered by more technical texts.

WOS, L., OVERBEEK, R., LUSK, E., and BOYLE, J. *Automated Reasoning: Introduction and Applications*, 2nd. ed. McGraw-Hill, 1992. A very accessible presentation and exploration of the techniques which enable certain computer programs to reason. Applications include the use of automated reasoning in designing logic circuits, proving program correctness and assisting in research in mathematics and formal logic. The book includes OTTER, a powerful resolution-based theorem prover.

BELL, J., and MACHOVER, M. *A Course in Mathematical Logic.* North-Holland, 1977. Besides a presentation of standard propositional and predicate logic, this excellent text contains chapters on Boolean algebras, model theory, recursion theory, axiomatic set theory and, most important, intuitionistic logic. Highly recommended to mathematically oriented students.

Metalogic

BERGMANN, M., MOOR, J., and NELSON, J. *The Logic Book,* 2nd. ed. McGraw-Hill, 1980. Since the logic systems, methods and notation presented in *The Logic Book* are almost identical to those of this text, it is the ideal reference for the metatheory of *Symlog*'s logic. In particular, it provides proofs for the completeness and soundness theorems for the natural deduction systems SD and PD and also for the truth-tree method.

LEBLANC, H., and WISDOM, W. A. *Deductive Logic.* Allyn & Bacon, 1972. Since the logic systems of *Deductive Logic* arc also vcry similar to those of *Symlog*, this text is also recommended for a study of *Symlog*'s metatheory.

BOOLOS, G. S., and JEFFREY, R. C. *Computability and Logic,* 3rd. ed. Cambridge University Press, 1984. A necessarily technical text which provides an excellent presentation of the fundamental theoretical results about logic: completeness, soundness, computability, representability, undecidability and definability.

Philosophy and History of Logic

QUINE, W. V. *Methods of Logic.* Harvard University Press, 1982. A lucid discussion of the fundamental notions of modern symbolic logic.

DELONG, H. *A Profile of Mathematical Logic.* Addison-Wesley, 1970. A nontechnical, clear and enjoyable exposition of mathematical logic, its metatheory and its philosophical implications.

KNEALE, W., and KNEALE, M. *The Development of Logic.* Clarendon Press, 1962. An extensive and excellent treatise on the development and history of logic.

BENACERRAF, P., and PUTNAM, H., eds. *Philosophy of Mathematics.* Cambridge University Press, 1983. A collection of seminal articles in the philosophy of logic and mathematics.

HEIJENOORT, J. VAN, ed. *From Frege to Gödel: A Source Book in Mathematical Logic, 1879–1931.* Harvard University Press, 1967. An excellent selection of some of the most influential papers in mathematical logic.

GABBAY, D., and GUENTHNER, F., eds. *Handbook of Philosophical Logic,* 4 volumes. D. Reidel Publishing Co. (Kluwer Academic Press), 1984. A succinct and technical presentation of the various areas of logic.

Index

General Index

Symlog Index

Screen Index

Learn Exercises Index

Symbol Index

SL TRUTH-TREE RULES

¬¬-Decomposition (¬¬D)

```
┌─────┐
│ ¬¬α │
└──┬──┘
┌──┴──┐
│  α  │
└─────┘
```

&-Decomposition (&D)

```
┌───────┐
│ α & β │
└───┬───┘
┌───┴───┐
│   α   │
│   β   │
└───────┘
```

¬&-Decomposition (¬&D)

```
┌───────────┐
│ ¬(α & β)  │
└─────┬─────┘
  ┌───┴───┐
┌──┴─┐  ┌─┴──┐
│ ¬α │  │ ¬β │
└────┘  └────┘
```

∨-Decomposition (∨D)

```
┌───────┐
│ α ∨ β │
└───┬───┘
 ┌──┴──┐
┌┴─┐  ┌┴─┐
│α │  │β │
└──┘  └──┘
```

¬∨-Decomposition (¬∨D)

```
┌───────────┐
│ ¬(α ∨ β)  │
└─────┬─────┘
   ┌──┴──┐
   │ ¬α  │
   │ ¬β  │
   └─────┘
```

→-Decomposition (→D)

```
┌───────┐
│ α → β │
└───┬───┘
 ┌──┴──┐
┌┴──┐ ┌┴─┐
│¬α │ │β │
└───┘ └──┘
```

¬→-Decomposition (¬→D)

```
┌───────────┐
│ ¬(α → β)  │
└─────┬─────┘
   ┌──┴──┐
   │  α  │
   │ ¬β  │
   └─────┘
```

≡-Decomposition (≡D)

```
┌───────┐
│ α ≡ β │
└───┬───┘
 ┌──┴──┐
┌┴─┐  ┌┴──┐
│α │  │¬α │
│β │  │¬β │
└──┘  └───┘
```

¬≡-Decomposition (¬≡D)

```
┌───────────┐
│ ¬(α ≡ β)  │
└─────┬─────┘
   ┌──┴──┐
 ┌─┴─┐ ┌─┴──┐
 │ α │ │ ¬α │
 │¬β │ │  β │
 └───┘ └────┘
```

PL TRUTH-TREE RULES

All the SL truth-tree rules and

∀-Decomposition (∀D)

```
┌─────────┐
│ (∀x)α   │
└────┬────┘
┌────┴────┐
│ (∀x)α   │
│ α(a/x)  │
└─────────┘
```

¬∀-Decomposition (¬∀D)

```
┌──────────┐
│ ¬(∀x)α   │
└────┬─────┘
┌────┴─────┐
│ (∃x)¬α   │
└──────────┘
```

∃-Decomposition (∃D)

```
┌─────────┐
│ (∃x)α   │
└────┬────┘
┌────┴────┐
│ α(a/x)  │
└─────────┘
```

Restriction:
The constant **a** must be
foreign to the branch.

¬∃-Decomposition (¬∃D)

```
┌──────────┐
│ ¬(∃x)α   │
└────┬─────┘
┌────┴─────┐
│ (∀x)¬α   │
└──────────┘
```